With very best wishes

A History of Music in the British Isles

Volume 2

Other books from The Letterworth Press
by Laurence Bristow-Smith

The first volume of
*A History of Music in the British Isles:
From Monks to Merchants*

and

Harold Nicolson: Half-an-Eye on History

A History of Music in the British Isles

Volume 2

Empire and Afterwards

Laurence Bristow-Smith

The Letterworth Press

Published in Switzerland by the Letterworth Press
http://www.TheLetterworthPress.org

Printed by Ingram Spark

ISBN 978-2-9700654-7-0

1 3 5 7 9 8 6 4 2

To
Peter Winnington
editor and friend for forty years

Contents

Preface to Volume 2 of *A History of Music in the British Isles*

This volume continues the story begun in *From Monks to Merchants*.

Writing about music in the nineteenth and twentieth centuries presents very different problems from writing about the music of earlier centuries. In the first place, there is so much more information. With Tallis and Byrd, with Purcell, even in the eighteenth century with Hook and Shield and Dibdin, I often had to hunt out the facts and piece them together to reconstruct the story. By the time I reached the Victorian era, the problem was the reverse. I had to sift through a mountain of facts, selecting and discarding in order to allow the story to emerge from what remained.

Then there is the problem that so much of the nineteenth and twentieth century is still with us – both physically and in terms of connected memory. Many of the monuments to musical life before the First World War are still standing and in use: Birmingham City Hall, the Royal Opera House, the Ulster Hall, the Colston Hall, the Albert Hall, the Wigmore Hall, the Cadogan Hall, the Usher Hall. For many people, venues such as these are part of their regular experience of listening to music on the radio or going to concerts. Sitting in my plush velvet seat, I always feel an extra sense of connection, thinking that Stanford or Parry, Wood or Beecham once conducted this same piece of music in this same hall. Of course, one can sit in Canterbury Cathedral and think that Tallis once sang there, but the feeling is less immediate.

That sense of connection with the (comparatively) recent past is enhanced by other, less physical, links. My grandfather drove the trams which took people to the Crystal Palace in the 1920s. My father watched it burn down in 1936. He saw Gus Elen perform and knew all the words to 'If It Wasn't for the 'Ouses in Between'. As an eleven- or twelve-year old, I saw Boult conduct. Boult had seen Richter and Nikisch conduct; he had known Holst and Vaughan Williams. I also saw Barbirolli, unshaven and in a scruffy tailcoat, conducting Elgar. Barbirolli had known Mackenzie and McEwen, and had himself been conducted by Elgar. That sense of a connection running back through time, a sort of apostolic succession, is important in music.

There is also the speed of change. As communications have improved and technology has developed, so music has changed ever more quickly. Musical styles and ideas which might in the past have taken fifty years to be worked through and gradually superseded can now become outdated within five or ten. That is not a criticism, just a recognition of modern culture.

At the same time, there has been a change in attitudes towards music; a change in how it is used, and what people think it is for. Music for its own sake is heard in live venues, on radio and television, on CDs, iPods and mp3 players. It is an essential component of major feature films and cheap TV sitcoms. It also there as background, as something to fill a space, in supermarkets and hotel lobbies, in television advertisements and when one is on the phone waiting to be connected to a call centre.

All these factors mean that the second volume of this work differs from the first. Popular music plays a much greater role in the story. There are more names of people and places, and more attention is paid to who knew who, when and where; there are more styles and genres to be defined and their place in the development of British music plotted; and, of necessity, there are more titles of songs, plays, films, and other works quoted as examples. As a consequence, and although it remains essentially chrono-logical, the narrative has to move back and forwards in order to keep track of the increasingly numerous strands of musical life.

Given all this, and in particular given the speed at which the story of music in the British Isles unfolds after 1800, it is important to emphasise the point I made in the Introduction to Volume One, that terms such as 'conservative' and 'progressive', 'forward looking' and 'backward looking' are used to position works and composers in relation to the broad develop-ment of music in Britain and in Europe. They are purely descriptive, not judgemental.

Laurence Bristow-Smith
Glenholme, Kirkcudbright
2017

Abbreviations Used

ABC   Associated British Corporation (a commercial television company)

BBC   British Broadcasting Company Ltd (from October 1922); British Broadcasting Corporation (from 1st January 1927)

CEMA Council for the Encouragement of Music and the Arts

ENSA Entertainments National Service Association

GPO   General Post Office

ISCM International Society for Contemporary Music

ITV   Independent Television

LPO   London Philharmonic Orchestra

LSO   London Symphony Orchestra

PRS   Performing Rights Society

RAM   Royal Academy of Music

RCM   Royal College of Music

RPO   Royal Philharmonic Orchestra

It is better to confront the issue of perceptions of British music during the nineteenth century at the beginning of the period rather than at the end. The most famous – or infamous – criticism came from the German writer, Oskar A. H. Schmitz, in 1914. His book, *Das Land ohne Musik: englische Gesellschaftprobleme* (*The Land without Music: English Social Problems*) asserted that 'the English are the only civilised nation without their own music (except street music).'[1] This was not the first such attack. Two other German writers on cultural matters, the activist Georg Weerth and the musicologist Carl Engel, both of whom had lived in England, had previously been equally dismissive of English musical awareness and ability. Even the poet Heinrich Heine, writing a newspaper article in 1840, gave it as his opinion that 'there is truly nothing on earth so terrible as English musical composition, except English painting.'[2] Why, one wonders, should such a perception have rooted itself so deeply in the German mind? And why did it concern them? The French and the Italians seem to have taken no comparable interest in the British musical soul. The answer is perhaps to be found in the huge divergence between the two musical cultures, best symbolised by the fact that in 1882 Germany saw the first performance of Wagner's *Parsifal*, whereas London in the same year saw the premiere of Gilbert and Sullivan's *Iolanthe*.

During the sixteenth and seventeenth centuries, the British looked upon Italy as the fount of musical inspiration. The madrigal, the concerto, opera – all originated in Italy. So, too, did the harpsichord, the violin and the piano. Over the course of the eighteenth century, perceptions began to change. The symphony was developed in Austria and Germany, and it was the symphony which, during the nineteenth century, came to be regarded (although not in Britain, and with Wagner, as always, an exception) as the supreme test of a composer's abilities. During the nineteenth century the German-speaking lands also produced a series of composers whose work utterly transformed classical music as we know it: Beethoven, Schubert, Mendelssohn, Schumann, Wagner, Bruckner, Brahms, Mahler. The British Isles produced no comparable figure and no comparable music.

This does not mean, however, that Britain was the musical desert of German imagining. In Volume One we saw how social conservatism (allied to the new, expanding, market economy) combined with musical conservatism (allied to the cult of Handel) to hold back change and innovation, except where new music with a proven record of popularity could be profitably imported from abroad. This situation had come about largely because of the vacuum left in British musical life – under William and Mary and the first three Georges – as the Court, the Chapel Royal and the Church of England gradually ceased to exercise the kind of leadership that had been their accepted role since Tudor times. We have seen also how various developments during the eighteenth century – the musical societies in provincial towns and cities, the Handel cult, glee singing and even Methodist-inspired hymn-singing – had began a process of democratising music, not only broadening its appeal, but also making it accessible to people from different levels of society, particularly among the new urban population.

What happened during the nineteenth century was that these various forces, and certain new ones, realigned themselves to bring about a transformation in British musical life. The nineteenth century, and the Victorian era in particular, was a time of almost continuous change – political, social and technological. It would be surprising if such a period had not also produced major changes in musical life, but they were not changes to match or parallel those in Germany or Austria or elsewhere. They went in an almost opposite direction. As the democratisation of music gathered speed and strength, it resulted in something like a popular revolution, which not only sparked off a wave of musical creativity in new areas and new genres, but also turned the middle and lower classes – the main consumers of music – into the arbiters of taste. What they wanted prevailed, and if that meant the novelty and vulgarity of music hall, the wit and spectacle of the burlesque, or the feminine allure of the ballet, rather than the expressive grandeur of Beethoven or Brahms, then so be it. Those who had traditionally controlled and directed British musical life might retain some residual influence, or they might behave as if nothing had happened, but with hindsight we can see that what they were facing was the arrival of a kind of multi-channel mass culture. From a German perspective, which saw high culture as all-important and discounted 'street music', the result was evidently deplorable, the equivalent of no music. Taking a different viewpoint, we can see much of what happened as innovative and exploratory, as a burst of creativity that marked the emergence of popular music as a significant cultural and economic force in British life – a position which, since that time, has strengthened with every new generation.

Critics and commentators, and even the concert-going public, have long regarded the work of nineteenth-century British composers – at least until the beginning of the so-called English Musical Renaissance at the end of the century – with a mixture of disappointment and exasperation: the 'could do better' of a potentially clever pupil's school report. There is certainly justification for this, but, as we shall see, the period did have many redeeming features. If there was no great music, there was much that remains worth listening to and exploring, and there were occasional moments of glory. Times were changing rapidly and composers naturally reflected those changes in their music, but that, of course, did not mean that the problems facing British music disappeared. The assumption that British music was necessarily second rate had become deeply entrenched in the national psyche and handicapped many who might have gone on to achieve more than they did. Some musicians accepted it as a fact and looked to Germany for a remedy. Others attempted to fight back. Still others seem to have tried, consciously or otherwise, to prepare for a time when British music could regain a degree of self-confidence.

Yet this is not to say that classical music was not popular; it was more popular than ever. Audiences grew – particularly for foreign music and foreign musicians. Well-meaning societies were established, dedicated to the promotion of music through lectures and through the commissioning of new works (although often from foreign composers). The first permanent orchestras came into being. Choral societies were established the length and breadth of the United Kingdom (with an emphasis, of course, on the oratorio). Brass bands became a feature of industrial towns. Music began to be taught in schools. The Tonic Sol-Fa System was invented to help people learn to sing. Very little of the music involved was new or challenging, but it was music, and it was reaching an unprecedented number of people. Many of those composers who have been criticised, fairly or otherwise, for not creating a 'new' British music were also energetic educators, committed, in their various and sometimes eccentric ways, to spreading knowledge and awareness of music as widely as possible. In contrast to Germany, where high culture ruled, British music became the handmaiden not of romantic idealism, but of adult education and local choral societies.

In 1800, however, all this was in the future. British music began the

3

century in a condition which can best be described as fragmented and uncertain. Germany was the leading musical power in Europe; fallout from the French Revolution and the Napoleonic Wars was affecting Britain in particular; but the single most influential individual was an Italian, at least by birth, although he spent at least as much of his life in England as did Handel, and his work has consequently to be seen in a British context.

Muzio Clementi (1752–1832) was born in Rome, the son of a silversmith. A child prodigy, he had composed several large-scale works by the age of fourteen, including a Mass that was performed in Rome to great acclaim. It may well have been this Mass that drew him to the attention of an English visitor, Peter Beckford, a passionate hunter and writer on hunting matters, and also a patron of the arts.[3] After some persuasion, Clementi's father agreed to allow the boy to go to England for a period of seven years, during which Beckford would fund his musical education. By the end of that time, spent mainly at Beckford's estate, Steepleton Iwerne, in Dorset, Clementi was ready to launch himself on the London musical scene. He became harpsichordist to the Italian Opera at the King's Theatre and gave virtuoso piano recitals. He rapidly established a reputation that spread beyond the confines of the British Isles and, in 1780, having received a number of invitations, set off on a European tour that lasted three years. In Vienna, he met Haydn, and, at the instigation of Emperor Joseph II, became involved in a musical duel with Mozart. Quite what happened we do not know. Clementi was always warm in his praise of Mozart, while Mozart, four years younger and perhaps feeling a little threatened, condemned Clementi's playing as mechanical and lacking in taste and feeling. Nonetheless, it was Mozart who borrowed from Clementi: the initial theme of Clementi's Sonata in B flat major, opus 24, no. 2, reappeared ten years later in the overture to *The Magic Flute*.

It seems that Clementi had already decided not to return to his native Italy, and from 1783 onwards he was settled in London, leading a busy life as a composer, conductor, performer, teacher and, later, businessman. In 1786, his Sonata in D, opus 16 ('*La Chasse*') appeared under the imprint of the music publishers and piano-makers Longman and Broderip. Clementi maintained a connection with the company, perhaps giving performances on their instruments, until it went bankrupt in 1798. At that point, he teamed up with James Longman, who was actually an organ-builder, bought the assets of the defunct company, and set up Longman, Clementi & Co, which later became simply Clementi & Co. The firm went through various changes of personnel, but Clementi remained a partner until 1831, the year before his death. He possessed considerable business acumen: during a second and even longer European tour, which lasted from 1802 to 1810, he negotiated the publication of a number of works by Beethoven, which proved extremely profitable. But the main reason for the tour, which took in Paris, Vienna, Berlin and Saint Petersburg, was to sell instruments, chiefly pianos – for which Clementi's talents made him a natural salesman (although, as we shall see, he had a equally talented assistant) – but also harpsichords, organs and harps.

The piano was changing. Johannes Zumpe's square pianos were rapidly being superseded by John Broadwood's invention, the grand piano, first seen in 1781. Broadwood soon went further, inventing and patenting the sustain and the soft pedals, and by 1810 extending the keyboard range to six octaves. All this made the piano much more flexible and responsive than the harpsichord, which gradually fell out of fashion with both composers and performers. The year 1795, when the grand piano replaced the harpsichord for the performance of the King's birthday ode, probably represents the tipping point in the relative fortunes of the two instruments. Clementi, combining a practical and technical understanding of the new pianos with a performer's instincts, was at the forefront of these changes. In the 1760s (as noted in Volume One, Chapter 46), Johann Christian Bach proclaimed that his sonatas could be played on the piano as well as the harpsichord. By the end of the century, such references to the harpsichord were rapidly disappearing. Clementi was the first to appreciate the expressive, even poetic, qualities of the new pianos and to apply them to the piano sonata. His Six Piano Sonatas, opus 2 – and particularly no. 2 in the set, often referred to as 'Clementi's Octave Lesson' – may well be the first true piano sonatas in that they appear to have been written with little or no consideration for performance on the harpsichord.

Clementi was a busy, but not prolific, composer. All together, he left some one hundred and fifty pieces for the piano – or for the piano and other instruments, mainly violin, cello, and flute. His real achievement, which had an impact on the development of classical music across the whole of Europe, was to demonstrate how what was now technically possible on the instrument could be applied in terms of style and form. Beethoven recognised this when he expressed his admiration for Clementi's piano sonatas – although, surprisingly, it was Broadwood, not Clementi, who in 1817 sent Beethoven a grand piano as a gift. Beethoven also praised Clementi's exercises and studies for students of the instrument. Works such as *Six Progressive Sonatinas* (1797), *Introduction to the Art of Playing on the Pianoforte*, opus 42 (1801), and *Gradus ad Parnassum* (1817), were the first of their kind.

As one might expect from someone who knew Haydn, Mozart and Beethoven, Clementi was also a composer of symphonies. These were works by which he set great store and they were popular in their day, but not as popular as those of Haydn, which is perhaps why he kept revising them, with the result that they were not published in his lifetime. Most of the symphonies were lost, the manuscripts possibly destroyed by Clementi himself, but musicologists have painstakingly reconstructed six of them from the fragments that remain, and they are certainly interesting works, with more than a touch of Haydn about them. The four later symphonies, reconstructed by the Italian musicologist, Pietro Spada, mix Haydn with an early romantic feel. They have scale, fluency and melody, but there is a lack of tension and sometimes direction. From the evidence that we have, based on what has been pieced together, it is clear that his symphonies were never going to rival his works for the piano in terms of intrinsic musical value or longer-term influence.

Clementi was also much sought after as a teacher: his methods and personality inspired a generation of composers and pianists across Europe, and a list of his pupils includes some of the best-known names in early nineteenth-century music. The Austrian Johann Nepomuk Hummel, who had previously been taught by Mozart, was one. Friedrich Kalkbrenner, who had been born in Germany but lived and worked in France, was another. During the 1820s, these two competed with each other to be recognised as Europe's foremost piano virtuoso. Yet another was Ignaz Moscheles, whom we have previously met as a distinguished visitor to the Glee Club and who will reappear as the teacher of many prominent nineteenth-century musicians, including Mendelssohn. He, too, was a piano virtuoso comparable with Kalkbrenner and Hummel. Then there was the prolific Czech composer, Carl Czerny, who taught Liszt, and developed what he learned from Clementi and Beethoven to the point where, through his own teaching, he became regarded as the father of modern piano technique. Nor should one forget the most successful opera composer of the century, Giacomo Meyerbeer.

Two of Clementi's British students also deserve mention. Johann Baptist Cramer (1771–1858), the son of William Cramer (see Volume One, Chapter

50), was actually born in Mannheim, but came to London at the age of four and made his career in Britain. He was another piano virtuoso, applauded by British audiences as 'Glorious John'.[4] The sheer number of such figures suddenly appearing is a testament both to the impact the new instruments were having in the world of classical music, and also to Clementi's influence. Beethoven, who saw a good deal of Cramer in Vienna in the winter of 1799/1800, considered him to be the finest technical pianist of the age. The two men were much the same age – Beethoven just a year older – and became firm friends. Cramer, perhaps taking his cue from Clementi, began to reduce his playing commitments after the age of forty and went into music publishing, first with Chappell & Co, and then, in 1824, setting up J. B. Cramer & Co, which continued as an independent company until 1964. Again like Clementi, Cramer managed to persuade Beethoven to sign a contract for the publication of a number of his works – among them the Piano Concerto no. 5. It is Cramer who is widely credited as having come up with the title *The Emperor*. Cramer's own compositions – and there were many, including two hundred or more piano sonatas and nine piano concertos – were popular enough while he remained a well-known figure, but soon slid into obscurity. From a modern perspective, they seem somewhat flat, somehow falling between the elegance of the Classical period and the passion of the Romantic. The one major exception is his *Studio per il Pianoforte*, opus 50. This comprises a total of eighty-four studies, published in four volumes (Books I and II, 1804; Books III and IV, 1810), which are still widely played by students today. Beethoven was sufficiently impressed to annotate the first volume for his nephew, Karl.

Cramer's career describes a pattern, even a template which, as we progress through the nineteenth century, we shall see repeated many times. A composer receives an excellent musical education; he is well connected; he is a more than competent, even an exceptional, instrumentalist. He travels in Europe to gain experience before returning to pursue a career in Britain. His talents propel him to public notice and a degree of celebrity; they provide him with a comfortable income, or, in some cases, a substantial fortune. He plays a role in promoting music for the benefit of the wider public (Cramer was one of the founders of the Philharmonic Society). He receives public recognition (in Cramer's case, not the knighthood that would become common later in the century, but an appointment to the board of the Royal Academy of Music). He also composes a considerable quantity of music, which attracts positive critical attention, if not actual acclaim, but which somehow fails to achieve the necessary flights of imagination or inspiration to propel it into the front rank. Of course, as we shall see, this pattern had many variations, some of them extreme, but it was there. Britain was definitely not a land without music, but it was a land where, for some reason, the highest flights of musical imagination were lacking.

Having identified a pattern, we must immediately draw attention to a major exception in the person of Clementi's second student, John Field (1782–1837), one of the greatest musicians ever to come out of Ireland. His father, Robert Field, was a professional violinist who played in the various orchestras that served Dublin's theatres. He saw his son's talent and was prepared to invest in it. He sent him for lessons to Tommaso Giordani (c.1730–1806), another of those wandering Italian opera composers who eventually settled in Dublin. At the age of ten, the young Field was performing in public concerts at Dublin's Rotunda Assembly Rooms. At the age of eleven, by which time the family had moved to London, he signed up for a formal, seven-year apprenticeship with Clementi – something which cost Robert Field, who was now a violinist with the orchestra at the King's Theatre, the not inconsiderable sum of one hundred guineas. Clementi was quick to see Field's abilities and within months had him playing in public at a benefit concert at the London Tavern in Bishopsgate. When Clementi went into business, Field became useful as a sales assistant, playing the pianos which Clementi sought to charm potential customers into buying. Some reports suggest that Clementi was a particularly demanding, even cruel master, but Field must have formed some kind of bond with the older composer, for when his apprenticeship formally ended in 1800, he continued to work for Clementi, making and demonstrating pianos. By now, he was performing in public regularly, giving programmes which included works by Bach, Handel and, of course, Clementi, as well as his own compositions, and meeting with growing appreciation. The high point of his early career came in 1801, when he performed his own piano concerto during a concert in Covent Garden to enthusiastic applause. He was still only nineteen.

The following year, Clementi set off on his eight-year European tour, the aim of which was business rather than performance. Field went with him in his role as sales assistant, but also gave successful concerts in Paris, Vienna and Innsbruck, which boosted his reputation. By the end of 1802, they had reached Saint Petersburg, where Clementi opened a piano showroom. Again, there are suggestions that Clementi did not always treat the young Field well. The German composer, Louis Spohr, who was in Saint Petersburg at the time, described Field as melancholy, shy and, speaking only English. This soon changed. In 1804, Clementi left Saint Petersburg, returning by slow stages to England where he remained for the rest of his career, eventually retiring to Evesham in Worcestershire. Field stayed on in the Russian capital and his career took off. He found a patron in the figure of General Markloffsky; he learned French, Russian and German; and he established a reputation for himself both as a concert virtuoso, and as a teacher, particularly of Russian aristocrats to whom he appeared an exotic figure. He was popular. He was making money. And he was soon the most celebrated pianist in Russia – a position he retained for over twenty years. His private life, however, was less happy. He started to drink too much, a habit which permanently damaged his health; and, while he survived a number of romantic scrapes with Russian ladies, his marriage, in 1810, to Adelaide Percheron de Mouchy, a French pianist and actress who had been his student, lasted only a few years, mainly because of his drinking.

Field was never a prolific composer, but what he did write has been hugely influential. His big works – the seven piano concertos – are often cited as an important stage in the development of the Romantic concerto, but, in reality, they are something of a mixed bag. Three of them – nos. 2, 3 and 7 – stand some way above the others. Even here, Field's sense of construction is suspect, although the structural failings are often obscured by his highly effective orchestration. He was far more at home working on a smaller scale and for solo piano. He wrote fantasies, *études*, and waltzes, but it is his sixteen nocturnes that are his claim to fame.[5] These are delicate, reflective pieces of great beauty and deceptive simplicity; they take Clementi's realisation of the poetic potential of the piano to a new and higher plane. Haydn had used the term 'nocturne' or '*notturno*' to describe a lyrical serenade for chamber orchestra, but it was Field who developed the genre and created the association with the piano. It is often stated, quite rightly, that without Field's nocturnes we would not have those of Chopin or Liszt, yet it would be wrong to see them as in some sense preparatory pieces, making sense only because they lead to something else. All sixteen are finished works in their own right, works of immense value and musical insight, which, had no one else ever written another nocturne, would still be regarded as masterpieces and would still justify the existence of the genre.

Field stayed in Russia, living first in Saint Petersburg and then – after the break-up of his marriage – in Moscow. He returned to London only once, at the request of the Philharmonic Society, arriving in 1831 and giving a concert early the following year. He played his Piano Concerto no. 4, which received a warm though not overwhelming reception, but the visit was overshadowed by his own ill health and by the death of Clementi, at the age of eighty-one. Field was one of the chief mourners at his funeral. He travelled on to Paris, Brussels, Toulouse, Marseilles, Milan and Naples, giving concerts to enthusiastic audiences, but in Naples his health gave way and he had an operation for cancer. He lay in a hospital there for nine months until a Russian family rescued him. He returned to Moscow by way of Vienna, where he stayed with Carl Czerny and gave three recitals. By the end of 1835, he was back in Moscow, where he revised some of his work and, the following year, played at a musical soirée organised by the German composer and pianist, Charles Mayer, who had been his student. It was his last public appearance. He died and was buried in Moscow in January 1837.

Field's career is the reverse of what we have come to expect. He was an export at a time when Britain was almost exclusively a musical importer. Italy, Austria and Germany were full of young British musicians learning whatever they could from whoever would teach them, before returning home to develop their careers. Field benefitted from his apprenticeship and employment with Clementi, but after leaving London seems to have had no instruction from anybody, preferring to rely on his own resources. Yet he built a European reputation, something which Purcell did not achieve and which no other British composer would manage until Elgar at the beginning of the twentieth century. Moreover, his development of the nocturne as a genre left a small but distinct mark on the European classical tradition in a way few composers of any nationality can match. And he achieved all this not in his native Ireland, nor in Britain, but in Russia.

55   Songs and Dances of the Napoleonic Wars

When Clementi died, he was given a public funeral in Westminster Abbey. He was not a musical giant, but he was widely respected, and his sonatas and his extension of what the piano could achieve had at least pushed at musical boundaries. Those British composers active during the early years of the nineteenth century – Dibdin, Hook, Shield, Kelly, Attwood, Samuel Wesley, Crotch – were all interesting, individual, even eccentric figures, but they did not have the same stature or authority. This is not to denigrate their achievement, but rather to reflect upon the nature of British audiences and critical opinion at the time. With Clementi, sheer longevity may well have played a part. For half-a-century he had been a significant presence on the British musical landscape. Like Handel before him and Mendelssohn later, he had become one of those foreign musicians accepted and adopted by the British public, but such sentiments were, in the end, only another aspect of British conservatism.

The twelve symphonies Haydn wrote to be premiered during his visits to London in the 1790s had aroused interest in the symphony as a musical form. While that interest fell away after his departure, Haydn was still popular and still regarded as Europe's leading composer. For British audiences, however, the oratorio remained the holy grail of composition, so when his great oratorio, *The Creation*, with an English libretto, received its London premiere at Covent Garden in March 1800, it might have been expected to take the city by storm. That it did not reflects, again, the conservatism of British audiences and the dead weight of Handel's reputation. *The Creation* was good, they said, but not as good as Handel. More performances followed, at the King's Theatre and at the Three Choirs Festival in Worcester, but *The Creation* never achieved wide popularity; and Haydn's second great oratorio, *The Seasons*, premiered in Vienna in 1801, was simply ignored. Perhaps this was because, in an increasingly correct moral climate, such profane matters were considered unsuitable for the great, sacred oratorio form; or perhaps Haydn was already beginning to slip into the obscurity that would be his lot for much of the nineteenth century. Other great classical works were given their first British performances around the same time. Mozart's *Requiem*, first heard at Covent Garden in April 1802, was described as an 'anthem' to avoid the Catholic and potentially alienating word 'Mass'. It was 'well performed', said the *Oracle and Daily Advertiser* for 21 February, but was 'in a style of musical composition to which English ears are less accustomed than to that of Handel.'[1] Insularity was now added to conservatism. Foreign musicians might be better than British ones, but only if they composed in the accepted manner. At the other end of the musical spectrum, however, insularity was proving a source of strength and inspiration.

From 1793 to 1815, with occasional tense interludes, Britain was at war with France. For a variety of reasons too complex and too far removed from music to come within the scope of this book, these years – and particularly the period from 1803 to 1815, when the enemy was Napoleon – had a far greater impact on the national psyche than previous wars against the French. One consequence was an outpouring of ballads and popular songs dealing with the war and its effects on society. War had always been a natural subject for ballads and songs. Clashes between the English and the Scots had given rise to ballads such as 'Flodden Field', 'Musselburgh Field' and 'The Battle of Otterburn'. The Spanish Armada inspired a number of ballads – none of them particularly distinguished, although one eccentric example, 'Skeltonical Salutation or Condign Congratulation and just vexation of the Spanishe nation', assures its audience that if they eat fish which have fed on the corpses of Spaniards suffering from venereal disease, they will not themselves become infected.[2] The Civil Wars generated propaganda songs, such as 'When the King enjoys his own again', which hammered home a message, rather than letting it emerge from the terms in which a battle or some other historical event was described. The War of Spanish Succession resulted in at least one classic ballad, 'Admiral Benbow' (*c*.1719), which is still widely sung and recorded; and throughout the eighteenth century there was a growing tradition of patriotic songs. 'Rule, Britannia!', as we have noted, was first heard in London in 1745. 'The Roast Beef of Old England', with words by dramatist (and novelist) Henry Fielding, first appeared in 1731, but is usually sung to a later tune by Richard Leveridge. 'Heart of Oak', with words by Garrick and music by Boyce, had its first public performance on New Year's Eve 1760 and later became the official march of the Royal Navy. Such songs retained their currency throughout the Napoleonic period, but the succession of wars which began in 1793 differed from previous periods in the number of ballads and songs they inspired, in the span of social issues and attitudes these songs addressed, and in the manner they addressed them.

'A New Patriotic Song', written in 1803 by Lieutenant Charles Durand in the East India Volunteers and sung to the tune of 'Rule Britannia', is typical of the cruder, rabble-rousing kind of song. The printed ballad sheet shows Britain represented by an angel and the dove of peace, while Napoleon is urged on by a devil, a snake and a skeleton.

> Britannia's kind angel with a smile
> Will now to Europe loud proclaim

That to defend our Heaven favour'd Isle
We teem with heroes seeking fame.

Slightly less crude were ballads such as 'The Battle of Trafalgar' and 'The Battle of Waterloo'.[3] Still full of patriotic rhetoric and celebrating the glory of British heroism, they nonetheless gave accurate details of the battles – the forces employed, the disposition of the armies, and the number of prizes taken or soldiers killed. The many ballads and songs that fall into this category represent what we might call the official view of history; and the broad popular appeal of this kind of patriotism meant that they were heard in the theatres as well as in the streets and taverns. The song 'The Arethusa', which tells of the fight between the British frigate *Arethusa* and the French *Belle Poule* in 1778, is an example of the kind of crossover that occurred. It came originally from a short opera, *Lock and Key*, first performed in 1794, with words by a librettist known as Prince Hoare, and music, adapted from a Morris tune called 'Princess Royal', by Shield. The song was a success in the opera, spread to the pleasure gardens, and was then printed as a ballad, creating the impression, which still persists in some quarters, that it was a traditional song.

Charles Dibdin went further than anyone else to exploit the appeal of bare-faced patriotism in the theatre. In 1803, he wrote and produced a comic opera (after the English model with much dialogue) called *The English Fleet in 1342*. Very loosely based on a British victory during the Hundred Years War, the production starred John Braham, whom we have met as Nancy Storace's partner, and another tenor, Charles Incledon, who had previously served in the Navy and whose inclusion in the cast was a crude but effective way of increasing patriotic appeal. But that was as nothing compared to *The Siege of Gibraltar* which Dibdin produced at Sadler's Wells the following year. Part of the stage was flooded. A hundred replica ships were constructed by shipwrights from the naval dockyard at Woolwich. Children representing Spanish sailors threw themselves overboard and were rescued. Gunfire and explosions rang out round the theatre. The details of both the ships and the action were surprisingly accurate, but it was the spectacle that the public loved – as they loved the aqua-dramas that followed: *An-Bratach*, representing Fingal's Cave, and *The Cataract of the Ganges*.

The ballad and folk-song tradition showed itself more subtle. We have already seen how anti-authoritarian tendencies had been evident from its early days – for example, in the Robin Hood ballads – and in the seventeenth and eighteenth centuries it was not uncommon for songs to circulate attacking a particular politician or protesting about a particular issue. Sir Robert Walpole and his ministry were frequently targeted. There were songs against slavery, such as 'The Negro's Complaint', originally a poem by William Cowper, and songs against taxation, such as 'Britannia Excisa'. Such songs naturally continued to be written and sung, as, for example, in this 1794 attack on the Prime Minister, William Pitt:

> But, say what you will, Pitt taxes us still—
> Our tea, our wine, and our drams;
> They have taxed our light, by day and by night,
> Our lawyers, poor innocent lambs.

But by the time of the Napoleonic Wars, we suddenly find not only a broader questioning of authority, but also a more fundamental questioning of the official view of history and all that went with it. One of several ballads called 'The Plains of Waterloo' is told from the point of view of a bereaved sweetheart. There is no patriotism or glory here: it is, quite simply, an anti-war protest song.

> My love he fell a victim 'mongst the thousands that they slew.
> Far from his own to hear him moan on the Plains of Waterloo.
> My love he lay the whole night long, my love he lay in pain.
> When the war was spread, he raised his head, and daylight came again.
> When that his comrades found him 'mongst the thousands that they
>
> slew ...
>
> ... they laid him in the cold clay on the Plains of Waterloo.

'The Banks of the Nile' deals with events in 1801 when British forces drove the French out of Egypt. The original probably dates from around that time, but the more common and better-known version must have been written later because of the reference to the Queen.[4] It takes protest a stage further, making it overtly political.

> The government has ordered, and the Queen she gives command.
> And I am bound on oath, my love, to serve in a foreign land ...
> Oh, cursed be those cruel wars, that ever they began,
> For they have robbed our country of many a handsome man.

Another ballad with the title 'The Plains of Waterloo' belongs to that particular class of ballads, explored in Volume One (Chapter 42), in which the returning soldier or sailor tests the loyalty of the girl he left behind by pretending to bring news of his own death, before revealing his true identity. There is a shift here, however, for even though the song has a happy ending, its message concerns the uncertainty and suffering of those left behind in wartime. The same emphasis on the impact of war on society at home is to be found in a number of songs dealing with the way soldiers were recruited. Songs such as 'The White Cockade' (or its variant 'The Blue Cockade') tell, again from the girl's point of view, how her foolish lover goes drinking with a recruiting party or press gang and is tricked into joining the army or navy. Versions may differ as to which of the services is involved, but they all contain the girl's astonishing outburst of bitterness at her young man's folly.

Well I hope you never prosper and I hope you always fail

At everything you venture, I hope you ne'er do well.

And the very ground you walk upon, may the grass refuse to grow,

Since you've been the very cause of all my sorrow, grief and woe.

The Irish song, 'Arthur McBride', looks at the same issue in a different way. Arthur and his cousin are accosted by a recruiting party with whom they first trade words – mocking the Sergeant's glowing description of a solder's life – and then blows. The expected order of things is reversed: it is the soldiers who end up looking cowardly and foolish, while the resisters, for all their self-interest ('You'd have no scruples to send us to France / Where we would be shot without warning'), appear as heroes.

On one level, these attitudes stemmed simply from unhappiness at the impact of the war. On another, however, they reflected a new spirit of idealism derived from popular understanding of the ideas behind the French Revolution and from works such as Thomas Paine's *Rights of Man*. This combination of social discontent and idealism enabled ballads and folk song to become recognised vehicles for protest; and this was a function that continued when the wars ended and the target for protest shifted to social and industrial conditions. It is worth noting that, later in the nineteenth century, when Kipling wanted to express the grievances of the ordinary solder in poems such as 'Tommy' or 'Danny Deever', he chose ballad form as the most appropriate means to do it. The fact that ballads and folk songs could take on this new function should not, of course, obscure the fact that lyrical and romantic songs with no element of protest about them continued to be written and to circulate in large numbers.

Society, even musical society, was divided. The issues that angered the ballad writers were not ventilated on the London stage and only rarely in the pleasure gardens. Nor, indeed, were there any protest glees. One area in which these divisions found oddly ambiguous expression was in the portrayal of Napoleon, who throughout the nineteenth century was the subject of more ballads and more songs than British heroes, such as Nelson or Wellington. The ruling classes, landowners, the majority of the merchant classes and, indeed, many working and enlisted men with traditional views saw Napoleon as a tyrant and menace to liberty. But there were others – many intellectuals, many in the northern industrial towns, many Catholics (particularly in Ireland), and men from all social classes who sought a new social order – who saw him, initially at least, in a positive light, as representing the ideals of the French Revolution. Even later, when he was at best a flawed hero, at worst a despotic warlord, he continued to fascinate. For those who still believed in the kind of social change that neither the endless Whig/Tory confrontations of British politics, nor George III with his recurrent bouts of mental illness, could deliver, Napoleon became a symbol of lost opportunity. So, on the one hand, patriots might gloat 'Let suff'ring Europe lift her head / Proud Bonaparte is humbled now', to the tune of 'Green grow the rashes, O!'; while on the other we have a song such as 'The Green Linnet', which takes the form of a heartfelt lament put into the mouth of Napoleon's second wife, Marie Louise. Although heavily partisan – the song is of Irish origin and many of the Irish saw Napoleon as a potential liberator – it has a subtlety quite alien to the patriotic outpourings of the British establishment. Napoleon himself is the linnet, a personification of a kind often found in Irish folktales, and also sometimes in Jacobite songs anticipating the return of the Young Pretender; and the poetic qualities of the lyric are matched with a tune which echoes a traditional Celtic lament. The effectiveness of the combination is demonstrated by the fact that the song has survived into the present day in the singing of artists such as Dick Gaughan and Martin Simpson.

Other ballads take a more balanced, even ambiguous, view of Napoleon and his life, which can make them more moving than the purely partisan efforts. A ballad such as 'Napoleon's Death' (also known as 'The Deeds of Napoleon') looks like a straightforward summary of Napoleon's life, but it is suffused with a sense of sadness not just for the loss of Napoleon, but for all those who died during the wars. It recognises his greatness, but also his failure, and does not seek to glorify or excuse.

> For Boney in a daze
> Beheld all Moscow in a blaze,
> And his gallant army melted
> Just like snow before the sun …

And when at Quatre Bras,
He let loose the dogs of war,
Many thousand Prussians there did fall
And there did die.

It avoids taking sides by insisting on the glory that is due to Lord Nelson – 'this Norfolk hero bold' – and the importance of 'great Trafalgar / Where he fell and where he bled'. And it ends in what can only be described as a spirit of forgiveness, supporting the idea that Napoleon's remains should be returned from St Helena to France:

Oh, bring him back again,
It will ease the Frenchmen's pain,
And in a tomb of marble
We will lay his body low.

'The Bonny Bunch of Roses' may also have had an Irish origin. It, too, is ambiguous in its presentation of Napoleon. It was certainly originally sung to an Irish tune, 'The Bunch of Rushes', which sounds as if it might perhaps have suggested the title. Like 'The Green Linnet', it makes use of the figure of Marie Louise, but this time she is in conversation with her son, Napoleon II. The son wants to imitate his father and raise an army in order to conquer the Bonny Bunch of Roses, a metaphor for the British infantry in their red coats. Once again, the song seems to admire the sheer scale of Napoleon's ventures, but Marie Louise reminds her son that death on St Helena was his ultimate reward, and she concludes on what British audiences would see as a strong, patriotic note: 'England she has a heart of oak / And England, Ireland, Scotland, their unity has ne'er been broke'.

This same ambiguity was also visible, although to a lesser extent, on the dance floors of the age. That Regency dancers should take the floor to such favourites as *Lord Nelson's Hornpipe, Nelson's Victory, Nelson's Waltz* or *Lord Wellington's Victory* was only to be expected. That a lady's dance card might also include *Bonaparte's Expedition, A Fig for Bonaparte*, or *Madame Bonaparte's Waltz* is rather more surprising. The title of a song is, naturally, of far greater significance than the naming of a dance. Nonetheless, the use of Napoleon's name suggests a remarkable degree of tolerance. One cannot imagine any dance named after Kaiser Wilhelm being danced during the First World War.

Today, Regency dance is almost an industry. Hundreds of societies exist in the United Kingdom, in the United States, and even in countries as disparate as Sweden and Nigeria, dedicated to reconstructing and enjoying the dances of an age noted for its elegance and its flirtatiousness. What they are really reconstructing is a period when dancing, at least in its formal manifestations, achieved a new level of social importance.[5] As we see in the novels of Jane Austen, it was not uncommon for families of all classes to stage small, private dances at home. Indeed, such functions were probably on the increase, materially assisted by the growing number of pianos and the growing number of young ladies who numbered piano-playing among their accomplishments. However, economic changes meant that the socially-ambitious mercantile middle classes could now participate in, and even host, the kind of balls and the large formal social gatherings that had previously been the preserve of the aristocracy.

Dances such as the gavotte and the minuet had long since fallen out of fashion, and although the most formal and aristocratic balls might still begin with a minuet, it was usually considered too slow. In the final decades of the eighteenth century, three kinds of dance predominated. Most common were the many varieties of the English 'longways' country dance, where couples faced each other and, in turn, performed a set of movements that took them down the line of dancers until everyone had returned to their original position. The cotillion, imported from France, although actually an adaptation of an earlier English dance, was based on dancers formed up in a square. Potentially more boisterous was the Scotch reel, where two or three couples performed a series of interlacing movements around each other. Depending on the venue and the nature of the company, music might be provided by a solo violin or a piano, a combination of instruments, such as violin, piano and flute, or even a string ensemble of six or eight players; while at the highest levels of society, at Buckingham House or in the great houses of the aristocracy, at Blenheim or Chatsworth, a string orchestra with added woodwind might be expected. The music itself was bright and tuneful, consisting of a combination of A and B lines with rhythmic variations appropriate to the particular dance, and was drawn mainly from an established repertoire of dance music. Later, somewhere around 1810, the quadrille made its appearance. As with the cotillion, couples formed a square, but it was a much more complicated dance with five, or sometimes six, separate sections which often speeded up towards the end to create a lively conclusion. The music, too, was more complicated, with the introduction of a C line, with different sections having wholly different time signatures, and with the introduction of tunes adapted from opera. As the century progressed, the quadrille became something of a craze, particularly in the upper echelons of British society. It was still popular enough in the 1860s for Lewis Carroll to satirise it with his Lobster Quadrille in *Alice in Wonderland* and expect to be understood.

The one thing all these dances had in common was that they involved no physical contact beyond holding hands. The waltz was different. It was current in parts of Germany in the 1770s, and had spread to Vienna by the 1780s. The name 'waltz' first appeared in Britain in 1791, together with a number of tunes in 3/4 time, but the movements associated with them do not seem to have differed significantly from a country dance. The waltz as we know it today, where the man puts his arm around the woman's waist, seems to have arrived in the early 1800s. It was clearly familiar to the cartoonist James Gillray by 1810 when he published a satirical sketch of two rather muddled couples on the dance floor; but it was only launched upon polite society in 1812 when the twenty-two-year-old Duke of Devonshire included it in a ball at his London house. Such physical proximity was scandalous; it was an incitement to flirtation or worse; and, of course, it was immediately wildly popular. Lord Byron, perhaps surprisingly given his reputation, fulminated against it; while Almack's Rooms, London's most exclusive and fashionable club, banned it. But to no avail. The newspapers were full of the Congress of Vienna, which negotiated by day and waltzed by night. The wife of the Russian Ambassador, Dorothea Lieven, one of the arbiters of fashion, publicly endorsed it. As a dance, of course, the waltz was simpler than other dances of the day, which no doubt added to its attraction. Musically, too, it was different. It depended on its rhythm, a consistent 3/4 (and sometimes 3/8) beat, rather than on a combination of rhythms and the repetition of melodic lines of a standard length. This made it more interesting to composers. They could exploit its flexibility and introduce subtleties that were not really possible in traditional country dance music. And there were few composers who, from 1815 onwards, did not try their hand at a waltz.

By 1814, Almack's was forced to lift its ban. By 1815, if we are to accept the evidence of Mr and Mrs Coles (who certainly belong to the socially-ambitious mercantile middle class) in Jane Austen's *Emma*, the waltz had become acceptable in provincial drawing rooms; and, in 1816, it received royal seal of approval, when it was included in a ball given by the Prince Regent. This event occasioned an incandescent outburst from *The Times*:

So long as this obscene display was confined to prostitutes and adulteresses, we did not think it deserving of notice; but now that it is attempted to be forced on the respectable classes of society by the civil examples of their superiors, we feel it a duty to warn every parent against exposing his daughter to so fatal a contagion.[6]

The newspaper, however, was out of step with the times. Thomas Wilson's *Description of the Correct Method of Waltzing*, published that same year, was a best seller. Wilson wrote a string of books and pamphlets about dancing – including *The Danciad*, a humorous description of the current state of English dance in rhyming couplets – and by 1822 he was running four separate dance academies in London, which taught the waltz as well as many other dances. Wilson was just one of London's many dancing masters, and the size of his business gives an indication of the importance of dance as a social movement in the years following the Napoleonic Wars.

In musical terms, Napoleonic ballads and the waltz have little in common, yet both have an important social dimension. Both show music reflecting and responding to pressures for change – and for change to happen quickly. The major musical developments of the eighteenth century that we examined – the burgeoning popularity of the oratorio and the glee, the emergence of the pleasure garden as a nationwide phenomenon – were important pieces in the changing jigsaw of British musical life, but they did not challenge anything. Wesleyan evangelical hymn singing may have implied social change, but did not directly promote it. By contrast, the idealism of wartime ballads and folk songs, and the adoption of the waltz as a badge of cosmopolitan modernity, were both, in their very different social and musical contexts, challenges to the established order of things. And, again in their very different ways, both gave an indication that in future music and musicians in the British Isles would find different ways to reflect and engage with society.

56 The Philharmonic Society, and the Royal Academy of Music

The Philharmonic Society was founded in January 1813. It was formed by musicians, not by a promoter or an impresario, and, although it would recruit subscribers to its concerts, its primary focus was on music, not profit. The first objective was to form a symphony orchestra. Despite all the excitement and the competition between orchestras generated by Haydn's visits in the 1790s, interest in playing major orchestral works had declined over the intervening years. The Professional Concert, successor to the Bach-Abel Concerts, had disbanded as early as 1793. The Antient Concerts continued to meet and perform, but it had become little more than a staid, aristocratic music club. Salomon and others had brought together various groups of musicians, but always on an *ad hoc* basis. Nor had twenty years of war against France helped matters. The economic consequences of the conflict were felt by musicians and music promoters as much as by anyone else. The net result was that by 1813 – the year in which Beethoven conducted the first performance of his Seventh Symphony and Schubert wrote his First – neither in London, nor in the United Kingdom as a whole, was there an orchestra capable of playing the kind of symphonic music that was being written on the Continent.

The group that came up with the idea for the Society included Johann Cramer; his brother Franz (also called Frank and François; 1772–1848), later Master of the Queen's Music; the violinist and pianist William Dance (1755–1840); the Scottish composer Philip Antony Corri (1784–1832), who later changed his name to Arthur Clifton and went to work in Philadelphia; and the journalist and promoter William Ayrton (1777–1858). Together, they drew up a manifesto pledging to encourage 'the superior branches of music' and to bring together 'the highest talents that can be procured, for the purpose of forming a full and complete orchestra'.[1] The manifesto attracted immediate support and among the other founding members was a host of well-known names we have already met – Clementi, Attwood, Salomon, Shield, Samuel Webbe – and others such as the conductor, Sir George Smart; the composer and violin virtuoso, Giovanni Viotti; and the composer of sacred music whose name is remembered in the music publishing house founded by his son, Vincent Novello.

There were to be up to fifty members, all professional musicians, who would make up the orchestra and give their services for free; an unlimited number of associate members, who could be called upon to add their skills as and when required; and, of course, subscribers who would pay to attend the Society's concerts. The Philharmonic was innovative in a number of ways, many of which stemmed from the fact that it was formed and governed by the musicians themselves. Particularly notable was its egalitarian spirit. Its constitution stated explicitly that 'there shall be no distinction of rank in the orchestra'.[2] Even with the search for subscribers, *The*

Spectator reported, 'there was no hunting after titled patrons or subscribers. No weak subserviency to mere rank. The most eminent members of the profession ... merged all claims of rank or precedence into one great object – the love of their art.'[3] Moreover, the society insisted that the audience remain silent during performances, something which, while not unknown in certain smaller music clubs, was comparatively rare at the time.

There were eight concerts during the Society's first season, all held in the Argyll Rooms, a converted house on Little Argyll Street. It had a capacity of only three hundred and competition for tickets was fierce. Later, in 1819, it was rebuilt and enlarged by the architect John Nash, becoming Britain's first purpose-built orchestral concert venue. Subscribers paid four guineas, with a concession that members of their family could pay only two. European music predominated. There were works by Haydn, Mozart, Cherubini, Johann Christian Bach and, of course Beethoven. The early seasons of the Philharmonic Society gave an immense boost to Beethoven's reputation in Britain. Although no longer regarded as mad or dangerous, his reputation was far from established. Well into the 1820s, the influential music magazine, *Harmonicon* – at one point edited by Ayrton, one of the Society's founders – was still publishing critical comments, often about the length of his symphonies. The Philharmonic, however, was his staunchest supporter. Indeed, their first concert, which Salomon directed, featured a Beethoven symphony (probably no. 1). At least two other symphonies were played that season and every programme had at least one Beethoven work. In 1816, the Society gave the London premiere of the Fifth Symphony. It was the first time that trombones and the contrabassoon had been heard in a symphonic context in London. There is an appealing story that during rehearsals Salomon at first lost his temper with the work, calling it 'rubbish', but then later apologised to the orchestra, retracting his criticism and saying he now regarded it as one of the greatest works he knew.[4] The Seventh Symphony had its British premiere the following year, and, in 1821, the pianist Charles Neate gave the first London performance of the Piano Concerto no. 1. Over the first twenty years of the Philharmonic's existence, from 1813 to 1832, Beethoven was far and away the dominant presence in its programmes. Two hundred and fourteen performances of his works were given, eighty-eight of them symphonies, while only fifteen of their one hundred and sixty concerts did not feature his name.[5]

The most famous interaction between the Philharmonic and Beethoven concerns the Ninth (*Choral*) Symphony. In 1817, the Society's directors offered Beethoven the sum of three hundred guineas for two new symphonies if he would come to London to conduct them in person. He was also offered the possibility of a benefit concert which would make him at least £500. Beethoven was very aware that Haydn's trips to London had freed him of all financial anxiety: he was tempted, but in the end decided he could not face the journey. He did, however, at a slightly later stage, accept £50 to write a new symphony. This work was much delayed, only arriving in London in December 1824, by which time it had already been premiered in Vienna. But it was the *Choral Symphony*, one of Beethoven's greatest and most radical works – indeed, one of the greatest of all symphonies – and the manuscript does bear a handwritten dedication to the Philharmonic Society. The first London performance was delayed, partly because the Society still hoped that Beethoven might be tempted to London to conduct it himself, and partly because Sir George Smart, the Society's chief conductor at the time, was slightly daunted by the score. In the end, Smart conducted a private, trial performance in February 1825, and a public performance the following month. *The Times*, reviewing the trial performance, was more perceptive than it had been about the waltz: 'A symphony by the celebrated Beethoven was tried for the first time on Tuesday evening.... In grandeur of conception, in originality of style, it will be found, we think, to equal the greatest works of this composer.'[6] However, *Harmonicon*, ever grumpy, said that 'we find Beethoven's Ninth Symphony to be precisely one hour and five minutes long; a frightful period indeed, which puts the muscles and lungs of the band, and the patience of the audience to a severe trial.'[7] We know the verdict of history.

The Society remained loyal to Beethoven right up to the end. In 1827, when he was ill and in desperate need of money, the directors sent him £100 which reached him just before his death. This was to redound to the Philharmonic's benefit forty years later. At the time of the centenary of his birth in 1870, a lady called Fanny Linzbauer, living in Budapest, offered the Society a bust of Beethoven in recognition of the generosity shown to him in his lifetime. But the bust, by the Austrian sculptor, Johann Nepomuk Schaller, was valuable. She would not send it; she would only deliver it into the hands of a member of the Society. Europe was still in the grip of the Franco-Prussian War. Nonetheless, the composer William Cusins, at that time conductor of the Philharmonic and recently appointed Master of the Queen's Musick, set off. In those days, of course, the journey had to be made by coach. Undaunted by massive troop movements, he arrived in

Budapest, collected the precious item and brought it safely back to London. It immediately became an icon. It was used as the model for the likeness of the composer that appears on the Society's annually-awarded gold medal; and it is still placed on the platform for all the Society's concerts.

The Philharmonic Society brought together the best players to play the best music. The orchestra was not perfect and attracted criticism from time to time, but it was a symphony orchestra where there had been none, and it stimulated a distinct improvement in the quality of music available to audiences in London in the years following its foundation and into the middle of the century. Equally significant was the organisational framework in which it operated. By and large, eighteenth-century concert promoters had a strong profit motive. That is not to say that they were not committed to the music they promoted, but rather to recognise the spirit of the times; and, of course, there were musical philanthropists: one only has to look at the £1,600 Lord Abingdon laid out (and lost) in supporting the Professional Concert. But the Philharmonic Society was fundamentally different. It was, by intention and design, a co-operative run by the musicians themselves, and it was also non-profit-making. The constitution states that 'after paying the expenses of each season, any balance that may remain shall be carried forward to the account of the succeeding year.'[8] It was, in short, an institution, in what would soon become the classic, Victorian sense of the term.

In 1822, just nine years after the foundation of the Philharmonic Society, a second important institution was established in London: the Royal Academy of Music (RAM) – although it did not receive its Royal Charter until 1830. The moving spirit was Lord Burghersh (1784–1859), later the Earl of Westmoreland, and an establishment figure if ever there was one. As a soldier, he had fought alongside Wellington during the Peninsular War and risen to the rank of General. With the war over, he became MP for Lyme Regis – a seat that was in the gift of his family – before taking a series of diplomatic appointments as Envoy to Tuscany, Envoy to Prussia, and then Ambassador to Austria. As a student, however, he had studied both the violin and composition, first at Cambridge, then in Zurich and Vienna; and, throughout his busy official life, he never stopped composing. He wrote six Italian operas, an English opera, a Mass, a setting of the Anglican Service, anthems, songs, glees and a host of other works, none of which are remembered today, probably with reason.

Burghersh, however, was just the man to mobilise the establishment of which he was a part. And his determination was backed up by logic. We have seen how it had become normal for promising British musicians to travel abroad to Italy or to Germany to study; and, on the face of it, the fact that London, the capital of an expanding British Empire, should not boast some kind of college or official academy dedicated to promoting musical excellence did seem strange – especially given the level of musical activity both in the city and in the British Isles as a whole. The reason such a body did not exist, of course, was because the idea behind it would have run counter to the essentially market-driven approach to music that had evolved over the previous century. The previous Royal Academy of Music, set up to produce opera between 1719 and 1728, typified the spirit of the eighteenth century in that it had been run as a joint stock company. Times, however, were changing and the new Academy was to be a charitable foundation. Meetings were held in the Thatched House Tavern. A constitution, based on that of the British Institution for Promoting the Fine Arts, which had been formed in 1805, was drawn up. George IV was approached and agreed not only to become the Academy's principal patron, but also subscribe a hundred guineas a year. Premises were taken in Tenterden Street, just off Hanover Square. Directors were appointed. A Board was appointed. Teaching staff were appointed. The names of those involved will by now have a familiar ring. The first Principal was William Crotch; the Board included Johann Cramer, William Horsley, Attwood, Shield and Smart; and among the professors were Clementi, Thomas Greatorex, and Franz Cramer. They were entrusted with the education of up to eighty students – forty male and forty female – and the whole organisation was to be funded by a mixture of annual subscriptions and student fees. The whole procedure was significantly more long-winded and cumbersome than that which had led to the formation of the Philharmonic Society, and, indeed, the whole venture was to prove much more troublesome to finance and to manage, but, at the end of March 1823, the Academy opened its doors. The first lesson, in piano, was given by Cipriani Potter (1792–1871) to a young man called Kellow Pye. Pye would go on to be a minor composer of church music in Exeter – his setting of Psalm 31, *In Thee, O Lord, have I put my trust*, is still heard – before returning to the Academy in an administrative capacity in the 1860s and later becoming a wine merchant.

The Academy went through a series of crises. As early as 1824, it was in debt, and, by 1827, the financial situation was so dire that only a combination of a public appeal, reduced salaries and increased fees enabled it to stay open. William Crotch resigned as Principal in 1832, to be replaced by Cipriani Potter, who was forty years old at the time and on the way to establishing a considerable reputation for himself as a composer. He had been another infant prodigy; his father, Richard Potter, was a piano teacher and the boy could play well by the age of five. He continued his piano studies with Joseph Wölfl, an Austrian pianist who had studied under Haydn and Mozart, and who was by then living in Marylebone. He also took instruction in composition and counterpoint from Crotch, Attwood and John Wall Callcott. He had his first success as a composer in 1816, when the Philharmonic Society commissioned him to write an overture for that year's concert season. Shortly afterwards, following the pattern expected of young and promising British musicians, he set off for Vienna. There, he got to know Beethoven, who apparently thought well of his abilities, and he was lucky enough to have some of his work performed. The reception was good and Potter moved on from Vienna for the obligatory tour of Italy. By 1821, he was back in London apparently determined to devote himself to composition, while keeping himself afloat financially by performing and teaching.

Potter wrote no less than ten symphonies, although one is missing and discussion of the others has been hampered in the past by the fact that he kept changing their numbers. Whatever else they are, these are not negligible works. They are large-scale compositions, written by a man clearly at the height of his powers and with a strong sense of the dramatic. As one might expect, Beethoven is a clear influence, particularly in moments such as the presentation of the main theme at the opening of the Third Symphony.[9] Mozart is present, too, but the symphonies are distinctly post-Mozartian in terms of the space Potter gives himself to develop his themes. His orchestration is impressively clear and controlled; and there are times when his use of repeated rhythmic patterns, especially when involving the brass, seems to look forward to the Berlioz of the *Symphonie Fantastique* and *Harold in Italy*. Potter's Symphony no. 8 is particularly enjoyable for its atmosphere of controlled drama and its at times almost humorous use of syncopated rhythms; Symphony no. 10 attracted warm praise from no less a figure than Wagner, when he visited London to conduct the Philharmonic Orchestra in 1855. Interest in these works has stirred in recent years and one or two recordings are now available, but one has to ask why, despite the encouragement of the Philharmonic Society, these symphonies were not appreciated at the time. Presumably, it was because Potter was

English (notwithstanding an Italian Christian name which came through his mother's side of the family), and English composers were not regarded as the equal of foreigners, especially when they wrote symphonies. Potter may, in fact, have materially reduced his chances of success by ignoring the choral bias of many British audiences. Quite unusually for the time, and with the exception of a long-forgotten cantata and a handful of songs, he confined himself to writing orchestral or instrumental music. His other major works included three piano concertos, and three large-scale overtures on Shakespearean themes – *Anthony and Cleopatra*, *Cymbeline*, and *The Tempest* – but none of them have generated any significant interest.

Somewhere around 1825, Potter composed a work for piano entitled *The Enigma: Variations and Fantasia on a favourite Irish Air for the Piano Forte in the Style of Five Eminent Artists, Composed and Dedicated to the Originals by Cipriani Potter*, which was published by a company at that time known as T. Boosey & Co. Both the title and the idea suggest Edward Elgar's 1899 masterpiece, and Percy Young has speculated, quite reasonably, that, as a boy, rummaging through the sheet music in the Elgar Brothers' Music Shop in Worcester, Elgar may have come across a copy of Potter's work and unconsciously stored the idea away for future use.[10]

Potter took over from Crotch as Principal of the RAM in 1832. He wrote the last of his symphonies in 1834 (although he did revise some of them later), his last piano concerto in 1835, and his last major orchestral work – *The Tempest* – in 1837. One has to ask why this was so. Had he run out of things to say? Was he dispirited by his lack public success? Or was it due to the pressure of his duties at the Academy? A combination of all three is the most likely answer, and there is no doubt that life at the Academy was far from easy. Finance was a constant source of worry, but more difficult still was Lord Burghersh. He had no egalitarian aims or sympathies. Having set up the Academy, he expected to control it. In 1837, a disillusioned student, Collet Dobson, published an article in the *Musical World* attacking the state of the organisation. Exempting the teaching staff from blame – 'they are fully competent to their duties … their lessons are very valuable … they are anxious for the improvement of their pupils' – Dobson pointed the finger directly at Lord Burghersh:

Director, conductor, dictator…. His introduction of his own compositions, to the exclusion of those of Handel, Haydn, and Mozart; his inattention to the real interests of the institution; his carelessness of every body's time and convenience; show most clearly that his object is not so much to improve the musical art, as to draw round him a circle of which he may be the principal attraction.[11]

It was this situation that Potter had to manage, and to his credit he managed it for twenty-seven years, until 1859. It was only when Lord Burghersh died that Potter himself felt able to retire as Principal, passing the reins to the cellist and conductor, Charles Lucas (1808–69). Even more to Potter's credit is that, despite these difficulties, the early years of the Academy produced several very talented composers.

Whatever their successes and whatever their faults and failings, the Philharmonic Society and the RAM represented change. They both stemmed from a recognition that something was rotten in the state of British music; and they were both indications of how British society would seek to manage what the Philharmonic unashamedly called 'the superior branches of music' during the nineteenth century. In broad terms, if the eighteenth century was a period of entrepreneurial promoters on the one hand and local music clubs on the other, then the nineteenth, by contrast, was an age of institutions. Classical music benefitted from the riches generated by the Industrial Revolution through expressions of burgeoning civic pride and a new spirit of philanthropy. Of course, the entrepreneurial impulse continued, especially where opera and theatre were concerned; and, of course, the great British choral tradition and festival culture had their roots in the eighteenth century; but the nineteenth century – and particularly the Victorian era – was qualitatively and, as far as choral societies and festivals were concerned, quantitatively different.

57   Oratorios and Festivals

In the 1850s, the population of the Shetland Islands lived mainly by fishing, whaling, crofting and spinning wool. True, communication had improved since the boats that linked the port of Lerwick to mainland Scotland had become steam-powered and consequently much more reliable, but it was still a particularly isolated community. Nonetheless, between 1848 and 1854, local singers and musicians were able to stage a quite incredible series of performances, beginning with Mendelssohn's *Elijah*. This in itself was remarkable. The oratorio had had a wonderful reception when premiered in 1846 at the Birmingham Festival, and it had been given for the first time in London in 1847, but it was still far from being widely known. After *Elijah* the islanders performed Handel's *Messiah*, *Judas Maccabaeus* and the *Dettingen Te Deum*, Haydn's *Creation*, Beethoven's Mass in C and his oratorio, *The Mount of Olives*, and then Mozart's *Requiem*. Three men seem to have been responsible for this remote flowering of musical enthusiasm. Thomas Barclay (1792–1873) was born on Unst, one of the northernmost of the Shetlands, and had been educated at Glasgow University. He was the Minister of the Church of Scotland in Lerwick and for a Scottish minister evidently took an extremely liberal view of music in church, allowing afternoon services to be concluded with the playing of an anthem. William Merrylees (1795–1859), from East Linton near Edinburgh, had married into a Shetland family. He was a shipping and insurance agent, as well as a talented amateur musician. He led and trained the choir at the parish church where Barclay presided. The key figure, however, was John George Glass (1816–54), a red-headed Englishman who taught at a school in Lerwick run by the United Brethren, also known as the Moravian Church. Glass was the man with the energy and determination to recruit and rehearse a choir – and, later, an orchestra – from the local community. He was also the one who directed the performances, which ceased following his death in 1854.[1] None of these three men achieved more than local recognition as musicians – although Barclay did go on to become a much-respected Principal of Glasgow University – but their activities demonstrate a number of characteristics crucial to an understanding of nineteenth-century music-making away from London and the big cities: the central role of the amateur, the formation of a community-based group or society, the element of self-help, and the continuing centrality of the oratorio.

It is difficult to overstate the importance of the oratorio throughout the British Isles during the whole of the nineteenth century. Even cynics recognised its centrality. Lady de Grey, a famous patron of the opera, dismissed English composers and musicians as people who wrote and performed oratorios in cathedral towns. The phenomenon is not easy to understand from the viewpoint of a later age, not least because it centres on the public profession of faith. The upheavals of the French Revolution and Napoleonic Wars, the self-examinations of the Romantic movement, and the writings of men such as Thomas Carlyle, John Stuart Mill, Charles Darwin and many others, all meant that this was not so much an age of faith as an age in which faith needed shoring up. Religion and morality were publicly examined and discussed more widely and more openly than ever before.

The Church of England was not well equipped to respond. It was battered by a series of crises over pluralism and the repeal of the Test Acts; it was challenged by evangelicals on the one hand and Anglo-Catholics on the other; and it was subject to reforms imposed by an unsympathetic Whig administration. One of the major strands of reform involved re-allocating resources from the grand cathedral foundations to small, often new, urban parishes. This was fully understandable in terms of demographic change and the church's mission, but it inevitably led to a further weakening of the position of music. The Anglican Church was simply in no condition to inspire great music.

As we noted in Volume One (Chapter 53), the talent of Samuel Wesley was largely ignored. William Crotch's church music was unremarkable. John Clarke-Whitfield (1770–1836) produced no less than four volumes of anthems, and contributed to the Handel cult by publishing the great composer's oratorios with piano accompaniment. He has been described as 'amiably unobjectionable.'[2] Sir John Goss (1800–80) composed extensively for the Church during the course of his long life. He is remembered today for his hymn tunes, including *Lauda anima* ('Praise, my soul, the King of Heaven'), but he also composed a large number of anthems. Although one or two of these are still heard, the majority combine a high degree of technical competence with a matching level of conventional musical sentiment: 'their well-ordered paths,' it has been said, 'are not disturbed by any special fire of inspiration.'[3] G. J. Elvey (1816–93) wrote a large amount of church music, most of which sounds like Handel. John Bacchus Dykes (1823–76) composed settings of the Service and anthems which continued to be heard until the end of the century but have since been largely forgotten. The Reverend Sir Frederick Gore Ouseley (1825–89), whom we shall come across again in Chapters 68 and 72, was a rich, aristocratic and technically-accomplished musician, who wrote books on *Harmony* (1868), *Counterpoint* (1869), and *Musical Form* (1875). In 1856, Gore Ouseley established his own college, St Michael's near Tenbury Wells in Worcestershire, which was to be dedicated to improving the standard of performance of Anglican church music. Unfortunately, this academic approach is what characterises his many settings of the Service (at least eleven) and even more numerous anthems (around seventy). It easy to be dismissive, and, of course, one can find moments of charm and interest in the works of all these composers – Gore Ouseley's short anthem, *O Saviour of the World*, for example – but it would be foolish to pretend that the bulk of the music written for the Church of England in the first sixty or more years of the nineteenth century was anything beyond adequate. Only two composers stand out: Thomas Attwood Walmisley and Samuel Sebastian (S.S.) Wesley. We will be looking at how they differ from the other church composers of the period in Chapter 60, but even their contributions (and Wesley's is considerable) cannot alter the broad characterisation of the church music of the period as solidly conventional.

All of this meant that those who wished to find a musical expression of their faith had to look elsewhere. Evangelical hymn-singing was one alternative. The oratorio was another. Both offered the emotional charge and sense of collective involvement that were lacking in the chill formalities of the Church of England. It is no accident that so many choral societies sprang up in industrial towns that were the heartland of Nonconformism, but the oratorio had a still wider appeal. It could reach all social classes, and it offered the potential to evoke a greater range of emotions. Inherent in the Victorian response to all 'serious' music, but to the oratorio in particular, was the concept of moral improvement – of the self and of others. In an autobiography which contains a chapter intriguingly entitled 'Music Means Morals', the Reverend Hugh Haweis encapsulates how the process was supposed to work where the lower classes were concerned:

> I have known the oratorio of the *Messiah* draw the lowest dregs of Whitechapel into a church to hear it, and during the performance sobs have broken forth from the silent and attentive throng.... I do not say that music will ever shut up all our prisons and workhouses, but I venture to believe that as a chief and sovereign means of rousing, satisfying, and recreating emotions, it would go far to diminish the number of paupers and criminals. It would help them to save, it would keep them from drink, it would recreate them wholesomely, and teach them to govern their feelings – to use, and not invariably to abuse, their emotions.[4]

The oratorio also had the advantage of scale and grandeur, both of which appealed to Victorian sensibilities, chiming with their sense of patriotism and Empire, as well as their sense of progress. This was not an age of miniatures. Big was beautiful, and big was effective. The five Handel Commemorations of 1784, 85, 86, 87 and 91 attracted a total audience of perhaps 80,000. The audience for the four Handel Festivals at the Crystal Palace in 1857, 59, 62 and 65 exceeded a quarter of a million.

The oratorio was a genuinely nationwide phenomenon. Choral societies soon covered the land. They tended to be institutional in character, and were often established with civic blessing. They were larger and more formal than the private, frequently all male, clubs of the eighteenth century. The Coventry Union Choral Society was founded in 1813; the Edinburgh Harmonists' Society in 1822. Blackburn Choral Society followed in 1829; Burnley in 1834; Huddersfield in 1836; York and Bedford in 1837; Stockport in 1840; and Glasgow in 1843. The trend took in major cities and rural centres, new industrial settlements and ancient cathedral towns. Wigan in 1847 was followed by Newcastle and Gateshead in 1850; Norwich in 1853; and then by Huntingdon and St Neots, and Carlisle the following year. By the end of the century, there were hundreds of them; and as the number of choral societies grew, so, too, did the number of smaller choirs, particularly in the industrial areas, where they were frequently based on chapels or workplaces, such as mills or banks or collieries. More choirs and more singers meant more music festivals. These had also begun in the eighteenth century, but now they spread rapidly. They were encouraged and supported by city and town councillors who saw a music festival as a way of putting themselves on the national cultural map. Yet even without festivals, the spread of interest in public and collective singing meant that remote spots – such as the Shetland Islands – might still manage a creditable programme of performances.

New festivals were good news for instrumentalists, for singers and for conductors; and it was not long before a festival circuit established itself. London remained the centre of British musical life, but the competition for orchestral work and for other musical engagements was intense, and the possibility of paid, often well-paid, work in the provinces was a godsend. Thomas Greatorex (1758–1831), was among those who made a speciality of directing regional music festivals and profited by it. In 1814, at a time when men working in the mills or on the land were lucky to get £40 a year (and women got much less), he was paid £105 for directing the Chester Festival; and he was also a regular conductor at festivals in Derby, York and Manchester. Greatorex was another solidly establishment figure, but fascinating for all that. A minor composer of church music, he was also conductor of the Antient Concerts, organist at Westminster Abbey, and a teacher at the RAM. At the same time, he was a champion archer, a respected astronomer, and a friend of the Young Pretender, whom he had met in Italy and who left Greatorex a number of valuable manuscripts in his will. His obituary, unsurprisingly, stresses his credentials as a gentleman of the old school.[5]

The other great festival director of the period was Sir George Smart (1776–1867), whom we met earlier puzzling over the score of the *Choral Symphony*. His musical pedigree was impressive and he worked hard in the cause of British music, but he was not, in any sense, an innovator. The son of an orchestral player and music publisher, he became a Chapel Royal chorister as a boy and was taught by Edmund Ayrton (1734–1808), father of William, the journalist who contributed to the Philharmonic Society manifesto. Smart also took lessons from William Cramer and Samuel Arnold. When young, he played the violin in Salomon's orchestra – although his main instrument at the time was the organ. There is a story that, having volunteered to deputise for an absent timpani player, he was given instructions by Haydn as to exactly how the composer wanted the timpani played in one of his London symphonies. Smart developed into a fine keyboard player with a solid, practical understanding of orchestral music. This led him to direct orchestras in the old-fashioned manner, from the piano or harpsichord. In 1811, his travels took him to Dublin, where he directed a series of concerts which so impressed the Lord Lieutenant of Ireland, the Duke of Richmond, that he awarded Smart a knighthood. Smart was a founder member of the Philharmonic Society and directed many of their concerts, including, as we have seen, the London premiere of Beethoven's Ninth Symphony. He was a great Beethoven enthusiast – even travelling to Vienna in 1825 to meet the composer – but for all that he was at heart an oratorio man and a Handelian. And this was why he became a fixture at so many provincial music festivals. Indeed, the list of the festivals over which he presided is staggering – Bath, Berkshire, Bristol, Bury St Edmunds, Cambridge, Derby, Dublin, Edinburgh, Hull, Leeds, Liverpool, Manchester, Newcastle-upon-Tyne, Nottingham and Norwich are all on record.[6] And, of course, they were rarely single visits: he never missed a Liverpool Festival between 1823 and 1836.[7] Smart's commitment was impressive, and so, too, were his earnings. His payment for the 1824 Newcastle Festival was £157 10s, while the boy choristers from Durham

Cathedral had to make do with £3 3s each, although even that was two-and-a-half times a local labourer's weekly wage.

It is perhaps worth noting that all this was before the arrival of the railways. All Greatorex's travelling to and from his provincial festivals, and most of Smart's, was done by horse-drawn carriage or stagecoach. It was slow and uncomfortable but there was no alternative. Once the railways came, travel was transformed. London was connected to Birmingham and Manchester in 1838. There was a line to Bristol by 1841; to Lancaster, Carlisle, Newcastle and, albeit circuitously, to Edinburgh by 1846. Even in their earliest and slowest days, trains would complete the journey in less than half the time of the fastest stagecoach. Train travel offered obvious benefits to high profile soloists travelling from festival to festival, and conductors like Sir Michael Costa (1808–84), who to some extent took over Smart's mantle as the festival director of choice, regularly conducting at Birmingham, Bradford, Leeds, York and elsewhere. It also allowed for larger numbers of people to travel, so groups of musicians, even whole orchestras, could now be moved around the country with comparative ease. Quicker communications, however, did not mean lower fees: for the 1858 Leeds Festival, Costa was paid three hundred guineas.

One might have expected, among this host of new choral societies and festivals, that there would be competition to offer something new or distinctive, but this appears not to have been the case. They seem rather to have competed to be the same. Handel continued to dominate: something that neither Greatorex nor Smart – who were in demand because of their credentials as Handel conductors – would have sought to change. Even Costa, who was regarded as something of a moderniser, went on to conduct the Handel Festivals at the Crystal Palace. For the ordinary people who joined the choral societies and choirs – as for their audiences – Handel was a quite simply a known quantity: beautiful, thrilling, uplifting, but above all familiar. And that made them happy. In the days before recorded sound, the annual repetition of *Messiah* was no stranger than a radio station playing a particular hit song every couple of hours. What we find strange is the length of time that Handel managed to remain at the top of the charts.

British composers were still wary of inviting comparison with the master; yet to write an oratorio was to arrive, and such was the pressure of expectation that most of them tried. Sadly, however, one is faced with another list of composers applying themselves, writing within a recognised structure, but for the most part achieving desperately disappointing results. A few examples will have to stand for many. Crotch wrote two oratorios: *Palestine* (1812) and *The Captivity of Judah* (1834). Of these, *Palestine* has attracted some interest: one slightly insistent chorus, 'Lo! star-led chiefs Assyrian odours bring', is occasionally resurrected during the Christmas season. However, the influence of Handel is only too apparent and only the most dedicated could sustain interest for a full two-and-a-half hours in what is not, in itself, a very dramatic narrative. Gore Ouseley's *Martyrdom of St Polycarp* (1854) can best be described as part imitation Mendelssohn and part imitation Handel. Even Costa had a go with *Eli* (1855) and *Namaan* (1864). Both were written for the Birmingham Festival, which was a recognised testing ground for new choral works right up to the early twentieth century when it premiered Elgar's great oratorios. Rossini's comment on *Eli* says it all: 'The good Costa has sent me an oratorio score and a Stilton cheese. The cheese was very good.'[8] Again, it is easy to be dismissive, but the one thing that all these oratorios share is a lack of conviction on the part of the composer. They do not sparkle. They trudge.

58 Foreign Oratorios, Spohr, and Mendelssohn

Foreign oratorios often fared somewhat better when they were introduced. Smart gave the London premiere of Beethoven's *Mount of Olives* at Drury Lane at the beginning of the Lent oratorio season in 1814, and he repeated it no less than nine times in the run up to Easter. He directed a further performance in Liverpool's Music Hall a few weeks later as part of a series of three benefit concerts. *Mount of Olives* was certainly not unpopular and continued to crop up regularly. It was played in Edinburgh in 1819, revived in Liverpool in 1823 and then revived in London several times during the 1830s. It was played in Manchester and, of course, in Shetland. But it did not disrupt the pattern of Handel-dominated performances. The German composer Louis (originally Ludwig) Spohr – remembered by many only for being sandwiched between Bach and Beethoven in W.S. Gilbert's attempt to make the punishment fit the crime in *The Mikado* – was more successful, at least at first.

Spohr's first visit to England was in 1820 at the invitation of the Philharmonic Society. His conducting, his violin playing and his compositions all attracted widespread but not extravagant praise. By the time of his second visit in 1839, his reputation had grown to the point where he was frequently spoken of in the same breath as Mozart and Beethoven. In the intervening nineteen years, his overture *Alruna, the Owl Queen (Alruna, die Eulenkönigin)* had attracted good audiences and been well received by the critics; excerpts from his operas *Faust* and *Jessonda* had been heard frequently on the concert platform; and arrangements of his works had proved popular among amateur musicians. But the main factor in the transformation of his reputation seems to have been the performance of his oratorio *The Last Judgement (Die letzten Dinge)*, first at the Norwich Festival in September 1830, and then at the Liverpool Festival the following month. 'This oratorio,' raved *The Spectator*, 'we regard as one of the most masterly compositions of the present day.... [It] shows the bold daring of a mind conscious of its own intellectual power, its imaginative resources, and its complete mastery of instrumental effects.'[1] *Harmonicon* agreed. The following year, *The Last Judgement* was given the signal honour of a performance at one of the Philharmonic concerts – the only oratorio ever to have been given there. Over the following six or seven years, it was given at all the Three Choirs venues and many of the major festivals – Dublin, Derby, Manchester, Oxford and York among them – receiving great acclaim all the way.

The Last Judgement was, in essence, a dramatised poetic narrative. The work that followed, *The Crucifixion*, was a sacred drama in which the performers took the role of biblical characters, including Jesus, Mary and the disciples. The first performance in Britain, at London's Hanover Square Rooms in 1837, was uneventful, but a subsequent performance at the Norwich Festival in 1839 was marred by controversy. Even though alterations were made so that Jesus' words were spoken by a narrator, one local vicar declared that anyone attending the oratorio would be damned. The actual performance was a success, but the oratorio was not taken up on the festival circuit for religious rather than musical reasons. The quarterly journal, *The Analyst*, not only complained that 'the author of the words has taken the most insolent liberties with the sacred text', but also that 'by selecting this subject for musical treatment, Spohr has brought himself into direct competition with the most complete of Handel's oratorios' – meaning, of course, *Messiah*.[2] Spohr's third oratorio, *The Fall of Babylon*, was given at Norwich is 1842, and then in London the following year, with Spohr himself conducting. Initial reviews seemed to suggest that his popularity remained unaffected. Indeed, some were positively hyperbolic, but *The Fall of Babylon* never attained the public following of *The Last Judgement*.

Considering the praise he had received, Spohr's reputation declined relatively quickly. In part, this was due to the growing popularity and influence of Mendelssohn, but there is no doubt that Spohr's musical achievements had been overrated. His oratorios continued to be heard in Britain, although nowhere else, right up to the end of the century, and from a later perspective, it is difficult to see why they were seized on with such enthusiasm. Spohr was a talented and often original composer, but in the end he was not a natural oratorio writer. His works for the violin – which was his instrument – are characterised by great smoothness and melodic delicacy, but that was not appropriate for the subject matter of the oratorios. There are some superb moments in *The Crucifixion*, such as when the earthquake strikes, but all too often, particularly in *The Last Judgement*, there is a mismatch between the seriousness of the subject matter and its musical treatment, and a tendency (which may, of course, have appealed to a Victorian audience) to drift towards sentimentality. In the end, Spohr was popular rather than influential. Mendelssohn, by contrast, was both: he influenced a generation of British composers and remained popular with British audiences for much longer. And, for many years, the central plank of that popularity was the one oratorio that came close to matching the appeal of *Messiah*.

Mendelssohn made his first visit to Britain in 1829 at the age of twenty. Articles about his precocious talent had already appeared in *Harmonicon* and the *Quarterly Musical Magazine and Review* so his name was not wholly unfamiliar to the musical public; and when he arrived Karl Klingemann, a diplomat at the Hanoverian Legation whom Mendelssohn had known in Berlin, and Ignaz Moscheles, his old piano teacher now resident in London, quickly engineered his introduction to London's musical and social elite. Within days of his arrival, Mendelssohn met Cramer, Attwood, Smart, the music publisher William Chappell, the Duke of Wellington, Robert Peel, and the Prussian Ambassador. After an initial misunderstanding with Smart, his First Symphony was given at one of the Philharmonic concerts in May, with Mendelssohn himself conducting from the piano. It was an immediate success with both the press and the public. Suddenly, he was a celebrity, almost overwhelmed by musical and social demands. Among many other engagements, he conducted his

Midsummer Night's Dream overture, appeared as soloist in Beethoven's *Emperor Concerto,* and visited the Glee Club, where he met William Horsley. In a matter of weeks, he had become the latest in London's succession of German musical heroes – following Handel, J.C. Bach, Haydn, and Spohr. It was an honour but an exhausting one and, after three months in London, Mendelssohn and Klingemann departed for a tour of Scotland, a journey which was to provide the inspiration for his concert overture *The Hebrides* (popularly known as *Fingal's Cave*) and for his Third (*Scottish*) Symphony.

Over the next eighteen years, Mendelssohn made another nine visits to Britain, embedding himself in both the musical and the social fabric of the country. He became an honorary member of the Philharmonic Society and appeared regularly at the Society's concerts, conducting his own works – among them, those he had written following his Scottish travels, the Fourth (*Italian*) Symphony, and his First Piano Concerto. He also conducted the works of other composers, including Beethoven, Schubert and, programmed for the first time at the Philharmonic, J.S. Bach. He presided at a command performance before Queen Victoria and Prince Albert. He heard William Sterndale Bennett play at a concert in Hanover Square and was so impressed that he went on to become the young man's friend and mentor. Mendelssohn was also invited to Buckingham Palace on a number of occasions where he played and sang together with the royal couple. The invitation certainly confirmed his status as a gentleman – in Victorian eyes, not all musicians were gentlemen – and he fell headlong for the image of the Queen and her Consort as the ideal married couple. It was Queen Victoria's enthusiasm for Mendelssohn that caused the 'Wedding March' from his incidental music to *A Midsummer Night's Dream* to become a fixture at British weddings: in 1858, she insisted that it be played at the marriage of her eldest daughter, Princess Victoria, to Prince Frederick William of Prussia.

Mendelssohn was born into a Jewish family which had converted to Christianity and was himself baptised as a Lutheran at the age of seven. He was not a man of deep religious convictions, but, commissioned to write an oratorio by the conductor and composer, Johann Scheible, he chose the subject of St Paul. Whether the idea of his family's conversion played any part in the choice is impossible to say, but the work did develop a personal significance, becoming a tribute to his father, who died while it was being composed. *St Paul* was premiered in Dusseldorf in May 1836. The first

British performance was at the Liverpool Festival that October, and it was repeated at the Birmingham Festival the following year with Mendelssohn himself conducting (by which time it had already crossed the Atlantic and been played in Boston). The fact that two provincial cities should play the work before it was heard in London no doubt represented a coup for the festival organisers, and it also shows once again how oratorio-centred such regional festivals were.

St Paul was just the kind of thing to appeal to amateur choirs and choral societies: a big work with a compelling narrative and a central role for the chorus. They are a chorus in the Greek sense, commenting on the unfolding of the plot; they are a mob, calling for Paul to be put to death; and, greatly daring, a chorus of women's voices speaks the words of God, asking Saul, 'Why persecutest thou me?' The involvement of the chorus in the drama of the piece recalls Handel; but there are elements of Bach, too, particularly in the way Mendelssohn uses chorale-like passages for emphasis or to move between scenes. This is perhaps not surprising, given Mendelssohn's passion for Bach, and the fact that, in 1829, he had revived the *St Matthew Passion* for the first time in fully a hundred years. In the end, however, *St Paul*, with all its strengths and weaknesses, such as a tendency to slip into easy, almost drawing-room melodies, is very definitely Mendelssohn's own. Perhaps its greatest strength, and the reason for its success in the 1830s, is the way in which it treats the developing narrative as a platform to mount a direct appeal to the religious feelings of the audience.

St Paul was a welcome addition to the repertoire, but Mendelssohn's great oratorio triumph was still to come. *Elijah* was commissioned by the Birmingham Festival, and the first performance was given in Birmingham Town Hall in August 1846. Mendelssohn himself conducted. For the city of Birmingham, it was a great civic occasion. A special train was put on to bring the best musicians from London to strengthen the orchestra. The chorus was nearly three hundred strong. By eleven thirty in the morning, over 2,000 people were in their seats and waiting expectantly. Mendelssohn took his place on the rostrum and the performance began. Eight movements were encored; the performance took over two-and-a-half hours; and the reception at the end was ecstatic. Birmingham had again stolen a march on London. Although his health was not good, Mendelssohn returned to England at the invitation of the Sacred Harmonic Society, the capital's leading choral society, to conduct the

London premiere of the work in April 1847. Again, the reception was rapturous, and one performance rapidly became four, the second of which was attended by the Queen and Prince Albert.

Elijah is both shorter and far more dramatic than *St Paul*. The narrative – a divine curse, a boy raised from the dead, a supernatural duel between God and Baal, an earthquake, Elijah ascending into heaven in a chariot of fire – could have come from a 1950s biblical epic, but it was just the kind of thing to appeal to Victorian audiences. There are a number of flowing arias – including the beautiful 'Hear ye, Israel' which Mendelssohn wrote with the Swedish soprano, Jenny Lind, in mind, although she never sang the role until after his death – and the recitative passages are handled with great imagination. But it is the choral writing that stands out. The choruses are fugal, often recalling Handel, and Mendelssohn creates a special inter-dependence, almost a merging, between the voices and the instrumental lines of the orchestra which is highly effective, especially in the more melodic and lyrical second part. It has been suggested that *Elijah* was tailored specifically to appeal to English taste. On the whole, this seems unlikely. Mendelssohn did not need to modify his style to win over English audiences. Written just a few years earlier in 1844, his anthem, *Hear my prayer*, with its iconic chorus 'O, for the Wings of a Dove' became extraordinarily popular in England, even more popular than *Elijah*. Every young lady of taste kept a copy of the piano arrangement on her instrument, and, in 1928, a recording by the choirboy Ernest Lough became the world's first million-selling record. Yet the anthem was originally written to a German text. Whether or not Mendelssohn had English audiences in mind when he wrote *Elijah*, the oratorio was a triumph, and soon became just as much a fixture at provincial festivals as *Messiah*. That he died just six months after its London premiere, giving a sense that it somehow represented the completion of his labours, may well have added to its popularity. Whatever the reasons, *Elijah* rapidly became far and away the most successful nineteenth-century oratorio.

British devotion to the oratorio continued right up to the end of the century. All the leading British composers – Macfarren, Stainer, Sullivan, Mackenzie, Parry, Stanford – wrote at least one, but the results rarely justified the effort and none came close to the success of *Elijah*. Not until Elgar's *Dream of Gerontius* in 1900 was there an English oratorio that deserved to be called a masterpiece. Ronald Pearsall has described the oratorio as 'a millstone round the neck of Victorian music', and it is hard not to agree.[3]

The strain on the composers was tremendous. Scouring their Bibles for tales which they could adapt, wrestling with librettos which were often stiff and unmusical, they were forced to write in a religious and improving manner, even when it did not suit them. Yet it is hard to see what else they could have done. The public view was that great art ought to be improving; it ought to be moral – even if many of the performers and many of the audience were not – and the oratorio was the best way to achieve this through music. It has been suggested that the strain on the audience was equally great: that many of them sat there, suffering agonies of boredom but dutifully maintaining a façade of interest because that was what family and society expected. No doubt there were a few such, but, even allowing for a degree of Victorian hypocrisy, no musical genre could have maintained such a level of public interest for so long under such circumstances: the oratorio was genuinely popular.

59   Foreign Visitors

Handel and Herschel both made a personal decision to come to England. Haydn was persuaded to come by an opportunist entrepreneur. The attraction was money. They all benefitted from an increasingly open, commercially-oriented economy, offering them opportunities that were simply not available elsewhere in Europe. The coming of the nineteenth century saw a quickening of the pace of industrialisation and social change. London was the heart of an expanding economy and an expanding Empire. It was by far the world's largest city – its population in 1830 was some 1,500,000, as against 785,000 for Paris and 230,000 for Berlin. The social and economic differences between Britain and the rest of Europe were growing and the potential rewards for visiting musicians were, or so it appeared, even greater. It was an indication of the changing times that the majority of such visitors – Mendelssohn was an exception – now came in response to an invitation from an established musical institution. Bodies such as the Philharmonic Society, the Italian Opera, the Royal Opera, or the major regional music festivals now had the resources to commission works, organise concerts and look after the musical and financial interests of those they had invited.

Gioachino Rossini (1792–1868) was undoubtedly the most famous opera composer of the day and it was something of a coup for Giovanni Benelli, the manager of the Italian Opera at the King's Theatre, to have persuaded him to come to Britain at all. Rossini's contract offered him generous terms to conduct eight of his operas during the season and to write two new works. Unfortunately, things did not go quite as planned. Crossing the Channel in a storm in December 1823, Rossini and his wife, the Spanish coloratura soprano, Isabella Colbran (1785–1845) were both severely sick – so severely in Rossini's case that, once in London, he took to his bed for a week. Once recovered, he and Colbran travelled down to Brighton where – courtesy of the Russian Ambassador, whom Rossini had known in Verona – they were presented to King George IV. London society took note. All doors were suddenly open to this jovial Italian and his beautiful wife. They were caught up in a time-consuming, and also lucrative, whirl of social and professional activity. They attended innumerable private parties where they sang and played the piano, charging their hosts £50 (and sometimes even more) for the privilege. Rossini travelled to Cambridge to appear at the festival there. He directed several benefit concerts at Almack's, and, as required by his contract, he conducted at the Italian Opera, where he won praise for the way he managed to improve the orchestral playing. But no new opera was forthcoming. Before long, the atmosphere began to sour: the press were beginning to mock Rossini's greed and to find some of his performances too histrionic. *Harmonicon* mocked 'the risque he encountered, and the inconvenience he endured, in crossing the abominable Straits of Dover.'[1]

Seven months after their arrival and richer to the tune of some £7,000, Rossini and Colbran abruptly departed for Paris where he had been offered a post at the Académie Royale. He left behind the manuscript of an unfinished opera, *Ugo, re d'Italia*, as surety for a return that never happened. Benelli went bankrupt six months later. From Rossini's point of view the visit had presumably been a success, but something in the way he was treated in England seems to have got under his skin. At least, his next opera, *Il viaggio a Reims*, written to mark the accession of the French King, Charles X, transparently mocks English musicality (or the lack of it) in the character of Lord Sidney, who only knows one tune, which is, of course, 'God Save the King.'

The Royal Opera at Covent Garden did only slightly better with their invitation to Carl Maria von Weber (1786–1826). They commissioned him to write a new opera and to come to London to conduct the premiere. The opera was *Oberon*, a three-act work with spoken dialogue after the English fashion. Weber had written nine previous operas, but his reputation rested on the success of *Der Freischütz* in 1823. He arrived in England in 1826, already suffering from tuberculosis and having undertaken the commission against his doctor's advice, because he believed that a success in London would solve his financial problems. Once again, however, things did not go according to plan. The premiere of *Oberon*, in April, was a success, although the composer was close to exhaustion. Unused to the ways of English performers, he had had to struggle to realise the opera on stage as he had written it. Then, a benefit concert on which Weber had been pinning his financial hopes was affected by rain and by competing concerts given on the same day. It raised less than £100. In the end, sadly, it did not matter. Weber died in the house of Sir George Smart, where he was staying, just over a week later. The Royal Opera had its opera, and a successful one despite a rather weak libretto, but it had lost its composer.

Just seven weeks before Rossini's rapid departure for Paris in 1824, the twelve-year-old Franz Liszt (1811–86) made his London debut in the Argyll Rooms, at a recital organised by the Royal Society of Musicians.[2] He returned a couple of weeks later to play Hummel's Piano Concert no. 3 under the direction of Sir George Smart. There was a larger concert at Drury Lane, and then Liszt and his father headed for Manchester where he played at the Theatre Royal. Reports of Liszt's precocious talent aroused the interest of George IV, who issued an invitation – effectively a command – for him to come and play at Windsor Castle. Liszt played for almost two hours with barely a pause. This was the first of a number of visits Liszt made to Britain between 1824 and 1841, during what are commonly called his virtuoso years, all characterised by an intense programme of touring and playing. The last of these tours, in 1840–41, was particularly gruelling. It took in no less than sixty-five towns and cities across England, Ireland and Scotland – everywhere from the Isle of Wight to Glasgow and from Kilkenny to Hull. Financially, however, it was not a huge success: the Dublin concert attracted an audience of 1,200 but one in Bridgewater only thirty. After 1841, there was a gap of forty-five years before he returned. By that time he was the doyen of European music, his every engagement reported in detail in the *Musical Times*.[3] He died just three months later.

Spohr, Rossini and Mendelssohn were received as composers who also played. Liszt's reputation as a composer only really developed in the 1850s. As a youth and then a young adult, he toured constantly for over twenty years before choosing to devote himself to composing and, later, taking holy orders. On his early visits to Britain, therefore, he was presented as a performer, a virtuoso pianist who both shocked and amazed. It is hard to reconstruct the piano style of a man who died before recording was possible, but the descriptions of Liszt's performances abound with adjectives suggesting just how different he was: wild, extravagant, loud, extreme, spectacular, violent, torrential, frenzied. Undoubtedly, he was a showman, and undoubtedly pianos broke under the physical force, the sheer violence, of his playing. It has been suggested that it was Liszt's playing that led piano manufacturers to change to metal rather than wooden frames. Undoubtedly also, he was one of the first international stars: some of his female admirers really did swoon with emotion and struggle to get hold of handkerchiefs or broken piano strings as souvenirs – although (*pace* Ken Russell's 1975 film, *Lisztomania*) this aspect of his celebrity has probably been rather exaggerated. His repertoire was varied. He did play some of his own compositions, but more often he played his own transcriptions of works by other composers – Schubert, Beethoven, Bellini, Donizetti, Berlioz, and many others. Liszt's unique style was such that (unlike Mendelssohn's piano works, for example) there was no boom in the sales of sheet music; and his major compositions were not written until he had ceased to perform in Britain. His oratorio, *The Legend of St Elizabeth*, was given during his last visit in 1886 – and in the presence of Queen Victoria – but Liszt himself did not conduct. That honour went to Sir George Smart. Liszt's influence on Britain, at least in his lifetime, was to change the way audiences looked at classical performance. Celebrity singers had been a feature of opera since Handel's time, and instrumental virtuosi were not new, but Liszt took the cult of musical stardom to a new level: he romanticised it. One only has to look at the way Paganini was presented when he made his first visit to London in 1831: he had been a political prisoner; he had been locked in a cell for twenty years with only a broken violin with one string to play on. None of it was true, of course, but the publicity turned Paganini into a romantic hero. As a result, he was mobbed in the streets and able to charge huge fees. Liszt made such things possible. Show business had arrived.

Richard Wagner (1813–83) made his first visit to Britain in August 1839. He was not responding to an invitation, but money was certainly on his mind: he and his wife Minna were fleeing from debts they had accumulated in Riga. The nine-day voyage to London was so stormy it actually inspired *The Flying Dutchman* (*Der Fliegende Holländer*). On arrival, Wagner tried to find Sir George Smart – to whom, two years previously, he had sent the score of his *Rule Britannia Overture* asking for it to be passed to the Philharmonic Society. He also tried to find Sir Edward Bulwer-Lytton, whose novel, *Rienzi*, he had already begun turning into an opera. Neither was in London. After a few days wandering around rather aimlessly, Wagner and his wife left for Paris. It was a singularly ineffectual visit.

Sixteen years later, in 1855, Wagner returned. This time he had been invited by the Philharmonic to conduct the season's eight concerts. It was a slightly grudging invitation. Costa had resigned; neither Spohr nor Berlioz were available; so Wagner was asked as a fourth choice. What he really wanted to do was finish scoring *Die Walküre*, but, as always, he was desperate for money, and he also hoped that the visit might lead to one of his operas being staged in London, so he accepted. Wagner was already a controversial figure, but by reputation only. Neither his music, nor his writings were at all well known. There was no compelling reason why he should not have become the next German musical hero. The first concert, which included works by Haydn, Mozart, Spohr and Mendelssohn, was received positively by the audience, and, although reviews were mixed, the balance was in Wagner's favour. After that, however, things began to go downhill. An article by James Davison, editor of the *Musical World*, raised the issue of Wagner's anti-Semitic views which, given that many people – including Davison himself – still venerated Mendelssohn, was bound to cause trouble.[4] The selections from *Lohengrin* and *Tannhäuser* that featured in the concerts were not well understood. They were not as shocking as many had feared or been led to expect, but to unaccustomed ears they were noisy, unmelodic, even dull. There were apparent strains in the relationship between Wagner and the Philharmonic Orchestra, based on his insistence on certain *tempi* which were often slower than what was considered usual. None of these issues need necessarily have been fatal to Wagner's cause had he taken the trouble to explain himself, or spell out his ideas, but he did not. And this points to another sign of the changing times.

The first half of the nineteenth century saw a huge growth in the consumption of printed material. Daily papers, evening papers, weeklies, and specialist magazines were all booming, and the opinions expressed in these publications influenced people's views, attitudes and even their actions to a new and unprecedented degree. By the time of Wagner's visit, both *Harmonicon* and the *Quarterly Musical Magazine and Review* had ceased publication, but new magazines had sprung up. Music critics had the opportunity to express their views – and at far greater length than would be normal today – and their views went a long way towards shaping the climate of critical opinion in the country as a whole. In this context, it was perhaps unfortunate that the two most influential critics were Henry Chorley of the *Athenaeum*, and James Davison, who was on the staff of *The Times* as well as the *Musical World*. Both men were distinctly conservative in their tastes – Chorley often grumpily so.

Wagner's concerts with the Philharmonic, and Wagner himself, were the subject of articles in, among others, the *Morning Post*, the *Daily News*, *The Times*, the *Sunday Times*, the *Illustrated London News*, *The Spectator*, the *Musical World* and the *Athenaeum*. Given the influence that music critics now exercised, it had become accepted (and sensible) for composers and conductors to meet them socially, to get to know them, to discuss forthcoming concerts and talk about the works which were to be performed. This Wagner refused to do, partly from a failure to understand what was expected of him and partly out sheer stubbornness. It is all very well for Wagner's biographer, Ernest Newman, to characterise the critics as 'men of ordinary intelligence brought face to face, for the first time in their professional lives, with a contemporary phenomenon that was extraordinary, and failing to see how much bigger it was than themselves,'[5] but Wagner did not help: he did nothing to make the critics less critical. At the end of the season, he left London in a climate of hostility and misunderstanding. As a result, appreciation of his music was set back many years: the first Wagner opera was not staged in Britain until 1870 when *The Flying Dutchman* was performed at Drury Lane – and even then, bizarrely, it was sung in Italian.

Wagner did return to London, twenty-two years later, in 1877, to conduct eight concerts at the Royal Albert Hall in a month-long Wagner Festival. The organiser was the great conductor Hans Richter. All accounts suggest that it was Richter's tact in handling the composer, together with his ability to give the orchestra a sense of what Wagner wanted from them when Wagner himself failed to do so, that held the Festival together. Wagner's earlier operas were better known by this time, but the newer works proved too difficult for many and there are accounts of the audience leaving the hall when faced with excerpts from *Das Rheingold*. In the end, the Festival was not actually a failure – at least, it did not lose money – but it did little to enhance Wagner's reputation in Britain. One person who was enthused, and would never forget the sight and the excitement of Wagner conducting, was a young, aspiring composer called Hubert Parry.

Wagner remains a figure of contradictions. In total, he spent no more than a few months in England, but he still managed to create controversy and alienate a substantial proportion of musical society. That did not, however, prevent him from going on to become a major influence on later generations of British composers. Hector Berlioz (1803–69), by contrast, spent much longer in the country, making a series of five visits during the 1840s and 1850s. He ruffled few feathers, but left no lasting influence. In one sense, this was surprising because Berlioz, in his day, was seen as almost as radical a composer as Wagner. Indeed, Wagner explicitly acknowledged the influence of Berlioz on his own work. *Harmonicon* gave its readers an indication of how Berlioz was regarded in 1828: 'The French journals tell us that a M. Berlioz ... had the courage to give a concert ... consisting entirely of his own compositions. The room ... was almost a desert. No wonder, when so wild an animal is master of ceremonies.'[6] The *Symphonie Fantastique* was first performed two years later in 1830, just six years after the premiere of Beethoven's Ninth. Its five-movement structure, programmatic narrative, and exuberant orchestration was genuinely new and, to some, genuinely shocking. By 1847, when he finally signed a contract to come to London, Berlioz was in his mid-forties and both he and the British press had perhaps mellowed. The contract was with Louis-Antoine Jullien, a former teacher at the Paris Conservatoire, who had been promoting promenade concerts in London and had now taken a lease on Drury Lane to promote opera (see Chapter 66). The contract was for six years. Berlioz would conduct the opera season at Drury Lane, conduct four additional concerts of his own works, and write a new opera for performance in 1849. That was the theory. As it turned out, he conducted some of the Drury Lane season and two concerts of his own works before Jullien was declared bankrupt and Berlioz found himself stranded.

Berlioz wrote no new music while he was in London, and the trip was certainly not a financial success, but he did come to know and understand London society better than many other musical visitors. England had had a special significance for him ever since 1827 when he had seen the actress Harriet Smithson playing Ophelia and Juliet in Paris. His obsession with Smithson led, eventually, to a disastrous marriage – which had broken up some years before his eventual arrival in London – but his devotion to Shakespeare never left him, and Shakespeare inspired some of his greatest works. Finding himself warmly welcomed by all sections of the capital's musical society, Berlioz was in a frame of mind to respond positively. On his return to Paris in July 1848, he told Liszt that he was 'in a very good position in England'; that he was 'carried in triumph by the entire press … [and had] left many supporters in London, a few friends, and many people with their mouths gaping.'[7]

A second visit followed in 1851. This was less musical than bureaucratic in character since he had been asked by the French Minister for Trade to be part of the international jury judging musical instruments at the Great Exhibition. During the trip, Berlioz wrote a series of five letters to the French newspaper, *Journal des Débats*, again taking a very positive view of English attitudes to music. A third visit, in 1852, was his most successful in musical terms. He signed a contract with Frederick Beale to give six concerts at Exeter Hall on the Strand for the first season of the New Philharmonic Society, which had just been set up, not so much to complete with the existing Philharmonic as to offer a somewhat more contemporary repertoire. Berlioz regarded the season, which included two performances of Beethoven's *Choral Symphony*, as an unqualified success. He returned in 1853 to conduct his opera, *Benvenuto Cellini*, at Covent Garden. This time, however, Berlioz was unlucky. The opening night became the subject of organised disruption and he withdrew the opera immediately. This had nothing to do with Berlioz, and everything to do with the financial situation of the theatre and rivalry between London's operatic cliques. Perhaps surprisingly, the experience did not embitter him as far as England was concerned, and he came back two years later. Again, the visit was slightly spoiled by feuding, this time between institutions and promoters. Berlioz conducted the New Philharmonic, while Wagner conducted the original Philharmonic. All went well and, although he turned down the post of conductor at the Crystal Palace, there was a suggestion at this stage that he might settle permanently in London. He returned to Paris, clearly intending to come back when he could, but somehow things got in the way and the 1855 visit was his last.

Berlioz did all the right things. He was friendly with Chorley, with Davison, and with George Hogarth, the Secretary of the Philharmonic Society and music critic of the *Daily News*. His concerts were well attended; apart from the debacle surrounding *Benvenuto Cellini*, his music was well received; and he seems to have been generally popular. Yet he left no obvious traces, no readily apparent influence on British music. Nor did

Chopin (1810–49), who came in 1848, already sick with tuberculosis, and desperate for money. He gave a handful of concerts in Edinburgh, Glasgow and London, but he was already a dying man, and his final concert in London that November, given for the Friends of Poland, was his last ever public performance. Nor, indeed, did a host of lesser-known figures whose names can be added to the list of musicians who came from abroad to live, to work, or just to visit: Jan Dussek (1760–1812), Ludwig Berger (1777–1839), Ferdinand Ries (1784–1838), Cesare Pugni (1802–70), Vincenzo Bellini (1801–35), Vinzenz Lachner (1811–93), Sigismund Thalberg (1812–71), and Ferdinand Praeger (1815–93).

The failure of any of these figures to make any lasting impact on musical life in Britain is, in one sense at least, less important than the fact that they came at all. Their motives may have been financial, but their presence undoubtedly added to the richness of the musical mix in the country. Britain did not produce composers of the stature of Wagner or Berlioz, or virtuosi with the genius of Liszt or Paganini, but it was certainly not a musical backwater. 'I am convinced that there is no city in the world where as much music is consumed as in London,' Berlioz wrote in one of his newspaper articles.[8] He was even, unlike some, complimentary about 'The London public [which] is very attentive and serious in its tastes.... I have been able to see for myself its excellent qualities.'[9] On the whole, British taste, whether in London or in the provinces, was conservative – which naturally threw men like Wagner into a rage. At the same time, regional music festivals and London music societies were just as ready – perhaps even more likely – to commission works from foreign composers as they were from British ones; and audiences throughout the country were thoroughly accustomed to concert programmes made up principally of music by leading Continental composers. Of course, there were gripes: the standard of orchestra playing came in for regular criticism, as did the attitude of some so-called patrons, whose interest in concerts and *soirées* was social rather than musical. Nonetheless, there was an openness, a richness and a depth to British musical life to match any country in Europe. The problem was what that meant for home-grown talent.

Music in Britain was flourishing. British music was not. Were British composers simply inferior? Or were they not given a chance in an environment that favoured foreign music and foreign musicians? In 1823, a concert series devoted to British music opened, but barely lasted the season. Its failure sparked debate in the music press of the day (in which the term 'English' was generally preferred to 'British'). *Harmonicon* was characteristically grumpy. There was nothing to stop English composers being heard as often as foreign ones. There were plenty of opportunities if they were good enough, but they were not. *Quarterly Musical Magazine and Review* was less sure. It carried articles entitled 'On the Present State of Vocal Art in England' (by 'An Englishman') and 'On the Present State of Music in England' (by 'An Observer').[1] Both were critical, but looked for reasons for current English failures: the need for a stronger national academy, or the neglect of church choirs. A few years later, in 1828, the same magazine, assessing the state of music in London, considered that 'the access of foreign professors, both vocal and instrumental, has been absolutely multitudinous – so much so indeed as to wholly eclipse, if not annihilate, the exertions of the native musician.'[2]

There is no doubt that there was a degree of prejudice against British composers on the part of both concert promoters and audiences. One only has to consider the comparative ease with which the newly-arrived and scarcely-known Mendelssohn, a composer with no track record in Britain, got his First Symphony played at the Philharmonic, and the reaction it provoked. Would a young British composer have received the same treatment and been received with the same enthusiasm? It must be highly doubtful. Faced with this kind of prejudice; overwhelmed by the number of foreign musicians; lacking the guidance and inspiration that had once come from the Church, the Chapel Royal and the Court; oppressed by the oratorio; still apprehensive of the essential foreignness of the symphony, and of the lack of a native tradition of symphony-writing, British music was, hardly surprisingly, at something of a low ebb. Yet there were composers whose music is worth considering – and, indeed, worth listening to – both for its own sake and for the pointers it offers for the development of British music throughout the rest of the century.

Thomas Forbes Walmisley (1783–1866) was a well-known London

organist and teacher. He was also a composer of glees – he became the secretary of Concentores Sodales and was elected a member of the Glee Club – and of church music. As a young man, he had been taught by Thomas Attwood, which explains why he chose to baptise his eldest son Thomas Attwood Walmisley. In fact, the Walmisleys were something of a clan. Thomas Forbes had twelve children – among them Frederick (1815–75), a well-known artist, and Henry (1830–57), a London church organist. He also had a brother, Edward, who was chorister in his youth and a recognised tenor when he grew older, but made his living as a parliamentary clerk. Edward, too, had a number of children, and, for some years, both families appear to have lived together in the same, presumably very crowded house in North Street, Westminster.

In all probability, Thomas Attwood Walmisley (1814–56) began learning music with his father, who was organist at St Martin-in-the-Fields for forty years, but his first formal lessons were with his godfather, Thomas Attwood, who managed a total of forty-two years as organist at St Paul's Cathedral. By the time he was eighteen, in 1832, Walmisley was an accomplished organist. He had also written two string quartets – which, considering the comparative newness of the form and the paucity of English examples, shows enterprise – as well as a symphony (of which Mendelssohn was dismissive), and two organ concertos. The manager of the King's Theatre, an eccentric Irishman named Monck Mason, who later became famous as both a balloonist and a theologian, tried to persuade him to write an opera, but Walmisley was not to be tempted. His musical enthusiasm was matched by a passion for mathematics and he decided to go to Cambridge University to study. A year later, aged nineteen, he was elected organist at Trinity and St John's College. He also took on the duties of organist at St John's College and at Great St Mary's, the University Church, playing for as many as eight services on a Sunday. Aged twenty, he composed his eight-part Service in B flat, which contains some fine dynamic passages in the *Nunc Dimittis* and the *Magnificat*, and which immediately marked him as a composer of more apparent conviction than most of his contemporaries. Aged twenty-one, he deputised for the Professor of Music, Dr John Clarke-Whitfield (1770–1836), writing an ode for the occasion of the installation of a new Chancellor of the University. The following year, aged just twenty-two, he was himself appointed Professor of Music, and he remained at Cambridge until his early death in 1856 – an event apparently hastened by a fondness for the college port.

The ode was by now a distinctly old-fashioned genre, but Cambridge University was a conservative institution and it was expected that the Professor of Music would write one to mark the installation of a new Chancellor. This happened three times during Walmisley's career, and his compositions show both his technical abilities and a degree of political awareness. On the first occasion, his ode was Handelian in character: a sensible choice for a young composer seeking to make a name for himself in a conservative institution. On the second occasion, 1842, he showed a gentle modernising tendency, taking Mozart as his model. The third time, in 1847, he took careful account of the known preferences of the new Chancellor, Prince Albert, and his ode clearly showed the influence of Mendelssohn. As Professor, Walmisley was distinguished by his advocacy of Bach, telling his students that Bach's Mass in B minor was the greatest musical composition ever written – an attitude which again put him well ahead of most of his contemporaries.

Walmisley's reputation today rests not on his odes or his teaching, but on a handful of works for the church, the main one being his *Evening Service in D minor*. This is a small gem. One senses the Anglican Service being lifted out of its eighteenth-century rut. The *Magnificat* alternates in a most effective manner between passages of serenity and of great, full-chorus grandeur; and the setting as a whole breaks new ground by giving greater thematic prominence to the organ. Parts of this Service, particularly the *Magnificat* and the *Nunc Dimittis*, are still heard today. Perhaps discouraged by Mendelssohn's reaction to his youthful symphony, Walmisley never really ventured into the field of orchestral music, but, in addition to his compositions for the church, he did leave two remarkable chamber pieces – sonatinas for oboe and piano, written for a Cambridge student and oboist called Alfred Pollock. These, by their nature, are small-scale pieces, but they are tuneful and intricate and demonstrate that, whatever held Walmisley back from writing more, whether it was college port or the oppressively conservative atmosphere of Cambridge, he did have a remarkable musical gift.

Samuel Sebastian Wesley (1810–76) was the son of Samuel Wesley, (whom we met in Volume One, Chapter 53) and is usually referred to as Sebastian to distinguish him from his father. Like his father, he was something of a child prodigy and grew into a remarkable composer – arguably the most original composer of church music since Purcell. However, he was also like his father in having strong personal beliefs, which he expressed directly and forcefully, and which, needless to say, did not go down well with the Church and musical establishment. He was a chorister at the Chapel Royal from the age of ten, and his solo singing earned praise from George IV. As a teenager, he held several appointments as organist at churches in and around London, and he also dabbled in incidental music for the theatre, but the Wesley sense of religious and musical conviction directed his career and, in 1832, he took up the post of organist at Hereford Cathedral. From Hereford in 1835 he moved to Exeter Cathedral, and it was during his seven-year tenure in Exeter that he took his doctorate in music at Oxford, for which he composed the anthem, *O Lord, thou art my God*. This is a large-scale work. It is full of changing textures, and builds through a series of impressive choruses, written for double choir and five voices, to a resounding climax. What is notable here, and in so much of Wesley's work, is his confidence in creating vocal effects that match and amplify the meaning of the text. From Exeter, in 1842, he moved on to Leeds Parish Church. In career terms, this may appear a step down, but Leeds, an increasingly important and wealthy city, had both an excellent church choir and a well-established choral society of which Wesley immediately became conductor. By this time, he was widely acknowledged as the best organist in the country, but his capacity for upsetting those in authority was beginning to show.

In 1845, having been passed over for the Professorship of Music at Edinburgh University – despite a glowing testimonial from Spohr – Wesley produced his Service in E, which, even more than Walmisley's D minor Service, exposed the shortcomings of most other Anglican church music of the age. Again, it is a big work, almost representing a return to the concept of the 'Great Service' as composed by Byrd and Tompkins. Like Walmisley, Wesley gives considerable importance to the organ, but the work stands out in comparison with other settings of the Service principally for its imaginative and dramatic qualities. It is full of big, uplifting melodies and climaxes that escalate in intensity as the work progresses, all supported by Wesley's characteristic precision in handling his text. He also drew on modern stylistic developments, such as those of Spohr, and largely ignored Handel. It was one thing to demonstrate the inadequacy of contemporary church and cathedral music in his compositions; it was quite another to spell out the Church's failings and his views on them in stark prose with detailed examples, but that is exactly what Wesley did in his Preface when the D minor Service was published. Four years later, he compounded the offence with *A Few Words on Cathedral Music*, a pamphlet which suggested that the Church's musical ills might be remedied if the authorities recognised the true status of cathedral organists and gave them appropriate financial rewards. Only then would there be a true revival of music in the Anglican Church.

Despite friction with the authorities, Wesley seems to have been happy at Leeds, but in 1849 he moved to Winchester, where he would stay for the next sixteen years. The salary was significantly lower, but as organist at Winchester College as well as the Cathedral he could educate his sons at no cost. Moreover, the advent of the railway meant that he could accept a concurrent position as Professor of Organ at the RAM while still living in Winchester. *Twelve Anthems*, which Wesley regarded as his most important publication, appeared in 1853 – although it is an indication of his poor standing with some in the church hierarchy that the Dean and Chapter of St Paul's refused to join the subscription list. In general, however, during the Winchester years, Wesley seems to have begun to lose interest in his work. He had always been a keen fisherman, but fishing and sailing began to take up more of his time, perhaps, as he later claimed, because he found Winchester society unsympathetic and lacking in good musicians. He certainly grasped the opportunity to move to Gloucester when it was offered in 1865. This allowed him to fulfil a senior role at the increasingly influential Three Choirs Festival, conducting his own work, some anthems by his father, and works by his friend Spohr. He also conducted the first performance outside London of Bach's *St Matthew Passion* – Bach's music being a passion apparently inherited from his father. One pointer to the future came at the Gloucester Three Choirs of 1868 when Wesley, who had a keen ear for new music as well as old, promoted the performance of a piece called *Intermezzo Religioso* by a wholly unknown – and at that stage amateur – composer called Hubert Parry. Some degree of official recognition came in 1873 when Wesley received a Civil List pension of £100 a year,[3] but by that time he was ill with a progressive kidney disease. He died just three years later.

Apart from the Service in E, Wesley composed a Short Service in F and a Chant Service, also in F. These works proved popular in the Church of England. Indeed, their popularity continued to grow well into the twentieth century, only falling off in the years after the Second World War.[4] He also wrote a number of attractive organ voluntaries, some small-scale organ works, and, of course, many hymn tunes, but he was never, or so it appears, tempted to write an oratorio. In the end, however, his reputation as a composer rests on his anthems, of which there are twenty-six. Throughout his life, Wesley insisted on the importance of cathedral music and most of his anthems reflect a Victorian notion of importance: they are designed to impress, in both conception and execution. *O Lord, thou art my God* and *Let us lift up our heart* are both some twenty minutes long and difficult to fit into any normal service. *Praise the Lord, O give thanks,* and *The Wilderness* are a little shorter but equally grand in conception. Wesley frequently makes use of recitative in his anthems, combining it with arias and big, often double, choruses to give a sense of the dramatic qualities of the text he is setting. If such a distinction can be made, his anthems appear to progress through illustration of the text rather than development of a musical theme. His emphasis on words and meaning included careful editing of the biblical text, so that he could focus on both the message and the drama that conveyed it. This is particularly clear in *The Wilderness*. There is also a strong sense – arguably not matched in any other composer of church music until Herbert Howells – that Wesley was writing with an awareness of the physical environment in which his music would be performed; that he knew how it would sound in the echoing nave of a cathedral or in a large parish church. Yet he did not have to compose on a grand scale to be successful or effective. *Cast me not away,* an unaccompanied six-part anthem which owes a great deal to his awareness of Renaissance polyphony, is a small masterpiece. Reputedly written while Wesley was recovering from a badly broken leg sustained in a fall while fishing for trout, it contains the words 'the bones which Thou hast broken', which are set to strange, unexpected chromatic chords.

Wesley stood out from the complacencies of the Church of England because of the quality of his music and his conviction that church music really mattered. His prefaces, pamphlets and outspoken attacks on the church authorities were heartfelt, but in the end had little, if any, effect – beyond perhaps reinforcing resistance to change on the part of those he attacked. When the revival of Anglican music for which he called so publicly did take place – beginning, as we shall see, in the middle decades of the nineteenth century – it was the result of a spiritual and doctrinal renewal within the Church and it took a different direction, favouring simplicity rather than the dramatic and imaginative complexities of Wesley.

Away from church music, it was very hard for young composers to stand out from the crowd, and even harder for them to get a hearing. From the early generations of students who attended the RAM two names stand out: William Sterndale Bennett and George Alexander Macfarren. Their careers have much in common. Both men had something to say musically and made their mark as composers at a comparatively young age. At the same time, both were passionately committed to raising standards of musical education and performance, a commitment that saw them rise to the top of Britain's musical establishment. The fact that neither of them achieved greatness as composers, and that their music is not well known today, may well be as much the fault of the times in which they lived as the result of decisions they made themselves.

John Bennett (1754–1837) was a Derbyshire tailor who played oboe in what seems to have been a West Gallery church band. He was also a fine bass, and the quality of his singing led to him being offered the position of lay clerk at King's College and Trinity College, Cambridge. Two of his six sons became choristers at King's, and the younger of those two, Robert Bennett (1788–1819), went on to study under Clarke-Whitfield. In 1811, he was appointed organist at St Peter's, the Parish Church of Sheffield – later to become the city's Cathedral – where he wrote songs and glees, taught piano and became part of the town's musical life. His third child and only son was William Sterndale Bennett (1816–75), born in Sheffield and into a family that was musical but in no sense influential.

Robert Bennett died when his son was only three and the boy was sent to Cambridge to be brought up by his grandfather. He became a chorister at King's, but his talent was such that at the age of ten he was sent to the RAM in London. He had a remarkable alto voice and Attwood frequently asked him to sing with the choir of St Paul's. He was also called upon to sing glees on less formal occasions. He could play violin well enough to be included in the Academy orchestra when it played for operas at the King's Theatre, but his real talent was for the piano and for composition. His piano teacher for the first seven years after his arrival in London was William Henry Holmes (1812–85). Composition lessons with Crotch did not last quite as long. Crotch was by now in his fifties and his teaching methods, which were geared towards church music, were highly conservative. Moreover, he disliked Mozart for whom the young Bennett had already developed an enthusiasm. A change of tutor became necessary. Cipriani Potter took over. He shared Bennett's enthusiasm for Mozart, and it was his encouragement that led directly to Bennett performing his Piano Concerto no. 1 in D minor at an Academy Concert at the Hanover Rooms in 1832. For a sixteen-year-old, the Concerto is a remarkably assured work. The influence of both Mozart and Beethoven is apparent, but there is genuine musical invention and an impressive control of the interplay between the soloist and the orchestra. There are some fine quiet passages in the Second Movement (Andante Sostenuto), and the Finale (Presto-Scherzo) has all the rhythm and vigour that was missing from most British music of the time. When the Concerto was repeated in June the following year, again at the Hanover Rooms, Mendelssohn was in the audience. He suggested that Bennett should study in Leipzig. Bennett had no money but, encouraged, he embarked on a period of what must have been almost frenzied composition. In the next three years, he wrote five symphonies, several concert overtures – including *Parisina* and *The Naiads* – and two more piano concertos. An indication of just how well he was regarded at this stage in his career – he was twenty in April 1836 – is given by the fact that both concertos were premiered at Philharmonic concerts, at a time when the Society was generally reluctant to programme works by new British composers.

In the autumn of 1836, Bennett eventually made his way to Leipzig, which was – and for the next fifty years would remain – the musical capital of northern Europe. In what may well have been one of the first examples of commercial sponsorship, the piano makers Broadwood had offered to meet his expenses for a year. Mendelssohn, with whom he had remained in close touch, was by that time musical director of the Gewandhaus Orchestra and had no difficulty in arranging for Bennett's music to be programmed. Bennett was soloist in his Piano Concerto no. 3 in C minor, directing the orchestra from the piano, and conducted his overture, *The Naiads*. The German audience, accustomed to the idea of Britain as musically backward, were surprised, even overwhelmed. Schumann, to whom Bennett was introduced by Mendelssohn, wrote fulsomely – perhaps too fulsomely – in his praise and even dedicated his own *Etudes Symphoniques* to the young Englishman. Once his year was over, Bennett returned to London to begin teaching at the RAM, but he was able to make a second visit to Leipzig in 1838. This time he played his Piano Concerto no. 4 in F minor and conducted another concert overture, *The Wood Nymphs*, again at the Gewandhaus. A third visit to Leipzig took place in 1842. This one seems to have been more significant for what he heard than what he played. He attended a series of chamber concerts put on by Ferdinand David, a violin virtuoso and composer, who was also Concert Master at the Gewandhaus. This inspired Bennett to organise his own series of chamber concerts in London, featuring solo piano music and piano ensembles. These concerts reflected his growing interest in promoting the work of lesser-known composers, which at the time included J. S. Bach – for Bennett was another of those who became fascinated by Bach's music – and, in 1849, he founded the Bach Society as a way of bringing together all those who shared his interest. He also used the concerts to introduce new artists, such as Jenny Lind, the violin virtuoso Joseph Joachim, and Clara Schumann, to London audiences.

There can be no doubt that Bennett enjoyed his success in Germany, but after 1842 he never returned there. His music continued to be played in Leipzig: between 1837 and 1857, there were only two seasons when at least one of his compositions did not feature on a Gewandhaus programme.[1] Back in Britain, however, he plunged into official musical life. He was Director of the Philharmonic from 1842 to 1848, and then again from 1856 to 1866; Director of Queen's College, London, from 1848; Professor of Music at Cambridge from 1856 to 1866; Principal of the RAM from 1866; and, of course, conductor at any number of musical festivals up and down the country. In 1853, he actually turned down an offer – quite unprecedented in that it had never been made to any foreigner – to become Concert Master at the Gewandhaus. He had become the pivot around which British musical life revolved, and his efforts were rewarded in 1871 with a knighthood. Yet, busy as he was, it is perhaps strange that a man in his position should not have made time to return to Germany, if he really wanted to.

What effect Leipzig had on Bennett is difficult to gauge, mainly because, after 1840, he composed very little for something like fifteen years. There were some songs (most with German texts), a few piano pieces, and a handful of anthems for formal occasions. It is usual to ascribe this sudden slowdown to the demands of his teaching and administrative commitments and, no doubt, they must have taken up a significant proportion of his time. But another possibility is that Bennett may have suffered some kind of loss of confidence. Having been prolific and successful in his youth, he was now faced with the hard realities of British musical life. Once he had become an established figure, British critics did not respond with the same enthusiasm as their German counterparts. It is even possible that the German connection provoked jealousy in some quarters. Bennett's overture *The Wood Nymphs*, to take just one example, was written for performance in Leipzig in 1838, where it was received with great applause and was praised to the skies by Schumann. When it was given in London, however, the critics dismissed it as noisy and incomprehensible. Then, in 1843, the year after his final visit to Leipzig, Bennett applied for the position of Professor of Music at Edinburgh University, but, despite the almost passionate advocacy of Mendelssohn, he did not succeed. Of course, he more than compensated in terms of official appointments in the years that followed, but he was a complex character, known to be intensely self-critical, and several commentators have pointed to the fact that, having lost his parents at a very early age, his nature was one which constantly sought approval. It would not be surprising if his confidence was affected when early successes met a sudden check.

When Bennett did return to composition in the mid-1850s, he was not the same force. Perhaps attempting to respond to public taste, he turned to choral music, composing a cantata, *The May Queen*, based on Tennyson's poem of the same name, for the opening of Leeds Town Hall in 1858, and an oratorio, *The Woman of Samaria,* for the Birmingham Festival of 1867. Both works were popular in their day, but they have little to recommend them to today's audiences. The sense of youthful energy that characterised his early works is, naturally enough, no longer there; it is replaced only by a superficial tunefulness, which, in the end, does not convince. Between the two choral works, after nearly thirty years, Bennett returned to the symphony. His Symphony in G minor was premiered in 1864 as a three-movement work. He added a fourth movement in 1867, but, again, while technically accomplished – and very Mozartian in style – the work seems to lack the drive that comes from a composer knowing what he wants to say. There were also two overtures, *Paradise and the Peri* (1862) and *Ajax* (1870). Only one small gem came from this later period: his Piano Sonata no. 2, given the title *The Maid of Orléans* because it was inspired by Schiller's poem. Here, too, there is much Mozart in Bennett's style, but the piece has the virtue of sounding unselfconscious – as if he were pleasing himself rather than a Victorian audience.[2]

Bennett always wrote best for his own instrument, and today it is the piano concertos that are most often heard, as well as *The Maid of Orléans* sonata, and a Caprice in E major, opus 22, dating from 1838. The extant symphonies – at least three of them are missing – certainly appear to have their merits, but they are not works that demand attention and most are unrecorded. Of his overtures, *The Naiads* and *The Wood Nymphs*, which are to all intents and purposes tone poems, are the best. Working outside a formal symphonic structure, Bennett is freer to follow where the music leads. Modern audiences may perhaps find a hint of Victorian sentimentality in certain passages, but of their time and of their kind they are attractive works, characterised by pleasing melodies and some controlled and highly effective orchestration. No one would claim Bennett was a great composer, but he remains an interesting figure, and his music, however many reservations one sounds, does represent a step forward in terms of his age. The piano concertos, in particular, are a genuine achievement, showing an understanding of the classical form and an ability to work within it that had previously eluded British composers. The demands of musical administration probably affected his composing, but his achievements in this respect were considerable. Above all, he was the saviour of the RAM. When Disraeli withdrew the government's annual grant in 1866, the directors saw no alternative to closure. Bennett stepped in and, supported by the staff and students, came up with a workable plan that kept the institution open. He was a highly respected teacher. Among his students were Sullivan, Parry, and Tobias Matthay, a great piano teacher and an even greater theorist of piano playing. Bennett also did more than any previous administrator to ease the path for women who wanted to study music – notably, by funding an annual prize for female students at the RAM. At a time when women with aspirations to become composers were not taken seriously, one of the students he taught and encouraged was Alice Mary Smith (1839–84).

In 1861, under Bennett's guidance, Alice Smith joined the London Musical Society – although as an associate only: women were not permitted to be full members – so that she might have a chance of getting her work heard. Two years later, at a Society meeting in November 1863, her Symphony in C minor was given its first performance. Thus she was the first British woman to write a symphony and have it performed. The critical response was favourable and she went on to write a Second Symphony in A minor, a Clarinet Sonata – of which the Andante second movement was later orchestrated as a separate piece – chamber works, and several concert overtures. By the end of the 1870s, the overtures, in particular, were receiving performances both in London and the provinces. In terms of style, Smith was very much another British disciple of Mendelssohn – with Bennett, and at a later stage Macfarren, as teachers, this is hardly surprising. Nonetheless, the two symphonies and the Andante for Clarinet, are composed with a light touch and have a very clean orchestral sound. They may lack rhythmic variation, but they certainly stand comparison with the male competition. There is no doubt that, as a woman entering what was very much a man's world, she had to work hard to overcome prejudice, but she had talent and determination, and she also had the support of her lawyer husband. Sadly, just as she was beginning to win through and be taken seriously as a composer, she caught typhoid and died, aged only forty-five.

The reception of Bennett's music in Germany raises again the issue of how British music was perceived on the Continent. Stephen Storace had had operas performed in Vienna, and John Field had developed a reputation as a composer while living in Russia. Bennett's achievement went beyond either. His reputation stood high in Germany, and particularly in Leipzig, for over twenty years; and there would be other composers whose work was well received there. But the success of a few individuals did not change the overall view of British music: they were seen as exceptions to the rule – and because they were exceptions to the rule, their music was sometimes over-praised. In Britain, the reaction to popularity and recognition in Germany varied. For the arbiters of musical taste, it was Germany that counted and recognition there often guaranteed acceptance by the musical establishment and a teaching post. It did not, however, guarantee popular success – German taste was often too 'advanced' for the conservative British public – while in some quarters the suggestion that the Germans necessarily knew more about musical matters than the British was liable to generate resentment. Young composers, however, were not deterred. For them, Germany was what Italy had been to previous generations, and there were many who now sought to study and start their careers there.

When Mendelssohn was in London, he often stayed with William Horsley, whom we have met previously as a composer of glees and who lived in an area then known as Kensington Gravel Pits and now called Notting Hill Gate. William Horsley's son, Charles Edward Horsley (1822–76) was a promising young musician, taught initially by his father and then by Moscheles. Mendelssohn encouraged him to go and study in Germany, which he did in 1839. He began in Kassel, where he spent two years with Moritz Hauptmann who, as well as being a sound teacher of music theory, was also a Bach scholar and an architect. Horsley then moved on to Leipzig where Mendelssohn took charge of him, giving him lessons or advice three times a week while refusing any payment. Like Bennett, the young Horsley responded to Leipzig, relishing an atmosphere in which music really mattered. He composed chamber music, an overture that was played in Kassel in 1845, and a Symphony in D minor which strongly recalls Mendelssohn. Horsley was never as original or inventive as Bennett, and when he returned to England he encountered even greater difficulties in gaining acceptance as a composer. While in Germany, he had concentrated on orchestral compositions. Now, he switched to oratorios which at least guaranteed him a hearing. *David* (1850), all three-and-a-half hours of it, was composed for the Liverpool Philharmonic Society. So, too, was *Joseph* (1850). *Gideon*, composed for the Glasgow Festival, followed in 1860. Two years later, he was offered an administrative role arranging the music for the London International Exhibition. This was not what he wanted. Feeling that he was getting nowhere, Horsley emigrated to Australia, where he became organist at Christ Church in South Yarra in Melbourne, and wrote an ode entitled *Euterpe* for the opening of Melbourne's new Town Hall. In 1872, he returned briefly to London before moving on to New York where he again took an organist's position and also became director of the Church Music Association. He died in New York in 1876.

Henry Hugo Pearson (1816–73) demonstrated even greater commitment to Germany than either Bennett or Horsley – to the extent that he eventually changed his name to Heinrich Hugo Pierson. An odd, rebellious personality, it is perhaps no surprise that some of his earliest compositions were settings of poems by Shelley and Byron. Despite parental opposition – his father wanted him to follow a medical career – he took lessons with Attwood and Greatorex before going up to Cambridge University, where he studied under Walmisley, but left in 1839 without taking a degree. He travelled to Germany, basing himself first in Darmstadt and then in Dresden, and taking lessons from the leading German teachers of the day. He visited Prague and studied briefly under Václav Tomášek. He travelled to Italy with Mary Shelley, before returning to Dresden where he seduced the wife of a well-known poet and painter, later marrying her after she had obtained a divorce. For a short while he adopted the pseudonym Edgar

Mansfeldt (her maiden name), apparently to deflect the impact of the scandal. Then, in 1844, after five years in Germany, Pearson applied for the Reid Professorship of Music at Edinburgh University. His candidacy was controversial from the beginning – he presented himself as the champion of a new and forward-looking approach to music, in opposition to the establishment candidates, which included Bennett – but he won. It was a prestigious post for a man still not yet thirty. The trouble was that he did not like Scotland – one version of the story emphasises the fact that he had a particular distaste for the bagpipes – and failed to carry out the duties associated with his post. After eight months, the university authorities prevailed upon him to resign and he returned to Germany, where he spent the rest of his life.

He had now become Pierson, but had not wholly given up the idea of success in Britain. His oratorio, *Jerusalem*, was staged at the 1852 Norwich Festival. It is a spiky, uneven work, something of a mix-and-match of styles drawn from Continental composers – Beethoven, Spohr, Schumann, Berlioz, Meyerbeer, even Wagner – highly romantic in its approach, and with only the barest of nods to Handel. What it does have is ambition and a sense of scale. Beginning with Christ's prophecy of the destruction of Jerusalem, it moves through an introduction, three acts and almost four hours, to Armageddon and a vision of the New Jerusalem that is to come. The choruses and recitatives have great vitality, although some of the arias are a little static. It was at least an attempt to do something different. Like Pierson himself, *Jerusalem* became the focus of debate between those who approved of what was termed 'the aesthetic school' – meaning an advanced version of 'romantic' – and those of a more conservative bent. The Norwich press was predictably enthusiastic. George Macfarren gave a more or less balanced preview of the piece in the *Musical Times*: he was clearly ill at ease with some aspects of the structure of the work, but applauded the move away from Handel and the originality of Pierson's execution. In an obvious reference to the ongoing debate about the status of British composers, he made it clear that Pierson is 'entitled to the support of his countrymen.'[3] The heavyweight London critics, however – Davison and Chorley – were hostile, not to say prejudiced, from the beginning. Davison's review in *The Times* managed to attack Pierson's sense of structure, rhythm, harmony, counterpoint, transition between keys, vocal writing and overall musical education, while throwing in a swipe at Wagner at the same time.[4] Pierson, who had come to England for the

Norwich premiere, returned to Germany and stayed there. He continued to compose, but did so with a view to pleasing German audiences, who increasingly saw him as one of their own. Norwich was the only location in Britain that gave him a hearing during his lifetime and two later works were also played there: his spirited incidental music for the second part of Goethe's *Faust*, and a second, unfinished oratorio, called *Hezekiah*. A concert overture, *Romeo and Juliet*, was heard at the Crystal Palace the year after his death – although clearly echoing Liszt and Berlioz, it was another example of Pierson's capacity to take an new and imaginative view of a familiar subject. He also wrote an opera, *Contarini*, which was given at Hamburg in 1872, and a large number of songs. His death in Leipzig in 1873 was the occasion for an outpouring of tributes, which emphasised the value German opinion placed on his music. By contrast, although his body was brought back for burial in Berkshire, the British press and the British musical establishment ignored his passing. One would not wish to over-praise Pierson as a composer, but he did at least try to break out of the straitjacket of the times. The fact that he was first demonised and then ignored for his presumption is a further illustration of the conservatism of British musical circles.

Another composer who dedicated himself to the German-speaking world, although in a very different way, was Robert Lucas Pearsall (1795–1856). A Bristol barrister with social ambitions, he liked to be known as Pearsall of Willsbridge,[5] and later began to style himself 'de Pearsall'. In 1825, he decided he no longer wished or needed to practice law and carried his family off to live in Mainz, where he took lessons with the Austrian composer and violinist, Joseph Panny. From Mainz, he moved to Karlsruhe, where he lived for twelve years, pursuing antiquarian musical interests and composing, among other things, a ballet-opera for a small theatre he had built in the grounds of his house. From Karlsruhe, he moved to the southern shore of the Wartensee in Switzerland where he bought and restored a derelict *Schloss*. There, when not composing, he wrote letters to friends and connections urging that his compositions be performed in England.

Pearsall was a leisured, expatriate amateur rather than a professional composer, and today his name is known, if at all, for his arrangement of *In dulci jubilo* which is heard every Christmas, but he also wrote a number of church anthems, all long since forgotten, and a remarkable ten-part arrangement of the old ballad 'Sir Patrick Spens'. His interest in early music led to a fascination with the madrigal. His aim was to reinvent the form, combining old-fashioned counterpoint with 'modern' nineteenth-century harmonies. An interesting, if eccentric experiment, it cannot be judged a success. Percy Young actually designated Pearsall's part-song, 'O who will o'er the downs so free', as the worst piece of music composed during the whole Victorian period.[6]

Bennett, Horsley, Pierson and (de) Pearsall all looked to Germany for their musical education and their inspiration. So did many other Victorian musicians who never set foot there. In a sense, this was inevitable. Over a century of Hanoverian kings and over a century of intermittent conflict with France, culminating in the Napoleonic Wars, had prepared the ground for the growth of German cultural influence. Germany was now seen by many (if not most) people, as the natural Continental reference point for British culture – an idea publicly symbolised by the marriage of Queen Victoria and Prince Albert in 1840. Despite Berlioz's visits to London, and the fact that Gounod lived and worked in London between 1870 and 1874, French influence on music was minimal. Italian influence was now confined to the opera, and even here it began to decline as the century progressed, faced with the onslaught of Wagner. German ideas, German music and German musical personalities would remain dominant for many years to come.

62   George Macfarren

George Alexander Macfarren (1813–87) was not one of those who studied in Germany, nor did he ever visit the country, although he seems to have begun his musical career accepting the prevailing wisdom that Mendelssohn was the model to follow. As he grew older, there are indications that he was moving away from this view. Perhaps, under other circumstances, he might have mounted a challenge to the idea of German supremacy, but such gestures as he made were largely tentative. Given the overwhelming conservatism of the British musical establishment – of which he himself was a part – this is not surprising, but it has undoubtedly affected his reputation in the eyes of subsequent generations and he is often dismissed, wrongly, as the epitome of all that was wrong with Victorian music. One significant difficulty in assessing his contribution and his legacy is that he simply wrote too much.

The arts featured in Macfarren's background in a very practical sense. His father, also George, began his professional life as a dancing master, but became better known as a dramatist and playwright, producing historical dramas and comedies, and adapting foreign plays for the London stage. He went to on to become a theatre manager and editor of the *Musical World*. He was also a talented violinist. Young George's instrument was always the piano, although he did play the trombone as well. His first music teacher outside the family was Charles Lucas, who, although only five years older than Macfarren, was already a well-known cellist and would go on to take over from Cipriani Potter as Principal of the RAM – to be followed by Bennett and then by Macfarren himself. Macfarren attended the Academy as a student from the age of sixteen, but trouble with his eyes, which had dogged him since early childhood, affected his ability to sight read. As a result, he was forced to concentrate on composition rather than performance, and his First Symphony was performed at an Academy concert in 1830. It was the beginning of an active and productive decade. A student from 1829 to 1834, he then taught at the RAM for two years, before taking up a teaching post on the Isle of Man. Less than a year later, in 1837, the Academy offered him a professorship and he returned to London. Somehow, he managed to combine his teaching commitments with sustained and intensive composition. By the end of 1840 he had written seven symphonies, four concert overtures, a piano concerto, five operas, two operettas, a masque, and a number of other theatrical pieces – although, of course, not all of this impressive catalogue was performed.

Of these many and various works, the Symphony no. 4 in F minor, written in 1833 and first performed a year later, was something of a breakthrough piece. Although clearly descended from Mozart and Mendelssohn, it is written with a sense of personal conviction. It is well structured and, both rhythmically and melodically, a very fluent work: themes evolve and transitions are made without any sense of stress or strain. There are times when the lilting melodies and the orchestral textures, particularly in the writing for brass, seem to anticipate Sullivan. Also written at this early stage of his career was *Chevy Chace*, which today is probably Macfarren's best known work. It began life in 1836, composed quickly following a commission to provide a prelude for a musical melodrama by the London playwright, James Planché (an Englishman despite his surname). The play told the story of a bloody land feud between the Percy and Douglas families and was based on the border ballad *Chevy Chase*. (The difference in spelling results from Macfarren's insistence that his own work be spelled in what he considered the original manner.) Both the Scottish and the folk music connection would have appealed to Macfarren – folk music was an interest that developed as his career progressed – but in the end the play was produced without his prelude. He claimed that the promoters were not giving him proper credit in the show's publicity, withdrew his music, and recast it as a concert overture – which turned out to be a wise decision. The piece was premiered in 1837 under the baton of the James Davison (whom we have previously met as a critic rather than a conductor). In 1840, its inclusion in a promenade concert was praised by the *Musical World* as evidence that at least some music by British composers was being heard, although it criticised the actual performance as under-rehearsed.[1] *Chevy Chace* also served to spread Macfarren's name abroad: Mendelssohn conducted it at the Gewandhaus in 1843 and wrote to Macfarren that it had been well received. Even Wagner, who conducted it at a Philharmonic Society concert in 1855, praised its 'peculiarly wild, passionate character', although he got the title wrong, calling it *Steeple Chase*, and was disobliging in his description of Macfarren (who was born in London) as a 'pompous, melancholy Scotsman'.[2]

In 1840, Macfarren joined the Musical Antiquarian Society and began working on an edition of Purcell's *Dido and Aeneas*. In 1844, he founded the Handel Society, which aimed to produce a full edition of all Handel's works. That same year, he married Clarina Thalia Andrae, a German opera singer and translator of German poetry, who became known as Natalia Macfarren. In 1845, he became conductor at Covent Garden. In 1846, his opera *Don Quixote*, with a libretto by his father, was given at Drury Lane. Still in his early thirties, he seemed, like Bennett, to be well on his way to becoming a pillar of the establishment, but in 1847 things changed. He fell out with the RAM over a new (and subsequently influential) theory of harmony proposed by Alfred Day. He resigned his professorship and he and his wife departed for New York. The main reason for the trip, which lasted eighteen months, was to seek new treatment for his eyesight, which continued to deteriorate. The treatment was unsuccessful, but by the time he returned he had completed *King Charles II,* his most ambitious operatic work to date. It was also the first work in which he thoroughly absorbed the changes that had been brought about in the operatic world over the previous fifteen years or so by John Barnett, Michael Balfe, and William Wallace – changes which we examine in Chapters 63 and 64. *King Charles*

II is a high-spirited, romantic piece with music that is appropriate, coherent, melodic and does not take itself too seriously. It ran for two seasons. The model for the opera as a whole is clearly Mozart, but Macfarren's use of madrigals and even Morris dance tunes shows an attempt – tentative, but nonetheless real – to create genuinely English music, something which would preoccupy Holst, Vaughan Williams and others fifty years later.

King Charles II showed Macfarren the way forward for his operatic writing: it would be English in character, and not in any sense Wagnerian. He was not exalting or mythologizing the English identity: he was having a little mild fun with it. Which explains *Robin Hood,* produced in 1860 at what was by then known as Her Majesty's Theatre, and undoubtedly Macfarren's finest operatic hour. The librettist John Oxenford created a three-act plot which was manageable on stage but incorporated all the key elements of the Robin Hood legend, albeit with rather too much stylised period dialogue. Macfarren matched it with music that is essentially simple and tuneful, and, again, wholly appropriate to the subject. By this time, his knowledge of English folk music had been deepened by working with William Chappell on a series of volumes entitled *The Ballad Literature and Popular Music of the Olden Time* (1855–59), and the score contains ballads ('The hunters awake'), romantic duets ('When lovers are parted'), part-songs ('The wood, the wood, the gay greenwood'), country dances ('Tilting at the quintain') and stirring patriotic songs ('Englishmen by birth'), all liberally scattered with folk motifs. The facility with which Macfarren mixes styles and the manner of his word setting again reminds one forcibly of Sullivan's music for the Savoy Operas. Equally, some of the lyrics – 'Yes, yes, we all agree,' sing the Greenwood Men – and the facetiousness of a finale entitled, 'We made a slight mistake', anticipate Gilbert. It may be a period piece, but it is nevertheless highly entertaining. George Bernard Shaw, reviewing Sullivan's one and only grand opera, *Ivanhoe*, in 1891, was clear that the score did not represent 'in any essential point an advance' on *Robin Hood*.[3] Three more operas in this English vein followed – *She Stoops to Conquer* (which has an appealing overture; 1864), *Helvellyn* (1864) and *Kenilworth* (1880; but unperformed). There were also two chamber operas in a somewhat more comic vein – *Jessy Lea* (1863) and *The Soldier's Legacy* (1864). But none of these recaptured the appeal of *Robin Hood*.

By the time he wrote *Robin Hood*, Macfarren was completely blind, and was forced to dictate his work to an amanuensis. Astonishingly, this had almost no effect on his ability to compose or the speed with which he produced new work. In fact, it was only as his eyesight worsened and then failed completely that he turned to large-scale choral writing. Between 1853 and 1887, he wrote seven cantatas and four oratorios. Of these, the best is probably the first, *St John the Baptist*, written for the Bristol Festival of 1873, and given again soon afterwards in London by the Sacred Harmonic Society. In oratorio-obsessed Britain, it was naturally praised as his greatest achievement, which it is not, but nor is it standard oratorio fare, for it shows signs of trying to break away from the dominance of Mendelssohn. It contains some fine choral writing – direct and, at times, deceptively simple – which hints at the way Elgar writes for the chorus in his biblical oratorios. And there are hints, too, buried in what is not a short work, of a different kind of Englishness from that represented by *Robin Hood*: an Englishness of the kind that would reappear in Parry and Vaughan Williams, based less on folk melodies than on hymn tunes and hymn tune tonalities. Such points of interest, however, cannot disguise a lack of propulsion and dramatic development. Macfarren was obviously at ease in the world of *King Charles II* and *Robin Hood*. He seems to have found the sustained seriousness required of an oratorio more constricting.

Like Bennett, Macfarren continued to pile up official appointments. He was reappointed to the RAM in 1851, and became its Principal, succeeding Bennett, in 1876. The previous year he had been elected Professor of Music at Cambridge, again in succession to Bennett. His knighthood, which under Queen Victoria became an almost routine award for senior figures in the country's musical life, came in 1883. Unlike Bennett, however, he never stopped composing. He composed his last symphony, his ninth, in 1874, and although he could not be considered a great symphonist, he was arguably the most persuasive British composer in the genre to that point. Indeed, there is scarcely a genre in which he did not write. There are six string quartets, spanning forty years of his life; a piano quintet; piano and violin sonatas; settings of the Service; anthems; a *Te Deum*, written for the opening of the International and Universal Exhibition in 1884; and several hundred songs, glees and part-songs. As he got older, he became less tolerant of change and of the new music that was gaining ground – he once famously expressed the wish that the earth would swallow up Bayreuth and everyone there – and was inevitably seen as old-fashioned. Yet during his lifetime he did move the musical debate forward. It was, as we have said, a tentative process. Macfarren was not a musical giant – he was more of a craftsman than an inspired creator – but, in the end, his main achievement was probably preparing the ground, nudging public opinion in a direction that would prove productive for the next generation of composers. His death, in 1887, was reported across Europe and around the world.

63   Early Nineteenth-Century Opera

Like British music in general, opera in Britain began the nineteenth century in a parlous state. Opera was mainly a London phenomenon. Some provincial theatres did stage performances, and the number of small touring opera companies grew during the 1840s and 1850s, but for many years performances of any quality outside the capital tended to be connected with regional music festivals and depended on London-based performers. Dublin showed more independence of spirit than most other cities. At the beginning of the century, the main venue was the Rotunda, opened in 1757, which could hold an audience of 2,000. It was here that the first Irish performances of Mozart's operas took place: *Cosi fan Tutte* in 1811 (featuring Michael Kelly), followed by *The Marriage of Figaro* and *Don Giovanni* in 1819. Then, in 1821, the possibilities were transformed with the opening of the new 3,000-seat Theatre Royal, which saw regular opera seasons including many new works: Weber's *Der Freischütz* in 1827 and his *Abu Hassan* in 1828; Auber's *Masaniello* and no less than five Rossini operas in 1829; Meyerbeer's spectacular *Robert le Diable* in 1832, only a year after its premiere in Paris. By 1829, there were companies of Italian musicians touring operas round Cork, Limerick and Belfast, stimulating the development of the Irish love affair with opera, so that over the course of the nineteenth century it became arguably the most popular and influential classical genre in Ireland. The early years of this Irish enthusiasm for opera were also the early years of Michael William Balfe (1808–70), who probably did more to enliven British opera than anyone else until the arrival of Gilbert and Sullivan in the 1870s.

The London operatic world presented a complex tapestry of restrictive licences, uncooperative companies, unscrupulous managements, under-rehearsed orchestras, alliances, betrayals, disfiguring adaptations, garbled translations, bankruptcies, early closures, fires, re-buildings, re-openings and occasional successes. Storace was dead; Shield wrote only one piece for the stage after 1800; Dibdin's operas had turned into showbiz spectaculars;

ballad opera as a distinct genre had long since faded away. Few new British operas, or 'English operas' as they were known, were being written; and when English works that had proved successful in the past were revived – such as *The Beggar's Opera*, Dibdin's *Lionel and Clarissa* or Arne's *Artaxerxes* – they were 'adapted', 'refurbished', or 'arranged'. Even operas by Continental composers – works which we would regard it as sacrilege to change – were 'arranged' to suit what theatre managements fondly imagined were public tastes. When *The Marriage of Figaro* was given at Drury Lane in November 1826, the performance was attended by a German traveller, Prince Hermann von Pückler-Muskau. The Prince is remembered today more for his skills as a landscape gardener – and because a particular German ice cream is named after him – than for his views on music. Nonetheless, his criticisms, of both the performance and the audience, were trenchant. Having been looking forward to 'the sweet tones of my fatherland', he was appalled

> at the unheard-of treatment which the master-work of the immortal composer has received at English hands!... Neither the Count, the Countess, nor Figaro sang; these parts were given to mere actors, and their principal songs, with some little alteration in the words, were sung by the other singers; to add to this, the gardener roared out some interpolated popular English songs, which suited Mozart's music just as a pitch-plaster would suit the face of the Venus de' Medici. The whole opera was moreover 'arranged' ... that is, adapted to English ears by means of the most tasteless and shocking alterations.... This abominable practice is the more inexcusable, since there is really no want of meritorious singers, male and female; and, with better arrangement, very good performances might be given ... [but] even if the stage were in good order, a second Orpheus would still be required to tame English audiences.[1]

It was the same year and against the same background that Weber drove himself to the edge of exhaustion as he struggled to get *Oberon* performed.

Across Europe, the Classical period, with its emphasis on tradition and progression, was giving way to the tenets of Romanticism: the primacy of the individual imagination, the expression of individual feeling, a love of nature. In operatic terms, this transition is perhaps best seen in the torrent of works that poured from the pen of Gioachino Rossini in the second decade of the century: from *Tancredi* (1813), through *Il barbiere di Siviglia*

(1816), *Otello* (1816) and *La Cenerentola* (1817), to *La donna del lago* (1819). Weber's *Der Freischütz* emerged in 1821 as the first fully-fledged expression of German operatic romanticism, with Meyerbeer's romantic spectacular, *Il crociato in Egitto* (1824), following shortly afterwards. To this brave new world, the British had nothing of remotely comparable quality to contribute. Indeed, the main British contribution to opera at the time was literary, rather than musical.

The poems and novels of Sir Walter Scott were a seminal influence on the Romantic Movement and over the years at least ninety operas have been based on his works.[2] The first wave of adaptations began in 1816, when the playwright Daniel Terry, with the help of Scott himself, adapted *Guy Mannering* for Covent Garden – although this appears to have been a play with musical interludes rather than an opera. The idea of turning Scott's romantic and heroic tales into opera spread rapidly across the Continent. Rossini got in first with his *La donna del lago*, premiered in Naples in 1819. But it was the French who showed the most enthusiasm, with Daniel Auber's *Leicester, ou, Le Château de Kenilworth* (1823), François Boieldieu's *La Dame Blanche* (1825), and Michele Carafa's *Le Nozze di Lammermoor* (1829) and *La Prison d'Edimbourg* (1833), all of them given in Paris. In Germany, Heinrich Marschner used *Ivanhoe* as the basis for *Der Templer und die Jüden* (1829), while the Danish writer Hans Christian Andersen produced a libretto for Ivar Bredal's *Bruden fra Lammermoor* (1832). Probably the best-loved and most popular adaptation of all Scott's works, Donizetti's *Lucia di Lammermoor*, was given for the first time in Naples in 1835.

The British themselves would probably have preferred straightforward stage adaptations, but such productions were subject to complicated licensing ('patent') regulations, which prohibited ordinary ('non-patent') theatres from mounting them. There were ways of getting round the regulations. The trick was to insert into any play with a normal three-act structure a minimum of five songs and (mis)describe it as a '*burletta*', or miniburlesque, which non-patent theatres were allowed to stage. The result was inevitably an inferior adaptation, whether judged dramatically or musically, but that was not the point. By the time the Theatres Act of 1843 came into force with new arrangements for licensing productions, almost all the Waverley novels and most of Scott's major poems had been adapted in some way or another. Charles Dibdin had composed the music for no less than eight adaptations for the Surrey Theatre alone, but more prolific in both this and almost every other area of theatrical music was Henry Rowley Bishop (1786–1855).

Henry Bishop's music has all but disappeared. The sentimental parlour ballad, 'Home! Sweet Home', originally from his opera, *Clari, or, the Maid of Milan*, has been widely recorded; a handful of glees and a few songs from Shakespeare's plays are still available; but little else. Given that he was responsible for the scores for something approaching a hundred and twenty theatrical works of varying kinds, this probably tells its own tale. He wrote operas, operettas, cantatas, incidental music, at least two odes, an unperformed oratorio and a large number of songs. He adapted many foreign operas for the London stage: indeed, it was his alterations and interpolations to *The Marriage of Figaro* which so outraged Prince von Pückler-Muskau. He had the ability to write simple, sentimental melodies, and the skill to ornament them sufficiently so that they might pass as operatic. As simple, sentimental melodies were exactly what the public wanted and would pay to hear, Bishop was in demand. At various times, he was chief conductor at Covent Garden, Drury Lane, The King's Theatre and Vauxhall Gardens. What he did not have, or so it appears, was any individual style or musical vision. A generation older than Bennett or Macfarren, Bishop was equally ubiquitous, but left no comparable mark or reputation behind him. Indeed, his works for the stage represent the low point of English opera. That did not prevent him from climbing high on the ladder of the musical establishment: he was a founder member of the Philharmonic Society; Professor of Music at Edinburgh for a short period; and then at Oxford, in succession to William Crotch. Queen Victoria gave him a knighthood in 1842 – presumably for his ubiquity – the first of those awards to senior musical figures which we have already noted becoming almost routine during her reign.

One of Bishop's many projects was to provide musical arrangements for the later volumes of a series known as *Moore's Irish Melodies*, which was published in ten volumes, with an additional supplement, between 1808 and 1834. The arrangements in the earlier volumes were by an Irish composer, Sir John Stevenson (1761–1833). The Moore of the title was the Irish poet, Thomas Moore (1779–1852), but the melodies, despite the title, were not his. They were traditional Irish tunes to which he had written some effective and romantic lyrics. Some of these songs – 'The harp that once through Tara's halls', 'Believe me if all those endearing young charms' and 'The Last Rose of Summer' – were among the most popular parlour ballads of the Victorian era and are still occasionally heard today. Moore, a would-be Irish revolutionary in his youth, crossed the sea to England, studied law and soon became a more-or-less respectable literary figure. He collaborated on two comic operas: *The Gypsy Prince* (1801), where his partner was Michael Kelly, and *The M.P., or, The Bluestocking* (1811) with Charles Edward Horn (1786–1849). But, as with Scott, his real contribution to opera was a literary one. Styled by its author 'An Oriental Romance', *Lalla Rookh* (1817) consists of a prose narrative linking four extended tales told in verse. Lalla Rookh, daughter of the Mogul Emperor Aurungzebe is on her way to marry the young King of Bucharia but falls in the love with the poet Feramorz, whose poetic stories steal her heart away. Eventually, it is revealed that the poet and the young King are one and the same and all ends happily. *Lalla Rookh* made a major impact, selling thousands of copies. Schumann based his cantata *Paradise and the Peri* on one of Feramorz's tales; and Bennett, as we know, wrote an overture with the same title. Operatic or quasi-operatic adaptations began with Gaspare Spontini's *Nurmahal* (1822). William Brough turned the work into a burlesque or pantomime in 1857; and further operas – Félicien David's *Lalla Roukh* (1862), Anton Rubinstein's *Feramors* (1863) and Charles Villiers Stanford's *Veiled Prophet* (1880) – testify to its continued popularity over a period of some sixty years.

Neither adaptations of Scott or Moore, nor the bland conventionality of Bishop's many theatrical excursions, could do anything to inject life into native British opera. Little of note happened before the 1830s. By that time, the pressure for reform of the patent/non-patent framework was urgent, and the public, growing tired of a diet of Rossini and Rossini imitations, was looking for something new. The Lyceum Theatre in Westminster, just off the Strand, had first opened its doors in 1798 under the management of Samuel Arnold. With his death in 1802, it passed to his son, Samuel James (S. J.) Arnold, who did his best to be innovative, staging, among other things, Moore's *The M.P.*, the first English version of *Der Freischütz*, and Marschner's *Der Vampyr*. Under his direction, the Lyceum became one of the first theatres in London to be lit by gas, which was considered safer than lanterns and candles. Nonetheless, it still burned down in 1830. When it reopened four years later, Arnold saw an opportunity and renamed it the New Theatre Royal Lyceum and English Opera House. Arnold's publicity stated that the theatre would be dedicated to 'the representation of English operas and the encouragement of indigenous talent.'[3] A total of five new

English operas were given that first season, beginning with *Nourjahad* by Edward Loder.

Nourjahad was originally a novel published in 1767 by Frances Sheridan, mother of the playwright Richard Brinsley Sheridan. Arnold had turned it into a play as long ago as 1813, when it had included some incidental music by Michael Kelly, but nothing more. Twenty years on, he resurrected and restructured the piece, cutting much of the dialogue, adding songs, duets and choruses, and turning it into an English-style opera. He approached the young composer Edward Loder (1809–65), who had just returned from Germany where he studied under Beethoven's former secretary Ferdinand Ries, to write the music. *Nourjahad* is set in the court of the Schemzeddin, Sultan of Persia, and mines the same vein of romantic orientalism as *Lalla Rookh*. With lavish costumes and scenery, it ran for twenty-nine performances in July and August 1834, with brief revivals later that year and in 1835. Loder's music received a lot more praise than Arnold's libretto, and he went to on to write a number of operatic and stage works, including *The Covenanters* (1835), a Scottish ballad opera on which he collaborated with Dibdin, and *The Wilis, or, The Night Dancers* (1846), based on a retelling of the Giselle legend by the dramatist George Soane. Loder's other claim to fame is that he tried to reinvent English art song on the model of the German *Lied*. So little of his work is currently available that it is difficult to judge how successful the attempt was, although critics have from time to time praised songs such as 'The Deep' and 'The Brooklet'. The Victorian public clearly preferred the parlour ballad.

The big success of the New Lyceum's first season, however, was not *Nourjahad*, but *The Mountain Sylph* (1834) by John Barnett (1802–90), with a libretto by Thomas Thackeray, a distant relation of the novelist, William Makepeace Thackeray. Barnett was of mixed German, Jewish and Hungarian parentage and, apparently, a second cousin of Giacomo Meyerbeer, but seems to have been all the more English as a result. As a child, he had a remarkable alto voice and sang on stage at the Lyceum in several productions until his voice broke. His early compositions were songs, praised and criticised in equal measure by the *Quarterly Music Magazine and Review*.[4] At least one of them was sung to great effect by John Braham. Barnett soon moved on to compositions for the theatre and adaptations of foreign operas, and seems to have been possessed of a genuine poetic-romantic musical talent. This, combined with his ambition to write a genuinely English opera, led to *The Mountain Sylph*.

The plot is not English at all, but a concoction derived from a French ballet, *La Sylphide* (1832),[5] and bits of German folk tales, all reassembled in a Scottish setting. With its supernatural comings and goings it was, in fact, sufficiently nonsensical to have provided Gilbert and Sullivan with the object of at least part of their satire in *Iolanthe*. The opera itself was halfway between English and Italian models in that, while it featured significant amounts of recitative, it also included dialogue. Barnett was clearly influenced by *Der Freischütz*, but he was clever enough to disguise the fact, and to earn critical praise, by giving the music a distinct Scottish accent. The overture sets a tone which is light and fresh, with some effective writing for the woodwind. The chorus of witches has some lively passages. The piece as a whole tells a more or less coherent story with some pleasant songs and an acceptable, if engineered, happy ending. Initial reviews were positive and, although there were one or two minor grumbles, the public poured in. It was performed over a hundred times in its first year, and continued to be revived in London until at least 1860. Outside the capital, it quickly travelled to Edinburgh, Birmingham, Norwich, and Liverpool, and as late as 1873 it was being toured in Scotland and Ireland. Moreover, sales of sheet music for home performance continued long after the opera ceased to be staged quite as frequently: even in 1880 the music publishers Boosey & Co were still reprinting the score. George Macfarren wrote that 'its production opened a new period for music in this country, from which is to be dated the establishment of an English dramatic school,'[6] and it possible to see the influence of Barnett's none-too-serious tunefulness in *King Charles II*, and *Robin Hood*, although they both have better plots and librettos. *The Mountain Sylph* was certainly tuneful and, while it lacked any real internal development, it at least had a plot and some identifiable characters. It was in no sense radical, but its great virtue was that it was seen as new, which speaks volumes for the state of English opera at the time. Despite its faults, *The Mountain Sylph* opened the way for a wave of what have become known as English romantic operas which would last for the next thirty years.

Barnett sought to follow up the success of *The Mountain Sylph* with *Fair Rosamond* (1837), which, as a love story with its origins in English history, might have come closer to the idea of an English opera. Unfortunately, it did not work like that. To say the libretto is weak would be an understatement. It has pantomime rhymes and a complete lack of subtlety. Equally unfortunate, according to *The Spectator*, was the fact that it ran to four acts.[7] Not even the greatest composer could breathe life into such a libretto or retain the audience's attention for such a long time. *Farinelli* (1839), which came next, was quite popular with the public and had fifty performances, but after that Barnett appears have lost interest or confidence or both. He withdrew from the opera world to teach singing and to write large numbers of songs, few of which were ever heard or published. But his success had given composers and theatre managers alike new belief in the possibilities of English opera. London was suddenly awash with new operas with intriguing titles – *Hermann, or, The Broken Spear* by John Thomson; *The Lord of the Isles* by George Rodwell; *Sadak and Kalasrade, or, The Waters of Oblivion* by Charles Packer. In the end, it was Michael Balfe more than anyone else who capitalised on what Barnett had achieved with *The Mountain Sylph*, and became the standard-bearer for English romantic opera. His first big success was *The Siege of Rochelle* in 1835. By that time, Balfe was in his late twenties and had already enjoyed an unusual, at times even picaresque career.

64   Balfe, Wallace, and Benedict

Michael William Balfe was born in 1808 in Pitt Street, Dublin – renamed Balfe Street in 1917 – to a Protestant father and a Catholic mother. His father, William, moved back and forward between Dublin, where he played violin at the Crow Street Theatre, and Wexford, where he was a dancing master. In his early years, Balfe seems to have picked up bits of musical knowledge from a number of people in the family circle, including a bandmaster in the Kerry militia. At the age of seven, he began to receive lessons from the Irish composer and violinist William O'Rourke (later anglicised to William Rooke for professional purposes), who was deputy leader of the orchestra in which William Balfe played. At the age of nine, Balfe made his first public appearance, playing violin at the Rotunda in Dublin. Then, when Rooke moved to London, where he went on to become leader of the orchestra at Vauxhall Gardens under Henry Bishop, Balfe continued his studies with another well-known Dublin violinist, James Barton.

Throughout his early career, Balfe seems to have been aided by a combination of luck and immense self-belief. When his father died in 1823, at the early age of forty, Balfe was just beginning his career as a professional violinist and the future must have seemed uncertain. Seeing the difficulties the family was facing, a wealthy relative of Balfe's mother offered to adopt him. The only condition was that Balfe should go and live in the West Indies, where the relative in question had large estates. Unwilling to give up his musical career, Balfe refused. However, at just that time, the singer Charles Edward Horn happened to be performing in Dublin. Horn had praised a song Balfe had written and, on that somewhat slender basis, Balfe asked to be taken on as an articled pupil. Horn agreed and Balfe went with him to London, where, when not studying, he played violin in the orchestra at Drury Lane and in other theatres, sending the money he earned back to his family in Ireland. Two years later, in 1825, he had another slice of luck. The story goes that he was dining out with a friend in London one night when he was introduced to Count Mazzara. The count was so struck with Balfe's resemblance to his recently deceased son that he offered to take him to Italy and pay for his studies. Balfe, not unnaturally, accepted this generous offer and accompanied the Count back to Rome, stopping briefly in Paris, where he met Cherubini. After a few months in Rome, Mazzara sent him to Milan to study singing – Balfe had a superb baritone voice – and composition. Here, he received his first commission. The manager of La Scala, an Englishman named Joseph Glossop, asked him to provide the music for a ballet, *La Pérouse* – which proved a modest success – and also promised him singing roles in the next season's operas.

Unfortunately, Glossop, who seems to have been a slightly shady character, was replaced without warning and the promised singing roles disappeared. Balfe decided it was time to move on and made his way to Paris, where his luck reasserted itself. He reintroduced himself to Cherubini, who not only recommended him to Rossini, but also arranged that a friend should pay for further studies which Rossini then arranged. In Paris, Balfe earned money and praise, singing Figaro in *Il barbiere di Siviglia* and taking the lead role in *Don Giovanni*. When he fell ill and needed to recuperate, he returned to Italy, where he met and married the beautiful Hungarian soprano, Lina Rosa. Returning to the stage, he then sang alongside Maria Malibran, the greatest soprano of the day. Only in 1834 did Balfe return to London, by which time he had written three operas, but was still principally known as a singer. Luck, self-confidence and letters of recommendation from Italy meant that all doors were open to him, and in no time at all he had received a commission for an opera from Arnold at the

Lyceum. Somewhere along the way, however, the venue and the management were switched, and it was eventually given at Drury Lane, which was then under the management of Alfred Bunn. The libretto, by the playwright Edward Fitzball, was based on the novel *Le Siège de La Rochelle* by Madame de Genlis, a subject apparently suggested by Balfe himself. The completed opera, with the title *The Siege of Rochelle*, was premiered in October 1835.

This was Balfe's breakthrough piece, running for seventy-three performances during its first season. During 1836 it was performed in regional theatres throughout England – including Bath, Liverpool, Manchester, Norwich, Sheffield, and York – as well as across the Irish Sea in Dublin. It was not, for some reason, played in Scotland until 1877. It continued to be played regularly, if not frequently, into the 1850s, and was revived successfully in the 1870s by the famous Carl Rosa Opera Company. (Rosa, a German-born violinist, conductor and impresario, was no relation to Balfe's wife.) Abroad, it reached New York in 1838 and Sydney in 1848. The plot and the libretto were criticised from the beginning for being thin and unconvincing, but Balfe's music carried the piece. The overture, the quartet from Act I, 'Lo, the early beam of morning', and the ballad from Act II, 'When I beheld the anchor weigh'd', were all popular on the concert platform as well as in the opera house.

Even in retrospect, it remains difficult to define precisely the characteristics of the new school of English romantic opera, but, whatever they were, Balfe was now established as their chief exponent. He followed up *The Siege of Rochelle* with *The Maid of Artois*, which is arguably his best work. Before leaving Italy for London, he had half-promised to write something for Maria Malibran; Alfred Bunn saw Malibran as a way of filling his theatre; so the two of them collaborated – Bunn contributing a libretto based on Abbé Prevost's *Manon Lescaut*, with a strong leading female part. Although still an English opera in that it mixes dialogue with music, *The Maid of Artois* shows Balfe edging towards a more Italian style. There is more recitative, and the solo pieces described as 'airs' in *The Siege of Rochelle* have become 'arias'. Written specifically for Malibran, the beautiful aria, 'Yon Moon o'er the Mountains' and the finale, 'The Rapture Dwelling', are very Italian in their style. So, too, is the duet from Act II, 'I have strength to hear'; while choruses such as 'These joyous sounds to hear' have clear echoes of Donizetti about them. After an initial run of twenty performances, Malibran went off to fulfil other engagements. Everyone expected she would return for a revival of *The Maid of Artois* and to star in Balfe's next opera, but she died suddenly and unexpectedly in Manchester in September 1836.

Catherine Grey opened at Drury Lane in May 1837, exactly a year after *The Maid of Artois*. This time Balfe went for a fully through-composed, Italian style opera, with recitative throughout and no dialogue. It ran for only four performances. This may have been because the new leading lady, the Scottish soprano Mary Ann Wood, could not meet the demands of a part written for Malibran (Balfe had a reputation for writing challenging parts for his soloists); it may have been because the score was held to lack originality (like many composers, Balfe did re-use passages of his own work, but on this occasion he was also suspected of borrowing tunes from Rossini); or it may have been because the illness of William IV had an impact on theatre-going (he died three weeks after the opening night). In any event, Balfe accepted the setback and set to work on his next opera, *Joan of Arc*. This opened in November 1837 at Drury Lane, but faced stiff competition from Covent Garden, first by a spoiler, an alternative version of *Joan of Arc*, described by the *Literary Gazette* as a 'new, grand historical and legendary drama';[1] and then by a lightweight piece called, *Amilie*. This must have been something of a surprise because the composer of *Amilie* was none other than William Rooke, Balfe's teacher from his early years in Dublin. In fact, Rooke had written *Amilie* twenty years earlier, at about the time he was teaching Balfe. It completely outsold *Joan of Arc* that season – even though *Joan of Arc* was still performed over twenty times. However, neither the competition nor the result had any effect on the continuing good relations between the two men: Balfe actually sang in the Dublin production of *Amilie* in 1838.

Perhaps learning the lesson that the London public preferred lighter works, Balfe followed *Joan of Arc* with *Diadesté*, a comic opera with an Arabian plot and a particularly nonsensical libretto by Fitzball. *Diadesté*, given at Drury Lane, was followed immediately by *Falstaff* for the Italian Opera at Her Majesty's Theatre. Both were premiered in 1838. Neither were failures, but neither repeated the success of *The Siege of Rochelle* or *The Maid of Artois*. Balfe had now written six operas in three years. He might well have continued writing at the same speed, but theatrical life in London, never the most stable environment, seems to have thrown up its usual delays, difficulties and shortages of cash, which culminated in manager Bunn being declared bankrupt. Balfe went back to singing. He took part in

Barnett's *Fair Rosamond* and *Farinelli*, and returned twice to his native Dublin, where – to a rapturous welcome – he sang not only in *Amilie*, but also in three of his own operas.

While Balfe was taking time out, other composers were producing romantic operas of their own: Macfarren's first and moderately successful essay in the genre, *The Devil's Opera*, appeared in 1838. So, too, did *The Gypsy's Warning* by Julius Benedict (1804–55). Born in Stuttgart of Jewish parents, Benedict had been a pupil of both Hummel and Weber. In his twenties, he had obtained positions as a conductor at theatres in Vienna and Naples. Then, in 1836, on the advice of Malibran, he made his way to London, where almost immediately he was appointed conductor at the Lyceum and then, in 1838, at Drury Lane. In his first decade in London, he wrote three operas for Drury Lane – *The Gypsy's Warning* (1838), *The Brides of Venice* (1844) and *The Crusaders* (1846) – but it was not until some years later that he scored his biggest – indeed, his only – major operatic success.

In 1840, Balfe returned to the fray, determined to go into theatre management himself in order to produce his new work, an Egyptian tale called *Keolanthe*. For once, however, luck seemed to desert him. After a series of financially worrying delays, *Keolanthe* was produced at the Lyceum, with Balfe's wife, Lina Rosa, in the title role. It was followed by an undistinguished piece by Edward Loder, *The Deer Stalker*. Neither captured the public imagination and Balfe, like so many theatre managers before and since, found himself running out of money. An invitation to compose an opera for the Theatre Italien in Paris came just at the right time. He put theatre management on hold and set off for France, but still things kept going wrong. He had nearly completed the opera when the whole project was cancelled, probably because the leading lady, Giulia Grisi – who had made a huge hit in London a few years earlier – fell pregnant.[2] Then, suddenly, his luck turned. He was asked to write something for the Opéra Comique. The result was *Le Puits d'Amour*, which was given its premiere in April 1843. Paris audiences responded enthusiastically. Balfe was naturally delighted, but he wanted his new success to be heard in London. The management of the Princess's Theatre in Oxford Street agreed to take it, but the need for an English translation and for consequent rewriting meant that *Geraldine, or, the Lover's Well*, as it became, would be delayed by some months. To cover the gap, it was decided to revive *The Siege of Rochelle*. Both operas were sufficiently successful for Balfe to focus his attention on London once again. Yet more good luck followed. Alfred

Bunn, bankruptcy notwithstanding, somehow managed to get himself re-instated as manager at Drury Lane. He appointed Julius Benedict as musical director, and approached Balfe for a new opera. As it happened, Balfe had something in the cupboard. It was a work he seems to have begun two or three years previously, but it still needed finishing and revising before it could be put into rehearsal. So the new season at the Lyceum began with London's second revival of *The Siege of Rochelle* within six weeks. Then, in November 1843, Balfe's new opera, *The Bohemian Girl* opened.

Looked at objectively, *The Bohemian Girl* is a slight piece. It has always been called an opera, but to call it an operetta would not be indefensible. The libretto, by Bunn, involves insulted honour, a kidnapped maiden, a wicked gypsy queen, a fugitive nobleman, and a happy ending. The music is uncomplicated, unashamedly emotional, and immediately appealing. Balfe was not a great composer, but he had a great musical talent. His strength was to recognise and respond to public taste. His personal preferences were probably better reflected in a work such as *The Maid of Artois*, which leaned more towards the Italian operatic model, but in *The Bohemian Girl* he captures precisely the public taste of the early years of the Victorian era. It is a fantasy with just that touch of the exotic that the audience liked – a Bohemian setting and a band of gypsies – but nothing too threatening. There are lively choruses with a hint of *tzigane*; a rather empty waltz and a gallop; but the musical high points are the ballads – they lean far more towards the parlour ballad than the operatic aria – and they display Balfe's Irish melodic gift to the full. This sort of attractive, unchallenging piece was clearly what the public wanted, yet it was Balfe's talent – at the risk of damning with faint praise – which prevented it from being anything worse.

The Bohemian Girl may be trite, but it is genuinely tuneful: at least two of the songs, 'I dreamt I dwelt in marble halls' and 'When other lips and other hearts', have developed a life beyond the opera itself. It may lack artistic or psychological depth, but it avoids the excesses of sentimentality which coloured many of the English romantic operas that followed in its wake. The silliness never becomes vulgarity. And it is difficult to argue with success. People were whistling the tunes in the streets just a few days after the first performance. There were over a hundred performances at Drury Lane during its first season, and that was just the beginning. It opened in Dublin, New York and Philadelphia in 1844; it reached Vienna and Sydney in 1846; and thereafter it spread rapidly to all corners of Europe – Prague,

Stockholm, Berlin, Trieste, Verona, Bologna, Zurich, Amsterdam, Rouen, Gothenburg, Paris, and the list goes on. By the 1870s, it was being played in Canada and New Orleans. By the 1880s, it had reached Mexico City and Cape Town. Until the arrival of Gilbert and Sullivan in the 1870s, it was far and away the most popular British opera of the nineteenth century. Moreover, its popularity was not limited to professional companies: it became a staple of the amateur dramatic and operatic societies that grew up during the second half of the century alongside the flourishing network of choral societies. It has been filmed at least three times – one version, bizarrely, a silent film; another a comedy adaptation starring Laurel and Hardy. It was revived for nineteen performances at Covent Garden in 1951, and is still performed in the twenty-first century.

Balfe never repeated the success of *The Bohemian Girl*, but he continued to work for the next twenty years, and his reputation as the most consistently popular opera composer in Britain remained unchallenged until his death in 1870. During those twenty years, he produced a string of operas too numerous to be assessed individually. The follow up to *The Bohemian Girl* was *The Daughter of St Mark* (1844), Bunn's libretto for which was probably the best Balfe ever had to work with. A through-composed work, billed as a grand *opera seria*, it suggests again that Balfe aspired to be a composer of 'real opera', but, even then, the one song to achieve widespread popularity was the Irish ballad-like setting of 'We may be happy yet'. *The Bondman* (1846), *The Maid of Honour* (1847), *The Rose of Castille* (1857), *Bianca* (1860), *The Puritan's Daughter* (1861), and *The Armourer of Nantes* (1863) all drew big enough audiences to be counted as successes. Many of them crossed the Atlantic; many were played in France, where King Louis Philippe awarded Balfe the Legion of Honour; and *The Bondsman* was given in Berlin at the personal request of the King of Prussia. At one point, Balfe travelled to Saint Petersburg, where his daughter married the British Ambassador. At home, he was one of the most respected conductors of opera and, from 1846 to 1852, he was Principal Conductor of the Italian Opera at her Majesty's Theatre – a particularly eventful few years, for they included the London debut of Jenny Lind and the first London performance of a number of Verdi's new operas, among them *Nabucco*.[3] In November 1863, Balfe's *Blanche de Nevers* was premiered at Covent Garden. It was the last new work to be performed in his lifetime. The following year he retired to Rowney Abbey in Hertfordshire where he worked on his own – and only – adaptation of Scott, based on *The*

Talisman and called *The Knight of the Leopard*. It was not performed until four years after his death when it was, for some strange reason, sung in Italian.

Balfe knew his limitations. Overtures and a few pieces of incidental music aside – and excepting also a few youthful indiscretions – he wrote hardly any instrumental music. As a singer himself, he understood the human voice and his talent was to write for it, which is why, in addition to his thirty operas, he left over two hundred and fifty songs. Balfe never forgot his Irish roots – he returned to Dublin on many occasions and also organised concerts to raise money for those affected by the famine – and his most successful songs manage to capture and reflect his Irishness in a manner that appealed to English audiences. Songs such as 'Hark to the wind upon the hill', 'Killarney', 'Don't let the roses listen', 'The Blighted Flower', his famous setting of Tennyson's 'Come into the garden, Maud', and the almost equally famous setting of Kingsley's 'The Sands of Dee' sold many thousands of copies of sheet music. Here again, Balfe's strength was to understand what his audience wanted; and he gave them well-crafted, melodic songs, which – like the airs, arias and ballads at the heart of his operas – could be sung at home and became part of the popular classical music of the day.

When Balfe died, he was commemorated by a statue in Drury Lane theatre, a window in St Patrick's Cathedral in Dublin, and a plaque on the wall in Westminster Abbey – a list of memorials which, from our perspective, might seem excessive. Yet he was genuinely popular – as an individual, as a singer, and as a composer. Although he avoided the overblown sentimentality of so many Victorian parlour ballads and the crude melodrama of so much of the Victorian stage, Balfe's work is often sentimental and does make the occasional excursion into what modern eyes interpret as almost camp melodrama. Yet the fault is not in Balfe – or, indeed, in any of his contemporaries whose work exhibits the same qualities. Such things were the cultural currency of his time. Balfe's works, like those of the Tudor madrigalists, are consciously artificial – in structure, in style, in characterisation, in the expression of emotion, in humour. Balfe's nineteenth-century sensibility may seem closer to us than that of Weelkes and Wilbye, but in both cases it requires a leap of imagination for modern audiences to penetrate the conventions of a different age.

If English romantic opera can be said to have begun with *The Mountain Sylph*, it reached its apogee with *The Bohemian Girl*. It did not die away immediately: it lasted for another twenty years, and there were at least three more major successes, but *The Bohemian Girl* defines the genre better than any other single work. Balfe, as we have seen, continued to compose, and many other composers produced new operas that sought to exploit this genre for which the public had such an appetite. Edward Loder's *Night Dancers*, mentioned earlier, was successful when produced at the Princess's Theatre for the 1846–47 season, and, following its London run, was given not only in cities around the country – Dublin, Manchester, Hull – but also in Sydney and New York. Loder's attempts to follow it up, however, were a disappointment. *Robin Goodfellow*, 'A Fairy Ballad Opera' (1848), barely qualifies as an opera at all, consisting of a string of solo ballads linked by dialogue and some incidental music; while *Raymond and Agnes*, a grand opera that opened in Manchester in 1855, closed after just a week. George Macfarren's successful operas, *King Charles II* and *Robin Hood* have already been discussed. They, too, belong to this same operatic family and are clearly intended to appeal to the same public. But Macfarren was, at heart, a more academic composer. That is not to say that he did not understand or write well for the stage – he obviously did – rather that his response to his material was more complex, recognising emotional nuances and ironies that many of his contemporaries would miss or ignore. As a result, his operatic music is more sophisticated. In the years after *The Bohemian Girl*, of all those who produced works that come within the broad definition of English romantic opera, only two had a level of success that even came close to rivalling Balfe.

Like Balfe, William Vincent Wallace (1812–65) was an Irishman, and his career also had a picaresque quality to it. His father was a Scot who had emigrated to Waterford, where he played the bassoon and led the local regimental band. The young Wallace was yet another musical prodigy, with a precocious ability to play not only the church organ, but also all the instruments in his father's military band. By the time the family moved to Dublin – where his father got a job in the orchestra at the Adelphi Theatre – he was in his early teens and had added the violin to the list of instruments on which he was proficient. By the age of fifteen, he was leading the orchestra of the Dublin Philharmonic Society; and, at the age of eighteen, he was appointed organist and Professor of Music at Thurles Cathedral in Tipperary. This was a welcome recognition of his talent, but from a young man's point of view Thurles was a small town in the middle of nowhere. He did not stay long. He married, returned to Dublin, and found employment playing the violin in the orchestra at the Theatre Royal. At this point, boredom seems to have set in. Wallace, his wife and his young children set off for Australia, which in 1835 was a serious undertaking.

Wallace initially settled in the bush, apparently intending to be a sheep farmer, but he was 'discovered' and persuaded to move to Sydney, where one of his early concerts was hailed as 'the commencement of a new era in the chronology of music in this Colony.'[4] He gave more concerts; he opened Australia's first Academy of Music; he started a business importing pianos; but then, in January 1838, he disappeared, leaving behind his wife and children, his brother and sister (who were working in his school) and debts of £2,000. What happened next is not clear. According to Wallace's own account, he went whale-hunting, fought Maoris in New Zealand, hunted tigers in India (and was mauled), travelled through Chile, Cuba, and Jamaica, and arrived in Mexico City, where he conducted the 1841 season at the Italian Opera. He then moved on to New Orleans and worked his way up the American east coast to New York, where he gave a number of concerts, before crossing the Atlantic to tour Germany and Holland. The details of such a progress cannot easily be checked and – given that Wallace has been described as 'charming but unprincipled' and habitually untruthful[5] – some of them must certainly be open to doubt. What we do know is that he was in New York by 1844, because in that year the New York firm of Firth, Hall & Pond published the first batch of the many piano pieces that he composed during the 1840s and 1850s. Wallace's name is usually associated with opera, but his piano works – the most famous of which is probably *La Cracovienne* – were popular right up to the end of the century. Another certainty is that Wallace was in London by May 1845, when he gave a concert at the Hanover Rooms that was greeted with great enthusiasm.

With luck apparently rivalling Balfe's, within a few days of arriving in London, Wallace bumped into an old friend from Dublin. The friend introduced him to Edward Fitzball, who had provided the librettos for *The Siege of Rochelle* and *Diadesté*. Wallace and Fitzball agreed to collaborate and in November that same year – just six months later – Wallace's opera *Maritana* was produced by Alfred Bunn's management at Drury Lane, with Benedict conducting. On this occasion, the expected strain of mild exoticism was provided by a setting in Spain. The plot involves an innocent gypsy girl, a king in disguise, an unjust imprisonment, a fake execution, many deceits and complications and, of course, a happy ending. That

Wallace was not a composer to equal Balfe is evident from the overture, which spells out 'Spain' and 'Drama' in the musical equivalent of capital letters. There are a number of light and charming melodies – 'Of fairy wand had I the power', 'It was a knight of princely mien', the 'Angelus' chorus from Act I – and Wallace's orchestration is vigorous and inventive enough to hide faults elsewhere, but the libretto is cumbersome, and the opera is flat in terms of dramatic development. Nonetheless, it was an outrageous success, both in London and then in Dublin the following year. It became particularly popular in the United States, reaching Philadelphia in 1848, and, although not given in New York until 1854, it was then revived every few years until the end of the 1860s. *Maritana* reached Australia in 1849 – although we have no record of Wallace's wife's reaction. Nor did its popularity at home die away. There was an extended revival at Covent Garden in 1848 – in which Wallace's sister took one of the lead roles – and it continued to be revived regularly right up until the 1930s. In 1873, when Carl Rosa[6] launched his new English Opera Company, which was to play a long-lasting and important role in taking English language opera to the provinces, he chose *Maritana* as his first production.

Wallace's second opera, *Matilda of Hungary* (1847) was not a success. Fitzball was particularly critical of the libretto – though as it was by Bunn and not him, he may have been jealous. There was then a gap of thirteen years while Wallace returned to the United States, made a second (and apparently bigamous) marriage to a pianist called Helen Stoepel, had two sons by her, helped found the New York Philharmonic Society, returned to London and set himself up as a fashionable piano teacher. Only then, in 1860, did *Lurline* appear. Wallace had begun the work much earlier and there may have been a partial performance in Germany in 1853, but the complete opera was played for the first time at Covent Garden by the Pyne & Harrison Opera Company in 1860. Lurline (a variant form of Lorelei) is the daughter of King Rhineberg, and the plot, which is comparatively simple, tells how with the aid of a magic ring and the spirits of the Rhine she overcomes various trials and tribulations to win the love and secure the hand of Count Rudolph. This, of course, is Wagner territory, although it predates *Das Rheingold* which did not receive its first performance until 1869, and Wagner would never have allowed a happy ending. *Lurline* was immensely popular. Productions in Dublin and Sydney followed within just two years of its first London run and, again, it proved successful in the United States. There are some attractive tunes – notably 'Flow on, O silver

Rhine' – but the true nature of *Lurline* is shown by the fact that within a matter of days of the first performance the main arias and duets had been published as parlour ballads with piano accompaniment in a volume entitled *The Vocal Gems of William Vincent Wallace's Grand Romantic Opera* Lurline. The work might be through-composed, and the theme might be mythical and grand, but in the final analysis, *Lurline* was less an opera than a string of well-constructed and melodic ballads woven around a romantic and mildly dramatic storyline.

Three more operas followed – *The Amber Witch* (1861), *Love's Triumph* (1862), and *The Desert Flower* (1863) – again produced by the Pyne & Harrison Company, but none of them amounted to anything. In his final years, Wallace became a somewhat tragic figure. His two sons by his New York marriage both committed suicide, and he himself became almost blind. He had also lost or spent all his money. His last months were spent in France, in a small village just north of the Pyrenees, where he died in 1865. His body was brought back to England and he was buried in Kensal Green Cemetery, only a few metres from Balfe, whose memorial is much the grander of the two.

As things turned out, it was Julius Benedict, not Wallace, who was the real beneficiary of the success of *Lurline*. Benedict had been making a name for himself. He had not only become one of Britain's most sought-after opera conductors – having directed the premieres of both *The Bohemian Girl* and *Maritana* – but had also distinguished himself as a conductor of orchestral music. He was particularly associated with the Norwich Festival, which he directed for over thirty years between 1845 and 1878. In the middle of this period, he conducted Jenny Lind's first appearance as a singer of oratorio; and, as a result and at her insistence, he acted as her pianist and conductor during an extensive, two-year tour of the United States organised by the showman and promoter, P. T. Barnum. During the two years he was away, no Norwich Festival was held. Earlier in his career, he had, as we have seen, written a number of none-too-successful operas, and after *The Crusaders* (1846), he appeared to have given up writing for the stage. Indeed, after 1850, he composed almost nothing for some ten years. Then a cantata, *Undine*, written for the Norwich Festival of 1860, was given a warm reception. After that, quite suddenly, whether directly inspired by the success of *Lurline* or for some other reason, he composed *The Lily of Killarney*. The plot was based on a melodrama, *The Colleen Bawn, or, The Brides of Garryowen*, by the Irish actor-manager Dion Boucicault. The play had opened first in New York in March 1860, and received its London premiere in September the same year, meeting with favourable reviews and enthusiastic audiences. It was clearly crying out for adaptation as an opera. Benedict chose John Oxenford, who had worked with Macfarren on *Robin Hood*, as his librettist, and the result of their collaboration was not only a success in itself, but seems also to have given renewed impetus to Benedict's career as a composer.

Balfe and Wallace, the two Irishmen, had gone to France, Bohemia, Spain and Germany for their operatic inspiration. Benedict, who was German and Jewish, chose Ireland. *The Lily of Killarney* concerns an Irish family faced with dispossession for debt. A bizarre catalogue of events concerning marriage plans and murder plots follows, culminating in the expected, if unlikely, happy ending. It is hardly social realism, but it is a great deal closer to some kind of reality than most of the other operas we have been considering. The libretto is particularly strong; and the score is more elaborate than most operas of this period – Macfarren being the exception. Benedict's music is permeated by Irish harmonies and rhythms which are a lot more subtle than Wallace's attempts to suggest Spain in *Maritana*. The work convinces from the beginning with an overture that is tuneful and controlled, but not overambitious, qualities which apply to the piece as a whole. And, of course, the Irish setting provides the perfect excuse for a series of crowd-pleasing ballads, such as 'Eily Mavourneen', 'The bloom is on the rye', 'It is a charming girl I know' and 'The moon hath raised her lamp above'. Benedict later produced a German version which toured widely in his native country; and, as one might expect, *The Lily of Killarney* proved popular in both Ireland and the United States. Of all the operas we have considered in this section, it is the one that is still performed with any frequency – the last recorded performance at the time of writing being in Dublin in 2015.

Unlike the majority of his peers, Benedict did not seek to follow up his success with more operas. He did write a short and unsuccessful operetta, but most of his creative energies were diverted into more academic compositions: two piano concertos, a number of concert overtures, two symphonies, several cantatas, and an oratorio based on the life of St Peter. The first of the symphonies, opus 101 in G minor, is one of the better English symphonies of the period – although its Englishness is diminished by the fact that its composer's German roots are clearly audible. Benedict also went on to conduct the Liverpool Philharmonic Orchestra, and to contribute regularly to the Birmingham Festival, for which he wrote several works. In 1871, he became a naturalised British subject and, at the same time, received one of Queen Victoria's musical knighthoods.

The Lily of Killarney was the last English romantic opera to achieve significant success. Many operas, as we have seen, were revived over the decades that followed, both at home and abroad, but the genre gradually faded away. One of the oddest ways of keeping residual interest alive was the attempt to market *The Bohemian Girl, Maritana* and *The Lily of Killarney* as an English, then later an Irish, Operatic Ring, in some undefined way analogous to Wagner's *Ring*. The idea seems to have arisen in the last quarter of the nineteenth century when opera companies sometimes played the three operas back-to-back on consecutive nights. The three operas have neither setting, nor storyline, nor even the nationality of the composer in common, but apparently it was hoped that by suggesting that they form some kind of unity, opera-goers might be persuaded to attend on all three nights. Surprising as it may seem, the idea continues to have some traction: the 2015 performance of *The Lily of Killarney* referred to above was billed as part of a concert performance of the 'Irish Ring'.

The British approach to music has never been theoretical. English romantic operas were composed during a thirty-year period that generated a lot of excitement, a lot of business – some profitable, some not – and a lot of entertainment. Whether they appeared in the theatre programme as airs or arias or ballads, it was always the songs that were the focus of both the composer's and the audience's attention. Overtures, orchestral passages and choruses were important, but it was the songs that counted; and many beautiful songs were produced. With one or two exceptions, the librettos were not strong; and the operas themselves, despite many an elaborate plot, were remarkable for the absence of sustained dramatic development. Occasional attempts were made to accustom audiences to through-composition and full recitative, but the public were not enthusiastic and gave every indication of preferring their operas in the English style with dialogue. It can be argued that, in many respects, little had changed since the days of the ballad opera, although one important consequence of the brief supremacy of the English romantic period is that it marked the end of the cobbled-together, pasticcio opera. What emerges is that, in opera as elsewhere, British music was again following its own path; working through its own response to the coming of Romanticism with little reference to Continental models.

Romanticism placed great emphasis on the value, even the nobility, of folk art and folk culture. This attitude, as it developed during the first half of the nineteenth century, was closely connected to a broader interest in the past – particularly the medieval past – and to a new interest in exploring national, cultural, and even ethnic origins. It manifested itself in many ways – in the rediscovery of Nordic and Celtic mythologies; in Scott's *Minstrelsy of the Scottish Borders*; in Wordsworth and Coleridge's adoption of ballad metre in their poetry and their idealisation of rural life; in Thomas Moore's use of traditional tunes as the basis for his appealing and richly emotional lyrics in *Moore's Irish Melodies*; in Wallace's choice of the Lorelei legend as a subject for an opera; in the warm public response to a Celtic story such as *Lily of Killarney*. And towards the end of the century, this same attitude would have a major impact on music throughout the British Isles as composers and folklorists began to collect folk songs and folk dances, using them to inform the classical tradition in a new and more direct way.

Yet the folk tradition that the exponents of Romanticism saw and valued was based on an idealised conception of the past. It had little connection with the harsh realities of rural life or the often even harsher realities of urban life. Such things either passed them by or proved too difficult to reconcile with their artistic aims. There were exceptions – or partial exceptions. Robert Burns, many of whose poems were written specifically for, or were later set to, music, evinces some awareness of social conditions (although Burns was not, as has at times been suggested, a full-blown socialist). George Macfarren, in writing part-songs about cricket and about the railways,[1] showed an awareness that his art did not exist in a world totally divorced from the everyday. But such flashes of awareness were limited and at best occasional.

Folk music is a partial mirror of the society from which it comes, and the folk music of the early 1800s was changing. Songs of rural love were still being written. Two well-known songs, 'Just as the Tide Was a-Flowing' and 'The Banks of Sweet Primroses', first appeared on broadsheets around 1830 and 1840 respectively, although both were almost certainly written earlier. Another kind of ballad that was still being written was the transportation ballad. Earlier songs such as 'Van Diemen's Land' or 'Young

Henry the Poacher' have their roots in the eighteenth century and their origins in the countryside, telling of young men sentenced to many years in Australia or Tasmania for what, the song implies, is the minor offence of poaching. Later transportation ballads often have an urban setting. 'We're Bound for Botany Bay', for example, which emerged in its final form in the 1880s, but has clear precursors in the 1820s, tells how the singer has been sentenced 'for bashing a bloke down our alley / And taking his ticker away.' As society changed, so the focus of folk music moved away from the rural world and from traditional occupations such as farming and hunting, towards urban and industrial life. A.L. Lloyd has suggested that by the 1850s the rural tradition of folk song composition had almost ceased.[2] This may well be true: the folk song collectors of the late-nineteenth and early-twentieth century all reported that the songs they collected were already regarded by their singers as old. None were contemporary and few, if any, were described as having come into the tradition in the lifetime of the singers from whom they were collected.

The new songs that escaped the attention of (or were ignored by) the collectors were work songs. These came from an urban world and often concerned life in the new industries. Many contained the same essential characteristics as the older rural songs, but, in line with the changes we saw emerging from the Napoleonic Wars, these newer songs tended to move folk music beyond stories of love and hardship, adding a social or political dimension, which might even become an explicit message or commentary on specific events. Weaving was one of the country's major industries that changed radically with the introduction of new technology. This, in turn, changed the lives of the weavers and textile workers; and the whole process was recorded in song. 'The Bury New Loom' was first published as a broadsheet by the Manchester printer, Swindells, in 1804. An itinerant weaver meets a young woman who asks him to help her set up her new hand-loom. It is, of course, a ballad of seduction, cleverly written so that the technical terms for the parts of the loom and the weaving process become physical and sexual metaphors.

My shuttle ran well in her lathe, sir, my thread it worked well up and
down,
My level stood close to her breastbone the time I was squaring her
loom.[3]

But the days of the hand-loom were numbered. Steam-driven power looms took over the industry. The skilled weaver working at home was replaced by the unskilled factory worker, and the transition is marked in a song called 'The Weaver and the Factory Maid'. The date is uncertain, not least because there are many versions of the text, some of them garbled, but the situation it describes relates to a period roughly between 1820 and 1850. The song is about sex, but sex within a clearly defined social context which the songwriter evidently regarded as important.

> I'm a hand weaver to me trade.
> I fell in love with a factory maid,
> And if I could but her favour win,
> I'd stand beside her and weave by steam.
>
> My father to me scornful said,
> How could you fancy a factory maid?
> When you could have girls fine and gay
> Dressed like unto the queen of the May ...
>
> Where are the girls, I will tell you plain:
> The girls have all gone to weave by steam,
> And if you'd find them you must rise at dawn
> And trudge to the mill in the early morn.[4]

Weaving and poverty went hand in hand throughout the century, and there were many songs that recorded the hardships of the weaver's life. They range from 'I am a poor cotton weaver', published as a broadside in Manchester about 1860, but probably written anything up to forty years previously, to 'Poverty, poverty knock', based on the noise made by the shuttle of the Dobbie Loom, a technology introduced in 1843, although the ballad itself may have been written as late as 1880 or 1890. The majority of these songs lack the sense of heroism in adversity which characterises so many rural ballads where tragedy plays a part. They do not lack emotion – there is sadness, anger, compassion – but, at the same time, they rarely offer any real sense of a solution: they are economic complaints, not calls for political change. One notable exception must be noted. 'The Hand-loom Weaver's Lament', written by John Grimshaw shortly after 1821 – and often sung to the tune of 'The Grand Old Duke of York' – is one of the first songs to threaten what appears as a class-based response to the weavers' sufferings:

> You tyrants of England, your race may soon be run
> You may be brought unto account for what you've sorely done.

A much bigger class of industrial ballads, and much more overtly political, is that dealing with mining. Coal mining ballads were certainly not new. The famous Tyneside song, 'The Collier's Rant', reflecting the old superstition that mining accidents were caused by the Devil, may well have been written as early as 1650; the more celebratory 'Bonny Pit Laddie' was current in many areas of the country well before 1800; and even Burns' song 'My Collier Laddie' was written in 1792. These were work songs and love songs of the old sort. Any social observation they contained was simply part of the setting of the song, and carried no additional message or meaning. In the period after the Napoleonic Wars, however, this began to change. Coal mining was growing in scale and importance; the coal owners were growing richer; but the miners were not. The 1830s and 1840s saw a series of strikes with the miners demanding better pay and safer working conditions; and the strikes, which often led to lockouts, were accompanied by a wave of new songs and ballads. Printed as broadsides by local printers and sold or circulated among the miners themselves and within the wider community, they were an important channel of communication, allowing the miners to make their case to the outside world – because, as A. L. Lloyd has noted, the mine owners all too often owned the local newspapers as well.[5] As a consequence, many ballads developed a polemical tone, exhorting the public, the miners, or some other group to listen, to stand together, or to take some form of collective action: 'Come all ye miners far and near, and let us all unite O'; 'Come all kind-hearted Christians and listen to my songs'; 'Come all you good people and listen a while'.

A strike in County Durham in 1844 gave rise to a number of interesting ballads, among them 'The Coal-owner and the Pitman's Wife', which takes the form of a dialogue. It not only communicates the miners' message, but goes further, using the metaphor of the Devil in Hell to conflate the moral issue of poor pay and conditions with a threat of direct action against the mine-owners. The pitman's wife tells Lord Firedamp that

> They're turning the poor folk all out of hell
> This is to make room for the rich, wicked race ...
> And the coal-owners is the next on command
> To arrive in hell, as I understand ...
> Now how can you think to prosper and thrive
> By wanting to starve your poor workmen alive.

An indication of how such ballads travelled among mining communities in different parts of the country is given by the fact that, although its origins are clearly traceable to County Durham, the ballad was actually collected from a miner in Lancashire. A lock-out in Northumberland in the same year is the probable origin of another impressive ballad, still sung today, which exposes a different aspect of the conflict arising out of the strikes. 'The Blackleg Miner' lays bare the threat of violence underlying the strike, and, by using real place names, emphasises its reality.

> Now dinna gan near the Seghill mine
> Across the way they stretch a line,
> To catch the throat and break the spine
> Of the dirty blackleg miner.

Strikes were not the only stimulus for ballads. New technology could sometimes be celebrated. 'The Haswell Cages', printed by George Walker in Durham in 1839, describes in great detail the new cages that carried both the coal and the miners themselves from the seam to the surface. It differs from many ballads in that it shows the miners' positive pride in what they did, despite the difficulties and the dangers. There is also what amounts to a separate subclass of ballads dealing with mining disasters. 'The Blantyre Explosion' is a moving piece concerning the Blantyre Colliery near Glasgow, where two hundred and ten miners died in October 1877. Musically, it takes the form of a Scottish lament and derives its emotional power from its concentration on the grief of one girl whose true love, Johnny Murphy, was killed in the blast. More famous is 'The Trimdon Grange Explosion', written in the wake of a disaster that killed seventy-four people in February 1882. The ballad was sung to the tune of a well-known parlour ballad, 'Go and leave me if you wish it', with words by the so-called collier bard or pitman poet, Tommy Armstrong. It was on sale within days of the explosion as a means of raising money to help the bereaved families

> Men and boys left home that morning for to earn their daily bread,
> Nor thought before that evening they'd be numbered with the dead.
> Let's think of Mrs Burnett, once had sons but now has none –
> By the Trimdon Grange explosion, Joseph, George and James are
> > gone.

As late as 1934, when some two hundred and sixty miners were killed at Gresford, near Wrexham in Wales, this kind of ballad was still being written. Although 'The Gresford Disaster' is less personal, taking a more bitter, journalistic approach, the fact that it was written at all is an indication that the mining industry, and more particularly the miners, continued to see balladry as an accepted, even necessary way of expressing their feelings and commemorating such disasters.

Even in the second half of the nineteenth century, there was still rarely any indication of what tunes were associated with individual ballads when they appeared. Just as in Elizabethan times, the name of a tune – usually an old or familiar one – might be printed under the title, but such references were not always reliable, so singers tended to choose any tune that fitted the music or could be easily adapted. It was not a matter of great importance, for here, unlike the classical or art music tradition, the music was not an end in itself: it was a vehicle of communication and influence. When they were composed, these songs would have had an urgent and present purpose, but as time passed they would have been stored away in the memory of the singers, to be brought out and sung on suitable occasions in order to recall, or connect with, past events. This was the origin of the long and proud tradition of ballad singing that flourished in the Mining Institutes and Working Men's Clubs and continued into the last decades of the twentieth century.

Mining ballads were written wherever there was a coalfield and a community, but the strongest tradition was in North East England, closely followed by Scotland. Ballads might be written by ordinary miners with a talent for words, by those we might now call activists, or by people in the local community. And these were not always men: the work of at least two women balladeers from the time of the 1844 lockouts survives. Jane Knight from Wingate in County Durham wrote 'The Pitmen's Grievances', and Elizabeth Gair, probably from North Shields, produced 'The Colliery Union', both urging support for William Roberts, the Chartist lawyer who championed the miners' cause. As the century progressed, however, urbanisation progressed with it. The institutes and the clubs grew bigger and more formal in their organisation. The outright amateur gave way to the semi-professional, the retired collier who did a turn as a singer-comedian, and ultimately the professional entertainer – men like Tommy Armstrong and Joe Wilson, who became spokesmen for their communities. The change put mining ballads on the same bill as comedy and light entertainment, linking them to the emerging power of music hall. This moved the tradition away from the working men with whom it originated, but at the same time allowed it to continue into the modern age. Ed Pickford's 1962 song, 'The Pound a Week Rise', with its direct and disobliging references to the Coal Board Chairman, Lord Robens, is a direct descendent of the 1844 ballads rehearsing the pitmen's grievances.

> Robens wouldn't give a pound, he wouldn't give ten bob
>
> He gave them seven-and-six and said, 'Now, get back to your job.'

So, too, is Billy Bragg's 'Which Side Are You On?', written in response to the 1984 miners' strike, but – indicating that folk music, like classical music, is international – based on a song by Florence Reece about a miners' strike in Kentucky in 1931.

The sea and sailors have been the subject of ballads and songs as far back as the folk tradition can be traced. With the end of the Napoleonic Wars, however, naval ballads naturally declined in importance. The image of a heroic Jack Tar defending his country, reflected in songs such as Shield's 'The Arethusa' and in Dibdin's patriotic spectaculars, could no longer be used to draw audiences to the theatre or to the pleasure gardens. The new seafaring ballads were songs of peace time, but they still emphasised the heroism of the sailors and the sufferings they faced. 'The Ship in Distress', which was probably based on a French original, deals with courage and self-sacrifice in the face of a storm. 'The Whale-Catchers' describes the hazards and hardships of whaling in the icy seas of Greenland. So does 'The Greenland Whale Fishery', which first appeared as a broadside before 1725, but, in updated and altered form, enjoyed great popularity during the nineteenth century and was reprinted on numerous occasions between 1819 and 1885. 'The Loss of *The Amphitrite*' laments the wreck of a convict ship lost in the English Channel on its way to New South Wales. 'A New Song on the Melancholy Loss of the Emigrant Ship *Anglo-Saxon*' is exactly what the title suggests. These songs and many others like them are not exactly objective – they can be emotional, even moving – but, even when voiced in the first person, they still give the impression of being written by an observer rather than participant. By contrast, it is in the drinking songs and the shanties that the voice of the sailors themselves seems to come through.

Songs such as 'New York Girls', sung to a polka beat (which was a new import from Central Europe in the mid-nineteenth century), and 'Go to Sea No More', a more traditional ballad, are both typical of a sub-class of songs that appear to regret, but secretly also celebrate, a sailor's night ashore:

> When first I landed in Liverpool, I went upon a spree;
>
> While it'll last I spend it fast, got drunk as drunk could be,

But before my money was all gone on liquor and the whores

I'd made up my mind that I was inclined to go to sea no more.

But it is the shanties that are central to the nineteenth-century folk tradition at sea. Shanties were not new. They had been outlawed in the Royal Navy during the Napoleonic Wars: sailors worked to the rhythm of a tune played on a fife or a fiddle instead. Now, however, they enjoyed a resurgence, becoming a more widespread phenomenon than ever before. Slave ships plying between West Africa and the West Indies, East Indiamen trading with India and Ceylon, narrow-hulled clippers linking Britain with China and Australia, all would have had a shantyman on board. His job was to have a store of shanties in his head, to shout out the verse, and to lead the chant as the work was done. At the height of their popularity in the middle decades of the century, there were hundreds of shanties in circulation. The most famous of all – 'What shall we do with a drunken sailor' – probably dates from the 1830s. The words might, as in that case, reflect a sailor's daily life, or the route the ship was sailing – 'We're bound for South Australia' – or almost anything at all. 'Leave her, Johnny, leave her' is about a sailor leaving his girl behind as the ship prepares to sail for home. 'Poor old horse', which is sung to a very similar tune, has a more obscure origin relating to an on-board ritual celebrating the end of a sailor's first month at sea. 'The Black Ball Line' takes its name from the company whose ships traded between Liverpool and Australia. Other lyrics, such as those of 'Haul away, Joe' are wittily irreverent.

King Louis was the King of France before the revolution

He went and got his head chopped off which spoiled his constitution.

But, of course, the words were not important. It was the rhythm that counted. The shantyman had to choose a shanty with a rhythm appropriate to the task on hand, and as different jobs had different rhythms, so there was a difference between a capstan shanty, a halyard shanty, and a pumping shanty. Different shanties were often sung, too, on outward voyages ('We're bound for the Rio Grande') and on homeward voyages ('Farewell and adieu to you, Spanish ladies'). In some ways, shanties were the ultimate kind of work song, binding a small community of men together in their work and attempting to ease the strain. By 1900, however, steam had largely replaced sail on the long routes across the world's oceans. There were no sails to raise, lower or trim; and the anchor was raised by steam power. Shanties gradually fell out of daily use and instead became items of interest to folk-song collectors.

Between 1815, the year of the Battle of Waterloo, and 1851, the year of the Great Exhibition, the population of the United Kingdom almost doubled. The population of London did double, while that of Manchester more than tripled. The 1851 census marked another milestone when it showed that, for the first time, over fifty per cent of the population lived in towns or cities. Massive population growth, rapid industrialisation, and equally rapid urbanisation all led to a major shift in the cultural and economic balance. In the space between the work songs of the weavers, miners and factory hands on the one hand, and the concerts of the Philharmonic Society or the productions at Drury Lane and Covent Garden on the other, there grew up a new and varied industry geared to providing entertainment for the urban masses. Provincial cities were growing faster than London, but even so, in 1851, London accounted for over thirteen percent of the population, which was more than all the other major cities in the country put together. The size of London's population created a market that allowed for change and innovation. Consequently, it was London that led the way, although the new trends that started in the capital spread throughout the country with ever-increasing speed.

The phrase 'Victorian popular music' immediately conjures up images of music hall, and the halls did, of course, come to occupy a central, even dominant position in the popular music of the second half of the nineteenth century. To begin with, however, they evolved as one strand of a much more complex picture of musical entertainment within a rapidly changing society. By 1815, Vauxhall Gardens was the last of the pleasure gardens that had played such a significant part in London's musical life to remain open. It tried to retain a high quality orchestra with leading players and conductors – men such as William Rooke and Henry Bishop – but music became less and less of an attraction, and the management resorted to non-musical events to attract an audience. These added a circus-like quality: there were equestrian performances, rope dancing, novelty light shows, balloon ascents, and even a re-enactment of the Battle of Waterloo involving 1,000 soldiers. These tactics were effective for a while, but, eventually, the Gardens ceased to attract the size and the quality of audience that had made it famous. Complaints about drunkenness, theft, and disorderly behaviour reached a level where, in 1859, Vauxhall was forced to close.

Several attempts were made to revive the pleasure garden ethos. In 1837, Rosherville Gardens opened in Gravesend with walks and a pseudo-medieval hall for dancing. Visitors had to take a steamboat trip down the Thames to get there, which was popular at first, but 1878 a boat returning to London was involved in a collision and over six hundred people drowned. After that, visitors travelled by railway. The Royal Surrey Gardens began life as a zoo, then in 1855 its owners built a huge 12,000-seat auditorium, which for a short while was successful in attracting audiences for musical and variety performances, but it burned down in 1861. Cremorne Gardens in Chelsea opened in 1845, offering a full range of fairground attractions as well as a huge pagoda that could hold a medium-sized orchestra and up to 4,000 dancers. It lasted until 1877. In the end, while these ventures provided opportunities for dancing and entertainment, none of them offered music of a quality to match the London gardens of seventy or eighty years previously. The musical significance of the gardens declined, and the gardens themselves gradually disappeared. However, the kind of audiences that had once flocked there to eat, drink, dance, and listen to anything from arias by Handel to symphonies by Boyce or songs by Shield and Hook, did not disappear. It was rather that, in a changed social environment, they could now choose between a wider variety of musical offerings.

Pubs, inns and taverns had long been the venue for meetings of amateur musical societies, singing clubs, glee clubs and the like. Now, in the 1820s and 1830s, these activities gradually gave rise to a new kind of entertainment: the saloon theatre or the song-and-supper room. These were gatherings – of men only to begin with – that took place in the large hall, often termed the 'ballroom' or 'clubroom', attached to an inn or tavern. To begin with, there was a strongly amateur flavour: two or three nights a week members of local music clubs and singers from the community might perform on a raised stage while, at long tables below, an audience of a hundred or more would be noisily eating, drinking and smoking. Gatherings such as these, known as 'free-and-easies', continued unchanged for many years in some places. Elsewhere, however, amateur performers were soon supplemented by professional entertainers paid for by the landlord. Performances became daily; premises were modified or extended; and the whole thing rapidly became a new kind of business.

One of the best-documented supper rooms was Evans's, not far from Covent Garden. W. C. Evans was a comedian and actor. In what had been the basement coffee room of the Grand Hotel, he set up a song-and-supper room and called it Evans's Late Joys. (Joys was the name of a previous owner.) The supper aspect of the venture was important. In the days before restaurants, Evans's served steaks, kidneys, chops and pies, oysters and rarebits throughout the day and well into the early hours. Under Evans's regime, the musical content of a given evening was likely to be good but haphazard – Evans himself might oblige with a rendition of his favourite song, 'If I had but a thousand a year'.[1] It was when he sold out to John 'Paddy' Green in 1846 that the place gained an enduring reputation for its musical entertainment.

There are many contradictions in Victorian attitudes to music and to popular culture as a whole. The music halls were criticised as dens of iniquity by some of the more robustly moral middle classes (although such criticism expressed in the parlour might not necessarily prevent the man of the house and his friends from attending). At the same time, Victorian attitudes to music in general could be remarkably unsnobbish. They were often far less compartmentalised than has since become normal. Victorians might recognise a difference in kind, and a difference in artistic value, between *Messiah*, *The Bohemian Girl*, a sentimental parlour ballad such as 'Home! Sweet Home!' and a comic song like 'The Ratcatcher's Daughter', but they would not think it odd or unusual to enjoy and appreciate all four. Thus Dickens, who had himself once written the libretto for an opera, *The Village Coquettes* (1836), was enraptured by Mendelssohn's songs and overcome with emotion at Gounod's *Faust*; yet he was also a regular at Evans's.

Under Paddy Green's management, the music would usually begin with a programme of glees, madrigals and operatic extracts. As a Catholic, Green also felt it his duty to smuggle in a piece of sacred music if he could. These pieces would be sung by the best choristers he could find – often from the Savoy Chapel, Westminster Abbey, or St Paul's Cathedral. The audience was encouraged to respect and applaud the performers, but still the smell of food, the clatter of plates and the noise of conversation would have been all around. This programme, which varied daily, would end round about midnight, after which singers of a different character took the stage.

The concept of a star performer had existed in the theatre since the early seventeenth century, and in opera since the beginning of the eighteenth. It was from the song-and-supper clubs, and the musical halls that evolved out of them, that the first real stars of popular song arose. At Evans's, the big star was Sam Cowell, the son of a British colonel and an American actress. His songs were acted as much as sung, and he was famous for a light-hearted forty-eight-verse epic about a vain good-for-nothing called 'Billy Barlow'. Another one of his was 'The Rat Catcher's Daughter':

> Not long ago in Vestminster
> There lived a rat catcher's daughter
> But she didn't quite live in Vestminster
> Cos she lived t'other side of the water
> Her Father caught rats and she sold sprats
> All round and about that quarter
> And the gentlefolk all took off their hats
> To the pretty little rat catcher's daughter.

His act would also feature Cockney retellings of *Hamlet* or *Macbeth*. Most popular of all was his Cockney ballad of two star-crossed lovers, 'Villikins and his Dinah', usually delivered with an exaggerated alliterative commentary on the action.

> (*Now this here is what the paternal parient said agin*
> *to the daughter, and tells you what the parricidal papa*
> *parenthetically and paragorically pronounced, with all*
> *the parabolical particulars*)
> Then go, boldest daughter, her parient replied
> As you won't agree to be this here young man's bride.
> (*He was a merchant pieman from Abyssinia, and*
> *exported baked taters to Timbuctoo for the Hottentots*)
> I shall leave your large fortune to the nearest of kin
> And you shan't have the benefit of one single pin.

Other regular performers at Evans's included Charlie Sloman, who rejoiced in the title of '*improvisatore*'. He made up songs or verses – almost in the style of a modern rapper – based on suggestions from the audience. Then there was Harry Perkins, who wrote over five hundred music hall songs, the most famous being 'Pretty Polly Perkins of Paddington Green'; and J. W. ('Jack') Sharp, who was known for his risqué ballads and his songs describing topical events. The fact that Sharp also sang frequently at Vauxhall Gardens is an indication of just how much the kind of music heard at the gardens had changed. At Evans's, he was paid £1 a night and allowed free drinks, though allowed to make money by selling copies of his songs. The drink became a problem and he died in the poorhouse at the age of just thirty-eight in 1856.

The song-and-supper rooms were a transitional phase, but nonetheless influential in determining what later became standard music-hall fare. The Coal Hole, just off the Strand, and the Cyder Cellars, between the Strand and Covent Garden, were known to attract journalists, artists and a slightly more intellectual audience. At the Coal Hole, W. G. Ross became one of the most popular turns of the day when he sang 'My name it is Sam Hall', the bitter, unrepentant confession of a murderous chimney sweep on his way to the scaffold; it was one of the best known of the murder ballads that were to prove popular throughout the century.

> Well, my name it is Sam Hall, Sam Hall.
> Yes, my name it is Sam Hall; it is Sam Hall.
> My name it is Sam Hall an' I hates you, one and all.
> An' I hates you, one and all:
> Damn your eyes.
>
> I killed a man, they said; so they said.
> I killed a man, they said; so they said.
> I killed a man, they said an' I smashed him in the head.
> An' I left him layin' dead,
> Damn his eyes.

At the Cyder Cellars, Thomas Hudson sang his satirical take on gossip and scandal, 'I Never Says Nothing to Nobody'. In 1851, the promoter, 'Chief Baron' Renton Nicholson, took over both establishments and moved the entertainment down market. His 'Judge and Jury' routines were mock trials of prominent or public figures – the charge usually being a sexual offence – in which the audience acted as the jury. The banter was crude and the singers were required to spice up their acts to match. The change was not popular: the audience dwindled and took itself off to the newly-established music halls. Both clubs soon closed.

One reason for the existence of song-and-supper rooms was the tangle of 'patent' regulations surrounding theatres and theatrical productions. Songs, sketches and comedy routines were fine, but when, in 1834, the Union Saloon in Shoreditch decided to put on a production of *Othello*, the management, cast, musicians and even the audience were all marched off to the local police station. The situation changed in 1843 with the new Theatres Act. Stripped of its complications, this led to a distinction between ordinary theatres, licensed by the Lord Chamberlain, where smoking and drinking were not allowed in the auditorium; and other theatres, licensed by local magistrates, where (with various provisos) they were. This change in the legal framework – it was certainly not a simplification – coupled with the growth and evolution of the song-and-supper rooms, led to the explosion – there is no other word – in music halls, both in London and across the country, which took place in the 1850s.

Burlesques were another strand in London's musical life. The Victorian burlesque was a theatrical production with a loose and variable structure. It consisted of a basic and necessarily simple plot – often adapted from Shakespeare or some well-known story – around which was woven a fabric of songs, dances, comedy routines, witty dialogue, and a few dramatic scenes. Burlesques were also distinguished by their elaborate scenery and their spectacular costumes and tableaux. In the end, they owed something to opera, something to pantomime, and something also to the Jacobean masque. Versions of burlesque had been around for years, but the new genre was really launched by Eliza Vestris with her *Olympic Revels* at the Olympic Theatre in 1831. Versions of *William Tell* and *The Golden Fleece* were soon on stage. Despite a life largely given over to bookish and anti-quarian pursuits, James Planché became the acknowledged master of the burlesque script. Planché – whom we have met before as the writer of the melodrama *Chevy Chase* which in the end did not feature Macfarren's music – produced works with titles such as *Amoroso, King of Little Britain*; *Sherwood Forest*; and *Orpheus in the Haymarket*. A burlesque script had to be full of wit, puns and wordplay, and many journalists and writers, includ-ing W. S. Gilbert, took a turn. Musically, it cannot be said that burlesques contributed anything new or significant. Their importance lies in their popularity. They had an advantage in that they could be performed in non-patent theatres and venues right across London. And once they proved profitable there, provincial theatres quickly cashed in. Burlesques were important, too, as a contributory factor in the rise of the music hall; and because they mined something of the same vein of satire, wit and inconse-quential humour which Gilbert later exploited so successfully in his part-nership with Sullivan.

Ballet was another musical form that saw a huge growth in popularity during the first half of the nineteenth century. It was initially an exclusive entertainment, centred on the King's (later Her Majesty's) Theatre, but by the 1870s and 1880s, some of the top music halls – notably the Empire and Alhambra in Leicester Square – felt able to mount spectacular productions, starring some of the most popular ballerinas of the day. The emergence of ballet in London followed on directly from the appearance in Paris of new ballets in the romantic style, giving greater prominence to the ballerina, to the aesthetics of dance, and also featuring specially written music, rather than assembling a pasticcio score. The key figure was Marie Taglioni (1804–84), generally regarded as the greatest dancer of the age. She was born in Stockholm to a Swedish mother, who danced with a local ballet company, and an Italian father who was a talented choreographer. Taglioni grew up surrounded by dance. She made her first professional appearance in Vienna at the age of eighteen. Five years later she made her Paris debut, and by 1830, the date of her first appearance in London, she was recognised as Europe's leading ballerina – a position which was not seriously challenged until her retirement in 1847.

More than anyone else, Taglioni created the role of the ballerina as we understand it today. In London, she danced *The Tyrolienne*, based on Rossini's *William Tell*, and *La Bayadère*, with music by Auber. She was an overnight sensation and two years later, when she returned to dance *La Sylphide* (the story of which provided the basis for Barnett's *Mountain Sylph*), she was paid £100 a night (at a time when £100 a year was considered a good income). Part of her success was that her dancing was graceful, but was not seen as sensual or suggestive. This helped transform not only ballet itself, but also British attitudes to ballet, which were rigid and generally disapproving. At the time, 'actress' was frequently regarded as a code word for prostitute, and ballet dancers with their tight, often revealing costumes were particularly morally suspect (although sometimes, it has to be said, with good reason). Taglioni's achievement, a considerable one in the circumstances, was to move ballet beyond such moral strictures.

She soon had rivals. First came the Elssler sisters, Fanny and Theresa. Fanny soon emerged as the more talented; she enraptured London with her athletic routines based on traditional Spanish dances. Then came Francesca Ceritto, who seems to have captivated Sir Michael Costa. He wrote a ballet called *Alma*, which she danced in 1842. That same year another new ballerina appeared. Carlotta Grisi was ten years younger than Fanny Elssler and fifteen years younger than Taglioni. And she had the advantage of being launched in London in a ballet that rapidly became one of the most popular ever written. Despite a somewhat gruesome storyline about young girls who have died before their wedding emerging from their graves to dance, and despite the music having been composed in just one week, *Giselle*, with its score by the French composer, Adolphe Adam, remains in the international repertoire to this day. It was premiered in Paris in August 1841. It was given its first London performance the following March and made an immediate star of Grisi. She followed it up with a second triumph two years later: *La Péri* by Théophile Gautier, to music by the German composer Johann Burgmüller, was another reflection of the contemporary craze for all things Oriental. Grisi was praised for creating two separate roles within the same ballet.

Following the pattern set by Taglioni, these ballerinas criss-crossed Europe, giving their spectacular performances and enjoying the rewards of stardom. Paris, Saint Petersburg, Vienna, Munich, Milan and London were among the most prestigious bookings, but it was in London that competing promoters exploited the rivalry between the ballerinas most effectively, creating a mass audience and, as a result, offering the greatest financial rewards. That rivalry came to a head in 1845 when Benjamin Lumley, manager of Her Majesty's Theatre, made a mess of his booking arrangements. He somehow contracted Taglioni, Ceritto, Grisi and the new Danish ballet sensation, Lucile Grahn, to appear in the same season. Pride and precedence were at stake. In the end, a solution was reached and a new *divertissement* was put together by the theatre's choreographer, Jules-Joseph Perrot, to music by the Italian, Cesare Pugni. This was the famous *Pas de Quatre*, one of the high points of romantic ballet. The piece was designed to give all four stars the opportunity to show off their particular talents and specialities; and there were to be just four performances. It worked. The *Pas de Quatre* was a hot topic of conversation and correspondence not only throughout the United Kingdom, but throughout Europe. It even featured in diplomatic correspondence. Still more significant in terms of the future image and reputation of ballet was the fact that Queen Victoria and Prince Albert attended the third performance. It was not quite the first time the Queen had attended a ballet – in 1843, she had expressed a wish to see Francesca Cerrito and Fanny Elssler, and a special *Pas de Deux* had been danced during the interval of *The Barber of Seville* – but this was the occasion that gave ballet the royal seal of approval. It also marked something of a tipping point. With ballet now officially respectable as well as popular, the music hall proprietors saw it as a something they, too, could put on. It would enhance their reputation for culture and respectability – which was constantly being challenged by the London County Council and other licensing bodies – and now it would do so without losing money. The prime mover in this process, which we will explore in Chapter 71, was Charles Morton (1819–1904), the man who would become known as 'The Father of the Halls'.

The slow demise of the pleasure gardens, coupled with the trend among those that survived towards concentrating on dancing and circus- or fairground-style entertainment, left a gap in the market for those who wished to hear classical music, but were not able or willing to expose themselves to the formality of the Philharmonic Society or the Antient Concerts. By the end of the 1820s, there were probably more outlets for classical music in the provinces – in cities such as Dublin, Bristol, Birmingham, Leeds and Newcastle, where tastes changed more slowly, where there were subscription concerts in the Town Hall, and where the local pleasure gardens still survived – than there were in London. The concert hall in the Hanover Rooms, built in the 1770s, was in constant use, but it was small. The Philharmonic Society had moved its concerts to Her Majesty's Theatre, which was not really a suitable venue. Exeter Hall, which could take an audience of up to 4,000, was reserved for meetings of a political or religious character rather than concerts. Not until 1852 did its shareholders allow something as frivolous as the Philharmonic's annual concerts to move there. There were simply no modern, purpose-built concert halls in the city.

The term 'promenade concert' had originated in the pleasure gardens where, in their heyday, orchestras had played music by composers such as Handel, Corelli, Scarlatti, Arne, and Boyce, as well as selections of songs and more obviously 'popular' works, to an audience that came and went and wandered around as it chose. In 1838, the management of the Lyceum saw a new business opportunity. They would adapt the idea, staging a season of indoor promenade concerts and, in order to add glamour and credibility, they would bring over the French conductor Philippe Musard, who had recently organised a series of successful outdoor concerts in Paris. It was a deliberate if potentially risky attempt to attract a mass audience for classical music. A professional orchestra of sixty players was recruited; the auditorium was boarded over to allow for a standing audience, and the price of admission was set at one shilling. Despite initial concerns, it was a success, and the Lyceum began to stage promenade concerts on a regular basis. Moreover, it set a trend. Smaller venues like the Crown and Anchor in the Strand, which still hosted Glee Club meetings, and larger ones such as the enormous neo-classical Colosseum in Regent's Park, put on their own concerts in the same format. So did the prestigious Almack's Assembly Rooms. For a short while everything went well, but then audiences began to thin out. In part, this was because there were too many concerts. In part, also, it was because the public seemed to favour classical programmes of the lighter kind – those that made room for dance tunes and allowed them to waltz or form up for the cotillion and the quadrille – as opposed to those featuring symphonies or works that required a degree of concentration. Promenade concerts seemed to have run up against the barrier of the fickle and essentially lightweight taste of the British public.

In 1840, however, the Drury Lane management announced a series of promenade concerts in the French style – *concerts d'été* – instigated by the orchestra leader Edward Eliason. Also involved was Louis-Antoine Jullien, whom we have previously met bringing Berlioz to London in 1847. Jullien (1812–60), who had fled to London from Paris leaving a trail of debts behind him, was initially the associate conductor of the new venture, but rapidly made a place for himself on the British musical scene by reason of his outrageous showmanship and his ability to read British audiences. By the time of the second season in 1841, he was conducting an orchestra of over a hundred in programmes that included Beethoven symphonies, in an auditorium that featured a fountain as a centrepiece and was decked out with flowers and potted palms. Rightly understanding that familiarity was the key to success with a British audience, he added a choir to the concerts, mixing symphonies with choral pieces, such as extracts from Handel, which he knew would be familiar and popular. Ticket prices were kept low – still just a shilling – which ensured that people of all social classes could attend. And they would also be treated to the spectacle of Jullien with his long, wavy black hair, wearing a flamboyant costume with embroidered lapels and an extravagant waistcoat, pulling on a pair of white kid gloves and conducting with a jewel-encrusted baton, often with his back to the orchestra so as to make eye contact with his audience.

By 1844, Jullien's promenade concerts had moved to Covent Garden and he had begun to divide them between more serious music in the first half and lighter, dance music in the second. In 1845, he began to conduct huge outdoor concerts at the Surrey Gardens, sometimes accompanied by fireworks. His personality and panache were such that he was able to carry off such bizarre oddities as the Beethoven Septet, opus 20, performed by no less than sixty players, or Beethoven's Fifth with four brass bands added to the orchestra. At the same time, he could successfully programme something as serious and intense as the *Kreutzer Sonata*. For all his showmanship – a gift for the caricaturists at *Punch* – Jullien insisted on high musical standards, and he was a genuine musical educator. He took his promenade concerts on extended regional tours, maintaining the same low prices and thus offering many working men and women in cities such as Bradford, Leeds, Birmingham and Belfast their first experience of orchestral music. There is an account of three members of a brass band from Keighley in Yorkshire walking ten miles to attend a Jullien concert in Bradford and ten miles back again.[2] Attempting to apply his showmanship to opera, however, proved a step too far and Jullien was declared bankrupt. He fought back, even taking his promenade concerts to the United States, but luck was against him. In 1855 the colossal auditorium at the Surrey Gardens burned down. The following year Covent Garden also burned down. Jullien tried to stage enormous festivals devoted to individual composers – Haydn, Rossini, Verdi – but these did not produce the much-needed profits. In debt, he fled to Paris, but his French creditors had not forgotten him. He was thrown into a debtors' prison, tried to commit suicide and was adjudged insane. He was then sent to an asylum where he died in March 1860 at the age of forty-eight. An indication of his popularity is the fact that in the August following his death, a Jullien Festival was held in the Royal Botanical Gardens in Belfast, one of the provincial cities that had benefit-ted from his activities. Jullien's orchestra was supplemented by the band of the Royal Antrim Rifles and conducted by a Russian prince. Over 5,000 people came and the proceeds were donated to Jullien's widow.[3]

67   Pianos, Parlour Ballads, and the Great Exhibition

The enduring image of a young lady seated at a piano in the family parlour, perhaps with an attentive young man at her shoulder ready to turn the pages, is somehow evocative of the Victorian era. Yet the period was one of constant change, in music as in almost every other area of life. When Queen Victoria came to the throne in 1837, ownership of a piano was largely confined to the rich and the affluent middle classes. By the time she died in 1901, the piano had become an item of mass production. Exact figures are impossible to obtain, but one estimate suggests that by 1910 there was one piano for every ten to twenty people in the country.[1] This massive expansion in piano ownership and piano-playing rested to a significant degree on mechanical and technological advances made during the first thirty years of the nineteenth century.

Britain had long led the field in piano manufacture. This was partly due to the strength of its economy, which made for a buoyant market, and partly to the fact that London was home to John Broadwood & Sons. From 1780 onwards Broadwood's developed a series of important innovations in piano technology; it remained a leading force in the music industry throughout the nineteenth century; indeed, it is still a going concern today. But as time went on, it began to face competition from other innovators. There were two French manufacturers: Sébastien Erard (who had actually spent a number of years in London avoiding the revolutionary and Napoleonic turmoil) and Ignaz Pleyel. Both patented further small but significant technical advances. And there was an American firm, Alpheus Babcock, which made another step forward by introducing an iron frame. There were, of course, many other manufacturers, but it was competition between these four that produced the kind of piano that we would now recognise, and that made it for possible Chopin, Schumann and Liszt to write and play as they did.

Even during the Napoleonic Wars, the British economy remained strong and a number of new piano manufacturers started up – some of which have already been discussed. Clementi (1798), Muir & Wood in Edinburgh (1798), Challen (1804), Chappell (1811) and Wilkinson (1811) all sought to exploit what they correctly saw as an expanding market. In fact, until the 1830s, the growth in piano sales seems to have been steady rather than spectacular. After that, however, it began to accelerate rapidly, to the point where, by 1850, some 25,000 pianos a year were being sold – equivalent to half the total worldwide production. One of the central figures in all this was Robert Wornum (1780–1852). More than anyone else, Wornum saw the musical and commercial possibilities of the upright piano; and he devoted most of his working life to patenting new ideas and producing a series of models – the Cottage Piano, the Piccolo Piano, and the Cabinet Piano – all of which are variants of the basic upright design. He even opened a music hall next to his factory as a means of advertising and sell-ing them. It was the upright, not the grand, that turned the piano from a luxury into mass-market item. It was cheaper to produce, cheaper to buy, and small enough to fit into a lower middle-class or working-class home or even into the bar of a street-corner pub.

There was, of course, a huge difference between Queen Victoria's sumptuous golden grand in Buckingham Palace (by Erard, bought in 1856, gilded and decorated with cherubs, animals and birds), and a small upright, bought on credit, squeezed into the corner of a front room of a terraced house in Huddersfield. Nonetheless, the piano was a unifying factor in Victorian musical culture – even though many Victorians would have struggled to recognise it as such. Another contributory factor to the piano boom was the fact that Britain also led the world in publishing and printing sheet music. In the 1840s, it was estimated that Britain produced more sheet music than the rest of Europe put together. Every kind of music was available: piano exercises, country dances, waltzes, polkas, songs and parlour ballads, hymns, classical piano pieces, piano arrangements of concert overtures and symphonies, piano scores of the great oratorios. Here, too, there was a sense of something shared across society. The piano duet that the Queen and Prince Albert played in Buckingham Palace, or the ballad the Queen sang, accompanied by one of her ladies-in-waiting, at Osborne House on the Isle of Wight where there were several pianos, could just as easily be played or sung in any other home in the kingdom. The Queen might attend the opera or the ballet in state, but at home her tastes and the after-dinner amusements she shared with her husband were much the same as those of any middle-class family.

There is no workable definition of a Victorian parlour ballad. Some of the most famous, as we have already seen – 'The harp that once through Tara's halls', 'Believe me if all those endearing young charms', even 'Home! Sweet Home!' – were extracted from operas. 'I'll sing thee songs of Araby' came from a cantata. Others, such as 'Love's Old Sweet Song' (often better known by the first line of the chorus, 'Just a song at twilight'), 'The Old Arm Chair' or 'The Rose of Tralee' were written purposely for the song market. Perhaps the most famous of them all, Arthur Sullivan's 'The Lost Chord', with lyrics by Adelaide Proctor, was written as a personal response to his brother's final illness. It went on to sell half a million copies. These songs, and a thousand others like them, are simply the kind of song that would have been sung, usually to piano accompaniment, in a Victorian home as part of an evening's entertainment. If they have an additional common factor, it is that they reflect the sentimentality which has so often been identified – and criticised – as a central characteristic of the Victorian era. Whatever we think of that kind of sentimentality, it is clearly what the Victorians sought, perhaps as a way of intensifying the communication of emotion and sincerity in response to the prevailing romanticism of the age.

We also know that in performance, it was expression – the tremolo in the voice, the emphatic chord, the ability to draw from the audience an emotional response – that was valued at least as much as technical ability. Sentiment was the language of the age, and one which, again, united the denizens of Clerkenwell with those of Buckingham Palace. When Victoria and Albert became engaged, he presented her with a three-volume set of his own *Lieder und Romanzen* – he was a good amateur composer – which are full of sentiment: 'The Last Words of a Poet', 'The Pain of Love', 'Say, Sleepest Thou, Love?' Two months later, he sent her 'Dem Fernen', about sending thoughts of love to a loved one far away.[2]

Yet sentiment and the image of the Queen and her Consort playing duets in the royal parlour are only part of a much more complex picture. Theirs was a genuine romance, and it was also in complete contrast to the domestic life of the two previous monarchs – George IV, who kept a string of mistresses and made no secret of it; and William IV, who left ten children but no legitimate heir. Victoria's reign saw a major change – indeed, several major changes – in the way the monarchy related to society. Projecting an image of morality and domestic harmony was part of it; so, too, was a change in the royal relationship with the arts. In terms of music, Victoria's predecessors had taken a genuine, if intermittent interest, frequently based on personal whim. All that would now change, and Albert would be the agent of change. The Queen could play the piano and sing, but Albert was an accomplished musician. He played the piano and the organ; he had strong tenor voice; and, as we have seen, he also composed – at his death, in 1861, he left over forty *Lieder*, a number of anthems and hymns, as well as one or two melodic pieces for violin. These were days long before the emergence of public relations, but Albert, almost like a medieval king, seems to have understood instinctively how music could be used to boost the standing of the monarchy.

George IV had maintained a private orchestra, but it had been genuinely private and paid for out of his own resources. This has to be distinguished from the monarch's official musicians, once called the King's Musick but by now known, confusingly, as the Queen's Private Band. This had declined to the point where it was no more than handful of wind players, who were occasionally called upon to play at court functions. Prince Albert reformed the Private Band. He transformed it into a small orchestra capable of giving proper concerts, and extended its repertoire beyond arrangements of songs from popular operas to include Mozart, Beethoven, Schubert, Spohr and, of course, Mendelssohn. He also, although it took much longer, arranged for the complete renovation of the ballroom at Buckingham Palace, so that royal balls and royal concerts took place in appropriately splendid surroundings. The duties of the Master of the King's (now the Queen's) Musick had been much reduced over time: they no longer involved composition, and he was, in reality, no more than an occasional conductor. Sadly, this was a situation which Prince Albert did not live long enough to reform.

The Queen loved music and she loved dancing. She was also particularly fond of opera – although it is said that she was equally fond of the crowd-pulling interval acts such as lion-tamers and jugglers – but it was Albert who persuaded her to become a formal patron of the English Opera at the Lyceum. This gave a struggling organisation the royal seal of approval at a time when many still regarded anything to do with the theatre as morally suspect. Albert himself became a director of the Concerts of Antient Music and also took an active interest in the Philharmonic Society. His public support for Mendelssohn was partly because he liked the German composer's music, but also because he hoped that Mendelssohn's example might be beneficial for British composers at a time when their reputation did not stand high, either at home or abroad.

The Great Exhibition of 1851 was one of the defining events of Queen Victoria's reign and, again, it was largely Albert's doing. He and his Commissioners triumphed over mockery, disbelief, obstructing tactics, and technical and financial difficulties. They created an international exhibition of unparalleled size, with twenty-eight countries participating, although the aim of the whole thing was unashamedly to demonstrate British technical and industrial superiority. Among the exhibitors were thirty-eight piano manufacturers from Britain alone, as well as many others from France, Germany and the United States. The models on display ranged from grand pianos and uprights to folding pianos suitable for taking on board a gentleman's yacht. There was a piano for four players, and a contraption that allowed one person to play a piano and a violin simultaneously. There were no less than five full-size organs on display. One monster was by Henry Willis of Manchester. It had three manuals, seventy-seven stops and 4,700 pipes. Willis did well out of the Exhibition. A recital on his organ, given in the presence of the Queen and Prince Albert – and tactfully including a piece entitled 'Schlaf, Schlaf, mein Kindelein' by the Prince himself – resulted in him receiving a contract to install an organ in St George's Hall, Liverpool. He was also asked, some years later, to build the organ in the Royal Albert Hall.

Thirty thousand people attended the opening ceremony on 1 May 1851. There were barrel organs and fiddlers playing for pennies in the streets leading to Hyde Park where the newly-erected Crystal Palace stood. There were brass bands playing in various parts of the park for the amusement of picnicking families. The Queen and Prince Albert drove in a procession of carriages from Buckingham Palace. A fanfare of trumpets greeted them as they descended from their carriages and entered the building. When they reached the ceremonial platform at its centre, the Great Organ in the South Transept – built by Gray and Davison, and not only bigger than Willis's, but claimed to be the biggest in the world – began to roll out the tune of the National Anthem. A thousand voices joined in. However, in view of the presence of diplomatic representatives from many countries, it had been decided to omit the potentially offensive second verse.

> O Lord our God arise
> Scatter her enemies
> And make them fall
> Confound their politics
> Frustrate their knavish tricks
> On Thee our hopes we fix
> God save us all

Prince Albert made a speech. The Queen replied. The Archbishop of Canterbury offered up a prayer. Then the organ, an orchestra of two hundred and a choir of six hundred – drawn from St Paul's Cathedral, Westminster Abbey, St George's Windsor, the Chapel Royal and from other churches all over London – launched into a full volume rendition of the 'Hallelujah Chorus'. This was music on a gargantuan scale, designed to impress, to shock, to make a statement. Even in an age of extremes, nothing could provide a greater contrast with the domesticity of piano duets in Buckingham Palace, but there is little doubt that Prince Albert's vision of the monarchy and of music encompassed both.

Perhaps because he was not British, Albert was one of few men in that age of emotion who could stand back and look at British society with a degree of detachment. He could see the weaknesses as well as the strengths of his wife's Empire. This enabled him to develop a long-term vision for the intellectual and artistic future of the United Kingdom, in which music played a central role. As early as 1853, he had the idea of using the profits from the Great Exhibition to create a complex of national institutions devoted to science and the arts on what was then the South Kensington Estate. At the time, the concept was widely mocked as 'Albertopolis', and Albert never lived to see it come to fruition, but today South Kensington is home to an unmatched collection of nationally important museums and colleges: the Natural History Museum, the Science Museum, the Royal College of Art, the Royal Geographical Society, Imperial College, and many others. On the northern side of this area stands the Royal Albert Hall, which many would still regard as the country's most prestigious musical venue; while just behind it, opening onto Prince Consort Road, is the Royal College of Music.

> Why is it that Germany, France, and Italy have national styles of music? Why is it that England has no music recognised as national? It has able composers, but nothing indicative of the national life or national feeling. The reason is not far to seek. There is no centre of music to which English musicians may resort with confidence, and thence derive instruction, counsel and inspiration.[3]

The words are those of the Prince of Wales on the opening of the Royal College (RCM) in 1883, but the vision is that of his father, Prince Albert.

68   Early Sullivan

Twenty years to the day after the opening of the Great Exhibition, on 1 May 1871, another major exhibition opened in London. Although neither as grand nor as iconic as its predecessor, the London International Exhibition of Fine Arts and Industry was not without significance. It was intended as the first of ten annual events, each focussing on scientific discoveries, on developments in the fine arts, and on particular categories of manu- factured goods. It was also the first major event to be hosted at what was officially known as the Royal Albert Hall of Arts and Sciences. The Albert Hall had been opened just over a month earlier, at the end of March, with a huge official ceremony, presided over by the Prince of Wales – Queen Victoria was present, but so overcome with emotion at the memory of her late husband that she was unable to speak. The musical centrepiece was

Sir Michael Costa's *Biblical Cantata*, which he himself conducted. The performance, with a full orchestra and 1,200 voices, was monumental, but the work itself has since been entirely forgotten. After the ceremony came a 'Grand Miscellaneous Concert', that began with *L'invocazione all'armonia* by Prince Albert and included an aria from Handel's *Rinaldo*, but otherwise featured nothing which could be considered British music – even by adoption.

The opening concert of the London International Exhibition was a different matter. The programme consisted of four pieces by contemporary composers, each representing a major European nation and each conducted by the composer. Italy was represented by Ciro Pinsuti, and France by Charles Gounod, both of whom were living and working in London. Germany's representative was Ferdinand Hiller, a friend of Mendelssohn's and pupil of Hummel's, whose claim to fame was that he had been at Beethoven's deathbed and heard Schubert perform *Winterreise*. The man chosen to represent Britain was Arthur Seymour Sullivan (1842–1900), who conducted his cantata *On Shore and Sea*, written specially for the occasion.[1] Sullivan was much younger than the others, only twenty-nine, and it was certainly a notable honour to be chosen, but he had for some years been marked down as the great hope of British music and had already come a long way in his career, both professionally and socially.

Sullivan was born in Lambeth in South London, but his parents were Irish, and his gift for a persuasive, lilting melody links him to that Irish strain that we have seen contributing to nineteenth-century British music – and particularly theatrical music – through composers such as William Rooke, Michael Balfe and William Wallace, although Sullivan's abilities and achievements were far greater than theirs. At the time of Arthur's birth, his father, Thomas Sullivan, was working as a clarinettist in the orchestra at the Royal Surrey Theatre. Under the management of the celebrated Mrs Frances Davidge, the Royal Surrey had a reputation for staging almost anything – from ridiculous musical adaptations of Dickens' novels to *The Beggar's Opera* or *Der Freischütz*. Such variety no doubt broadened Thomas Sullivan's musical horizons, but it was demanding work and in 1845 – when Arthur was three – he was delighted to be offered a new post as Bandmaster at the Royal Military Academy at Sandhurst. The new job meant tutoring band members, conducting the band, and selecting and arranging the music they played. It was the perfect appointment. By 1857, his reputation was such that, when the Commander-in-Chief of the British

Army, the Duke of Cambridge, decided to establish the Royal Military School of Music at Kneller Hall in Surrey, Thomas Sullivan was appointed Professor of Brass Instruments.

Arthur Sullivan thus grew up, like William Wallace, learning to play all the instruments in his father's military band. He later claimed that the only wind instruments on which he did not become fully proficient were the oboe and the bassoon. He also developed a beautiful singing voice, and it seems to have been his own idea that he should become a chorister at the Chapel Royal. His father, initially at least, was not keen for him to follow a musical career, but the boy insisted and, although slightly over the normal age limit, was eventually admitted in 1852 on the recommendation of Sir George Smart. By now in his late sixties, Smart was Composer to the Chapel Royal and represented the musical old guard. An authoritative and commanding figure, his recommendation to the Master of Choristers, the less than inspiring and less than inspired figure of the Reverend Thomas Helmore, was law. Standards at the Chapel Royal were not what they had been a generation or two earlier when Smart himself had been a chorister, and membership of the Chapel was no longer the guarantee of a successful musical career that it had once been. Nonetheless, Sullivan made the best of the opportunities available to him: he not only advanced musically, but also gained access to areas of society that would otherwise have remained beyond the reach of someone from his lower-middle-class background.

Sullivan had charm. From his earliest years, he had an ability to get on with, and obtain the good opinion of, people who could be useful to him. This was not sycophancy – although to our eyes it might seem at times to run close – but rather an old-fashioned sense of deference and respect, combined with a naturally open temperament. So it was that Smart not only agreed to conduct the thirteen-year-old Sullivan's anthem *Sing unto the Lord* at the Chapel Royal, but to do so in the presence of Prince Albert, who expressed his approval. So it was also that Thomas Helmore, a known martinet whose musical interests and teaching methods were solidly old-fashioned, discovered and actively encouraged Sullivan's interest in composition. Of course, Sullivan had talent and a superb singing voice, but not every talented boy managed to get the same level of encouragement and opportunity.

In June 1853, the Chapel Royal choir assembled in the chapel at Buckingham Palace for the christening of Queen Victoria's latest (and last) son, Prince Leopold. The Queen's Body Guard – also, and significantly in view of Sullivan's later history, known as the Yeomen of the Guard – were on parade. The Queen, the Prince Consort and their children were naturally present. So, too, were the King of Hanover, the Prince of Prussia (and future German Emperor), the Prince of Hohenlohe-Langenburg and a generous scattering of Dukes and Duchesses, both British and German. The Archbishop of Canterbury officiated. Sir Michael Costa had written an anthem, *Suffer the Little Children*, for the occasion, and the treble solo was sung by the eleven-year-old Arthur Sullivan. In 1854, the rich and aristocratic Sir Frederick Gore Ouseley hired the choristers of the Chapel Royal, including Sullivan, to sing the oratorio, *The Martyrdom of St Polycarp*, which he had written as his doctoral submission, at Oxford. In 1856, Gore Ouseley mounted a huge inauguration ceremony for his newly-established St Michael's College at Tenbury Wells. The royal choirs of the Chapel Royal and St George's, Windsor, were supplemented by those of five cathedrals – Exeter, Oxford, Hereford, Worcester and Gloucester. Sullivan led the trebles. The following year saw another royal christening – that of Princess Beatrice – at Buckingham Palace, again heavily laden with ceremonial and European royalty. Such events gave Sullivan an early sight of the upper levels of Victorian society and may well have planted the seeds of social aspiration. At the same time, he was also exploring the musical landscape of London, discovering the opportunities available to a young musician, and making his first acquaintance with figures who would be important in helping him make a musical career.

The most obvious legacy of the Great Exhibition was the Crystal Palace, which the whole country adopted as a symbol of British technological innovation. After the Exhibition, which lasted six months, it was bought by a consortium of businessmen, removed from Hyde Park and re-erected in a much enlarged form at Sydenham in South London. Queen Victoria formally reopened the building in June 1854, with Michael Costa presiding over musical forces which were, once again, on a gigantic scale: the choir alone was 1,500 strong. The new Crystal Palace rapidly became London's most popular musical venue. There were two main reasons for this. The first was the sheer size of the new venue – it could accommodate an audience of 4,000, all seated – which meant that ticket prices could be kept low. The second was the work of two men, August Manns (1825–1907) and George Grove (1820–1900), whose careers we will examine in the next chapter. For the moment, it is enough to note that concerts at the Crystal Palace were immensely popular – so popular that at weekends special trains were laid on to bring people from central London – and that the young Sullivan was frequently in the audience. He attended Manns' Saturday concerts and would surely have responded to the fact that between them Manns and Grove were not only introducing works by less familiar Continental composers – Schubert, who was still largely neglected, and Schumann, who was regarded as dangerously modern – but also trying to provide a much-needed platform for works by British composers. He also found himself singing there, as part of the chorus for the 1857 Handel Festival, when the size of the orchestra and chorus (850 and 2,000 respectively) reached new heights.

Sullivan was in the audience when Wagner conducted the 1855 season at the Philharmonic. Wagner, too, made an effort to promote British composers, programming symphonies by Cipriani Potter and Charles Lucas, but when Bennett took the podium in 1856, the emphasis switched back to German music – Mendelssohn, Spohr and Schumann. It was Schumann's *Paradise and the Peri* that had the greatest effect on the young Sullivan, at least in so far that he, too, took inspiration from *Lalla Rookh* for one of his early (and now lost) orchestral works, *The Feast of Roses*. *Paradise and the Peri* featured Jenny Lind as the soprano soloist. Hearing her sing for the first time was an experience Sullivan never forgot. By contrast, he saw Anton Rubinstein play and was not impressed.

In 1856, Sullivan was the first person to be awarded a Mendelssohn Scholarship, which allowed him to study at the RAM and then, two years later, took him to Leipzig. The existence of such a scholarship was the result of the ever-growing influence of German music in general and what has been described as the 'virtual beatification' of Mendelssohn in particular.[2] Sullivan's name was put forward by John Goss, another of those influential, establishment figures who responded to Sullivan's charm and went out of their way to help him. When Sullivan started at the Academy, Goss taught him harmony, while among his other teachers were Cipriani Potter, Bennett, and the Scottish composer, Frederick Jewson (1823–91), all of whom were also, in their different ways, representatives of the musical establishment. Talented and well meaning though such men were, they spent half their time battling to keep the Academy alive and functioning in the face of political and social indifference, often – as we have seen in the case of Potter and Bennett – at a cost to their own creative endeavours.

The situation in Leipzig, when Sullivan arrived there in September 1858, still aged only sixteen, could not have been more different. Mendelssohn had been dead for over ten years, but it was still his city. He had set up the Conservatorium, where Sullivan would study, and his nominees, Moritz Hauptmann and Julius Riecke, were still in charge at the Thomaskirche and the Gewandhaus. Not only was the relationship between these institutions positive and cooperative, but they were actively supported by the Leipzig authorities, who saw the arts, and music in particular, as a matter of civic and public pride. This was a far cry from London and the haphazard state of music and musical education among British institutions. The standard of teaching at the Conservatorium was high. Moscheles (back from his sojourn in London) and Hauptmann were there. So, too, were Ferdinand David (1810–73), Ferdinand Becker (1804–77), and the influential composition and choral teacher Karl Reinecke (1824–1910). They may not be household names today, but, as teachers, they were a cut above those Sullivan had known at the Academy. Among his fellow students were John Barnett, soon to be known for *The Mountain Sylph*, Walter Bache, who became Britain's leading proponent of Liszt's music, and a shy Norwegian called Edvard Grieg.

The original intention of the scholarship committee had been that Sullivan should study in Leipzig for a year. In the end, because he worked hard and received glowing reports from his tutors, he was able to stay three. These were formative years. Leipzig was at the hub of the debate that was raging between those who upheld the musical tradition of Beethoven and Mendelssohn and the supporters of the 'new music', represented by Schumann, Liszt and Wagner. Sullivan kept a foot in both camps. Mendelssohn's influence never left him, but he continued to appreciate and to persuade others of the merits of Schumann. And, as ever, Sullivan made friends and connections. Moscheles took a special interest in him. Mendelssohn's sister-in-law looked after him and introduced him to Konrad Schleinitz, the municipality's director on the board of the Conservatorium. Schleinitz later arranged for him to be excused tuition fees during his third year. At an evening party given by Ferdinand David, Sullivan met Hans von Bülow (1830–94), one of the greatest of Germany's nineteenth-century conductors, then played cards and walked home in company with Liszt.

At the Conservatorium's Spring Concert in May 1860, Sullivan conducted his *Feast of Roses* overture. Reviewers were optimistic for the composer's future but found the work itself too close to Mendelssohn in style. The following April, just days before his final departure from Leipzig,

his suite of music for *The Tempest* was given as part of that year's gradua-
tion concert. Sullivan was praised for his ability to handle the orchestra.
His future as a composer was not in doubt. The work was held to be imaginative, charming, attractive. Only one small note of caution was added:
the composer needed to think more deeply about the meaning of his work.
But then, he was still not quite nineteen.

Returning to London in April 1862, Sullivan's prospects were bright. He
had his own natural talents – both musical and social. He had been a
chorister at the Chapel Royal, linking him to the great, if now moribund,
tradition that had shaped so many English composers. He had received the
best musical education that Britain and Germany could offer. He had the
support of the British musical establishment. He had every possible advantage for a successful musical career, and there were not a few who believed
that he would turn out to be the great composer that Britain had for so
long failed to produce.

In reality, of course, coming home meant finding a job. He put an adver-
tisement in the *Musical World* and began to give lessons. He also took
lessons himself – on the organ, something not provided in Leipzig; and
before long he joined another great British musical tradition by becoming
a church organist – at St Michael's Church in Chester Square, a position
which Helmore seems to have found for him. The salary of £80 a year was
reasonably good, but, in terms of the future, possibly the most significant
aspect of the appointment was that Gerald Road police station was nearby.
All members of the constabulary based at the station were required to
attend Matins every Wednesday morning and to be members of the church
choir, so Sullivan regularly found himself conducting a chorus of policemen.

69   Grove, Manns, and Sullivan

George Grove's greatest claim to fame is his *Dictionary of Music and
Musicians*, the first edition of which was published in four volumes
between 1879 and 1889. However, by the time he came to compile that great
work, he had already had two different careers – neither of them remotely
connected with his father's business, which was that of a fishmonger and
venison dealer in London's Charing Cross Road. Born in 1820 and given a

good basic education at Clapham Grammar School, Grove was apprenticed to Alexander Gordon, a civil engineer based in Westminster. This was the beginning of the railway age and Grove's first practical engineering experience was on the new lines that were being built the length and breadth of Britain. In 1841, he was sent to Jamaica and Bermuda to supervise the erection of prefabricated cast-iron lighthouses. When he came back in 1846, he worked with Edwin Clark and Robert Stephenson on the Britannia Bridge across the Menai Straits to Anglesey. Only in 1850, at the age of thirty, did he change direction. On the recommendation of three powerful figures – Stephenson, Isambard Kingdom Brunel and Sir Charles Barry – he became Secretary to the Society of Arts, and then, two years later, Secretary to the Crystal Palace Company. It was in this second position, once the building was re-erected and reopened, that Grove began to exert an influence on the musical life of the country. He had always been passionately interested in music, but he knew he was not a composer or performer. He was a manager, an organiser and a scholar, and to make the best of the opportunities offered by the new Crystal Palace, he needed a partner who was a practising and practical musician.

August Manns arrived in London in 1854, having already enjoyed a varied musical career. The son of a glassblower in what is now Gdansk in Poland but was then part of Prussia, and one of ten children, Manns learned his music the hard way. He began as an apprentice to a local town musician, worked his way up to become the bandmaster of a crack Prussian regiment, and then went on to be conductor and violin soloist at Kroll Gardens – Berlin's equivalent of Vauxhall. The invitation to London came from Henry Schallehn, who had formed a military-style band to play at the Crystal Palace and wanted an assistant conductor. The two quickly fell out and Manns left, but Grove, having investigated the dispute, sacked Schallehn and called Manns back from Amsterdam where he had taken a temporary job. A powerful partnership was born. Under Manns' leadership and with Grove's support, the wind band was transformed into a small orchestra, and the small orchestra soon became a full symphony orchestra. Between them, they organised a vast range of musical activities, but most popular of all were the Saturday concerts, which began in 1855 and continued until Manns' retirement in 1901. Grove's role was more than just managerial and administrative support. He and Manns jointly developed their ideas on what kind of music the Crystal Palace should promote and which works should be programmed. And it was Grove who wrote the extensive and detailed programme notes – which, of course, paved the way for his *Dictionary*.

They began with Beethoven, Mozart and Mendelssohn, but not always the familiar pieces. Their aim was educational in a very Victorian sense: they wanted to make what they considered good music available to large numbers of people at low cost; and they sought to edge their audience towards a deeper and wider appreciation of composers and their works. The centenary of Mozart's birth in 1856 was a perfect opportunity. The all-Mozart centenary concert mixed arias from the operas with orchestral music and even a piano sonata. And the public responded. Another all-Mozart concert was so popular that, despite nine hundred seats being available, six hundred people had to be turned away. By the end of 1856, Grove and Manns were able to programme works such as Schubert's C major Symphony (*The Great*), Schumann's Fourth Symphony – neither of which had previously been heard in Britain – and even extracts from Wagner's *Tannhäuser*, secure in the knowledge that such novelties would attract an audience. They educated their audience in other ways, too, politely requesting people to remain in their seats during the performance and to move about only during intervals.

Another aspect of their partnership was the policy of encouraging and programming new works by British composers. We have noted previous attempts to do the same thing, but Grove and Manns were truly persistent. When Grove left the Crystal Palace – which he did in 1873, after more than twenty years of unremitting effort – it was a policy that Manns continued alone. And by the time he retired, he had conducted works by no less than one hundred and three British composers. For many of them, facing institutionalised disbelief in the value of British music and the practical difficulties of getting a hearing, this was nothing short of a lifeline. The first Crystal Palace concert devoted solely to works by British composers was given in April 1861, just a week after Sullivan's *Tempest* had had its premiere in Leipzig. Those represented were Balfe, Bennett, William Wallace, Macfarren, John Hatton (1809–86) – an aspiring opera composer who in the end found light, popular songs more profitable – and Henry Leslie (1822–96) – usually better known for his choirs than his compositions. It was a bold initiative and recognised as such by London's increasingly influential music press. It was also an initiative that came at just the right time for Sullivan.

Sullivan's ability to get on with influential people, however different their views might be from his own, is evident in the fact that he quickly became friends with Henry Chorley, the conservative and often acerbic music critic of the *Athenaeum*. It was Chorley who introduced Sullivan to Grove; and it was Chorley who arranged a private performance of *The Tempest* at his London home. Grove was impressed and decided to programme the music at a Crystal Palace Saturday Concert in April 1862. It was a breakthrough moment. The audience and the press were enthusiastic, and the piece was repeated the following Saturday when, as it happened, Charles Dickens was in the audience. In March 1863, the Crystal Palace staged a special concert to celebrate the marriage of the Prince of Wales and Princess Alexandra of Denmark. The programme featured two new compositions by Sullivan; the *Princess of Wales' March*, based on Danish folk songs, and a song, 'Bride from the North'. After the concert, he was introduced to the Prince of Wales and the Duke of Edinburgh. A few weeks later, *The Tempest* was played in Manchester at the famous Free Trade Hall by Charles Hallé and his equally famous, eponymous orchestra. *The Manchester Guardian*, like the London press, was fulsome in Sullivan's praise. Suddenly, he was the darling not just of the British musical establishment, who had – in a manner of speaking – already put their shirt on him, but also of a broader section of fashionable society.

In this new and unfamiliar situation, it was probably gratitude and inexperience that led Sullivan to put his faith in Chorley. Asked by the Pyne & Harrison Opera Company to consider an opera, Sullivan turned to Chorley for a libretto. Although Sullivan tried his best, what Chorley produced was almost impossible to set, and *The Sapphire Necklace* was never performed. Costa, another his powerful backers, commissioned a ballet for Covent Garden. Sullivan worked quickly and *L'Ile Enchantée* was given in May 1864, with moderate success. But when, on Costa's recommendation, the Birmingham Festival commissioned a work from Sullivan, he again turned to Chorley for a text. *Kenilworth*, a cantata in the now hallowed tradition of adaptations based on Sir Walter Scott's novels, was the first setback of Sullivan's career. It fell flat, largely because the libretto itself was flat and lacked any dramatic or character-based opportunities for the composer to exploit. In fact, the only time Sullivan enjoyed success with Chorley's lyrics was with a part-song, the drearily sentimental 'The Long Day Closes', published in 1868.

Sullivan was not a man to repine. He took himself off to Ireland in what appears to have been a journey of exploration into his Irish heritage. By the time he returned, he had written his *Irish Symphony*. In 1866, for an Englishman, or, indeed, an Irishman, to produce a symphony was rare enough. Macfarren had not written symphonic music since the 1840s. Alice Mary Smith had written one in 1863. Bennett had had three movements of his G minor Symphony played in 1864. It was not a crowded field, but that was the problem. Promoters did not believe in British symphonies, and it took no less a person than Jenny Lind to persuade the normally willing Manns to programme Sullivan's. The *Irish Symphony* was played at the Crystal Palace in March 1866 and repeated a month later at the Musical Society of London. It was a great success with both the audience and the critics, although a third performance, by the Hallé in Manchester that December, was less well received. It seemed that Sullivan might have broken the British jinx on the symphony, but hindsight does not support that view. What we see is a work that is immensely fluent and melodic, with some finely-judged woodwind passages. It is lyrical and wistful in an Irish way – although Sullivan does not slip into Irish folk idiom or make use of Irish tunes. It begins beautifully with a slow, evocative hunting call, and its several themes are technically well developed – although the final movement has its faults and the concluding fanfare section is rather derivative. It is probably Sullivan's most successful orchestral work, and yet, in the end, there is something missing. The warning sounded by the Leipzig reviewer comes to mind: compared with Continental models, the *Irish Symphony* lacks depth and a sense of purpose. Nonetheless, at the time, it boosted Sullivan's reputation and, buoyed up by his success, he decided to write a cello concerto. As with the symphony, this was a bold, and not an obvious choice. Vivaldi and Haydn had written cello concertos, but neither were well known – if known at all – and, apart from Schumann's, written in 1850, there were no recent examples in the repertoire; and it was hearing the Italian cellist Carlo Piatti perform the Schumann that inspired Sullivan to write his own. He worked quickly and the piece was ready for performance at the Crystal Palace, again by Piatti, in November 1866. The premiere went well enough and the critics were polite, but the piece was not repeated. Sullivan seems to have accepted that it was not a success. In any case, by that time, he had moved off in a different direction.

Earlier that year, Sullivan had received a commission to write a piece for the Norwich Festival. A few days later, his father died. Sullivan was still only twenty-four; the family had always been close; his father had always been there as a source of advice and support. His grief came out in the work he wrote for Norwich. The concert overture *In Memoriam* was popular with the Victorian audiences but has damned him in the eyes of critics ever since. It was, quite simply, a descent into the worst kind of sentimentality, with weak tunes which are treated in a manner at once empty and bombastic. Despite its popular success, *In Memoriam* marked the beginning of the end of Sullivan as a composer of orchestral music. In 1867, he wrote another overture, *Marmion*, based on Scott's epic poem, which was performed several times but never published. It was only five years since Sullivan had first been hailed as the future of British music, but the gloss was already wearing off. He had worked hard, but he had not achieved the musical greatness that had been predicted. Reservations were being heard. *Marmion* was praised as 'eminently picturesque'. A visit to Leipzig promised well, but when *In Memoriam* was played at the Gewandhaus the reception was tepid.

Sullivan now began to focus on choral and theatrical music, and naturally, like all composers of the time, he wanted to try an oratorio. *The Prodigal Son* was premiered at the Worcester Three Choirs Festival in 1869 and given again at the Crystal Palace shortly afterwards. It was heard in Manchester, Hereford and Edinburgh during 1870. It was an oratorio; it was by Sullivan; it had some fine tunes; and so, in the short term at least, it gained a popular following. But Goss, Sullivan's old teacher, saw through the well-orchestrated surface and warned him of a lack of commitment to his music. As if to relax after the seriousness of *The Prodigal Son*, Sullivan worked with the dramatist and writer of comic sketches, Francis Burnand, on a one-act comic opera, *Cox and Box*. It received its first professional production in 1869 and ran for three hundred performances. His music for this light-hearted piece of comic nonsense may not have shown the commitment Goss was asking for, or the depth that other critics sensed lacking in his work, but it did show his abilities as a highly practical composer of theatrical music. So, too, the following year, did *Overture di Ballo*, which was to be the last major orchestral piece he ever wrote. *Di Ballo* has attracted much attention because of its liveliness and orchestral colour; and it is great fun, completely different from *In Memoriam* or *Marmion*. Sullivan may have written it as a concert overture, but it sounds like a piece of musical theatre. For all its technical facility, it comes over as if it was meant to be played before curtain-up at one of London's better music halls. It was these practical and theatrical skills that would dominate the second half of his career.

The trouble was, of course, that this was not what Sullivan's supporters expected. Nor was it what he himself expected. He was caught in a trap, and not one of his own making. His talent was universally recognised and, even before the age of thirty, he had been widely accepted as Britain's leading composer. The field was not crowded, but it was nonetheless an achievement. In the Victorian age, however, such a position was expected to encompass moral as well as musical leadership. He was expected to produce high art with a moral purpose – what we might term 'the oratorio ethic'. Had it been otherwise, Queen Victoria would never have entrusted him with the almost sacred task of editing Prince Albert's compositions (or asked to receive copies of all his works – only Mendelssohn had previously been so honoured). The difficulty lay in the fact that both his talents and his personality steered him in a different direction. Dr Benjamin Papperitz, who taught harmony and counterpoint at Leipzig Conservatorium and had been impressed by Sullivan as a student, blamed 'commercial England' and accused him of prostituting his gifts:

> Compare Sullivan and Brahms. Of the two I think Sullivan had the greater natural musical talent; but Brahms will not write a note he doesn't think is worthy of his gift.... As for Sullivan, he settles in London, and writes and publishes things quite unworthy of his genius.[1]

Yet it is not correct to suggest that Sullivan 'sold out'. The massive success, both popular and financial, of his collaboration with Gilbert (of which more in a moment) came from following his instincts, not his wallet. It reflected what he was actually good at, rather than what he thought he should be good at. As a result, his life as a composer developed an odd duality. On the one hand, he enjoyed the success and the recognition the Savoy Operas brought him. On the other, he felt guilty that he was not devoting himself to 'serious' music and felt a constant pull to return to it – because, in line with the oratorio ethic and like the good Dr Papperitz, he felt popular music to be necessarily less worthy.

A similar division marked Sullivan's attitude towards his position in society. A man of his standing was expected to teach and, as we have seen with so many other composers, to take a leading role in the country's musical institutions. Sullivan disliked teaching and fought shy of taking on official positions. Early in his career, he had agreed to become 'Professor of Pianoforte and Ballad Singing' at the Crystal Palace School of Music, which had been set up by Manns, who was not alone in considering that the RAM was inadequate as a national school. Unfortunately, the majority of the students Manns' school attracted were lady amateurs, and Sullivan's appointment was not a great success. In 1875, he reluctantly accepted a position as Professor of Composition on the staff of the RAM, but lasted only two years. Given his celebrity, it was only natural that he should be seen as a candidate for major appointments. Rumours began to circulate that he was interested in becoming Principal of the RAM or Professor of Music at Cambridge. He wrote to the *Athenaeum* and the *Musical World* denying that they were true, but the rumours continued and, in 1876, he was forced into a corner. Dissatisfaction with the RAM had come to a head. With the support and personal involvement of the Duke of Edinburgh, Queen Victoria's second son, a National Training School for Music was to be established. Sullivan was offered the job of Principal. He declined. The Duke personally requested him to reconsider. He agreed. In the end, he served five years and seems to have been popular but largely ineffective. When the Training School was reformed and remodelled into the RCM, he resigned with some relief.

What Sullivan did enjoy, however, was Society. He liked being flattered by the Duke of Edinburgh. He liked having long conversations with the Prince of Wales. He liked be known as someone who moved in royal circles. He liked being bracketed with the rich and famous. He enjoyed luxury and pleasure in a variety of forms. He was a great gambler, whether at London card tables, in French casinos, or at the races (in later life he became a moderately successful racehorse owner). He would spend large sums of money on carriages, hotel rooms and restaurants. He also had a string of love affairs – although he never married – details of which he sometimes recorded in his diary. These pursuits, however, did not arouse the guilt he felt when he gave himself up to the composition of popular music.

70 Sullivan and Gilbert

William Schwenk Gilbert (1836–1911) and Arthur Sullivan could scarcely have been more different from each other if they had tried. Sullivan was brought up in a close, warm, Irish family. Gilbert had a strict upbringing at the hands of parents who fought with increasing ferocity and whose marriage eventually fell apart. Sullivan was affable, friendly, and generally got on with people. Gilbert was a good friend to many, but was also quick-tempered and frequently confrontational. Sullivan's whole life was spent in music. Gilbert was a civil servant, a soldier and a barrister before becoming a full-time writer and dramatist. It was their contrasting lives and characters that eventually broke the partnership, but the same combination of contrasts also created a series of comic operas that occupy a unique place in British musical history.

Gilbert's first successes were pantomimes and burlesques of well-known operas and plays. From these, he moved on to farce-like musical entertainments, such as *No Cards*, produced in 1869 at a theatre known as The Gallery of Illustration, with music by the proprietor, Thomas German Reed (1817–88). Later that same year, he wrote *Ages Ago*, a more complex piece, much closer to comic opera, with music by Frederic Clay (1838–89). Gilbert and Clay continued to collaborate until 1875, producing a series of light comic operas – *The Gentleman in Black* (1870), *Happy Arcadia* (1872), *Princess Toto* (1875). These show Gilbert learning how to put together a libretto and Clay as a perfectly competent tunesmith. It was during a rehearsal for *Ages Ago* that Clay first introduced Gilbert to Sullivan. The meeting was polite but nothing came of it. If Sullivan was Britain's leading composer, Gilbert, by this stage, was not far behind as a writer of dramatic scripts and, in 1871, John Hollingshead at the Gaiety Theatre on the Strand was delighted when Gilbert sent him the script of his two-act comic opera, *Thespis, or, The Gods Grown Old*. It was an original idea – the gods on Olympus, now aged and out of touch, exchange places with a troupe of actors – written by a man secure enough in his education to make fun of the classics. Hollingshead, perhaps seeing parallels with Offenbach's *Orpheus in the Underworld,* which had had its first London performance seven years earlier in 1864 and was still extremely popular, immediately passed the script to Sullivan. The commission was welcome. Sullivan had enjoyed the success of *Cox and Box* – although his other comic opera, *The Contrabandista* (1867), had been a failure. He was sceptical of the singing abilities of some of the proposed cast for *Thespis,* but it certainly promised a change from the solemnity of *On Shore and Sea* and the opening of the Royal Albert Hall that March, so he agreed to provide the music.

The first performance, just before Christmas 1871, was severely under-rehearsed and overran by more than an hour, but lessons were learned and cuts made. The critics praised Sullivan's music, though not for the last time suggesting that theatrical scores of this nature were beneath such a lofty talent. Gilbert's libretto was generally appreciated, although those critics and members of the audience who had expected a traditional pantomime were disappointed, while others who lacked a classical education did not get the joke. Nonetheless, *Thespis* ran for sixty-four performances, one of which was attended by Sullivan's friend the Duke of Edinburgh, before being taken off at the beginning of March.[1] Given that the Gaiety was known for pantomimes and burlesques which usually survived for no more than a month, this was a perfectly acceptable run. The piece was certainly not a failure – as some commentators assert – but nor was it the kind of success that made a follow up from the same combination of writer and composer a foregone conclusion. Gilbert returned to working with Clay, while Sullivan extracted one song, 'Little Maid of Arcadee', for publication and returned to serious music.

That same winter, while audiences were enjoying *Thespis*, the Prince of Wales was slowly recovering from a serious bout of typhoid, the disease that had killed his father. His recovery was cause for national celebration, and the Duke of Edinburgh was the moving spirit behind a huge event at the Crystal Place in May 1872, the musical centrepiece of which was the first performance of Sullivan's *Te Deum*. As with many of Sullivan's bigger works, it was immediately branded a masterpiece, only to see the level of enthusiasm wane with the passage of time. The opening bars and the entry of the chorus suggest Handel, but Handel is quickly followed by the slow rhythms of a hymn tune and descants reminiscent of Christmas carols. There are wonderful explosions in the brass, several rather odd, rhythmically jolly passages that suggest the Savoy Operas, and the piece ends with a series of overblown variations on 'Oh God, Our Help in Ages Past'. It has a scale and a grandeur that inevitably link it to the great days of Victorian imperialism and give it a kind of honest vulgarity. It is not a masterpiece, but remains enjoyable today precisely because it *is* such an over-the-top mixture of styles. Encouraged by his success, Sullivan wrote a second oratorio, *The Light of the World*, inspired by the Pre-Raphaelite painting by William Holman Hunt. When first heard at the Birmingham Festival in 1873 with Sullivan himself conducting (the Duke of Edinburgh again present), it was received with overwhelming enthusiasm – Gounod called it a masterpiece. Again, however, the tide of critical opinion has since receded. *The Light of the World* is characteristic of a certain type of Victorian music that attempts to express its moral or religious purpose by moving slowly. There are occasional flashes of surface brilliance of the kind one expects from Sullivan, but, taken overall, the work is heavy and un-dramatic.

Sullivan returned to the theatre with some incidental music for *The Merry Wives of Windsor*, first performed in Manchester in 1874, but it was not until the following year that he and Gilbert worked together again. The impulse was wholly practical. Richard D'Oyly Carte, the manager of the Royalty Theatre in Soho, wanted to cash in on the popularity of Offenbach by putting on his comic opera *La Périchole*, but *La Périchole* was too short for a full evening's entertainment, so he asked Gilbert to consider a short, comic piece to act as a curtain-raiser. Gilbert had originally published a version of *Trial by Jury* in his collection of verse, *The Bab Ballads*, in 1869 – but had since rewritten and extended it. He proposed music by Carl Rosa, who had started his company devoted to opera in English just a couple of years previously, but Carte had the wisdom to see that Sullivan was the only composer capable of matching Offenbach musically. He also saw Sullivan as a name that might make the venture a commercial success. Carte sent Gilbert round to Sullivan's flat where, in front of a blazing open fire, Gilbert read the script out loud. To Gilbert's surprise, Sullivan agreed on the spot. He wrote the music in just three weeks. Carte, realising the quality of the work, switched things round so that instead of being a curtain-raiser, *Trial by Jury* brought the evening to triumphant climax. The first performance was at the Royalty Theatre in March 1875. Between that opening night and May 1877, it moved theatres twice and notched up three hundred performances.

The critics were inclined to give Sullivan the lion's share of the credit, and there is no doubt that he not only captured the spirit of Gilbert's text, but that, in terms of comic opera, his through-composed score was simply a cut above anything that had previously been heard in London. Nonetheless, *Trial by Jury* was really Gilbert's success. It was his idea, his structure, his libretto, and he was responsible for some of those features – the strong characterisation and the active role played by the chorus – that made it different from run-of-the-mill burlesques and musical entertain-ments. In terms of the actual performance, it was Sullivan's brother Fred, as the judge, who brought in the crowds. Contemporary accounts suggest that his performance, particularly his diction, was masterly. Indeed, it was Fred Sullivan's sudden illness that brought an end to *Trial by Jury*'s initial run. Sullivan himself was distraught at his brother's illness and subsequent death; and the story goes that he wrote his single most famous song, 'The Lost Chord', at Fred's bedside. Sullivan seems to have lacked judgement when it came to assessing what was a good or settable text, and he certainly lacked the ability to transform a bad text into a good song. 'The Lost Chord' is a case in point. The banality of Adelaide Anne Proctor's poem served only to bring a bland and sentimental setting from Sullivan. These days, the song is little more than a monument to Victorian sensibility. By contrast, Gilbert's words for *Trial by Jury*, and for the other comic operas he and Sullivan worked on together, are on a knife edge. With the wrong setting, they could have become knockabout farce or heavy-handed comedy, but Sullivan responded to Gilbert's brilliance: the music and words hold each other in balance.

Richard D'Oyly Carte (1844–1901) was a Londoner, born in Soho. As a young man, he worked in his father's music-publishing and instrument-making business in the Charing Cross Road. He tried his hand at a musical career: he composed several comic operas and conducted a touring opera company in performances of *Cox and Box* and works by Offenbach. However, he soon realised his limitations and set up a management agency, specialising in musical, operatic and lecture tour appointments. His client list was impressive, including Gounod, Offenbach, and Clara Schumann, and, on the non-musical side, Matthew Arnold, James McNeill Whistler, and Oscar Wilde. He also, as we know, went into theatre management. Carte's strengths were his sure commercial judgement – which was impressive for a man only just in his thirties – and his London background which provided him with an extensive network of contacts.

Even after *Trial by Jury*, further Gilbert and Sullivan collaborations were not inevitable. It was Carte who took the initiative and the risk, leasing the Opéra Comique Theatre, and, together with a number of interested music publishers, setting up the Comedy Opera Company. He arranged that Gilbert and Sullivan should have control of casting and production, and he paid them a two-hundred-guinea advance. *Trial by Jury* had been satirical. *The Sorcerer* goes further into the world of what audiences soon learned to call 'Topseyturveydom', but was less obviously satirical. It was based on one of Gilbert's short stories, *The Elixir of Love*, and there are moments in the score – for example, the trumpet part in 'With heart and voice' – which suggest that Sullivan might have been thinking of Donizetti's *L'elisir d'amore*. George Grossmith was recruited to take the role of John Wellington Wells, the sorcerer who wreaks havoc in the village of

Ploverleigh – which would have been taken by Fred Sullivan had he lived. Grossmith went on take the lead role in all the major Gilbert and Sullivan operas. *The Sorcerer* marked the first appearance of a full-blown patter song, an expected feature of future works, and was also the first to feature a magic potion. Gilbert's addiction to plots involving magic was to be a source of friction with Sullivan in the future. *The Sorcerer*, first played at the Opéra Comique in November 1877, did not quite repeat the success of *Trial by Jury*, but with a hundred and seventy-five performances it was successful enough to ensure that there were would be a follow up. Gilbert and Sullivan were launched.

H.M.S. Pinafore, in May 1878, was their first real blockbuster. It returned to satire – on unqualified people in powerful positions, on the Royal Navy, on the class system – and it ran for five hundred and seventy performances. It was so popular that it sparked a string of unauthorised or 'pirate' productions, particularly in the United States. For this reason *The Pirates of Penzance* was given its first full performance in New York in December 1879, whereas in London it opened the following March. *The Pirates*, a satire on serious opera, on respectability, on the police, on English attitudes in general, was the first opera produced by the new D'Oyly Carte Opera Company, the directors of which were Carte, Gilbert, and Sullivan. It was also the last to be staged at the Opéra Comique. *Patience*, which took aestheticism as its target, was premiered in April 1881 at Carte's newly-constructed Savoy Theatre in the Strand. *Iolanthe* followed in 1882, the fully-electrified Savoy permitting the introduction of new special effects, which the audience loved. *Princess Ida*, satirising women's education and the 'new woman' of the 1880s, was less successful than its predecessors, and strains in the partnership were beginning to show. Gilbert's proposal for their next opera involved a magic lozenge. Sullivan was fed up with magic potions and magic lozenges and said so. After a period of stalemate, Gilbert came up with a storyline that avoided magic or the supernatural, but satirised bureaucracy and absurd laws, while at the same time exploiting the current British craze for Japanese art and aesthetics.[2] *The Mikado* in 1885 was their biggest hit to date. By the end of 1888, it was approaching eight hundred performances in London alone; it was being performed by over a hundred companies across the United States; and Carte had taken it on tour right across Europe from Spain to Russia, including the operatic capital of Vienna, where it was a raging success.

After *Ruddigore* (1887) and the more serious *Yeomen of the Guard* (1888), the relationship between the two principals was at best tense. Sullivan wanted to write a grand opera. Gilbert did not – or rather felt that he could not do it successfully. Sullivan felt that his music was sacrificed to Gilbert's words. Gilbert felt his words were taking second place to Sullivan's music. At this stage, Gilbert seems to have been the more emollient of the two and suggested that Sullivan should write a serious opera – which became *Ivanhoe* – with another librettist if they did a further comic opera together. Sullivan agreed and Gilbert came up with *The Gondoliers*, perhaps the sunniest of the canon. Sullivan liked the Venetian setting and, perhaps because he was writing serious opera concurrently, recovered his enthusiasm for comedy. He made his point about their partnership by ensuring that the opera began with almost twenty minutes of unbroken music. Gilbert made his point by having the two gondoliers, Marco and Giuseppe, reign jointly as Kings of Barataria – the relevance of which was not lost on those in the audience and the many critics and commentators, including the cartoonists of *Punch*, who had heard the reasons for the quarrel on the London grapevine. *The Gondoliers* was premiered at the Savoy in December 1889 to enthusiastic notices, and peace seemed to have been restored. It did not last long. The following spring came the celebrated carpet quarrel. Gilbert accused Carte of charging himself and Sullivan too much for the carpet in the foyer of the Savoy. Sullivan sided with Carte and a huge row broke out. Gilbert seems to have been in the right, but, especially given the fact that he knew Sullivan to be ill, his conduct was aggressive and insensitive, and the matter ended in court. They appeared to be heading in opposite directions. Sullivan achieved moderate success with a light opera called *Haddon Hall* (1892) with a libretto by Sydney Grundy. Gilbert produced some none too successful plays. It was only when Thomas Chappell, the music publisher – and a man whose business had profited greatly from the partnership – intervened that the two men agreed to cooperate again. But too much had been said and done, and the spark had gone. *Utopia Limited* (1895) was a modest success, but *The Grand Duke* (1896) lasted for only a hundred and twenty performances and was the only one of their operas not to make a profit. They never worked together again.

Sullivan's collaboration with Gilbert had brought him wealth and world-wide fame, but it was not the only strand to his working life. From 1880, he had been director of the Leeds Festival, and it was for Leeds that he wrote his 'Sacred Music Drama', *The Martyr of Antioch*, based on a poem by

Henry Milman, the Dean of St Paul's. This is a strangely mixed work, combining passages of outstanding dullness with others, such as those dealing with the sun-worshippers, when the liveliness and the fun of *Pinafore* or *The Pirates* seem to creep through into what was intended as a serious work. Sullivan's big cantata, *The Golden Legend* (1886), was also written for Leeds. With a libretto by Joseph Bennett, the influential music critic of the *Daily Telegraph*, this was a composition for which Sullivan had great hopes. There is some evidence that he saw it as a kind of trial run for the grand opera he would write later. It is, however, a sadly muddled work, mixing brilliant orchestral writing with unconvincing, rather episodic drama and equally unconvincing characters – notably Elsie, the heroine, whom one struggles to take entirely seriously. Out of respect and civic loyalty, the Leeds audience greeted the great man – he had been knighted in 1883 – and his work with enthusiasm. Posterity has been less kind.

Then came *Ivanhoe*. This was intended to be a great moment in British musical history. Carte had spent a fortune building a new theatre, the Royal English Opera House – today the Palace Theatre – on Cambridge Circus, which was to be devoted to English opera. The orchestra was enormous; the scenery correct in every architectural detail; the company fully rehearsed. The Prince and Princess of Wales, Princess Victoria, Princess Maude, and the Duke and Duchess of Edinburgh were all in attendance. Scott, as we have seen, was fertile ground for operatic adaptation, and the choice of *Ivanhoe*, in which noble Saxons, assisted by Robin Hood, help Richard Cœur-de-Lion triumph over his wicked brother seemed to contain all that was necessary for a great English opera. On the first night, 31 January 1891, the reception was, as might have been expected, overwhelming. Most of the initial reviews were positive, although it was noted from the beginning that, while there were some tuneful choruses, there was no great aria or march to inspire the audience. George Bernard Shaw, however, writing just four days after the first night, saw through the glitter: Julian Sturgis's dialogue was 'fustian' and Sullivan's music was 'gentlemanly'.[3] Only when *Ivanhoe* was played in Germany, where Sullivan had received his musical education and whence he had derived his musical inspiration, were the really hard words said. It was given at the Berlin Opera in the presence of Kaiser Wilhelm II. The opera was 'unremarkable, but the sumptuous décor [made] it worth seeing.' The music was 'so negative and dreary in invention, so conventional in its make-up, so destitute of any ... originality, that it can worthily stand beside the libretto.'[4] In truth,

Ivanhoe is not that bad, but, like Sullivan's other large scale choral works –
the oratorios and cantatas – it lacks the spark that is so evidently there
in *The Pirates*, *The Mikado* and *Iolanthe*. *Ivanhoe* ran for one hundred and
fifty-five performances, a record for a grand opera, but it did not restore
Sullivan's reputation as a composer of serious music. Worse still, Carte's
new and expensive opera house began to haemorrhage money and by 1894
it had become a music hall.

Sullivan died in November 1900. He was only fifty-eight, but for many
years he had suffered from a recurrent kidney complaint that had given
him periods of intense and debilitating pain. From today's perspective, it is
hard to appreciate what a hugely important figure he was in his own time.
For thirty years, in the eyes of the press, the public and the Royal Family, he
personified British music. Not since Purcell had a British musician occupied such a central and dominant position in the country's musical life –
and Purcell was not subject to constant news items and reviews in the
national and international press. Nor had any musician previously scaled
the social heights that Sullivan attained. If Burney was the first musician to
be accepted as a gentleman, Sullivan was the first to become a close friend
of princes. At least once, following a bout of illness, he was invited to recuperate at Sandringham with the Prince of Wales. In the words of *The Times'*
obituary, 'he ranked with the most distinguished personages, rather than
with ordinary musicians.'[5]

Sullivan desperately wanted to be a great composer, by which he meant
a serious composer after the German model. That he did not succeed
was partly due to his temperament, and partly due to his reverence for
the German musical tradition (which was shared by Victorian society).
Composers such as Elgar, Delius, Vaughan Williams, and Holst would
soon take British music in new directions, but it was easier for them at
the end of the nineteenth century than it was for Sullivan. He grew up in
a world where German cultural influence was dominant – indeed, he
received his Mendelssohn Scholarship because of it – and it was not in his
nature to break away. He was not a deep musical thinker. He found it hard
musically to sustain a tragic or deeply moral purpose – and it shows. Nor
was he a rebel. He was too easy-going, and, having risen through hard
work and application from a poor background to riches and social
eminence – an achievement which should not be underestimated – he was
naturally inclined to value the rewards offered by the status quo.

Where Sullivan did succeed was in elevating the status of music as pure entertainment. In the age of the oratorio, his best music, and the music on which his reputation now rests, was sheer, light-hearted fun, with no deeper or hidden meanings. If one wishes to be critical, one can say that the Gilbert and Sullivan operas have a tendency to be formulaic, both in terms of the characters and the music employed to bring them to life. Yet, after nearly a century-and-a-half, their popularity remains undiminished. Professional companies know that a Gilbert-and-Sullivan will always attract an audience. So, too, do amateur companies. Gilbert-and-Sullivan societies now spread right across the English-speaking world. At the time of writing, there are at least sixty-two in the United Kingdom. And there are 'G & S' societies right across North America – from Toronto to Galveston, from New England to Seattle. They exist throughout Australia and New Zealand. There is one in Cape Town, and even one in Bermuda. Not even *Messiah* has drawn so many amateur performers onto the stage.

71   The Golden Age of Music Hall

Music hall was the great popular music phenomenon of the Victorian and Edwardian era. People flocked in their thousands to hear oratorios. They flocked in their tens of thousands to attend the mixture of song, dance, comedy and variety acts that constituted music hall. It was a phenomenon that began in London, evolving, as we have seen, from the song-and-supper clubs and saloon theatres attached to some of the city's larger taverns. The first 'Theatre of Varieties' was the Regency in Tottenham Street, which had once been the home of the Concerts of Antient Music. Another early example was The Grecian Saloon (later Theatre), attached to the Eagle Tavern, on the City Road.[1] The Grecian was purchased and demolished in 1882 by General Booth, founder of the Salvation Army, but he was unable to prevent smaller-scale music hall performances continuing in the Eagle itself; and it was here at a free-and-easy that Marie Lloyd made her debut, probably in 1884.

The man who developed music hall as a successful commercial enterprise was Charles Morton, the 'Father of the Halls'. In 1849, inspired by the example of W. C. Evans in Covent Garden, he bought the Canterbury Arms in Westminster Bridge Road. The entertainments he put on were so successful that, in 1852, he built a new seven-hundred-seat hall at the back of the tavern, admitting women as well as men. This was the first purpose-built music hall. Four years later, he replaced it with a new 1,500-seat hall. Success bred imitation and, in 1859, a rival entrepreneur, Henry Weston, opened Weston's Music Hall – later to become the Holborn Empire – on the site of what had been the Six Cans and Punch Bowl Tavern in High Holborn. Morton retaliated by building the architecturally adventurous, 1,800-seat Oxford just a few hundred metres away in Oxford Street, on the site of the Boar and Castle, an old coaching inn. It burned down twice, was rebuilt and enlarged, and remained one of London's most popular and profitable halls until replaced by a Lyons Corner House in 1927. Morton later took on the management of the Alhambra in Leicester Square and the Tivoli in the Strand. In 1891, he actually announced that he would retire, but changed his mind when presented with an irresistible challenge. Richard D'Oyly Carte had invested huge sums of money in his Royal English Opera House, but, as we saw in the previous chapter, following an initial, limited success with Sullivan's *Ivanhoe*, the theatre had run into financial difficulties and Carte was forced to sell it at an enormous loss. Converted into a music hall, it reopened as the Palace Theatre of Varieties in 1894 with Morton as manager; and it ran at a profit until his death in 1904 at the age of eighty-five.

In the meantime, music halls were spreading all over London. The Old Mogul in Drury Lane (the 'Old Mo') was renamed the Middlesex Music Hall and became the first to use footlights. The London Pavilion opened in 1859 behind the Black Horse Tavern in Piccadilly. The South London Palace, built in 1860 at a cost of £8,000, was the first of the 'Palaces', and also the first music hall to be designed along the lines of a traditional theatre with a proscenium arch. Sam Collins, a former chimney sweep, opened the Marylebone Music Hall before going on to establish Collins' in Islington. There was the Swallow Street Hall, the Gaiety, the Metropolitan, and the Star of Bermondsey. By 1865, there were thirty-two licensed halls with a capacity of between five hundred and 5,000 in London alone, as well as an estimated two hundred smaller ones. By 1878, when the Trocadero in Great Windmill Street (which boasted the Prince of Wales as one of its regular patrons) opened its doors, those figures had grown to seventy-eight large halls and over three hundred smaller venues. After 1878, new licensing restrictions meant that only larger theatres opened, like the Empire in Leicester Square in 1887, the Tivoli in the Strand in 1891, and the 2,300-seat Chelsea Palace in 1903.

The success and rapid spread of music hall was made possible by a series of social changes. The most obvious was urbanisation. The second half of the nineteenth century was a period when the United Kingdom's towns and cities were growing at an unprecedented speed. While this created many social problems, it also created catchment areas of a size necessary to make large-scale music halls profitable. Then there was transport. By the 1860s, when Morton was building the Oxford and music hall was on its way to becoming big business, the railway network made it possible for performers to travel around the country quickly and in comparative comfort. Appearing before different audiences in different towns not only boosted their income, but, in the days before recorded music, also encouraged the sale of profitable sheet music. In the 1870s, before her London debut, the young Vesta Tilley was able accept a schedule of engagements which included Nottingham – where her father was chairman at the St George's Music Hall – Birmingham, Liverpool, Derby, Leicester and Hull, confident that she could move between the cities with ease and on time. Contemporaneous improvements in printing technology meant that sheet music was of better quality and cheaper, at least in relative terms, and also that advertising became cheaper and more effective.

Even then, the speed with which music hall spread across the country was impressive. There was a local version of music hall in Connell's Monster Saloon in Dublin as early as 1855. In 1859, the big hall on the first floor of the Wheatsheaf in Newcastle-upon-Tyne's Cloth Market opened as the Royal Music Saloon. In 1862, it was renamed Balmbra's Music Hall – under which name it is mentioned in Geordie Ridley's famous song 'Blaydon Races', first performed there that same year. Music hall reached Edinburgh in 1861 when a stockbroker called William Paterson took over the Dunedin Hall, which had previously been used for circuses, and turned it into the Alhambra Music Hall. Just down the road, working-class Leith had its first purpose-built hall in 1865, and a total of four by 1888. As music hall grew in popularity across the country, so it threw up syndicates and business empires. The biggest and most powerful involved three men: Edward Moss, who had built up a group of halls in Edinburgh and Manchester; Oswald Stoll, whose halls extended from Liverpool to South Wales; and Richard Thornton, who operated in Newcastle and the north-east. In 1899, they formally came together as Moss Empires, owning 'Empire' halls throughout the country, including a large number in the London suburbs, and going on to build three impressive, flagship venues in

London itself: the Finsbury Park Empire and the London Hippodrome in 1900, and the London Coliseum in 1904.

In the early years of music hall, the biggest stars were a group of young men known as the *lions comiques*. Although they worked independently – and were often great rivals – they represented an attitude which struck a chord in society. Up to that point, the standard music hall turn had been a working-class figure conveying a cloth-cap-and-overcoat image. The *lions comiques*, although in reality working class themselves, cultivated an upper-class image, wearing white tie and tails, and singing songs which praised drinking, womanising and a life devoted to pleasure. The first of the *lions comiques* was the Great Arthur Lloyd, a Scottish actor who made his music hall reputation at the London Pavilion. It was Lloyd who coined the word 'swell' to describe the kind of man-on-the-make depicted in his many songs. 'Immensikoff (the Shoreditch toff)', based on the name of a kind of fur-lined overcoat, was one of his most popular songs, but the only one remembered today is probably 'Married to a Mermaid'. After Lloyd came the Great Vance (Arthur Vance; 1839–88), who also made his name at the Pavilion. Vance developed the image of the swell with songs like 'The Style, by Jove!', 'The Young Man of the Day', 'The Languid Swell' and 'The Dancing Swell'. It was Vance who coined and popularised the word *zoo*, for what had previously been called *zoological gardens,* in his song 'Walking in the Zoo'.

Greater than either the Great Arthur Lloyd or the Great Vance was a former sailor, the Great MacDermott (Gilbert Hastings Farrell; 1845–1901), whose songs often contained contemporary references. 'Master Dilke Upset the Milk' referred to divorce proceedings involving the Liberal MP and cabinet minister, Sir Charles Dilke. 'Would You Be Surprised to Hear?' was based on a famous legal case where a London butcher's son pretended to be the missing claimant to the Tichbourne baronetcy. MacDermott's greatest moment of fame came in 1878 when he sang the patriotic, and at the time anti-Russian, 'We don't want to fight, but by Jingo if we do'. The song was so successful, he was asked to sing it in private audience with the Prince of Wales and subsequently became known as the 'Statesman of the Halls'.

However, the most successful *lion comique* of all was George Leybourne (1842–84), born in Gateshead and an engine-fitter by trade. He began his stage life under the name Joe Saunders, but reverted to his birth name when he appeared at London's Bedford Music Hall in 1863. His breakthrough came three years later in Leeds when he gave the first performance of the song which was to shape his career: 'Champagne Charlie'. It had such an impact on sales of champagne that the importers actually gave him free champagne to the tune of £20 a week to continue singing it. The same year also saw him singing the other song for which he is remembered: 'The Daring Young Man on the Flying Trapeze', inspired by the immense success of the trapeze artist Jules Léotard (who gave his name to the one-piece exercise garment that he knitted for himself). In 1868, Leybourne was taken on at the Canterbury at £25 per week, but within a very short time he was earning £120 or more – at a time when a farm labourer might earn £45 a year and a senior clerk perhaps £250. As music hall developed, the most popular artists would give three, four, or even five 'turns' at different theatres in the course of an evening. In this way, all the *lions comiques* earned huge sums of money, but, true to their 'swell' image, they spent it on what we might now call a rock'n'roll lifestyle. Only Arthur Lloyd survived beyond the age of sixty.

In the 1870s, tickets for the Tivoli cost between one and five shillings. In what were then the suburbs, halls such as Collins' in Islington, charged between tuppence and one shilling and sixpence. An evening's programme might last four hours and feature twenty or more acts, sometimes sepa-rated by interludes of popular classical music or well-known arias. Gradually, however, as competition increased and audiences became more demanding, programmes became more concentrated. It was the Moss, Stoll and Thornton syndicate that moved away from the traditional arrangement, where a ticket bought a whole evening's entertainment, insti-tuting instead a system based on two shows a night as a way of meeting the enormous costs of their big 'Empire' halls.[2] The combination of bigger halls and two shows a night also changed the character of music hall acts. They became more professional, with less room for improvisation and interac-tion with the audience. This disappointed many who had grown up with the early halls; nonetheless, the general consensus remains that the period from 1890 to 1914 was the golden age of music hall.

The later decades of music hall saw an increase in the number of female performers. One of the earliest big female stars was Vesta Tilley (Matilda Alice Powles; 1864-1952). Tilley was a male impersonator, who made her first stage appearance at the age of five, dressed as a boy. There were other male impersonators, such as Nellie Power (1855–87) and Bessie Bonehill (?–1902), but Tilley's act was different because it was based on precise observation and meticulous preparation. Men admired her because her clothes were stylish; women admired her because her act mocked and satirised men and their egos. Her most famous character was the middle-class swell who appears in 'Berlington Bertie', but she appeared in a whole range of different guises, including a judge, a clergyman, a policeman, a town councillor and a soldier. Her act stood out also because it avoided the double entendres and sexual innuendo characteristic of Marie Lloyd, Florrie Forde and many other stars, both male and female. During the 1890s, songs like 'After the Ball' and 'Following in Father's Footsteps' made her the highest-paid woman music-hall star. Her popularity endured right up to the First World War when she sang 'Jolly Good Luck to the Girl Who Loves a Soldier', which proved a useful recruiting song – although it was also partly intended as a riposte to another male impersonator, Hetty King, who sang 'All the Nice Girls Love a Sailor'. Tilley retired in 1920, following a year-long farewell tour, during which she donated all her earnings to children's charities. She went on to become Lady de Frece, wife of the Conservative MP for Blackpool.

Florrie Forde (Flora May Augustus Flanagan; 1876–1940) was born in Australia and did not make her music hall debut in Britain until 1897. In complete contrast to Vesta Tilley, Forde was a big, busty woman, which she exploited and made fun of in her act. She specialised in glamorous, sequined costumes, and elaborate, often plumed headgear. She also carried a bejewelled cane which she used to encourage the audience to join in the choruses. She was an energetic performer with a better voice than many music hall singers, and she enjoyed a string of popular hits, including 'Has Anybody Here Seen Kelly?', 'Hold Your Hand Out, Naughty Boy', 'Oh, oh, Antonio', 'My old man said follow the van', and 'Down at the Old Bull and Bush' – songs which, with their mixture of sentiment, vulgarity and melody seem to contain the essence of music hall. During the First World War, it was her popularity that helped songs such as 'Goodbye-ee', 'Pack Up Your Troubles in Your Old Kit Bag', and 'Take Me Back to Dear Old Blighty' to achieve iconic status among British and, indeed, Australian troops.

The greatest music hall star of them all, of course, was Marie Lloyd (Matilda Alice Victoria Wood; 1870–1922), introduced to audiences in her days of fame as 'The One and Only'. The eldest of eight children, she was born into a working-class family in Hoxton in London's East End. Her father made artificial flowers and worked as a part-time waiter at the Eagle Tavern; and it was on the stage at the Eagle, just a few months after her fourteenth birthday and calling herself Bella Delmere, that she seems to have made her first public appearance.[3] A few weeks later, she appeared at the Falstaff in Old Street. She was spotted by an agent. She changed her stage name. Appearing at Sebright's in Hackney, she sang 'The Boy I Love Is Up in the Gallery', which was to become one of the trademark songs of her career, but she did so without the permission of Nellie Power, for whom it had been written. This was a potentially serious matter because singers relied on their popular numbers to secure them bookings. Marie Lloyd, as she had become, pleaded innocence and ignorance and got away with it. Within two years, she was earning £100 a week.

Marie Lloyd was not good looking – she had protruding teeth and a rather dumpy figure – and her vocal range was limited, but she had charisma, perfect diction and a sense of fun. Pantomime did not suit her, although she appeared at Drury Lane three years running in the early 1890s. Music hall did. It gave her the opportunity to improvise, to respond to the audience with her famous ad libs. Like many of the music hall greats, her success was due to her ability to become the character singing the song, whether it was a sentimental young girl with a sweetheart in the gallery, a lady of quality ('When I Take My Morning Promenade'), or a gin-sodden old wreck ('One of the Ruins that Cromwell Knocked about a Bit'). Lloyd's popularity – and her notoriety – also depended on her skill in seeming to make even the most innocent lyric suggestive. There is a story that a lady called Laura Ormiston Chant, acting on behalf of the Social Purity Alliance, reported Lloyd to London County Council for what were described as lewd performances. Summoned before the committee dealing with theatres and music halls, Lloyd performed several of her songs, including 'Oh, Mr Porter!' and 'She Sits Among the Cabbages and Peas' (which, after protests, she retitled 'She Sits Among the Cauliflowers and Leeks'), in the most innocent manner imaginable. She then sang Tennyson's 'Come into the Garden, Maud' turning it into a minefield of sexual innuendo. It was, she said, all in the mind. Songs like 'Every Little Movement Has a Meaning of its Own' and 'She'd Never Had Her Ticket Punched Before' were not so very different from folk songs like 'Bonnie Black Hare' and 'The Cuckoo's Nest', and they were just as popular. They belonged to that same strand of British humour that later generations would appreciate in the *Carry On* films or the *Benny Hill Show* in the 1960s and 70s. Yet there was a serious subtext. Lloyd's songs and her act asserted female sexuality, and the right of women to exercise their sexuality – 'A Little of What You Fancy Does You Good' – which was something denied, at least in public, in Victorian England. Respectable opinion (or parts of it) may have been outraged, but Lloyd's public loved it; and they loved it even more because she exposed the hypocrisy of respectable opinion.

At the height of her fame, Marie Lloyd was earning £500 a week. She toured France – at the invitation of the French government; she toured Australia; and she toured the United States. Her personal life, however, was less successful. She married three times, but all three of her husbands had drink problems, and two of them beat her so seriously that the police had to be called in. Yet she was always ready to help others. During the 1907 music hall strike, she was a passionate advocate of higher wages for the rank-and-file performers. She did not need the money herself, but she disliked unfairness, so she stood out against the owners and managers who refused to pay a decent wage, among them Oswald Stoll. Payback came in 1912, by which time music hall was becoming respectable. George V agreed to the idea of a royal command performance. It took place at the Palace Theatre on Cambridge Circus that July. The idea had originally been Edward Moss's, but he died before the event took place, and it was left to Stoll to organise and choose the participants. Lloyd, who was at the height of her fame, was on an early cast list, but not among the acts finally chosen. Was it because her act was too risqué for royalty? Or because she had mocked Stoll and his colleagues during the strike? Probably a combination of both. But Lloyd was 'The One and Only'. She hired the London Pavilion, just a few hundred metres away, for the same evening and played to a packed house, claiming her performance was 'by command of the British public.' It was a characteristic response.

Compared with performers such as Tilley, Forde and Lloyd, the male stars of music hall's golden age included more jokes, monologues and sketches in their acts. They tended to be entertainers as much as singers. In financial terms, the most successful was undoubtedly Harry (later Sir Harry) Lauder (1870–1950). For his first ever performance at Larkhall, just south of Glasgow, in 1891, he received five shillings. He spent a number of years building a reputation in Scotland and in the music halls of northern England before moving south to London in 1900. By 1913, he was the highest-paid entertainer in the world, receiving £1125 for a single appearance at the Glasgow Pavilion. Lauder also had one of the better music hall voices and wrote many of his own songs, the best known of which are 'I Love a Lassie', 'Roamin' in the Gloamin', 'A Wee Deoch-an-Doris', 'Stop Your Tickling, Jock', and 'The End of the Road'.

There were other performers from the regions. Will Fyffe (1885–1947) was another Scots act. Best known today for the song 'I Belong to Glasgow', he caught only the tail end of the great years of music hall and during the 1930s and 40s became a successful film actor. George Lashwood (1863–1942), known as 'The Beau Brummel of the Halls' because of his fine costumes, and singer of 'Goodbye Dolly Gray', was a builder's son from Birmingham. Mark Sheridan (Frederick Shaw; 1864–1918), who had huge success with 'I Do Like to Be Beside the Seaside' and with the wartime song 'Belgium Put the Kibosh on the Kaiser', was a dockworker from Sunderland. Billy Williams (Richard Isaac Banks; 1878–1915), who sang 'When Father Papered the Parlour', was Australian. But music hall was an urban phenomenon and it was inevitable that London, the largest urban centre in the world, should dominate.

Dan Leno (George Wild Galvin; 1860–1904) was a Londoner, and one of the leading music hall stars during the 1890s. Originally a clog dancer, he developed an act based on a series of invented characters – firemen, policemen, shop girls, huntsmen, hairdressers, pantomime dames, beefeaters at the Tower of London – into whose monologues on everyday subjects he would inject unexpected, even surreal observations. His songs, with titles such as 'The Railway Guard', 'The Shopwalker', and 'The Boiled Egg and the Wasp' were largely defined by the content of his act and few are now remembered. It was not just London that held the centre of the music hall stage: it was Cockney London. And it was Dan Leno's main rival, Albert Chevalier (1861–1923) – actually christened Albert Gwathveoyd Louis Onésime Britannicus – who is credited with inventing the so-called 'coster' style, meaning that his stage act was based upon the lives, characters and accents of costermongers, the Cockney term for those who sell fruit and vegetables, usually from a street barrow. The scenario Chevalier used for his most famous song, 'My Old Dutch', shows just how music hall could reflect real working-class experience. An elderly couple came on stage, apparently heading for the workhouse where, according to the rules, they would be accommodated by gender. The song was the man's plea that they should not be separated: 'We've been together now for forty years'.

Gus Elen (Ernest Augustus Elen; 1862–1940) was the probably most successful of the 'coster' comedians. He was another performer whose comedy contained surreal images. His best-known song, 'If It Wasn't for the 'Ouses in Between' describes how on a Sunday a costermonger decorates his backyard 'Wiv the turnip tops and cabbages / Wot people doesn't buy' and 'Wiv tomatoes and wiv radishes wot 'adn't any sale' to make it look like the country. Another popular Cockney figure was Harry Champion (William Henry Crump; 1865–1942). It was his songs, with titles such as 'Any Old Iron' and 'Boiled Beef and Carrots', that helped establish the image of Cockney life – however unrealistic and stylised – that remained current in the media for many decades. Champion's signature tune was 'I'm Henery the Eighth, I am', about a man whose wife has been married seven times before. He was also responsible for popularising the anarchic mixture of monologue and song, 'When the Old Dun Cow Caught Fire', written by Harry Wincott in 1893 and still heard today in folk clubs and bar sing-songs throughout the country.

In the bigger halls, performers would have been accompanied by an orchestra of anything between sixteen and thirty players – strings, wood-wind, brass and percussion, often with the addition of a piano and some-times a banjo. In the smaller or more remote halls, it might just be a piano, or piano and accordion. Sheet music, an important source of revenue for performers and writers alike, was naturally arranged for the piano, to allow for home performance. In strictly musical terms, the value of the songs that emerged from the sixty years during which music hall thrived was limited. They are simple in structure, repetitive, strophic, and often written for performers with a limited vocal range. Yet they were also effective, witty, often dramatic, and phenomenally popular. Music hall bred hundreds of singers and entertainers – only a very few of them can be mentioned here – and it produced thousands of songs. During its heyday – from the 1850s until about 1920, after which it was in marked decline – it was a significant cultural force. Performers could make politicians and public figures look ridiculous, whip up popular opinion against Russia or Germany, or have a measurable impact on enlistment, just by singing a few lines of what was effectively doggerel. In this respect, music hall edged aside the folk tradi-tion. As the product of an increasingly urbanised society, it was better equipped to reflect and communicate the concerns of the urban masses, who now made up the majority of the population. The folk tradition did not die out during the great years of music hall – it found other outlets, often allying itself to the direct expression of political or industrial grievances – but it was diminished. Popular song and folk song became distinct entities.

Even after its demise, music hall remained an influence. In the 1950s, singers like Lonnie Donegan and Tommy Steele released songs that consciously recalled music hall. In 1965, Harry Champion's 'I'm Henery the Eighth, I am' was actually revived, becoming a hit for the pop group Herman's Hermits. And the music hall image of the cheeky Cockney played a part in the success of another early 1960s group, Joe Brown and the Bruvvers. In 1953, BBC television hit on the idea of presenting a music hall from the Victorian-Edwardian golden age. Filmed at Leeds City Varieties and chaired by Leonard Sachs, *The Good Old Days* proved hugely successful with the viewing public, although presumably mainly with the older generation. It ran for thirty years. In 2004, Wilton's Music Hall reopened its doors – the trust that owns it having spent several million pounds on restoration – and is now a venue for variety acts and concerts of various kinds. In part, of course, all this can be explained by nostalgia, but music hall songs have an appeal and have entered folk memory for a reason. Just as we can see certain similarities between the rhythmic banter of some music hall lyrics and the patter songs of Gilbert and Sullivan's Savoy Operas, so it is possible to see the best of what music hall produced as another expression of the British genius for matching words and music.

72   Musical Education, and the Anglican Revival

By the beginning of the twentieth century, most areas of British music were in a healthier state than they had been half-a-century earlier. The reasons for this, and how much can be attributed to what is usually referred to as the English Musical Renaissance, is something we must leave for a later chapter, but it is clear that, from the middle of the nineteenth century onwards, there were a number of factors that were driving change and improvement.

One factor was the provision of new concert halls and new concert series. We have focussed on the Crystal Palace, which was the largest and most spectacular venue, but by no means the only venture of its kind. In 1858, two music publishing firms – Chappell & Co and Cramer & Co – came together to build St James's Hall in Piccadilly, with a seating capacity of 2,000. Arthur Chappell started a series of concerts designed to be accessible to ordinary people with ticket prices (like those for Jullien's promenade concerts in the 1840s) of just one shilling. Although they concentrated on chamber music, Chappell's 'Monday Pops', as they became known, regularly drew audiences of 1,500. Outside the capital, the Reid Concerts in Edinburgh – named after General Reid who endowed the Professorship of Music at the University – had started in 1841. In 1859, they moved into the new Reid Concert Hall, where they have continued to maintain a regular programme of high quality music ever since. The Liverpool Philharmonic Society had been founded in 1840, and in 1849 moved into the purpose-built Philharmonic Hall, which claimed to be among the best venues in the country. In 1850, Charles Hallé started his 'Gentlemen's Concerts' in Manchester. They were so successful that, in 1858, he founded the Hallé Orchestra and gave his own shilling-a-head concerts for the less well off in the newly constructed Free Trade Hall. Many concert series like these became permanent institutions, offering classical music played to a good standard in appropriate surroundings.

Musical education was another area of change. The RAM continued to lead a troubled life. The students resented the harsh levels of discipline imposed by the controlling Board. The teaching staff resented interference by Board members with no musical knowledge. Finance was a constant problem. Bennett did his best to pull things together after the financial crisis of 1866, but a Royal Society of Arts report was critical of the way the institution functioned and the Duke of Edinburgh became involved. He called for a new music school to be set up as part of Albertopolis in South Kensington, a key feature of which would be the provision of scholarships to be made available for students from the provinces. One attempt had already been made to create a National College of Music. Organised by Henry Leslie and a group of influential music professionals, it had opened in 1864 but lasted barely a year. This new initiative, with royal backing, promised to be more successful and led, in 1876, to the establishment of the National Training School for Music, with Arthur Sullivan as its reluctant Principal. Unfortunately, royal backing did not guarantee funds and within just two years, the Training School was in trouble. A proposal to merge with the RAM was rejected by the RAM Board – much to the relief of teaching staff at the Training School. The Prince of Wales became involved and, in 1882, organised a meeting to which he invited potential financial backers, Lords-Lieutenant from the English counties and provincial mayors from up and down the country. The Prince's plan was to set up a Royal College of Music, and the one man who did more than any other to get the project off the ground was George Grove. He travelled the length and breadth of the kingdom raising funds; and then, when he was appointed Director of the new college, brought his formidable administrative abilities to bear, developing a curriculum and engaging the best teaching staff he could find. At the inauguration ceremony in May 1883, the Prince of Wales was at pains to emphasise the egalitarian principles of the College, pointing out that the first scholarship recipients included 'a mill-girl, the daughter of a bricklayer, the son of a blacksmith, and the son of a farm labourer.'[1] He also awarded Grove a knighthood. That the College grew and quickly achieved the reputation it did was due to Grove's tireless efforts as an administrator, and to the teaching staff he had recruited, which included many who were already, or who were to become, recognised musical figures – men such as Hubert Parry, Charles Villiers Stanford, Walter Parratt, Frederick Bridge, and Ernest Pauer. Grove remained Director until 1894, when Parry took over.

In the meantime, in 1880, with far less fuss and far less fanfare, the City of London opened the Guildhall School of Music. The Principal was Thomas Weist Hill (1828–91), a violinist, a former teacher at the RAM and, briefly, musical director of a major new venue in north London, the Alexandra Palace – briefly because it burned down just sixteen days after it opened. Hill and his staff were less well known than their peers at the RCM, but the venture was no less successful: after just four years, it boasted over 2,000 students. Elsewhere, the same impulse towards musical education was being felt and acted upon. In Dublin, the Irish Academy of Music was founded in 1848 by a group of musicians that included Charles Stanford's father, John. It moved to new and much larger premises in 1871 and received its Royal Charter the following year. In Birmingham, the Midland Institute began 'Elementary Instruction in Singing' in 1859. It took twenty years to mature, but by 1879 a full, professional music curriculum was available. Degrees in music became available from London University in 1879, from Durham in 1889, Edinburgh in 1893, the University of Wales in 1894, and Birmingham in 1905. In 1893, much to the annoyance of Grove, Manchester also gained a Royal College of Music. The initiative, as one might expect, came from Hallé, who, despite his German origins, had become an honorary Mancunian and was determined that anything London could do Manchester could do at least as well.

The teaching of music in schools, seen by some – including the Reverend Haweis, whom we met earlier – as a tool for moral improvement, became the subject of public debate. Certain public schools led the way. At Harrow School, John Farmer (1836–1901), who had studied in Leipzig, became the first official music master and began singing contests to stimulate interest on the part of the boys. At Uppingham School in Rutland, Paul David, the son of Ferdinand David, Mendelssohn's friend and Sullivan's tutor, was brought in to stimulate and develop the school's musical life. Then, in 1864, the Clarendon Report on the public schools recommended that music should be an integral part of the curriculum. Six years later, the 1870 Education Act made attendance at school compulsory for all children between the ages of five and thirteen. It did not make musical education compulsory, but, in practice, largely because of the involvement and influence of the Church of England, music was taught in most of the nation's schools, often to a surprisingly high standard. A significant step forward maintaining and developing those standards still further was made in 1872 with the appointment of John Pyke Hullah (1812–84) to Her Majesty's Inspectorate of Schools as the new Inspector for Music.

By the time he was appointed, Hullah was sixty years old and had already had a varied career. He was a bit of a late starter, not beginning his musical education until the age of seventeen when he took lessons with William Horsley. In 1833, at the age of twenty-one, he was admitted to the RAM, and during the 1830s, went on to write three operas – including *The Village Coquettes* (1836) for which Dickens wrote the libretto. None were absolute failures, but nor were they runaway successes. In 1839, Hullah took himself off to Paris to investigate French methods of music teaching. On his return, he got a job as music teacher at the Battersea Training College for Pupil Teachers. The college's founder was Sir James Kaye-Shuttleworth, who also happened to be Secretary to the Privy Council Committee on Education. Hullah saw an opportunity, lobbied Kaye-Shuttleworth and, in due course, came to exercise an important influence on the philosophy underlying the 1870 Act. In addition to his official teaching commitments, Hullah also began his own music school, using the Tonic Sol-fa technique to teach singing. This method – which substitutes syllables (doh-re-me-fa-so-la-ti-doh) for conventional notation – was the invention of a lady from Norwich called Sarah Glover; Hullah, who seems to have been almost as tireless an administrator as George Grove, turned it into a popular phenomenon. Between 1840 and 1860, it is estimated that the movement he started taught some 25,000 people to sing. The trouble was that the system was inflexible: it could not cope with sharps or flats, so everything had to be transposed into the key of C, which was impractical to say the least. A slightly more flexible variant of Tonic Sol-fa was produced by John Curwen (1816–80), and it was this system that the government decided should be taught in schools – and which Hullah, to his mortification, was responsible for enforcing. By 1863, some 180,000 people were using Curwen's version to learn to sing. In 1869, a Tonic Sol-fa College was established, offering a basic level of training and issuing a certificate to those who completed the course. Over 250,000 people received them. All in all, and despite its inherent limitations, there is no doubt that the Tonic Sol-fa system taught many thousands of children and adults to sing and, quite possibly, to love music. Whether, as Hullah and Curwen fondly imagined, it therefore acted as a force for moral progress and social improvement is quite another question.

Church music was also entering a period of change and renewal. The Church of England had been at a low ebb for some time and church music, as we have seen, was consequently lacking in inspiration – the one notable exception, Sebastian Wesley, being effectively sidelined. The revival of Anglican church music, when it came, was the result of a movement for reform that arose from within the Church and, initially at least, had little to do with music.

The Oxford, or Tractarian, Movement was an attempt by a group of theologians to address what they saw as shortcomings within the contemporary Church of England. They sought to counteract secularisation on the one hand, and the increasing influence of evangelical clergy on the other, by taking liturgical practice back to its roots, reintroducing ritual and reviving certain religious practices, such as making the sign of the cross and lighting candles on the altar, which dated back to medieval times. The name Tractarians came from a series of 'Tracts for the Times' published between 1833 and 1841, which held, among other things, that beauty was an essential element in worship; that both churches and the services that were held in them should seek to reflect the beauty of God's creation. This meant vestments for the clergy; art, fabrics and furnishings throughout the church; and, of course, music during services. All this was highly controversial and for nearly half a century the reformers – who became known, generically, as Anglo-Catholics – found themselves and their practices subject to debates in Parliament, challenges in the courts, wild accusations of 'Popery', and even violence in the streets. Yet their influence spread and, with it, their attitude to and practice of music in church.

Most cathedrals and a handful of Oxford and Cambridge colleges had maintained the tradition of choral services down the years since the

Restoration; with the advent of the Oxford Movement, the musical component of these services was significantly strengthened. Prayers were intoned, psalms and canticles chanted, and hymn singing became an integral part of worship. As time went on and Anglo-Catholicism grew in influence, these practices spread across the country – although not without opposition in some quarters – bringing new life to services in parishes where church music had all but disappeared. And many of these practices revived as a result of the Oxford Movement remain current today. The fact that every cathedral and most parish churches will have a choir, that members of the choir wear surplices, sing the responses and chant the psalms, is a direct consequence of the Anglican Revival. As part of this same process of renewal, Gregorian chant was reintroduced; Merbecke's metrical psalms were rediscovered; and so, too, particularly in the great cathedrals, were works by other composers from the Tudor period, notably Tallis and Byrd. This use of Tudor music in Anglican Church services during the 1860s and 1870s represented the first stirrings of a more fundamental rediscovery and reappraisal of early music that took place at the end of the century and exercised considerable influence on British music as a whole.

Before the Anglican Revival, hymn singing was regarded by many in the Church of England as inappropriate, even suspicious, because it was associated with Methodism and Evangelical Non-Conformism. Consequently, hymns had disappeared from many, if not most, parish churches. As things turned out, however, the emphasis placed on hymn singing by the reformers proved an important factor in attracting worshippers back to church. Such was the response from congregations up and down the land that Anglican enthusiasm for hymn singing and hymn writing now rivalled that of the evangelical Methodists. Indeed, probably the best-known product of the Oxford Movement and the Anglican Revival is *Hymns Ancient and Modern*, that most iconic of hymnals, first published in 1861. It was the brainchild of two clergymen, Francis Murray (1820–1902) and William Denton (1815–88) both of whom graduated from Oxford in the 1840s. Murray enlisted the assistance of another clergyman from the same Oxford generation, Sir Henry Baker (1821–77), and they were joined by the organist, choirmaster and composer, William Henry Monk (1823–89), who became the hymnal's first editor. Together, the four of them collected and edited existing hymns, as well as writing and arranging new ones. The resulting volume was intended to stand alongside *The Book of Common Prayer* and it did, indeed, become the standard hymn book for generations of churchgoers and schoolchildren. *Hymns Ancient and Modern* has gone through a number of editions over the years, its contents evolving slowly to match changes in the Church and society, but it remains by far the most popular English-language hymnal ever published. In 2011, one hundred and fifty years after its first appearance, its publishers estimated that they had sold 170 million copies.

The Anglican Revival, as the name indicates, revived music and musical practices from former times. It spread the use of music in church through-out the country and improved standards of performance. What it did not manage to do was improve the standard of contemporary church music. Goss and other members of the older generation continued to write their regulation services and anthems well into the 1870s, presumably aware of, but apparently untouched by the Oxford Movement. Gore Ouseley was an enthusiastic supporter of the Oxford Movement, but his main contribution lay not in his compositions, but in the college he founded at Tenbury Wells, which did much to drive the improvement in performance. A slightly younger man, and another strong Oxford Movement supporter, was John Bacchus Dykes, whom we met earlier as a composer of services and anthems which reflected the prevailing sentimentality of the age. He was also a prolific hymn writer. Among his more than three hundred hymn tunes are several that are still popular, including *Nicaea* ('Holy, holy, holy, Lord God Almighty'), *Lux Benigna* ('Lead, kindly light') and *Melita* ('For those in peril on the sea'). Joseph Barnby (1838–96) had a genuine talent for writing for voices and worked together with Gounod to form the Albert Hall Choral Society in 1872. He was a prolific composer, much influenced by Gounod, who wrote significantly more sacred than secular music, but his sacred music, even more than Dykes', is strongly marked by contempo-rary secular influences. He developed a particular style for his secular part-songs – perhaps best exemplified by an excruciatingly sugary setting of Tennyson's 'Sweet and Low'[2] – which carried over into his services and his anthems. These, as a result, are constantly changing tone and expression in a way which simply does not work, making them sound trivial or obvious. He, too, wrote a large number of hymn tunes, among them *Merrial* ('Now the Day is Over') and *Sine Nomine Sarum* ('For all the saints').

Perhaps awareness of what was required by Papperitz's 'commercial England' helped when it came to writing successful hymn tunes. Certainly, Arthur Sullivan showed himself adept at coming up with popular and memorable melodies. His hymn tunes include *St Gertrude* ('Onward!

Christian soldiers'),[3] *St Nathaniel* ('God moves in a mysterious way'),[4] and *Bethlehem* ('While shepherds watched their flocks by night'). Yet in the 1860s and 1870s, when he came to write a series of anthems for the Church, he was less successful. A story, reportedly told by Sullivan himself, illustrates the problem. He was writing the scene in *The Golden Legend* – described by one critic as 'glutinous in its sentiment'[5] – where the heroine, Elsie, is confronted by Lucifer and prepares to sacrifice herself to save the life of the hero, Prince Henry. 'Have you thought well of it?' says Lucifer. 'I come not here to argue, but to die,' responds Elsie. Sullivan confessed that he had to fight back the impulse for the chorus to sing 'No, she don't come here to argue, but to die' in the manner of a Savoy opera. And it is this spirit of the theatre that creeps into his writing for the Church. He does his best, but there are passages in anthems such as *I sing the birth was born tonight, Sing O Heaven O God, Who is like unto Thee,* and *Thou art worthy to be praised* which simply do not sound like church music.

Other composers managed better. George Garrett (1834–97), for example, a pupil of Sebastian Wesley, wrote a number of well-regarded settings of the Anglican services. His Full Services in D and in F are still heard occasionally. Both follow Wesley in giving prominence to the organ as a separate and independent part of the composition, and, significantly, both also feature music for the Office of Holy Communion, which was celebrated far more frequently with the coming of the Oxford Movement. Charles Steggall (1826–1905), who took over as editor of *Hymns Ancient and Modern* from William Monk, deserves a mention for the little-known but intensely beautiful four-part anthem *Remember now thy creator.* So, too, do Langdon Colborne (1835–89), organist at Tenbury Wells and at Hereford Cathedral, whose Evening Service in D is still heard from time to time; and Ebenezer Prout (1835–1909), Professor of Composition at the RAM and later Professor of Music at Dublin University, whose Services in D and F remained popular right up to the end of the nineteenth century.

The best-known composer of church music during this middle period of the century, however, was Sir John Stainer (1840–1901). Although a traditionalist in that he spent his career holding a series of important positions in the musical hierarchy, Stainer was also, in his own way, an instigator of change. At the age of nine, he became a chorister at St Paul's, and at the age of sixteen was picked by Gore Ouseley to serve as organist at Tenbury Wells, a position which also required him to supervise the choir and give piano lessons to students who were only a few years younger than he was.

Aged twenty, he was organist at Magdalen College, Oxford. Four years later he received his BA, and two years after that his doctorate. He was incredibly conscientious and hard-working, in part because, like Sullivan, he came from a poor background – his father was a cabinet maker – and he saw music as a way to improve his social status. Unlike Sullivan, however, Stainer was prepared to climb the ladder of establishment appointments. In 1871, he became organist at St Paul's Cathedral. A string of offices and honours followed: Honorary Fellow of the RAM, musical director of the London Madrigal Society, Inspector of Music on the School Inspectorate (he took over from Hullah in 1882 and continued in the job until his death in 1901), Senior Adjudicator at the Welsh Eisteddfod, Professor of Music at Oxford, and Chevalier of the *Légion d'Honneur*. He received his knighthood from Queen Victoria in 1888.

Stainer wrote some forty anthems, often quite ambitious in scope but less successful in execution. *I am Alpha and Omega* contains some well-balanced contrasting passages, though one is left at times wondering about Stainer's sensitivity to the rhythm of the words he is setting. *Lord, Thou art God* attempts a particularly grand scale and ends with a version of the National Anthem. His best anthem is certainly *I saw the Lord*, an impressive eight-part piece, probably written in his late teens, which is both dignified and uncomplicated. Although written in several movements, it has a musical unity that is reinforced by effective word-setting of a kind he does not often achieve elsewhere.

A word must also be said about Stainer's oratorio, *The Crucifixion*, written in 1887, which, although not strictly church music, is probably the work for which he is best known – and it is a work that divides critics as sharply today as it did when it was first performed. Stainer wanted to write what he called *A Meditation on the Sacred Passion of the Holy Redeemer*, and based the structure of the work on the *St Matthew Passion* – he was another of those who played a part in rediscovering and popularising Bach. At the same time, he wanted to make it a work that a parish choir could sing. Such an approach, while true to the ideals of the Oxford Movement, would inevitably be musically limiting. Unfortunately, he was limited further by the libretto, assembled by the Reverend William Sparrow-Simpson, Librarian of St Paul's, which manages to reduce the story of the Passion to little more than doggerel. Stainer had to overcome this and there are undoubtedly passages where he did. The crucifixion scene – 'When Jesus Therefore Saw His Mother ' and 'Is It Nothing To You?'– is handled with great emotional power. His insertion of several hymn-like passages – 'The Misery of Divine Humiliation', 'The Mystery of the Intercession', and the final 'For the Love of Jesus' – to encourage the participation of the congregation can be, if carefully handled, a master stroke. It has to be said, however, that there are other numbers – 'Processional to Calvary' and 'So Liftest Thou Thy Petition' to name but two – in which the music fails to rise above the libretto and dissolves into trite sentimentality. For all that, *The Crucifixion* remains one of only a handful of nineteenth-century oratorios that are still heard in the twenty-first.

In the final analysis, Stainer is like many of the post-Oxford Movement generation of composers in that his most interesting work is to be found in his settings of the Anglican Service. None of them rise to heights of greatness, but they are much better than those of his contemporaries. Moreover, they were works which, in the context of his appointments at Magdalen College and at St Paul's, had a practical application. They were the expression of his belief in the value of choral music in a religious setting; they were intended to be both beautiful and expressive; and they were also written with a view to training and developing the choirs for which he was responsible. (When he took over the choir of St Paul's it was in a particularly poor state.) His Morning and Evening Service in E flat is probably his best. It is consistently dignified and tuneful, with a directness and a clarity that is maintained throughout. The Service in B flat – the *Nunc Dimittis* and the *Magnificat* from which are still heard – is also interesting in that it was written with a specific acoustic, that of St Paul's Cathedral, in mind. The idea of composing for the acoustics of a particular edifice was something that would not recur until the work of Herbert Howells half a century later.

Although not well known today, Stainer was a major musical figure in his lifetime: composer, performer, teacher, educator, choirmaster, and also musicologist. He did not write many hymn tunes, but he was fascinated by carols and, together with another musicologist, Henry Ramsden Bramley (1833–1917), he published *Christmas Carols, New and Old* (1878). Now almost as iconic as *Hymns Ancient and Modern*, and with every carol prefaced by an appropriately atmospheric engraving, *Christmas Carols, New and Old* brought a number of carols now regarded as old favourites to public attention for the first time – among them 'The First Noël', 'God Rest You Merry Gentlemen', 'The Seven Joys of Mary', 'See, Amid the Winter's Snow', 'Once In Royal David's City', and 'The Holly and the Ivy'.

Stainer also published at least ten books on matters connected with the theory and history of music. Musicology as such is beyond the scope of this book, but it is worth noting the number of those directly or indirectly involved in music – composers, conductors, and critics – who felt impelled to record their ideas and put them before the public. Goss, for example, published half-a-dozen volumes on psalmody and church music. Gore Ouseley, as we have seen, published a string of technical treatises. John Hullah's publications amount to a small library. The first volume of *Grove's Dictionary* appeared in 1879. Ebenezer Prout published nine books on aspects of musical theory. The study of music was another growth area which was also, in its own way, driving change.

73   Alexander Mackenzie

The three most prominent members of the musical generation that followed Sullivan were a Scotsman, an Englishman, and an Irishman: Alexander Campbell Mackenzie, Charles Hubert Hastings Parry, and Charles Villiers Stanford. Together they are often referred to as the architects of the English Musical Renaissance – a notion that we shall look at in more detail in later chapters. The term 'generation' is perhaps misleading as all three were born during the ten years following Sullivan's birth, but they *feel* as if they belong to a later musical generation. This is partly because Sullivan's career took off at such a young age – by the time any of the three were composing works of any significance, he had already embarked on his career-defining partnership with Gilbert – and partly also because Sullivan's reputation, the Savoy Operas excepted, slumped dramatically after his death. Many reasons have been suggested for this – among them a conspiracy by musical intellectuals, including the three above-mentioned, who resented his popular success – but the most likely explanation is simply that music had moved on. Tastes had changed. The new generation were not interested in Mendelssohn; they were interested in Liszt, Wagner and Brahms. And because Sullivan, with his active and persuasive personality, had been such a presence on the music scene, it took his death to make people realise that his work had been over-praised.

Alexander Mackenzie (1847–1935), the eldest of the three, came from a family of hard-working musical professionals. His grandfather had been a violinist; his father, another Alexander, was also a violinist and led the orchestra at Edinburgh's Theatre Royal. By the age of eight, the young Mackenzie could play violin well enough to sit in with his father's band on a regular basis. At the age of ten, he was sent to the small German principality of Schwarzburg-Sondershausen in Thuringia where he studied at the conservatory and also played second violin in the orchestra of Duke Günther Friedrich Karl II. By the time he was fifteen, he was in London, studying at the RAM, and playing in music halls and theatres to pay for his studies. Mackenzie senior had died while his son was still in Germany, and an important reason for choosing the RAM seems to have been that it allowed young Alexander to study under Prosper Sainton, who had taught his father. Mackenzie had one or two youthful compositions performed while he was at the Academy, but, at this stage, he seems to have thought of himself as a performer rather than a composer.

Back in Edinburgh and still only eighteen, Mackenzie threw himself into work. He taught in local colleges and institutions; he gave private lessons; he gave chamber concerts; he commuted between Edinburgh and Glasgow, playing first violin in orchestras in both cities; he became conductor of the Scottish Vocal Music Association; he became Precentor of St George's, Charlotte Square, an Edinburgh church noted for its music; he played in four consecutive Birmingham Festivals (1864, 67, 70, and 73), where he got to know both Costa and Hans von Bülow. As if this were not enough, he also got married, became a father, and began to think seriously about composing – despite, or perhaps as a result of, being told very directly and in person by the great Russian pianist, Anton Rubinstein, that Britain had no composers. A first glimmer of success came in 1877 when his concert overture, *Cervantes*, was given its premiere in Sondershausen under the German conductor, Max Erdmannsdörfer. More important, however, was the fact that von Bülow then took up the piece and gave it at a 'Scottish Night' concert in Glasgow.

Given his workload, it is not surprising that Mackenzie had some kind of breakdown. The result was the decision, in 1879, to take himself and his family off to Florence, where the living was cheap and he could concentrate on composition. It was to remain his base for most of the next ten years, and it was during this time that most, although not all, of his best work was written. It was also during this time that the expatriate Scot began to build a Scottish dimension into his music. His *Rhapsodie Ecossaise* (1879) uses the tune of Burns' 'There was a lad was born in Kyle', while the

Second Scottish Rhapsody (1880), a work of controlled romanticism, is actually titled *Burns*. Both pieces were given their first performance in Scotland – in Edinburgh and Glasgow respectively. Although Mackenzie never became an aggressively nationalist composer, Scottish themes and ideas are at the heart of many of his best works.

Italy also gave him time to concentrate on larger-scale compositions. Over the course of his career, Mackenzie wrote a dozen large-scale choral works, and it was his cantata, *The Bride*, given at the Three Choirs Festival in Worcester in 1881, that first brought him acclaim as a composer. *The Bride* was followed by *Jason* for the Bristol Festival the following year, but his most successful and most popular choral work was *The Rose of Sharon*, commissioned for the Norwich Festival of 1884. The libretto, telling the story of King Solomon's love for the Shulamite woman in the Song of Songs, was put together by Joseph Bennett of the *Daily Telegraph*, and the piece was billed as a 'dramatic oratorio'. As interpreted by Mackenzie and Bennett, this came to mean 'almost an opera'. The libretto contains details of setting and costume that are, in effect, stage directions. The prominent role given to the orchestra, and the use of something not too far from leit-motifs (Mackenzie had learned a lot about Wagner while he was in Germany), together with the long, connected, developing scenes and the use of dialogue, all suggest opera – and are reminders that most of Mackenzie's early musical experiences were in the orchestra pit. After the first performance, which he had returned from Italy to conduct, Mackenzie was showered with roses by the audience. The *Monthly Music Record* stated that it was an 'epoch-making' work, in tune with 'the spirit of [the] age', while still reflecting 'the traditions of the past'.[1] Others said it was the best thing since *Elijah*. It was not. In an age of dull oratorios, Mackenzie responded to the oriental theme with music that was fluid and tuneful and had sufficient ornamentation to characterise but not to swamp the action. It was also, as with all Mackenzie's work, superbly orchestrated. If the oratorio as a whole does not reach the heights, it is because, as so very often in the history of nineteenth-century oratorio, the libretto does not contain enough actual drama to maintain tension and interest to the end – but the work remains of more musical interest than many other contemporary examples of the genre.

Mackenzie was unlucky with his librettos. In part, this was probably his own fault. He was content to rely on journalists such as Joseph Bennett, or Francis Hueffer of *The Times* (successor to James Davison), rather than on poets, or playwrights, or classic texts. In his autobiography, *A Musician's Narrative* (1927), he claims that he never received a completed libretto before having to start composition: the final text was always assembled as he went along – which must have made it extraordinarily difficult to give a sense of coherence to the work in question. In the end, none of his subsequent major choral works, nor any of his operas – of which there were six, two of them written while he was in Italy – attracted anything approaching the interest of *The Rose of Sharon*. *Colomba*, a Corsican revenge drama based on a novella by Prosper Mérimée, was the first and probably the most successful of his operas. It enjoyed a short run in London in 1883, produced at Drury Lane by the Carl Rosa Opera Company, and was also – most unusually for a British opera – given in Germany, in Hamburg and Darmstadt, the following year. *The Troubadour* (1886), his attempt at grand opera, was generally held to be dull. *His Majesty, or, the Court of Vignolia*, his attempt at comic opera, was written some years later, in 1897. With the Gilbert and Sullivan partnership having finally collapsed, Carte was desperate to find something to take its place. He put together a team comprising Mackenzie, Burnand (who had written the libretto for *Cox and Box*), and Rudolph Lehmann, a well-known contributor to *Punch*. Mackenzie's score was professional, appropriate, and even at times witty, but critics found the plot 'confused'. The piece ran for sixty-one performances and was taken on tour later, but it was clearly not an experiment Mackenzie felt he wanted to repeat. The irony, of course, is that Mackenzie was among those who had criticised Sullivan for wasting his time on comic operas. One might-have-been in Mackenzie's operatic career lies in the fact that Lewis Carroll wrote to him in 1883 suggesting that he should consider *Alice in Wonderland* and *Through the Looking-Glass* as the basis for an operetta. Mackenzie seems to have been interested, but Carroll never produced a libretto.

Mackenzie completed one other major work while in Italy, his Violin Concerto in C sharp minor, which is probably his finest composition. Given his background, it is hardly surprising that he wrote well for the violin. The piece was commissioned for the Birmingham Festival of 1885 and took six months to write. The Victorians loved celebrities and they loved virtuoso instrumentalists. Mackenzie had intended the concerto to be premiered by Joseph Joachim, the great Hungarian virtuoso. In the end, however, Joachim withdrew and the piece was taken up and given at Birmingham by the Spanish virtuoso, Pablo de Sarasate,[2] who afterwards became a close and lifelong friend. The Concerto retains a conventional three-movement structure, but Mackenzie allows himself the freedom to adapt the form to suit his needs and to give the soloist maximum exposure. The expected development section in the first movement is replaced by a cadenza; the statement and response between orchestra and soloist in the second movement contains some extended and elaborate violin responses; and the finale, despite some wonderfully rich virtuoso passages, maintains the balance between soloist and orchestra. It is not one of Mackenzie's overtly Scottish pieces – the finale is said to be based on a Polish dance – but there is still a detectable Celtic flavour in certain passages, notably at the beginning of the second movement. These connect with the more explicitly nationalist *Pibroch Suite for Violin and Orchestra*, which followed a few years later in 1889. This is another romantic and virtuoso piece, which, initially at least, gives the impression of being loosely put together, but is, in fact, very carefully structured. It moves from a cadenza-like opening through a tightly-knit set of variations, and concludes with a second, more high-spirited set of variations. Several soloists have seen the *Pibroch Suite* as a natural companion piece to Bruch's *Scottish Fantasy* which was written just a few years previously in 1880. Both were premiered by Sarasate.

There is a sense of theatricality in Mackenzie's music, which, oddly, comes across more naturally and more effectively in his Scottish music and in orchestral pieces, such as the Violin Concerto, than it does in his cantatas, oratorios, and operas. It is particularly evident in his other major orchestral work, the *Scottish Concerto* for piano and orchestra, which was first performed at a Philharmonic concert in 1897. The soloist on this occasion was another famous virtuoso – and later Prime Minister of Poland – Ignacy Jan Paderewski, and the reception was so enthusiastic that he was obliged to repeat the finale. The piano concerto was, of course, the romantic genre *par excellence* and Mackenzie builds his big romantic structure on a foundation of three Scottish folk songs – 'The Reel of Tulloch', 'The Waulking o' the Fauld', and 'Green Grow the Rashes O'. The use of these songs is fundamental to the work, not just in terms of themes, but also in terms of its character. Mackenzie does not shy away from exploiting a beautiful tune, but nor is he prepared to bow to convention and allow overblown romanticism or images of heroic Scotland to dominate. The big themes are qualified, sometimes undercut, by lively, even cheeky, orchestration and more than a hint of self-mockery. Given its quality and its strength of character, it is remarkable that this work was not recorded until 1998.

The longer Mackenzie lived in Italy, the greater was the demand for his presence in Britain. He was constantly returning to fulfil conducting engagements, particularly at regional festivals, but the decision to return permanently was not made until 1888 when, following the death of George Macfarren, he was offered the post of Principal at the RAM. The appointment was somewhat two-edged. It was an honour to be asked, but, although the RAM was not in the same kind of financial straits as in the 1860s under Sterndale Bennett, it was definitely in need of a modernising hand. Macfarren had been in charge for nearly twelve years and, towards the end of his life, had become resistant to change of any description. Moreover, the RAM was rapidly becoming overshadowed by its newer and, for the moment, more prestigious rival, the RCM. Although an 'insider' in that he had studied at the RAM, Mackenzie was also an 'outsider', having lived in Italy, away from the cliques and factions of London musical life. His belief that such divisions were actually harmful to the cause of British music was shared by Grove at the RCM. As a result, the two of them were able to work together, becoming friends as well as colleagues, a circumstance aided by the fact that they both lived – were, in fact, near neighbours – in Sydenham, the South London suburb that was home to the Crystal Palace. This was a first step towards the kind of co-operative relationship we saw operating in Leipzig and elsewhere in Germany; and the first tangible result was the establishment, in 1889, of the Associated Board of the Royal Schools of Music to administer exams on behalf of both institutions – as, indeed, it still does today.

Something else that Mackenzie and Grove agreed upon – although it was an area where Grove had more experience – was the need to get the musical press on the side of British music, at least as represented by the two colleges. The arch-conservatives Henry Chorley and James Davison were dead. Henry Lunn (1817–94), former editor of the *Musical Times*, was one of Grove's allies. He shared many of Grove's ideas: he opposed conservative attitudes to music; he believed in the educational value of music; and he saw state funding as necessary to stimulate the process of change. By the time Grove and Mackenzie began working together, however, Lunn was ageing and no longer the influence that he had been. Of the newer generation, both Joseph Bennett of the *Daily Telegraph* and Hueffer at *The Times* were, as we have seen, connections of Mackenzie's. They were also progressive in their views, particularly on the divisive figure of Wagner. Hueffer's role was limited by the fact that there were personal issues between him and Grove, but when he died unexpectedly in 1889, his place at *The Times* was taken by John Alexander Fuller Maitland (1856–1936), a close colleague of Grove's – already designated as the next editor of his *Dictionary* – and a dedicated supporter of the RCM. Together, Grove and Mackenzie embarked upon a simple, even primitive, public relations campaign, but one that was important in changing the negative perceptions of British music that had plagued British composers for so long.

Once installed at the RAM, Mackenzie began the process of reforming the syllabus, recruiting new staff, and generally raising the profile of the institution. In the course of time, he organised and oversaw the process of moving to a new and more suitable building on the Marylebone Road. Nor was he content to be a figurehead and administrator. He continued to teach composition and orchestration, as well as conducting the student orchestra. Busy as he was at the RAM, he also found time for conducting engagements, notably at the annual concert series of the Philharmonic Society between 1893 and 1899, introducing new works by Tchaikovsky and Borodin, as well as his own *Scottish Concerto*. And on one occasion, in 1903, at the invitation of Charles Harriss, he went on a extended tour of Canada.

Charles Harriss is an interesting example of the way a musical career could work in the age of the British Empire. A graduate of Gore Ouseley's college at Tenbury Wells, he held a series of jobs as choir director in Wrexham, organist at Reading and then at Welshpool, before, in 1882, moving to Canada to take up an appointment – for which Gore Ouseley had apparently recommended him – as organist at the Church of St Alban the Martyr in Ottawa. In 1883, he moved to Montreal to become organist and choirmaster at Christ Church Cathedral and later also at the Church of St James-the-Apostle, holding both posts until 1894. Meanwhile, he founded a glee and madrigal club, toured the west coast of the United States giving organ recitals, married a wealthy woman, and gradually made a name for himself in the wider musical world. He became Honorary Director in Canada for the Associated Board of the Royal Schools of Music; he became the first director of the McGill Conservatory in Montreal; and he began to promote a series of tours and ever more grandiose musical projects, some in Canada, some in Britain. He was behind the decision to start Empire Day Concerts in London in 1907. He founded the 4,500-strong Imperial Choir, which went on to form the core of the 10,000-strong choir heard at the Empire Day concert in 1911 and then again at the peace celebrations in 1919. His last major role was as Director of Music for the 1924 British Empire Exhibition at Wembley.

Among Harriss's earlier projects was what he called 'The Cycle of Musical Festivals of the Dominion of Canada'. Reduced to essentials, this meant that Mackenzie – by this time Sir Alexander Mackenzie – would spend six weeks giving thirty concerts in fifteen Canadian cities, some of which had never seen a full-scale symphony concert before. Local choirs spent two years learning and rehearsing a programme which – at Mackenzie's insistence – included mainly British composers: Sterndale Bennett, Samuel Coleridge-Taylor, Elgar, Parry, Stanford, and Sullivan, as well as works by Mackenzie himself and even a piece by Harriss. The three symphony orchestras involved travelled up from the United States. Most of the soloists came from London, although one came from Paris and another from Boston. It was a undertaking on an imperial scale – and a great success.

Administration, teaching and conducting inevitably meant that Mackenzie would have less time for composition after his return from Italy, but he did continue to produce new work throughout the 1890s and into the 1900s, and several pieces from the period are worth considering. The *Pibroch Suite* and the *Scottish Concerto* have already been noted. The incidental music to *Twelfth Night*, composed in 1888, immediately after his return to London, and that for *Coriolanus* written in 1901, show again how strongly Mackenzie responded to the theatre. The *Twelfth Night* music is particularly effective. Mackenzie seems to balance his sympathy for the characters with an enjoyment of the absurdity of their behaviour, turning ideas on their heads and playing with the listener's expectations in a way that reflects the action of the play. The *Third Scottish Rhapsody: Tam O'Shanter* is another occasion when Mackenzie lets himself go with a good tune and spirited orchestration. Other works, it has to be said – cantatas such as *Veni Creator Spiritus* and *The Witch's Daughter*; the opera, *The Cricket on the Hearth*, and a handful of occasional orchestral pieces – do not appear to have sparked the same degree of enthusiasm in him.

Although less well known than Parry or Stanford, Mackenzie's role as an agent for change in late Victorian music should not be overlooked. He was forty-one when he took on the job of Principal of the RAM and seventy-seven when he retired. Towards the end of those thirty-six years, he became more conservative in his approach and famous for his unpredictable and eccentric dislikes, the most oft-cited being his horror of the music of Ravel. Nonetheless, the value of his work in maintaining standards and stability at the Academy as the world outside moved by stages from high Victorianism to a radically-altered environment in the aftermath of the First World War should not be underestimated. Yet he was first and foremost a musician. *The Bride, Jason*, and *The Rose of Sharon* made him famous. In nineteenth-century Britain, a composer seeking to establish himself had to write choral music and Mackenzie did so with some success, but, in the final analysis, choral music was not his forte. He was an orchestral composer, and a better one than most of his contemporaries. It was his orchestral writing that overwhelmed the young Edward Elgar, playing in the back desk of the violins, when *The Bride* was premiered at Worcester in 1881. Background was an important factor in this. Mackenzie was not precisely an outsider, but he differed from Parry and Stanford in that he did not come from the upper-middle classes or have a university education. Although he studied at the RAM, his formative musical experiences – with his father's orchestra in Edinburgh, with the Duke's orchestra in Schwarzburg-Sondershausen, and with the music hall and theatre bands of London in the early 1860s – were practical ones. While he might not be able to write music with the extraordinary ease and facility of a man like Sullivan, he knew what worked or what could be made to work. Mackenzie always aimed high – even when writing something like his *Britannia: A Nautical Overture*. This is an unashamedly popular work, composed for the seventieth anniversary of the RAM, but it is superbly put together. His own themes are woven together with two immediately recognisable seafaring tunes – the hornpipe 'Jack the Lad', and Arne's 'Rule Britannia' – to create a work that is not only professionally-crafted and beautifully orchestrated, but also witty, unexpected and, again, has a touch of self-mockery. Mackenzie had judgement. Flag-waving patriotism, like extreme romanticism, had to be qualified. And there is judgement also in the fact that, whether in his choral or in his orchestral works, he never slipped over into that sentimentality which dogs so much Victorian music. That alone made him an example worth following.

Among the wave of emigrants who left Germany for the United States in the 1840s was the Dannreuther family from Strasbourg. They settled in Cincinnati, where Dannreuther senior began making pianos. He tried to persuade his son, Edward, to take advantage of the opportunities in the brave new world where they now found themselves and become a banker. Edward, however, resisted and, in 1859, at the age of fourteen, managed to return to Germany. He enrolled in the Leipzig Conservatorium, where he studied piano under Moscheles and took lessons in music theory and composition from Hauptmann and Hans Richter. At the beginning of 1863, he arrived in London with an introduction to George Grove, who arranged his London debut at the Crystal Palace that April – a concert that featured the first British performance of Chopin's Second Piano Concerto. Dannreuther soon established himself as a leading soloist – he gave the British premieres of both Grieg's Piano Concerto (1874) and Tchaikovsky's First Piano Concerto (1876) – as well as a teacher, writer on musical matters, and champion of new music. He developed a close and long-lasting friendship with Grove, for whom he proved an essential source of advice, particularly on Beethoven, when it came to compiling the great *Dictionary of Music and Musicians*.

In 1873, Dannreuther received a request from the rich art collector, Thomas Gambier Parry, to give private lessons to his son, Hubert. At this stage, Hubert Parry (1848–1918) was still, reluctantly, an amateur musician. From an early age he had shown considerable musical talent. While at Twyford School, he had been exposed to the playing of Sebastian Wesley (then organist at Winchester Cathedral); when he moved on to Eton, he was encouraged to take lessons with George Elvey, organist at St George's Chapel in nearby Windsor Castle. Elvey, a prolific writer of anthems, chants and church music generally, is today remembered only for the hymn tunes *Diademata* ('Soldiers of Christ, Arise!') and *St George's Windsor* ('Come, ye thankful people come!'). Still at Eton, and aged just seventeen, Parry entered and passed Oxford University's Bachelor of Music exams – the youngest person ever to do so. But when he went up to Exeter College, Oxford, in 1867, he studied law and history, not music. This was the result of family pressure.

Although his father Gambier Parry's principal focus was the visual arts, he also had musical interests. He played the French horn, tried his hand at a few small-scale compositions, and was one of the most important patrons of the Three Choirs. Having purchased a large country estate, Highnam Court, in Gloucestershire, he took an interest in the Festival and donated large sums of money to keep it going. When he died, his generosity was recognised by a special performance of Sullivan's *In Memoriam* at the Gloucester Three Choirs in 1889. Gambier Parry's musical tastes were conservative – Handel, Mendelssohn, Spohr – and so, too, were his social attitudes. Music might be acceptable as a pastime for a gentleman, but it was not a suitable career for a son. That was a mistake he had made once already: Hubert's elder brother, Clinton, had been allowed to study music, together with history, but had disgraced the family and been expelled from Oxford for a series of offences involving sex, drugs and drink. Hubert's chances of a musical career looked slim.

While at Oxford, Hubert did his best to keep up his musical interests. He participated in various university musical societies and spent the summer vacation of 1868 in Stuttgart, studying with the now fully Germanised Heinrich Hugo Pierson. In the end, however, parental pressure triumphed. He took his degree and in 1870 became an insurance underwriter at Lloyd's of London. This seemingly self-sacrificial gesture kept the family peace, but there was another motive. He had secretly become engaged to Lady Elizabeth Maude Herbert and was eager to prove to her family that he would be acceptable as a son-in-law. Her family, however, and in particular her mother, regarded Parry as unsuitable and Parry the musician as unthinkable. His decision to join Lloyds prompted a change of heart. They withdrew their objections and the wedding took place in 1872.

Insurance did not preclude music entirely. Parry took lessons in counterpoint from Macfarren and in composition from Sterndale Bennett, whom he felt was too nice to offer the criticism he felt he needed.[1] But it was Dannreuther who recognised his potential and helped shape his development as a composer. Dannreuther had also had to overcome parental opposition to both his musical career and to his marriage, and so understood something of the pressures Parry was facing. Under Elvey's influence while still at Eton, Parry had begun producing anthems and motets, songs, choral pieces, and solo pieces for organ and piano. He had written an anthem, *O Lord, Thou hast cast us out*, for his Bachelor of Music degree. At Oxford, he had written chamber music and also the *Intermezzo Religioso* for strings that Sebastian Wesley had introduced at the 1868 Three Choirs

Festival. These pieces showed promise but were otherwise more or less conventional. Once he had been to Stuttgart, however, Parry's musical thinking became more adventurous, moving away from Mendelssohn towards Brahms and Wagner. Dannreuther encouraged this, and also encouraged him to continue working at songs and chamber pieces. These were then played at concert evenings which Dannreuther gave at his home in Orme Square, Bayswater – evenings which were renowned for featuring advanced or modern music. Dannreuther particularly pressed the claims of Wagner to represent the future of music. In 1872, he had founded the Wagner Society and, in 1876, gave Parry tickets for the first full performance of *The Ring* at Bayreuth. The following year, when Wagner came to London for the month-long Wagner festival, he actually stayed at Orme Square and Parry was able to meet the great man in person. Dannreuther also made other important introductions – to Hans Richter, who was to conduct many of Parry's compositions; and to George Grove who, while less musically exalted than the other two, was to prove highly influential in Parry's life. It was Grove who, in 1877, having begun work on his *Dictionary* and realising that he needed a sub-editor, turned to Parry.

Parry was nearly thirty. He hated the insurance industry. He was not making much money. His marriage was proving unhappy – Lady Maude, as she was known, did not actually care for music. The decision to leave Lloyd's was the outward expression of a rebelliousness that had been growing for some time. Success as a musician did not come immediately, but, had he not made the move, it would not have come at all. An overture, *Guillem de Cabestanh*, was performed at the Crystal Palace in 1879, and the following year both Richter and August Manns conducted his Piano Concerto in F sharp with Dannreuther as soloist. But the first work to attract widespread attention was a cantata, entitled *Scenes from Shelley's 'Prometheus Unbound'*, written for the Gloucester Three Choirs in 1880. For Parry himself, the work represented an important step forward. It was not only the largest work he had ever written, it was also another small act of rebellion. By choosing to set Shelley, he was setting the work of an atheist and a political radical (and also, perhaps not incidentally, a man who stated that it was wrong for a couple to remain married when they had ceased to love one another). This put Parry in opposition to his father, a deeply religious man who was genuinely upset by his son's adoption of an atheist viewpoint. It also put him at odds with the Three Choirs' authorities, who would not allow Shelley's words to be heard in the Cathedral. The cantata was, therefore, given as part of a secular concert, the first in the history of the Three Choirs, held in Gloucester Shire Hall.

Prometheus Unbound is, unsurprisingly, heavily influenced by Wagner. It uses leitmotifs and adopts aspects of Wagner's rhythmic and declamatory style in a way that works well with Shelley's words. The orchestral textures – especially in the prelude – show Parry absorbing Wagner's cumulative method of developing a theme or an idea. It was bold; there are some brilliant passages; and it appeared to offer something new in terms of setting English words; but, at the same time, it was a work of promise rather than fulfilment. Parry's style lacks coherence: one catches hints of Mendelssohnian melodies mixed in with the Wagner, and there is at times a curious sense that Handel is not far away. Nor is it in any sense harmonically adventurous. Once again, this is not surprising given that Parry had never before attempted a work on this scale, but the fact that *Prometheus* is not a mature work requires emphasising because of the significance it has acquired in retrospect.

The initial reception was, at best, mixed. Some condemned it as incomprehensibly avant-garde – a judgement that is hard to understand; it was probably born of prejudice against Wagner and all his works. Others, Grove and Stanford among them, saw it as a genuinely modern work, although the praise was directed as much at the intellectual boldness of the idea as at the music itself. Herbert Howells, who was Parry's pupil in the years before the First World War, maintained that Parry had intended *Prometheus* as a radical or revolutionary gesture, and it is possible to see Parry, once again like Wagner, attempting to present a myth-based alternative to traditional Christian philosophy; but the music itself is certainly not revolutionary and the work has never gained a popular following or been regularly performed. And yet the first performance of *Prometheus* rapidly came to be seen as a pivotal moment, a kind of starting gun for the English Musical Renaissance. This may have begun with Fuller Maitland who, in 1902, wrote that *Prometheus* contained 'the first evidence of a touch that had not appeared before in English music'.[2] Certainly, it was accepted by Ernest Walker, who, in 1907, could write: 'If we seek for a definite birthday for modern English music, 7 September 1880 when *Prometheus* saw the light at Gloucester … has undoubtedly the best claim'.[3] Thereafter, the idea became embedded in critical consciousness, even though, as Meirion Hughes and Robert Stradling point out in *The English Musical Renaissance 1840–1940*, those who accepted and repeated this piece of received wisdom had not always heard the work or even read the score.[4] Objectively, it is hard to see why *Prometheus*, despite its positive qualities, should be invested with such significance. It is worth adding that, at the time of writing, no modern recording is available.

At the very least, *Prometheus* got Parry noticed, and the praise of those whose opinion he valued encouraged him to continue. A flurry of new compositions followed. He conducted his Symphony no.1 in G at the Birmingham Festival in 1882, and it was given again by Manns at the Crystal Palace the following year. In fact, 1883 was the year in which Parry's career really took off. Stanford, whose career, unhampered by parental opposition, was running ahead of Parry's, was particularly supportive. He used his influence at Cambridge University to commission both Parry's incidental music for Aristophanes' *The Birds* and a Second Symphony in F, which naturally became known as the *Cambridge*. That summer saw Parry conduct a second commission for the Three Choirs, again at Gloucester. This was an ode, *The Glories of our Blood and State*, to a text by the seventeenth-century poet James Shirley. He was also appointed Choragus, or choirmaster, of Oxford University; and, perhaps most important, he was invited by Grove to join the teaching staff at the new RCM.

In many ways, the appointment at the RCM spelled the end of Parry's brief period of rebellion. He had rebelled, or so it seems, in order to join the musical establishment. Having done so, he sought to consolidate his position with an opera, *Guinevere*. This was a mistake. There were huge problems with the libretto and, although Parry spent nearly two years on the work, it was turned down by Carl Rosa, the most influential opera producer of the day, and has never been performed. It was, at least, not a public failure. Parry bounced back with a much shorter piece, again commissioned by Stanford. It was Grove who suggested that he consider Milton's poem 'At a Solemn Musick' which celebrates the joy of choral music. *Blest Pair of Sirens* was premiered at a concert celebrating Queen Victoria's Golden Jubilee in 1887. Intellectually, it was far less challenging than *Prometheus* – Milton's words are essentially an assertion of the moral and spiritual value of music – but Parry obviously responded to the dignity of Milton's language and the work was an immediate success. It was given at the 1888 Three Choirs in Hereford and was taken up by choirs and choral societies across the country. One can see why. It a celebratory piece. The orchestral and choral writing is broad and open, and it builds, without inhibitions, to an intense and emotional choral climax. It may not have been new, but it was a glorious, even liberating, celebration of the British choral tradition.

As before, success led Parry to attempt forms to which his talents were not really suited. Regional festivals up and down the land commissioned new works and he was drawn into that graveyard of so many nineteenth-century musical hopes, the oratorio. He wrote three in six years – *Judith* (Birmingham, 1888), *Job* (Worcester, 1892), and *King Saul* (Birmingham, 1894) – and all three are, frankly, dull. He did not wish to turn down commissions and he understood that festivals required oratorios on biblical themes, so he chose stories that he believed could support a universal and humanist interpretation as well as a religious one. The attempt seems to have squeezed out the music. *Job* is probably the best of the three, but it offers little to a modern audience. *Judith* was the most popular in its time; and it is from *Judith* that one tune has survived and established a life beyond its original context. Originally intended for the aria 'Long since in Egypt's plenteous lands', it is better known these days as the hymn tune *Repton*; so called because, in 1924, a music teacher at Repton School in Derbyshire used it for the hymn 'Dear Lord and Father of mankind'. Two other choral works from the period are more interesting. *L'Allegro ed Il Penseroso* (1890) is a return to Milton to whom Parry was evidently drawn, while *De Profundis* (1891) sets a Latin text in twelve parts. Both show that, when fully engaged with a text, Parry was a fine choral composer; and both also suggest that he was better writing for shorter formats.

Despite bouts of ill health – he had suffered from angina since his university days – Parry's capacity for work was tremendous. His Symphony no. 3 in C (*English*) and Symphony no. 4 in E minor were both written in or around 1889. He wrote no more formal symphonies, but his *Elegy for Brahms* (1897), *Symphonic Variations* (1897), and *Symphonic Fantasia* (1912; sometimes referred to as his Fifth Symphony) are all substantial orchestral works. Parry's contemporaries would undoubtedly have seen them as of secondary value compared with his choral works. Today, the situation is less clear cut. The symphonies and the other significant orchestral works have all been recorded and have attracted a good deal of attention. The *Elegy for Brahms* and the *Symphonic Fantasia* were given Proms performances in 2010. Modern orchestras and modern conductors frequently seek for rarely heard works to revive and it is right that they should. Revivals of Parry's orchestral works, however, seem to promise, but, in the end, disappoint. The four symphonies are attractive, conventionally-structured works, much influenced by Brahms, with some fine, melodic passages; but something is lacking. They sometimes suggest a film soundtrack or a choral work with the chorus missing. The thematic material does not grip the listener, and the orchestration, while clearly the work of an accomplished musician, lacks any distinctive quality. The later orchestral works have more in the way of emotional commitment about them – particularly the *Elegy for Brahms*, which, perhaps revealingly, was written as a personal tribute and not performed for some twenty-one years. Such judgements may sound harsh, but even with the later works, one only has to listen to contemporaneous compositions by Elgar, Delius, or Vaughan Williams to realise that Parry's orchestral writing lacks inspiration.

In 1894, Grove retired as Director of the RCM and the College Council were unanimous in appointing Parry to replace him. Despite his health worries – and the pressures of a continuing unhappy marriage – Parry worked unstintingly on behalf of the College. Even when he went sailing, which was almost his only relaxation, he was never away for long. He continued Grove's policy of working closely with Mackenzie at the RAM. He cared deeply about the well-being of both staff and students, and he had an ability to get on well with both – with one exception. Stanford, who had hoped for the appointment himself, seems to have been reluctant to accept Parry's increased authority and their friendship cooled – although it is fair to add that some of Parry's budget cuts may have antagonised Stanford. Increased responsibility at the College did nothing to diminish his output as a composer. In 1895, he collaborated with the poet Robert Bridges on an ode, *Invocation to Music*, which was performed at the Leeds Festival to mark the two hundredth anniversary of Purcell's birth. Another ode with words by Bridges followed for the Gloucester Three Choirs in 1898. *A Song of Light and Darkness*, written for soprano voice, chorus and orchestra, was the first in a series of works, which in terms of their structure are really odes, but which are often loosely referred to as 'ethical oratorios' or 'ethical cantatas'. Six more followed – *War and Peace* (1903), *Voces clamantium* (1903), *The Love that Casteth Out Fear* (1904), *The Soul's Ransom* (1906), *A Vision of Life* (1907), and *Beyond These Voices There Is Peace* (1908) – with texts drawn from the Bible and interspersed with passages by Parry himself. These took the idea underlying his earlier oratorios a step further in that they were an attempt to establish a choral form that could give expression to his complex humanitarian views. Audiences were unconvinced. Traditional biblical oratorios based on a story with which they were familiar were one thing; abstract philosophical ideas set to music were quite another. A number of musicians spoke up for Parry's ideas – among them Elgar and Vaughan Williams, both of whom, in their different ways, were concerned with the intellectual structures underlying their music – yet, as with *Prometheus*, the praise seems to have been for the concept and the attempt as much as for the execution. Yet if we look ahead to the twentieth century, we see in the works of composers as diverse as Holst, Foulds, Britten and Tippett an increasing use of music to express personal philosophies. In that sense at any rate, Parry was a pointer to the future.

Parry, like many nineteenth-century composers before him, had become a public figure: knighted in 1898; Professor of Music at Oxford in 1900; created a baronet in 1902. It was not surprising, therefore, that he was asked to write an anthem for the Coronation of Edward VII, also in 1902. *I was glad* was meant to be sung as the King entered Westminster Abbey. In fact, it was sung twice: once too soon because of a breakdown in the signalling system, and once when the King actually did arrive. It has been sung at every coronation since. Apart from *Jerusalem*, it is Parry's best-known work. It is not subtle – nor, as a celebration of monarchy written at the zenith of British imperial power, would one expect it to be – but it is controlled and concise. Less than eight minutes long, it uses massive forces – choir, full orchestra and organ – and builds to an equally massive choral and orchestral climax.

Parry was a lifelong admirer of Germany and German culture. His work and his ideas represent the high point of German influence on British music. Even before 1914, a younger generation of composers – men such as Delius, Vaughan Williams, Holst, and Ireland – were seeking alternative models in the folk tradition and elsewhere, but the First World War, when it came, completely disrupted patterns of cultural life as well as everything else. For Parry, it was traumatic. Nonetheless, he carried on. He helped to found and then chaired an organisation called the Committee for Music in War Time. Then, in 1916, his former pupil, the Welsh composer and conductor Walford Davies, wanted a piece for another wartime movement, Fight for Right, founded by Colonel Francis Younghusband, who had led the British invasion of Tibet in 1904. Robert Bridges suggested Blake's *Jerusalem*. Parry, who was busy, put the song together in a day and apparently gave it to Davies, saying, 'Here's a tune for you, old chap. Do what you like with it.'[5] Parry was less than happy about the aims of Fight for Right and later withdrew his support, but was delighted when *Jerusalem* was taken up by the women's suffrage movement. For all his status as a public figure and country landowner – he had inherited the family estate at Highnam in 1898 – his politics had never lost their liberal edge. In the 1920s, the copyright passed to the Women's Institute, which subsequently became nicknamed 'Jam and Jerusalem'. In the 1950s, Sir Malcolm Sargent introduced it to the Last Night of the Proms, where it has remained a fixture ever since. And in recent years, *Jerusalem* has taken on broader significance, being claimed as the unofficial national anthem of England and sung by fans at every cricket match where the England team are playing.

Another wartime composition – indeed, one of the last works he completed – and one that could not be more different from *Jerusalem*, was *Songs of Farewell* (1918). This consists of six unaccompanied part-songs for between four and seven voices. Perhaps influenced by the trauma of the war, the music seems more consciously English than is normal for Parry. The choice of 'Never Weather-Beaten Sail' looks back to Campion, and there is a clarity in the arrangements that recalls Tudor polyphony. Parry was seventy in 1918, and not in good health. The choice of poems such as John Donne's 'At the round Earth's imagined corners' and Henry Vaughan's 'My soul, there is a country' make it clear that he is thinking about the end of his life; and the final song, the only formally religious text, is a setting of Psalm 39, 'Lord, let me know mine end'. The tone is serious, but not dark or despairing; the vocal textures are open and expressive, but controlled. It is certainly one of Parry's finest compositions, demonstrating the clarity he could bring to English choral writing, and suggesting again that he was at his best when working within the discipline of a shorter form.

The one aspect of Parry's work which remains to be considered – and which yet again demonstrates his strength working in shorter musical forms – is his songwriting. He wrote songs throughout his compositional life, but they seem to have taken on greater importance as he grew older. Interest in them has revived over recent decades, and they may eventually come to be seen as his major contribution to British music. Composers had, of course, always written songs of differing kinds – in the Victorian period, as we have seen, the parlour ballad was dominant – but there was no established tradition of what we would now call the art song. Edward Loder was probably the first to try to write English songs on the model of German *Lieder*; Hugo Pierson and Sterndale Bennett also made the attempt; even Sullivan tried; but the idea did not catch on. It was Parry who over the years, and by a process of trial and error, established the parameters of the English art song. In the 1870s, he experimented with Shakespeare's lyrics and sonnets and with texts by other Elizabethan and Jacobean poets. It is an indication of how he went about his task and the importance he attached to German techniques that with the sonnets, he began by setting German translations, only later adapting his settings to the original text.

In 1885, Parry published *English Lyrics Set I*, the first of twelve such volumes that were to occupy him for the rest of his life, the last two being published after his death. They represent the heart of his achievement as a songwriter. There are seventy-four songs in all, drawn from a range of sources. He began with Sidney, Shelley and Scott, returned to Shakespeare, and then began to mix contemporary texts with Elizabethan and Jacobean poetry, translations from Greek and even Welsh. *Set V* is devoted to women writers; *Set VI* to men. Two contemporary poets feature strongly: Mary Coleridge, to whose work *Set IX* was devoted (and whose poems were also set by Stanford); and Julian Sturgis, the American-born writer who had provided the libretto for Sullivan's *Ivanhoe*. Over twelve volumes and thirty years, Parry's technique naturally varies and develops. What shines through is his belief – reflected so strongly in his ethical cantatas – that music can both enhance the emotional component of a text and elucidate meaning. Some songs are strophic; some are through-composed; some are a mixture of both. Sometimes the accompaniment can seem awkward, angular, or lacking in ornamentation, and his piano writing is certainly less fluent than some of the art-song writers who followed him. But however he expresses himself, Parry is always responding directly to the text. The mood is almost always serious – indeed, he has been criticised for a lack of humour, irony and general light-heartedness – and not all the songs work. But there are some wonderful examples of the songwriter's art. 'Willow Song', 'When icicles hang by the wall' and 'Take, O take those lips away' are among the best of the Shakespeare settings. Scott's 'Proud Maisie' from *Heart of Midlothian* and the anonymous 'Low in the grave, I'll lie' are highly effective treatments of short lyrics. And among the contemporary poems, Parry's settings of Sturgis's 'Through the ivory gate', Mary Coleridge's 'Three aspects', Langdon Mitchell's 'Nightfall in winter' and Harry Warner's 'When the sun's great orb' are all fine works. Parry's achievement was to find a musical language that allowed him to express both the essence of the poem and his response to it.

Parry died in October 1918, a month before the Armistice, not of the angina from which he had suffered for so many years, but of the Spanish flu, in the pandemic that claimed almost as many victims as the war itself. Stanford, rising above the personal differences that had dogged their relationship, arranged for him to be buried in St Paul's Cathedral. Parry's reputation as a composer was largely swept aside by the cultural upheaval of the war and the changes in attitude and musical language that followed it. There is no doubt that as a composer of choral works and as a writer of art songs he offered something new. Just what the following generations made of his legacy is something we shall examine when we have looked at the work of the other leading composers of his generation and can assess their impact as a group. What has never been in doubt, however, is Parry's influence as a teacher. The list of younger composers who passed through his hands is truly staggering: Arthur Somervell, Gustav Holst, Vaughan Williams, Walford Davies, Samuel Coleridge-Taylor, Frank Bridge, John Ireland, George Butterworth and Herbert Howells are some of the better-known names. Vaughan Williams was among those who testified to his open-mindedness: how, when dealing with students who were propounding theories or writing music which was not to his taste, he would set aside his own ideas, and try and see the student's point of view. And it was not just his influence on individuals that counted. It was the direction that he gave to the RCM through the twenty-three years of his directorship; and also his generosity in helping others. When Augustus Jaeger of the music publishers Novello & Co was keen to get Hans Richter to introduce a new work by a rising English composer, Parry came to his aid and persuaded the great conductor to agree – even though he had never seen the score of the *Enigma Variations* and had only met Elgar briefly.

75   Charles Villiers Stanford

Charles Villiers Stanford (1852–1924) was an Irishman, and Irishness was a fundamental part of both his personality and his music. He had an Irish accent, an Irish temper, and an Irish gift for melody. He arranged Irish songs and incorporated Irish melodies into his compositions well before the Folk Revival and the work of collectors such as Francis Child, Lucy Broadwood, Sabine Baring-Gould and Cecil Sharp who brought folk music to the centre of British musical life. However, this essential Irishness was checked – even compromised – by two other factors. Socially, the world into which he was born, and in which he was educated up to the age of eighteen, was upper middle-class Dublin. It was cultured and intellectual. It was also Protestant. It believed firmly in the value of British rule in Ireland and took its cultural lead from London. Musically, therefore, the belief that the young Stanford absorbed from the world around him – and from his first music teacher, his godmother, Elizabeth Meeke, who had herself been taught by Moscheles – was that German music was the best in the world and represented the only real model for an aspiring British composer to follow. He was Irish, but his relationship with Ireland and its culture was a complicated one.

Dublin was a musical city. In British terms, it was second only to London as a centre for opera, and Stanford's love of opera was formed by frequent visits to the Theatre Royal, where visiting companies put on thirty or forty performances a year. His father, John Stanford, was one of the city's leading amateur musicians, a fine bass singer – he took the part of Elijah when Mendelssohn's oratorio was premiered in Dublin in 1847 – and also a cellist. His mother, Mary, was a talented amateur pianist, good enough to play Mendelssohn's First Piano Concerto at a Dublin Musical Union concert. One of John Stanford's close friends was Joseph Robinson (1815–98), a Dublin-based organist and composer of church music and songs. Robinson founded the Dublin Antient Concerts Society and, together with John Stanford, was one of the co-founders of the Royal Irish Academy of Music. In 1846, the two men made the journey to the Birmingham Festival where they not only heard the premiere of *Elijah*, but met and dined with Mendelssohn. Robinson even played the organ with him. In the Stanford household, this naturally reinforced the ascendancy of German music and of Mendelssohn in particular.

Charles Stanford ('Charlie' as he was familiarly known) was not sent away to school, but given a strongly traditional – that is, classical – education at a one-man establishment run by Henry Tilney Bassett, just a short walk from the family home in Herbert Street. His musical education was given over to a series of private teachers, whose histories demonstrate just how full of musical talent Dublin was. When Elizabeth Meeke left the city, her place as his piano teacher was taken by Henrietta Flynn, who had been taught by both Moscheles and Mendelssohn; and when she left, Michael Quarry, a third Moscheles pupil, stepped in. It was Quarry who directed

Stanford's first piano recitals, the programme for which, unsurprisingly, was almost exclusively German. Violin lessons came from Richard Michael Levey (1811–99), a veteran of the Crystal Palace Handel Festivals, a friend of William Wallace and Michael Balfe, and Professor of Violin at the Royal Irish Academy. Levey, whose real name was actually O'Shaughnessy, composed some fifty overtures and large quantities of incidental music for productions at the Theatre Royal, where he directed the orchestra. He also published two collections of traditional Irish folk tunes.

However, it seems to have been his organ teachers that were the greatest influence on Stanford. The first of these was the family friend Joseph Robinson, who was also responsible for introducing the young Stanford to the virtuoso Joseph Joachim, thereby launching a friendship that would last many years. The second was Robert Prescott Stewart (1825–94), one of Ireland's leading composers in the second half of the nineteenth century. Stewart left a large body of church music, secular choral works and songs. He also fulfilled a range of high profile musical posts with the Dublin Choral Society, the Dublin Philharmonic Society, the Belfast Philharmonic Society, the Royal Irish Academy, and Trinity College, Dublin, where he was Professor of Music. Largely forgotten today, Stewart composed works for the Birmingham Festival – notably an *Ode to Shakespeare* (1870) – and was noted for his organ recitals which included lengthy improvisations. Lessons with Stewart involved playing the great organ in St Patrick's Cathedral, and Stanford found him an inspirational teacher. When Stanford went up to Queen's College, Cambridge, it was as an organ scholar.

Before then, however, there were summers spent in England with his father, broadening his knowledge by attending concerts at the Crystal Palace, and making useful contacts with Grove and Sullivan. He also had his first lessons in composition – with Arthur O'Leary, another Irish composer, principally of piano music, whose studies in Leipzig in the 1840s had been partly funded by John Stanford. The result was that by the time he arrived in Cambridge in 1870, Charlie Stanford was both well advanced in his musical education and well connected in the musical world. A musical career seemed inevitable. John Stanford, who had wanted his son to follow him into the law, did not object, but stipulated that he should have a general education to fall back on in case of need. Charlie studied Classics and in 1874 duly got a third class degree. By that time, however, it scarcely mattered.

At Cambridge, Stanford helped revive the University Music Society. He became its conductor and, against opposition, brought about the admission of women. His organ playing achieved such renown that when the position of organist at Trinity College became vacant, he was offered the place. It carried a stipend of £100 and permission to spend one term and the summer vacation studying abroad. His first trip was to the Schumann Festival in Bonn, where he met Brahms, whom he all but idolised. On the recommendation of Sterndale Bennett, later trips in 1874 and 1875 – after he had taken his degree – were to Leipzig, where he studied with Reinecke and Papperitz, both of whom had taught Sullivan over a decade earlier. Stanford found Leipzig disappointing. It was now nearly thirty years since Mendelssohn's death and it was not the city that it had been, so in 1876, at Joachim's suggestion, he went to Berlin, where he studied under Friedrich Kiel at the recently-founded *Hochschule für Musik*. Kiel, who was well known for both his teaching and his piano and chamber works, was his last formal teacher and Stanford considered him the best.

No one could have been better prepared for a musical career, but, unlike most of his contemporaries, he did not immediately gravitate to London. Cambridge became his power base. He kept his position at Trinity College – it was made permanent in 1877 and the salary increased to £250 – and he continued to mould the University Musical Society into a force he could use. Trinity College received visits from some of Britain's leading organists, men such as Walter Parratt, Frederick Bridge, and Charles Harford Lloyd (all of whom we will meet in due course). The Trinity choir benefitted from the effort he put into training them, and much of his early church music, including the 1879 Service in B flat, with its splendid *Magnificat*, was written for them. By 1876, the once almost moribund Musical Society was able to perform Brahms' *Requiem*, and the following year it gave the first British performance of Brahms' First Symphony. Under Stanford's direction, it gained a reputation for performing works by the new generation of British composers, such as Mackenzie, Parry, and Frederick Cowen. He used it to give hearings of works by friends such as Robert Stewart, and, of course, to perform his own compositions, including the premieres of his early oratorio *The Resurrection* (1875); his five-movement setting of Psalm 46, *God is Our Hope and Strength* (1877); and his *Three Intermezzi* for clarinet and piano (1880). Stanford also exploited his connections to attract star international performers such as Joachim, Dannreuther, and Richter. The University authorities might ignore his enthusiastic and ambitious plans to create a conservatoire on the German model, but they could not ignore the fact that Cambridge was no longer a musical backwater. When Macfarren died in 1887, Stanford's claims to become the University's Professor of Music were too strong to be overlooked.

Stanford eventually left Cambridge in 1892. He resigned his post as organist at Trinity, citing the pressure of other commitments, although he stayed on as conductor of the Musical Society until 1893, in order to preside over its fiftieth anniversary. This occasion was marked by the university awarding honorary doctorates to Tchaikovsky, Saint-Saëns, Bruch, Parry and Mackenzie. Grieg, unfortunately, was not able to be present. No one but Stanford could have put together such a gathering. He also remained as Professor of Music until just before his death in 1924 – which, given his regular explosions of temper when faced with regulations or official attitudes which he considered unreasonable, was a miracle in itself – but, from 1892 onwards, his focus was London. This was inevitable. When Grove had put together his team at the RCM in 1883, Stanford was appointed Professor of Composition. As the College had grown in both size and prestige, it had demanded more of his time. And he had also added to his own workload by introducing an opera class and an annual opera production. London was also the home of the Bach Choir, of which he was conductor from 1886 until 1902; and living in London made it easier to travel to additional commitments – such as conducting the Leeds Philharmonic (1897–1909) and the Leeds Festival (1901–10) – in other parts of the country.

Stanford was a contradictory character. He could be helpful and generous one moment, quick-tempered and irascible the next. He transformed the Leeds Festival. He introduced rarely-heard works by Bach and Handel, as well as new works by his beloved Brahms, by Verdi, Richard Strauss and Dvořák, and by a long list of new British composers from Elgar and Vaughan Williams to Rutland Boughton and Granville Bantock. However, when he took exception to the behaviour of the Festival Secretary, Frederick Spark, the association ended in a blaze of angry correspondence. Nor did Stanford make life at the RCM easy for those about him. He infuriated and exasperated Grove and his falling-out with Parry has already been mentioned. Yet even those he antagonised recognised his talent and ability. He was undoubtedly more suited to teaching composition at the RCM than the more general curriculum required of him at Cambridge. It was his work at the College that formed the basis of his legacy as a teacher; and it was the impact he made as a teacher on the next generation of composers that has led him to be described as one of the architects of the English Musical Renaissance. His list of students included all those taught by Parry and many more – among them Rutland Boughton, George Dyson, Ernest Farrar, Arthur Bliss, E. J. Moeran, Ivor Gurney and William Hurlstone. The last two he regarded as among the most brilliant he ever encountered. Gurney's descent into madness and Hurlstone's early death saddened him greatly. Stanford's teaching style was the antithesis of Parry's broad-minded approach. He saw his pupils individually and he challenged them relentlessly. He remained devoted to Brahms, which meant that by the last decade of the nineteenth century his approach was a conservative one. (Both musically and politically, he was more conservative than Parry.) The ideal that he set before his students was the classical expression of German romanticism. Any deviation from this was 'ugly', 'vulgar' or 'slovenly' – three of his favourite critical terms. His judgements were often intuitive (perhaps this was the Irish in him); he could provoke anger, self-doubt, even tears; but he would never let his students get away with anything superficial, sentimental, or poorly put together. If this drove some of them to rebel – and it did: the majority of them took musical paths that led away from Brahmsian principles – then at least they had a visceral understanding of what they were rebelling against. And that spirit of rebellion, as George Dyson suggested after Stanford's death, may well have been the greatest gift he could have given them.[1]

Stanford's knighthood came in 1902 – four years after Parry's – and he collected the string of honorary doctorates expected for a man in his position. Trinity College Dublin was the last major university to acknowledge his contribution, in 1921. He continued to teach and to compose, but during his later years there was a sense of disappointment, of being misunderstood and left behind. In 1894, Parry, not he, became Director of the RCM; and that same year he was passed over for the Professorship at Trinity College Dublin, which went to Ebenezer Prout. In both appointments, Stanford's temperament went against him; although it is undeniable that Parry was the better administrator and Prout the better theorist and lecturer. He was furious when Richard Strauss praised Elgar as the first truly progressive British composer; and two years later, in 1904, when Elgar was appointed as the first Professor of Music at Birmingham, Stanford wrote him an aggressive letter. He fell out with Richter over an imagined slight to one of his students. The First World War had a greater impact on Stanford than on Parry. It exploded the cultural values that had guided his whole life, and the deaths of Butterworth and Farrar upset him deeply. Unlike Parry, he was not equipped to explore the consolations of philosophy, and the years after the war saw his anger and his conservatism becoming increasingly evident. In 1921, he gave a lecture to the Royal Musical Association, 'On Some Recent Tendencies in Composition,' which was bitterly hostile to almost everything that had happened in music in the previous forty years. By that time, however, his health was beginning to decline. In March 1924, he suffered a stroke and died a few days later. He was buried in Westminster Abbey.

Above all, Stanford wanted to be a composer. He wrote music all his life, in just about every possible genre, and he probably wrote too much. Of his ten operas, seven were performed during his lifetime, but none was truly successful. He seems to have been dogged by bad luck and some strange decision-making. His first opera, *The Veiled Prophet of Khorassan*, based on Moore's *Lalla Rookh*, has distinct echoes of Meyerbeer, whose *Le Prophète* Stanford had seen in Paris. It was written to an English libretto, but translated into German for its premiere in Hanover in 1881. There were one or two follow-up performances in provincial German opera houses, but it was not given in London until 1894 when a production at Covent Garden – in Italian – was not a success. *Savonarola* (1884) was again premiered in Germany, this time in Hamburg, but an under-rehearsed and scrappy performance at Covent Garden – in German – prevented it from achieving popularity. *The Canterbury Pilgrims* (1884), given by the Carl Rosa Opera Company, sounds too much like *Die Meistersinger*. The comic opera *Shamus O'Brien* (1896) was his most successful stage work, running for over sixty performances at the Opéra Comique and being exported to Australia and the United States. *Much Ado About Nothing* (1901) had a very good libretto by Julian Sturgis and some interesting, Italian-sounding passages. It probably deserved to last more than two performances. *The Critic* (1916), based on Sheridan's play, was farcical, satirical and witty, with a score woven round quotations from other composers. The critics of the day were impressed, but the public was not. Stanford's last opera, *The Travelling Companion*, based on a story by Hans Christian Andersen, appears to be a rather mixed work, and was performed only after his death.

None of these are 'bad' operas. Stanford lived by the principles he drummed into his students: he did not write anything that was slipshod or poorly worked through; he did not, in the terms of Dr Papperitz's criticism of Sullivan, write a note that was not worthy of his gift. Unlike most of his contemporaries, he had been exposed to opera since his early years, and this may be reflected in the fact that, however progressive he may have tried to be in musical terms – at least in British musical terms – the structures within which he chose to work were largely conventional. *The Critic* attempted to do something new, although its musical humour, based on the recognition of musical quotations, has an in-crowd quality that would not have been sustainable as a model for the future. The problem is that, for all the work he put into it, and for all its undoubted quality, Stanford's operatic music seems tentative. It seems to lack some essential connection with the story. The work that stands out is *Shamus O'Brien*, not because it is a great opera, but because the idiom is at least Stanford's own. George Jessop's libretto makes full use of the humorous potential of Irish English.[2] Around it, Stanford weaves a light, well-judged score, conveying both humour and emotion, which is based on and suffused with the characteristics of Irish folk melodies. It is not musically profound, but it shows Stanford at ease with what he is doing; and it shows that George Bernard Shaw's suggestion that Stanford should replace Sullivan as the composer for D'Oyly Carte's Savoy Operas was not at all unreasonable.

Something of the same pattern is evident in Stanford's symphonies. Between 1876 and 1911, he wrote seven in all, although the first was only performed once during his lifetime. All seven are in the classical four-movement form, with Brahms as the main influence. But Stanford is not Brahms and one is left with the sense that his choice of symphonic form actually limits his natural musical invention. In the Third Symphony, he tried to get round this by introducing some Irish themes, but he failed to integrate them in the way that – to quote a contemporary example – Dvořák did with such success. With Stanford, the effect is artificial and distorts the symphonic structure. In the Fifth and Sixth Symphonies he attempted a loose programmatic structure. The Fifth is based on Milton's poem *L'Allegro ed Il Penseroso*, while the Sixth was intended as an elegy for the artist G. F. Watts, whose big allegorical paintings on cosmic themes Stanford admired, but in neither case does the programme unify the work. The symphonies contain ample evidence of Stanford's natural musicality and many lyrical passages where his skill in orchestration obscures broader problems. In their day, they were widely played and widely praised. The Third Symphony, premiered by Richter in 1887, enjoyed great popularity. Gustav Mahler included it in his concert programmes. The Fourth Symphony was commissioned by the Berlin Philharmonic and premiered at an all-Stanford concert in the German capital, an honour not previously enjoyed by any British composer. Yet, when we consider the works of contemporary symphonists like Bruckner, Tchaikovsky, Dvořák and Mahler himself, we can only conclude that Stanford never solved some basic issues of form and content, perhaps because he did not really think on a symphonic scale.

Did Stanford realise this? Was it the reason he devoted so much time and effort to his six *Irish Rhapsodies*? He clearly viewed his Irishness as a musical strength and wanted very much to bring Irish themes into his orchestral work. A rhapsody, which, in so far that it has a musical definition, concentrates more on emotion than form, had the potential to allow him to do this. The *First* and *Second Irish Rhapsodies* are based around Irish folk tales. The *Third*, a richly lyrical and emotional work for cello and orchestra, centres on a tune by Carolan. *The Fourth* is based on fishing and marching songs. The *Fifth* is a wartime piece dedicated to the Irish Guards; while the *Sixth*, for violin and orchestra, was Stanford's last completed work and has a strong elegiac quality to it. The emotion is certainly there, but, perhaps because it was such a serious matter for him, Stanford never managed to deploy his Irish material with the same easy naturalness that Mackenzie achieved with his Scottish tunes. Nonetheless, the rhapsodies are attractive works, with some genuinely beautiful orchestral writing, and one can see why they attracted an immense popular following in their day – Stanford heard the *First Rhapsody* so often that he claimed to regret ever having written it – and are still revived today.

Like Parry, Stanford was better working on a smaller scale. Large choral works, like the Mass in G (1893), the *Requiem* (1897), and the *Te Deum* (1898), tend to be self-consciously grand. As a consequence, they often lose their way in passages of over-rich orchestration and echoes of Verdi and Berlioz, although the *Stabat Mater* (1907) fares somewhat better. Even by the standards of the Victorian oratorio, Stanford's *Eden* is uninspired. It is hard to see how such a gifted composer could produce a work that actually says so little. One reason for this seems to be that, again like Parry, Stanford needed a text with which he could engage – the essential difference being that while Parry's engagement was intellectual, Stanford's was emotional and instinctive.

This may well go some way to explaining the success of his music for the Anglican Church. To be brought up a Protestant in Dublin was much more than a matter of faith: it was a matter of culture and identity. Protestants overwhelmingly supported the Act of Union which bound Ireland to England, Scotland and Wales as part of the United Kingdom. Stanford's Protestant belief was thus an integral part of his loyalty to Queen and country, and his church music was an expression of the British rather than the Irish side of his character. Here was an established form that suited him; it came with a text that was part of his upbringing and identity; and it allowed him to produce music with a freedom and sense of conviction that is simply not present in the operas or the symphonies. The early B flat Service has already been mentioned. The Evening Service in A which followed in 1880, and was later completed as a Full Service with the addition of the Morning Canticles and Communion Service, is both beautiful and powerful; and it shows how, in this context, Stanford *was* able to give a sense of unity and completion to his work. The component parts of the Service develop from one to the next, producing a musical whole which has actually been described as symphonic.[3] This approach to an overall structure was repeated in the less complex Service in F (1889), which does not necessarily require an organ accompaniment, and again in the Service in G (1904), which features one of Stanford's deft imaginative touches. He imagines the Virgin Mary as little more than a girl at the time of Christ's birth and pictures her at a spinning wheel, so the *Magnificat* becomes not an exultant celebration, but a light treble solo with choral and organ accompaniment. It is, however, the Service in C (1909) that is the best known of Stanford's settings, and rightly so. No one has ever sought to write a symphony after the manner of Stanford, but the C major Service influenced a generation of composers, including among others Charles Wood, George Dyson, Herbert Howells and Gerald Finzi. The word-setting is precise – and reinforced by equally precise dynamic markings – yet the whole piece seems natural and unforced, far away from the self-consciousness of the big choral works. Stanford creates that sense of serenity, spirituality and yearning that we have seen as a recurring characteristic of British music; in this context, it harks back to the great Tudor Masses of Taverner and Tallis. If one had to choose a single composition by which to remember Stanford, this would be it.

Stanford also wrote a range of other choral music for the church, including motets – his *Three Motets* (1905), dedicated to the Trinity College choir, has been rightly singled out – and a number of distinctive and memorable anthems. *If ye then be risen with Christ* is a cleverly-constructed and wonderfully tuneful piece, based on part of the hymn tune *Easter Hymn*

('Jesus Christ is risen today'). *The Lord is my Shepherd*, possibly his best, is a wonderful example of his responsiveness to a text, the mood of the anthem following the spiritual journey of the psalm's narrator. The pastoral beginning – 'green pastures'; 'still waters' – gives way to mounting mystery, foreboding, and then full-blown terror at the 'valley of death'. The tempo slows and the harmonies settle as faith in the protection of the Lord restores a sense of security, and the piece ends with a feeling of quiet triumph. *Lo, I raise up that bitter and hasty nation* was a response on Stanford's part to the First World War, and shows the same degree of responsiveness but to a far less well-known text. Beginning in anger and violence – 'They are terrible and dreadful.... Their horses also are swifter than leopards ... more fierce than the evening wolves ...' – it passes on to a quietness that could be peace, or could be death: 'let all the earth keep silence before Him.'

The British Stanford is also present in many of his songs. The recurrent naval theme, reinforcing an imperial stereotype, may account for the popularity of his settings of Tennyson's *Revenge* (1886), and of poems by Sir Henry Newbolt in *Songs of the Sea* (1904) – which includes the famous 'Drake's Drum' – and *Songs of the Fleet* (1910). These were popular in their time and, apart from his church music, are still among his best-known works today. Stanford, much more than Parry, needed concrete imagery to sustain his writing, and in many of his art songs and part-songs, he finds this in heroic themes that are bound up with ideas of British imperial greatness. Such choices can cause a sense of unease in a twenty-first-century audience, but the songs live precisely because, as with the church music, he believed in the message conveyed by the words he was setting. Overall, however, both the selection and the mood of the poetry he chose was wider and more varied than Parry's. It ranged from big, serious narratives such as *La Belle Dame sans Merci* to miniature settings of limericks by Edward Lear; and, of course, the heroic, English songs were balanced by his many Irish songs. He was a fine, if at times erratic, songwriter. He wrote songs all his life and over two hundred survive. His technique was in general simpler than Parry's. He believed it was the job of the vocal line to carry the song, without interference or too much elaboration from the orchestral or piano accompaniment, the role of which was to create what he called 'atmosphere'.[4] 'The Faery Lough' from the *Irish Idyll* collection, an exercise in mood creation based on a Irish dialect poem, shows just how effective this technique could be.

Stanford's Irish songs bring us back to the question of his Irishness. Poems such as those by Moira O'Neill in *An Irish Idyll,* and by Winifred M. Letts in *A Fire of Turf* and *A Sheaf of Songs from Leinster,* are of poorer quality than most of his English choices, principally because they dwell too much on misty Irish nostalgia. As a result, no matter how imaginative and atmospheric his settings, the songs tend to suffer. Indeed, it seems odd that someone so much on the look out for poor workmanship, and so conscious of his own Irishness, should have accepted such a watery and stereotypical view of his native land. Was it simply a question of giving the public what they wanted? Or was it that the Ireland that tugged at his heart was, in fact, a version imagined by the Protestant Dublin boy whose religion and social position cut him off from the real Ireland? And might this, in turn, help explain the difficulties he faced when trying to integrate Irish material into his compositions? Stanford's best Irish songs work because they have an empathetic quality which goes beyond their origins. 'A Broken Song', from *An Irish Idyll,* uses the question and answer technique that was to become a feature of English song over the next fifty years, particularly in settings of A. E. Housman's 'Is My Team Ploughing?' 'Poor Mary Byrne' from *A Sheaf of Songs from Leinster* sets a colloquial and conversational text with economy and sympathy, but without sentimentality. 'Skies', the song of an Irish exile in London, clearly had a personal application and shows much more emotion than Stanford usually allowed himself to express. Songs like these demonstrate what Stanford could achieve as a songwriter and they had a direct influence on the next generation of songwriters, most of whom he taught.

76   Parratt, Lloyd, Alcock, Corder, and Cowen

Mackenzie was the orchestrator, the practical musician; Parry the intellectual with a gift for choral and vocal writing; Stanford the demanding teacher and master of the Anglican Service. They represented a concentration of talent at the top of British music that was probably unprecedented. Whether they constituted the basis for, or were the architects of, an English Musical Renaissance is quite another matter. Their pre-eminence was not unquestioned. Between 1888 and 1894, George Bernard Shaw was music critic first of the *Star* and then of the *Nation,* styling himself 'Cornetto di

Basso'. He saw the three composer-teachers as a self-congratulatory and self-reinforcing club, producing what he called 'sham classics'.

> If you doubt that *Eden* is a masterpiece, ask Dr Parry and Dr Mackenzie, and they will applaud it to the skies. Surely Dr Mackenzie's opinion is conclusive; for is he not the composer of *Veni Creator*, guaranteed as excellent music by Professor Stanford and Dr Parry? You want to know who Parry is? Why, the composer of *Blest Pair of Sirens*, as to the merits of which you only have to consult Dr Mackenzie and Professor Stanford.[1]

Shaw's strictures are harsh. As a group, the three of them undoubtedly did exercise a significant and beneficent influence on British music, but they were not the only talented or influential figures of their time. There were many others. The 1880s and 1890s were certainly a period of change and, if we are looking for instigators of that change at a domestic level, then we cannot overlook the role of Grove. He was not a composer or a performer, but it was his understanding and judgement that created the team at the RCM which has been credited with leading the English Renaissance. Parry and Stanford have received the lion's share of the attention, but no account of the influential early decades of the RCM would be complete without considering some of the others who taught there.

From a modern perspective, it is easy to forget just how important the organ was in late-nineteenth-century music. In an age before recorded sound, and when churchgoing was far more common than it is today, the organ was the instrument most frequently heard by a large proportion of the population. Cathedrals and churches had organs; so, too, did town and city halls, theatres and musical halls, universities and major public venues, such as the Royal Albert Hall and the Crystal Palace. A College of Organists was founded in 1864, receiving its Royal Charter from Queen Victoria in 1893 – twenty years before the Philharmonic Society received its 'Royal' seal of approval. Organs were an essential component in oratorios, and in major choral pieces such as Parry's *I was glad*. The eighteenth century was the high point of composition for the organ, but the second half of the nineteenth century was the time when virtuoso organ recitals reached their peak. These might include classic works for the instrument by Bach, Handel or Mendelssohn, as well as contemporary organ works, such as Parry's *Fantasias* or Stanford's Toccata and Fugue in D minor (1907). There would often be transcriptions of symphonies or well-known orchestral pieces designed to show off the organ's capabilities, and – very popular with Victorian audiences – extended virtuoso extemporizations allowing the organist to show off his talents. Recitals by men such as Walter Parratt, Basil Harwood, Charles Harford Lloyd, or Walter Alcock could attract audiences in their thousands.

Thus, when the RCM was founded in 1883, the choice of Professor of Organ was an important one. The job was given to Walter (later Sir Walter) Parratt (1841–1924), who, though his role is rarely mentioned today, rapidly became the third member of Grove's inner circle alongside Parry and Stanford. As a child in Huddersfield, Parratt had shown such exceptional talent that he was given his first paid position, as organist at St Paul's Church, Armitage Bridge, when he was just eleven. For the next twenty years, his career built slowly. He went to a London choir school; he played in churches in and around Huddersfield; he came to the attention of Sir Frederick Gore Ouseley, who arranged for him to become private organist to the Earl of Dudley; he was organist at All Saints' Church in Wigan. But it was not until 1872 that he attained a position of real importance. He succeeded Stainer as organist at Magdalen College, Oxford, and, using this as a springboard, threw himself into Oxford musical life, conducting the choirs and directing the University Choral Society as well as the musical societies of five different colleges. He also began to give solo recitals and to develop a national reputation. In 1873, he gave a recital at the Royal Albert Hall and the following year played with Sebastian Wesley at a concert recital given to mark the opening of Bristol's new concert venue, the Victoria Halls.

Then, in 1882, Sir George Elvey, who had been organist at St George's Chapel, Windsor, for forty-seven years – and, briefly, tutor to Arthur Sullivan – decided it was time to retire. Parratt replaced him, and the following year was snapped up by Grove at the RCM. A string of establishment positions and honours followed. In 1892, he was knighted and, in 1893, became both Queen Victoria's private organist and Master of the Queen's Musick – a position he retained under Edward VII and George V. There were honorary doctorates from Oxford, Cambridge and Durham, and additional honours (Member of the Victorian Order; Commander of the Victorian Order; Knight Commander of the Victorian Order); he became Dean of the Faculty of Music at London University; he succeeded Parry as Professor of Music at Oxford; he was President of the Royal College of Organists.

He had become the establishment figure *par excellence*, but Parratt was never conservative. At Windsor, he insisted on high musical standards, and both expanded and modernised the repertoire, which had stagnated under Elvey's regime. At Buckingham Palace, where he was responsible for the music heard on official and state occasions, he again transformed both the standard of musicianship and the repertoire. He was not himself a significant composer. His best-known works are probably a setting of the Funeral Service and the anthem, *Comfortare*, which was composed for the Coronation of Edward VII in 1902 and played again at the Coronation of George V nine years later. But, at the RCM, he was regarded as one of the most effective teachers on the staff. He was progressive in his tastes, promoting the works of César Franck, Max Reger and Charles-Marie Widor rather than those of Mendelssohn, Gounod and Liszt, although he stood out against the contemporary practice of trying to make the organ sound like an orchestra. Like Stanford, he loathed anything slovenly or vulgar. He sought to instil in his students taste and technical mastery, constantly urging them to be 'clean' in their playing.[2] This he saw as the only way to address the decline in British church music. One of his most important roles was to act as a link and channel of communication between the RCM and the Court. It was because of Parratt that the music of young British composers – Elgar, Holst, Ireland, Dyson, Bliss and others – began to be heard at Buckingham Palace. And his position enabled him to influence, if not actually decide, the selection of candidates for important organ appointments up and down the country. Over the four decades during which he was organist at Windsor and Master of the Queen's Musick, the majority of such positions were filled by those who had been his pupils. He died in March 1924, just two days after Stanford.

Parratt was responsible for recruiting other famous organists who worked with him at the RCM at various times; men such as Frederick Bridge (1844–1924), Charles Harford Lloyd (1849–1919), and Walter Alcock (1861–1947). Having determined at an early age that he wanted to be a cathedral organist, Bridge was appointed to Manchester Cathedral in 1869 at the age of twenty-four, and to Westminster Abbey at thirty. At the Abbey, he was responsible for the music at a series of major royal events – Queen Victoria's Silver and Diamond Jubilees; Edward VII's Coronation and funeral; George V's Coronation – and was knighted for his pains. Despite holding such a prominent post, his playing was regarded as suspect and critics put much of his success down to having the genuinely brilliant

Walter Alcock as his assistant for twenty years. Similarly, although Bridge wrote a number of oratorios and cantatas, he was not a distinguished composer; and reports from students at the National Training College and then the RCM where he taught counterpoint suggest that, while personally popular, he was not the most effective of teachers. He was, however, a respected administrator, scholar, editor, writer and fundraiser; and it was these skills that made him a force for change in the musical world of the time. He restructured musical practice at Westminster Abbey and oversaw the construction of a new choir school; he ran festivals devoted to Purcell and Gibbons and restored Handel's original orchestration for *Messiah*; he edited hymn books and wrote text books on counterpoint. He also founded the Organists' Benevolent League. In an age that set great store by institutional positions, he became the first King Edward Professor of Music at London University, President of the Musical Association, and musical director of the Royal Choral Society. He too died in March 1924, within days of Stanford and Parratt.

Lloyd, by contrast, was primarily a performer, famed for his recitals and particularly for his extravagant extemporizations, although he also achieved some recognition as a composer and choirmaster. In 1876, he succeeded Sebastian Wesley as organist at Gloucester Cathedral, a position which brought with it important responsibilities in relation to the Three Choirs. It was Lloyd who played the organ for the first performance of Parry's *Prometheus Unbound* at the 1880 Three Choirs, and most his own music was written for the festival. He wrote a series of cantatas, with a bias towards Nordic subjects, such as *The Song of Balder* (1885), *The Longbeards' Saga* (1887), and *The Ballad of Sir Ogie and the Ladie Elsie* (1894), although his most successful work was *Hero and Leander* (1884). Lloyd also wrote a number of settings of the Anglican Service, but his compositions are rarely heard today. From Gloucester, he went on to teach at the RCM and Eton College, finishing his career as organist at the Chapel Royal.

Walter Alcock was also primarily a performer and recitalist. His teachers were Sullivan and Stainer and he himself went on to be a highly influential teacher during the early years of the RCM. Alcock had the distinction of playing at three coronations – Edward VII, George V, and George VI – as well as contributing to the new era of broadcast sound when, in 1932, he was one of three organists who played the organ at the opening of the BBC's new Concert Hall in Broadcasting House. He was knighted the following year.

Meanwhile, not far away in Marylebone, Mackenzie, as Principal, was labouring to restore the prestige of the RAM, and in that role has been seen as making an important contribution to the Renaissance. But he did not work alone. He, too, was building a team, which, although less obviously prestigious than that at the RCM, contained a number of figures whose progressive ideas can be traced in the careers of the people they taught. Tobias Matthay (1858–1945) was among the most influential piano teachers of the age. Born in Germany, he moved to London with his parents when he was young. In 1871, he won a scholarship to the RAM where he studied piano under Sterndale Bennett, Sullivan and Macfarren. He stayed on at the Academy, and in 1880 Macfarren appointed him Professor of Piano, an appointment Mackenzie subsequently confirmed and which Matthay retained until 1925. Matthay did give recitals and he also composed, but his reputation rests on his teaching and on his pioneering of a scientific approach to the mental and physical aspects of playing the piano, an approach first outlined in his book, *The Art of Touch* (1903). His pupils included some of the leading British pianists of the twentieth century – Irene Scharrer, Myra Hess, Moira Lympany, Harriet Cohen, Clifford Curzon – and the composers York Bowen and Arnold Bax, both of whom were also talented pianists.

Another member of Mackenzie's team, and one whom he appointed immediately on taking over as Principal in 1888, was his Professor of Composition, Frederick Corder (1852–1932). Corder had studied at the Academy under Sterndale Bennett and won a Mendelssohn Scholarship which took him to Cologne for three years, where he studied with Ferdinand Hiller. From Cologne, he went to Milan for two years to develop his knowledge of opera which, at that stage, was his main interest. Returning to England in 1879, he embarked on a period of intense composition. During the 1880s, he wrote two full-scale operas, three operettas, five orchestral works, a symphonic ode and two cantatas. Of his operatic works, only *Nordisa* (1887), which was commissioned by the Carl Rosa Opera Company and had its premiere in Liverpool in 1887, achieved any success. Even then, once it transferred to London, it lasted only a single season. Corder had hoped to be able to become a full-time composer. The appointment at the RAM seems to have marked his acceptance that that particular dream was over. After 1890, he composed no more operas and only a handful of choral and orchestral works, choosing to devote himself to teaching and also to writing. He was a great Wagner enthusiast and, together with his wife Henrietta, had already produced some of the earliest translations of Wagner's librettos – their version of *The Ring* appeared in 1882. Now he wrote a series of books on harmony, composition and orchestration that were based on his work at the Academy. These were followed by books on Wagner, Beethoven and Liszt. Corder failed as a composer because his version of Germanic late Romanticism was simply not distinctive enough and was diluted by attempts to appeal to popular taste, but his strong character and analytical skills made him a good teacher. His list of students is not as impressive as that of some of the professors at the RCM, but it still includes a number of figures who were at the heart of the next musical generation: John Blackwood McEwen, Granville Bantock, Joseph Holbrooke, York Bowen and Arnold Bax.

The RCM and the RAM have long been seen as the leading schools of music connected with the English Musical Renaissance, but they were not the only ones. The Guildhall School of Music, as we have seen, was founded in 1880 and expanded rapidly. By 1886, it had outgrown its original premises, a disused warehouse next to London's Guildhall, and moved to Blackfriars. It was further strengthened in 1896 by the appointment of a new Principal, W. H. Cummings (1831–1915), who had been Professor of Singing at the RAM for the previous fifteen years. Cummings presided over a further expansion of the Guildhall's premises in 1898. London's Trinity College of Music had been founded in 1872 by Henry Bonavia Hunt. The initial aim was to train choirmasters and thus improve the quality of church music, but within a few years it was teaching a full musical curriculum. It was pressure from Trinity College that, in 1876, led the University of London to begin awarding degrees in music, for which students from Trinity and elsewhere could sit the examinations. The University did not have its own Faculty of Music until 1903. Outside London, Edinburgh University formally established a Faculty of Music in 1893. Thus, whatever the genesis of the English Musical Renaissance, and whatever form it actually took – issues we shall examine in the next chapter – it developed out of a musical world that was already in a state of flux, responding to social and cultural change.

Another area where things were changing was the willingness of promoters to give British composers a public hearing. We have noted how, earlier in the century, they were often reluctant to programme works, and particularly new works, by British composers in the belief that they would simply not attract an audience. In subsequent decades, the Grove-Manns partnership at the Crystal Palace, the dedication of men such as Sterndale Bennett and Macfarren, the work of Charles Hallé in Manchester, the efforts of Prince Albert and the Duke of Cambridge, even Wagner's season with the Philharmonic Society, had already all gone a long way towards changing attitudes. It was still not easy to get a hearing – complaints that no one wanted an English composer would be heard into the 1920s – but it was getting easier. This, of course, was of fundamental importance for it was no use the RAM, the RCM, Trinity College, the Guildhall, Oxford, Cambridge and all the other universities offering degree courses in music and training composers if their works were never to be heard.

The man who selected the works to be programmed, whether for a one-off concert, a concert season or a festival, was usually the conductor. Where a festival or a concert society such as the Philharmonic was concerned, the conductor was usually also the musical director, and while a committee might sometimes also be involved in the selection process, the conductor/musical director was the most powerful voice. The whole idea of having a conductor, rather than someone who directed the orchestra from a keyboard or while leading the violins, was comparatively new. It became accepted practice only during the early years of the nineteenth century – even then, Smart in the 1820s, and Mendelssohn and Bennett in the 1830s were among those who frequently directed from the piano. In Britain, the first generation of celebrity conductors were all foreign, and as often as not, German – Spohr, Mendelssohn, Jullien, Costa, Berlioz, Wagner, Manns. These gave way to a second generation, also dominated by Germans – Richter, von Bülow, Charles Hallé, Arthur Nikisch. Of course, men such as Sullivan, Mackenzie, Parry, Stanford and others around them conducted regularly, and frequently achieved high standards, but – Sullivan excepted – they had teaching and other commitments that reduced the time available for conducting. And in British eyes, the same sense of glamour and prestige attached itself to foreign conductors as to foreign composers and foreign music.

The career of Frederick Hymen Cowen (1852–1935) demonstrates how this was beginning to change. The Cowen family were living in Jamaica when Frederick was born and remained there until he was four. On their return to England in 1856, Cowen's father, also named Frederick, became private secretary to the Earl of Dudley and, at the same time, Treasurer to the Italian Opera at Her Majesty's Theatre. This gave young Frederick something of a musical advantage, especially as he was a precocious child capable of writing a waltz, which was actually published, at the age of six. He gave his first public concert, playing the piano, at the age of eleven, and played together with Joachim at a concert at Dudley House at the age of twelve. Frederick's talent was undeniable. His father paid for studies in Germany – interrupted briefly in 1866 by the war between Austria and Prussia – where his teachers included Moscheles, Hauptmann and Reinecke. Having a generous and well-connected father was an advantage. Frederick senior also paid for a concert in London which effectively launched his son as a composer. It took place at St James's Hall, the venue for Chappell's 'Monday Pops', in December 1869, and included both young Cowen's Piano Concerto in A minor and his First Symphony.

Cowen wrote four operas – *Pauline*, commissioned by the Carl Rosa Opera Company and first performed in 1876, was the most successful – five oratorios, and numerous cantatas, notably *The Corsair* (1876) for the Birmingham Festival and *The Deluge* (1878) for Brighton. He also wrote operettas, incidental music, a large number of orchestral works and some three hundred songs. However, if you had asked him, he would almost certainly have said that he regarded himself as a symphonist. He composed six. The Sixth (*Idyllic*) Symphony, from 1897, is an attractive work, which has its adherents even today, but the one that stands out is the Third or *Scandinavian Symphony*. Premiered in 1880 at St James's Hall, it rapidly became the most frequently-performed of all British symphonies and remained so until eclipsed by Elgar's First Symphony in 1908. It certainly has character, and some interesting themes; it is quirky and entertaining, although not, in the end, completely coherent. Quite why it should have achieved the popularity it did – beyond that of symphonies by Parry or Stanford – is not immediately obvious, but its popularity was not limited to Britain: there were many performances in France, Germany, Austria, Hungary and in the United States.

As a composer, Cowen lacked depth and imagination; he did better when he attempted less. Even then, some of the lighter works, such as *Indian Rhapsody* or *The Butterfly's Ball*, can sound like the soundtrack from a 1950s romantic comedy. Like Sullivan, he preferred (and largely managed) to avoid teaching, and as a consequence concentrated on his career as a conductor. This was to prove his real legacy. From 1880, when he succeeded Sullivan as conductor of the promenade concerts at Covent Garden, until 1923, when he appeared at his eighth and last Handel Triennial Festival at the Crystal Palace, Cowen travelled the length and breadth of Britain, gaining a reputation for careful programming, championing British music, and thoughtful musical interpretation. In addition to the Handel Festival, he was at various times conductor and musical director of the Philharmonic Society, the Hallé (following the death of Sir Charles Hallé in 1895), the Scottish Orchestra, the Liverpool Philharmonic, the Bradford Festival, the Bradford Permanent Orchestra, the Scarborough Festival, and the Cardiff Festival. And there were innumerable appearances as guest conductor at other festivals and concert series. He was known for raising orchestral standards by paying attention to detail; and he insisted on orchestras having adequate rehearsal time – something that got him sacked from the Philharmonic Society in 1892, although he was later reappointed. Cowen's conducting was effective rather than extrovert. He was criticised by Shaw for being undemonstrative, although praised by Elgar. Showmanship would come with the next generation of conductors for whom Cowen was opening the way. They would be the first generation of British conductors who were not also composers, and would establish a genuinely British tradition of conducting: men such as Landon Ronald, Henry Wood, and, of course, Thomas Beecham.

77   The Idea of a Renaissance

We have met Joseph Bennett before. He was a librettist: he collaborated with Sullivan on *The Golden Legend*, with Mackenzie on *The Rose of Sharon* and a number of other works, with Cowen, and with Frederick Bridge. He was also chief music critic for the *Daily Telegraph*, a position he held from 1870 until 1906. In both roles, he was an energetic champion of British music, so it would have been no surprise when, on its appearance in 1882, he offered fulsome praise for Parry's First Symphony. The work, he claimed was 'proof that English music has arrived at a renaissance period.'[1] Precisely what Bennett meant by his choice of word we shall never know, but the idea of a musical Renaissance caught on – although, as we have seen, the starting date shifted to the first performance of Parry's *Prometheus Unbound* in 1880. Francis Hueffer at *The Times* picked up the idea, and Bennett himself developed it, but often in relation to works, such as Cowen's *Scandinavian Symphony*, Mackenzie's opera, *Columba*, or Stanford's *Savonarola*, which, heard today, seem to disprove rather than demonstrate his idea. The real early proponent of the concept of an English Musical Renaissance, however, was Hueffer's successor at *The Times*, John Fuller Maitland. In *English Music in the XIXth Century*, published in 1902, he makes his case by dividing both the century and the book into two parts: 'Before the Renaissance' and 'The Renaissance'. Five years later, Ernest Walker's *History of Music in England* contained a chapter entitled 'The English Renaissance', without further comment or explanation. The Renaissance had become an accepted fact; and it featured as a fact in articles, radio and television programmes throughout the twentieth century. It also provided the theme for a string of books, including, among others, Frank Howes' *English Musical Renaissance* (1966), Peter J. Pirie's book of the same title (1979), and Michael Trend's *Music Makers* (1985).[2] It was left to Meirion Hughes and Robert Stradling in 1993 to present an alternative viewpoint in *The English Musical Renaissance 1840–1940*, a book that was attacked in some quarters for its sceptical stance.

A rebirth of British music was, of course, the grail which many composers, teachers, scholars, commentators and even members of the Royal Family had been seeking for the previous half century or more – so to be told that it had arrived was cause for celebration, not a matter for doubt. The word 'Renaissance' was well chosen also in that it suggested a link between contemporary music and the age of the Taverner, Tallis and Byrd, the period when Britain had produced composers and music of European significance. Greatness, it implied, had returned. The initial promoters of the idea of an English Musical Renaissance were all supporters of the Grove-Mackenzie, and later Parry-Mackenzie, alliance which allowed the RCM and the RAM to work together. And the fact that the public perceptions of the Renaissance, formed by commentators such as Fuller Maitland, were from the first centred on the two institutions, with the RCM seen as the more influential of the two, has to be seen as a triumph for the public relations campaign launched by Grove and Mackenzie in support of British music. It was an idea promoted by the critics and the musical press, and it became to some extent politicised within the musical world — but what was the reality behind it?

The last two decades of the nineteenth century undoubtedly did usher in an extended period of significant change in British music and the structures around it. The next two, even three, generations of composers went off in musical directions inconceivable to their predecessors, and some of them produced works of a quality superior to anything seen for two hundred years. The two royal colleges naturally played an important part in all this, but, as we saw in the previous chapter, the causes and driving forces of change involved other individuals, institutions and influences as well. In this context, the all-enveloping term 'English Musical Renaissance' may be useful as a shorthand reference to a particular period in the history of British music, but it is misleading if taken to suggest that there were shared values, a shared sense of direction, or any unity of purpose among the composers of the time. Certain individuals or groups may have thought and worked along the same lines, but the Renaissance was in no sense a movement, let alone a homogeneous movement.

Certain questions immediately arise. Was it an English or a British Renaissance? It has always been referred to as English. Musical life centred on London and so did the Renaissance. It is true also that most of the leading composers associated with the Renaissance, from Elgar to Britten and beyond, were English by birth. However, the involvement of Mackenzie and Stanford, who drew on their native folk traditions in their work and also taught so many of the Renaissance composers, suggests that there was from the beginning a non-English component. And, while most of the leading composers may have been English – Delius being the obvious exception – there were lesser figures who were not. William Wallace,[3] Learmont Drysdale, Hamish MacCunn, and John Blackwood McEwen were Scottish. Granville Bantock, who was English, drew his inspiration from Scottish seascapes and Celtic mythology. Charles Wood and Hamilton Harty were Irish. E. J. Moeran was half Irish; Arnold Bax was English but adopted an Irish personality; and both of them leaned heavily on Irish music and musical forms. Nor, of course, was the impact of the Renaissance limited to England. So while it is probably too late to change the traditional appellation, we can at least resist the notion that it was either a coherent movement or wholly Anglo-centric.

Just how radical was the music that came out of this period of rebirth? And how was the 'new' British music viewed elsewhere in Europe? Music has always been international, and composers have always taken careful account of developments in other countries, but by the end of the nineteenth century there had been a step change in communications. Trains, steamships, the telegraph, even the advent of recorded music (primitive though it was, first on cylinder, then on disc), made it easier to keep track of what was happening elsewhere in Europe or even across the Atlantic. Developments in British music did not happen in a vacuum. We shall, of course, look at the lives and works of individual composers in future chapters, but, in assessing the impact of the English Musical Renaissance as a whole, it is necessary to have some sense of its international context. From Parry and Stanford to Michael Tippett and Benjamin Britten may seem a huge leap, but in France, for example, the same period saw a progression from Fauré and Widor to Poulenc and Messiaen; while the Germanic world travelled from Mahler and Hugo Wolf to Schoenberg, Berg and Webern. There may have been works produced in Britain by composers associated with the Renaissance which can be seen as revolutionary in their own terms; they may have helped establish a new direction and a new sense of identity for British music within its own confines; but they were not necessarily radical or revolutionary in the broader scheme of things.

Similarly, and contrary to what is often stated or implied, the Renaissance does not seem to have resulted in any across-the-board increase in awareness or appreciation of British music on the Continent. Balfe, William Vincent Wallace and Benedict had had operas performed in Germany, France, Italy, the United States, even in Australia. Pierson, Horsley, Sterndale Bennett, Sullivan, Mackenzie and Stanford had all had their works premiered and played abroad, particularly in Germany. The new generation of composers received a certain amount of international attention, but overall probably neither more nor less than their predecessors. Of course, certain works did receive a particularly enthusiastic response – Elgar's *Enigma Variations* and his First Symphony were both hugely successful in Europe and elsewhere; and, as a result, Elgar naturally developed an international reputation. Holst achieved international recognition with *The Planets*; and Vaughan Williams gradually became recognised as a symphonist of international significance. But the success of individual works and individual composers was on the whole shortlived and did not transfer to or boost the reputation of British music as a whole or in the long term.

It was not a movement; it was not, in a European sense at least, revolutionary; nor did it significantly boost the perception of British or English music abroad. So, one could be forgiven for asking, what was it? What was all the fuss about? Acknowledging that it is easier to reach a balanced assessment of a historical period when time has passed and the dust has settled, and that early assessments of the Renaissance were notably enthusiastic, a twenty-first century perspective allows us to see that the Renaissance was a period during which English music – to stay for the moment with the traditional terminology – began to distance itself from the uncertain German imitations of the past and gradually evolved a new and, in time, recognisably English identity. Certain components of this new identity, most notably the rediscovery and the integration of folk music, were common to the often more radical developments taking place on the Continent. However, English music, as it had done before at times of change, went its own way. If we count the Renaissance as a revolution, it was, like most English revolutions, essentially conservative in character. British composers were not attracted by serialism and twelve-tone music. They were not theoretical in their approach. They were – and this is something we have identified as a British characteristic more than once before – essentially pragmatic and geared towards melody in its various forms. The composers of the Renaissance era asserted – or, taking the long view, reasserted – the individuality of British music through a mixture of elements that we shall see recurring regularly in the period up to and beyond the Second World War. These included folk song, Tudor music, pastoral evocation and description of the natural world, and an expansion of the potential of the art song tradition. But they did not take the world, or even Europe, by storm.

78   Edward Elgar

One of the problems for those seeking to take ownership of the Renaissance on behalf of the two royal colleges is the fact that its first two significant exemplars were complete outsiders: neither Edward Elgar (1857–1934), nor Frederick Delius (1862–1934) fitted the mould. Writing in 1916, Stanford and Cecil Forsyth launched an attack on Elgar that can only be described as vitriolic. He 'reaped where ... others had sowed.' He was 'cut off from his contemporaries by the circumstances of his religion and his want of regular academic training'. His subjects lacked distinction; he himself lacked humour and was not interested in English music. Delius, by contrast, was merely dismissed as 'English by birth, but Dutch-German-French by heredity, taste and residence.'[1] Composers had attacked each other and each other's music before. The difference now was that such attacks were increasingly political in nature, focussing on who could legitimately claim to represent what was coming to be seen as 'national music'.

Elgar, of course, was wholly English. The name goes back to the Domesday Book. However, he stood out from his contemporaries not only because he was a Roman Catholic – his mother converted before he was born and brought up all her children in her new faith – but also because of his social origins. His father, William Henry Elgar, was a piano tuner and teacher, who, with his brother, went on to run a music shop in Worcester High Street, not far from the Cathedral. Elgar himself was born in the village of Lower Broadheath just outside the city, and his love for his native countryside would become a recurring theme in both his life and his music, but for most of his early years he lived in rooms above the shop. He eventually became a baronet and a member of the Order of Merit, but for much of his early career his social origins held him back. When in 1889, he married Caroline Alice Roberts, the daughter of a major-general, she was considered to have married so far below her station in life that a number of friends and acquaintances dropped her altogether.

Elgar's father played a full part in Worcester's musical life, whether singing among friends at impromptu gatherings or playing violin at the city's Glee Club, and, although he himself had little time for religion, he was also organist at the Catholic church. (It was this appointment which had resulted in his wife's conversion.) He made sure that his children had a good, basic musical education with local teachers, but much of the young Edward Elgar's musical education was the result of his own efforts. The Cathedral was at the heart of the city and of the city's music. Elgar went there to listen to the choir and the organ. He borrowed books and scores from the Cathedral library. In 1866, when he was nine and Worcester was preparing to host the Three Choirs, his father – one of the second violins – arranged for him to attend a rehearsal. It was the first time he had heard a full orchestra, an experience he never forgot. He naturally spent a lot of time in the family shop, studying the books and sheet music there. He even found a set of Vivaldi concertos that had once belonged to Daines Barrington, an eighteenth-century amateur player, who had been present when Mozart visited London in 1764 – something else that fired his imagination.

Elgar's skills developed rapidly and, by the age of eight, he was playing the piano – a Broadwood from the very beginning of the century – and giving occasional recitals at the house of Dr Davison, a canon at the Cathedral. Yet the piano was never really Elgar's instrument. He tried the organ and was soon able to play with some facility, but it was not what he was looking for. At the age of twelve, however, having found that Reicha's *Orchestral Primer* described the violin as the king of instruments, he begged one from the stock held in the shop and taught himself to play. Within a few months, he had joined his father as a member of the band at the Glee Club. He also began to write music. When the Elgar children decided to put on a play, Edward provided the incidental music – resurrecting and orchestrating the tunes many years later for his two *Wand of Youth* suites (1907 and 1908). He tried a fugue; he composed a setting of a poem written by his mother. It was an education based on trial and error.

W. H. Elgar was no great businessman and the family was not well off, so at the age of fifteen Elgar would not have been surprised, though probably still disappointed, to be told that there was no money to send him to study in Leipzig. Instead, he became the office junior in a Worcester solicitor's office. He lasted a year before leaving, in June 1873, to become his father's assistant in the music business. He began giving violin lessons. He took on occasional orchestral work, playing in the small orchestra that accompanied visiting opera companies or alongside his father in the second violins at the Three Choirs Festival. He played in Gloucester in an orchestra directed by Charles Harford Lloyd. In 1879, he took charge of a small band made up of staff at the Worcester County Lunatic Asylum, later known as Powick Hospital, where an enlightened regime believed that music was good for those with psychiatric illnesses. He was paid £30 a year for one day a week, with extra payments for dances he composed himself.

It was a living, but the real story of those years was the slow expansion of his musical knowledge and experience. He substituted for his father at the Catholic church, extemporising voluntaries and making arrangements of Mozart to vary the normal diet. He heard Sebastian Wesley play the new cathedral organ. He rang the bells at St Helen's Church. He put together his own group of musicians, based on family and friends, and began writing pieces which they played in one of the sheds at the back of the music shop. He played in the orchestra for Spohr's *Last Judgement* and, in May 1876, for Mendelssohn's *Elijah* – an important moment in Elgar family history for the son was now placed among the first violins, while the father remained in the seconds. He scraped together the money to go to London for lessons with the violinist Adolphe Pollitzer. He was given an introduction to Manns which allowed him to attend rehearsals for concerts at the Crystal Palace. He became director of an amateur orchestra in Worcester. He played in the Three Choirs Orchestra for Mackenzie's *The Bride* – a revelation for him in terms of how an orchestra could be used. With much effort, he saved enough to go to Leipzig, not to study but to spend a couple of weeks there attending rehearsals and concerts and absorbing the atmosphere. He played in the Birmingham orchestra when Dvořák conducted his *Stabat Mater* and Sixth Symphony.

And so on, throughout the 1880s. His reputation was growing, but only very slowly. He wrote dances for his asylum band; he wrote a few songs and chamber pieces. In 1883, he had a short orchestral composition, *Intermezzo moresque* performed in Birmingham; the following year, a Spanish-influenced work, *Sevillana*, was played by Manns at the Crystal Palace. Then, in 1886, he began giving piano lessons to Alice Roberts. In 1888, he dedicated a short, romantic piece for violin and piano to her. It was called *Salut d'Amour*.[2] They married the following year. She was nine years older than him, and her surviving relatives (both her parents were dead) regarded the marriage as wholly unsuitable because of Elgar's background in trade and because she chose to convert to Catholicism. Yet Alice knew her own mind: she believed in him and his dream of writing great music; she would offer him the emotional support he needed. It would be a long road, but his fortunes began to look up almost at once.

The concert overture, *Froissart*, was commissioned for the Worcester Festival in 1890. It was his first major orchestral work. Then came *The Black Knight* (1893), which he had begun before *Froissart*. Based on Longfellow's translation of a German poem, Elgar called it a choral symphony, but the publishers called it a cantata. It was bigger than anything he had attempted before and, while not a great work, it is full of interesting melodic ideas and shows the beginning of his fascination with the relationship between chorus and orchestra. Other choral works followed. *The Light of Life* (1896), with a libretto assembled from biblical texts by Edward Capel-Cure, a Worcester-based curate and amateur cellist, told the story of Christ healing a blind man. *Scenes from the King Olaf* (1896), a cantata based on an episode from Longfellow's *Tales from a Wayside Inn*, was his first major work not written for Worcester. This time he asked a Malvern neighbour, Harry Acworth, to help adapt the text. The story of Olaf's Christian hero-ism clearly inspired Elgar. The music has a matching heroic quality which goes beyond mere romanticism, and the piece ends with a moving, unac-companied choral epilogue. It was a significant step forward and its recep-tion at the North Staffordshire Festival was enthusiastic, but Elgar, as often happened after the first performance of a major new work, was depressed.

He was approaching forty and still, to all intents and purposes, a provincial musician.

His first London premiere came in 1897 with the undistinguished *Banner of St George*, a ballad for chorus and orchestra. His *Imperial March*, played in the same year by Manns at the Crystal Palace, is more interesting. Both works were written for Queen Victoria's Diamond Jubilee, and the *Imperial March* is the first glimpse of the imperial Elgar that would emerge over the next decade and colour his future reputation. With his provincial background, it was natural that Elgar should be an old-fashioned imperialist and supporter of the Queen – and marriage to the daughter of a major-general in the Indian Army would not have diminished those convictions. That same background meant that he was in many respects less sophisticated than men such as Parry and Stanford. They would not – perhaps could not – write with the emotional directness that characterises many of Elgar's compositions. His emotions are the actual subject of his music, and they are often confused, uncertain, even tortured. But where the Queen and the Empire were concerned his feelings were straightforward and unambiguous and he wrote with an openness, flamboyance, and excitement which avoided sentimentality and embarrassment because it was natural.

His next work, which, by virtue of his contributions to the Jubilee celebrations, he was allowed to dedicate to Queen Victoria, was *Caractacus*: a big, ninety-minute cantata for soloists, chorus and orchestra, again with words by Harry Acworth. Elgar himself conducted the premiere at the Leeds Festival in 1898. Seen from today's perspective, we would probably agree with the lone critic who expressed reservations and suggested that the scale of the work and Elgar's immensely effective orchestration obscured a lack of thematic invention. At the time, however, the work was a success with both the audience and the press. Extracts arranged for orchestra were soon being played at Crystal Palace concerts. Elgar was now a rising star, but he was still depressed. For all the hard work he had put in, he had no money. *Caractacus* was a success, but he still had to return to Malvern and violin teaching to make ends meet.

The next few years would change everything – except Elgar's mood swings, which intensified as he grew older. The story of the genesis of the *Enigma Variations* – how Alice drew his attention to a tune he had not even realised he was improvising – has often been told, and the work itself has become so familiar that it is easy to forget how original it was. Variations on pre-existing or original themes were nothing new; and, as we have seen (page 27), there had already been at least one *Enigma* in which the variations imitated the styles of eminent composers. Elgar's use of music to express the personality traits of fourteen friends and associates (including himself), and the humour he brought to the concept, made it something new. Of course, there was the additional enjoyment of an in-joke for those in the know, but as Elgar himself recognised when describing the idea to his friend August Jaeger, this would not in any way hinder an uninstructed audience from enjoying the music. Jaeger had been Elgar's contact at his publishers, Novello's, since 1896, and had rapidly become both a trusted adviser and a friend. It was Jaeger who, gently but determinedly, pressed Elgar to strengthen the ending of the *Enigma*, and it was Jaeger who invoked Parry's help to get Richter to premiere the new score.

Richter conducted the first performance at St James's Hall in June 1899. A revised version, the one usually heard today, was played in Worcester that September. There was some minor carping about the hidden identity of the subjects, but the quality of the work and of Elgar's orchestration was recognised immediately. No British composer had written anything to approach it for generations. *Caractacus* had been inspired by a conversation with his mother on the Malvern Hills and it contained passages that were a direct expression of his love for his native countryside. The *Enigma*, too, is redolent of the English countryside: the variations seeming to present individuals in the context of the natural world so clearly conjured up in the main theme.

Before the idea for the *Enigma* unexpectedly cropped up, Elgar had promised to write something for the contralto, Clara Butt, to sing at the Norwich Festival that same October. He came up with the song cycle, *Sea Pictures*. Although he wrote many songs, Elgar was not a great songwriter, partly because of his belief that it was better to set mediocre poems. The five poems he sets in *Sea Pictures* are far from distinguished, but the songs work because his music gives them coherence and makes them into a cycle. The work was a huge success in Norwich and was repeated just two days later in London at St James's Hall where it was sold out. Even Jaeger could not get a seat. Elgar had arrived.

Then came *The Dream of Gerontius*, composed for the Birmingham Festival in October 1900. The text is taken from a poem of the same title written some thirty-five years earlier by John Henry Newman, one of the leaders of the Oxford Movement, who converted to Catholicism and later became a Cardinal. It follows the thoughts and prayers of a man as he anticipates death and then awakes after death to face judgement. Elgar took this poem, condensed it, and turned it into a work of quite astonishing power. In one sense, *Gerontius* is the apotheosis of the Victorian oratorio, a tired and wearisome form taken to unexpected new heights. Yet it is barely an oratorio as traditionally understood – its structure is continuous, unbroken by set piece arias and recitatives – and Elgar's musical idiom went so far beyond the parochial English (or even Mendelssohnian) oratorio that even Hans Richter struggled to understand it at first, and the Birmingham choir and chorus master were completely lost. As a result the premiere was little short of a disaster. Its modernity was such that Elgar was faced with accusations that it was unplayable – until it was played in successive years to packed houses at the Lower Rhine Festival in Düsseldorf. It was after the second Düsseldorf performance in 1902 that Richard Strauss toasted Elgar as the first English progressive composer – the statement which so infuriated Stanford. Only then was *Gerontius* given again in Britain, in Manchester in 1903 by Richter, and later the same year in Hanley with Elgar himself conducting.

Gerontius has no natural drama; its subject is a theological one and, as such, its action is a progression through abstraction. Yet it not only works, it is a masterpiece. It works because for Elgar, as a Roman Catholic, the theology of Newman's poem was important. It genuinely mattered, and his belief and commitment come across in the music. Neither his emotions nor the intensity of the music are dampened by the fact that the 'story' takes place in the realm of abstraction, or that much of the momentum of the piece comes from disembodied choruses of devils and angels. And it works because Elgar's understanding and belief welds all the elements of both poetry and music – purpose, meaning, atmosphere and expression – into a complete unity. On the last page of the manuscript, he wrote: 'This is the best of me.' He was right.

Even before *Gerontius*, Elgar had had the idea for a gigantic oratorio that would tell the story of the beginnings of Christianity from the calling of the Apostles by Christ to the establishment of the Christian Church outside Palestine. In time, this concept – very Victorian in its belief in the value of sheer size – became a plan for a cycle of three oratorios: *The Apostles, The Kingdom,* and *The Last Judgement.* Elgar himself conducted the first performance of *The Apostles* at the 1903 Birmingham Festival; and it was given again the following year by Richter as part of a three-day Elgar Festival in London. *The Kingdom* followed in 1906, again in Birmingham.

These are massive works, with librettos drawn from the Bible and put together by Elgar from the Bible, almost Wagnerian in their scale and their use of leitmotifs. Any critical assessment has to take into account the fact that Elgar never wrote *The Last Judgement*. Had he done so, had he completed the cycle, it might perhaps have done something to bring a greater sense of cohesion and unity to the works that we have. As things stand, however, the two completed oratorios are structurally and musically episodic, which means that Elgar is driven to orchestral special effects to cover the gaps. There are some magnificent moments, but none of the structural coherence and musical unity which characterises Gerontius. After *The Kingdom,* Elgar wrote only one more choral work of any scale: T*he Music Makers,* a setting of a truly dreadful poem by Arthur O'Shaughnessy ('With wonderful deathless ditties / We build up the world's great cities'), in which, by reusing tunes from earlier works, he identifies himself with those artists whose art has helped shape the world.

The first decade of the new century saw Elgar turning decisively towards orchestral compositions. The confident and expansive overture, *Cockaigne (In London Town)* appeared in 1901, and looks forward to the symphony that was to come. The same year also saw *Pomp and Circumstance no. 1*, the first of a series of five marches that expressed his loyalty to Queen and Empire and provided some very substantial royalty cheques. It was at the suggestion of King Edward VII that Elgar sought words for the tune in *no. 1* that is now almost universally recognised as 'Land of Hope and Glory'. Elgar's acceptance of this suggestion and the success of the resulting song, first performed by Clara Butt in 1902, no doubt contributed to the award of a knighthood in 1904. We have seen how, during Queen Victoria's reign, it had become usual for senior musicians to receive knighthoods – Parratt had received his in 1892, Mackenzie in 1895, Parry in 1898, and Stanford in 1902 – but for Elgar, the son of a provincial shopkeeper, whose wife's friends had dropped her because of his origins, the honour was that much greater because he had come that much farther. A holiday in Italy over the winter of 1903/04 led to the overture *In the South (Alassio).* This was followed by a work that is now recognised as a small masterpiece, *Introduction and Allegro for Strings* (1905). Written for string quartet and string orchestra, it is a multi-faceted and exploratory work. Deeply imbued with Elgar's love of the English landscape, it manages to be polyphonic, neo-classical and deeply romantic at the same time. While complete in itself, it can also be seen as preparing the ground for the First Symphony, which was premiered by Richter and the Hallé Orchestra at Manchester's Free Trade Hall in December 1908.

The music writer and broadcaster, Stephen Johnson, has suggested that some of the rhythms of Elgar's First Symphony are derived from the rhythm of cycling which Elgar adopted as a pastime in 1900 and which, for a few years, became his main way of experiencing the Worcester and Hereford countryside.[3] Whether true or not, the suggestion points to the essential difference of Elgar's First Symphony. We have followed British composers over almost a century as they tried to write a breakthrough symphony that would attract and maintain international attention and respect. Here was a symphony in the traditional four-movement structure (although in the slightly unusual key of A flat major), written for a normal symphony orchestra, yet it did not sound like previous British symphonies. The distinctive, opening theme – given Elgar's favourite marking 'nobilemente' – is established with apparent confidence, but then seems almost to disappear. The work moves into a different key (D minor) and the main theme hovers in the background, reappearing in different guises, changing and evolving, and then eventually returning, transformed, for the final, triumphant conclusion. From its opening bars, the symphony moves forward with an assurance that makes those of Parry and Stanford sound tentative. Elgar was a nervous man, rarely in good health. For years he had dreamed of writing a symphony. When he finished it, he collapsed with depression, but the symphony itself was a monument of confidence. With its grandeur and its optimism, it is not hard to see why the First Symphony has been taken as a kind of hymn to the glories of the Edwardian era, although Elgar himself insisted that there was no programme beyond the expression of his experience of life and his optimism for the future. Perhaps it was an unconscious expression of some kind of zeitgeist. The work enjoyed unprecedented success. Within weeks, it was being given across the United States, in Saint Petersburg, and in the great centres of German symphonic culture – Vienna and Leipzig. Within a year of its premiere, by Richter and the Hallé in Manchester in December 1908, it had been performed over a hundred times.

Elgar's next work was his Violin Concerto, a big romantic composition, which even he admitted was intensely emotional. With the famous Fritz Kreisler as soloist, it was premiered in London in 1910 to yet more public and critical acclaim. The violin, of course, was Elgar's own instrument and the concerto remained one of his favourite works. In his later years, he became one of the first composers to take a serious interest in recording his own music and in 1932, at the studios of His Master's Voice in London's Abbey Road, he conducted the London Symphony Orchestra with the sixteen-year-old Yehudi Menuhin as soloist. It proved to be one of the first great recordings of a classical piece and is still available today.

The Violin Concerto was the last of Elgar's works to be received with such overwhelming public enthusiasm. The Second Symphony, premiered in May 1911, was dedicated 'to the memory of His late Majesty King Edward VII'. It was greeted with respect, but with less excitement than before and there were rumblings among the critics. The mood is almost the opposite of the First Symphony. At the beginning of the score, Elgar quotes Shelley's line, 'Rarely, rarely, comest thou, Spirit of Delight!', and a sense of melancholy, even sadness, pervades the whole work, although the overall effect is of dignity and resignation rather than tragedy. It is less obviously melodic than the First Symphony, perhaps because it lacks the same emotional certainty, and Elgar deliberately and cleverly heightens the sense of uncertainty with instances of chromaticism and the use of a full tone scale. The Second Symphony took a long time to establish itself with British audiences and orchestras and has never achieved anything like the popularity enjoyed by its predecessor in Europe. Nor was this change in public attitude limited to the Second Symphony. Two years later, his tone poem *Falstaff*, a much more accessible score with an explicit programme based on scenes from Shakespeare and some very fine orchestral writing, received the same respectful but far from overwhelming welcome. Success, fame and a knighthood had come to Elgar with the arrival of the Edwardian era. Now, with the passing of Edward VII, Elgar's popularity had passed its peak.

The outbreak of the First World War found the Elgars on holiday in Scotland, where they were stuck for a couple of days because all available transport had been commandeered to rush troops to France. Elgar's musical orientation was German and he had numerous German friends, but his unambiguous approach to matters of country and patriotism meant that the war was less traumatic for him than for Parry or Stanford. Once back in London, he volunteered to become a special constable and began composing a series of patriotic works: *Carillon* to encourage support for the Belgians; *Polonia* to do the same for the Poles; *The Spirit of England*, which set poems by Laurence Binyon; *The Fringes of the Fleet*, a musical entertainment based on Kipling's work of the same title. Competent and professional like everything Elgar wrote, these works were by their nature born of duty rather than inspiration, and served to reinforce his connection with the political and social establishment in a way that would damage his reputation in the longer term.

Elgar's profession tied him to London, but his heart was in the country. The journey back to Worcester and Malvern was long and tiring, so in 1917, Alice tried a new solution. She rented a cottage called Brinkwells, near Fittleworth in West Sussex. Here, over a two-year period, Elgar composed his last important works. Inspired by the woodlands around Brinkwells, and also as a reaction to the very public nature of his wartime music, he fulfilled a long-held wish to write chamber music. The Violin Sonata, the String Quartet and the Piano Quintet were written in sequence. None of the three could be described as adventurous – the Piano Quintet is perhaps the least conservative – yet, while lacking the assertiveness and challenge of some of his earlier works, they are rounded, accomplished and deeply rewarding pieces, with a reflective quality that is not quite introspection. One has the sense of Elgar writing music to satisfy himself.

With no pause at all, he moved on to the Cello Concerto. The cellist Felix Salmond had played in the first performances of both the String Quartet and the Piano Quintet at the Wigmore Hall in May 1919. Elgar was sufficiently impressed to ask him to be the soloist when the Concerto was premiered at London's Queen's Hall that October. This is a big, confident, passionate work. Highly unusual in that it begins with a solo cello recitative, it moves through a conventional three-movement structure – again featuring Stephen Johnson's bicycling rhythms – to a decisive, almost sudden ending. Within that framework is contained all Elgar's romantic lyricism, his love and longing for the English countryside, and his deep, searching melancholy. That is how we see the work today, when it is widely regarded as a national treasure. The first night audience heard only an anxious soloist trying to cope with an under-rehearsed and muddled orchestra. As Elgar premieres went, it was even worse than *Gerontius*. In 1928, he conducted a recording with the London Symphony Orchestra and Beatrice Harrison as soloist, but it did not approach the power of the Violin Concerto with Menuhin. The Cello Concerto did not really become popular in Britain until the 1960s when it was played by Jacqueline du Pré.

Alice Elgar died in April 1920. She had supported him loyally over thirty years. She had been his helper and his inspiration, and when she could not help, she had not stood in the way of others – usually, but not always, women – who were able to give him friendship and encouragement. He had composed his first large-scale work just after their marriage and his last, the Cello Concerto, was completed six months before her death. He continued to compose songs, piano pieces, occasional pieces and incidental music right up until 1933, the year before his own death, but he wrote nothing of any scale in those years and nothing that would make the world think any differently of the man or his music. The one work that might have made a difference, the Third Symphony, was left unfinished. About half of it was sketched out at the time of his death. It has since been carefully and cleverly completed by Anthony Payne, but because it is a hybrid – and particularly because the ending is wholly Payne's creation – it is hard to regard it as more than a fascinating sidelight on Elgar himself.

Elgar was very English. He composed from emotion, not theory. His music is full of colour and melody, with an essential admixture of romantic yearning. And he was more genuinely a product of the English countryside that inspired so much of his music than any other composer of his age. Yet in other ways he does not fit the pattern of an English Renaissance composer. Mackenzie, Parry and Stanford were all believers in the value of folk music. Mackenzie made use of folk tunes in his work; Parry published two volumes of *Characteristic Popular Tunes of the British Isles* (1900); Stanford arranged over one hundred and fifty folk songs and published several collections, the best known of which is *Songs of Erin* (1901). A belief in the importance of folk music was something they passed on to their students and it became embedded in the work of the next generation of composers. Elgar, however, did not care for folk music. He neither made use of it, nor arranged it, nor published it. Once, when questioned, he is supposed to have made the regal retort, 'I am folk music', a statement that has been much analysed, but was probably no more than a means of deflecting the question. Nor did Elgar share that other interest common to almost all other composers of the period – and which we shall examine in due course – the revival of Tudor music. He acknowledged the genius of Purcell, but Tallis and Byrd did not speak to him at all. Indeed, he is reputed to have called them 'museum pieces'.[5] Elgar left school at fifteen and had no further formal education, either musical or academic. As a consequence – and beyond the occasional article, which was frequently more autobiographical than musical – he never tried to write about music. The series of lectures he gave following his appointment as Professor of Music at Birmingham in 1904 was a shambles. He had decided views on many musical issues and was not shy of giving them, but, as a lecturer, he lacked the education and the experience to organise his thoughts, with the result that he became long-winded, disorganised and repetitive. This again set him apart from almost all the other English Renaissance composers, who, coming from better-off, middle-class backgrounds, were better educated and better able to express themselves, whether verbally or on paper.

Elgar had good, although certainly not close, relations with Mackenzie, Parry and Parratt (who had known W.H. Elgar slightly). Stanford was friendly at first – it was he who pushed for Elgar to be awarded an honorary doctorate at Cambridge – but the relationship deteriorated rapidly. Stanford seems to have been jealous of Elgar's success, and, in particular, of the Birmingham professorship. Elgar had never liked Stanford's music and was anything but placatory, appearing to attack Stanford in his lectures. Whatever the rights and wrongs of the case, they remained at odds for the rest of their lives. They shook hands formally at the unveiling of a memorial to Parry in 1922, but it was not the kiss of peace and Stanford's disciples, notably E.J. Dent, Professor of Music at Cambridge from 1926 until 1941, carried on the war against Elgar after Stanford's death and into the 1930s. This mutual dislike may have been one reason why he remained at a distance from the royal colleges. Or were there still social reasons? Even quite late in his life, Elgar could be extremely sensitive about the way people reacted to 'the shop' in his background. The fact is that neither the RAM or the RCM ever really opened their arms or their doors to him. So we are left with a puzzling situation where the most successful composer to emerge during the Renaissance period – and the composer who arguably did more for the profile of English music on the Continent than anyone else – did not subscribe to a number of the musical interests held to be central to the development of that Renaissance, and was never fully accepted by the individuals and organisations usually regarded as having brought it about.

79   Frederick Delius

Frederick Theodore Albert Delius (1862–1934) was a different kind of outsider. Nowadays regarded as one of the great innovators of British music – and here we must insist on the term British – he was, like Elgar, slow to come to musical maturity, and throughout his creative life he remained at an even greater distance than Elgar did from the British musical establishment as represented by the two royal colleges and their professors. Yet whereas Elgar's musical vision centred on his Englishness and his Catholicism, that of Delius, while it could and at times did express an intense appreciation of pastoral England, offered a much broader vision of the natural world and the transience of human existence.

The family was German, from Bielefeld in Westphalia, but they had settled in Bradford and taken British nationality long before Fritz – as he was christened – was born. It was not until he was forty that Delius decided to anglicise his name to Frederick. His father, Julius, was in the wool business and very successful. Theirs was a well-off, cultured household where music was encouraged. Young Delius learned the violin and the piano, and developed a preference for Grieg and Chopin over the German classical masters. At school – Bradford Grammar School and then the London College of the International Education Society, London's first international school – he was good at cricket, but showed no particular academic ability. Leaving school in 1880, aged eighteen, he did what was expected of him and joined the family wool business. It was not a success. Sent to Germany, he neglected business for music lessons. Sent to Sweden, he became involved with the theatre. Sent to Paris, he went on holiday to the Riviera. Fritz had become the family problem. Julius Delius decided to send him further afield, to Florida, to manage a run-down orange plantation called Solana Grove. There, Delius heard the work songs of the black plantation workers and the crews on the boats that passed up and down the St Johns River. His *Appalachia: Variations on an Old Slave Song* (1893, rewritten 1903) is reputed to have been based on the singing of one of his servants who had once been a slave. In nearby Jacksonville, he heard black waiters singing spirituals and playing banjos. Also in Jacksonville, he met Thomas Ward, a Brooklyn-born organist who had come to Florida because the climate was supposed to be better for his tuberculosis. Ward taught him counterpoint and composition, lessons Delius later claimed were the only useful ones he ever had.[1] Delius stayed in Florida for just over a year. Then, in 1885, he put his negro foreman in charge of the plantation and moved north to Virginia, where he taught music in a local girls' school and gave violin and piano lessons to private students. This lasted another year, by which time Julius Delius, perhaps recognising a determination to match his own, agreed to fund his son's musical education in Leipzig.

Delius studied at the Leipzig Conservatorium from 1886 to 1888. Musically, it probably left less of a mark on him than Florida, although studying there with teachers such as Reinecke – who had taught Sullivan, Stanford and Cowen – must have knocked off some of the rough edges, and in 1887 he had his first orchestral work, the *Florida Suite*, given at a private concert. More important was the fact that he made friends with the small colony of Norwegian music students – among them Christian Sinding, Johan Halvorsen and Halfdan Jebe – and through them he met Grieg, who would be a lifelong friend. Delius had visited Norway when working in Sweden for his father, but now, his understanding of the country mediated by his new Norwegian friends, it became a kind of spiritual home, the atmosphere and the landscape acting as a source of inspiration that would last for the rest of his life. And it was Grieg who intervened to ensure that Delius's father accepted his son's vocation and settled on him, however grudgingly, a small annual income.

With this new freedom, Delius went to live in Paris, where he slowly extended his skills and his abilities. He concentrated on opera – *Irmelin* (1892) was followed by *The Magic Fountain* (1895). Both were written to Delius's own, essentially banal librettos, and, although *Irmelin* contains some fine music, neither was performed until the second half of the twentieth century. There were orchestral works, too, and when a now forgotten orchestral suite, *Paa Vidderne*, was given in Oslo in 1891, it marked the first public performance of a work by Delius. These years saw him socialising with a number of influential musicians, artists and writers: Gabriel Fauré, Maurice Ravel, Paul Gauguin, Edvard Munch (who became another close Norwegian friend) and August Strindberg. These were people he knew, people who followed a similarly relaxed, bohemian lifestyle, but they were not collaborators or influences. Delius's creative life was always a very private matter: he developed his own music in his own way. It was also in Paris, probably in 1895, that he contracted the syphilis that would eventually kill him.

In January 1896, at a Parisian dinner party, Delius met a German art student named Helena Rosen, but known to everyone as Jelka. Her mother was the daughter of Ignaz Moscheles, whose name has featured so often in these pages. She was a painter, studying at the Académie Colarossi, which was considered much more go-ahead in its attitudes than the École des Beaux-Arts. When not studying in Paris, she rented a house in the village of Grez-sur-Loing not far from Fontainebleau, which for some years had been home to a colony of Scandinavian artists. When the owner of the house, the Marquis de Cazeaux, decided he wanted to sell, Jelka bought it, with help from her parents. In the summer of 1897, Delius moved in with her. They married in 1903 and, except when they fled to England during the First World War, lived there for the rest of their lives. They evolved a largely self-contained existence, receiving visits from friends, often travelling to Norway in the summer, sometimes to Paris, but on the whole removed from the busy artistic and musical world.

It was a life that encouraged composition but did little to get Delius's music known among conductors and promoters. In 1897, at Elberfeld in Westphalia, Hans Haym played the fantasy overture, *Over the Hills and Far Away*, an attractive piece which later became a favourite of Thomas Beecham's. Not until 1899 was anything by Delius heard in Britain. Even then it was only because he decided to sponsor a concert of his own music out of his own pocket. It took place at London's St James's Hall under the baton of the German conductor, Alfred Hertz. The programme consisted of seven works, including *Over the Hills and Far Away; Five Danish Songs; Mitternachtslied Zarathustras*, a large-scale choral piece based on Nietzsche's *Also Sprach Zarathustra*; and extracts from Delius's opera *Koanga*, a story of passion and slavery on an eighteenth-century Louisiana plantation, which allowed him to draw on his knowledge of black American music. The audience was large and well disposed. The performance was good. The critics were certainly not hostile: they recognised that Delius had something to say and that his harmonic language was new and individual, but beyond that they were slightly mystified. The event was not a failure, but, in the year of the *Enigma Variations*, that was not sufficient to get the work of a new and unknown composer onto concert programmes. It would be eight years before his music was again played in England.

Back in France – resigned rather than disappointed, and certainly poorer, for staging the concert had cost much more than he had expected – Delius returned to composition and produced his first major work. *Paris, Song of a Great City* was written in 1899, but not premiered until 1901 when it was again given by Haym in Elberfeld. Called a nocturne and divided into seven contrasting sections, it is rich and impressionistic, moving through a range of moods to create a cumulative portrait of the city Delius loved. Unfortunately, it was neither understood nor well reviewed, and a Berlin performance the next year fared even worse. Gradually, however, with performances in Paris – with Haym conducting again – and then in Liverpool, opinion began to turn. *Paris* marked a significant shift in Delius's development as a composer, and the period between its first performance and the outbreak of the First World War saw him producing a series of often highly innovative works – although the perceived difficulty of Delius's music, coupled with his almost reclusive lifestyle and a reluctance to speak publicly about his work, meant that they were frequently not performed until several years after their composition.

The first of these works was *A Village Romeo and Juliet* (1901), the best and undoubtedly the most intense of his six operas, in which the human tragedy of the young lovers unfolds against a background of an unchanging and ever-renewing natural world. The balance between the two finds expression in the interlude between Scenes Five and Six, known as 'The Walk to the Paradise Garden', which is frequently played as a separate orchestral piece. *Sea Drift* (1904) is based on 'Out of the Cradle Endlessly Rocking', a poem from Walt Whitman's *Leaves of Grass*. Often considered Delius's finest work, it shows a boy coming to an acceptance and understanding of the transience of life as represented by a pair of mocking birds – although reduction to such a bald summary cannot do justice to the way in which the composition transcends the poem by fusing a range of differing, even conflicting, emotions into a deeply-felt spiritual unity. The following year came *A Mass of Life*, a huge, atheist testament in which the music again expresses the course of man's spiritual development. Delius took his earlier *Mitternachtslied Zarathustras* and built it into a massive statement of Nietzschean engagement with life and courage in the face of death, requiring four soloists, double choir and a large orchestra. In works such as these, turning musical expression into overt philosophical statement, Delius was doing something no other British composer had ever done in the same way. Elgar's angst was personal; so, too, were Parry's ethical cantatas. Delius was dealing with metaphysics on a cosmic scale. Wagner would have understood; and Mahler; so, too, perhaps might Richard Strauss (although Delius regarded Strauss's *Also Sprach Zarathustra* as a failure). And there were other Continental composers who were beginning to think along the same lines; but Delius was certainly among the leaders.

After *A Mass of Life*, Delius changed direction. *Songs of Sunset* (1907) is a song cycle based on eight poems by Ernest Dowson, where the sensuousness always present in Delius's music was now mixed with a sense of decadence and melancholy. *Brigg Fair* (1907), a set of variations on the tune of an old Lincolnshire folk tune collected by Percy Grainger a couple of years earlier, was the first in a series of orchestral works. There followed *In a Summer Garden* (1908), *A Song of the High Hills* (1911) – orchestral but for a wordless chorus, one of Delius's specialities – *On Hearing the First Cuckoo in Spring* (1912), *Summer Night on the River* (1912) and the very fine *North Country Sketches* (1914). It was as if he had said all he could say about the human condition in the abstract and was now seeking new truths in the emotional responses to landscape and the natural world. The stimulus might come from his garden in Grez, from the Norwegian mountains, or from the Yorkshire moorlands he knew as a boy, but in these works Delius took his personal brand of lyricism and sensuousness to new heights. They are all comparatively short; they do not develop so much as evolve; and the fact that the motive force resides within the composer's emotions rather than the musical structure can obscure how musically concise they are.

All this time, Delius's music was slowly gaining the attention of German conductors, particularly Fritz Cassirer, who had been introduced to Delius's music by Hans Haym and went on to conduct the premieres of *Koanga*, *Appalachia*, *Sea Drift* and *A Village Romeo and Juliet*. It was Cassirer who reintroduced Delius's work to Britain. He conducted *Appalachia* at a concert in St James's Hall in 1907. Thomas Beecham's new Symphony Orchestra had been hired for the occasion and Beecham himself attended the concert. Unlike most of the audience who, just as eight years previously, were impressed but mystified, he became an immediate convert. With characteristic energy and enthusiasm, he set about promoting Delius in Britain. Indeed, he did much more than that. In 1914 when Delius and Jelka, fearing the German advance, fled to England (burying a thousand bottles of their best wine in the garden before they did so), Beecham was able to offer them a rent-free place to stay; and because Delius had no money – his publisher being German, income from his works had naturally dried up – he also provided much-needed financial assistance. In the event, the war never reached Grez, and Delius was eventually reunited with his home, his garden and his wine. Another person working hard on Delius's behalf in Britain was the young Peter Warlock. He had been captivated by *Songs of Sunset* as a schoolboy and did all he could to promote Delius, particularly in print. He published the first study of Delius's music in 1923.

Whether because of the war or for some other reason, Delius made another change of direction. He began writing in more traditional forms: a Violin Sonata (1914), a Cello Sonata (1916), and a String Quartet (1917), the slow movement of which is entitled 'Late Swallows'. These pieces effectively blend Delius's characteristic sensuousness with a more formal discipline than he had previously applied in his work. But his concertos – the Double Concerto for Violin and Cello (1915), Violin Concerto (1916) and Cello Concerto (1921) – while containing passages of great beauty, are less satisfactory. Delius's world, even in his chamber music, was one of overpowering emotions which ebbed and flowed. He was not the man to manage the delicate balance between soloist and orchestra. One other work from this period should be mentioned: *Eventyr*, meaning 'adventure' in Norwegian, was written in 1917 and premiered by Henry Wood in 1919. Inspired by the atmosphere of the Norwegian folk tales as told by Peter Christian Asbjørnsen, it plays out a kind of fantasy drama between darkness and fear and light and resolution. It was his last really original work.

By this time, Delius's health was declining as the syphilis took hold. He wrote the incidental music for James Elroy Flecker's verse drama, *Hassan*, which was produced at Her Majesty's Theatre in 1923. The play ran for nearly three hundred performances and provided Delius's first, indeed only, commercial success. By that stage, however, he had to be carried into rehearsals, and had to rely on Percy Grainger to write last minute additions to the score and Peter Warlock to help with the copying. By 1928, he was blind and almost completely paralysed. Then, hearing of his plight, a young Yorkshireman named Eric Fenby wrote and offered to act as his amanuensis. Fenby later wrote about the experience in his book *Delius as I Knew Him*. It was hard enough trying to understand what Delius was trying to dictate, but there were other problems. Delius could be difficult, mocking Fenby's Catholicism, and as time went on Fenby became as much nurse as amanuensis. Nonetheless, a clutch of valuable late compositions emerged from their collaboration – including *Cynara*, a setting of Dowson's poem; *Songs of Farewell*, based on five poems from Whitman's *Leaves of Grass*; and *A Song of Summer*, an orchestral piece which Delius described to Fenby as expressing the feeling of sitting on cliffs overlooking the sea while seagulls flew past on the breeze. Delius died in 1934; Jelka a year later.

The trouble with Delius is that neither in life nor in death did he quite fit the mould. In life, he remained individual and independent. He wrote what he wanted to write: he was not driven by commissions or requests. He did not teach; he did not have disciples; and he never became a significant or lasting influence on other composers. In his lifetime, he never attained great fame or success; conversely, his reputation did not suffer the kind of decline that many composers suffer after their death. In 1946, as soon as cultural life began to recover after the Second World War, there was sufficient interest and commitment on the part of his supporters to stage a seven-concert Delius Festival led by Thomas Beecham. Delius's music also attracted interest in the United States, helped by the fact that he had lived in Florida. Elsewhere, however, it was a different story. Neither in Germany nor in France has his music ever regained the popularity it enjoyed before 1914. There is a story that, as late as 1970, Nadia Boulanger, who grew up in Paris during the pre-war years, claimed never to have heard of him.

Delius fits the model of an English Musical Renaissance composer no better than Elgar. That the guardians of the idea of a Renaissance disowned him is evident from Stanford and Forsyth's dismissal of his work quoted in the previous chapter. Delius spent little of his life actually living in Britain. Like Elgar, he was not greatly interested in music of the distant past. His major influences were Continental: Wagner, Richard Strauss, Grieg, and to a lesser extent Debussy, and from them he forged a style that was very much his own. He was prepared to make use of folk music when it suited his purposes, although he was probably more affected by Scandinavian folk music than English. His passionate response to landscape and the natural world included, but was not limited to, the English countryside. His message to his contemporaries, in so far that he had one, was that it was possible to be original or different and not to worry about it. He was lucky in that men like Thomas Beecham, Henry Wood and, later, Malcolm Sargent very definitely saw him as part of the broad and developing picture of new English music. How did Delius see himself? He was not a patriot in the Elgarian mould. He was at home in France and felt a spiritual connection with Norway, but he did have residual feelings for Britain. He was prepared to pay to get his music heard in London and – perhaps the most telling piece of evidence – he asked to be buried in an English country churchyard.

History is written with hindsight, and it is inevitable that a survey such as this should concentrate on the contribution made by composers whose work has survived into the present day and is seen – with hindsight – as having pushed styles or boundaries forward. At the same time, the generation to which Elgar and Delius belonged produced many composers whose music is interesting, at times challenging, and was quite often more popular than theirs in its day. Neglected or forgotten now, their music is important because it provided the background against which contemporary composers and contemporary audiences had to assess the works with which we are now more familiar and value more highly. Also, given that no one knew how styles and fashions would develop, their music offers glimpses of what might have been had British music followed a different course.

Following the brief and not wholly satisfactory flowering of English romantic opera under Balfe, Wallace and Benedict, British opera struggled along in much the same way as before. Gilbert and Sullivan had been a huge success, of course, although frowned on by certain serious-minded commentators. Mackenzie, Stanford and Cowen had all written operas, all broadly after the German model, sometimes successful, sometimes rewarded with a German performance, but never approaching the kind of breakthrough for British opera that Elgar managed for the symphony. Delius's *Village Romeo and Juliet* represented a different approach, but it was, in the end, probably too idiosyncratic to form the basis of a new operatic movement.

Ethel (later Dame Ethel) Smyth (1858–1944) was another who sought to find a way forward for British opera. Smyth had to fight to become a composer. Her father, like Alice Elgar's, was a major-general. He disapproved of women having a career at all, and doubly disapproved of a musical one, but his daughter proved at least as tough as he was. She got her way and, in 1877, went to Leipzig to study. This gave her a degree of freedom she would never have enjoyed had she studied in London, but it also meant that she absorbed perhaps too much German romanticism. Most of her early works – string quartets, string quintets, cello and violin sonatas – are strongly Germanic in style; and at least half her songs and choral works have German lyrics. Her music was not heard in Britain until 1890 when a piece called *Serenade* and her concert overture *Anthony and Cleopatra* were performed at the Crystal Palace. A more ambitious *Mass in D* followed three years later.

Smyth wrote six operas. Her second, *Der Wald* (1902), was premiered in Berlin in 1902, when it faced vocal opposition based on a combination of prejudice against women and anti-British feeling aroused by the Boer War. Subsequent performances in London and Stockholm were more successful. *Der Wald* is a one-act tragedy of peasant life set against an eternal and unchanging natural world. The essential idea, if not the music, is not far from that of *A Village Romeo and Juliet*. Her best and best-known work, however, is *The Wreckers* (1904), again premiered in Germany, this time in Leipzig. Thomas Beecham gave the first London performance at Covent Garden five years later. It is a distinctive and dramatic work set in a wrecking community on the Cornish coast, with music that is strongly evocative of both the characters and the powerful presence of the sea (the latter a particular strength in all her work). One critic has claimed that it is the most important British opera between Purcell and Britten.[1] While this is perhaps an enthusiastic judgement, *The Wreckers* has never achieved the place in the repertoire that it probably deserves. Her later attempt at a comic opera, *The Boatswain's Mate* (1914), is less successful because it attempts to combine a ballad-opera-style first act, incorporating folk songs that do not quite fit, with a through-composed second act (which Beecham saw as almost Wagnerian in its method). Nonetheless, she deserves credit for at least trying, as her career progressed, to incorporate British social themes and musical styles and to move away from the German that she had absorbed in her youth.

Smyth was closely involved with Emmeline Pankhurst and the suffragette movement. She wrote a rousing piece, 'The March of the Women' – to, it has to be added, excruciating lyrics – which became the movement's anthem. In 1913, she served two months in Holloway Prison for breaking windows in the service of the cause. One of her regular visitors while she was in prison was Thomas Beecham, who told the story of arriving there to find her fellow suffragettes marching round the prison yard singing their song, while Smyth conducted their performance from an upper window with a toothbrush. Beecham described her as stubborn, indomitable and unconquerable.[2] In later life, she went deaf, and became famous for wearing wigs and a kind of tricorn hat.

Another opera composer of the same period was Edward German

(1862–1936; real name German Edward Jones). Much more of an establishment figure than Ethel Smyth, Edward German should really have been the
natural successor to Sullivan, at least as far as operetta was concerned. A
student at the RAM and a visitor rather than a student in Germany in the
late 1880s, he wrote early works in a number of genres, including two
symphonies, but it was in 1888, when he was appointed musical director of
London's Globe Theatre, that he found his métier. His incidental music for
Shakespeare's plays, some of it later arranged into orchestral suites, is a
kind of stylised version of what Tudor music might have sounded like, and
proved immensely popular. Although less academic in his approach than
most of the other British composers who were influenced by the revival of
interest in Tudor music in the period before and after the turn of the
century, Edward German's music was a product of the same impulse – a
successful, imperial nation looking back and reassessing its past as a means
of shaping its future. His response was theatrical rather than scholarly.

In 1899, attempting to fill the gap left by the end of the collaboration
between Gilbert and Sullivan, Carte commissioned a comic opera from
Sullivan to a libretto by a former army captain called Basil Hood. *The Rose
of Persia* was a moderate success and Sullivan had already begun writing a
follow up, *The Emerald Isle, or, The Caves of Carrig-Cleena,* when he died.
German was asked to complete it and did so with some success. It ran for
over two hundred performances at the Savoy Theatre in 1901 and was given
successfully in New York the following year. But whereas *The Rose of Persia*
had been a pale imitation of Gilbert and Sullivan – even down to a patter
song – German's undeniable feel for the theatre turned *The Emerald Isle*
into something lighter and less satirical with a strong sense of Irish music
and dance; something, although the distinction is a fine one, closer to
operetta than comic opera.

German's next work, again with a libretto by Hood, was the one which
has perpetuated his name, *Merrie England* (1902). The score combines
all the 'mock Tudor' features of his incidental music, with fine melodies
and clever tunes – some catchy ('It is the Merry Month of May'), some
romantic ('The English Rose'), some stirring ('The Yeoman of England') –
and highly effective orchestration. The story is set at the court of Queen
Elizabeth I and asserts its Englishness through English springtime lyrics
and a plot that manages to include every English mythical figure from St
George to Herne the Hunter and Robin Hood. It is a charming piece of
nonsense which was hugely popular both in London and on tour in the

provinces. Like many of the Gilbert and Sullivan operas, which it naturally resembles to some extent, it was taken up enthusiastically by amateur companies and remained popular among them right up to the 1950s. In 1953, the year of Queen Elizabeth II's Coronation, it has been estimated that there were at least five hundred amateur productions. The follow-up, *Tom Jones* (1907), based on Henry Fielding's eighteenth-century novel, has a better plot, a better libretto and a greater sense of musical coherence. It was premiered in Manchester before transferring to London's Apollo Theatre, but, while a more sophisticated and satisfying work, it did not achieve the long-term popularity of *Merrie England*.

Like Elgar, who is known to have admired his music, Edward German's period of greatest popularity coincided with the Edwardian era. He collaborated with Gilbert on *Fallen Fairies* (1909), but the piece was a failure and after that he composed very little. He did, however, remain a very visible and popular figure, both through his conducting and because of his interest in the new discipline of recorded music. An indication of how influential he remained is given by the fact that he was knighted in 1928 and awarded the Royal Philharmonic Society's Gold Medal in 1934. German's orchestral music is very rarely heard, but pieces such as *The Seasons* (1899), *Theme and Six Diversions* (1899) and *Welsh Rhapsody* (1904), while they lack the depth of Elgar's music, do hint at the same romantic and pastoral yearning. If he had been born twenty years later, German would almost certainly have composed film music. As it is, his neat, effective, tuneful compositions look forward to the school of British light orchestral music, which would become popular and commercially successful in the first half of the twentieth century with the works of men such as Charles Ancliffe (1880–1952), Eric Coates (1886–1957) and Frederick Curzon (1899–1973).

In the traditional view of the English Musical Renaissance, Ethel Smyth is seen as at best peripheral, and Edward German is rarely mentioned at all. Yet, in their different ways, their operas – particularly, *The Wreckers* and *Merrie England* – show the beginnings of an impulse to establish, or perhaps disinter, a native tradition of English music. This impulse, the first stirrings of the concept of 'national music', was something new. However much his music might express the idea of Englishness, creating a national music was not something that would have motivated Elgar. Delius, with his more cosmopolitan outlook, would no doubt have been aware of the idea, but he was simply too cosmopolitan for it to take a place in his thinking. It would, however, become a significant factor in the works of younger composers – men such as Granville Bantock, Holst, Rutland Boughton, George Butterworth, and, above all, Vaughan Williams. Yet within the British Isles, it was the Scots – always more at ease with their national identity – not the English, who led the way in this respect. Mackenzie did not begin the process of incorporating Scottish folk tunes into classical music, but he certainly moved it forward, and, in doing so, provided an example and a stimulus to a series of younger, and now largely neglected or forgotten, Scottish composers.

81   Scotland, Ireland, and Wales

William Wallace (1860–1940) studied medicine in Edinburgh, Glasgow, Paris and Vienna, qualifying as an ophthalmic surgeon and practising for short while in London before, in 1889, giving up the medical profession for music. He spent a year at the RAM – his only formal training – shortly after Mackenzie was appointed Principal, and thereafter devoted himself to composing and writing about music. He was much influenced by Liszt and Wagner, and at a time when the debate between the merits of 'programme' and 'abstract' music was raging, he was very much a programme composer. Almost all his works have descriptive titles and, if not the first British composer to write a symphonic poem, he was the first for whom it was the natural mode of expression. Two of his most successful essays in that particular genre – *The Passing of Beatrice* (1892) and *Villon* (1909) – have subjects drawn from medieval European culture, while many of his other works draw on Scottish themes, making use of Scottish tunes and Scottish harmonies. These include the symphonic poem based on the life and reputation of his namesake, *William Wallace 1305–1905* (1905); the overture, *In Praise of Scottish Poesie* (1894); and various choral and vocal works, *Freebooter Songs* (1899), *Jacobite Songs* (1900), *The Outlaw* (1908), and *The Massacre of the Macpherson* (1910). Wallace's *Creation Symphony*, premiered in 1899 at one of Granville Bantock's concerts in New Brighton (of which more later), deserves to be better known. Bantock regularly tried to give a hearing to works which the royal colleges and their professors saw as too modern or too progressive. The *Creation Symphony* certainly fitted the bill. Influenced by both Wagner and Wallace's study of numerology, it is a fascinating work, uneven perhaps but, given that it was written ten years before Elgar's First Symphony, showing considerable courage and invention. Wallace's orchestral works can also recall Mahler, but it is doubtful whether he would have heard any of Mahler's work at the time he wrote them.

Learmont Drysdale (1866–1909) began his musical career as a church organist in Edinburgh's Greenside. In 1887, he moved to London and took an organist's position in Kensington so that he could study at the RAM under Corder and Mackenzie. He returned to Scotland in 1904 and taught briefly at Glasgow's Athenaeum School of Music, but died five years later, aged just forty-three. Forgotten now, Scottish-inspired works such as the ballade, *The Spirit of the Glen*, and the overtures, *Through the Sound of Raasay* and *Tam o'Shanter*, were all premiered between 1889 and 1890, and were widely praised at the time. His tone poem, *A Border Romance* was commissioned by Henry Wood for one of his 1904 Queen's Hall Promenade Concerts.

Hamish MacCunn (1868–1916) came from a rich and influential background: his father was a prosperous shipowner while his mother had been taught by Sterndale Bennett. He attended the RCM from its opening in 1883, but left without taking a diploma, although he did later become Professor of Harmony at the RAM under Mackenzie. After Sullivan's death in 1900, he became the chief conductor at the Savoy Theatre, presiding over the first performance of Edward German's *Merrie England*. MacCunn's chief source of inspiration seems to have been the works of Sir Walter Scott, and he took on the role of a nationalist composer – in a cultural not a political sense – exploiting a particular lyrical and romantic vision of Scotland which is not dissimilar to that of Scott. This is reflected in orchestral works, such as *The Dowie Dens of Yarrow* and *Highland Memories*; in vocal and choral works, such as *Bonny Kilmeny*, *The Lay of the Last Minstrel*, and *Four Scottish Traditional Border Ballads*; and in the opera, *Jeanie Deans* (1894), based on *Heart of Midlothian*, which is sometimes spoken of as MacCunn's best work. The work for which he is best remembered today is the light, romantic overture, *The Land of the Mountain and the Flood* (1887), the title of which is taken from Scott's *Lay of the Last Minstrel*. Although in some respects a rather thin work, *The Mountain and the Flood* benefits from an attractive and memorable – if poorly developed – main theme, and in some quarters has become almost an anthem of Scottishness.

John (later Sir John) Blackwood McEwen (1868–1948) was born in Hawick in the Scottish Borders. Initially, he went to Glasgow to study, but then moved to London to attend the RAM. Returning to Scotland, he worked as an organist and taught at the Glasgow Athenaeum before, in 1898, being called south again by Mackenzie, who appointed him Professor of Harmony and Composition at the Academy. In 1924, he succeeded Mackenzie as Principal, a position he held for the next twelve years until his retirement. He gained the knighthood and the doctorates that went with a successful musical-academic career; and he was also a much-respected teacher – Arnold Bax was one of his students. Such academic respectability should not, however, obscure the fact that he was an ambitious, skilled and prolific composer. He was a more finished composer than the other three Scots that we have considered so far in this chapter, and, although he never achieved the recognition he sought, it was with him that this upwelling of Scottish music, sometimes called the Scottish Revival, reached its high point.

McEwen kept away from the operatic stage, but wrote extensively in most other genres. He was at his most effective when writing orchestral and chamber music. Like the other three Scots, he was a romantic, but his was a controlled romanticism. The influence of Liszt and Wagner is apparent; so is that of Dvořák, and sometimes also Debussy, but McEwen developed a style of his own, richly harmonic, often reflective, and, in the larger works, characterised by a wonderfully visual sense of orchestration. Much of his inspiration came from the Scottish landscape, particularly the landscape of the Scottish Borders where he was born, although both his piano and his chamber music do also sometimes draw on his love of France. McEwen's best orchestral works are his tone poems, music which is descriptive of mood and location rather than offering a strict programme. *Grey Galloway* (1908) is particularly successful in this respect, with a tight-knit, three-part structure based on original but Scottish-sounding themes, evoking the natural beauty and drama of the Galloway hills and coastline. Together with its earlier, although less convincing, companion pieces, *The Demon Lover* and *Coronach*, it forms part of *Three Border Ballads*, in which McEwen was clearly moving towards the idea of a symphonic unity based on his evocations of mood and place; only *Grey Galloway* and *Coronach* were ever performed in his lifetime. In 1909, he took this concept a stage further with *A Solway Symphony*, an impressive and imaginative work, also with a three-part structure, each movement of which has a title ('Spring Tide', 'Moonlight', 'The Sou'west Wind'), inspired by the landscape and the coast of South-West Scotland. Sadly, the symphony went unplayed until

1922, a failure which seems to have had a serious impact on his confidence and may have contributed to a nervous breakdown. Indeed, after *A Solway Symphony*, he wrote only two major orchestral works: *Hills o' Heather*, written towards the end of the First World War, a deeply reflective and elegiac piece for cello and orchestra, again highly evocative of landscape, which stands up well in comparison with Stanford's *Third Irish Rhapsody*; and *Where the Wild Thyme Grows*, another landscape-inspired tone poem.

McEwen's best chamber music is to be found in his string quartets, of which he wrote seventeen, and the best of these were written after he had failed to make headway with his orchestral works. His String Quartet no. 6 (*Biscay*; 1913), written in France where he went to recover from his break-down, is an attractive work in his preferred three-movement form, each movement having a descriptive title: 'Le phare', 'Les dunes', 'La racleuse'. His next string quartet, no. 7, entitled *Threnody* and written in 1916, is another wartime work. Dark, moving, deceptively simple, and with a last movement based on the old Scottish lament, 'Flowers of the Forest', it is a neglected gem of string-quartet writing.

It is perhaps too much to describe these four composers as constituting a distinct 'Scottish school' – not least because they were all forced to go down to London in order to make a successful musical career – but their careers and their music do demonstrate an essential difference between Scotland and England at the time. Both countries went through a period of musical revival to which traditional music and aspects of folk culture were important contributing factors – the Scottish revival to some extent predating that in England. Scotland, however, as we have already noted, was more at ease with its national and cultural identity. Traditional music was more widely known, played and accepted as a normal part of the cultural life of the country. As a result, the use made of it by Mackenzie, Wallace, Drysdale, MacCunn and McEwen represented development and continuity rather than revolution or radical change. While this made it easier for them to establish their own national – and essentially Romantic – idiom, it also meant that their work had less of a transformational impact than parallel developments in England.

Irish national music was, initially at least, embodied in Stanford, and in men such as Joseph Robinson, Arthur O'Leary, and Charles Wood (1866–1926), the songwriter and composer of church music, who taught at both Cambridge University and the RCM, numbering Vaughan Williams, Herbert Howells and Arthur Bliss among his students. Their music was culturally, rather than politically assertive. However, as time moved on and the Irish situation grew ever more volatile, the political element began to grow. In Ireland alone of the four nations of the United Kingdom, certain composers began to associate music with the struggle for independence. Robert O'Dwyer (1862–1949), for example, although born in Bristol, became one of the leading Irish nationalist composers. His *Eithne*, completed in 1909, was the first full-scale opera written in Irish Gaelic, and he also wrote many Gaelic choral works. Thomas O'Brien Butler (1861–1915; his original surname appears to have been Whitwell), also wrote an Irish-language opera, *Muirgheis*. Yet these were minor figures. No Irish composer ever came close to the kind of identification with the national identity or the national struggle achieved by Grieg, Dvořák or Sibelius.

Wales, too, had its own music. There was a strong choral tradition, based on Methodism and, later, reinforced by the temperance movement, which led to the foundation of the Temperance Choral Union in 1854. The involvement of ordinary people was stimulated by the Tonic Sol-fa movement, which was particularly strong in South Wales. The choirs that came out of these movements held festivals and competitions, concentrating on hymns and other religious music. At the same time, beginning in the 1850s, a revival of interest in traditional Welsh music and traditional Welsh musical forms led to the foundation in 1860 of the National Eisteddfod Society. Regional and even national eisteddfodau had been held in the past, but the Society provided a new focus for Welsh music. Its first event was held in Aberdare in 1861 and a National Eisteddfod has been held almost every year since. The main focus of such gatherings is on traditional Welsh forms that are often closely associated with poetry – forms such as *penillion* or *cerdd dant*, where words in strict metre are improvised over a folk melody – but during the 1890s and the first decade of the twentieth century, oratorios, cantatas and orchestral works were also performed. The eisteddfod tradition spread to the United States where the Welsh emigrant population used music as a way of expressing and maintaining its identity.

An important figure in reviving and raising the profile of Welsh music was the harpist, John Thomas (1826–1913), who taught at the RCM and the Guildhall School of Music, and was, from 1872, Queen Victoria's official harpist. Thomas was also a composer. Among his compositions were two harp concertos and two cantatas, *Llewellyn* and *The Bride of Neath Valley*, both of which became popular with Welsh choral societies. He also published a series of four volumes entitled *Welsh Melodies, with Welsh and*

English Poetry, in collaboration with the Welsh poet and architect John Jones. Joseph Parry (1841–1903)[1] was another important figure. Born in Merthyr Tydfil, he was a child labourer in the coal mines from the age of nine and spent his adolescent years working in an iron works in the United States. These were desperately unpromising beginnings, but he managed to obtain an education in music through the eisteddfod tradition. He eventually received a doctorate in music from Cambridge University and went on to become Professor of Music at Cardiff University, where he was known as 'The Great Doctor'. Among his many compositions was the opera, *Blodwen* (1878), the first ever written to a Welsh-language libretto. In the period up to the turn of the twentieth century, it was performed over five hundred times, mainly in Wales and the United States, although there were several performances in London. He also wrote the music for the famous Welsh ballad 'Myfanwy'.

The composer and conductor David Protheroe (1866–1934) came from a younger generation. Born in Cwmgiedd near Ystradgynlais, he, too, emigrated to the United States when still young. He received a doctorate from the University of Toronto and helped develop Welsh music in North America. Although he never returned to live in Wales, he visited frequently, became an important figure in the eisteddfod movement and wrote a number of Welsh-language works. Yet, despite figures such as these, Welsh music remained inward-looking. It never found a champion of the stature of Stanford or Mackenzie or McEwen, and, as a consequence, never achieved the kind of synthesis with the broader classical tradition that Scottish and Irish music did. Traditional Welsh music certainly benefitted from the National Eisteddfod Society, but in Britain – as in the United States – interest was largely confined to Welsh communities.

After the First World War, Walford Davies (1869–1941) was one of the most active figures in promoting musical life in Wales. In the twenty years before 1914, he had been an active and prolific composer, particularly of large-scale choral works. After the First World War, his main concerns tended to be academic and organisational. From 1919 to 1926, he was Professor of Music at Aberystwyth; and he was Chairman of the Welsh Council for Music from its inception in 1918 until his death in 1941. One feature of the 1920 Eisteddfod, with which he was involved, was an attempt to inject new life into Welsh music by holding a competition for a tone poem, or a work for chorus and orchestra. Walford Davies and Vaughan Williams were the judges, but the results were disappointing. Looked at from a contemporary perspective, the main, lasting Welsh contribution to British music during this period is really to be found in hymn tunes, such as *Cwm Rhondda*, written by John Hughes (1873–1932) and sung as 'Guide me, O thou great Jehovah';[2] or Joseph Parry's *Aberystwyth*, which provides the tune for Charles Wesley's words 'Jesus, Lover of My Soul' and also the basis for the South African national anthem, 'Nkosi Sikelel' iAfrika'.

82   National Music

The issue of 'national music' and its emergence at the zenith of British imperial power in the years on either side of the turn of the twentieth century was both complex in itself and complicated by external factors. In Continental Europe, national music as an aspect of the rising tide of cultural nationalism was already a recognised phenomenon. British musicians and British audiences would have known the work of a number of composers who made use of folk tunes, folk tales and mythologies to create music with a distinct national character: Smetana and Dvořák in the Czech provinces of the Austro-Hungarian Empire; Grieg in Swedish-ruled Norway; Sibelius in the Finnish provinces of the Russian Empire; Albéniz in Spain. In Britain, national music emerged out of the Renaissance period (and here the Renaissance has definitely to be seen as British, not just English). It was a part of the Renaissance in that it represented a shift of musical focus, and might even be described as a second stage – although, given the overlapping lives of the generations of musicians, chronology is not a good guide. By putting a new value on roots and origins, the idea of national music certainly sought to establish a new and different continuity from that which had previously underpinned British classical music; and in so doing, it went a long way towards defining the musical agenda for subsequent generations.

National music from the Continent was widely heard in Britain from the 1880s onwards. Grieg's music became popular at that time. The Piano Concerto was premiered by Dannreuther at the Crystal Palace as early as 1874. Manns, Hallé, Richter, Henry Wood, and Dan Godfrey, the founder of the Bournemouth Municipal (later Bournemouth Symphony) Orchestra, all promoted his music, and by the time he gave his first concert at the London St James's Hall in May 1888, his name was enough to guarantee packed houses. In all, Grieg made five visits to Britain between 1888 and 1906 – several more were cancelled because of his poor health – and the Piano Concerto, the *Holberg Suite*, and the *Peer Gynt Suite no. 1* all appeared regularly on concert programmes. Dvořák was another 'nationalist' composer whose music was widely known. Enthusiasm for his music began in 1883, when Joseph Barnby (whom we have met as a composer of church music during the Anglican revival) conducted a performance of the *Stabat Mater* at the Royal Albert Hall. This was followed a few months later by a performance of the Piano Concerto under Manns with Oscar Beringer as soloist; and the following year, Dvořák made the first of his nine visits to Britain. His popularity was even greater than Grieg's. All the leading conductors – Manns, Mackenzie, Hallé, Wood, Richter – programmed his works. The cantata, *The Spectre's Bride*, was written for the Birmingham Festival in 1885; the oratorio, *St Ludmila*, for Leeds in 1886; the great Symphony no. 7 in G for the Philharmonic Society in 1890.[1] All his major works, including the symphonic poems based on Czech folk tales – *The Spinning Wheel*, *The Water Goblin*, *The Noon Witch* – were heard in Britain in the period up to the end of the century. Albéniz lived in London between 1889 and 1893. He gave orchestral concerts in the capital and toured widely as both pianist and accompanist. His heavily Spanish-influenced programmes were seen as exotic and proved very popular, but his attempt at operetta, *The Magic Opal* (later *The Magic Ring*) was not a great success. It attracted moderate audiences in the provinces, but in London it flopped, losing its backers a lot of money. Sibelius, whose music was (or was interpreted as) more overtly politically nationalist than that of Grieg or Dvořák, attracted significant attention and interest in Britain, beginning with a performance of his incidental music to the play *King Christian II* given by Henry Wood at the 1901 Proms. He visited four times in the years before the First World War – his tone poem, *Luonnotar*, was given its world premiere at the 1913 Three Choirs Festival under Sir Herbert Brewer – and once more in 1921. His particular champions were Granville Bantock, Henry Wood, and the critic and Wagner biographer, Ernest Newman. The British public was well disposed towards Sibelius's music. His more romantic works – the First and Second Symphonies, and the tone poems, both those drawn from Finnish mythology such as *Pohjola's Daughter* and *The Swan of Tuonela*, and those with a less defined programme such as *Finlandia*, *En Saga* and *The Oceanides* – gave audiences what they expected and were immediately popular. Other works –

the neo-classical Third Symphony, and the dense, much bleaker Fourth – were greeted with respect rather than enthusiasm.

There is no doubt that such nationalist composers had an influence on music in Britain. Grieg influenced both Delius and Percy Grainger, who, though an Australian, played an important role in shaping the English Folk Revival. Dvořák's influence was less than his popularity might lead one to expect. It can be heard at times in Elgar's orchestral works, but the British composer who most resembled Dvořák, both in his quest for a balanced romanticism and in his ability to write with equal power for both orchestra and string quartet, was probably McEwen. However, it was Sibelius, with his capacity to evolve themes and his unique sound world, who had the greatest influence on British composers in the early decades of the twentieth century – on Vaughan Williams, Granville Bantock, Arnold Bax, E.J. Moeran and Edmund Rubbra, among others. Such influences were naturally a factor, in some cases an important factor, in the development of British music, but their impact was diminished by the very different social and political context in which British composers worked.

By 1900, German music had been the dominant influence on British music for longer than anyone alive could remember. What Handel and the Hanoverian kings had begun, Mendelssohn and Prince Albert had perpetuated, but they were long dead, and it was now simply time for a change. A new generation of composers had grown up secure in the knowledge that Britain was the world's greatest imperial power, and now sought, consciously or unconsciously, to demonstrate the riches and the relevance of their own culture. At the same time, political assertiveness on the part of the new German Empire was beginning to affect Anglo-German relations – the German pro-Boer stance which affected the premiere of Ethel Smyth's *Der Wald* was just one small example – leading to a sense that it was time to assert Britain's cultural and musical difference. As we have seen, that difference emerged differently in each of the four nations of the United Kingdom, according to their individual character and circumstances.

In England, the emergence of national music was a slow process – certainly slower than in Scotland or Ireland. In part, this was because German musical dominance was more marked in England than elsewhere; but in part also it was because England, as the dominant partner among the four nations making up imperial Britain, was less certain of the identity it wanted national music to express, and because it had a different and more complex relationship with its folk tradition. We have already seen how folk songs and ballads played an important part in reflecting social change during the Napoleonic Wars and the period of industrialisation that followed. And it was continuing social change in the urban and industrial areas of the country that provided the basis for growth and evolution of the folk tradition – at least until the second half of the century when it was gradually eclipsed, and its function as an expression of social conditions overtaken, by music hall. Late nineteenth-century romanticism, however, did not recognise the value of – or in many cases the existence of – an urban aspect to the folk tradition, focussing all its attention on rural song and dance and craft, moribund though they were rapidly becoming. It was on this rural tradition that the English folk-song collectors, whose approach was romantic rather than sociological or scientific, concentrated; and it was from this tradition that the majority of the younger English composers, whose approach was also essentially romantic, drew their inspiration.

The rediscovery of folk music was fundamental to the development of national music in England. Just as Thomas Hardy chronicled the decline of the old rural ways in his novels, so the collectors and composers noted down and published details of the rapidly disappearing old songs and dances. In both cases, the effect was not only to preserve much which might otherwise have been lost, but also to spread some level of awareness and knowledge of these traditions among other sections of society. Most of Hardy's readers were from the urban middle classes; so, too, were those who played the carefully-arranged folk songs or danced the reconstructed folk dances. This was the beginning of what was to prove a long process of breaking down the barriers of class and snobbery that had placed a greater distance between the folk tradition and middle class audiences in England than in other parts of the United Kingdom.

83   The Folk Revival, and the Tudor Revival

The Reverend John Broadwood (1798–1864), a grandson of John Broadwood the piano maker, was the first of the new breed of collectors. Ballads and folk songs had, of course, been collected for generations. The difference was Broadwood's attempt, in his slim, 1847 volume *Old English Songs*, to make a precise record of what he heard. The title page proudly proclaims the tunes to be 'exactly as they are now sung, to rescue them from oblivion and to afford a specimen of genuine Old English Melody', and the words 'in their original Rough State with an occasional slight alteration to render the sense intelligible.'[1] John Broadwood's niece Lucy Broadwood (1858–1929) was inspired by his example and began to make her own contribution in the 1890s. She republished her uncle's work; she collected songs in Cornwall with the Reverend Sabine Baring-Gould (1834–1924); and she worked with Fuller Maitland on the highly influential volume, *English County Songs* (1893). In 1898 she was one of the founders of the English Folk Song Society and became a leading administrator of the new folk music establishment. She later also helped organise Vaughan Williams's Leith Hill Festival in Surrey. Best known these days for the words to 'Onward! Christian Soldiers!', Baring-Gould was another stalwart of the new folk establishment; so was the Leeds-based collector Frank Kidson (1855–1926); but the central figure in the rediscovery and market-ing – for that is what it amounted to – of traditional music and traditional dance was undoubtedly Cecil Sharp (1859–1924). It was not a position he attained by being first in the field, or even by any particular claim to origi-nality, but rather by sheer sustained effort and the almost missionary fervour he brought to his work.

Sharp received a good basic musical education at Uppingham School but was neither an infant prodigy nor a musical genius. He read mathemat-ics at Cambridge, although music (everything from studying Wagner to playing the ocarina) seems to have occupied much of his time. He gradu-ated in 1882, whereupon his father – a London slate merchant with histori-cal and artistic interests – packed him off to Australia to make his own way in the world. Arriving in Adelaide, he cleaned hansom cabs, worked in a bank and then in a lawyer's office, but gravitated ever closer to the musical world, directing choirs and choral societies and eventually becoming joint Director of the Adelaide College of Music. He made a couple of return trips to England (during one of which he had a serious bout of typhoid) when he tried, and failed, to find a job that would support him while he studied music properly. At the end of 1891, even though he was no nearer achieving his aim of a full-time musical career, he decided to leave Australia for good. Back in London, he inhabited the fringes of the musical world, trying to compose, which he did without great success, apparently imitating Schumann, until in 1893 he took up teaching, first at Ludgrove School and later at Hampstead Conservatoire of Music.

By his own account, Sharp's awakening to folk music involved two road-to-Damascus moments. The first was on a snowy Boxing Day in 1899 when, staying in the village of Headington just outside Oxford, he encountered the local Morris men dancing 'Laudanum Bunches', 'Constant Billy' and 'The Rigs of Marlow'. By the end of the nineteenth century, Morris dancing, essentially a rural practice and consequently much affected by rapid industrialisation, was in deep decline – so much so that no more than half-a-dozen sides (as they are known) can claim to have existed and performed throughout the nineteenth century without interruption. Sharp's subsequent championing of the Morris marked the beginning of a period that saw the revival of old sides and the formation of new ones. By 1934, the movement had grown to the point where a national association, the Morris Ring, was formed; and the decades since the 1950s have seen interest in all forms of folk dancing rise to new heights. The Morris Ring is now an association of a hundred and fifty Morris, sword-dancing and mummers clubs, which jealously guards standards of music and performance. Yet even that figure does not truly represent the level of involvement and enthusiasm. There are over seven hundred sides practising the kind of dances represented by the Morris Ring, and many others which promote and practise Scottish and Irish dancing. Traditional Welsh dancing, like traditional Welsh music, has its adherents, its champions and its practitioners in Wales, but has not developed a wider following.

Sharp's second epiphany took place in Hambridge in Somerset, when staying at the home of his friend, the Reverend Charles Marson (the history of the Folk Revival is littered with enthusiastic vicars) in September 1903. Marson's gardener was singing 'The Seeds of Love' as he mowed the lawn. Sharp noted down the tune and the words, harmonised the song and it was performed that same evening around the Reverend Marson's piano. It was on this occasion that one of the audience likened Sharp's arrangement to putting the song into evening dress. At the time, the remark was not intended to be derogatory, but it is often used to describe the process by which classical arrangers of folk song – musicians as diverse as Vaughan Williams, Grainger, Moeran and Benjamin Britten – manage to distance folk song from its origins by formalising it. Such a criticism cannot be wholly denied, but does not diminish the quality of the music. Nor does it answer the point that without the folk-song collectors and arrangers a vast amount of folk music would almost certainly not have survived in any form at all.

Sharp's subsequent career was an almost unbroken sequence of lectures, campaigns, collaborations, new societies, travelling, song collecting and publishing – all in the service of the cause. In 1905, Mary Neal, a friend and disciple of Sharp's, began teaching Morris dancing to the girls in her Espérance Club, an organisation that aimed to improve the lives of working girls in London. The initiative was a success and gave Sharp the confidence to begin publishing his *Morris Book* (in five volumes, 1907–13). This was followed by *The Country Dance Book* (six volumes, 1909–22) and *Sword Dances of Northern England* (three volumes, 1909–13). In 1911, he founded the English Folk Dance Society, which was intended to parallel and complement the Folk Song Society; the two organisations merged in 1932 to become the English Folk Dance and Song Society, which still flourishes and has its headquarters in Cecil Sharp House just north of London's Regent's Park. No one since John Playford, in the seventeenth century, had taken such a close interest in English dance forms. Indeed, *The English Dancing Master* provided the basis for parts of *The Country Dance Book*, but Sharp was both more systematic and more detailed in his approach.

In the aftermath of the First World War and through the interwar years, folk dancing achieved a level of popularity that would have seemed impossible in the pre-war years. It became a symbol of hope and renewal after the horrors of the war. It was part of the rehabilitation programmes for wounded soldiers. It featured in the Peace Day celebrations in Hyde Park. It became part of YMCA programmes. It was encouraged by the clubs, organisations and communal movements, many of them connected with outdoor activities, that were fashionable in the 1930s. In part, this was obviously a question of zeitgeist, but it would not have happened without the relentless popularising efforts of Sharp and his collaborators.

At the same time as he was studying and recording dance forms, Sharp was also collecting folk songs: initially in Somerset, then across Dorset and other parts of West and South-West England. In the twenty years between his Hambridge awakening and his death in 1924, he collected almost 5,000 songs. Nearly 3,000 were from England, while of the remainder more than 1,500 came from the United States; in particular, from the Appalachian Mountains where Sharp, accompanied by his collaborator (and later biographer) Maud Karpeles, spent a year travelling in remote areas and often under difficult conditions.

Sharp's Appalachian trip broke new ground: it produced a rich harvest of new songs, as well as many versions and variants of songs already

collected in England, and over the years it has provided material for count-
less academic studies, but song-collecting was not what initially led him to
visit the United States. His first visit, in 1914, was at the invitation of the
actor, director and critic, Harley Granville-Barker, who was mounting a
production of *A Midsummer Night's Dream* in New York and wanted
Sharp's assistance to ensure the authenticity of the songs and dances. In
this, Granville-Barker was probably influenced by the fact that the United
States was enjoying its own version of the Folk Revival. A key figure was
Elizabeth Burchenal (1876–1959). Her passion for all kinds of folk dancing
led to Scottish and Irish dances being taught in American schools, and to
huge dance festivals, such as that staged in Brooklyn's Borough Park in 1910
involving 10,000 schoolgirls. The English Folk Revival had also made itself
felt in the United States in the years before 1914 through the Fuller Sisters –
a trio of young English girls who toured widely, performing programmes
of songs and dances put together by their brother, Walter Fuller, who had
himself been inspired by Sharp's 1907 publication, *English Folk Song: Some
Conclusions*.[2] The result of all this was that when Sharp arrived, although
barely aware of American folk songs (he had to be told about them by
Rosalind, one of the Fuller Sisters), he found a section of the American
public already receptive to his ideas, so he was able to spread the word and
earn much-needed money giving public lectures.

Sharp's approach was that of a teacher and an academic. He was also a
creator and supporter of institutions. And the broader folk movement – to
distinguish it from the impact on classical musicians – flourished through
institutions. Sharp was an enthusiast, a missionary. He could harmonise a
song, and he might perform in order to illustrate a lecture, but his influence on British music – which was, and continues to be, immense – derives
from the huge number of songs he collected, arranged and published. Of
the many composers of the period who were influenced by folk music –
and whose work we shall consider in subsequent chapters – some came to
the folk tradition independently and some through the work of Sharp and
his collaborators, but they all acknowledged the value of his contribution.
Sharp's name featured more prominently than any other collector in what
has been termed the Second Folk Revival in the 1950s, 60s and 70s. Yet he
has not been an uncontroversial figure. The second half of the twentieth
century saw an extended and sometimes heated debate about the true
nature of the folk tradition, as well as about the impact and social implications of the collectors and their work. Sharp, as the most prominent among

them, has attracted more criticism than the others.[3] The details of such a debate are outside the scope of this study. It is enough to note that during the early decades of the twentieth century, the Folk Revival, whatever its essential nature, exerted an influence both on the classical tradition and on music at the most basic, popular level. Just as it became normal for composers to arrange folk songs and to draw on folk tunes in their orchestral works, so it became commonplace to find folk music on the school curriculum, featuring in Boy Scout sing-songs, and used as the basis for dance classes up and down the country.

At the time that the Folk Revival was gaining momentum, so, too, was what is generally referred to as the Tudor Revival, although it also encompassed music from the early Stuart period. This was a revival of a very different character in that it had little popular application. For the most part, its impact was limited to church music, composers in the classical tradition, and scattered groups of madrigal singers. Interest in the music of earlier centuries had been growing for some time. We have seen how a string of composers from Attwood to Stanford had pressed the claims of Bach (reflecting both Bach's genius and the German orientation of British music throughout the nineteenth century). There were stirrings of interest in early British music as far back as the 1840s when the Musical Antiquarian Society had published a series of volumes of works by Byrd, Gibbons, Dowland, Wilbye, Morley, Purcell and others. But it was the publication of *Grove's Dictionary* that really changed things. The articles Grove commissioned, and sometimes wrote, created an awareness of what we now call early music, and in particular of sixteenth- and seventeenth-century British music – and of its historical importance – that had simply not existed before.

The impact was profound and rapid. The last volume of the *Dictionary* was published in 1889. In 1893, Fuller Maitland published his *English Carols of the Fifteenth Century*; a year later, he published the first of two volumes of *The Fitzwilliam Virginal Book*, jointly edited with Barclay Squire. The second appeared in 1899. Both projects were ground-breaking. By 1896, Richard Runciman Terry (1865–1938), a former Cambridge choral scholar, had converted to Catholicism and become Director of Music at Downside, the famous Benedictine school in Somerset. There, he set about bringing back the Latin liturgical settings of composers such as Taverner, Tallis and Byrd, as well as those of Continental masters. These works were eventually made available in choir-friendly arrangements as *Downside Motets* (1901) and *Downside Masses* (1905). In 1901, Terry became the first Master of Music at the newly-built Westminster Cathedral, where his work was hugely influential. Plainsong and polyphony, the works of English, Italian and Flemish composers from the sixteenth century, were all now regularly heard at services in central London. Stanford famously told his students that they could hear Palestrina for tuppence: the cost of a bus ticket from the RCM to Westminster. Yet, for all his scholarship and commitment to the music of the past, Terry was not in any sense opposed to modern music. Many of the new generation of composers – Vaughan Williams, Holst, Bax, Herbert Howells – were influenced by what he was doing and wrote music for the Westminster Cathedral choir. Terry played a major role in changing attitudes to early music, but he was also a difficult and combative personality and was eventually forced to leave Westminster Cathedral because of his increasingly erratic behaviour.

While Terry was reviving the church music of the sixteenth and seventeenth centuries, Edmund Horace Fellowes (1870–1951) was doing the same for the secular music of the period. Fellowes was a less imaginative man than Terry, but made up for it by sheer application and hard work. Between 1913 and 1924, he published *The English Madrigal School* in thirty-six volumes, making works by Morley, Weelkes, Wilbye, Gibbons, Tomkins and others accessible once again. This was followed, between 1920 and 1932, by *The English School of Lutenist Song-Writers* in thirty-two volumes. And as if that were not enough, he also published works on Gibbons and Byrd, wrote what became the standard historical work on English cathedral music, and was one of the editors of the seminal, ten-volume edition of *Tudor Church Music*, which was published in 1929. (Terry was the original series editor, but was replaced after he suffered a breakdown.) Fellowes was more academic in his approach than Terry, and more narrowly focussed on English music, but was certainly no less influential. Both received official recognition for their work: Terry received a doctorate from Durham University and a knighthood; while Fellowes, closer to the establishment by virtue of serving as a canon at St George's Chapel, Windsor, for fifty-one years, and also by not being a Catholic, received a string of fellowships and doctorates and became a Companion of Honour. He was also interested in cricket and, in 1930, added a history of cricket at Winchester, his public school, to his already long list of publications.[4]

The figure of Arnold Dolmetsch (1858–1940) is important at this point. He provided the initial impetus for the interest in period sound and period instruments that has grown steadily in importance since the 1960s. Dolmetsch was French by birth, but it was in England in 1893, while teaching music at Dulwich College, that he became interested in reconstructing instruments from previous eras. He began with a lute, then – encouraged by members of the Arts and Crafts Movement, notably William Morris and Roger Fry – progressed to harpsichords, clavichords, recorders, viols and other 'lost' instruments. As an instrument maker, he was naturally interested in early music of all kinds, not just that from the Tudor and early Stuart period. However, he was personally responsible for reviving works written for consort of viols by William Lawes, John Jenkins, Matthew Locke, and others. Dolmetsch's insistence that, when rediscovering the music of the past, the sound of the instruments and nature of the performance were just as important as the music on the page, was new at the time and has resonated with musicians ever since. It formed the basis of his *Interpretation of the Music of the XVII and XVIII Centuries* which first appeared in 1915. Dolmetsch spent periods of time in both France and the United States, but returned to England on the outbreak of the First World War. In 1917, he set up a studio, workshop and music centre in Haslemere in Surrey, where an educational foundation still exists and an early music festival is held annually to perpetuate the ideas and ideals for which he worked.

Like the Folk Revival, the Tudor Revival developed its own momentum, continuing into the 1920s and 30s, merging with the ever-growing interest in Bach, Palestrina, Monteverdi and other early music, and becoming part of the fabric of British musical life. Dom Anselm Hughes (1889–1974) was one of those at the academic heart of that movement. He conducted detailed research into medieval polyphony, and, among many other volumes, published the series of *English Gothic Music* (1941–61), jointly edited with Percy Grainger, as well as *The Fayrfax Series of Early English Choral Music* (1949–61). William Gillies Whittaker (1871–1944) was another important figure. A musicologist, professor and composer of forgotten and now inaccessible works, he founded the Newcastle Bach Choir and, in 1924, gave the first performances of Byrd's *Great Service* for over three hundred years. He also conducted all of Bach's cantatas in a series of concerts, first in Glasgow and then in Newcastle-upon-Tyne. One of those inspired by Whittaker was Cuthbert Bates (1899–1980) who, in 1923, founded a choir called the Tudor Singers. Supported by Vaughan Williams, the choir pioneered early music on the BBC, giving broadcast performances throughout the 1930s. In the years before the Second World

War, Bates also ran what were known as Madrigal Summer Schools. Later, in 1946, he founded the Bath Bach Choir and, in 1950, the Bath Bach Festival. Men such as these, and the choirs and instrumental groups and concerts they inspired, laid the foundations of what is now a thriving early music sector, of which Tudor and early Stuart music is an integral part. The fact that BBC Radio 3 has a weekly *Early Music Show*, that York is home to the National Early Music Centre, that Scotland has its own Early Music Forum, that Galway and East Cork both host annual festivals of early music, is proof enough that what started as a minority interest has become a genuinely popular strand of musical culture throughout the British Isles.

84   Exoticism, Bantock, and Foulds

The concept of national music, the Folk Revival and the Tudor Revival were all trends or movements that evolved and grew to exercise considerable cultural influence during the period of the English Musical Renaissance. They were not the only reasons why British music was able to take new directions and develop a new identity, but individually and collectively they were clearly major contributing factors. Their influence varied widely from composer to composer. Elgar, as we have seen, was interested neither in folk music nor in the Tudor Revival; nor, however patriotic some of his works might be, did he ever seek to write music in a national style or reflecting a national identity. Vaughan Williams, on the other hand, was an active participant in the Folk Revival, was inspired by the rediscovery of Tudor music, and in 1934 wrote a book called *National Music and Other Essays*. What we can say is that all three movements were broadly contemporaneous, that they were in varying ways interrelated, and that they were all active, and often powerful, factors in the lives of the generation of composers that followed Elgar and Delius.

Born, with one or two exceptions, between 1870 and 1890, these were composers who grew to maturity, or had at least formed their view of the world and begun their careers, before the First World War. They were romantic in a very British way – something that has drawn criticism from those making comparisons with what was happening on the Continent. Their romanticism contained a strong sense of the pastoral, as well as strains of mysticism and transcendental longing, sometimes drawn from

Tudor church music, sometimes from Celtic myth and music, and sometimes from more remote oriental sources. As a generation, they were often
prolific. They excelled at the art song, at rhapsodies and romantic orchestral colouring; even those who did not espouse religion in any traditional
sense wrote sacred music; but, despite a number of gallant attempts, they
did not produce operatic works of enduring appeal and quality. They were
also numerous – too numerous for many to be given more than passing
notice in a study such as this. Taken together, their collected works may
not equal what was happening in Europe in the age of Mahler, Strauss,
Sibelius, Schoenberg and Stravinsky, but in British terms they represent a
body of musical achievement unmatched since Tudor times.

Within that broad definition, there were, of course, as many variations
of theme and style as there were individuals, but certain trends emerge.
The music of Granville Bantock (1868–1946), the oldest of this generation
of composers, shows a mixture of oriental and Celtic inspiration. Born in
London, the son of a highly-respected surgeon and gynaecologist, Bantock,
like so many other composers we have considered, had to overcome paternal opposition to a musical career. Destined first for the Indian Civil
Service and then forced to study chemical engineering, he seems to have
got his own way through sheer stubbornness, entering the RAM in 1888 at
the age of twenty. He studied under Frederick Corder, who was sufficiently
impressed to agree to write the libretto for Bantock's one-act opera,
Caedmar, set in 'Ancient Britain'. This was one of two student works taken
up by August Manns and played at the Crystal Palace. The other was the
overture to Bantock's dramatic cantata, *The Fire Worshippers* – yet another
work based on Thomas Moore's *Lalla Rookh*. However, on leaving the
Academy in 1892 Bantock found employment hard to come by. He started
the *New Musical Quarterly Review*, and then found a job as musical director with the Gaiety Company, touring light musical comedies such as *A
Gaiety Girl* and *In Town* round the provinces. Musical comedies were a
highly popular genre during the 1890s. The tour was a success. Bantock
was promoted to conductor; more comedies were added to the company's
repertoire – *The Shop Girl* and *Gentleman Joe* – and they set off on a fifteen-
month tour of the Unites States and Australia.[1] Returning to England, his
prospects seemed no brighter. He continued to conduct light music for
touring theatrical companies and, together with his brother Leedham,
wrote a music hall hit – 'Who'll Give a Penny to the Monkey?' In 1896,
swinging to the other extreme, and probably with financial help from his

father, he staged a concert of his own works at the Queen's Hall, presenting himself in the programme notes as the champion of new and radical English music. The following year, he was appointed musical director of the Tower Orchestra at New Brighton near Liverpool.

New Brighton was a tourist resort just across the River Mersey from Liverpool, and, on the face of it, this was another light music appointment, but Bantock seized his opportunity. He turned the local band into an effective orchestra, sometimes borrowing musicians from the Liverpool Philharmonic. He infiltrated Beethoven, Mozart, Wagner, Dvořák and Tchaikovsky into programmes that normally consisted of dances, romantic songs and seaside holiday music. He even gave concerts wholly devoted to new British music, including, as we have seen, the premiere of Wallace's *Creation Symphony*, as well as works by Stanford, Parry, Mackenzie, Elgar, Corder, Edward German, and Holbrooke. It was a brave agenda, and one which finally brought his qualities to the attention of the British musical establishment. In 1900, he took up a post as Principal of the Birmingham and Midland Institute School of Music, rejecting an offer to teach at the RAM in London. Birmingham was to remain the hub of his career. He succeeded Elgar as Professor of Music at Birmingham University in 1908, retaining the position until 1934. He played a decisive role in founding the City of Birmingham Symphony Orchestra, which gave its first performance in 1920 – the programme included Bantock's own overture *Saul* – and was to rise to prominence in the 1980s under Simon Rattle. Only in 1934 did he return to London – to act as Chairman of the Board of Trinity College of Music – returning to Birmingham again shortly before his death in 1946.

Bantock composed throughout his adult life and was immensely prolific. He was extremely well regarded by his fellow composers – both Sibelius and Elgar dedicated works to him – and he had fewer difficulties getting his music heard than many of his contemporaries. After about 1930, however, his music gradually fell out of fashion and remained neglected until recent years when there has been a revival of interest. He wrote very little abstract music. His work is almost always inspired – by a story, a place, or an atmosphere. He wrote works based on biblical and classical themes, such as his *Pagan Symphony*, his musical vision of Arcadia; some pieces were inspired by Shakespeare; but much of his music is characterised by a fascination with the exotic in one form or another. For some time following its composition between 1906 and 1909, Bantock's most famous work was his massive, three-part *Omar Khayyám* for soloists, chorus and orchestra. To modern ears it can seem somewhat over-long and melodramatic, but it enjoyed great popularity in its day and illustrates the fascination that oriental subjects held for him. *Two Orchestral Scenes from The Curse of Kehama* was based on an epic poem by Robert Southey concerning Hindu mythology; and the tone poem, *Thalaba the Destroyer,* was based on another Southey epic dealing with the Islamic world. There was an early opera called *The Pearl of Iran,* a choral work called *The Burden of Babylon,* a setting of James Elroy Flecker's *Golden Road to Samarkand,* a song cycle, *Five Ghazals of Hafiz,* and a suite of piano pieces called *Arabian Nights* which was dedicated to Gustav Holst. Other works, generally later in his career, took their inspiration from the Far East: poems by Ezra Pound were the basis for *Suite from Cathay,* and poems by Chinese writers for *Songs from the Chinese Poets* and *A Feast of Lanterns.* This was one strain of Bantock's exoticism. The other, closer to home, but no less exotic for a Londoner living in Birmingham, drew on the Celtic world, and in particular on the folk tales, land and seascapes of Scotland.

Bantock's enthusiasm for all things Scottish first took hold about 1910. How much was due to the fact that his paternal grandmother was Scottish (which was his preferred explanation) and how much to the spirit of the age – this was the period of W. B. Yeats and the Celtic Revival – is difficult to say, but his response was emotional, imaginative and romantic, and it produced some of his finest music. His *Hebridean Symphony,* written in 1913, is a single-movement work, rich in Celtic imagery and making use of several Scottish tunes. The music seems to emerge almost tentatively from mist and sea, gradually gathering itself into a storm and a full orchestral climax before subsiding once more into the mist. The symphony was followed by a series of works for full or string orchestra – *Scottish Rhapsody* (1913), *Scenes from the Scottish Highlands* (1913), *The Land of the Gael* (1915), *Coronach* (9181) – which culminated in *The Sea Reivers* (1920), a feisty 'Hebridean Sea Poem' inspired by the idea of sea-borne raiders out among the Western Isles, and evidently owing something to Bantock's theatrical experiences. He also arranged a number of Hebridean folk songs and wrote chamber music with Scottish themes, notably the beautiful *Pibroch* for cello and harp (1917). For many of these works, Bantock drew upon tunes he found in Marjory Kennedy-Fraser's three-volume collection, *Songs of the Hebrides* (1907, 1917, 1921). Kennedy-Fraser's work has been heavily, and rightly, criticised for altering and distorting traditional songs, almost in the manner of an eighteenth-century collector. Bantock was undoubtedly aware of this, but it did not affect the way in which he transformed and absorbed the source material into his own personal Celtic sound world. He returned to Scottish themes towards the end of his life, particularly with a second Scottish symphony, his *Celtic Symphony* (1940), written for string orchestra and six harps. In part based on a Hebridean song called 'Sea Longing', this is another remarkable and imaginative work, which one commentator has suggested should be seen alongside Elgar's *Introduction and Allegro for Strings* and Vaughan Williams's *Fantasia on a Theme of Thomas Tallis* as one of the landmarks of the Renaissance period.[2]

John Foulds (1880–1939) was another whose music contains mystical elements drawn from both Celtic and oriental sources. Born in Manchester, he began his career as a cellist in the Hallé Orchestra under Hans Richter, before moving to London to pursue his ambitions as a composer. Like Bantock, he was forced to rely on writing incidental music for the theatre, including the score for the first London production of Shaw's *Saint Joan* in 1924. He also wrote light music of the kind that was popular with radio audiences once the BBC began regular broadcasting in the 1920s: his over- tures *Carnival* and *Le Cabaret* were broadcast regularly, as were other pieces with a Celtic inspiration (although Foulds always used the spelling 'Keltic'): *Keltic Melodies for Strings and Harp; Keltic Suite; A Gaelic Dream Song*. He was not immune to the influence of jazz, or to English pastoral. Indeed, he manages to blend the two with great effect in his remarkable Cello Concerto (1908). Theatre scores, light music and Celtic suites were his bread-and-butter work, but Foulds' real interest was in the music and culture of the Indian subcontinent. This informed many of his more seri- ous works – the works that he hoped would make his name as a composer – and derived in part from his long relationship with Maud MacCarthy, an expert on Indian music and mysticism, whom he met in 1915 and eventu- ally married in 1932.

Foulds nearly made the breakthrough to success with his *World Requiem*. This is a massive, ninety-minute composition in twenty movements for orchestra, soloists and a huge choir: the premiere, at the Royal Albert Hall on Armistice Day 1923, required 1,250 performers. It was intended to commemorate and honour the dead of all nations, and the text, compiled by Maud MacCarthy, combines passages from the traditional Christian Requiem, the Bible, and *Pilgrim's Progress,* with extracts from the fifteenth- century Indian mystic poet Kabir. The music, in similar fashion, is based in the western classical tradition but contains passages which clearly draw on both Celtic and Indian styles. For four years, the *World Requiem* was given as part of the British Legion's annual Festival of Remembrance, but was then dropped. Foulds, disappointed, subsequently went to live in Paris, but found it no easier to make a living there, and, at one point, was reduced to improvising piano accompaniments for silent films. By the time he returned to Britain, his moment had passed. But then, in 1935, together with Maud MacCarthy and their children, he moved to India and his career began to look up. All India Radio employed him as their Director of European Music. He founded an orchestra and began writing works which blended western and eastern musical forms. Sadly, he was struck down by cholera and died in Calcutta in 1939.

In many respects, Foulds was a hippy thirty years too early, but he was also a genuinely original talent. His music has enjoyed a revival in recent years, largely due to the efforts of the Finnish conductor Sakari Oramo. The *World Requiem* was revived in 2007 and a number of Foulds' other works have been recorded. *Three Mantras* is built round complex, essentially mystical concepts of Hindu philosophy, and manages to incorporate Indian *raga* forms into music that, in the 1920s, was already seen as daring in its approach to rhythmic and harmonic structures. *Lyra Celtica* is another, and in some ways even more remarkable, example of Foulds' east-west fusion. Cast in the form of a concerto for voice and orchestra – although only two movements were completed – it draws (like Bantock's work) on Hebridean sources. It has a strong otherworldly quality, leaving the listener with a sense that Hebridean and Indian music are actually not too far apart.

Gustav Holst (1874–1934), whose life and music we shall examine in more detail in Chapter 86, was also influenced by Indian religious literature. Early in his career, he spent the years from 1899 to 1906 working on a three-act opera called *Sita*, based on the *Ramayana*, which has never been staged. Although he later dismissed the work as 'good old Wagnerian bawling',[3] his daughter Imogen Holst has suggested that the composition of the opera over such an extended period was in fact the process by which Holst gradually moved himself away from Wagner towards a style of his own. This is partly borne out by his next opera *Savitri*, finished in 1908 but not performed until 1916.[4] Based on a story from the *Mahābhārata*, *Savitri* is a chamber opera, still an uncommon form at the time, and the first work to suggest what a powerful and genuine talent Holst had. With just three singers, a wordless chorus and an orchestra of twelve players, the scale is anything but Wagnerian; and although one can still hear echoes of Wagner in some of the vocal writing, the music has a simplicity and a directness that suggests but never quite sounds like folk music. Holst also wrote musical settings – some for voice and piano, some for chorus and orchestra – to five groups of hymns from the Sanskrit *Rig Veda* which he translated himself. These settings experiment with Indian scales and harmonies, but Holst never approached Foulds' attempts at a genuine east-west musical fusion. For him, unlike Foulds, Indian influence was not an end in itself. It was important enough for him to attend classes at University College, London, in an attempt to learn Sanskrit, but it was nonetheless a phase through which he passed, a way of getting a different perspective on the western classical tradition that would help him develop his mature musical personality. Well before the First World War, his intellectual focus was shifting elsewhere – although he retained an interest in other forms of mysticism, including astrology.

85 Celtic Connections, Bax, and Boughton

Whether mediated through English poetry or the result of more direct exploration of Islamic, Indian or Chinese culture, oriental influence was more evident among British composers at the beginning of the twentieth century than among their Continental contemporaries. It reflected an interest that was essentially a by-product of Empire, but, although widespread, it never approached the importance of Celtic culture as an influence on the generation of composers we are considering. Indeed, the impact of Celtic culture sometimes went well beyond music.

Arnold Bax (1883–1953) was a case in point. The origins of the Bax family were Dutch, but by the time of Arnold's birth they had been English for three hundred years. They began as farmers, invested their capital wisely and became a classic example of a wealthy Victorian mercantile middle-class family – with the consequence for Arnold that at no stage in his life did he ever need to work for a living, something that set him apart from the majority of his colleagues and contemporaries. He and his brother Clifford, who became a well-known playwright, poet and journalist, were brought up at Ivy Bank, a large house in Hampstead, which was then on the northern edge of London. When not playing cricket in the extensive gardens, they went to Crystal Palace concerts and meetings of the local choral society with their father, or listened to their Uncle Ernest talk about his conversations with William Morris and George Bernard Shaw. Their mother, who doted on them, had a generous nature and was given to grand philanthropic gestures. She would hold elaborate parties for children from the local area, or open the family home to people who found themselves in difficulties. It was an idyllic late Victorian upbringing.

Arnold Bax's musical abilities developed rapidly during his teenage years. At the age of thirteen, he was acting as accompanist to his father's choral group. By the age of fifteen, it was clear that a musical career was a possibility and he was sent to Hampstead Conservatoire, then under the direction of Cecil Sharp. Bax failed to respond to Sharp's passionate advocacy of folk song. Indeed, he regarded Sharp as a fanatic. His work shows an acute awareness of Celtic musical styles and harmonies, but the influence of English folk music is wholly lacking – he is reputed to have told Holst on one occasion that English folk songs were either bad, or Irish. In 1900, he took and passed the entrance exam for the RAM. Corder was his composition teacher, but the institution took its tone from Mackenzie, who had been Principal for twelve years and would remain so for the next twenty-four. Here, for five intense years, Bax worked on his compositional technique and studied the music of Liszt, Wagner and Tchaikovsky (of whom his teachers approved), as well as Elgar, Richard Strauss and Debussy (of whom they did not). Bax himself was a fine pianist, particularly renowned for his sight-reading skills, and his fellow students included the pianists Myra Hess and Irene Scharrer. Other future composers studying at the RAM during Bax's time included York Bowen, Benjamin Dale, Eric Coates, and the composer and violinist W. H. Reed, who became a friend close of Elgar's. On leaving the RAM, Bax spent a short period in Dresden in 1906; there he revelled in Wagner, in Strauss's *Salome* and *Rosenkavalier,* but failed to appreciate Mahler.

Yet the discovery which probably did more than any other to shape his music was unconnected with his musical education. From his boyhood, Bax had loved poetry. In 1902, he came across W. B. Yeats's *Wanderings of Oisin* and was immediately captivated. That same year, he made his first visit to Ireland, accompanied by his brother Clifford and his sister Evelyn. Thereafter, he went alone. Ireland, and especially the wild, romantic western coast, became the focus of his imagination. From 1904 until 1930, he visited the remote Donegal village of Glencolmcille whenever he could, often twice a year and often for extended periods. He immersed himself in Irish culture. He studied Ireland's history, myths and folklore. He learned Irish Gaelic. He even adopted an Irish persona, calling himself Dermot O'Byrne and publishing poems, stories and plays under that name. Ireland and Irish culture also gave him direction as a composer, although only once did he use an existing Irish tune in his work.[1]

In the 1930s, Bax turned his attention to the west coast of Scotland, with the village of Morar, just south of Mallaig, supplanting Glencolmcille as the place to which he would retreat and write. This represented a shift of focus rather than an actual diminution of his Celtic interests. He never became Scottish in the way he had become Irish, but Scotland offered new landscapes and another perspective on the Celtic world. It also allowed him to make a connection with Nordic music and mythology in which his interest had been growing for some time, stimulated in part by the music of Sibelius. It was in Morar that he wrote most of his Sixth and Seventh Symphonies, the high points of his symphonic writing. Only after the Second World War, when his music no longer fitted the prevailing fashion and the creative urge began to fail, did he lose some of his Celtic focus. Sir Arnold Bax, as he had become in 1937, was Master of the King's Musick but, apart from a few ceremonial pieces, composed very little. He spent much of his time in Sussex, where he lived in rooms above a pub in Storrington, more interested, at least according to William Walton, in going up to London to watch a cricket match than to attend a concert and hear his music played.[2] He died in 1953 on a visit to Ireland and was buried in Cork.

For over thirty years, music poured out of Bax. He wrote in almost every genre except opera and oratorio. He did actually begin an opera based on the story of the legendary Irish heroine, Deirdre, but never finished it, recycling the music into his early tone poems. He wrote a lot of solo piano music, much of it dedicated to Harriet Cohen (1895–1967) for whom he left his wife and children, and with whom he had a long and complicated relationship. Central to Bax's piano compositions are his four sonatas. The First, which shows the influence of Scriabin, was written in 1910, the year in which, having fallen in love with a Russian girl, he followed her to Saint Petersburg, Moscow and the Ukraine. Romantically, the trip was a disaster, but he learned much about Russian music along the way. The Second, written in 1919, is one of his finest piano works, introspective yet dramatic without ever losing artistic focus.

Bax wrote extensively for various chamber ensembles. The First String Quartet (1918) is a brilliant combination of Celtic-inspired melodies and classical quartet structure. The Second (1925), equally impressive, is a much harder-edged piece, more demanding on both players and audience. The Viola Sonata (1922) is another very focussed work; and the Concerto for Flute, Oboe, Harp and String Quartet, written in 1936 although not recorded until 1998, again shows Bax's ability to apply Celtic inspiration and Celtic instrumentation within a classical structure. A word must also be said about Bax's choral music. Although he was not a great choral composer, one work stands out: his 1921 *Mater, Ora Filium*. In terms of the rest of his output, this comes from nowhere. He composed little sacred music and wrote rarely for unaccompanied chorus, yet this is an undoubted masterpiece. Scored for double chorus with a tenor solo, it has echoes of Byrd, and of pre-Reformation polyphony, but the whole is unmistakeably modern and contrapuntal, anticipating the late twentieth- and early-twenty-first century sound world of John Tavener and James Macmillan.

For all that, it is on his orchestral works – on the seven symphonies, the tone poems, and the two big works for piano and orchestra: *Symphonic Variations* (1918) and *Winter Legends* (1930) – that Bax's reputation really rests. Both the piano works are very fine compositions, but neither is a concerto in the traditional sense. *Symphonic Variations* is divided into two parts, each made up of named sections, beginning with 'Youth', ending in 'Triumph', and seeming to pivot about the first section of Part Two, 'The Temple'. Was Bax mapping out the life of some legendary Irish hero? Or an Irish hero of his own imagining? The answer has never been revealed. *Winter Legends* has a more-or-less traditional structure of three movements and a coda. Here, Bax made the link with heroic literature, this time of the north, explicit, but did not reveal whether he had a particular work or story in mind. Both works have difficult piano parts, but in neither does the piano play the virtuosic role expected in a concerto: it is rather first among equals in an ensemble piece which aims at creating a mood or an atmosphere.

That aim is what relates the piano works to the tone poems, which today are probably Bax's best-known works. *Into the Faëry Hills* (1909) was inspired directly by Yeats's *Wanderings of Oisin*. *The Garden of Fand* (written 1913, orchestrated 1916) is intended to evoke the atmosphere of a particular Celtic legend, Fand's story being part of the Cuchulain saga, and her garden the sea. Then came *Tintagel* (written 1917, orchestrated 1919), which was played regularly and kept his name before the public during the 1960s and 70s when he was otherwise out of fashion. It is a big romantic outpouring, written at the beginning of his affair with Harriet Cohen, and using myth-laden Tintagel as a vehicle for the expression of personal emotion. *November Woods* (1917), with its wonderfully pictorial orchestration of wind among the trees, came next. After *The Happy Forest* (1922), he wrote fewer tone poems – although *The Tale the Pine Trees Knew* (1931) and the two *Northern Ballads* (1927 and 1934) are still notable works – and focussed on his symphonic writing.

All of Bax's seven symphonies have a three-movement structure and all were written between 1922 and 1939. In them, Celtic inspiration is less overt than in the tone poems – there are no titles to suggest the mood or the origin of the inspiration – but it is nonetheless fundamental to the music. There are other influences at work, too. Bax acknowledged the influence of the sagas and dark northern winters on the Third Symphony (1929), but the delicate tracery of the bassoon and clarinet opening of the first movement, the sprightly rhythms, and the oboe, clarinet and harp sound of the epilogue are all surely Celtic in origin. The Fifth Symphony (1932) is the least characteristic. It attempts to evolve themes in the manner of Sibelius (to whom it is dedicated), and ends on a bolder, more triumphant note than is characteristic with Bax. Yet even here, Lewis Foreman, the leading Bax scholar, has linked the opening of the second movement to Bax's attachment to 'the natural grandeur of the West of Ireland.'[3]

It is easy to forget that in the 1930s, Bax's music – especially the Fifth Symphony – was felt to be new and difficult. He reached his symphonic peak in 1935 with the Sixth Symphony, an immensely powerful work, which is hard to characterise, encompassing as it does a vast range of emotions within a controlled and brilliantly orchestrated symphonic structure. By this point, Bax was widely considered to be Britain's leading symphonist – Vaughan Williams, the only other contender, produced his Fourth Symphony that same year – but Bax himself was feeling the strain. He became increasingly melancholic and said he wanted to retire 'like a grocer.'[4] The elegiac, beautiful and deeply emotional Seventh Symphony did not appear until 1939. It was his last work of any real significance, but a fitting conclusion to his career as one of Britain's greatest symphonists.

A wholly different version of the Celtic obsession is demonstrated by the career of Rutland Boughton (1878–1960). In no sense as important a composer as Bax, Boughton did at least try to give operatic shape to some of the myths and stories that formed such an important and influential part of the Celtic Revival. His was an anglicised Celticism: he did not make regular visits to Ireland or Scotland or assume an Irish persona, and the operas he produced had, for the most part, what one might call an English tone. Nonetheless, like Bantock and Bax, Boughton looked to the Celtic world for the material that he believed could revive British music.

Boughton's family was far from rich. His father was a grocer and, even though it was obvious from an early age that young Rutland was musically gifted, there was no money to spare for his education. Eventually, through a chain of connections, an early composition reached the hands of Stanford at the RCM. He persuaded the MP for Aylesbury, where the Boughtons lived, to raise a fund for the boy's education, and Boughton was able to enjoy a short period of formal tuition at the RCM. Even then, life was difficult. Between leaving the College in 1901 and being offered a teaching post by Bantock at the Birmingham and Midland Institute, he struggled to make ends meet, even – by his own account – going without food. But Boughton was one of those irrepressible, resourceful people, and he fought his way through.

With his head full of Wagner and William Morris-style socialism, Boughton wanted to create music drama for England as Wagner had done for Germany, but with a social purpose. In collaboration with a young poet and writer called Reginald Buckley, he planned a cycle of Arthurian operas to rival *The Ring*. The first, *The Birth of Arthur*, was written in 1908. The problem was getting it produced – a problem complicated by the fact that he had left his wife and was living with an art student, which, given the mores of the time, alienated many potential supporters. Nonetheless, he persisted. Having obtained the endorsement of Elgar and Bantock and the backing of a number of local dignitaries, Boughton succeeded in staging the first Glastonbury Festival in August 1914: even the outbreak of the First World War could not stop him. The centrepiece of the first festival was not *The Birth of Arthur*, but *The Immortal Hour*, a two-act opera finished the previous year and based on a verse drama published some years earlier by Fiona Macleod (who was in fact a man called William Sharp). The production was basic – in the local Assembly Rooms with makeshift costumes and piano accompaniment – but it launched an opera which would go on to break records in the years after the First World War.

With just a couple of exceptions during the war and another in 1923, the Glastonbury Festivals were held three times a year for the next twelve years.

In that time, hundreds of works were produced, including several by Boughton: among them *The Birth of Arthur; The Round Table*, the second part of his Arthurian cycle; *Bethlehem*, a folk opera based on English carol tunes; and *The Queen of Cornwall*, another heavily Celtic work, a version of the story of Tristan and Isolde (here, Tristram and Iseult), based on the play by Thomas Hardy. Both *Bethlehem* and *The Queen of Cornwall* proved popular, but it was *The Immortal Hour* that was to make Boughton's reputation. The 1922 Glastonbury production was taken on to Birmingham where, although only a few performances were scheduled, it proved such a popular success that it was immediately transferred to London, opening at the Regent's Theatre, formerly a music hall, that October. It ran for two hundred and sixteen consecutive performances. Revived just a few months later, it ran for one hundred and fifty-three more. The plot is simple – the malevolent Dalua bewitches the beautiful Princess Etain and uses her to bring about the downfall and death of the High King Eochaidh – but around it swirl the indefinable mysteries of Celtic mythology, and music which is simple, Celtic in style, restrained and neither sentimental nor melodramatic. The public kept coming back for more. By 1932, there had been over a thousand performances and it had attracted praise from Elgar, Ethel Smyth, Bax, Holst and Vaughan Williams and many others.

In the United States, however, the fated tragedies of the Celtic world had less appeal. In 1926, *The Immortal Hour* opened in New York, but was taken off after four weeks. That same year, Boughton contrived to bring about his own downfall. Having recently become a Communist, and appalled at what he saw as the unjust outcome of the General Strike, he mounted a new production of *Bethlehem* for that year's Glastonbury Festival. The Christ story became a socialist parable: the stable was a miner's cottage and Herod a cigar-smoking, top-hatted capitalist. This was too much for the good people of Glastonbury and the festivals came to an end. The third part of the Arthurian cycle, *The Lily Maid*, was staged in Stroud in 1934, but the remaining two, *Galahad* and *Avalon*, although completed during the Second World War, have never seen the light of day. By that time, Boughton was living on a small farm in Gloucestershire. He continued to write music – including symphonies, an overture to the Arthurian cycle, concertos for oboe and flute, and chamber music. He also wrote books and articles, which, despite their musical subject matter, were often vehicles for his staunchly left-wing views. But he never regained the public or musical profile that he had enjoyed in the early 1920s.

These various oriental and Celtic influences are reflected in the work of many composers, not just the handful we have considered here. They make it clear that, for all the 'English' and 'national' influences operating on them, the composers of 1870–90 generation were not wholly insular or parochial in their outlook. That said, ideas of England and Englishness in particular, whether they derived from landscape, history, poetry, plays, myths or other forms of folk culture, were immensely important. Indeed, they were central to the work of the generation as a whole.

What all these sources of inspiration had in common was that they were largely non-musical. Again, looking at this generation and their work as a whole, we can see a shift away from the traditional genre-plus-number kind of compositions (String Quartet no. 2; Piano Sonata no. 3). In their place, as we find looser, less defined forms and an increasing use of titles to indicate a mood, image, or programme underlying the music. String quartets and piano sonatas continued to be written, as did concertos and symphonies (and sometimes they, too, were given a title and a programme), but tone poems, rhapsodies, mood pieces and other titled compositions became far more common. They were the natural forms of expression for the kind of late Romanticism that characterised the music of this generation both in Britain and also on the Continent. In Britain, they had a particular appeal. They reflected both a continuing movement away from German classical models and the German tendency towards abstraction, and a corresponding broadening of horizons to include the influence of composers such as Sibelius, Dvořák, Richard Strauss, Ravel and Debussy. They also allowed for a much greater engagement with literature, particularly poetry, and with composers' own ideas and philosophies.

Gustav Theodore von Holst came from an intensely musical family. His great-grandfather, Matthias, taught the harp at the Russian Imperial court in Saint Petersburg. His grandfather, Gustavus, fled from Russia in 1799, apparently for political reasons, arriving in London where he, too, taught the harp, as well as composing fashionable salon music. It was Gustavus who adopted the prefix 'von' to give an impression of aristocratic descent (Holst dropped it in 1918). Holst's father, Adolph, was an organist in Cheltenham, while his mother, Clara, was a gifted pianist and singer. All of which meant that it was natural for Gustav to receive a musical education. He learned the piano, which he enjoyed; the violin, which he did not; and the trombone as therapy for his asthma. With such a musical heritage behind him, it was equally natural for him to respond to accepted models. As a teenager, he admired Mendelssohn, Chopin and Sullivan. Then, in 1892, he saw Mahler conducting *Götterdämmerung* at Covent Garden and fell under the spell of Wagner. Much of the next twenty years was to be spent breaking free of these influences and establishing his own musical voice.

Holst began composing before receiving any formal training and one or two of his early efforts were given amateur performances in and around Cheltenham. At the age of nineteen, and at the second attempt, he was admitted to the RCM, where he was taught by both Parry and Stanford, although without making any particular impression. Perhaps the two most important events of his student years happened in 1895: he attended the first modern performance of Purcell's *Dido and Aeneas* (conducted by Stanford), and he met Vaughan Williams. The first had a major impact on his understanding of how English should be set to music. The second provided a lifelong friendship and probably the greatest single influence on his music.

Even while he was studying, Holst had to work to make ends meet, sometimes playing on south coast pierheads with Stanislav Wurm's White Viennese Band. On leaving the RCM in 1898, he embarked upon a career as a professional trombonist, taking freelance work, joining the Carl Rosa Opera Company and, later, the Scottish Orchestra.[1] This was invaluable experience, giving him the same kind of understanding of an orchestra from the inside that had benefitted both Mackenzie and Elgar, but it was a life which he felt offered too little time for composition. In 1903, he turned to teaching, first at James Allen's Girls' School in Dulwich, where he succeeded Vaughan Williams, and then, two years later, at St Paul's Girls' School in Hammersmith, where he remained until his tragically early death in 1934.

In some ways, the outward circumstances of Holst's life tell us less than the story of what he was studying and thinking. He was very much an idealist, but at the same time highly eclectic in his approach. We have already noted how his interest in Indian religious literature helped him move away from Wagner and develop his own musical style, but oriental-ism was only one of his intellectual interests. He was deeply affected by both the socialism of William Morris and the transcendental philosophy of Walt Whitman; and when introduced by Vaughan Williams to folk song, it was not just the music, but what he saw as the essential purity of the folk idiom that moved him.

Nor were these interests in any sense exclusive. At the same time as he was learning Sanskrit and wrestling with the composition of *Sita*, he was tramping the country in company with Vaughan Williams, collecting songs and discovering folk music – a discovery that his daughter Imogen believed gave him his real direction as a composer. As early as 1900, he had written the romantic and pastoral *Cotswold Symphony* – it was premiered at Bournemouth in 1902 – a rather bland work, and interesting only because of how Holst developed later. The first real product of his enthusiasm for folk music was *A Somerset Rhapsody* (1907), an attractive if not particularly exciting pastoral piece. It was based on four songs collected by Cecil Sharp and probably much influenced by Vaughan Williams, with whom Holst used to enjoy 'Field Days' when they scrutinised each other's work. Vaughan Williams paid tribute to the absolute integrity of Holst's assessments, and integrity was an essential part of his make-up. He led an ascetic life, neither drinking nor smoking, and was given to strenuous walking holidays. One of these holidays, in 1908, was in Algeria. This opened another avenue and led to the *Beni Mora Suite* – a much more original work, combining North African rhythms and riffs with western orchestral textures, and giving a foretaste of his later technique.

Beni Mora was first played during a series of eight concerts devoted to new British music at the Queen's Hall in 1912 and 1913. Others whose music was heard included Delius, Vaughan Williams, Bax, Percy Grainger, Cyril Scott and Roger Quilter. The concerts were financed by Henry Balfour Gardiner (1877–1950). A musician and composer himself – known principally for his setting of the *Evening Hymn* (1908) and the light-hearted *Shepherd Fennel's Dance* (1911) based on a Hardy short story – Gardiner's real contribution to British music was the way he employed his substantial personal fortune to support other composers. When, towards the end of his life, Delius was facing financial problems caused by his illness, it was Gardiner who bought the house in Grez-sur-Loing so that Delius and Jelka could carry on living there. And it was Gardiner who, in 1918, just before Holst was sent off to Greece to organise musical education for soon-to-be-demobbed troops, financed a private premiere of *The Planets*, conducted by Adrian Boult, at the Queen's Hall.

The Planets, written between 1914 and 1916, is now such a popular and familiar work that it is worth recalling how challenging and unfamiliar it seemed when it was first performed. Boult included it in a public concert in 1919, but insisted on cutting two of the movements because he thought the public would not be able to cope with such a large work in such a new musical language. Holst's original title was *Seven Pieces for Large Orchestra*, but, having been introduced to astrology – a subject which, characteristically, he took very seriously – by Arnold Bax's brother, Clifford, he came up with the idea of *The Planets*. Each movement is named after a different planet and represents musically the characteristics which astrology associates with that planet. The structure is clear and complete in itself, but in no sense symphonic. Holst's practical versatility is evident in his ability to come up with contrasting themes and contrasting patterns of orchestration, from the intensely rhythmic 'Mars' to the great, striding tune of 'Jupiter'. The work also displays a vast range of influences from Berlioz and Tchaikovsky to Stravinsky and Schoenberg, but the result is an original voice that is also unmistakeably English. Holst later adapted the central 'Jupiter' theme as a hymn tune, *Thaxted*, which became the tune for the patriotic song 'I Vow to Thee My Country'.

The Planets was a success and made Holst's name, but he came to feel that its very popularity distracted attention from his other works. Even before *The Planets* was performed, he had gone off on another tack. *Hymn of Jesus*, written in 1917 but not performed until 1920, is based on the Acts of John, part of the New Testament Apocrypha. Characteristically, he learned Greek so that he could work on the text. Written for two choruses, a semi-chorus and orchestra, it is a world away from the solemnity and sentimentality of the Victorian oratorio. Holst's version of the Christian revelation is full of Gnostic philosophy, dancing and ecstasy. This demanding, highly original work impressed the critics, but it was not the sort of thing to appeal to choral societies and, while often praised, has not been heard, or indeed recorded, as often as it deserves.

Holst then turned his attention to opera. *The Perfect Fool* took four years to write and received its premiere at Covent Garden in 1923. It is an odd work. It might be an operatic satire on opera, or it might have some hidden symbolism which no one has ever quite penetrated, but it was certainly a failure. Only the ballet music, which Holst turned into an attractive orchestral suite, is still regularly heard. *The Perfect Fool* was followed in 1924 by *At the Boar's Head* which takes the tavern scenes from Shakespeare's *Henry IV* and sets them to traditional English tunes. It is clever; it is fun; but it is hardly an opera. The next year, 1925, saw a return to orchestral music with his *Choral Symphony*, drawing its text from the poetry of John Keats. Again, it was an unsatisfactory work. The second movement, a setting of 'Ode to a Grecian Urn' is perhaps the best, but overall the work does not develop as a symphony should and there is no real resolution.

These larger works from the mid-1920s clearly lack direction, and to concentrate on them is to risk a partial view of Holst's achievement. His philosophical interests, the influence of folk song, and perhaps also his experience as a teacher and educator seeking to convey the essence of music to his students and to amateur musicians, all led him to prize simplicity – which does not always come across in his larger works, but does characterise many of his other compositions. It is there in works such as the *St Paul's Suite* (1913) for string orchestra, in some of his vocal and choral pieces, in his folk song arrangements, and in the many settings of English poetry he made throughout his life. Holst is not one of the great songwriters, but the breadth of his choice of poetry is both impressive and eclectic – including writers as diverse as Whitman, Tennyson, Thomas Hood, Robert Bridges, Thomas Heywood, Robert Herrick, William Morris and Humbert Wolfe – again indicating the importance of literature and ideas as both guide and inspiration. His setting of songs from Tennyson's *Princess,* the Six Choral Folk Songs written for W. G. Whittaker's Newcastle choir, and his arrangement of the folk ballad 'Diverus and Lazarus', show him at his best. On the surface, they are simple and direct, but the simplicity derives from Holst's carefully calculated use of rhythm, harmony and occasional dissonance, which creates and conveys an intensity and a sense of spirituality more often associated with church music.

In 1927, Holst composed what was to be his last major orchestral piece, *Egdon Heath*, a representation of Thomas Hardy's mysterious, imagined landscape in *The Return of the Native*. Holst considered it one of his finest works, an opinion seconded by Vaughan Williams, although critics have not always agreed. Elemental and brooding – and including a strange, otherworldly dance, which might reflect Hardy's mummers – *Egdon Heath* combines a simplicity of approach with a deep sense of Englishness in music that is far more challenging than the normal pastoral idyll. It seemed that Holst had rediscovered his sense of direction, an impression confirmed by his next major work. This was *The Wandering Scholar*, another chamber opera, with a libretto by Clifford Bax based on a novel by Helen Waddell. A neatly-structured, one-act comedy, featuring four well-drawn characters and, again, a notable simplicity of approach, this is undoubtedly the most stage-friendly of his operas. Holst finished it in 1930 and it was produced in Liverpool in 1934. Sadly, by that time he was too ill to attend. Musically, there was every reason to suppose he was on the verge of even greater things, but his health, which had never been good, began to deteriorate. He was an invalid from 1932, and he died of heart failure after an operation in 1934.

In worldly terms, Holst was far from a success – Balfour Gardiner gave him regular financial help and also paid for medical care at the end of his life. Musical ambition was what drove him – he was an experimenter, in many ways the most progressive composer of his generation, something reflected in the number of his works which do not quite succeed. Yet for all his eclectic intellectual interests, it was poetry that inspired him: actual poetry, the poetry of folk song, and poetry he found elsewhere. Even his response to Indian religious texts, such as the *Ramayana* or the *Rig Veda*, to works on astrology, and to something like the Acts of John, was essentially a poetic one. The abstract ideas fascinated him; the words and images moved him.

87   Somervell, Quilter, Ireland, and Dyson

This kind of response to poetry and poetic imagery is a characteristic of many English composers of the late Victorian and Edwardian periods, and was, of course, an essential element in the rise to prominence and popularity of the art song – a phenomenon which often overlapped with the popularity of folk song settings. Parry and Stanford in their different ways raised standards for setting English poetry to music, and, as exponents rather than teachers, their influence in this area was considerable. Arthur Somervell (1863–1937) studied under Stanford at Cambridge, spent two years in Berlin, and then returned to the RCM where he was a private pupil of Parry's. Although he did write other forms of music – including an elegy for Scott of the Antarctic as part of his *Thalassa Symphony* – it is as a songwriter that he is remembered. His songs are still very much in the German *Lieder* mode and can hardly be described as adventurous; but they are immensely fluent, with a genuine feel for both the pulse and the emotion of the lyrics. His setting of the anonymous poem 'Sweet Kate' is a good example. He wrote settings of Blake and lyrics from Shakespeare, including 'O Mistress Mine' which stands up well beside Gerald Finzi's much more famous version. Central to his work were his song cycles. *Maud* (1898), based on Tennyson's 1855 volume, was the first real song cycle in British music and deserves to be heard more often. There were two subsequent cycles based on Browning – *James Lee's Wife* and *A Broken Arc* – and, in 1904, the first ever setting of poems from Housman's *Shropshire Lad*, a volume that was to become a favourite quarry for composers over the next twenty years. Somervell's *Shropshire Lad* has been eclipsed by much more frequently heard versions by Butterworth and Vaughan Williams, but it remains a fine work, made up of effortless, unassuming melodies that allow the poems to speak for themselves.

Roger Quilter (1877–1953) wrote an opera and some light orchestral music, but is rightly regarded as a specialist songwriter – he wrote over a hundred, as well as arranging some twenty folk songs. He, too, was educated in Germany, and the flavour of Brahms' and even Mendelssohn's *Lieder* is detectable in his work. Although some fourteen years younger than Somervell, he seems at times to belong to an earlier era. His folk song arrangements, made at various times during his life, are very different from those of Vaughan Williams or Holst. Quilter arranged folk songs as if they were parlour ballads, which can make them attractive, but to modern ears can also give them an obvious, even camp quality. They were eventually collected in *Arnold's Book of Old Songs*, a volume dedicated to his much-loved nephew, Arnold, who died in the Second World War. His setting of poetry can be erratic, but the poems themselves are carefully chosen and his settings, when successful, show real judgement. *To Julia* (1906) is a short, even miniature, cycle of six songs to poems by Robert Herrick. None lasts much longer than two minutes, but they are unified by common musical themes and form a neat, satisfying unity. His *Three Shakespearean Songs* (1905) and *Songs of Sorrow* (1907) to poems by Ernest Dowson, apparently a very personal work reflecting his problems with depression, also show a real understanding of the words being set. But the high point of Quilter's achievement is *Seven Elizabethan Lyrics* (1908). The choice of poetry probably reflects an awareness of the Tudor Revival, which was beginning to make itself felt at the time, although Quilter's music is not obviously influenced by Tudor styles. The settings are less musically inte-grated than in *To Julia*, but the texts (one by Campion, one by Ben Jonson and five anonymous) are carefully ordered and combine with his simple, fluid accompaniments to give the sense that this is a genuine song cycle, complete in itself.

The response of John Ireland (1879–1962) to poetry and to poetic stimuli was, if anything, even more intense. In part, this may be because he came from a literary background – his father was a newspaper editor, his mother the biographer of Jane Welsh Carlyle – but it also fits with his character, that of an intensely private and often unhappy man. His father was seventy when he was born and died before Ireland entered the RCM in 1893. His mother died the following year, leaving him to face the emotional and practical demands of making his way in the world alone – a circumstance not improved by what he felt to be Stanford's hectoring, confidence-sapping teaching methods (although Ireland did later acknowledge how much he learned from Stanford). Moreover, he was in all probability wrestling with the knowledge that he was homosexual, and the attendant feelings of shame and guilt. His attempt at marriage in 1926 with a student thirty years younger than himself ended after little more than a year, apparently unconsummated.

For Ireland, music and poetry were bound up with the need to confront his fears and insecurities, and also with his search for some kind of spiritual home – which was itself reflected in a powerful sensitivity to the spirit of place. Chelsea, the Channel Islands, Maiden Castle in Dorset, and the Sussex Downs around Chanctonbury Ring were among the places which at various times captivated him in a manner that he tried to express in his music. Sensitivity to place and to the ancient associations of place led Ireland to become an admirer of the writer and mystic, Arthur Machen; and these intense, almost pantheistic, feelings inspired at least three compositions, all of them in a distinctly romantic vein. The tone poem, *The Forgotten Rite* (1913), is Ireland's imaginative response to Jersey and its ancient past. *Mai Dun* (1921) uses the ancient name for Maiden Castle to evoke the presence of its vast earthworks on the Dorset landscape. Ireland called it a symphonic rhapsody, although tone poem would be just as accurate. *Legend* (1933), for piano and orchestra, was based on a mystical experience Ireland had on the South Downs and is actually dedicated to Machen.

Of Ireland's larger works, the finest is certainly his Piano Concerto (1930), which is romantic without being indulgent, and has deservedly become increasingly popular in recent years. But he was more at home in smaller forms, and these make up the greater part of his output. His first success came with chamber music, notably the Violin Sonata no. 2 (1917), which won him a prize of forty guineas and a concert performance by the

English virtuoso Albert Sammons at the Aeolian Hall in Bond Street. Ireland claimed that the next morning he woke up famous. However, it is in the piano music and the songs that lie the heart of his achievement. The piano works are largely miniatures, almost all with titles indicative of place or mood. *Decorations* (1913) is characteristic. Subtle and impressionistic in style, it consists of three short pieces, with both the music and the poetic titles of each section ('The Island Spell', 'Moonglade', 'The Scarlet Cere-monies') clearly intended to conjure magical or mystical associations. *London Pieces* (1920) has the same three-part structure and begins with 'Chelsea Reach', an impressionistic evocation of a part of London that he loved and where he lived for over twenty years. In 1939, Ireland moved to Guernsey and *Sarnia: An Island Sequence* (1941), is another evocation of place. Again in three parts ('Le Catioroc', 'In a May Morning', 'Song of the Springtides'), it is a slightly longer work and slightly looser in form. It was begun in Guernsey, but completed after he was evacuated: he was on one of the last boats to leave ahead of the German invasion in 1940.[1]

Ireland was in his thirties when he began setting poetry. By that time, the influence of Beethoven and Brahms that he had absorbed at the RCM had been diluted by that of Ravel, Debussy and even Bartok. The German *Lied* is consequently more distant than in Somervell or Quilter and the prevailing style is an English version of impressionism. Ireland's ninety or more songs are drawn from the works of over twenty poets and include some of his finest work. Among his early settings, John Masefield's 'Sea Fever' has long been regarded as a classic. Its open melody and accessible harmonisation fit the words perfectly, and it has a sureness of touch that has made it deservedly popular. Other early settings are less successful and display his weaknesses. Masefield's 'Bells of San Marie' and Hardy's 'Great Things', both of them drinking songs, seem artificially bright, while Arthur Symons' 'Santa Chiara' is an example of Ireland slipping into a sentimental-ity usually foreign to his nature, but which does occasionally creep through.

In general, the tone darkened and became more personal as Ireland grew older. As with many of his generation, Housman, with his distinctly melancholy streak, was among the poets that brought out the best in him. Ireland wrote his fine *Shropshire Lad* cycle, under the title *The Land of Lost Content,* in 1921; and a second shorter Housman cycle, *We'll to the woods no more,* in 1928. This second work, consisting of two thematically linked poems and finishing, unusually, with a solo piano piece, is an expression of sadness and loss, perhaps reflecting on the failure of his marriage. *Songs*

Sacred and Profane (1931) and *Five XVIth Century Songs* (1938) both contain some excellent songs and one should not ignore two famous miniatures: Thomas Lowell Beddoes' 'If there were dreams to sell' and Ernest Dowson's 'When I am dead, my darling'. At his best, Ireland is among the leading songwriters of the twentieth century, but he can be uneven, and the difference seems to be in the level of his engagement with the poem. The more personal or profound the response, the better the song.

Sensitivity to poetry and to literary stimuli did not, of course, always guarantee a concentration on art song or folk song, as the career of George Dyson demonstrates. Dyson (1883–1964) was born into a working-class family in Halifax – his father was a blacksmith and his mother a weaver. His musical background was the local Baptist church and the local choral society, where they sang Handel and Mendelssohn. He first heard Wagner played by a brass band. Talent and hard work gained him a scholarship to the RCM in 1900. More hard work gained him the Mendelssohn Scholarship which allowed him to travel to Florence, Rome, Vienna and Berlin, where he met Richard Strauss, albeit briefly.

Back in England in 1907, Dyson was recommended by Parry to be Director of Music at the Royal Naval College at Osborne on the Isle of Wight. For a man with Dyson's background, this was a huge achievement. In 1911, he moved on to Marlborough College, but with the coming of the war in 1914 he joined up, becoming a temporary 2nd Lieutenant in the Kensington Battalion of the Royal Fusiliers. He was appointed a grenade officer, even writing a training manual on the subject, before serving on the front line in France. Having experienced the trenches at first hand, he wrote to a friend that Dante's conception of hell was amateurish and that he could improve on it.[2] In 1917, a shell exploded under his horse and, although physically unhurt, Dyson was invalided out of the army with severe shell shock. He did reappear briefly as a Major in the Royal Air Force, organising military bands, but it was not until three years after the war that his career properly resumed. In 1921, he took a teaching post at Wellington College in Berkshire and, the same year, was appointed a Professor at the RCM. In 1924, he moved to Winchester to take up an appointment at the school there. Both the school, founded in 1394, and the city appealed to Dyson's sense of history. He called Winchester his 'spiritual home' and lived there happily for thirteen years until the need to be closer to the RCM forced him to move to London. He worked at the RCM for a total of thirty-one years, the last fifteen as Director, keeping the

College open throughout the Second World War in the face of government pressure to close, and coping with huge administrative burdens in the years of reconstruction that followed. When he retired in 1952, he moved back to Winchester.

In many ways Dyson was the antithesis of Holst. Although nine years younger, his tastes and attitudes were less far adventurous. Musically, they came from the same generation, but although he had ambition, Dyson was less driven than Holst. Coming from a poor background, it was perhaps natural that he should become a man of institutions, seeking to balance the uncertainties of a musical career with a steady job and a steady income. He certainly followed a professional path that was already looking old-fashioned: writing a significant amount of church music; producing choral pieces for provincial festivals and for the coronations of George VI and Elizabeth II; receiving a knighthood in 1953. To this was added a highly practical outlook: he could repair cars, design schemes for land drainage, and his first concern, on taking over as Director of the RCM, was to refurbish the lavatories.

As a composer, Dyson developed slowly. Little of his early music survives – although his Morning and Evening Service in D from 1907 is still regularly sung in the Church of England. So, too, is his later Service in F, which includes some inventive writing for treble and bass soloists. His first major work was *In Honour of the City* (1928), a setting of the poem of the same name written somewhere around 1500 by the Scots poet, William Dunbar – Dyson himself having turned the text into modern English. This was the first real indication of his ability to write for chorus and orchestra and of his preference for poetry from the more distant past. Then in 1931 came what has to be regarded as Dyson's masterpiece, his setting of the Prologue to Chaucer's *Canterbury Tales*.

Musically, *The Canterbury Pilgrims* may not be progressive, but it is not backward looking. There are shades of Wagner in some of the writing for brass and for strings; there are echoes of Richard Strauss and Ravel in the orchestration. What Dyson creates is a style that leans heavily on tradition, yet is at once unmistakeably of the twentieth century and wholly suited to setting a medieval text. The opening section is calm and atmospheric with medieval dance rhythms leading into a choral passage suggestive of Tudor church music. The host's scene-setting is gently authoritative. Then comes a series of brilliant, theatrical character sketches – the noble knight, with more than a hint of Elgar; the ironic bombast of the merchant; the rough assertiveness of the shipman; the suppressed sexuality of the Wife of Bath emphasised by the Spanish-sounding dance rhythms. Dyson's characterisation and word-setting are precise, and in perfect sympathy with the detachment, irony and sympathy of Chaucer's own descriptions. Lewis Foreman has even suggested that the rhythm of each section is intended to suggest the kind of steed that that particular character might be riding.[3]

The Blacksmiths followed in 1932. It is a setting of an alliterative medieval lyric and Dyson probably wrote it in memory of his father. Unusually rhythmic and percussive, it is again wholly appropriate to its subject and its text. But it is in *Quo Vadis*, finished in 1939 after a gestation period of almost ten years, that the true intensity of his feeling for poetry comes through. *Quo Vadis* is two-hour song cycle for soloists, chorus and orchestra, with a libretto assembled by Dyson himself from poets as diverse as Henry Vaughan, Cardinal Newman, Robert Herrick, Shelley, Wordsworth and the psalm translator Thomas Sternhold. It may not be Dyson's finest composition, although there are some superb passages, but it is a deeply spiritual work, Dyson's reflection on the nature of human existence. As such, it deserves to be placed alongside Vaughan Williams's *Sancta civitas* and *Dona nobis pacem*, Howells's *Hymnus Paradisi*, and Finzi's *Intimations of Immortality*, all of which we shall look at in due course.

During the Second World War, Dyson was weighed down by practical and administrative concerns and naturally wrote less, although in 1942 he did complete a Violin Concerto that was generally appreciated by the critics. However, in the early 1950s when he retired from the RCM and from his other teaching posts, he enjoyed a late resurgence of creativity. There were some more short settings of Herrick, and three other notable works. The first, in 1954, was *Sweet Thames, Run Softly*, an adaptation of Edmund Spenser's *Prothalamion*, for baritone, chorus and orchestra, in which Dyson coveys the pastoral river scenes with appropriate sensuousnesss. The second was *Agincourt*, a much larger work in six sections, this time for chorus and orchestra without soloists, but equally English in conception, taking its text from *Henry V* and concluding with the *Agincourt Hymn*.[4] Dyson clearly enjoyed the theatricality of the ships crossing the Channel to France and the eeriness of the night before the battle. Neither work marked a stylistic move forward – although *Agincourt* showed awareness of both Vaughan Williams's *Sea Symphony* and Walton's music for Laurence Olivier's *Henry V* – but, as ever with Dyson, the music was apt for its purpose and full of fluent and effective choral writing.

The third work of Dyson's late period is very different. *Hierusalem* is a setting of words taken from an eighteenth-century translation of St Augustine. This was his last major composition, completed in 1956, and a work of intense feeling and beauty. Written for soprano solo, chorus, string orchestra, string quartet and organ, it takes us once again into that emotional heartland of so much English music, with the soprano voice expressing a yearning to reach the mystical beyond, represented in this case by the chorus. Like Holst, Dyson was a spiritual rather than a religious man; and, again like Holst, he was inspired by poetry to use music to explore the spiritual aspects of the human condition. Holst ranged far and wide in the search for inspiration, and was more intellectual in his approach, risking more, and opening up musical possibilities which he never lived to explore. Dyson was less of a risk taker, although that does not mean his work is as conservative or backward-looking as has sometimes been suggested. The essential difference is that Dyson's starting points were traditional sources (although he was barely touched by folk music) and traditional frameworks. From these – and sometimes within these – he created a personal idiom that was warm, accessible, often theatrical, and, above all, well suited to the texts he chose to set.

88   Coleridge-Taylor, Bridge, Scott, and Grainger

As noted earlier, the generation born between 1870 and 1890 was both numerous in itself and prolific in its output. Whether, by the time its members reached maturity, there was more music being produced than ever before is perhaps arguable, but certainly more of it has survived, not least because many careers that began in the world before 1914 lasted into the era of film, radio, and recorded music. So there are other composers whose careers must be touched upon, not in an attempt to be comprehensive, but because they all gained some degree of public notice in their lifetime, with the result that their names still appear in critical discussions or on concert programmes. Moreover their music illustrates the increased diversity and complexity of musical life in the early twentieth century.

Samuel Coleridge-Taylor (1875–1912) was born in Holborn in London to an English woman and a doctor from Sierra Leone who were not married. He thus began life with a double disadvantage: being illegitimate and of mixed race were not small handicaps in late Victorian Britain. These difficulties were, to some extent at least, overcome by his musical talent, which was evident from a very early age. He gained admission to the RCM at the age of fifteen; he was helped by August Jaeger at Novello's and, as a result, by Elgar, who recommended him to the Three Choirs Festival. His Ballade in A minor was played at Gloucester in 1898, and that same year he completed the work which made his name, the cantata *Hiawatha's Wedding Feast*. It received its first performance under Stanford's baton at the RCM. Its air of exoticism and Coleridge-Taylor's clever management of Longfellow's repetitive rhythms seemed to offer something new and it was a huge popular success – although the composer never received any royalties from it, having sold the rights for a mere fifteen guineas. Two further cantatas followed – *The Death of Minnehaha* and *Hiawatha's Departure* – and the completed trilogy was given its first performance in 1900.

Once he had achieved success, Coleridge-Taylor was able to turn his racial heritage to advantage. He continued to compose in the classical, Brahmsian tradition that he had absorbed from Stanford, modified by his own passion for Dvořák, but he also wrote a number of works that drew on his African heritage – works such as *Twenty-Four Negro Melodies*, *Toussaint l'Ouverture* and *Symphonic Variations on an African Air*. He believed that making people aware of black culture was one way of restoring the dignity of black people, and in this context he made three visits to the United States and was even received at the White House by Theodore Roosevelt. Indeed, he is still highly regarded in the United States as a pioneer of black consciousness, if not as a composer. None of his later compositions achieved anything approaching the success of *Hiawatha*, perhaps because he was trying too hard and writing too much. He died of pneumonia brought on by overwork and exhaustion at the age of just thirty-seven.

His music might have been forgotten altogether, but for his son – Hiawatha Coleridge-Taylor (1900–80) – who was determined to stage *Hiawatha* at the Albert Hall. In 1924, he succeeded. The idea caught on and was massively and unexpectedly popular. From then on, for two weeks every year, the *Hiawatha* trilogy was produced at the Royal Albert Hall with costumes and scenery, as if it were an opera rather than a cantata. Many of the performances were conducted by Malcolm Sargent. Audiences dressed up, often competing to wear the most authentic costumes. Native American chiefs came from the United States to participate and, on several occasions, members of the Royal Family attended. These festivals ended with the coming of the Second World War and, apart from the occasional revival of *Hiawatha*, Coleridge-Taylor's music is now rarely heard.

The career of Frank Bridge (1879–1941) presents a complete contrast. Yet another student of Stanford's at the RCM, Bridge became a noted string quartet player and conductor before making his mark as a composer. He was also a highly-respected teacher of violin and viola, although he only ever had one composition student. That student was, of course, Benjamin Britten, who repaid the debt some years later with his *Variations on a Theme of Frank Bridge*. Bridge was an individualist, whose work was barely touched by either the Folk or Tudor Revivals, and his career is best approached through his writing for string quartet. The *Phantasie Quartet* of 1905 and the String Quartet no.1 from 1906 both show his practical knowledge of how chamber music works from the inside. They are romantic but with great clarity of texture and sound. The Second String Quartet from 1915 marks a definite move towards a more modern approach, still tonal, and oddly reminiscent of Dvořák at times, but distinctly more questioning. These works can be linked to the four-movement orchestral suite *The Sea* (1911), probably still his most famous composition. They represent an Edwardian Bridge who had learned from Stanford, but was now absorbing other influences, taking his music forward by stages while still remaining on the edge of English pastoralism.

Several theories have been advanced as to what happened next. One is that Bridge, a strong pacifist, was so disturbed by the First World War that he was forced to rethink his musical philosophy. Another is that he was deeply affected by the childlessness of his marriage. Whatever the reason, the 1920s saw a significant change. In 1922, he could still make a jaunty arrangement of the old country dance, 'Sir Roger de Coverley', but by 1924 he was moving in a different direction, signalled by the powerful Piano Sonata and *In Autumn*, a group of starkly impressionist piano pieces. The Third String Quartet (1927) is a strong, spiky work, quite possibly the best thing Bridge ever wrote, showing how closely he – unlike most British composers of the time – was following developments in Vienna where Schoenberg and his followers were moving away from romanticism to a form of expressionism. In orchestral terms, Bridge's new technique was reflected in the tone poem, *Enter Spring*. Possibly inspired by Bax's *Spring Fire*, *Enter Spring* is hypnotic and modern with clear echoes of *The Rite of Spring*. Today, it does not seem a difficult work, but when it was first performed at Norwich in 1927 – with Bridge himself conducting the Queen's Hall Orchestra – the reviewer in the *Musical Times* seemed uncertain how to approach it.[1]

By this stage, the audience that Bridge had attracted in the years before 1914 was disappearing, apparently put off by the seriousness and modernity of his later music. He was considering increasing his teaching load in order to make ends meet when he was lucky enough to be offered financial support by the American patron of music, Elizabeth Sprague Coolidge. This allowed him to write his Piano Trio no. 2 (1929) and his Fourth (and last) String Quartet (1937). Both works are now recognised as among his best, although both attracted criticism at the time. The Fourth Quartet is another striking work, even more modern in technique, and even closer to Berg, whom Bridge much admired, and the composers of the Second Viennese School. Critics have disagreed about how deep and how radical the changes in Bridge's style were during the 1920s, but the fact remains that, in British terms at least, he was breaking new ground, writing intensely personal music that was not calculated to appeal to the audience of the day – and his reputation suffered as a result. Later works on a larger scale, such as *Oration* (1930) for cello and orchestra, and the *Rebus Overture* (1940), show impressive technique but do not have the same drive or thematic interest as the quartets. Bridge died in 1941 and his music was neglected for many years. Although interest has revived, he still remains on the periphery, in many ways a musician's musician.

If Bridge is attracting more attention today, it is precisely because he failed to do so in the 1920s and 30s: he was looking forward, looking beyond the English pastoral-national style of the time. All one can say is that the reputation of many of his contemporaries who did not attempt a comparable leap forward has fared worse. Both Joseph Holbrooke (1878–1958) and Cyril Scott (1879–1970) achieved early success and seemed destined for great things. Holbrooke studied at the RAM under Corder, where he was considered a gifted virtuoso pianist as well as a potentially fine composer, and won a string of prizes. His first real success was in 1900 when his tone poem, *The Raven* (he was fascinated by Edgar Allen Poe), was accepted by Manns and given at a Crystal Palace concert. Henry Wood, Beecham, Richter and Dan Godfrey at Bournemouth all played his works. For a brief period he worked alongside Bantock in Birmingham. Then, in 1909, came an opera, *Dylan, Son of the Wave*, the first in a trilogy of works based on legends from the *Mabinogion* as retold by T. E. Ellis, the nom de plume of Thomas Scott-Ellis, 8th Baron Howard de Walden. The second opera, *The Enchanter*, followed in 1914 and the third, *Bronwen*, in 1924. The whole, massive trilogy – the idea for which appears to have arisen independently of Boughton's Arthurian cycle – is known as *The Cauldron of Annwn*. Although not Welsh himself, Holbrooke was inspired by Welsh landscape and Welsh legends, and his music does at times show the influence of Welsh folk tunes, but much more evident is his affection for Tchaikovsky and the influence of Brahms and Dvořák.

The decline in Holbrooke's fortunes began after the First World War. In part, this was because the appeal of his rich, late-Romantic style had diminished and critics were inclined to see musical weaknesses previously obscured by his ebullient style and lush, Richard Strauss-like orchestration. In part also it was because he was a determined publicist and self-publicist. For all the right reasons, he campaigned tirelessly and vociferously on behalf of British composers (including himself), but he managed to offend as many people as he persuaded. There were some performances of his operas – by the Carl Rosa Opera Company, even in Vienna and Salzburg – but he found it more and more difficult to get his music played, and his attacks on the musical establishment, including the BBC, became more and more aggressive and, in the end, self-defeating. He continued to compose – operas, ballets, ten symphonies, a large number of orchestral works, piano pieces and songs – and Lord Howard de Walden stood by him financially, but despite his many talents, Holbrooke's career stalled because his music did not develop. He composed almost nothing after 1940.

At one time or another, Debussy, Ravel, Richard Strauss and Stravinsky all praised Cyril Scott. So did John Ireland and Percy Grainger. The slightly younger English composer and conductor, Eugene Goossens (1893–1962), once called him the 'father of modern British music'.[2] It is perhaps only fair to add that Alban Berg considered his music 'mushy',[3] but the consensus was overwhelmingly positive. Scott studied in Frankfurt at the same time as Percy Grainger, Roger Quilter and Balfour Gardiner. His early orchestral works included two symphonies, both written before he was twenty-four. These were taken up and played by Richter, by the Dutch conductor Willem de Haan and by Henry Wood, an indication of how highly Scott was regarded, although he was not satisfied with either work: he withdrew one and radically restructured the other. His pre-First World War success was based on his piano music – a Piano Quartet, premiered in London in 1901; a Sextet for Piano and Strings, first given in 1903; and series of romantic and impressionistic pieces for solo piano, to which he gave suitably romantic and poetic titles (*Vesperale, Chimes, Lotus Land, Columbine, Water-Wagtail*). These were followed by a Piano Concerto, again romantic but not overblown, given by Beecham in 1915 with Scott himself as soloist.

Scott was a fine pianist and interpreter of his own work. He was also considered extraordinarily good-looking in a brooding, Byronic manner, and at least a part of his early success was based on image, something he did not apparently disdain. The problem was that he had too many talents. By the 1920s, he had begun to take a serious interest in Indian philosophy, describing himself as a 'Vedantist'. This led on to a belief in the occult and reincarnation (something, probably coincidentally, that he shared with Eugene Goossens). He also wrote poetry in a rather 1890s style, publishing six volumes of his own work and two of translations. Eventually, he published some thirty books on a vastly diverse range of subjects from the occult to constipation and including two volumes of autobiography. And in his spare time, he designed his own furniture and painted.

Scott was now composing on a large scale – moving from solo piano works to opera, big orchestral pieces, and concertos for piano, cello and violin – but the romantic style and the romantic image had begun to seem dated. His 1933 tone poem on the sinking of the *Titanic*, initially called *Disaster at Sea* and later retitled *Neptune*, was slated by the critics, among them Constant Lambert. In fact, during the inter-war years, Scott was probably more popular in Germany than he was in Britain. Many of these works were published there and his one-act opera, *The Alchemist*, was given in Essen in 1925. He sought to revive his reputation in Britain with two large-scale choral works: *Let us Now Praise Famous Men*, written for the Norwich Festival in 1936, and *La Belle Dame sans Merci*, written for Leeds in 1937, but his moment had passed. He continued to compose inter- mittently into the 1960s, but by that stage he was largely unknown and unheard.

A last name in this section, illustrating again the range of different approaches to composing art music or classical music during the early decades of the twentieth century, is Percy Aldridge Grainger (1882–1961). Grainger was born in Melbourne and spoke of himself as an Australian composer. He arrived in London in 1901 and lived in Britain for only thir- teen years, leaving for the United States in 1914 and basing himself there for the rest of his life. Nonetheless he has to be included here because the nature of his work, the friendships he established and the influence he exerted constitute a significant piece in the jigsaw of British musical life at the time.

The nineteen-year-old who arrived in London in the year of Queen Victoria's death was already a distinctive, even odd personality. Up to the age of thirteen, he had been educated at home under the supervision of his powerful, controlling mother, Rose Aldridge. One feature of this education was immersion in Norse myths and Icelandic sagas. As a result, Grainger maintained a lifelong commitment to northern and Nordic culture – to the point where, later in life, he would insist on using words which had no Latin or French component. Thus a composer became a 'tone-wright', an audience a 'folk-host', while a crescendo would be marked 'louden' and a diminuendo 'soften'. Grainger had already made his public debut as a pianist when he and his mother left Australia for Frankfurt in 1895. After six years at the Hoch Conservatory, he was an accomplished soloist and a budding composer. He also had some very strong prejudices against southern and central European music. London was where he chose to launch his career.

Grainger's concert style was musically intense and physically athletic. With assistance from the Australian community in London and also, like Cyril Scott, helped by exceptionally good looks, Grainger was soon establishing himself as a new and exciting figure on the musical scene. He gave concert performances and recitals; he accompanied the great soprano Adriana Patti on a tour of Britain, and Ada Crossley, who had been one of Queen Victoria's favourite singers, on a tour of Australia. Queen Alexandra attended his concerts. He met Elgar and Strauss and Vaughan Williams. He had a short but productive friendship with Grieg, which ended with the Norwegian composer's unexpected death in 1907. That same year, he met and became friends with Delius, with whom he had a number of tastes, views and prejudices in common. All the while, he was composing, but not publishing or playing his compositions in public. It was part of his (or perhaps his mother's) career strategy that he should establish himself as a performer before revealing himself as a composer. The great moment came in 1911, when his first works were published. The following year, he gave a concert devoted entirely to his own works in London's Aeolian Hall.

Six years prior to that concert, Grainger had attended a lecture in London given by Lucy Broadwood. Inspired by what he heard, he started collecting folk songs, beginning around the Lincolnshire town of Brigg – where he collected 'Brigg Fair', which he later passed to Delius. The early folk-song collectors transcribed the tunes and songs they heard into note-books. Grainger was one of the first to record them onto phonograph cylinders. These travelled around with him for the rest of his life. Perhaps his finest folk arrangement is *Lincolnshire Posy*, a six-movement suite writ-ten for the American Bandmasters' Association in 1937, and consisting of songs he had collected thirty years previously. Grainger was a busy and uneven composer. He arranged folk songs; he arranged works by other composers; he wrote original works. Each work has a distinguishing title – he eschewed accepted musical forms, such as sonatas or concertos – and almost all are short, very few of them longer than seven or eight minutes. As with Holst, the discovery of folk music seems to have been a crucial development, giving his compositions a sense of direction. One of his most appealing, and lesser-known, folk arrangements is *La Scandinavie*, a four-movement suite of Scandinavian folk tunes for cello and piano, composed as early as 1902. Others, such as *Molly on the Shore* and *Shepherd's Hey*, are well known, and *Country Gardens* has become the victim of over-exposure. The tune for *Country Gardens* was provided by Cecil Sharp but not arranged until Grainger enlisted as a bandsman in the US Army during the First World War. It was published in 1919 and it made Grainger rich, but – as with Holst and *The Planets* – he came to dislike the work that had made his name. Grainger's original compositions range widely – from the light-hearted *Handel in the Strand* and *Mock Morris* (folk-inspired with just a hint of ragtime), to settings of poems by Kipling (whose work and Anglo-Saxon orientation Grainger admired) and the megalomaniac *Warriors (Music to an Imaginary Ballet)* which requires three conductors and a one-hundred-and-ten-piece orchestra with the addition of three pianos.

Grainger's eccentricities increased as he grew older. Ideas about beatless music, free music, tonal strands, elastic scoring and music without human intervention poured out of him and found their way into experimental pieces, few of which were ever publicly performed. He loved technology and often used strange instruments, such as the theremin, or machines of his own construction. To one of these, which can be seen as a distant ancestor of the synthesiser, he gave the name Kangaroo-Pouch Tone-Tool.

Grainger's mother had always exercised a stabilising influence on him, but her mental health deteriorated and in 1922 she committed suicide by throwing herself from the window of a New York skyscraper. Grainger was badly affected, and without the presence of his mother in the background both his musical and non-musical ideas grew gradually more and more extreme. His belief in Nordic cultural and racial superiority and his anti-Semitic attitudes make uncomfortable reading. While they never quite veer into Nazi territory, they make it evident that Grainger's individualism came at a price. He died at his house in White Plains, just north of New York, in 1961.

89   Vaughan Williams

The one composer of this pre-First-World-War generation whom we have yet to look at in detail is, of course, Ralph Vaughan Williams (1872–1958). He has been left until last not just because of his longevity and his prolific output, but also because his career and the role he played in British musical life encapsulate the central issues and difficulties surrounding any assessment of the period. Hindsight tells us that Vaughan Williams was the outstanding figure of his generation, yet it was not until the 1930s, by which time he was in his sixties, that anyone would have recognised him as such. Some of the works which we now regard as familiar, concert programme staples were, in their day, genuinely radical, and although he was never as obviously adventurous a composer as Holst, he was in his own way perhaps a greater force for change.

He was born at Down Ampney in Gloucestershire where his father was the vicar, but at the age of three, following his father's death, he and his mother moved back to her family's home at Leith Hill Place in Surrey. The family were distinguished – his mother was a member of the Wedgewood family and a niece of Charles Darwin – and liberal in outlook, but not aristocratic. They were also wealthy and throughout his life Vaughan Williams, like Bax, had a private income sufficient for him to live on. His education was conventional for someone with his background. It began at home, and continued first at preparatory school in Rottingdean in Sussex, and then at a public school, Charterhouse, in Surrey, where he went when he was fourteen. Even though he wrote his first composition at the age of six and took a correspondence course in music from Edinburgh University when he was eight, his determination to pursue a musical career when he left Charterhouse met with opposition from his family. He wanted to concentrate on the viola and become an orchestral player. They doubted he had the talent and felt that if he had to be a musician, he should adopt the more respectable profession of organist. A compromise was reached: he agreed to learn the organ, and was allowed to spend two years at the RCM before going up to Cambridge.

Vaughan Williams was eighteen when he entered the RCM in 1890. The talent was there, but the technical knowledge and wider knowledge of music was lacking. He studied basic harmony; he took composition classes with Parry, who pushed him to study Beethoven and Brahms; he went to hear *Carmen*, Verdi's *Requiem*, and *Tristan*, all for the first time. In 1892, he went up to Trinity College, Cambridge, to study music and history. The Irish composer Charles Wood, noted for his settings of the Anglican Service and his anthems, tutored him for his music degree; while Alan Gray (1855–1935), another church music specialist, helped with his laborious progress at the organ. And throughout his three years at Cambridge, he travelled down to London every week to continue his classes with Parry. In 1895, having satisfied his family by gaining a degree in music and another in history, he returned to the RCM.

This time his composition teacher was Stanford. Vaughan Williams later claimed that he respected Stanford as a teacher, but at the time the relationship was a combative one. His compositions may have been clumsy – Stanford dubbed them 'ugly' and 'rot' – and he may not have known precisely where he was heading musically, but he at least knew that it was not where Stanford wanted him to go. This second period at the RCM saw the beginning of his close and long-lasting friendship with Holst. It also saw him on the stage as a member of the chorus in Stanford's epoch-making production of *Dido and Aeneas*. At the same time, he applied and was accepted for the post of organist in the large, neo-Gothic church of St Barnabas in South Lambeth. He was a competent organist. Neither Parratt at the RCM nor regular duties at St Barnabas managed to get him beyond that, but St Barnabas did teach him a great deal about the practical side of church music.

In 1897, Vaughan Williams married Adeline Fisher. She played piano and cello and was a cousin of Virginia Woolf. Their honeymoon consisted of several months in Berlin, where – among other things – they experienced the *Ring* cycle and he took lessons from Max Bruch. Returning to London, they set up home in Westminster. Vaughan Williams continued to compose, but still in the tentative manner of a student rather than a fully-formed composer; he played in amateur string quartets and other groups; and he worked for his Doctorate in Music, which he was awarded in 1899. But it was 1901, and he was twenty-nine, before he had any music published.

He was, as must be evident from this chronology, a slow developer, and it is at least arguable whether, if he had not had a private income from his family, he would have been able to develop as a composer in the way he eventually did.

That first published work was 'Linden Lea', a setting of a poem by the Dorset poet, William Barnes. It was and remains deservedly popular. It is not a folk song – it still leans on German models – but it sounds as if it should be. 'Linden Lea' was followed in 1904 by *The House of Life*, a setting of six sonnets by Dante Gabriel Rossetti, of which 'Silent Noon' is the outstanding piece; and by *Songs of Travel*, a cycle of poems by Robert Louis Stevenson. These works were the first real evidence of his gifts – of his ability to find tunes, to set words, and to express contrasting moods without a sense of conflict. The same year also saw both the appearance of *In the Fen Country*, a Delius-like tone poem, evoking the East Anglian landscape, and his agreement to take on the job of editing a new hymn book, *The English Hymnal*. This lasted two years and Vaughan Williams considered it a better musical education than studying fugues or sonatas. The final volume included several tunes that he had written himself, two of which are still popular in the Church of England today: *Down Ampney* ('Come Down, O Love Divine') and *Sine Nomine* ('For All the Saints').

In the meantime, like Cecil Sharp a few years earlier and Grainger a few years later, Vaughan Williams was discovering folk song. In December 1903, after a parish tea at the village of Ingrave in Essex, he was introduced to a labourer called Charles Pottipher, who sang 'Bushes and Briars'.[1] Vaughan Williams was already aware of folk song: he had given lectures on its importance in British music and he knew Lucy Broadwood. 'Bushes and Briars', then, was not quite the road-to-Damascus revelation experienced by Cecil Sharp, but it did nonetheless galvanise his interest. His next major composition, *Norfolk Rhapsody no. 1* (1906) was based on folk songs, some of which he had collected himself from Norfolk fishermen in a pub called the Tilden Smith in King's Lynn.

Vaughan Williams's first major choral work, *Towards an Unknown Region*, based on a text from Walt Whitman's *Leaves of Grass*, was premiered in 1907 at the Leeds Festival. Despite clear echoes of Wagner, the piece is unmistakeably English. Vaughan Williams extends and expands the techniques employed in his earlier songs, and he includes a flavour of the hymn tunes on which he had been working. More important, however, is the way in which the transcendental mood of the text – the unknown region is, of course, death – is expressed musically. Vaughan Williams is clearly working towards that sense of mystical yearning which we have already identified as a central characteristic of English music. Critics and public alike recognised that *Towards an Unknown Region* marked an important step forward, but Vaughan Williams himself was not satisfied. He went to Paris and spent three months taking lessons with Ravel, who helped him reduce the Germanic influence in his writing and adopt a lighter touch in his orchestration. The first results were heard in his *Shropshire Lad* song cycle, *On Wenlock Edge* (1909), which mixes folk song and Ravel as influences in more or less equal measure. Six poems do not necessarily make a major work. In this case, however, Housman's deceptively simple lines were set to themes that Vaughan Williams managed to develop and dramatise even within the short space of a poem, so that each setting and the cycle as a whole are resolved, making the whole work seem bigger than it actually is. Vaughan Williams felt that the pendulum had swung too far and that the cycle was too French in approach; and it was the subject of an outspoken attack by the critic and Wagner biographer, Ernest Newman; nonetheless, *On Wenlock Edge* remains a popular and frequently-recorded work.

The autumn of 1910 marked a turning point in Vaughan Williams's career. In September, he conducted the *Fantasia on a Theme of Thomas Tallis* in Gloucester Cathedral as part of the Three Choirs Festival; in October, on his thirty-eighth birthday, he conducted *A Sea Symphony* at the Leeds Festival. Applause, in those days, was not permitted in churches or cathedrals, so the premiere of the *Tallis Fantasia* ended with silence. The young Herbert Howells and Ivor Gurney who were in the audience were so stunned by what they heard that they wandered the streets of Gloucester unable to sleep. Fuller Maitland in *The Times* famously said, 'Throughout its course, one is never sure whether one is listening to something very old or very new',[2] which was surely the point. The majority of the press and the audience, however, were simply bewildered. It offered no obvious models. It was certainly not German, but there was nothing of Ravel either. The scoring – for two string orchestras and a string quartet – was unusual to say the least. Here was the Tudor Revival in full force. Here was certainly yearning, both pastoral and mystical, and an intense concentration on musical texture. Elgar was trying to remake English music in accordance with Continental models; Vaughan Williams was clearly going in the opposite direction, searching for new models to fit English music into.

At the time, the first performance of *A Sea Symphony* seemed the more important event. A massive choral work with an explosive opening, setting texts from Walt Whitman's *Leaves of Grass* and lasting some seventy minutes: this, not the *Tallis Fantasia*, was the work which to the public of the day announced the arrival of Vaughan Williams as a significant musical force. *A Sea Symphony*, despite being in four movements, is only loosely symphonic in structure. Vaughan Williams knew that. He quite probably called it a symphony to make a point: the title, the integrated chorus and the programmatic text, all seem intended to distance the work from the traditional (and largely Germanic) symphonic tradition which he felt had become too rigid and self-regarding. And, of course, calling it a symphony was also a way of attracting attention. The *London Symphony*, first performed at the Queen's Hall in 1914, is a less adventurous work, but raises similar issues. Vaughan Williams himself insisted that it should be considered abstract or absolute music, yet the title, the inclusion of street cries and the Westminster quarter chimes, and the picturesque, descriptive qualities of the work all point to at least some programmatic intent.

Vaughan Williams was forty-two in the October of 1914, but he still joined up. He became a private in the Royal Army Medical Corps, serving first in France, where he brought the wounded and dying out of the trenches, and then in Greece. In 1917, he took a commission in the Royal Artillery and returned to France. When the fighting ended, he was appointed Director of Music for the First Army, which meant organising musical activities among troops who were waiting to be demobilised. It was not until 1920 that his musical life really re-established itself, and the most important event of that year – at least in retrospect – was the first performance of *The Lark Ascending*, which he had written in 1914.[3]

A hundred years after it was composed, *The Lark Ascending* has become astonishingly popular. In 2014, 2015 and 2016, it was voted Britain's favourite piece of classical music. Yet it has also attracted criticism for its romanticism, its nostalgia and for the way in which the undoubted religiosity of Vaughan William's music is associated with pastoral England in what has been seen as a kind of chauvinism.[4] The title is taken from a poem by George Meredith, and the music closely follows the attributes of the lark and its song as described in the poem. The opening theme sounds like a folk song, which is obviously what Vaughan Williams intended, but is actually one he wrote himself; and all the other themes of the work, including the lark's song, either evolve from it or are variants of it. The theme and its treatment are undoubtedly romantic and ethereal, but there is much more to *The Lark* than nostalgia and what Stephen Johnson has called 'images of cream tea England'.[5] Vaughan Williams was writing as an English composer, which is what he was, but his purpose was broader than any kind of national chauvinism. He was making a statement about the spiritual relationship between traditional society, as represented by the folk-like theme, and the natural world, as represented by the lark. The inspiration for the piece came while he was walking on the cliffs above Margate in 1914 in the days immediately following the beginning of the war, so one must assume that it contains a some degree of reflection on, or contrast with, the state of affairs at the time. Yet that connection remains implicit. *The Lark*, for all its English pastoralism, aims at universality.

The 1920s and 1930s saw a series of major works which established Vaughan Williams as Britain's leading composer in succession to Elgar, who wrote nothing of any real consequence after 1919. *A Pastoral Symphony* was first heard at the Queen's Hall with Adrian Boult conducting the Royal Philharmonic Orchestra at the beginning of 1922. 'Elegaic' would have been a better title. Its pastoral tones are shot through with a melancholy that is not present in *The Lark* and, while there is no actual programme, it is evidently a work that looks back to the war. Vaughan Williams stated that it was conceived in northern France and that it was inspired by the sound of a bugler practising. This experience is reflected in the trumpet cadenza in the second movement, which, together with the solo soprano voice over timpani at the beginning of the fourth movement (recurring at the end without the timpani), is one of the defining moments of the symphony, concentrating its sense of grief and loss.

There followed a series of remarkable choral works, composed over a period of fourteen years, which show a fascinating intellectual and musical progression. The first was his powerful, unaccompanied *Mass in G* which reaches back to the age of Byrd and English polyphony. Vaughan Williams said that he saw no reason why an atheist could not write a perfectly good Mass and he was as good as his word.[6] *Mass in G* was premiered at the end of 1922 in Birmingham and first sung in a liturgical context, as the composer intended it should be, under the direction of Richard Terry at Westminster Cathedral. Having expressed himself in the most traditional of all religious musical forms, Vaughan Williams moved on to *Flos Campi* (which translates as *Flowers of the Field*), which is very much *sui generis*. First heard in 1925, it is a six-movement suite for viola and small orchestra with a wordless chorus, but the fact that each movement is headed with a verse from *The Song of Solomon* indicates an underlying religious or spiritual intent. The work has a strong sensuous quality, as much mysterious as mystical. At the same time, Vaughan Williams, quite unusually, steps away from his Englishness to employ rhythms and tonalities suggestive of the music of the Near East. Was he looking back to the kind of music that would have been heard at the time of Christianity's origins, in a manner perhaps analogous to Holst's rediscovery of the ecstasy and dancing of the Christian revelation in *Hymn of Jesus*? His next work, in 1926, was *Sancta Civitas*. Vaughan Williams called it an oratorio but beyond a biblical text – taken from *The Book of Revelations* – it has nothing in common with the Victorian oratorio tradition. It is short and urgent, and, in spirit rather than musically, again recalls Holst's *Hymn of Jesus*. It is also socially relevant. Shorn of its symbols and metaphors, the text confronts the issue of private as against public responsibility – a very live issue in Britain at the time. Coincidentally but tellingly, *Sancta Civitas* was given its first performance at the Sheldonian Theatre in Oxford during the General Strike. The next work of comparable scale and purpose came ten years later in 1936. *Dona Nobis Pacem* is called a cantata, but its tone, its purpose and its intensity are those of an oratorio. It is a big work, far removed from the pastoralism of earlier years. It opens with an 'Agnus Dei', normally the concluding part of the Mass, bringing a message of peace and forgiveness, but here carrying the threat of war. The second, third and fourth movements take texts from poems by Walt Whitman. 'Beat! Beat! Drums!' dwells on 'ruthless force'; 'Reconciliation' on sadness in the face of inevitable death in war; 'Dirge for Two Veterans' is told by a woman who has lost both her husband and her son. The fifth movement quotes the famous 'Angel of Death' speech given in Parliament by the Quaker orator John Bright when opposing the Crimean War. The soprano voice that sings 'Dona Nobis Pacem' in the 'Agnus Dei' returns regularly throughout, pleading for peace but seemingly powerless. Only in the last movement, a succession of biblical verses, is there any glimpse of optimism. *Dona Nobis Pacem* was very much a tract for the unsettled 1930s, but it also has both a universal and a personal quality, seeking the peace of the soul as well as international peace.

It was works such as these that led the adjective 'visionary' to be applied to Vaughan Williams and his work. In early life, he claimed to be an atheist. Later, he called himself a cheerful agnostic and then a Christian agnostic. He was, in fact, a cultural Christian, loving the language of hymns and the Bible, loving church architecture and the long tradition, both historical and mystical, of the Christian religion, but never an actual believer. These works certainly reflect that spiritual side of his character. However, 'visionary' also implies someone whose ideas are removed from daily reality. This was simply not true of Vaughan Williams. Inspired, like Holst, by the arts-and-crafts-style socialism of William Morris, he devoted a huge amount of time and energy to helping and promoting amateur music-making. He conducted the Leith Hill Music Festival for nearly fifty years; he formed soldiers into choirs and ensembles; he worked with local groups, with the English Folk Dance Society, with the Surrey Education Committee, Rural Schools Music, the Federation of Women's Institutes and many other organisations. These activities stimulated much of his functional or occasional music – which has been likened to Hindemith's concept of *Gebrauchsmusik*[7] – the mass of small, original pieces and often player- or group-specific arrangements that stand at the opposite end of the spectrum from his big 'visionary' works.

As early as 1922, when the *Pastoral Symphony* appeared, a younger generation of composers, including Constant Lambert (who had been Vaughan Williams's student) and Peter Warlock, had begun to snipe at his pastoral style. The Fourth Symphony, the first without a title, put paid to such criticisms, at least for a while. It is tense, violent, and dissonant, with an explosive opening, a highly expressive second movement and an epilogue that is almost savage. It had its premiere in 1935, the year before *Dona Nobis Pacem*, and one is tempted to see it as another, less focussed and more angry response to the troubles of the 1930s. In later life, Vaughan Williams said he was not sure that he liked it, but that it was what he meant at the time. The Fifth Symphony, which was premiered during the 1943 Proms at the Royal Albert Hall, eight years after the Fourth, is a complete contrast. It is quiet, slow-moving and follows the methods of Sibelius – to whom it was dedicated – in that its themes evolve from almost nothing into swelling climaxes. Although seen by some as a return to his earlier pastoralism, the Fifth is a work of considerable depth, where moments of serenity, elation and pride are mixed with tension and doubt – again seeming to reflect the outer world, in this case the conflicting and contrasting emotions of wartime. The Sixth Symphony consists of four movements played without a break: the first three noisy and dramatic, the finale slow, quiet and almost desolate in tone. When it was premiered in 1948, it was widely interpreted as another war symphony, with the violence of the war itself giving way to post-war desolation at the end. Vaughan Williams seemed to deny this when he quoted Prospero's farewell – 'We are such stuff / As dreams are made on, and our little life / Is rounded by a sleep' – in relation to the last movement. But what did that mean? Was he was about to retire? He was seventy-six and it was a perfectly reasonable supposition. It is more probable that he was indicating that he wanted the work to be seen as having a universal application. Retirement was not on his agenda.

Vaughan Williams was a patriot, but his was not a flag-waving, institutional patriotism like Elgar's. It was a community-oriented, mucking-in, and above all self-effacing kind of patriotism. Hence his decision in the First World War to enlist as a private soldier. During the Second, he was far too old for active service, but took his turn fire-watching and became involved in helping refugees and interned alien musicians. It was as a result of his desire to do more to help the war effort that he allowed himself to be persuaded to provide music for the film *49th Parallel*, which sought to influence public opinion in the then still neutral United States. After *49th Parallel* came *Coastal Command*, about Sunderland flying boats hunting for U-boats, the first in a series of Ministry of Information propaganda films for which he provided the score. Writing for films was a new skill and one that paid dividends after the war.

In 1946, he wrote the score for a full-length Ealing Studios' feature, *The Loves of Joanna Godden*, and then, two years later in 1948, came *Scott of the Antarctic*, starring John Mills. Vaughan Williams was certainly not the first 'serious' composer to write for films – William Walton already had a number of film scores to his credit, including Laurence Olivier's wartime *Henry V*; and earlier that same year David Lean's *Oliver Twist* had featured an impressive soundtrack by Arnold Bax – but he was certainly not slow in realising its potential. *Scott of the Antarctic* was a tale of man against nature, a tragedy of human ambition and courage overwhelmed by elemental forces. For a man with Vaughan Williams's temperament and imagination, this was fertile territory and the film score became the basis of his Seventh Symphony, *Sinfonia Antartica*, in 1953. There is, however, a fundamental distinction between film music, which works through short, illustrative passages, and a symphony which is (or should be) a continuous musical argument. It is a distinction that *Sinfonia Antartica* does not overcome. It is a powerful work, imaginatively scored to include a piano, a celesta, an organ, gongs, vibraphone, xylophone, and a wind machine. It conveys the cold, the immensity of the barren landscape, the struggle and the heroism of Scott and his men, but it remains linked to their narrative. It is not a symphony. In fact, it is even less symphonic in form than *A Sea Symphony*.

The post-war years were not a vintage period for Vaughan Williams. He showed no signs of slowing down but the works he produced tended to be in some way unusual, written for specific occasions or individuals or perhaps just to please himself. *An Oxford Elegy* (1949) is a heavily nostalgic piece, based on a text drawn from Matthew Arnold's poems *The Scholar Gypsy* and *Thyrsis*, and unusual in that the text is spoken by a narrator. Even more unusual was *Romance for harmonica and orchestra* written for the American harmonica player, Larry Adler; and there was also a Tuba Concerto written for Philip Catelinet of the London Symphony Orchestra. The most important and, from Vaughan Williams's point of view, the most disappointing premiere of the period was of his opera – although he preferred to called it a 'morality' – *The Pilgrim's Progress* in 1951.

Vaughan Williams had always been interested in the stage. His ballet *Job* – which he called *A Masque for Dancing* – was choreographed by Ninette de Valois and became one of the first productions of the new Vic-Wells Ballet in 1931. (The company's name and origins are explained on p.346.) It contains some dark but impressive music. He wrote at least four other masques or ballets during the course of his career. He also wrote no fewer than five operas. *Hugh the Drover*, completed in 1910, when he was still heavily influenced by folk music, but not performed until 1924, is a pastoral ballad opera set in Napoleonic times. *Sir John in Love*, which had an amateur performance in 1929 and a professional one in 1946, is based on Shakespeare's *Merry Wives of Windsor*, drawing on both folk song and Tudor music. In both cases, one can see what Vaughan Williams was trying to do, but neither opera is ultimately successful. *Riders to the Sea*, finished in 1932 and first performed in 1937, is wholly different and a much more impressive work. In the first place, it is a tragedy. Based on J. M. Synge's play, it tells the story of an Irishwoman who has already lost her husband, her father-in-law and four sons to the sea. Now she loses her last two sons. Secondly, it is short, lasting barely forty minutes. The vocal writing is tense and follows Synge's dialogue closely. There is no room for arias or choruses. On stage the central character is Maurya, but she shares that centrality with the sea, which is ever present in the music, rising and falling, menacing and threatening. It is a somewhat surprising piece for Vaughan Williams to have written and represents his only real excursion into the Celtic world where so many of his contemporaries found inspiration.

The work for which Vaughan Williams wanted to be remembered, however, was *The Pilgrim's Progress*. The idea of turning Bunyan's allegory into a stage work came to him before the First World War; the premiere of the completed 'morality' came six years after the end of the Second. Its failure was perhaps the biggest professional disappointment of his life. It was the longest work he ever wrote – in four acts, and well over three hours in performance – and reflects again his philosophical position as a cultural Christian. He deliberately altered the central character's name from Christian to Pilgrim to give a sense of universality, and for the same reason he wanted the work performed in a theatre not a church. There are wonderful moments, such as Act IV, scene ii – 'The Shepherds of the Delectable Mountains' – but the work as a whole is so dependent on a progression of abstract ideas that it is extremely difficult to inject sufficient dramatic progression to make it a good opera. Again, one sees what Vaughan Williams intended and why he insisted on the term 'morality' rather than opera. A 2012 production by English National Opera overcame at least some of the difficulties, but it is a work that remains at best problematic. Elgar, Bax, Vaughan Williams, and – by that time – William Walton, had produced symphonies of undeniable quality, but the great British opera remained elusive.

In 1952, Vaughan Williams turned eighty. That same year his wife Adeline died after many years of frail health. Vaughan Williams himself showed no diminution of energy. The following year came not only the premiere of *Sinfonia Antartica* but also a second marriage. His last years saw a number of new works. The Eighth Symphony, given by Sir John Barbirolli and the Hallé Orchestra in 1956, was coolly received and deservedly so. It is his weakest, largely because the four movements seem neither fully developed, nor musically integrated. However, his return to songwriting – something he had all but abandoned since the 1920s – was more successful. *Ten Blake Songs* (1957), for tenor voice and oboe, is remarkable for its combination of absolute simplicity and real poetic understanding. It was followed by *Four Last Songs* (1958), to poems by his new wife, Ursula, an often stark meditation on loneliness and death. But the jewel of this late burst of composition was the Ninth Symphony. Written when the composer was eighty-five and given its premiere in 1958 just five months before his death, the Ninth has often been described as enigmatic. It is natural to want to see the work as some kind of leave-taking, but the Ninth has none of the elegiac quality of Bax's Seventh or the spirit of acceptance found in Dyson's last major work, *Hierusalem*. Vaughan Williams himself claimed it was inspired by Hardy's *Tess of the d'Urbervilles* and there is some evidence from the original sketches that this is true, but the symphony as we have it is not programme music. It is the work of a composer who is still prone to anger, uncertainty and doubt, still experimenting with ways of expressing himself and unsure where his experimentation will lead. It is not a settled work, not an easy work, but it is a masterpiece.

By the time he died in 1958, Vaughan Williams was the Grand Old Man of English music, a bulky figure in country tweeds often referred to – disparagingly by his critics – as 'Uncle Ralph'. By that time, also, debates about national music were antediluvian, and the English Musical Renaissance was a subject for historians. He had outlived all the composers of his own generation and most of those in the next. As a consequence, both the public and the critics came to see him as representative of an entire musical era – which may explain why, when his music and that of his contemporaries had fallen out of fashion in the 1960s and 1970s, he was so often singled out for criticism that seemed almost ideological in tone. Since then, the balance of critical opinion has largely reasserted itself and Vaughan Williams is now recognised as one of Britain's most original composers. However, when we come to consider British musical life as it developed from the 1930s onwards, it is important to recognise the status acquired by Vaughan Williams during that period. It went beyond that of a respected national figure, achieved by Elgar. Unlike Elgar, he was both strongly academic in orientation and highly articulate. What he said and thought about music – and the interpretation placed on it – acquired an almost symbolic importance for younger generations of composers and, indeed, for the critics.

90   The Proms, Henry Wood, and Thomas Beecham

In August 1895, just two weeks before Vaughan Williams's twenty-third birthday and shortly after he had returned to the RCM to wrestle with Stanford as a composition teacher, a young British conductor gave the first of a new series of promenade concerts at London's Queen's Hall. His name was Henry Joseph Wood (1869–1944). Promenade concerts, as we have seen, had their origins in the pleasure gardens and achieved nationwide popularity as a result of the showmanship of Louis-Antoine Jullien. From 1844, London's promenade concerts had been staged at Covent Garden.

Sullivan had been the chief conductor for a couple of years before handing over to Frederick Cowen in 1880; and it was Cowen who conducted the last of the Covent Garden concerts in 1893. They were being moved because London had a new concert venue, the 2,500-seat Queen's Hall in Langham Place, just north of Regent Street. Cowen conducted the inaugural concert at the new venue, but was not engaged to conduct the new series of promenade concerts, partly because he was taking over as chief conductor of both the Hallé in Manchester and the Liverpool Philharmonic following the death of Sir Charles Hallé, and partly because the manager of the new hall, Robert Newman, had decided the series needed a revamp.

Newman was a keen amateur singer who had made money in the City before becoming an impresario. He wanted to return to the spirit of the original promenade concerts. They should be cheap, so that the hall would be full in August and September, a time when Londoners did not usually attend concerts; and they should be informal, so smoking, eating and drinking were to be allowed during performances. Wood at this time was a *répétiteur*, singing teacher and aspiring conductor with a growing reputation for opera – he had worked for the Carl Rosa Opera Company and had conducted the British premiere of Tchaikovsky's *Eugene Onegin* when the Saint Petersburg Imperial Opera Company visited London in 1892. It was Wood who introduced Newman to Dr George Cathcart, an ear, nose and throat specialist from Edinburgh who had moved to London a few years previously. Cathcart agreed to finance the new concerts but made two conditions: he wanted Wood to conduct all the concerts, and he insisted that the pitch should be lowered to what was known as 'Diapason normal' or 'Continental Pitch'. At the time, English concert pitch was a semitone higher than was normal on the Continent, and in the course of treating professional singers, Cathcart had come to the conclusion that the higher pitch was damaging their voices. To the lay reader this may sound highly technical, but, once other orchestras followed the lead of the Queen's Hall, it represented a significant step forward for practical musicianship, bringing Britain into line with Continental norms.

Wood was only twenty-six, but he knew an opportunity when he saw one and he seized it. He recruited a new orchestra for the Queen's Hall and set about imposing new levels of discipline on the players. He would not tolerate lateness at rehearsals. He would not allow them to nip outside for a smoke during a movement in which they were not required. And he took on the deputy system. At that time, orchestral players were employed on a casual basis. If a player accepted one engagement, but then received the offer of another that paid more, or perhaps came from a conductor or a promoter who might offer more work in the future, it was customary for him or her to nominate a deputy to fill in at rehearsals or even for the concert – with inevitable consequences for the standard of performance. In 1904, Wood, with Newman's backing, refused to accept any more deputies. Forty players resigned, but they were replaced and both the Queen's Hall Orchestra and the promenade concerts carried on as before. As it happened, Wood's actions had positive consequences which went well beyond the improvement of Queen's Hall performances. A group of those who resigned decided to form their own orchestra, run by the players themselves as a co-operative. This was the beginning of London's first permanent symphony orchestra – the London Symphony Orchestra (LSO).[1] They gave their first concert that June with Arthur Nikisch conducting. The following year another group of players followed their example and formed the New Symphony Orchestra (later known as the Royal Albert Hall Orchestra).

The first season of Robert Newman Promenade Concerts, as they were known, lasted ten weeks. Programmes were far longer in those days – often twice as long as a modern symphony concert – which meant that there was a huge amount of music to rehearse and perform. Promenade concerts usually consisted of light classical and orchestral works, popular arias and songs by recognised composers. The first programme featured a *Hungarian Rhapsody* by Liszt, a *Serenade* by Schubert, extracts from *Carmen* and *I Pagliacci*, and songs by Saint-Saëns, Gounod, Rossini and Haydn. Almost immediately, Wood began introducing more demanding works – Beethoven, Schubert, Tchaikovsky, Richard Strauss – and during the 1896 season he instituted all-Beethoven programmes on Monday nights and all-Wagner programmes on Fridays. As time went on, he grew bolder, giving performances of Mahler's First Symphony (1903) and his Fourth (1905). Both works were widely regarded as incomprehensible at the time. In 1912, he also gave the British premieres of Scriabin's *Prometheus* and Schoenberg's *Five Orchestral Pieces*. If the audience found such works difficult, there was always something more popular on the bill to make up for it. His policy was one of educating and entertaining. In the same spirit, he began to introduce works by contemporary British composers, something which remains a feature of the Proms as we know them today. In the years before 1914, he included pieces by Mackenzie,

Stanford, Edward German, Coleridge-Taylor, Elgar, W.H. Reed, Joseph Holbrooke, Landon Ronald, Granville Bantock, York Bowen, Havergal Brian, Cyril Scott, Learmont Drysdale, Eric Coates, Walford Davies, Vaughan Williams, Delius, Hamilton Harty, Foulds, Quilter, Frank Bridge, and Arnold Bax. The list is not exhaustive, but Wood and the Queen's Hall promenade concerts clearly played a very significant role – and one that grew in importance as their reputation increased – during the English Musical Renaissance period by offering British composers a platform for their works at the centre of British musical life.

Musically, the concerts were a great success. Financially, they were a disaster – at least for Newman, who was so committed to his mission that he failed to see bankruptcy looming. The axe fell in 1902. The Proms were only saved by the intervention of Sir Edgar Speyer, a financier and philanthropist, who founded the company that built London's Northern, Bakerloo and Piccadilly underground lines, and who also acted as fundraiser for Captain Scott's ill-fated expedition to the South Pole. Speyer formed a syndicate to run the Queen's Hall, allowing Newman to remain as manager, but financed the Proms from his own pocket, claiming later that he did so only to please his wife. In recognition of Wood's popularity as a conductor, the concerts were renamed the Henry Wood Promenade Concerts, under which name they continue to this day.

Wood was not the only up-and-coming conductor as Britain entered the Edwardian era. Hamilton Harty (1879–1941) was born in Hillsborough, just outside Belfast. A church organist by the age of twelve, he came to London when he was twenty to pursue a career as an accompanist and composer. His early compositions, notably his *Irish Symphony*, which he conducted himself in Dublin in 1904, and his arrangements of Irish songs proved popular, and his *Comedy Overture* was given at the Proms in 1907. His London conducting debut came in 1911 when the LSO gave his tone poem *With the Wild Geese*, which, like much of his work, has an Irish lyricism very similar to Stanford's. A return engagement with the LSO the following year was less successful, and an engagement to conduct *Carmen* and *Tristan and Isolde* at Covent Garden in 1913 drew criticism from the press. Nonetheless, he was gaining experience and gaining a following. In 1914, he made his debut with the Liverpool Philharmonic and then with the Hallé, the orchestra that was later to make his name.

Thomas Beecham (1879–1961), who was the same age as Harty, rose to prominence much more noisily. It helped, of course, that the family was rich – his grandfather had invented Beecham's Pills, the well-known laxative, and his father, Joseph, had built up the business to the point where, in 1899, his income was estimated at £85,000. That was also the year in which Joseph decided to organise and pay for a concert to mark the beginning of his second term as Mayor of St Helen's. He imported the Hallé and their new conductor, Hans Richter, from Manchester for the occasion – except that Richter was ill, so the baton was taken by the self-taught, twenty-year-old Thomas Beecham. That evening laid the foundation stone of his career.

Shortly after these events, Joseph Beecham committed his wife to a mental home. Young Thomas Beecham was outraged and said so. As a consequence, he was estranged from both his father and the family fortune for the next ten years. This meant that during the early stages of his musical career, he had to make his own way. In 1902, he was recruited by Kelson Trueman as one of two conductors for a tour by the newly-formed Imperial Grand Opera Company. Unfortunately, the tour extended only to five London suburbs, but it was nonetheless his professional debut. In 1906, he became conductor of the New Symphony Orchestra, an association that lasted until 1908, when they parted company, largely because of Beecham's objections to the deputy system. Unable to find an orchestra that would do his bidding, he decided to found one. The Beecham Symphony Orchestra gave its first concert at the Queen's Hall in September 1909. It was an orchestra of huge and sometimes explosive character. Beecham himself was only thirty, and the average age of the players was about twenty-five – young enough for them not to have had time to become blasé about their calling. The viola section for that first concert included both Lionel Tertis (1876–1975) – for whom Bax, Bridge, Bliss, Holst and Vaughan Williams all wrote works – and the composer Eric Coates.

Beecham was talented, dynamic and headstrong. He insisted on programming works that he liked, not works that would attract audiences. This was good in that the musical public up and down the country – for the orchestra was soon on tour – was exposed to works they would otherwise not have heard: Borodin, d'Indy, Lalo, Smetana, Debussy, and César Franck all featured on Beecham Symphony programmes. There was also a plentiful selection of works by British composers: Elgar, McEwen, Granville Bantock, Holbrooke, Balfour Gardiner, and Vaughan Williams, but above all Delius, whose work Beecham promoted tirelessly from their first meeting in 1907. The Beecham Symphony featured *Sea Drift* in its inaugural concert and, in 1910, gave the first full performance of *A Mass of*

Life. The downside of all this was the Beecham Symphony was soon in financial trouble.

Disaster was averted by a rapprochement between Beecham and his father, which was engineered in 1909 by Ethel Smyth, while Beecham was conducting *The Wreckers* at His Majesty's Theatre. Rapprochement meant access to the Beecham money; father and son, who appear to have had very similar characters, decided to take on the British musical establishment in what Beecham's biographer has called 'an orgy of opera'.[2] In 1910 alone, they promoted one hundred and ninety operatic performances. Beecham conducted most of them, but among his guest conductors were Richard Strauss and Bruno Walter. Over the next three seasons, the Beechams gave the British premieres of no fewer than five Richard Strauss operas – among them *Elektra* which, with its concentration on hatred and violence and strong sexual overtones, caused a sensation. They premiered *A Village Romeo and Juliet*. They played Offenbach's *Tales of Hoffman* which, together with Johann Strauss's *Die Fledermaus* proved highly profitable at the box office. They played Humperdinck's *Hansel and Gretel* and Massenet's *Werther*; they revived Stanford's *Shamus O'Brien* and Sullivan's *Ivanhoe*; there was a Mozart season; there was *Carmen* and *Tristan und Isolde*. London had never seen so much opera.

And there was more to come. Nineteen thirteen was the year of 'Joseph Beecham's Grand Season of Russian Opera and Ballet' at Drury Lane. With a century of hindsight, that month-long season seems the stuff of myth. Three Russian operas – Mussorgsky's *Boris Godunov* and *Khovanshchina*, and Rimsky-Korsakov's *Ivan the Terrible*[3] – all had their London premieres, starring the fabled bass, Feodor Chaliapin, who was paid £400 a night. The ballet company was Diaghilev's celebrated Ballets Russes with Nijinsky and Tamara Karsavina in the leading roles and Pierre Monteux conducting. They gave *Les Sylphides* with Glazunov's orchestration of Chopin's music; they gave Debussy's *L'après-midi d'un faune* which many considered dangerously erotic; and they gave the first British performance of Stravinsky's *Rite of Spring*, just two months after its premiere in Paris had provoked a near riot.

The following year saw seven more Russian operas – including British premieres for Borodin's *Prince Igor* and Stravinsky's *Nightingale* – as well as *Der Rosenkavalier*, *The Magic Flute* and Joseph Holbrooke's *Dylan*. There were fifteen ballets, including Ravel's *Daphnis and Chlöe* and Stravinsky's *Petrushka*, which Beecham, Monteux and just about everyone else much preferred to *The Rite of Spring*. Thomas Beecham was already on his way to becoming a conducting legend, particularly among his players. Joseph Beecham was spending a fortune to educate the musical public – but it was worth it: Edward VII made him a baronet and Czar Nicholas II awarded him the Order of St Stanislaus. The season ended with him being dragged on stage after a performance of *Petrushka* to accept the grateful applause of the Drury Lane audience. Ten days later, Britain was at war with Germany.

91 The War Dead

Tensions between the European powers had been growing for some time, but even the political classes were surprised by the speed with which war burst upon them. To the musical world, it came as a complete shock. Suddenly, the whole emotional and intellectual basis of British musical life was under threat. German music had been the dominant influence for two hundred years. That influence had been diminishing since the 1890s, but it had not disappeared. Young British composers had fallen under the influence of Celtic music, Indian philosophy and the Folk and Tudor Revivals, and were consciously seeking to write English, Scottish or Irish music, but Germany remained in the background. It was like a gravitational field from which these young composers were seeking to escape.

Overnight, anti-German feelings rose to fever pitch and anything that had German origins was suspect. German players fled from concert halls and theatre pits. There were stories of German pianos being thrown from windows, burned, or used for impromptu patriotic sing-songs. Edward German had to announce publicly that his real name was Edward German Jones. Anti-German pressure forced Sir Edgar Speyer and his wife to withdraw from public life and eventually to leave for the United States – which left the Proms without a sponsor until Chappell & Co agreed to step into the breach. There were calls to ban German music, although the Proms, which continued throughout the war years, managed to resist and, after an initial wobble, even continued to stage the weekly Wagner night. The more extreme manifestations soon died away, but anti-German sentiment remained constant throughout the war years, even causing George V to change the royal family's name from Saxe-Coburg-Gotha to the more patriotic-sounding Windsor.

Shortly after the outbreak of war, Sir Frederick Cowen chaired a meeting in the Queen's Hall to discuss what seemed at the time a very bleak outlook for those involved in music. A Music in Wartime Committee was set up but seems to have had little impact, being chiefly concerned to root out 'enemy' musicians. During the Second World War, there was a government policy on classical music and there were government-funded commissions to boost morale and keep musical life alive. The First World War saw nothing so imaginative. Classical music was left to its own devices although, in the end, it did not suffer too badly. Covent Garden became a furniture store for the Ministry of Works. Many provincial festivals were cancelled, among them the Three Choirs, which did not restart until 1920; and, as the war continued, there were fewer privately-sponsored concerts. However, like the Proms, both the Royal Philharmonic Orchestra and the London Symphony Orchestra continued with their concert programmes, and regional centres which had a tradition of classical concerts – towns such as Bath, Cheltenham, Harrogate, Manchester, Liverpool and Edinburgh – benefitted from an influx of tourists and music enthusiasts who would otherwise have gone abroad. The exodus of foreign players and the fact that many younger musicians joined up or were conscripted left gaps in orchestral ranks, which led to a significant increase in the number of professional women players. Although there was no actual ban on German music – as there was across the Atlantic when the United States entered the war in 1917 – fewer German works were being performed and, as a consequence, British composers found it easier to get a hearing.

Reactions to the war varied widely. Stanford, as we have seen, was devastated. The German classical tradition, and Brahms in particular, had provided the intellectual and practical basis for his own work and his teaching for nearly forty years. Suddenly, it was regarded with hostility. Several of his former students were killed in the trenches. And then came the Easter Rising of 1916, which to a Unionist like Stanford seemed nothing short of a complete betrayal by his fellow Irishmen. Parry, if anything even more German in orientation than Stanford, was equally devastated, but managed to carry on, serving on the Music in Wartime Committee and becoming involved in activities that sought to keep musical life going. Elgar, equally German in his musical sympathies but less intellectual in his approach, was too old to enlist but joined various volunteer organisations and wrote patriotic works. Delius left Grez and ended up staying in Watford, but took little interest in the war. Dyson joined the Royal Fusiliers.

Vaughan Williams became a private in the Royal Army Medical Corps. Hamilton Harty joined the Navy. Holst wanted to enlist but was declared medically unfit. Bax, also declared unfit, was not much interested in the war; but he was outraged by the violent suppression of the Easter Rising, which he supported and sought to celebrate in a book of bad, incendiary verse that was subsequently banned by the British censor. Percy Grainger left for New York. Edgar Bainton (1880–1956), a composer of church music and Principal of Newcastle-upon-Tyne Conservatory of Music, was visiting Bayreuth when the war broke out and was interned near Berlin for the duration. So, too, were the composer Benjamin Dale (1885–1943) and the noted art-song writer Frederick Keel (1871–1954).

Then, of course, there were those who enlisted but never came home. The best known of these is George Butterworth (1885–1916). He died on the Somme, aged thirty-one, leaving behind just a handful of compositions. In many ways he was the archetypal English gentleman of the Edwardian era. He came from an ancient English family; his parents were comfortably off (his father was a solicitor who became General Manager of the North Eastern Railway); he attended Eton College and Oxford, where he read Classics; he was a keen cricketer. Like so many others, he had to overcome parental opposition to a career in music, but he seems to have done so without great difficulty. While at Oxford, between 1904 and 1908, he made friends with Vaughan Williams; with Cecil Sharp; with Hugh Allen (1869–1946), who became Professor of Music at Oxford and then Director of the RCM; and with Reginald (always known as 'R.O.') Morris (1886–1948), one of the finest music teachers of his generation. In such company, it is no surprise that he became a convert to folk music, sometimes making collecting expeditions with Vaughan Williams, but also collecting over four hundred and fifty songs himself, mostly from Sussex. After leaving Oxford, he spent one year as a teacher at Radley College and another as a student at the RCM, where Parry and Charles Wood both encouraged him, but he did not complete the course, apparently feeling that he was not suited to an academic environment. He also acted as an assistant music critic on *The Times*, working under Fuller Maitland. He joined Cecil Sharp's English Folk Dance Society as soon as it was founded in 1911, and was regarded as an expert dancer, becoming a member of the Society's first Morris side.

Butterworth appears to have been a strong character, impatient with views that ran counter to his way of thinking and generally restless in his approach to life. That restlessness is not evident in the compositions which survive – although he seems to have burned a lot of his early work before embarking for France in 1915. The orchestral works – *Two English Idylls* (1910–11), *A Shropshire Lad* (1912), and *The Banks of Green Willow* (1913) – are romantic, elegiac, English, and pastoral. *A Shropshire Lad*, which Butterworth called a rhapsody, is remarkable for the ease with which its themes develop and for its command of orchestral texture. Like *The Lark Ascending*, it does not draw directly on folk song, but it is quite obviously inspired by traditional music. The other two works are both based directly on folk songs Butterworth had collected in Sussex and show how effectively, even at such an early stage in his career, he could use folk material to create something that was more than just an elaborate medley. Butterworth's real claim to be remembered rests not on his orchestral works, but on his two collections of Housman songs – *Six Songs from 'A Shropshire Lad'* (1911), and *Bredon Hill and Other Songs* (1912). Setting Housman was, as we have seen, almost a requirement for aspiring songwriters at the beginning of the twentieth century, but Butterworth's have acquired an almost iconic status. There are only eleven of them but their directness, utter simplicity and rejection of the trappings of romantic song-writing have made them classics of the English song repertoire.

What musical direction Butterworth might have taken, especially given the contrast between the rich romanticism of his orchestral pieces and the simplicity of the Housman songs, is a matter for speculation. But he was not the only young composer killed in the war who might have made a difference to the future of British music. Gustav Holst's 1919 setting of words by Whitman, *Ode to Death*, is dedicated to 'Cecil Coles and the fallen'. Coles (1888–1918) was a Scot, born in the village of Tongland, near Kirkcudbright, where his father was a landscape painter and archaeologist. His mother died when he was young and at some point Coles's father moved himself and his five children to Edinburgh, where Coles was educated. He enrolled in Edinburgh University but in 1906 won a composition scholarship to the London College of Music, which was then an independent conservatoire in Great Marlborough Street. The work he submitted for the scholarship may have been part of the three-part suite, *From the Scottish Highlands*, which he seems to have completed in 1907. In London, Coles was desperately poor, but received help from a Miss Brooke who worked at Morley College. It was she who introduced him to Holst, with whom he became friends. They later went walking in the Alps together.

There is no doubt that Coles was talented. In 1908, he won another scholarship, this time from Edinburgh's Reid School of Music, which allowed him to go and study in Stuttgart. There, he composed his *Scherzo for Large Orchestra* and his *Overture: The Comedy of Errors*. The latter in particular, for all its mixture of Wagner and Mahler, is a surprisingly mature work for a composer in his very early twenties. It was probably in Stuttgart that he composed his *Four Verlaine Songs* for soprano and orchestra; they seem not to have been performed at the time and may have been revised later. Again, we can hear Wagner and Mahler, but the songs are not derivative. They show both a clear vision and an ability to manage orchestral resources. Coles stayed on in Stuttgart with an appointment as assistant conductor at the Royal Opera House there, which allowed him to meet and have dealings with Richard Strauss. He continued to write songs, including settings of Alfred de Musset, and also some delicate piano miniatures, *Fünf Skizzen für Klavier*. In 1913, probably because of the deteriorating political situation, he returned to London where he acted as chorus master for the Beecham Opera Company and taught at Morley College, sometimes deputising for Holst who was also teaching there. Early in 1914, he completed *Fra Giacomo,* a large scale setting of a poem by William Buchanan. Wagner is again the dominant influence, although the music shows great maturity, developing thematically in parallel with the action of what, it has to be said, is a rather melodramatic text. In 1915, Coles was sent to France as a Bandmaster Sergeant with the Queen Victoria Rifles. He continued writing when he could, sending his manuscripts back to Holst. He was killed by a German sniper on the Somme in April 1918 while trying to retrieve wounded soldiers from no man's land. At the time of his death, he was writing the four-part suite called *Behind the Lines,* only two movements of which survive, the rest having been destroyed by shellfire. Coles was almost unknown as a composer until his daughter discovered his manuscripts in the 1990s.

Coles, unlike Butterworth, continued to follow German models, but, with his dramatic sense and his operatic experience, could he have been the man to transform British opera? Could William Denis Browne (1888–1915) have had a significant influence on English song? Browne sailed for Gallipoli in 1915 aboard the *Grantully Castle.* The poet Rupert Brooke and the former Olympic rower and aspiring composer, Frederick Kelly (1881–1916), were on the same ship. Both Browne and Kelly were among the pallbearers for Brooke when he died of blood poisoning and was buried on the island of Skyros in April 1915. Browne was killed during an attack on the Turkish trenches six weeks later. Kelly survived Gallipoli, despite being wounded twice, and while recuperating wrote an elegy for strings and harp dedicated to Brooke's memory, but he was then killed on the Somme that November. As a critic, Browne had a progressive outlook on music. He was a great supporter of *The Rite of Spring* which he saw during the Beecham Festival of 1913; and he railed against what he considered the outdated German and Brahmsian school of music. As a composer, he wrote very little. Some short orchestral pieces and an unfinished ballet, *The Comic Spirit*, survive. His reputation, such as it is, rests on a small handful of songs – 'Arabia', a setting of Walter de la Mare's poem; 'Diaphenia', to a lyric by the Elizabethan playwright Henry Chettle; 'Epitaph on Salathiel Pavy', a poem by Ben Jonson; and 'To Gratiana, Singing and Dancing', a lyric by Richard Lovelace. It is an incredibly slender legacy but one which has never been lost sight of by later song composers.

Then there was Ernest Farrar (1885–1918). Educated at Leeds Grammar School, he won a scholarship to the RCM where he studied organ with Parratt and composition with Stanford, who thought highly of him. He was a member of the so-called Vagabonds Club, which included fellow students Frank Bridge and the future musicologist, Marion Scott. He also became friends with Vaughan Williams. Six months as organist at the All Saints' English church in Dresden was followed by two difficult years at St Hilda's Church in South Shields, where he was desperately poorly paid. In 1912, he obtained an altogether more suitable appointment as organist and choirmaster at Christ Church, Harrogate. The town even had its own Municipal Orchestra, conducted by Julian Clifford, known for his flashy style, with whom Farrar made friends. It was Clifford who in 1915 recommended Farrar as a suitable teacher for the young Gerald Finzi, an association which lasted until Farrar enlisted in the Grenadier Guards a year later. As early as 1908, Stanford had conducted Farrar's orchestral setting of Rossetti's *Blessed Damozel* in Leeds; and after Farrar arrived in Harrogate, Julian Clifford premiered several of his works, including *The Forsaken Merman* (1914) and the *Variations on an Old British Sea Song* (1915). Farrar also wrote songs, notably *Vagabond Songs* (1911), settings of Arthur Symons, Dante Gabriel Rossetti, and Robert Louis Stevenson. His last major work was *Heroic Elegy (For Soldiers)* which he conducted himself at Harrogate while on leave from France in July 1918. He was killed by machine gun fire that September on his third day at the front. Two other orchestral works, *English Pastoral Impressions* (dedicated to Vaughan Williams) and the *Three Spiritual Studies*, were published posthumously. Farrar's music tends towards the English pastoralism of the time, but there is a vitality in his work which suggests the possibility that he might have developed in a different and more robust direction. As with Farrar, so with the composer of organ and piano works Frank Maurice Jephson (1886–1917); or Herbert Howells' promising young friend Francis Purcell Warren (1895–1916); or the New Zealand-born, RAM student Willie Manson (1896–1916); or the art song composer and Morris-dancing friend of Butterworth, George Wilkinson (1885–1916): we shall never know.

92   Wartime Melodies

One of the most popular marching songs at the beginning of the First World War was 'We are Fred Karno's Army'. A characteristically ironic and self-deprecatory British lyric ('We cannot fight, we cannot shoot / What bloody use are we?') in which the troops likened themselves to music hall performers employed by the impresario, Fred Karno, was sung to the tune of the hymn 'The Church's one foundation'. This was an exception. Most of the songs that the troops sang as they marched off to war were first heard in the music halls – although, once adopted by the troops, the words were frequently altered and coarsened. 'It's a Long Way to Tipperary' had been written in 1912, reputedly for a bet, but was adopted by the Connaught Rangers in 1914 and subsequently recorded by the Irish tenor, John McCormack. 'Pack Up Your Troubles in Your Old Kit Bag' was written by two Welsh brothers and made popular by Florrie Forde. 'Take Me Back to Dear Old Blighty', another song from 1916, was first sung by Dorothy Ward, and then also by Florrie Forde. The following year came 'Good-bye-eee', based on a catch phrase used by the comedian Harry Tate and again sung by Florrie Forde.

If they caught on, the sheet music of jaunty, patriotic, crowd-pleasers such as these could sell anything up to a million copies. At the beginning of the war, when patriotic feeling was running at its highest, Paul Rubens, better known as a writer of musical comedies, wrote 'Your King and Country Need You' featuring the famous line 'Oh, we don't want to lose you, but we think you ought to go.' It was designed to encourage recruitment and Vesta Tilley sang it at recruiting rallies throughout the country.

The sheet music, published by Chappell & Co at one shilling, stated that all profits would go to Queen Mary's 'Work For Women' Fund. It made half a million pounds. Such sales reflect the centrality of the piano – in the home, in pubs and clubs and restaurants – as the way in which millions of ordinary people experienced music. The war years also saw a significant rise in the popularity of the gramophone, which would soon come to challenge the piano. (Originally, the word *gramophone* was used by the Gramophone Company to distinguish its products from rivals such as 'phonograph' and 'graphophone', but in 1910 a British court ruled that it had already become a generic term.) Although gramophones had been available in the years leading up to 1914, they were generally regarded as little more than a novelty. During the war, both at home and, more particularly, among solders in the trenches and elsewhere, they provided a cheap and portable source of entertainment. Gramophone companies made more records, and more records meant more money for singers and musicians and for music publishers and songwriters. It was the beginning of a new industry that would enjoy its first boom during the 1920s.

In 1914, music hall was still the most widespread form of popular musical entertainment, but the revue was definitely making inroads. Whereas music hall consisted of a succession of different acts, revues offered a blend of song, dance and sketches based (however loosely) around a central story or theme. They could be produced to tour as a package; and there were fewer star turns, which made them cheaper for managements to stage. By 1918, almost all the big music hall stars – Harry Tate, George Robey, Violet Loraine, Harry Lauder – were appearing in revues. Only Marie Lloyd refused to change the way she worked. Revues divided broadly into two categories. Intimate revues, such *Odds and Ends*, produced at the Ambassador's Theatre in 1914, by the impresario C. B. Cochran, were witty and stylish. Spectacular revues, such as Albert de Courville's *Flying Colours*, produced at the London Hippodrome in 1916, relied for their appeal on elaborate staging and large-scale production numbers. One of the most popular revues of the war years was *The Bing Boys Are Here*, presenting a picture of life in London through a series of musical sketches. It opened at the Alhambra in 1916, with George Robey and Violet Loraine as the star turns. Their duet, 'If You were the Only Girl in the World', was a smash hit.

If revues were popular, so, too, were light musical comedies. Before the war, London's most popular entertainments in this genre – Franz Lehár's *Merry Widow* (1907) and *The Count of Luxembourg* (1911); Oscar Straus's

Chocolate Soldier (1910) – had been written by Austrians. Managements now found themselves searching for alternatives with more acceptable origins. The most successful of all wartime musical entertainments was *Chu Chin Chow*. Written by Oscar Asche, with music by Frederic Norton, it opened at His Majesty's Theatre in August 1916. A stage up from a revue in that it tells a more-or-less coherent version of the story of *Ali Baba and the Forty Thieves*, it remains pure make-believe. Its costumes were lavish and colourful, its stage sets exotic, and its dance routines dazzling and elaborate. Altogether, it provided the perfect escapist contrast to a world of khaki uniforms and wartime gloom. It was certainly expensive to stage. Asche, who produced as well as writing it, laid out over £5,000 before the first performance, but the gamble paid off. *Chu Chin Chow* ran for five years and 2,238 performances. 'The Cobbler's Song', sung by Baba Mustafa in Act II, and later made popular in a recorded version by the Australian bass-baritone, Peter Dawson, is probably the only song from the piece to provoke any degree of recognition today.

More sophisticated both musically and dramatically was *The Maid of the Mountains*, which had a short out-of-town trial in Manchester before opening at Daly's Theatre, just off Leicester Square, in February 1917. Harold Fraser-Simson and James Tate wrote the music, while Frederick Lonsdale wrote the book and Harry Graham most of the lyrics. Its two outstanding songs were 'A Bachelor Gay am I', also recorded by Peter Dawson, and 'Love Will Find a Way', sung in the production by the female lead José Collins, and later recorded by Joan Sutherland. Where *Chu Chin Chow* was spectacular and exotic, *Maid of the Mountains* was romantic and dramatic – a tale of love, jealousy and betrayal among a bandit community high in the Alps – but it mined the same vein of escapism. Its run of 1,352 performances ended only when José Collins felt she could no longer continue in the role. *Maid of the Mountains* has been revived more often than *Chu Chin Chow*, particularly in the 1940s, repeating its function as wartime escapism, and there was a West End production as recently as 2006. An indication of the importance of the musical theatre industry to cultural life during the war years is given by the number of new productions (revues and musicals) launched in London, many of which went on to tour the provinces. In 1915, the first full year of the war, there were eighteen; in 1916, twenty-eight; in 1917, twenty-three; and in 1918, twenty-one.

For the world of popular music, much more than for the classical world, the war acted as a catalyst for change. It was not just soldiers and sailors, but everyone in society – shipyard workers, munitions workers, nurses, civil servants, railwaymen, farmers, the families left behind – who were affected by war and its often tragic repercussions. Popular music offered them an easily accessible alternative world of hopes, dreams, love and romance. As a result, it thrived, providing musicians and writers with new opportunities, building platforms for future careers, and creating new stars. José Collins, for example, was an up-and-coming singer and actress, but *The Maid of the Mountains* turned her into a star. George Grossmith junior was the son of the George Grossmith who had played the comic lead (Major-General Stanley, the Lord Chancellor, the Lord High Executioner) in many of the Savoy Operas. Grossmith junior had appeared in a number of plays and musicals during the Edwardian period, but the war turned him into both a successful producer and a writer. His most popular productions included shows such as *Tonight's the Night* (1914) and *Theodore & Co* (1916), and he wrote the book for *The Bing Boys Are Here* and for a series of sequels, such as *The Bing Girls Are There* and *The Bing Boys on Broadway*. After the war, he continued to write, produce and act for London's musical stage before, in the 1930s, moving into films. *Theodore & Co*, with a run of just over five hundred performances at the Gaiety Theatre, was one of the war's more successful shows, but its main importance is that it launched the career of David Ivor Davies, better known as Ivor Novello, as a theatrical composer.

Novello (1893–1951) was born in Cardiff and had his first taste of success as a boy when he sang at an Eisteddfod. His mother was a singing teacher and wanted him to become a classical composer, so when the family moved to Gloucester, he took lessons with the distinguished but conservative composer and organist Herbert Brewer (1865–1928). Brewer dismissed any possibility of a musical career for him, but nonetheless, he managed to win a scholarship to Magdalen College School in Oxford, where he sang treble in the College choir. Novello himself claimed that it was these early experiences of dry, classical music that turned his mind towards lush romanticism. Whether or not this was true – he seems always to have had a gift for melody and published a romantic song at the age of fifteen – when he arrived in London in 1913, it was to the world of popular music that he looked. Unlike so many others, he was immediately successful. In 1914, to words by the American lyricist, Lena Guilbert Ford, he wrote 'Keep the Home Fires Burning', which vies with 'It's a Long Way to Tipperary' for the title of most popular song to come out of the First World War. It brought him huge royalties. *Theodore & Co* was Novello's first revue. He wrote most of the songs – the others were written by the young Jerome Kern – and got himself noticed. By the end of the war, despite spending two years working at the Air Ministry, he had contributed to four more revues and in doing so laid the foundations of his future career. After the war, as we shall see later, Novello continued to write revues, developed a career as an actor – first in silent films and then on the stage – before returning to musicals in the mid-1930s with a series of successful and in some ways underrated works.

Like the gramophone, film was a medium that saw a huge increase in popularity during the war years. The need for silent films to have musical accompaniment was recognised from the beginning. The image of an impoverished musician hammering away on an old upright piano or vamping an accompaniment on a cinema organ was accurate enough in the early days of cinema and remained current in the more remote parts of the country into the 1920s. However, as the content and the production values of silent films grew more sophisticated, both film-makers and cinema managers realised the importance of appropriate accompanying music. The bigger cinemas, both in London and in the provinces, soon began to employ bands of musicians. There were wide variations, but even during the war a typical band might consist of two violins and a cello, a piano and a percussionist, perhaps also a double bass and a harmonium. For special occasions or particularly prestigious films – such as the London premiere of *The World, the Flesh, and the Devil*, the first ever full-length colour film in 1914; or the American silent epic, *Birth of a Nation*, which appeared in 1915 – twenty- or thirty-piece orchestras might be assembled.

Very often pieces from the classical repertoire would be played to accompany a film – Mendelssohn was popular; so, too, were orchestral extracts from Italian operas which could be relied upon to be suitably dramatic – but such works brought their own problems. Apart from the issue of whether a cinema band could actually play Rossini or Verdi to a standard that would not actually detract from the film, classical works rarely fitted the mood or the action on the screen. It was obvious that *She Stoops to Conquer* (1915), based on Goldsmith's play, would require a different kind of accompaniment from the swashbuckling adventure *Rupert of Hentzau* (1915) or the documentary *Battle for the Somme* (1916). So film distributors began to issue guidance in the form 'cue sheets', which described the film, gave its overall length and the length of certain key scenes, and indicated the kind of music that could be used as an accompaniment. They also sometimes drew attention to specific incidents – thunder, gunfire, an explosion, a clock striking, a train whistle – which might be illustrated by appropriate sound effects. Music publishers, seeing a lucrative opportunity, began to commission pieces of various lengths and moods, which could also be adapted for ensembles of different sizes and combinations of instruments, so as to build up libraries of film music.

One composer who benefitted from this system – which remained in place until the coming of the 'talkies' in the late 1920s – was Albert Ketèlbey (1875–1959). A Birmingham-born Englishman despite the name (his biographer suggests that he added the grave accent himself in order to convey a sense of distinction),[1] Ketèlbey initially trained with the intention of becoming a composer at the classical end of the spectrum. In the event, however, he became not only the most popular composer of light music of his day, but also one of the first seriously to adapt to the new technologies of recorded sound and film. He was a gifted child and at the age of fourteen won a scholarship to Trinity College in London – beating the young Gustav Holst into second place – where he studied under Frederick Corder. On leaving college in 1895, he gave piano recitals and then, in order to make ends meet, began conducting for a touring light-opera company. This was followed by a period as musical director of the Opéra Comique. In 1900, his comic opera called *The Wonder Worker* was politely but not enthusiastically received. Money was short and he took what was generally regarded as hack-work, arranging and scoring for music publishers. Then, in 1907, he was offered a job with the recently-established Columbia Gramophone Company. He conducted for recording sessions, learning how orchestras and ensembles needed to be arranged around the microphone and how players should adapt their performance to get the best recorded sound. Eventually, he became the company's musical director.

Ketèlbey's breakthrough year was 1915. It was J. H. Larway, one of London's smaller music publishing houses, which agreed to take *In a Monastery Garden*, a work he had written the previous year. Massively romantic, complete with swelling melodies, lush orchestration and even a chorus of monks, *In a Monastery Garden* took the English pastoral idyll to extremes. It has its adherents even today, and was played (perhaps slightly tongue-in-cheek) at the Last Night of the Proms in 2009, but the First World War public found in its idealised picture of rural England another and deeply emotional escape from grim daily reality. They responded with the same enthusiasm they showed for *Chu Chin Chow* and

The Maid of the Mountains. The sheet music of *In a Monastery Garden* sold a million copies in five years. A post-war companion piece, *Bells Across the Meadow*, published in 1921, proved almost as popular. To modern ears, *In a Monastery Garden* sounds overblown and clichéd, reminiscent of romantic film scores from the 1930s and 40s, but, of course, Ketèlbey was one of the originators of those soundtrack clichés. Nineteen-fifteen was also the year in which he published *Kinema Music*, a collection of mood pieces specifically intended as film accompaniments. Titles included 'Quiet River Scene', 'Love', 'Romance', and 'Mexican or Spanish'. The following year, he published his *New Moving Picture Book*, a similar collection, which contained 'Plaintive', 'Oriental Music', 'Hurry Music' and 'Mysterioso'. Pieces such as these were exactly what the film distributors and the cinemas were looking for and, again, the sheet music sold in huge quantities. Ketèlbey, like Novello, would build on these wartime successes in a post-war career which saw his music remain popular into the 1940s.

93   War Damage

Inevitably, the aftermath of the First World War saw major readjustments in British musical life. In the classical world, the generation of composer-teachers that had dominated the late Victorian and Edwardian eras had already seen their influence diminished by the sudden alienation of Germany and its culture. Now, one after another, their careers came to an end. Parry, struck down by flu in 1918, did not live to see the end of the war. Stanford, having become increasingly and aggressively conservative in his last years, died in 1924. Parratt also died in 1924, having resigned his professorship at the RCM the previous year. That same year, Mackenzie resigned as Principal of the RAM. He had become an arch-conservative in the eyes of many and was out of sympathy with the times. Although he lived on until 1935, he composed almost nothing new during those years.

In the years before the war, British music had been developing an identity of its own. As ever in Britain, this was not a matter of manifestos, isms, or theories; it was rather a collection of influences or characteristics that composers shared or did not share according to their own particular interests and musical ideas. A concentration on melody was central. Other characteristics, as we have seen, included a strong pastoral strain; an intense and often poetic response to landscape and the natural world; an intense response to poetry itself; and often, though not always, the influence of the folk tradition – both myth and music – and of what we now call early music. After the war, the men in whose music these characteristics had found expression were suddenly faced with a changed world, one in which national music and pastoral idylls seemed somehow devalued and irrelevant. How should they react? How could they adapt themselves and their music? Vaughan Williams developed his pastoralism into a much more complex, expressive and personal style, which allowed him to respond effectively to the changed world. Dyson, while creating a musical style that was a mix of ancient and modern, sought reassurance in the literary and cultural traditions of the past. Bridge attempted a radical change of direction. Ireland resolutely followed his own personal concerns. Holst, after the brave, even defiant *Hymn of Jesus*, lost his way for a while. There were as many approaches as there were composers.

And what of the next generation – those born after 1890? They had a particular problem. The music they had absorbed in their early years and that coloured their musical education was that of the Edwardian era, yet by the time they were ready to begin their careers it was a radically-changed, post-war world that confronted them. Attitudes had been shifting before the war, but after 1918 when this new generation of composers sought to establish their individuality and their position in the musical world, they frequently found the ethos of the teaching they had received inadequate, or irrelevant. And in more than a few cases the difficulties they faced were complicated by the fact – and the knowledge – that they had been physically or mentally damaged by the war. Again, there were as many solutions as composers.

Arthur Bliss (1891–1975) was half-American – his father came from Massachusetts – but his upbringing and education could scarcely have been more English: Rugby School and Cambridge University, where he studied Classics but took lessons in composition and counterpoint from Charles Wood. This was followed by a year at the RCM, where he found Stanford out of touch with the contemporary music in which he and his fellow students were interested – the music of Stravinsky, Debussy, Ravel and the even more challenging works by composers from the Second Viennese School, such as Schoenberg and Webern. His year at the RCM ended in the summer of 1914. Bliss joined the Royal Fusiliers, later transferring to the Grenadier Guards. He served in France – he was one of those who took a portable gramophone to the front with him – was wounded twice and gassed once. His elder brother, Kennard, was killed on the Somme, near Thiepval. Bliss's memories of the war haunted him for the rest of his life, although he repeatedly tried to exorcise them through his music.

Bliss's career as a composer really began in 1918, the year in which he converted to Roman Catholicism, a conversion which may well have been related to the emotional and psychological traumas of the war. His early compositions were experimental in style, perhaps self-consciously so. *Madame Noy* (1918) is a slightly bizarre song about a Cornish witch, with a solo soprano voice soaring, swooping and floating over an odd, half-humorous accompaniment provided by flute, clarinet, bassoon, harp, viola and double bass – a work, it should be noted, that predates Walton's *Façade*. *Rout* (1920) is a ballet in one scene, where the soprano voice sounds non-sense syllables over a ten-piece ensemble. *Conversations* (1920) is a suite for flute, oboe, violin, viola, and cello, its five movements having titles such as 'In the Committee Meeting' or 'On the Tube at Oxford Circus'. All this was a declaration that Bliss was aware of what was happening in France with Cocteau, Satie and the composers who called themselves *Les Six*.[1] In Britain, such works were seen as avant-garde and perhaps a little shocking. Bliss gained a degree of notoriety and, in accordance with the spirit of the times, made a number of idealistic statements about music and the duties of musicians in the modern age.

Ironically, it was the conservative Elgar who brought about the next stage in his career. Bliss had been impressed by *Gerontius* at school, had actually met Elgar while at Cambridge, and had remained in touch with him during the war. Now Elgar, whose kindness to young composers is often overlooked, arranged for him to receive a commission for a major work to be played at the 1922 Three Choirs Festival. The result was *The Colour Symphony,* a four-movement work with each movement based on a colour – purple, red, blue and green – and its heraldic significance. Bliss struggled at first, but received help and encouragement from Vaughan Williams, at whose Chelsea house much of the symphony was written. *A Colour Symphony* is bold, vivid, and colourful in orchestration as well as concept, but it is far too episodic to qualify as a true symphony. Elgar did not actually regret his decision to help, but did speak of the work as 'disconcertingly modern'[2] Other reviews at the time spoke of its ugliness and ultra-modernity and questioned whether such a work was suitable for performance in a cathedral,[3] but from a later perspective it is hard to understand such extreme reactions. *A Colour Symphony* is certainly less experimental than the works which preceded it.

In 1923, Bliss moved to the United States, where he composed less and conducted and played the piano rather more. Returning to England in 1926, he returned also to composition with two important commissions for American orchestras: *Introduction and Allegro* for Leopold Stokowski and the Philadelphia Orchestra, and *Hymn to Apollo* for Pierre Monteux and the Boston Symphony. These works marked a distinct shift in style. Bliss was realigning himself with the English melodic and romantic tradition – the title *Introduction and Allegro* was an obvious homage to Elgar – and this direction of travel continued with his *Quintet for Oboe and Strings* (1927) and *Pastoral: Lie Strewn the White Flocks* (1928), a choral work, originally written for an amateur choir. *Pastoral* is dedicated to Elgar, and uses texts which span the centuries: from Theocritus and the Florentine Renaissance poet Poliziano, to Ben Jonson and John Fletcher, right down to the contemporary poet Robert Nichols. Its subject matter – shepherds in the spring honouring Pan and stories of love from the classical world – might perhaps seem to echo Cocteau and the Ballets Russes, but the music is, as one would expect from the title, a version of English pastoral; more self-conscious than the pre-war variety, but pastoral nonetheless.

Bliss continued to attach himself to the musical mainstream by writing a series of works for leading virtuosi: the *Quintet for Clarinet and String Quartet* (1932) for the clarinettist Frederick Thurston (1901–53); a Viola Sonata (1933) for Lionel Tertis; and a Piano Concerto, premiered by the British piano virtuoso known as Solomon (1902–88) at the New York World's Fair in 1939. Bliss also wrote ballets, the most notable being *Miracle in the Gorbals* (1944), a disturbing version of the Christ story set in Glasgow; and ventured into films, his best score probably being his first – for the 1936 science fiction film based on H. G. Wells' *The Shape of Things to Come*. His finest work from these middle years of his career was *Music for Strings* (1935), first played by the Vienna Symphony Orchestra under Adrian Boult. Heavily indebted to Elgar's *Introduction and Allegro* and with the reputation among players of being a difficult work, it is from a listener's point of view lively, accessible, and richly melodic. He had certainly come a long way from the *enfant terrible* of fifteen years earlier.

The issue with all these middle-period works, and with so much else that Bliss wrote, lies in the relationship between the composer and his material. Bliss's music seems to lack the depth conveyed by personal involvement:

when faced with emotions, it is descriptive rather than expressive. That this stems from some kind of reaction to the traumas of the First World War is a possibility raised by *Morning Heroes*, a work written in 1930 with the explicit intent of exorcising the memories of the trenches that were still giving him nightmares more than twelve years on. Described as a choral symphony, and including a significant part for a narrator as well as a choir and orchestra, *Morning Heroes* is really more of a requiem: it is dedicated to the memory of his brother, Kennard, and 'all other comrades killed in battle.' As with *Pastoral*, the text is taken from a variety of sources – including Homer, the Chinese poet Li Tai Po,[4] Walt Whitman, Wilfred Owen and (again) Robert Nichols. It is without doubt a heartfelt work with a clear, five-part structure, but Bliss's approach is more romantic than angry or sad; and the work as a whole, despite some fine moments, fails to end with the sense of catharsis that its length and purpose seem to demand.

During the Second World War, Bliss worked at the BBC, becoming Director of Music between 1942 and 1944. It was in this role that he produced his 'Music Policy Statement', which looked at the future of music broadcasting in the United Kingdom and articulated the basic principles that would to lead to the launch the BBC's Third Programme (the predecessor of today's Radio 3) in September 1946. In this, he can fairly be described as visionary. As a composer of opera, which was what he tried his hand at when he left the BBC, he could not. *The Olympians*, with a libretto by J. B. Priestley, was first performed in 1949. The plot has similarities with Gilbert and Sullivan's *Thespis* in that it concerns the Greek gods who have become a group of travelling players. It was poorly rehearsed and poorly received. In the aftermath of the First World War, Bliss's experimental pieces, whether successful or not, had managed to capture the spirit of the age; in the aftermath of the Second, *The Olympians* singularly failed to do the same. It was too remote, too classical in inspiration, too old-fashioned for a newly-democratic age.

Bliss was knighted in 1950 and succeeded Arnold Bax as Master of the Queen's Music in 1953. He took the role very seriously, composing fanfares, royal toasts, music for the investiture of the Prince of Wales, as well as soundtracks to film and television programmes on royal subjects. Such works did little to enhance his reputation. The fact that he was now seen as a member of an older musical generation is illustrated by the way in which two of his works – both more interesting than royal commissions – were eclipsed by parallel compositions from Benjamin Britten.

In 1960, the BBC commissioned Bliss to write an opera for television. It was the sixth commission of its kind: the first two had been Arthur Benjamin's *Mañana* and Malcolm Arnold's one-act *Open Window* (both 1956), and these were followed by works by Joan Trimble, Richard Arnell and Guy Halahan. Bliss's *Tobias and the Angel,* with a libretto by Christopher Hassall, was far superior to *The Olympians,* and marked a distinct step forward in terms of adapting opera to suit television techniques. The BBC spent a lot of money on the commission and the work received good, even enthusiastic reviews, yet it has never been rebroadcast. Ten years later, Britten wrote *Owen Wingrave,* again following a commission from the BBC. It is not one of Britten's best operas, but it is the work that today seems to define television opera as a genre for critics and audiences alike. Similarly, Bliss was commissioned to write a work for the reconsecration of Coventry cathedral in 1962. This was *The Beatitudes,* with a text that mixes the Sermon on the Mount, the Book of Isaiah, Henry Vaughan, George Herbert and Dylan Thomas. Yet from the first it was overshadowed by Britten's *War Requiem,* also commissioned for the occasion. Indeed, Bliss's work was effectively demoted in that it was performed in the Coventry Theatre rather than in the Cathedral.

Bliss's post-war career did, however, yield two works of real quality. *Metamorphic Variations* dates from 1972, just three years before his death. It was inspired by a triptych, *Tantris,* painted by the surveyor, music critic, photographer, artist and sculptor, George Dannatt. It is imaginative, richly scored, and carefully structured, with each of its fourteen movements having a title indicative of the prevailing mood – 'Assertion', 'Interjections', 'Contemplation', 'Funeral Processions' (again a reference to the First World War) – but it cannot be compared with a work like the *Enigma Variations* because, as elsewhere in Bliss, it remains essentially episodic in structure. Simpler in concept and much more effective is *Meditations on a Theme by John Blow,* written for the Birmingham Symphony Orchestra in 1955. This is a work that achieves a sense of completion and catharsis not often found elsewhere in Bliss. The theme in question was part of Blow's setting of Psalm 23, 'The Lord is My Shepherd', and Bliss's musical treatment can best be described as tense pastoral: even when it appears playful, there is a sense of feelings being held in check. That control is maintained right up to the seventh movement – 'Through the valley of the shadow of death' – when we realise that once again war and a desolation of the spirit hover in the background.

How much was Bliss damaged by the First World War? His career trajectory from slightly wild, youthful experimenter to fullly paid-up member of the musical establishment was not an unusual one, but there is a sense that the war was the inescapable background to the rest of his life, and it must be the probable explanation for the lack of emotional engagement in so much of his music. The career of Ernest John Moeran (1894–1950) took a different path entirely, but he was another whose experience of war never left him. Educated until the age of eighteen at Uppingham School, where his music teacher was the grandson of Sterndale Bennett, he went on the RCM. It was a time of revelations. Having been brought up in the then comparatively remote region of north-east Norfolk, he had never before heard so much music. In particular, the music of Elgar and Delius (whom he also met at one of Balfour Gardiner's concerts) was new to him. But the revelations were interrupted. In 1914, Moeran joined the Norfolk Regiment as a motorcycle despatch rider. In 1917, at Bullecourt during the Battle of Arras, he received a shrapnel wound, which left fragments of metal too close to the brain to be removed and resulted in his having a metal plate inserted in his head. This affected his physical and mental health for the rest of his life, and he was later awarded a disability pension in compensation. Remarkably, by the beginning of 1918, he was back with his battalion, although as a non-combatant, and posted to Boyle in County Roscommon. It was his first experience of Ireland (which was his father's country) and, despite the political tensions, he fell in love with the landscape and the culture and began collecting folk songs. This vision of Ireland informed his first published work, *Three Pieces for Piano* ('The Lake Island', 'Autumn Woods' and 'The Horse Fair') in 1919.

Once demobbed, Moeran returned to the RCM, where he studied composition under John Ireland, and where he remained until 1923, by which time he was nearly thirty. He also put a lot of energy into riding motorbikes at high speed, even winning a gold medal for a London-to-Land's-End speed trial. His first major works began to appear – a Piano Trio, full of Brahms and Ravel, who were Ireland's major influences; his String Quartet no.1, again very much modelled on Ravel. Then, in 1921, came his first orchestral work, *In the Mountain Country*: the title echoes both Vaughan William's *In the Fen Country* and Delius's *Song of the High Hills* and reveals the composers whose ideas were most in his mind at the time. Throughout his career, it is almost always possible to read the influences that were operating on Moeran at any given moment, yet this does not detract from the quality of his music or prevent him from being highly original at times. In 1924, Hamilton Harty was sufficiently impressed by what he heard to offer Moeran the chance to have a symphony played by the Hallé. Moeran almost finished the work, but was not satisfied and the opportunity was lost. It was in these post-war years that Moeran returned to the Norfolk countryside which he loved and toured the pubs, collecting and recording well over a hundred folk songs.

Then came a decisive change in his life. In 1925, he went to live in Kent, sharing a house with Peter Warlock in the village of Eynsford. Their chaotic, riotous and alcohol-fuelled lifestyle was particularly damaging for a man who had had a serious head injury.[5] It may have been fun at the time, but it dried up Moeran's creativity – he wrote almost nothing for three years. It also exacerbated the latent mental instability that was the legacy of his head wound, and it left him with an alcohol problem that dogged him for the rest of his life. The ménage eventually broke up and Moeran started composing again. He began with songs, which we will look at later, but his next orchestral writing, published in 1931 following a period of illness and reassessment, consisted of two pieces: *Lonely Waters* and *Whythorne's Shadow*. While musically unrelated in terms of their origins – the first is a version of a Norfolk folk song; the second based on an Elizabethan part-song – they are both in the classic English pastoral vein; and they were the last he was to produce in that style. Indeed, it is possible that they were written earlier, for two other works from this time, the Sonata for Two Violins (1930) and the String Trio (1931) show the different, somewhat sparser texture that was to characterise his later work.

In the 1930s, Moeran spent a lot of time in Ireland. His chosen spot was the town of Kenmare in County Kerry. As with Bax, Ireland became the core of his inspiration. The fact that the bar in the hotel where he stayed was later named after him gives an indication of at least one facet of that inspiration. It was in Kenmare that he rewrote and completed the Symphony in G that he had abandoned over decade previously. Much has been made of the fact that it is deeply influenced by Sibelius and contains echoes of other composers including Bax and Elgar, but in the end it is Moeran's own Irish-tinted vision that comes through. It is his finest orchestral work, although the 1944 *Sinfonietta* runs it close.

The Second World War was a productive time, interspersed though it was with bouts of self-doubt and drinking. The Symphony had got him noticed and he began to receive commissions and requests from conductors and soloists. The Violin Concerto, requested by Henry Wood and premiered by Arthur Catterall as the soloist, was completed in 1942. It is another Irish-inspired work full of Moeran's folk-sounding themes. Although more interested in folk music than Bax was, he rarely made use of an existing folk tune. The *Rhapsody no. 3 for Piano and Orchestra* was written at the urging of his new publishers, J. & W. Chester and premiered by Harriet Cohen in 1943. The *Sinfonietta* followed in 1944, apparently inspired by the Herefordshire landscape around the town of Kington close to the Welsh border where his family was now living. In the last days of the war, Moeran married the English cellist, Peers Cotmore, and it was for her that he wrote his last major works, the Cello Concerto (1945) and the Cello Sonata (1947). These later works continue to show a qualified, pared back, occasionally spiky romanticism. Moeran was one of the later exponents of folk- and landscape-influenced style that had come into being around the turn of the century. He modified it, but he remained at heart an English romantic; and if one needs proof of the fact, one needs only to look at his folk-song arrangements and his songwriting.

Moeran's thirty or so folk-song settings are drawn from Norfolk, Suffolk and County Kerry. They are arranged with thoughtful simplicity; and, whether we listen to 'Down by the Riverside' from the 1923 collection, *Six Folksongs from Norfolk,* or 'The Dawning of the Day' from *Songs from County Kerry* in 1950, they are unashamedly romantic. Those that are not – 'The Sailor and Young Nancy', 'The Jolly Carter' – have a bar-room, sing-along bawdiness that reflects the other side of Moeran's character. Moeran's art songs also span his whole career. As one might expect, he set a number of *Shropshire Lad* poems, including the favourite 'Loveliest of Trees', but his Housman settings, while accomplished, do not have the appeal of those by Butterworth, Vaughan Williams, or John Ireland. The high points of his song-writing career can be found in four collections. *Songs of Springtime* (1930) consists of settings of Shakespeare, Fletcher, Herrick and others; while *Phyllida and Corydon* (1939) is a suite of madrigals, pastorals and airs using sixteenth and seventeenth century texts. These reflect Moeran's association with Warlock, who was something of an expert on Elizabethan and Jacobean verse, and also associate him firmly with the Tudor revivalists. More important are *Seven Poems of James Joyce* (1929), written as he was recovering from living with Warlock, and *Six Poems of Seamus O'Sullivan* (1944). Both are very fine collections, displaying a range of moods and textures unified by his natural affinity for the Irishness of the poetry.

Moeran died of a cerebral haemorrhage – probably caused by his wartime injuries – in Kenmare in 1950. There can be no doubt that his life after 1917 was lived in the shadow of those injuries and their consequences. War does not feature in his work, except for a few bland references in some of the folk songs, but one wonders whether this and his romanticism constitute a case of looking the other way. In the end, it was alcohol that ruined his life: it broke up his marriage and led to what his biographer has called 'inevitable physical and mental disintegration',[6] and it would be foolish to deny the connection between his alcoholism and his physical and psychological war wounds.

Ivor Gurney (1890–1937) was born in Gloucester where his father was a tailor. The family was neither well off nor particularly well educated, but Gurney received encouragement and support from his godfather, the Reverend Alfred Cheesman. As a boy, he was a chorister at Gloucester Cathedral, and when his voice broke he stayed on as an articled pupil under the organist, Sir Herbert Brewer. Brewer's other pupils at this time were Ivor Novello, whom, as we saw, he tried to discourage from pursuing a musical career, and Herbert Howells, whose work we shall look at in the next chapter. It must have made for an interesting organ loft. Gurney won an open scholarship to the RCM, where Stanford considered him potentially the most talented of all his students, while recognising that he was at the same time not receptive to being taught.[7] Gurney was independent-minded and saw himself as modern and forward-thinking. He found himself up against a vastly experienced teacher who would not compromise on musical principles and standards that Gurney saw as old-fashioned. Gurney failed to see how much he needed the discipline Stanford demanded, but still longed for Stanford's approbation. It could be an image of his relationship with the world as a whole.

Gurney began songwriting before the war. *Five Elizabethan Songs*, setting familiar lyrics by Shakespeare, Fletcher and Thomas Nashe, was completed in January 1914 and shows already a talent for word-setting and fluent, effective timing. By this stage, even before the war, Gurney had already suffered and recovered from his first, apparently mild, breakdown. There was a history of mental instability on his mother's side so we cannot say that his subsequent problems were wholly due to his wartime experiences, but, as with Moeran, it would foolish to deny any connection. Gurney joined the Gloucester Regiment in 1915 and served in France. His first volume of verse, *Severn and Somme*, was written while he was at the front and unable to write music. He was shot; he was gassed; he suffered battle fatigue and shellshock; and was invalided back to Bangour Hospital, not far from Edinburgh, to begin his recuperation. He fell in love with one of the nurses, Annie Drummond, and she with him. For a time all was well, but the relationship failed; his father was ill with cancer; he himself was still suffering from the after-effects of gas and agonies of self-doubt about his future. It all triggered a major breakdown. His suicide attempt a few months later never got further than sitting on the bank of a canal in Warrington but it was a clear indication of his state of mind.

Gradually, Gurney appeared to recover. He was discharged from the army in October 1918 and returned to the RCM, where Vaughan Williams proved a more sympathetic teacher than Stanford. Again, as with Moeran, discharge from the army was followed by a brief period of apparent recovery and success. A second volume of verse, *War's Embers*, was published, as were several volumes of songs, beginning with two collections of Housman poems, *Ludlow and Teme* and *The Western Playland* (both 1919). Yet this was not enough to boost his waning self-belief. He left the College without completing his course and returned to Gloucester, where he was looked after by his family. He failed to find work, but wrote obsessively, both poetry and songs. He was convinced that the world had turned against him. His behaviour and his mental condition deteriorated rapidly. By 1922 his family felt they had no choice: they committed him to Barnwood House mental hospital. He was later moved to a mental hospital in Dartford in Kent where he died in 1937, having spent his last fifteen years in institutional care.

Gurney was both a poet and a songwriter. He left little instrumental music of significance: his one full-scale orchestral work, *A Gloucestershire Rhapsody*, is in the full, pre-war pastoral vein that the title implies. In the eyes of posterity, his poetry is generally more highly regarded than his songs – as a war poet, he ranks alongside Wilfred Owen and Siegfried Sassoon – but he regarded himself as first and foremost a musician. Of the two hundred and fifty songs that survive, over half were written, or at least sketched, in the four-year period between leaving the army and being committed to the asylum. Only a small proportion were published in his lifetime. Many more have been published as editors – among them Gerald Finzi – have laboured to interpret his chaotic manuscripts. His choice of poetry, as with so many of the songwriters of the period, was wide and discerning. Inevitably, as we have seen, there were collections of Housman poems. There were a number of successful settings of Yeats – among them 'Cathleen ni Houlihan', 'Down by the Salley Gardens', 'The Fiddler of Dooney' and, best of all, 'The Folly of Being Comforted'. Yeats, it should be remembered, was at the time the doyen of the Celtic Revival and had not yet entered on his later mystic phase. Another Irish poet chosen by Gurney was Joseph Campbell, whose 'I will go with my father a-ploughing' is the basis for a memorable, jaunty, folk-like setting. Gurney seems, however, to have had a particular affinity for the poets of the so-called Georgian School – as evidenced by his settings of Wilfred Gibson's 'The Black Stitchel', Walter de la Mare's 'The Scribe', Edward Shanks' 'The Singer' and Edward Thomas's 'Lights Out'.

Gurney's career was cut short, so we can only speculate as to what he might have achieved or how he might have developed. The songs that we have look back to the nineteenth century. Their musical language is closer to that of Stanford than Vaughan Williams. And although he was at the RCM at the same time as Bliss and Moeran, Gurney shows no awareness of Stravinsky, Debussy, Ravel or any other of the more assertively modern Continental composers. He wrote so much so quickly, and often in such a disturbed state of mind, that the quality of his work is inevitably uneven. Yet the agony in his mind does not transmit itself to his music. Even in songs such as Robert Bridges' 'When Death to Either Shall Come' or Edward Thomas's 'Lights Out', the emotion is controlled. Gurney is not a natural tunesmith like Quilter or Butterworth; and there are a great many songs that are technically flawed, where the accompaniment seems to lumber along, or quite simply does not work. But his great strength is his occasional, almost instinctive ability to illuminate a poem, creating a connection between the music and the words which develops as the song itself develops. When that happens, he is among the finest of the English romantic songwriters.

94   Howells, and Warlock

Looked at in broad terms, the story of those composers who began their professional careers in the aftermath of the First World War all comes down to a struggle to find a style suitable for the times in which they were living. The English national-pastoral style had served its purpose. It would, of course, as we have seen, go on serving the purpose of the generation with which it originated. It allowed them to express a common strand of feeling and it served as an effective lever to loosen the hold of German influence. To many younger musicians, however, it was a style that did not seem compatible with the post-war world as they perceived it. Bax, just eight years older than Bliss and eleven older than Moeran, felt able to respond defiantly, channelling his own 'brazen' (his word) romanticism into music on a symphonic scale. That option was not really available to the younger men. Their problem was how to escape from the English neo-romanticism or at least develop it into a persuasive and popular style that suited their purposes. Bliss, despite flexing some youthful muscles imme-diately after the war, never quite managed to escape from the prevailing late-romantic orthodoxy or to mould it to his own ends. With Moeran, we have the sense of a man struggling so hard with the problems of self-expression that he never quite managed to build the platform on which he could develop in his own way. And Gurney, sadly, never reached the start-ing line. None of these three, in the end, managed to move the musical debate forward – which is not to denigrate their achievements, but rather to recognise the complexity of the situation in which they found them-selves.

Herbert Howells (1892–1983) was one of those who did manage to create a style of his own and music that went beyond the orthodoxies in which he was educated. It was Howells whom we saw walking the streets of Gloucester with Gurney after hearing the first performance of Vaughan Williams's *Tallis Fantasia*. In terms of background, the two had much in common. Howells was the youngest of eight children born to a painter-decorator-builder in the small town of Lydney on the edge of the Forest of Dean in Gloucestershire. An inspiring father but a bad businessman, Oliver Howells went bankrupt. The disgrace and the humiliation inflicted on the family at the time left Howells with a sense of insecurity which continued to surface in later life. As with Gurney, who was helped by his godfather, Howells received assistance from Charles Bathurst, the local landowner and squire. Like Gurney, he won an open scholarship to the RCM, arriving there in 1912 where he studied under Stanford and Charles Wood.

More biddable than Gurney and also exceptionally talented, Howells got the very best out of the RCM. He never experienced Stanford's bad temper, while the background presence of Parry, a Gloucestershire man like himself, added the sense of security he needed. That first year in London he composed a *Mass in the Dorian Mode* for Richard Terry at Westminster Cathedral and, in 1913, Stanford conducted his Rachmaninoff-influenced but still extremely assured First Piano Concerto at an RCM concert. The golden future predicted by all was suddenly at risk when he was diagnosed with Graves' disease and given six months to live. He was saved by a specialist at St Thomas's Hospital who offered him injections of radium twice a week, an experimental technique that had never been tried out on any human being before. It worked. He lived to be ninety. His illness also saved him from military service.

Even during his treatment – which lasted two years – and the extended convalescence that followed, Howells kept working. He completed his Piano Quartet in A, a work of real depth: pastoral yet assertive, full of touches he had learned from Ravel and full also of the Gloucestershire countryside. The dedication is to Gurney, and refers to Churchdown (or Chosen) Hill outside Gloucester which was of special significance to them both. He also completed the *Phantasy String Quartet* (1917), and wrote the first draft of his Third String Quartet, which he then managed to leave on a train. It was rewritten several times in the 1920s and seems to have been finished about 1930 when it acquired the title *In Gloucestershire*. Richly melodic, and again full of the Gloucester countryside, but still with an assertiveness and directness of approach, it must count, along with the Piano Quartet, as one of Howells' early masterpieces. Also written at this time was *Elegy* (1917), for viola, string quartet and string orchestra, which he dedicated to the memory of his friend, Francis Purcell Warren, killed on the Somme the previous year.

During his convalescence, and no doubt with help from the RCM, Howells received a grant from the Carnegie Trust which allowed him to spend three years at Westminster Cathedral editing Tudor church music under the supervision of Richard Terry. The impact of the affinity he developed with Tudor music would not really become evident until the 1930s, but when it did, it would help him reach new heights as a composer. By 1920, he had recovered from his illness and had married Dorothy Dawe, who came from the village of Churchdown. He began teaching at the RCM and, later, followed Holst as Director of Music at St Paul's Girls' School in Hammersmith. These and other administrative functions reduced the time available for composition, but the real damage was done at the Queen's Hall premiere of his Second Piano Concerto in 1925. It is not his best work, but it did not deserve to be the subject of a public outburst by a hostile critic: Robert Lorenz of the *Musical Times* apparently stood up and announced, 'Thank God, that's over!' Howells was mortified. The incident provoked a crisis of confidence which meant that he composed very little for ten years – and most of what he did compose was left in a drawer. One small-scale but important work that was composed and published during that period, however, was *Lambert's Clavichord* (1929). Named for a Bath instrument maker who lent him a clavichord, it consists of twelve pieces, which, without pastiche, set out to recreate the spirit of Tudor keyboard music. It was the first evidence that Howells was using his accumulated knowledge of Tudor music in an original and, in this case, highly entertaining way. Two similar works, *Master Tallis's Testament* (1940) and *Howells' Clavichord* (1961), were to follow in later years.

The watershed of Howells' career came in 1935 and, initially, had nothing to do with music. His nine-year-old son, Michael, contracted polio and died within the space of three days. He was buried at Churchdown. Howells was distraught. Eventually, he began to channel his grief into composition and, between 1936 and 1938, wrote *Hymnus Paradisi*. This is a big work, in six movements, calling for tenor and soprano soloists (the soprano part is particularly demanding), choir, orchestra and organ. Despite its size, it is intensely personal. Howells takes himself and his audience on a complex journey from the anguish of grief and loss to a sense of consolation – the journey beginning with the fourth-century poet Prudentius, and then drawing on the Psalms and the Burial Service. Howells felt the work to be so personal that he did not disclose its existence until 1949, when he showed it to his friend, the Gloucester organist Herbert Sumsion. Only when Sumsion enlisted the support of Finzi and Vaughan Williams did Howells agree to it being performed at the 1950 Three Choirs Festival. Since that time, its reputation has continued to grow, and not just because of its emotion and personal intensity. The setting of the text, the handling of choral and orchestral polyphony, the expression of and transition between contrasting moods, all mark *Hymnus Paradisi* as one of the great pieces of English choral music, rivalling *Gerontius*.

After the composition of *Hymnus Paradisi* – but long before its performance – Howells returned to choral and organ music. He published *Four Anthems* (1941) which included the stately yet serene *O, Pray for the peace of Jerusalem*. Then he deputised as organist at St John's College, Cambridge, from 1941 to 1945. From that time onwards his output of church music became a flood. An initial stimulus came when the Dean of King's College challenged him to write a set of canticles. The result became known as *Collegium Regale* (begun 1945, completed 1956), and, together with his *Gloucester Service* (1946) and *St Paul's Cathedral Service* (1951), it is one the most often-quoted examples of Howell's brilliance as a composer of sacred music. Yet he wrote no less than sixteen settings of the canticles, usually for specific locations – St George's Chapel at Windsor, Chichester, Winchester, Worcester, Hereford and York – frequently making careful adjustments to his arrangement so that it would suit the acoustics of the chapel, church or cathedral where it was to be sung. Since the death of his son, Howells had become increasingly introverted, and the Anglican Service, especially Evensong, celebrated in a church or cathedral became the perfect environment for him to express the sense of loss and nostalgia that he experienced. The music is not unadventurous – his harmonic language can be original and challenging – yet what Howells did was more than a matter of technique. He built a style that could rediscover the real emotions – ecstasy, agony, glory, longing, peace – conveyed by the language of the liturgy but long obscured by use and by time. His achievement in this respect was no less than Stanford's half-a-century or more earlier: his music and his innovations would carry Anglican church music forward for the next half century and longer.

In the wake of *Hymnus Paradisi*, Howell's growing confidence led him to write two large-scale works. The first was *Missa Sabriensis* (1954), a reference to the River Severn, which runs close to Lydney where he was born and through the city of Gloucester which played such a major part in his life. The second was his *Stabat Mater* (1965). Both are dramatic, contrapuntal works, with some glorious choral moments and a command of soft dissonant textures. Both also express a very personal emotional vision – the *Stabat Mater*, in particular, lamenting the death of a child, had an obvious personal application for Howells and the work ends with a sense of absolute exhaustion and hopelessness. Both works have developed a reputation for difficulty, particularly among amateur choirs, but perhaps, as Howells' music becomes better known, they will be better understood. A more accessible and popular late work is the superb, unaccompanied anthem, *Take Him, Earth, For Cherishing* (1964) which became associated with the worldwide response to the death of President Kennedy and is now regarded one of Howells' finest works.

In his later years, Howells collected the usual honours (CBE;

Companion of Honour), fellowships and doctorates. He also became an effective communicator, giving radio talks on music that proved popular. Yet he remained a very private man who claimed that he wrote music solely because he wanted to create beauty. The paradox of his career is that his greatest successes were brought about by a personal tragedy which stayed with him to the end of his life.

At the opposite end of the spectrum in almost every way is Philip Heseltine (1894–1930), better known in musical circles as Peter Warlock. He was born to a prosperous family – indeed, he was actually born in London's Savoy Hotel where his parents were living at the time. Perhaps because his father died when he was only two, Heseltine had an intense and complex relationship with his mother. Even when she remarried – to another equally wealthy man – she remained exceptionally possessive. Heseltine had every advantage. His interest in music was encouraged by his mother and by his teachers at his prep school in Broadstairs. He disliked Eton but found at least one teacher who saw promise in him. It was this teacher, Colin Taylor, who in 1911 arranged for him to meet Delius, for whose music Heseltine had developed a teenage enthusiasm. The meeting led to a close friendship in which, to Heseltine's mother's fury, Delius played a fatherly role, advising the young man on his future and on his music.

After a few months in Cologne, where he failed to make much progress learning German, but did manage to write his first songs, Heseltine went up to Christ Church, Oxford, to study Classics. That lasted just a year. In October 1914, he moved to London University to study literature and philosophy, but that lasted only five months. Emerald Cunard, one of London's leading hostesses, helped him get a job as music critic on the *Daily Mail*. That lasted four months. He spent time in the British Library editing Elizabethan musical manuscripts. He fell in love with an artist's model nicknamed Puma, because of her temperament. He moved to Worcestershire and scandalised the locals by riding his motorbike naked. He moved to Cornwall to be near D. H. Lawrence, but returned to London when they fell out.[1] He declared himself a pacifist and managed to get an exemption from war service. He met the Dutch composer, Bernard van Dieren, whose music he promoted tirelessly. He had a child by Puma and another by a Swiss girl.[2] That takes us to 1916 when he married Puma, began to use the pseudonym Peter Warlock for his musical and critical activities, and began to write music seriously.

Warlock (as we shall now call him) was a miniaturist and, apart from his *Capriol Suite* (1926) – a reworking of some sixteenth-century French dance music for string orchestra – is known almost exclusively for his songs and a few choral pieces. His first notable work was a short collection called *Saudades* (1917), using texts from Li Tai Po, Shakespeare, and Callimachus. These are his most consciously modern settings and in some ways his least characteristic. Perhaps reflecting the influence of van Dieren, two of them have neither key signatures nor bar lines. In 1917, he moved to Ireland to avoid a review of his exemption from military service. There he became involved in various occult practices, including the invocation of demons. After a while this mellowed into an interest in theosophy, through which he met W. B. Yeats. It was during this period that Warlock found his voice as a songwriter, although some of the songs he began in Ireland were not finished until after his return to London in 1918. At that point he revisited musical journalism, culminating in a brief but ultimately unsuccessful period as editor of the magazine *Sackbut*: he was considered too aggressive and combative in his approach.

Songs from this period include 'My gostly fader' attributed to Charles d'Orléans, 'Lullaby' by Thomas Dekker, and another lullaby, 'Balulalow', a translation of a text by Luther made by the Scottish Wedderburn brothers in the sixteenth century. Warlock always took immense care over the selection of the poems he set. Of his one hundred songs, there are no epics and very few with any narrative component. He concentrates on simple lyrics conveying a mood or a moment – which is why his carols, such as 'Tyrley Tyrlow', 'Where riches everlastingly is', 'A Cornish carol' and 'Bethlehem Down', with their jaunty, singable tunes are so effective. 'Corpus Christi', slightly different in that it was composed for string quartet accompaniment, was also written during this early period. It is the best of his carols and one of his finest choral works.

Warlock's unstable and turbulent history – his inability to settle and his unerring ability to fall out with those who tried to help him – was partly the result of what we might now call a rock'n'roll lifestyle. He was aggressively extrovert and egotistical, given to all sorts of outrageous public stunts, wild sexual exploits (the marriage to Puma lasted no time at all), extended drinking binges, sometimes boosted by cannabis, cocaine and other drugs. But in the background was another Warlock: withdrawn, studious almost to the point of obsession, and not infrequently depressed. This duality suggests a throwback to someone like Thomas Weelkes – and, of course, it was to the sixteenth and early-seventeenth century that he looked for his inspiration, both musical and literary.

In 1921, with empty pockets and no job, Warlock returned to the family home in Wales and relied on the generosity of his mother and stepfather. Over the next three years, he wrote some of his best work: the collections he entitled *Lilligay* and *Peterisms I* and *II;* the collection of nursery rhymes, *Candlelight;* and settings such as John Fletcher's 'Sleep' and the fifteenth-century lyric 'Adam lay ybounden'. Warlock had written a version of 'Cloths of Heaven' in 1916, but his association with W. B. Yeats had not resulted in any new settings of the poet's work until now. It was while he was in Wales that he wrote *The Curlew*, his only genuine song cycle and his finest work. A setting of four poems with an instrumental interlude, it is bleak in the extreme, full of nostalgia, disillusion, and lost love, with the cor anglais representing the voice of the curlew and evoking the desolate moorlands and lakes of the Irish countryside. The extent and depth of the melancholy recalls Dowland. The music may seem simple but it works on (at least) two levels: it contains a variety of ideas and textures illustrating individual words and phrases, while at the same time creating and maintaining the unifying mood of the whole piece.

Warlock's turbulent lifestyle finds no echo in his music which is orderly, controlled, even precise, and shows a concern with detail that, from the outline of his biography, one might not expect. Where it does show through is in the nature of some of his songs. The drinking songs he wrote during his Welsh years and the Eynsford period when he shared a house with Moeran are a world away from *The Curlew*. Songs like Sir John Squire's parody-tribute 'Mr Belloc's Fancy', John Masefield's 'Captain Stratton's Fancy' or his own 'Peter Warlock's Fancy' praise drink and women in a manner that would have been perfectly recognisable in the age of Tobias Hume, Dowland and Robert Johnson, but the settings are always musically exact.

When the Eynsford household broke up in 1928, Warlock again returned to his family in Wales. In 1929, at the invitation of Sir Thomas Beecham (who had been knighted in 1916), he returned to London to help in the preparation and organisation of a Delius Festival. This was a useful stopgap, but did not compensate for the fact that he was writing less and that what he did write was receiving less attention. He was struggling to find the creativity that had sustained him over the previous ten years. The year 1930 saw two remarkable works: the carol 'Bethlehem Down' and one his finest songs, 'The Fox', both settings of texts by his friend Bruce Blunt. It was not enough. There are moving accounts of his state of mind. Van Dieren describes being unable to reach him in his depression. In December 1930, Warlock was found dead in his Chelsea flat with the gas turned on. The inquest could not decide whether it was suicide or an accident, but it seems as certain as anything can be that he took his own life.

Love songs, drinking songs, lullabies, dirges, songs of hope, songs of despair, elegies, nonsense songs, medievalism, mysticism – Warlock's range of expression was truly immense and the art song was his chosen medium. That he could have worked in larger formats is suggested by the structure and success of *The Curlew*. Perhaps his lack of formal training held him back. Perhaps he simply did not wish to become 'a composer' in the traditional mould. He said that the essence of songwriting was the unaccompanied tune, not the accompaniment; and he kept his tunes simple, avoiding melisma and frequently sticking to the 'one syllable, one note' formula promulgated by Cranmer – another sixteenth century connection. His harmonies were adventurous, even risky at times; he had an ability to play off vocal colour against rhythm; and, even when the words were nonsense – as in the wonderful 'The bayley berith the bell away' – he paid close attention to their rhythm and phrasing. He was influenced by Delius, and perhaps also by Stravinsky (whom he affected to despise). He was a great admirer of Bartok, and also of van Dieren (the latter not a view endorsed by posterity). These were strands he wove together with his own detailed knowledge and understanding of sixteenth- and seventeenth-century music, creating a style that was a unique mixture of old and new, and might – if one had to choose a phrase – be described as sophisticated simplicity. The link between Warlock and Howells is the way in which they both drew upon sixteenth- and seventeenth-century models as the basis for their own contemporary style.

What happened at the end is impossible to know. Had his creativity just dried up? He had created a style that was unique. Or could that have been part of the problem? Was his style was so uniquely his own that it was impossible to emulate or develop? He was scholar enough to realise that. As a songwriter, Warlock stands with Dowland – some have even said with Schubert[3] – but in terms of his own time Warlock's hard-won style, unlike that of Howells, did not lead anywhere.

American influence on popular music in Britain was in evidence as early as 1903 when the revue *In Dahomey* opened at London's Shaftesbury Theatre. This was the first all-black revue, with music by the African American violinist, Will Marion Cook, who had been one of Dvořák's students during the composer's time as Director of New York's National Conservatory of Music in the 1890s. After London, *In Dahomey* went on to make a successful provincial tour, returning to the capital for a command performance at Buckingham Palace to celebrate the ninth birthday of the future Edward VIII. The show introduced 'The Cakewalk' as a dance, and ragtime as a musical style. Both were quickly picked up by the musical halls and their popularity in the years leading up to the First World War was reflected in songs such as Irving Berlin's 'Everybody's Doing It' and 'Alexander's Ragtime Band'. The impresario Albert de Courville (who was born in Croydon, despite his name) was among those who cashed in on the craze. In 1912, his big, American-style spectacular revue, *Hello, Ragtime!*, opened at the London Hippodrome and ran for over four hundred and fifty performances.

American involvement in the war provided a commercial opportunity for publishers and gramophone companies alike. Songs like 'Ragtime Cowboy Joe' and 'Over There', with its chorus, 'The Yanks are coming', were used to whip up and trade on pro-American sentiment. Many American songs became popular hits in Britain. Some like 'There's a Long, Long Trail a-Winding' and 'K-K-K-Katy' continued to be popular long after the war, whereas others, including 'Your Lips are No Man's Land But Mine' and 'We Don't Want the Bacon (What We Want is a Piece of the Rhine)', survive only as curiosities of their particular time. A common language, a common purpose and more direct personal contact with Americans than ever before, all created a basis of familiarity on which American popular culture was able to launch itself in Britain when the fighting ended.

The arrival in London of The Original Dixieland Jazz Band (originally 'Jass Band') in April 1919 marked the beginning of the so-called Jazz Age. Some copies of their recordings, particularly their biggest hit 'Tiger Rag' had already crossed the Atlantic, but this was the first time that jazz had been heard live in Britain. The group made their debut at the London Hippodrome in a scene specially inserted into a revue called *Joy Bells*. They moved to the London Palladium, toured the provinces, and were then asked to play for the Victory Ball at the Savoy Hotel, which marked the signing of the Treaty of Versailles. Up to that point, jazz and its arrival in Britain had proved controversial in some quarters. London's evening newspaper *The Star* was among a number of journals that accused the band of murdering music,[1] but to be asked to play at such a momentous, historic occasion was a definite publicity coup. The audience included King George V, assorted European royalty, Marshal Pétain, Marshal Foch and General Pershing. King George was observed enthusiastically applauding 'Tiger Rag'. Jazz caught on.

In October 1922, Marie Lloyd gave her last performance. She was playing the Edmonton Empire. She sang 'One of the Ruins that Cromwell Knocked about a Bit', collapsed backstage and died three days later. Over 100,000 people lined the streets of Golders Green for her funeral. It was not the end of music hall, but it was a symbolic moment in what was already an irreversible decline. During the war years, as we saw earlier, the popularity of music hall had been eroded by revues and musicals. Now the 1920s saw the rise of other competing forms of entertainment: film – at first silent and then, by the end of the decade, the 'talkies' – the dance band, the gramophone, and also, of course, radio.

Over two hundred and fifty new musical shows opened on the London stage during the 1920s. It was a boom that threw up many new talented writers and performers whose careers would continue through the interwar years and beyond. Among them was Vivian Ellis (1904–96), who, although little remembered these days, was one of the leading stage composers of his generation. The product of a musical family, he studied piano under Myra Hess at the RAM and seemed destined for a classical career, but in 1922 he was offered the chance to contribute to a revue called *The Curate's Egg*. It was a career-changing moment. Over the next thirty-six years, he contributed to some seventy shows – at least half of them during the 1920s, and many of them produced by the great impresario C. B. Cochran. Most have long since been forgotten, although *Mr Cinders* (1929), a version of *Cinderella* with the sexes reversed, may perhaps be remembered for the song 'Spread a Little Happiness'. In the 1930s, Ellis teamed up with the lyricist Guy Bolton for a series of productions including *Jill Darling* (1934), *Under Your Hat* (1938) and *Running Riot* (1938), which starred three of the leading comedians of the day – Leslie Henson, Fred Emney, and Richard Hearne (who later achieved fame as Mr Pastry).

After the Second World War and service as a Lieutenant-Commander in the Navy, Ellis returned to writing for the musical stage. The old-style British musical was now looking decidedly old-fashioned alongside American imports such as *Oklahoma!* and *Annie Get Your Gun*, but with a new collaborator – the novelist, playwright and MP, A. P. Herbert – Ellis came up with *Big Ben* (1946). It was a musical tribute to the resilience of Londoners in wartime and, with one hundred and seventy-two performances, was accounted a moderate success. During the writing of *Big Ben*, Ellis was travelling to Margate (or possibly to Taunton, the story varies) when the rhythm of the train inspired him to compose the tune 'Coronation Scot', which was taken up by the BBC and used as the theme tune for the long-running radio detective series, *Paul Temple*. *Big Ben* was followed by the biggest success of Ellis's career, *Bless the Bride* (1947), which was popular both because of its songs – 'La Belle Marguerite' and 'This is My Lovely Day' were both best-sellers – and because its Victorian setting provided a complete contrast to the prevailing diet of American musicals. It ran for nearly nine hundred performances at the Adelphi Theatre and was for many years a favourite with amateur musical societies. *Bless the Bride* did not mark the end of Ellis's career, but it was the last great British musical of the kind which stretched back to *The Maid of the Mountains* and beyond.

Another and much more prodigious talent to come into its own during the 1920s was that of Noel Coward (1899–1973). The image of Coward that is now fixed in the public mind is that of the urbane, witty, well-educated Englishman with a cigarette holder, not unlike the character of Captain Kinross which he played in the film *In Which We Serve*. That image, and the myth that went with it, took a long while to create. In reality, Coward came from a struggling middle-class family, and his education was disrupted both by his own poor behaviour – he once bit a teacher – and by the efforts of his doting but ambitious mother to get him a theatrical career. Coward's first stage appearance was in a children's play in 1911 when he was just twelve. His first appearance in a musical was in *The Light Blues* in 1916, but unfortunately the show ran for only twenty performances. Nonetheless, he – and his mother – persisted and by 1920 he was starring in his own play, *I'll Leave It to You*.

Coward was multi-talented. Although he began as an actor, he regarded himself as primarily a writer. From an early age, he was writing plays and short stories, but it was not until 1923 that he had his first success as a composer. *London Calling!* was produced by André Charlot, a French actor-manager-impresario, who was possibly the only man to rival C.B. Cochran in terms of influence on the London stage at the time. It opened at the Duke of York's Theatre that September and proved something of a landmark production. Coward wrote most of the songs and sketches and took the male lead, playing opposite Gertrude Lawrence in her first singing role. Fred Astaire, then working down the road at the Shaftesbury Theatre in *Stop Flirting!*, helped with choreography and taught Coward to tap dance. 'Parisian Pierrot', a characteristic Coward tune, became the show's most popular song and his own first hit.

Coward would continue to write songs and scores for the musical stage for the next fifty years. *On with the Dance* (1925) featured 'Poor Little Rich Girl'; *This Year of Grace* (1928) included 'Dance Little Lady' and 'A Room with a View'; *Bitter Sweet* (1929) – which came about because Coward and C.B. Cochran were forced to share a cabin on the SS *Berengaria* while returning from the Unites States – featured 'I'll See You Again'. *Private Lives* (1930) was a play rather than a revue, but Coward wrote his own incidental music and included the song 'Someday I'll Find You', which became one of his biggest hits. Characteristically, he poked fun at his own score with the line 'Extraordinary how potent cheap music is'. His series of successes continued throughout the 1930s, was interrupted by the Second World War, then resumed during the 1950s and 60s. For a man with no formal musical education, it was an amazing achievement – especially as he was writing non-musical plays and taking acting roles in the theatre and on film at the same time.

Coward said that he was 'born into a generation that still took light music seriously'.[2] He drew on music hall, jazz, ragtime, blues, operetta, wartime popular song, anything that worked; and whatever the tone of a song – romantic, sentimental, comic – it was always theatrically effective. He had the immense advantage of being his own lyric writer, but it was the music, usually a simple vocal line, which came first. At the same time, his tunes are always tailored to reinforce the meaning of the lyrics. In this respect, his lack of formal musical training may have been an advantage in that it forced him to concentrate on the effect that he wanted to achieve. His romantic and sentimental songs – 'I'll Follow My Secret Heart', 'London Pride', 'Sail Away', 'Dearest Love' – had a simplicity and a direct emotional appeal to which the public responded. His comic songs – 'The Stately Homes of England', 'Mad Dogs and Englishmen', 'There are Bad Times Just around the

Corner', 'Mrs Worthington' – showed an exceptional command of language and an ability to send up established conventions and institutions in a way which, again, appealed to the British public (and recalled the patter songs of W. S. Gilbert). They also displayed masterly comic timing with every syllable precisely matched to the rhythm of the tune.

Today, we see Coward as a quintessentially English figure, which he was – although that was also the image he liked to project, and an important reason for the popularity of his one-man shows in the United States in the 1950s and 60s. In the 1920s, however, he was frequently seen by London reviewers as having absorbed too many American influences. In reality, he was something of a patriot. A show such as *Cavalcade* (1931) dealt in old-fashioned (and no doubt profitable) patriotism, but was nonetheless genuinely felt. Yet he was also, in his own idiosyncratic way, a moderniser. He took what was on offer and what was successful – whether it was American, European or British – and made it his own, pushing the limits of what was musically and theatrically possible. Hence *Cavalcade*, while telling the story of thirty years of British history seen through the lives of a quintessentially English family, the Marryots, could also feature the song 'Twentieth-Century Blues'.

Of the two hundred and fifty new shows put on in London during the 1920s, most were British, with music composed by a now long-forgotten generation of theatrical and light music composers, such as Jack Waller (1895–1957), Joseph Tunbridge (1886–1961), Haydn Wood (1882–1959) and Alfred Reynolds (1884–1969). Looking back from a twenty-first-century viewpoint, however, it is the American shows, the American writers and the American stars that have impressed their names on musical posterity. Various composer-lyricist combinations – names that would remain famous well into the post-Second World War era – made their first London appearances during the 1920s, either in person or through shows that transferred from Broadway. George and Ira Gershwin contributed to *Lady Be Good* (1926) and *Funny Face* (1928) – as well as *Stop Flirting!* (1923), already mentioned as starring Fred Astaire. Richard Rodgers and Lorenz Hart, who were riding a wave of popularity in the United States, saw at least five of their musicals transferred to London, including *The Girlfriend* (1927), *One Damn Thing After Another* (1927) and *A Yankee at the Court of King Arthur* (1929).

Most of these shows told romantic stories, were vehicles for particular stars, and contained one or two songs that stood out and were promoted through sheet music and gramophone records. *Showboat* was different. Written by Oscar Hammerstein II and Jerome Kern, it opened at the Theatre Royal in Drury Lane in May 1928, and featured songs which are still heard today. 'Make Believe', 'Ol' Man River', 'Can't Help Lovin' Dat Man' and 'Bill' (with a lyric originally by P. G. Wodehouse) exposed British audiences to a new African-American style of music and, in particular, to gospel-influenced music; while the setting on a Mississippi riverboat in the southern states introduced themes of racial prejudice and segregation, and in doing so expanded the possibilities of musical theatre. It ran for three hundred and fifty performances.

A number of musicals traded on the fascination of exotic locations. *Desert Song* (1927), featuring the sinister, cloaked character, Red Shadow, was written by Hammerstein, though this time his partner was the Austro-Hungarian operetta composer, Sigmund Romberg (1887–1951). Romberg, in collaboration with lyricist Dorothy Donnelly, was responsible for *The Student Prince* (1926), set among cheerful, thigh-slapping, beer-drinking German students. Hammerstein, the Czech composer Rudolf Friml (1879–1972) and one or two others wrote *Rose-Marie*, set among trappers and hunters in the wilds of Canada, which included the famous 'Indian Love Call'. *Lilac Time* (1922), originally produced in Vienna and consequently closer to operetta than to musical or revue, was an absurdly romantic reimagining of Schubert's life with a pasticcio score based on his music by the Hungarian Heinrich Berté (1858–1924).

It will be obvious from such a summary that musical theatre had rapidly become a big and increasingly transatlantic industry. Only a few of those productions that crossed the Atlantic to Britain also made it to Continental Europe. One that did, however – indeed, it opened in Paris before London – was the all black revue, *Blackbirds* (1926). It starred Florence Mills, who famously burst out of a birthday cake in the opening scene before singing her first song, 'Silver Rose'. *Blackbirds* also marked the first appearance of the Black Bottom dance on the London stage. The Charleston had already caught on – Fred Astaire had recorded 'I'd Rather Charleston' in 1924, and there were Charleston sequences in both *Lady Be Good* and *Funny Face*. The Foxtrot had made its way across the Atlantic with the troops during the war, and was soon the most popular dance around. The Tango and the Waltz were still popular. By the late 1920s, the Quickstep arrived. The 1930s brought the Rumba and the Jitterbug. Dancing was all the rage. A gramophone might serve at home or among friends – especially after 1926 when the new technique of electric recording drastically improved sound quality – but a proper dance required a dance band.

Suddenly, there were dances everywhere. There were tea dances and dinner dances. There were debutante balls and charity balls. There was dancing in hotels everywhere – in London, in provincial cities and in seaside resorts. There was dancing in night clubs, and there were new dance halls opening up all over the country. Glasgow had twenty, more than any other city – the Albert Ballroom held six dances a week; the Locarno on Sauchiehall Street was known as a place to dance the Charleston. The Regent in Brighton opened in 1923 and could hold 1,500 dancers. The Grafton in Liverpool opened the following year and could hold 1,200. Belfast had the Plaza, which had begun life before the war, and the wonderfully art deco Orpheus which opened in 1932. The 1920s saw the emergence of a generation of bandleaders and dance band musicians who would remain popular throughout the interwar years and into the post-Second-World-War era. A few examples will have to represent the many who enjoyed nationwide popularity during the period.

There was Benjamin Baruch Ambrose (1896–1971), whose family emigrated to London from Warsaw when Poland was still under Russian rule. He actually began his career in New York, but returned to London to work in the Embassy Club and the May Fair Hotel throughout the 20s and 30s. Known familiarly as Bert, his stage name was simply 'Ambrose'. He was responsible for promoting Vera Lynn in the early stages of her career. She joined his band in 1937 and went on to become an iconic figure among British troops during the Second World War. There was Harry Roy (1900–71), a clarinettist and saxophonist, who formed a small band, the Darnswells, with his brother on the piano. The Darnswells played at the Coliseum, the Café de Paris and the May Fair throughout the 20s, as well as touring as far afield as South Africa and Australia. In the 1930s, Roy went on to form a big band – Harry Roy and His Orchestra – and then, during the war, toured with a smaller group, Harry Roy's Tiger Ragamuffins. Jack Hylton (1892–1965) was slightly older than Ambrose or Harry Roy. He had been a regimental bandleader during the First World War and gone on to direct and record with the Queen's Dance Orchestra (the name implied no royal connection). Then in 1923, he formed his own band which rapidly became one of the most popular in the country, known for its strongly jazz-influenced dance music. This allowed him to persuade Duke Ellington to visit Britain and play not only in London, but also in Birmingham,

Liverpool and Glasgow. This was a musical coup; it was also good business, and Hylton was a shrewd businessman. He began the process of making dance band music respectable. Jack Hylton and his Orchestra moved out of the hotels and dance halls where other bands played and began appearing in theatres, opera houses and concert halls usually reserved for classical concerts. Hylton also made sure that they recorded as much of their material as possible. Even in 1929, at the height of the Great Depression, he is credited with selling over four million records. During the Second World War, he worked with the London Philharmonic Orchestra, his major triumph being to recruit Sir Malcolm Sargent to tour the blitz-damaged cities of northern England giving classical, promenade-style concerts. After the war, he became a promoter and produced many London musicals – notably the British production of Cole Porter's *Kiss Me Kate* – and later became involved with television.

Nothing illustrates the speed of change more clearly than the way in which the dance bands chose to promote themselves. Gramophone and record sales boomed in the 1920s. Record labels proliferated – Columbia, Monarch, Oriole, Vocalion, Decca, Regal, Homochord – and record sales rapidly became essential for any dance band seeking national or international success. Records were made of a brittle, shellac-based compound. They were either ten inches in diameter, lasting about three-and-a-half minutes, or twelve inches, lasting between four-and-a-half and five minutes. Quality was improving but they still produced a large amount of surface hiss. There were, as we have seen, classical musicians, such as Elgar, and recording companies, such as His Master's Voice, who were prepared to record classical music, but, in practice, jazz and dance band music with shorter playing times and a narrower dynamic range fitted better within the technical constraints. Selling records meant advertising and publicity. Getting music played in the dance halls and getting reviews in newspapers and magazines were both important, but by the second half of the 1920s the key to recording contracts and record sales was the new medium of radio.

The newly-formed British Broadcasting Company began transmitting from Savoy Hill in 1922. Transmissions and technology were primitive to begin with but improved rapidly. The new station's call sign – 'This is London calling' – provided the title of Noel Coward's revue the following year. As early as January 1923, the new company (it did not become a Corporation until 1927) transmitted its first outside broadcast. It came from Covent Garden where the equally newly-formed British National Opera Company were performing *The Magic Flute*. The event required the Royal Opera House to be connected to the BBC's Savoy Hill studio by a quarter-mile-long, lead-sheathed cable. It was a success, and more operas were broadcast that week, including *I Pagliacci* and parts of *Siegfried*. The ten-day experiment concluded with a performance of *La Bohème* starring Dame Nellie Melba. Harrods kept its restaurant open late into the evening so that customers could listen.[3] Outside broadcasts may have begun with opera, but relays of dance music from London's clubs and hotels soon followed and were much more popular. The Savoy Hotel, where the band was called the Savoy Orpheans, was favoured because of its proximity to the BBC's studio, but there were also regular broadcasts from the Dorchester, the May Fair and the Café Anglais. A major disadvantage for Ambrose working at the Embassy Club was the fact that it considered itself so exclusive – the Prince of Wales was among its regular guests – that it would not allow broadcasting from the premises. One regular broadcaster was Jack Payne (1899–1969) who, from 1925, led the house band at London's Hotel Cecil. In 1928, the BBC decided to form its own band – the sixteen-piece BBC Dance Orchestra – and appointed Payne as its leader and the Corporation's Director of Dance Music. The Orchestra broadcast daily for forty-five minutes from 5.15 to 6 p.m., always ending with Payne's signature tune, Irving Berlin's 'Say It with Music'.

Payne left the BBC in 1932 and was replaced by Henry Hall, who had been the bandleader at the prestigious Gleneagles Hotel in Scotland and subsequently recruited musicians and organised the music for a large chain of hotels run by the London, Midland and Scottish Railway. It was Hall's insistence that the celebrations to mark the Gleneagles Hotel's opening night in 1924 should be broadcast – it was Scotland's first ever outside broadcast – that brought him to the BBC's attention. He took over Payne's nightly slot, using his own 'Here's to the Next Time' as a signature tune. He introduced a Children's Spot into the programme, which led to a record of 'The Teddy Bear's Picnic' being issued with Val Rowsing as vocalist. It sold over a million copies. Another of Hall's innovations, based on programmes he had heard while visiting the United States, was *Guest Night*, in which celebrity entertainers joined the band to sing or play or do comedy routines. Guests, whose names were not announced beforehand, ran the whole gamut from the comedy duo, Flanagan and Allen, to the operatic tenor, Richard Tauber. The programme was a huge success. By 1936, technology had improved to the point where outside broadcasts could be made from a ship at sea, and Hall was invited to conduct the on-board band during the maiden voyage of Cunard's RMS *Queen Mary*. He left the BBC in 1937, taking the band with him. They went on to tour widely and to entertain troops during the war, although Hall himself continued to present *Guest Night*, a concept he was able to transfer to television as *Face the Music* in the 1950s.

During the 1920s, popular music became an international industry. The stage musical, the dance bands with their signature tunes, the gramophone, the radio – all in their different ways interrelated – provided the basis for a boom in musical entertainment that would last for the next thirty years. An extra dimension would be added and the boom would intensify, first in the 1930s as silent film gave way to films with synchronised soundtracks, and then in the 1940s as cinema entered what is often refered to as its golden age; but the essential components of the industry would remain recognisably the same until the sudden and overwhelming impact of television and youth culture in the 1950s.

96   William Walton

It was January 1924. A painted curtain had been drawn across the L-shaped living room of a Chelsea house. In the middle was the mouth of a huge megaphone – actually called a Sengerphone[1] – behind which a young woman prepared to read her poetry, while a very young composer prepared to conduct the four-piece band (trumpet, clarinet, cello, percussion) that would provide the accompaniment. It was to be a private premiere, the audience consisting of twenty-to-thirty invited guests. The poetry was intensely rhythmic and tightly-rhymed, allusive, eccentric, influenced by nonsense verse and nursery rhymes. The music kept close to the rhythms of the verse. It featured jazz sounds, a hornpipe, a tango, and a parody of 'I do like to be beside the seaside'. The poet was Edith Sitwell; the composer was nineteen-year-old William Walton; and the occasion was the first performance of *Façade*, described as 'An Entertainment'. *Façade* was modern; it was avant-garde; it embodied the spirit of the new Jazz Age. Or so it appeared. But in reality, immensely entertaining though the piece remains, Edith Sitwell's poems were not as 'modern' as those of T. S. Eliot or Ezra Pound, and Walton's modernistic idiom only served to obscure his true musical nature – in much the same way that Bliss's early works belied his.

William Walton (1902–83) was born in Oldham, where his father was a music teacher and church organist. Walton was ten – or so the story goes – and his mother was just about to take him to Christ Church Cathedral School in Oxford for an audition, when she discovered that her husband had spent the train fare in the pub the previous evening. She borrowed the money from a local grocer, but arrived after the auditions had ended. Only her special pleading and Walton's extraordinary talent got him accepted. The story may well be true – Walton was extremely lucky in finding help and support in his early years – but, like many incidents concerning his early life, it seems almost designed to contrast the rough, Lancashire-speaking lad from a poor background with the urbane and sophisticated composer that he became.

Dr Thomas Strong, the Dean of Christ Church, who would later act as Vice-Chancellor of the University during the First World War, took Walton under his wing. Strong found bursaries and funds that allowed Walton to stay on after his voice broke, and in 1918 arranged for him to be admitted to the University, even though he was not yet seventeen. Walton worked hard at his music, both with his tutor, Hugh Allen, and by himself, but he did not study the non-musical subjects required by the University. He failed the necessary exams three times and in 1920 left Oxford without a degree. That spring, however, on the strength of a gift of £50 from Dr Strong, he was able to accept an invitation from his new friends Osbert and Sacheverell Sitwell to accompany them to Italy. For the boy from Oldham, the trip itself proved a life-changing experience, but the Sitwells offered more: they offered him somewhere to stay when he was forced to leave Oxford and could not face returning to Oldham. By his own account, he went to stay with them for a few weeks and did not leave for fifteen years.[2] Walton was lucky. The Sitwells, Dr Strong, and the composer and former diplomat Lord Berners (whom we shall meet in Chapter 98), all recognised his talent and contributed funds so that he had an income just sufficient to allow him to concentrate on composition without needing to get a job.

When not having his artistic and social horizons broadened by the Sitwells, Walton composed obsessively. He was introduced to Stravinsky and Gershwin. He listened to jazz and dance band music, particularly at the Savoy Hotel. He had written a romantic piano quartet while at Oxford;

now he wrote an experimental string quartet that was played in Vienna in 1923, alongside works by Berg, Janáček, Bartok, and Hindemith. The reception was not overwhelming, but Alban Berg was interested enough to take Walton and Berners to meet Schoenberg. *Façade* provided his first success, even if it was a *succès de scandale*. Most of the reviews were critical, but that barely mattered because the Sitwells got a kick out of notoriety and Walton was happy to benefit from any publicity going. What did upset the Sitwells, however, particularly Edith, was Noel Coward's parody in *London Calling!* where the three siblings appeared thinly disguised as the Swiss Family Whitlebot – Hernia, Gob and Sago. Walton found it funny.

Façade was fun; it was formative; but it was a dead end musically. The work that began the path of development towards his mature style was the overture *Portsmouth Point* (1925), inspired not by the place but by the artist Thomas Rowlandson's caricature of goings-on on the Portsmouth waterfront during the Napoleonic Wars. Energetic, boisterous, brassy, dissonant, percussive, with echoes of Stravinsky's *Petrushka* and hints of sea shanties and hornpipes, *Portsmouth Point* was certainly very different from *Façade*, but it could only confirm his reputation as one of the new bad boys of British music. Ballet was very much in vogue in the 1920s. Walton had helped Constant Lambert (another bad boy) orchestrate his *Romeo and Juliet* which was danced by Sergei Diaghilev's Ballets Russes. Now he tried to write a ballet himself, but Diaghilev rejected it. At Lambert's suggestion, he turned the score into a three-movement *Sinfonia Concertante with Piano Obbligato*. This is a less assured work than its predecessors, a mix of unassimilated influences: Stravinsky, Rachmaninoff, Borodin, Ravel, perhaps Poulenc, certainly jazz. What it does do, however, is show Walton moving, albeit a little uncertainly, away from energetic dissonance and towards a kind of qualified lyricism. That direction of travel was confirmed in his next major work – the Viola Concerto (1929). It was written for Lionel Tertis, who had done more than anyone else to raise the profile of the viola as a solo instrument, but Tertis rejected the piece as too modern. Walton was deeply upset, but the composer Paul Hindemith who was also a violist stepped into the breach and played the concerto under Henry Wood during the 1929 Proms. From our perspective, Tertis's decision is inexplicable – and, indeed, it was one he soon regretted. The Concerto is certainly modern in tone, but for all its mixed and syncopated rhythms, it is a work born of emotion, for the first time showing Walton as both an original composer and a romantic. As Walton's biographer Michael

Kennedy has shown, the work it most closely resembles is Elgar's Cello Concerto.[3]

In 1929, the BBC broke new ground with its first commissions of classical music. Three composers were involved: Walton, Constant Lambert, and Victor Hely-Hutchinson. They were asked to write works for soloists, chorus and orchestra, using forces small enough to be suitable for broadcasting (given the limitations of radiophonic equipment at the time). This was the genesis of Walton's oratorio *Belshazzar's Feast*, although the subject was chosen not by him but by Sacheverell Sitwell, who also wrote the libretto. The work grew in the composing to the point where it was far too big for the BBC commission.[4] It eventually required a large orchestra with four percussionists, an organ, a chorus capable of division into eight parts and a baritone soloist – as well as two seven-piece brass ensembles. These, it is said, were added following a comment by Beecham who somewhat contemptuously told Walton that he would never hear the work again after the premiere so he may as well throw in a couple of brass bands. Beecham, who was the musical director of the Leeds Festival where the work was premiered in 1931, had no faith in it and passed it to Sir Malcolm Sargent for the first performance. The choir had difficulties learning what they saw as some very demanding passages, but in the end everything came together and the work was a huge success, hailed as a landmark in British choral music. *Belshazzar's Feast* fuses its ten separate sections into one thirty-five minute movement. It is noisy, exciting, full of fanfares, quivering strings, moments of tension and shouted declamations; and it remains deservedly popular. Yet, for all the drama, the brilliant orchestral tricks and techniques, underneath it is in many ways more traditional, more obviously descended from Elgar, Strauss and even Wagner than, for example, *Hymn of Jesus* or *Sancta Civitas*. Only the authorities at the Three Choirs were shocked. Presumably blinded by Walton's reputation as an *enfant terrible*, and despite the text being drawn wholly from the Bible, they found the work unsuitable for performance in their cathedrals – a ban which lasted until 1957.

Walton continued to find patrons and financial backers. Siegfried Sassoon helped him; in 1931, Mrs Samuel Courtauld left him a legacy of £500 a year for life; and between 1929 and 1934 he lived at least part of the time in Switzerland with a wealthy young widow, Baroness Imma von Doernberg. Their affair, passionate and stormy, is generally held to have been the inspiration for Walton's First Symphony. The symphony was originally promised to Hamilton Harty for performance in 1933, but Walton found himself unable to complete the Finale. Harty and the LSO performed the first three movements in 1934, and Walton eventually completed the work in 1935. By that time, he had broken up with van Doernberg and moved almost seamlessly into a relationship with Lady Alice Wimborne, a married woman over twenty years his senior. Critics have seen his change of relationship as accounting for a marked change of tone within the work: the questioning mood of the first three movements seems to contrast with the positive, almost triumphal fourth. They have also seen the influence of Sibelius – something which Walton always denied. Nineteen thirty-five was the year of Bax's powerful Sixth Symphony and Vaughan Williams's violent Fourth. Walton's First Symphony certainly stands up in such company, yet it also stands apart. His music is, as ever, deeply emotional, but what is important is that the symphony describes an emotional progress that is complete in itself: from the tentative horn call at the beginning of the first movement right through to the thunderous and triumphant resolution of the Finale. In this, and despite immense stylistic differences, one might see again Elgar as the symphony's true progenitor.

The story of the 1930s is really that of Walton gradually moving ever closer towards membership of the British musical establishment. While he was still struggling with the symphony, he wrote his first film score, *Escape Me Never* (1935), adapted from a play by Margaret Kennedy. It was the first of many. Film work was lucrative and Walton was keen to establish his financial independence, having become estranged from the Sitwells, who disliked Alice Wimborne. The Coronation of George VI in 1937 was the occasion for *Crown Imperial*, a work of unashamedly patriotic and emotional intent, and a worthy successor to Elgar's *Pomp and Circumstance*. This was followed by a Violin Concerto written for Jascha Heifetz in 1939, which is a well-constructed if somewhat nostalgic piece, lacking the depth of his Viola Concerto.

During the Second World War, Walton concentrated on writing scores for patriotic films such as *The First of the Few* and *Went the Day Well?* – the former resulting in his famous *Spitfire Prelude and Fugue*, another piece in the emotion-stirring *Crown Imperial* mould. Then, in 1944, he was called upon to write the score of Laurence Olivier's innovative film production of *Henry V*. This resulted not only in Walton's finest film score but one of the most successful musical interpretations of Shakespeare of all time. With the ending of the war, and as a deliberate contrast to six years of composing film music, Walton composed his String Quartet no. 2. This is his finest piece of chamber music and clearly an intensely personal work, full of rhythmic energy and, unusually for a string quartet, giving a leading role to the viola.

Alice Wimborne died in April 1948. Their relationship had lasted thirteen years and Walton was genuinely and deeply affected, but his emotional life was always one of strange twists and turns. That December, during a visit to Argentina, he fell in love with and, within a matter of weeks, married Susana Valeria Rosa Maria Gil Passo, who was twenty-four years his junior. He had already agreed with the BBC that he should write an opera, and had chosen *Troilus and Cressida* – Chaucer's version rather than Shakespeare's – as the subject, and Christopher Hassall as the librettist. Much of the opera was written on the Italian island of Ischia, where Walton and his new wife eventually settled and built a house. In the end, it took Walton over seven years to complete *Troilus and Cressida*, but when it was premiered at Covent Garden in December 1954 it failed to inspire much enthusiasm. In part, this was because the original team – Olivier to direct, Henry Moore to design the sets, Elisabeth Schwarzkopf to sing the lead role – all backed out; in part also it was because Walton's music could not disguise that fact that Hassall's characterisation was often weak and the drama often sluggish; but more significant was the fact that this was now the post-*Peter Grimes* world. British music and British opera had moved on and Walton's work, despite its undoubted qualities, belonged to a period that had now passed.

Troilus and Cressida did not mark the end of Walton's career, but it marked a realisation in the public and the critical mind that he was no longer at the cutting edge of music. For many, this was confirmed by the Cello Concerto, written in 1956 for the Russian cellist Gregor Piatigorsky. It is not a great concerto; nor is it one of Walton's best works; and in the self-consciously modern 1950s it undoubtedly appeared dated, although Malcolm Sargent defended it passionately. The three-movement *Partita* that followed, written in 1957 for George Szell and the Cleveland Orchestra, was a virtuoso, occasional piece, showing just what a witty and brilliant orchestrator Walton could be, but that in itself only strengthened the connection with past glories rather than the future. The Second Symphony, premiered at the 1960 Edinburgh Festival, divided critical opinion. Some saw it as little more than an exercise, lacking the emotional content of its predecessor. Others saw it as a genuine extension of Walton's musical language. Something was clearly driving Walton, for the work is terse, compressed – Michael Kennedy uses the word 'elliptical'[5] – and characterised by a sense of tension. It does not have the sense of emotional completion that marks the First Symphony, but probably deserves to be heard more often than it is. There was a second opera – a one-act 'Extravaganza' based on Chekov's *Bear* – in 1967, but for the most part Walton's later compositions were limited to short choral works, fanfares and other occasional pieces.

His seventieth birthday was marked by a dinner at 10 Downing Street hosted by the music-loving Prime Minister of the day, Edward Heath, and an all-Walton concert at London's Royal Festival Hall conducted by André Previn. When he died in 1983, there was a memorial service in Westminster Abbey. Walton had certainly put Oldham and his Lancashire childhood a long way behind him. Although for many years he was a major figure on the musical landscape, *Belshazzar's Feast* and the First Symphony were the high points of his achievement. His reputation declined in the last decades of his life and has never really recovered. This is probably because, for all his early reputation for experimentation, he now seems to us to be a composer who stands at the end, not the beginning of a tradition; a man without any obvious followers, whose work was quickly overtaken by the likes of Britten and Tippett.

97   Gerald Finzi

It may seem odd to follow an assessment of Walton with one of Gerald Finzi, but the comparison has value, not least in demonstrating the tendency of British music to go its own way regardless of trends and schools of thought. Finzi (1901–56) was ostensibly a minor composer, at least by comparison with someone like Walton. His output was comparatively small and his range was limited; his work was utterly English (not British) and ignored Wagner, Strauss, Debussy, Ravel, Sibelius and all the other composers whose influence was widespread in the early decades of the twentieth century. It also ignored contemporary influences such as jazz, the dance bands, film and theatre music. Yet Finzi's reputation, unlike Walton's, has not only survived, it has grown immeasurably.

Gerald was the fifth child and fourth son born to Jack and Lizzie Finzi.

Both parents were Jewish but neither was religious and, throughout his life, Gerald identified with England, wrote music for the Anglican Church, and set English poetry without any sense of conflict. Only during the Second World War did a sense of Jewishness come to the surface, and even then it was less a statement of identity than of personal opposition to Nazi doctrines. Before he was eighteen, Finzi's father had died of cancer; one brother had died of pneumonia; a second had committed suicide while working on an Assam tea plantation; and a third had been shot down over the Aegean during the First World War. He had also lost his first proper music teacher, Ernest Farrar, on the Western Front.[1] One can only speculate about the impact of so many deaths on his young mind. It may well have intensified a natural tendency to introspection. In his music, an elegiac and meditative strain is rarely far from the surface; it also characterises many of the poems he chose to set – whether by William Drummond, Thomas Traherne, Wordsworth, or Hardy.

Finzi's formal musical training was limited to a year with Farrar at Christ Church, Harrogate, which was brought to an end when Farrar joined the army; and then five years with Edward Bairstow, organist at York Minister – although he did have a few lessons in counterpoint from R. O. Morris some years later. Bairstow was strict teacher, traditional in his approach and his musical tastes, and Finzi was unhappy at first. Gradually, however, he recognised that the discipline Bairstow imposed was what he needed and Bairstow came to recognise and encourage his pupil's talent. After the war, Finzi spent a week at Rutland Boughton's 1919 Glastonbury Festival, hearing among other things Vaughan Williams's *On Wenlock Edge*, which became an almost talismanic work for him. He and his mother took holidays in Gloucestershire, on one occasion calling at the vicarage where Vaughan Williams, who had become Finzi's hero, had been born. Then Finzi discovered Gurney's *Five Elizabethan Songs*. 'Sleep' was the one that moved him most. It was a trigger. In 1922, he and his mother moved from Harrogate, staying briefly at Chosen Hill Farm on Churchdown (or Chosen) Hill, which has already appeared in these pages, before settling in the village of Painswick. It was a statement on Finzi's part of what kind of composer he intended to be. His first compositions began to appear: the richly pastoral *Severn Rhapsody*, very clearly derived from Vaughan Williams; and a cycle of six Hardy settings, *By Footpath and Stile*, for baritone and string quartet. Throughout his career, Finzi remained dedicated to the art of setting English poetry to music, and showed a particular devotion to Hardy, who is also central to the *Requiem da Camera*, which he probably composed about 1924. A restrained work dedicated to the memory of Ernest Farrar, although with no religious dimension beyond the title, it was never performed in Finzi's lifetime. At its heart is a setting of 'In time of "The Breaking of Nations"'; it contains many of the rhythmic and vocal features that were to become characteristic of his mature compositions.

Finzi loved the English countryside and hated London, but in 1926 he accepted that a young composer seeking to make his way needed to be there. He found a house near Sloane Square and for the first time began to mix regularly with other musicians, among them the composers Robin Milford (1903–59) and Howard Ferguson (1908–99), with both of whom he developed lifelong friendships. He also came to know Edmund Rubbra (1901–86), one of his most constant advocates. Finzi was a great reviser of his work, so it is not always easy to tell when a given piece was written, but his first years in London seem to have been busy and productive – although interrupted by a period in a sanatorium when he developed tuberculosis. He wrote *Three Short Elegies*, which are elegant a cappella settings of texts by the Scots poet, William Drummond; *Two Sonnets by John Milton*, highly accomplished settings for tenor soloist and orchestra; and began two more Hardy cycles – *A Young Man's Exhortation*, first given in 1933, and *Earth and Air and Rain*, published in 1936 but probably completed two or three years earlier. He also wrote a Violin Concerto, which he withdrew after the first performance, keeping only the central movement which he renamed *Introit*.

In 1930, Vaughan Williams found him a job teaching at the RAM; in 1933, he married Joyce Black and they started a family; in 1935, they left London for Wiltshire; and in 1938, they bought some land at Ashmansworth in Hampshire where they designed a house to suit their needs. During this period, Finzi began collecting and editing eighteenth-century music – William Boyce, John Garth, Richard Mudge; became involved in organising and editing Ivor Gurney's manuscripts; and started collecting and growing various varieties of apple tree. Not unnaturally, given this level of activity, his composing suffered, but in 1939 he did complete *Dies Natalis*, a cantata for solo voice and string orchestra, with a text drawn from the seventeenth-century mystic, theologian and poet, Thomas Traherne. *Dies Natalis* was his first big, mature composition, a natural and evocative enriching of Traherne's poetry. It is melodic, engaging and deservedly still popular. The premiere, intended for the Three Choirs at Hereford, was cancelled because of the outbreak of the Second World War, and a lower-key first performance took place in the Wigmore Hall in 1940.

During the war, Finzi worked extremely long hours at the Ministry of War Transport in London, where he was popular but not particularly effective. He continued composing when he could – the wonderful Shakespeare settings, *Let Us Garlands Bring* (1942), and the apparently pacifist *Farewell to Arms*, based on texts by two other seventeenth-century poets, George Peele and Ralph Knevet, both belong to these years. During those periods when he could escape to Ashmansworth, Finzi managed to set up his own amateur orchestra, The Newbury String Players, which he conducted until his death and which then passed to the direction of his son, Christopher (or 'Kiffer'). The end of the war ushered in a rich period: he wrote anthems, including *Lo, the Full and Final Sacrifice* (1946); he wrote four songs and ten pieces of incidental music for *Love's Labour's Lost* (1946); and, in 1949, he wrote the Clarinet Concerto which, while unlike much of his other work, has become possibly his most instantly recognisable composition. In 1950, he completed *Intimations of Immortality*. This was the most ambitious work he ever contemplated, a setting of nine of the eleven verses of Wordsworth's ode of the same name, yet despite (or because of) fourteen years of thought and planning, it does not really work. For once, Finzi's music fails to get to the heart of the poetry. His upward progress as a composer had been slow but steady: this was his first real setback.

A worse one was to follow. In 1951, aged fifty, he was diagnosed with non-Hodgkinson's lymphoma. He carried on working. He finished his still-popular anthem *God Has Gone Up*; and he continued to set poems by Hardy, many of which were heard only after his death. He also wrote *In Terra Pax* (1954), one of his finest works, in which a baritone soloist sings the words of Robert Bridges' 'Noel: Christmas Eve 1913', while a soprano sings the words of the angel from St Luke's Gospel. Finzi traced the genesis of the piece to a moment of personal revelation when he first moved south from Harrogate and climbed Churchdown Hill on Christmas Eve to hear the church bells ringing out across the Gloucestershire countryside. The desperate irony is that it was Churchdown Hill which he climbed with Vaughan Williams during the Three Choirs in 1956, showing the older composer where he had once lived, and meeting both the sexton of the church there and his children, one of whom had chickenpox. The contact was brief, but Finzi, already weakened by his illness, quickly developed shingles, which became encephalitis. He died that September, the evening after the first broadcast performance of his Cello Concerto, his last completed work.

At Ashmansworth, Finzi and his wife created not just a home, but a way of life. They grew vegetables, tended their apple trees, and lived in a manner that was as simple and detached from the urban norms of the time as they could reasonably make it. In music, too, Finzi followed his own individual path. His style derives from Parry, Elgar and Vaughan Williams: he actively disliked much modern music, including that of Benjamin Britten. It was a conservative idiom, but a deliberately chosen one. From an early age, as we have seen, he chose to attach himself to the English pastoral tradition. It suited him because it was the medium best suited to the expression of his other great passion: English poetry. Finzi was a literary as well as a musical scholar – at Ashmansworth, he amassed a library of some three thousand volumes, more than half of them poetry. Word-setting was his great strength. He developed clear ideas about how to set verse, largely by intuition. Like Howells, his instinct was for each syllable to have its own note. The rhythm of the language and the rhythm of his music worked closely together in support of meaning and emotion; so that even moments of passion or drama could be expressed without long melismatic emphasis, simply because the words and music had built up to that point together. Hardy was always his favourite: he completed more than forty Hardy settings and left another twenty-five unfinished. But whether it was Hardy, Shakespeare, Traherne or Edmund Blunden, Finzi had an ability to penetrate the poet's meaning, to respect it, and to enhance it musically in a way that, despite his undeniable limitations as a composer, is unmatched in British music.

98   Lambert and Berners, Ballet, and Opera

Hindsight allows us to see the 1920s and 30s as a period of transition. The mixture of grief and elation that followed the end of the First World War gave way to a socially polarised world where the lives of the Bright Young Things contrasted with those of striking miners; and this in turn gave way to the more politicised polarisations of the 30s, between communists and fascists, communists and Catholics, appeasers and re-armers. In music, as in literature, it was a period of upheaval and uncertainty in which differing styles and approaches – as ever, the British fought shy of schools and isms

– jostled for a hearing and for public and critical approval. At the time, this sense of multiple possibilities, of having no agreed agenda or direction, would only have heightened the prevailing sense of uncertainty.

We have considered the careers of the established composers, those who continued to compose and develop throughout the decade: men such as Vaughan Williams, Bax, Bliss and Walton, who were, or who came to be seen as, the leading figures of the time. We have looked at others who have since been recognised as important figures: men like Ireland or Finzi, who followed their own path, aware of what was going on around them, although not greatly influenced by it. Yet such categorisations simplify a complex picture that actually includes the many composers and musicians who may have seemed influential in their time, but who in the end did not significantly shape or alter the main current of British music, as well as important changes to the financial and administrative structures surrounding music and its performance.

We have yet to consider ballet, which was extremely popular in London during the 1920s. Building on the interest generated by the Beechams' Russian seasons in 1913 and 1914, Diaghilev and his Ballets Russes made regular visits to the capital. They performed ballets to music by Stravinsky and Prokofiev, Satie and de Falla, Cesare Bossi and Cimarosa, Gounod and Chabrier, but only two to music by British composers – the first was *Romeo and Juliet* by Constant Lambert (1905–51); the second, *The Triumph of Neptune* by Lord Berners (1883–1950).[1]

Lambert was only nineteen when *Romeo and Juliet* was commissioned, an indication that he was a young man from whom great things were expected. He had studied at the RCM under Vaughan Williams, Dyson and R. O. Morris, but showed an early independence of mind, being more interested in French and Russian music, and in jazz more than folk song or English pastoral. He loved Chabrier and the modernist French composers, such as Poulenc and Milhaud, but he also admired Mussorgsky, Borodin, Glazunov and the Russian romantics. Ballet attracted him from the first. He wrote two before he was nineteen: *Prize-Fight* has a satirical tone that shows he was very aware of Eric Satie's work, while *Mr Bear Squash-You-All-Flat* was supposedly based on a Russian folk tale. (It is worth noting that Lambert's father was born in Saint Petersburg.) Lambert's taste for modernism and mild iconoclasm is reflected in his friendship with the Sitwells and their set; and the Sitwells knew Diaghilev, so the commission to write for the Ballets Russes was not completely a bolt from the blue.

Romeo and Juliet received a lukewarm reception on its premiere in Monte Carlo in 1926; it became the object of a surrealist-inspired riot in Paris; and then gained a warm but not effusive welcome in London later the same year. Lambert's next work proved to be the high point of his composing career and again it involved the Sitwells. *Rio Grande* (1927) was a highly elaborate setting of Sacheverell Sitwell's poem of the same name. Lambert takes an alto soloist and choir in a more-or-less classical mode and sets them up against a piano-led orchestra with a greatly expanded percussion section playing what can only be described as Gershwin-influenced symphonic jazz. The combination was genuinely new and the fact that its premiere was a BBC radio broadcast added to the sense that it was modern and adventurous. Harty gave the first concert performance with the Hallé in 1929, and the work proved immensely popular. Surprisingly then, the ballet *Horoscope*, which followed in 1930, appeared to ignore the achievement of *Rio Grande* and reverted to a romantic, even conventional style. With a scenario based on the oppositions and attractions inherent in zodiacal signs, *Horoscope* apparently reflected his feelings for the ballerina Margot Fonteyn with whom he had an affair that lasted several years.

During the 1930s, Lambert began to drift away from composing and devoted himself more to conducting, particularly with the Vic-Wells and Sadler's Wells Ballet. His still very readable critical work, *Music Ho!* (1934), shows a deep knowledge of literature and art as well as music, but it also shows a growing pessimism about the future. Lambert was a complex character. He was given to violent likes and dislikes which he could express with great vehemence, and there was a self-destructive side to him. Alcoholism, chain-smoking and diabetes all contributed to his early death. That he never sought to develop the ideas and the synthesis that he achieved in *Rio Grande* raises a minor 'What if?' of musical history.

Eccentric, aristocratic, multi-talented, well connected and homosexual, Gerald Hugh Tyrwhitt-Wilson became Baron Berners on the death of his father. He also became extremely rich. Berners had been interested in music from childhood. As a young man, he took a few lessons with the composer and musical theorist Donald Tovey (1875–1940), who had a firm belief in the inner aesthetics of music, but his first career was as a diplomat. He was posted to Constantinople, and then to Rome. And it was in Rome during the First World War, by which time he was over thirty, that he began composing seriously. Taking advice from Stravinsky and the Italian composer Alfredo Casella, he began with piano pieces. These are French both in style and title, but with an added witty, parodic element which is decidedly English. The three pieces that make up *Trois petites marches funèbres*, for example, are 'Pour un homme d'état', 'Pour un canari', and 'Pour une tante à heritage'. After the war, compositions such as the two short orchestral pieces, *Trois Morceaux* and *Fantaisie Espagnole* (both 1919), began to attract notice. So, too, did his songs – sometimes to the oddest of texts, such as John Masefield's 'Theodore, or the Pirate King'[2] and E. L. Duff's 'The Green-Eyed Monster' – settings which, while comic, never lose the sense of being carefully thought out and controlled.

Berners was another member of the loose, self-consciously modern group that revolved around the Sitwells and passed, in Britain, for the avant-garde. Like the Sitwells, Berners knew Diaghilev, having met him in Rome at the same time as Stravinsky. So, again, it was no surprise that Berners should propose *The Triumph of Neptune* for the 1926 London season of the Ballets Russes. Berners' ballet – which Diaghilev preferred to an idea put forward by Walton – had a storyline and a design concept suggested by Sacheverell Sitwell. Walton, although presumably disappointed at the rejection of his proposal, was nonetheless pressed into service by Berners (as he had been by Lambert) to help score the work in time for its first performance. And anyway, Berners was one of his major benefactors, so Walton was in no position to complain. The avant-garde was a very small world.

The plot of *The Triumph of Neptune* concerns a journalist and sailor who journey to fairyland through a magic telescope that has been set up on London Bridge. Fleet Street newspapers compete for their story; the sailor's wife has an affair with a Dandy; and a drunken negro sailor called Snoball upsets the telescope, trapping the travellers in fairyland. Sitwell's costumes were based on the old-fashioned 'penny-plain, tuppence-coloured' toy theatre prints. Berners' music does full justice to all this inconsequentiality. It has classical moments, a polka, a schottische, extracts from 'The Last Rose of Summer' and 'Rule Britannia'. The whole thing seems to sum up the British musical avant-garde of the 1920s: witty, clever, technically accomplished, but whimsical rather than deep and ultimately lacking a central purpose.

Berners went further than many of his 'classical' colleagues in seeking to engage with a wider audience. His next ballet, *Luna Park*, a short one-act piece, was performed as part of C. B. Cochran's *1930 Revue*. It is a story of performers in a freak show: a three-headed man, a three-armed juggler, a man with six legs and a one-legged ballerina are all revealed to be normal human beings. They abandon the showman who has been exploiting them, leaving him to open the curtain on a deserted stage. The story recalls Stravinsky and *Petrushka*, but Berners' score suggests that he had learned a lot from Tchaikovsky's ballets, particularly in terms of characterisation. The experiment of including a ballet within a revue was successful enough for Cochran to repeat the idea in his 1935 production, *Follow the Sun*. On that occasion, however, the ballet was Walton's *First Shoot*, this time with a storyline by Osbert rather than Sacheverell Sitwell.

Nineteen thirty-one saw the foundation of the Vic-Wells Ballet and Ballet School. The name 'Vic-Wells' was a combination of the Old Vic and Sadler's Wells, two theatres owned by the manager and producer, Lilian Bayliss, while the technical expertise was supplied by the former Ballets Russes dancer, Ninette de Valois (1898–2001). From the beginning, de Valois worked closely with Constant Lambert, who became the company's musical director, and with the dancer and choreographer, Frederick Ashton (1904–88), who created the ballet of *Façade*. Ashton was confirmed as resident choreographer of the new company in 1935 and eventually succeeded de Valois as Artistic Director in 1963 (by which time the company was known as the Royal Ballet), a position he held until 1970. Over the course of his long career – his final work for the company was *Nursery Suite* in 1986 – he probably did more to shape the look and the style of British ballet than any other individual.

It was Ashton who choreographed Berner's 1937 ballet, *A Wedding Bouquet*. Based on a play by Gertrude Stein, it is a sad piece set in a French village, telling the story of Julia who is to be married to Webster, a notorious womaniser, who has seduced her. The uniqueness of the work lies in the fact that it is a 'choral ballet' – with a chorus, or in some productions a narrator, giving an oblique, sometimes comic, sometimes atmospheric, commentary on the action. Here, even more than in his previous works, Berners demonstrated his talent for short, focussed descriptive pieces which are tightly meshed with the action and the characters. It was probably the high point of his career. He did write two further ballets – *Cupid and Psyche* (1938) and *Les Sirènes* (1946), both choreographed by Ashton – but neither was successful. *Cupid and Psyche* lasted only four performances. In a politically-charged age, Berners' choice of classical subjects held little appeal. During the 1940s, he wrote several film scores, including one for the 1947 version of *Nicholas Nickleby* that received excellent reviews, but for his clever, witty, mannered music, so redolent of the 1920s, there was little demand.

Ballet was perhaps not the musical form most suited to reflecting or expressing the tensions and troubles of the 1930s, although the composer Alan Bush (1900–95) tried to do just that. His *Pageant of Labour* (1934), and his two ballets, *His War or Yours* and *Mining*, were written in 1935 for the London Workers' Ballet. All three featured scenarios created by the young Michael Tippett. Bush came from a middle-class household in Dulwich in south-east London. He was a student at the RAM, and studied composition under Corder and Ireland, and piano with Benno Moiseiwitsch. He looked set for a career as an international pianist, and a number of his early compositions, and in particular his string quartet, *Dialectic*, were also considered promising. Then in 1929, he went to study at the University of Berlin where, in addition to furthering his piano technique with Arthur Schnabel, he met a number of radical thinkers, including Bertold Brecht. It was a formative experience. In 1935, he joined the British Communist Party and founded the Workers' Music Association, which attracted support from Bantock, Boughton and the young Benjamin Britten. Bush's attempts to make his music directly political were, and remain, exceptional in British musical history. They were well intentioned and evoked a sympathetic response from some of his fellow composers, but, despite the vicissitudes of the 1930s, they failed to gain any kind of popular following.

Bush's Marxist experiments were peripheral and short-lived, but by the end of the 1930s, British ballet had developed a structure for itself which would last through the Second World War and provide a foundation for development in the post-war world. The Vic-Wells Ballet became Sadler's Wells Ballet in 1939, moved to the Royal Opera House in 1946 and became the Royal Ballet in 1956. In 1946, Sadler's Wells also established a sister company which eventually became the Royal Birmingham Ballet. British opera did not manage to organise itself in any comparable fashion. The Beecham Opera Company, founded by Thomas Beecham in 1916 with the purpose of promoting English opera and opera in English, lasted only until 1920, when complex legal proceedings forced it into liquidation. Members of the Beecham Company then formed the British National Opera Company, which began operating in 1922. It staged several seasons at Covent Garden, before moving to His Majesty's Theatre, getting into financial difficulties, and eventually closing in 1929. In 1927, as an attempt to provide a more stable financial basis for opera, Beecham launched the grandly-named Imperial League of Opera. It did not succeed. Various unsatisfactory syndicates based on Covent Garden came and went. Financing opera in Britain seemed even more difficult in the 1930s than in Handel's time. At one stage, in 1937, things got so bad that the opera house was sublet to a company that staged a twice-nightly ice ballet. One major problem, as George Bernard Shaw pointed out, was that in most countries opera was subsidised, whereas in Britain it was actually taxed: ticket sales were subject to something known as 'Entertainment Duty'. By the time war came in 1939, no satisfactory solution had been reached. Covent Garden became a dance hall and the various leagues, syndicates and schemes simply melted away. Only the Carl Rosa Opera Company, now seventy years old, carried on, lurching from crisis to crisis but at least maintaining a degree of continuity.

These were the years in which Rutland Boughton was probably the biggest name in British opera; in which Holbrooke was completing his *Cauldron of Annwn* cycle; in which Holst's *At the Boar's Head* and *The Wandering Scholar,* and Vaughan Williams's *Hugh the Drover, Sir John in Love,* and *Riders to the Sea* were first heard. Yet there were many other attempts, now largely forgotten, by British composers to make their mark on the operatic world. Donald Tovey, a survivor from an earlier generation – he had played his own piano concerto under Henry Wood's baton in 1903 – had his *Bride of Dionysus* premiered in Edinburgh in 1929. Eugene Goossens, usually regarded more as a conductor than a composer, saw his one-act *Judith* performed at Covent Garden in 1929, and the full-length *Don Juan de Mañara* in 1937. Both had librettos by the novelist Arnold Bennett and both sank without trace. *Don Juan de Mañara* survived for only two performances. Albert Coates (1882–1953) had made his name as a conductor with his interpretations of Wagner and Puccini during the Beecham-promoted Covent Garden season of 1914. In 1936, he formed his own opera company, the British Music Drama Opera Company, with a view to promoting and performing his own opera, *Pickwick*. It proved a short-lived venture. George Lloyd (1913–98) is usually better known for his twelve symphonies, but he also wrote three operas. *Iernin* (1934) recalls Boughton and Holbrooke in that its Cornish setting draws heavily on the myths and images of Celtic Britain. Critical reaction at the time was broadly positive, but it is in fact a rather static and uninspired work. Its successor, *The Serf* (1938), which takes place in the reign of King Stephen, failed to excite anyone's enthusiasm. His third opera, *John Socman,* written after the Second World War and set against the background of war with France and religious controversy in fifteenth-century England, is probably the best of the three, but to modern ears they all sound somewhat derivative, with Verdi as the main influence. It was not a happy period for British opera.

99   Between the Wars

In terms of orchestras and orchestral playing, the 1930s was a period of improving quality and growing confidence. Since 1924, the BBC had had its own small Wireless Orchestra, playing six concerts a week under the baton of its first Director of Music, Percy Pitt. Then in 1927, the Corporation took over responsibility for the Proms. A BBC Symphony Orchestra was the obvious next step. The idea occurred to two men at much the same time.

Thomas Beecham's restless intelligence was always looking for ways to improve the condition of British music. His Imperial League of Opera had proved a failure and he had accepted the post of musical director of the Leeds Triennial Festival – an appointment that resulted in some spectacular performances of Delius, Verdi, Berlioz, and Walton among others – when he came up with the idea that the BBC should sponsor a full-scale symphony orchestra. The BBC's Director General, Sir John Reith, reached the same conclusion by a different route. Reith's guiding principle was that the BBC existed in order to enlighten and educate its audience: a symphony orchestra was a logical consequence of that conviction. The conductor Landon Ronald, by that time Principal of the Guildhall School of Music, brought the two of them together to discuss the idea.

Reith and Beecham, both natural autocrats, were very different characters and could not agree on the nature of the new orchestra. However, this failure led to the creation of two new orchestras rather than none. The BBC pressed ahead with its own scheme and the BBC Symphony Orchestra came into being in 1930. Adrian Boult became its principal conductor and also took over from Percy Pitt as the Corporation's Director of Music. The new orchestra rapidly gained a reputation for high quality performances and for introducing new and challenging music, including works by

Schoenberg, Poulenc, Bartok, Berg and Mahler (whose later symphonies were still regarded as strange and unfamiliar). In the meantime, Beecham had been approached by the up-and-coming conductor Malcolm Sargent with the idea of forming an entirely new orchestra. With the backing of a number of wealthy individuals – among them the industrialist Samuel Courtauld (whose wife's will provided Walton with £500 a year) and the philanthropist Robert Mayer – they set up the London Philharmonic Orchestra (LPO), which gave its first concert at the Queen's Hall in 1932. Again, the new orchestra quickly established a reputation for high quality musicianship, and, as with all Beecham's orchestras, it soon embarked on a series of regional tours.

Outside the capital, developments involving regional orchestras were, in general, similarly positive. Hamilton Harty had become permanent conductor of the Hallé Orchestra in 1920 and over the next twelve years raised its reputation to the point where it was widely considered to be the best orchestra in the country. He introduced new works such as Mahler's Ninth Symphony and Shostakovitch's First, as well as playing works by Bax, Bantock, Moeran, Bliss and Constant Lambert. Harty even tried to stage Havergal Brian's massive, two-hour *Gothic Symphony*, but the resources required were too great and the work remained unperformed until 1961. When Harty left the Hallé in 1933, the orchestra preferred to work with a series of guest conductors rather than appoint a new permanent director, and they developed a special relationship with Malcolm Sargent which was to assume particular importance during the Second World War.

In Edinburgh, Donald Tovey had been appointed Reid Professor of Music at Edinburgh University in 1914 and had founded the Reid Orchestra, later the Reid Symphony Orchestra, during the First World War. He nurtured the orchestra through the 1920s and 30s until his death in 1940. Under his direction, it developed a wide repertory, generally more conservative than that of the London orchestras, though still including occasional works by Mahler and Schoenberg, and by British composers such as Holst, Ireland and Bridge, and, of course, Tovey himself. His finest composition, his immensely long Cello Concerto, written for and played by Pablo Casals, was given its premiere by the Reid Orchestra in the Usher Hall at the end of 1934. Tovey regarded himself primarily as an educator and under his stewardship 'Professor Tovey's Sunday Concerts' became a popular fixture in the calendar. The Reid Symphony remained Edinburgh's only professional orchestra right up until 1970.

When Adrian Boult joined the BBC, his role with the Birmingham Symphony Orchestra was taken by Leslie Heward, who had spent a number of years with the South African Broadcasting Corporation and the Cape Town Municipal Orchestra. Heward raised the Birmingham orchestra's national profile by allocating resources to frequent broadcasting and recording. In 1934, Dan Godfrey retired, having spent forty years building up the Bournemouth Symphony Orchestra. His place was taken by Richard Austin, who expanded the annual Bournemouth Music Festival, inviting a range of high profile guest conductors, including not only Beecham and Henry Wood, but also Stravinsky and Rachmaninoff. In 1935, the BBC, having taken a first step with the BBC Symphony Orchestra, went on to found regional orchestras in Scotland and Wales. In Liverpool things were more difficult. The Philharmonic Hall burned down in 1933 and for six years until its reopening – over which Beecham presided – the Philharmonic Orchestra was homeless, although it did manage to maintain a surprisingly full programme of performances in borrowed premises.

New orchestras and better playing were both welcome developments. As far as younger composers were concerned, the chances of getting a work into the concert hall, and of it receiving a decent performance once it got there, were naturally increased. But while the creation of new orchestras and the strengthening of existing ones might get them a hearing, it could do little to give them a sense of direction. Those whose works were first performed during the 1930s may have shared an awareness of the social and political difficulties of their time, but, in terms of their music, they remained essentially a collection of individuals pursuing their own, often very different ends.

Edmund Rubbra (1901-1986) was among the leading talents to emerge during the period. His musical abilities were obvious from early childhood. He discovered the music of Debussy and Cyril Scott while still at school, but family circumstances compelled him to leave school at fourteen to work as a clerk at the local railway station. He studied, played piano and made his first attempts at composition in his spare time. At the age of seventeen, he organised a chamber concert of Cyril Scott's music in the lecture hall of Northampton library, playing the piano himself. The local vicar told Scott, who agreed to take Rubbra as a pupil, and Rubbra's life was transformed. Two years later, he was at Reading University studying composition under Holst; three years later, he was at the RCM studying under Holst, R. O. Morris and sometimes Vaughan Williams.

By the time he was conscripted into the army in 1941, Rubbra had completed four symphonies, a number of chamber works and songs, and was being regarded in some quarters as the natural successor to Vaughan Williams as the champion of English music. There was a certain logic to this. Rubbra's music is profoundly English, even though it is often difficult to tell precisely where that Englishness lies. He admired Vaughan Williams, but he was not a member of the English pastoral school, nor was he particularly interested in folk song. In his songs, his choice of English poetry runs from the medieval to the twentieth century, although with an evident fondness for Shakespeare and his contemporaries, but he was equally happy to set Latin and French texts, or translations from Icelandic and Chinese. In his 1960 book *Counterpoint*, Rubbra stated his belief that the western classical tradition had evolved from melody and the interaction of melodic lines. Such a theory certainly places him in the British musical tradition that has always upheld the primacy of melody; this is borne out by his music, which is led by melody and counterpoint rather than harmony. He said that he composed without a plan, by letting musical ideas develop themselves, so that he was never quite sure what the end point would be until he got there. This was a strength in that it allowed him to create powerful musical structures that were held together by their own internal logic; but it could also be a weakness, leading him to place too much emphasis on the thematic core of a given work at the expense of harmony and orchestration – and one criticism that has been regularly levelled at Rubbra's symphonies is that the orchestration has a tendency to lack clarity.

Rubbra's output of eleven symphonies is impressive for a twentieth-century composer. The First and Second (both 1937) are densely contrapuntal and contrast strongly with the Third (1939) and Fourth (1941), which are more relaxed, as if the composer had grown into his own technique and was now allowing themes to establish and develop themselves. The Fifth (1948) was written after the war and after he had been received into the Roman Catholic Church. With a particularly beautiful slow movement and a horn solo at the beginning of the scherzo that stays fixed in the memory, it proved one of his most popular works. It was premiered by Boult (now Sir Adrian) and the BBC Symphony Orchestra at the beginning of 1949 and was taken up by Leopold Stokowski and the New York Philharmonic. Few composers have been less interested in what was going on in the musical world about them than Rubbra, so he never sought or pretended to be in any sense 'modern'. That counted against him in the 1950s when modernity was often a critical *sine qua non*. Both the Sixth and Seventh Symphonies (1954; 1957) were well received by the critics, but his music fell out of fashion. Of the later symphonies, the one that stands out is the Ninth (*Sinfonia Sacra*, 1972), a large-scale work for three soloists and orchestra. During the 1950s and 60s, Rubbra had written a large amount of choral music associated with his Catholic faith – works such as *Nine Tenebrae Motets; Laud Sion,* a setting of words from St Thomas Aquinas; and *Inscape,* setting poems by Gerard Manley Hopkins. *Sinfonia Sacra* blends his symphonic and choral techniques, telling the story of the Resurrection in what has a claim to be considered his most important work. The Tenth and Eleventh Symphonies (1974; 1979) are dense, single-movement works, giving the sense that Rubbra's symphonic thought had come full circle. He was a prolific composer and, although he kept away from opera, he wrote symphonies, concertos, choral works, chamber music and songs, achieving a measure of success in all of them. Despite this, he remains something of an outsider, perhaps because, although an intensely spiritual man – he was interested in Buddhist thought as well as Catholic doctrine – his music is more cerebral than that of many British composers, lacking the emotional and dramatic qualities of men such as Vaughan Williams, Howells or Walton.

Patrick Hadley (1899–1973), by contrast, represented a continuation of the folk-song, landscape and pastoral school. He was a slightly tragic figure, who had served in the trenches but lost both a leg and his brother during the final weeks of the war; he sought to cope with the resulting physical pain and depression by drinking too much. That did not stop him from becoming a highly-respected teacher, first at the RCM and later at Cambridge where he was an unconventional and somewhat boozy Professor of Music for some sixteen years. An indication of just how highly his technical expertise was regarded is the fact that Bax, Howells, Moeran, Walton and Lambert all at various times asked his advice on their work. He was also a composer of some distinction, principally of choral music, although his name is rarely heard today. His best work is *The Trees So High* (1931), a four-movement composition (called a symphonic ballad, though it could just as easily be called a symphony), based on Somerset folk songs. His setting of Keats's *La Belle Dame sans Merci* (1935) and *The Hills* (1944), another symphonic-scale piece that he wrote in memory of his parents, are also impressive. Like Moeran, Hadley was inspired by the Norfolk countryside and although he wrote little after the Second World War, he did produce one major work, *The Fen and the Flood* (1955), which commemorated the devastating storm and floods that hit the Norfolk coast in January 1953.

Philip Sainton (1891–1967), another largely forgotten composer of essentially romantic works, was the grandson of the violinist Prosper Sainton, who taught Mackenzie at the RAM and led Michael Costa's orchestra at Covent Garden in the 1840s. Sainton became principal viola in Henry Wood's Queen's Hall Orchestra after the First World War and some of his early works – *Sea Pictures* (1923) and *Harlequin and Columbine* (1925) – were taken up not only by Henry Wood, but also by Hamilton Harty and the Hallé. If remembered at all today, it is for his fine romantic tone poem, *The Island* (1944), which seems to hark back to McEwen's Galloway-inspired works, or for the rich evocation of the sea in his score for John Houston's 1956 film of *Moby Dick*.

These were figures who had begun to establish themselves before the Second World War, but there were many others, new names in the 1930s, whose careers did not take off or assume recognisable shape until after 1945. Although obviously musical as a child, Lennox Berkeley (1903–89) took a degree in French and philology at Oxford before beginning to study music in his early twenties. He then spent six intense years in Paris where he was helped by Ravel and drilled in counterpoint by Nadia Boulanger. He got to know Stravinsky, Poulenc, Milhaud, Honegger and many of the other musicians living in France at the time. He also became a Roman Catholic. Returning to Britain, he came to public notice in 1934 with the pleasant and stylish *Polka for Two Pianos* (1934). This was followed by a change of direction: *Jonah*, an oratorio, was given its first performance in a BBC broadcast in 1936, and given again the following year at the Leeds Triennial Festival with Berkeley himself conducting. *Jonah* divided the critics, some seeing it as undiluted modernism, others appreciating its neo-classical style (echoing Stravinsky) as a valid way of approaching the daunting British oratorio tradition. Benjamin Britten, who was to prove a major influence on Berkeley's career, was among those taking the positive view. The two had met the previous year and for a short while shared a house at Snape, in Suffolk, the village where Britten was to live for the rest of his life. In 1939, Berkeley went off in yet another direction with his *Serenade,* opus 12, for string orchestra.[1] This was a much more accessible piece, in many ways comparable to Britten's *Variations on a Theme of Frank Bridge*, which had been written two years previously. It proved an immediate success and has remained a regular feature of concert programmes ever since. It was his last important composition before the war.

During the early years of his career, Alan Rawsthorne (1905–71) was also seen as a purveyor of modernism and Continental ideas. He did not begin formal musical training until the age of twenty when he entered the Royal Manchester College of Music – having overcome parental pressures in favour of dentistry and architecture. He went on to study piano in Poland and then in Berlin, returning to Britain in 1932 and taking up a teaching position at Dartington Hall in Devon. Rawsthorne's early successes as a composer had an international dimension to them. His piano piece *Bagatelles* was first heard on the Norwegian Broadcasting Corporation network in 1938, while his *Theme and Variations for Two Violins* was given at an International Society for Contemporary Music (ISCM) concert in London the same year. In 1939, just months before the outbreak of war, he had a much larger work, *Symphonic Studies*, consisting of five linked movements, performed at an ISCM concert in Warsaw.

Gordon Jacob (1895–1984) was a slightly older figure, who had organised a scratch orchestra in a prisoner-of-war camp during the First World War. By 1939, he was over forty, well ensconced at the RCM and had already composed a dozen or so reasonably substantial works. These included his First Symphony (1929), written in memory of his brother who died on the Somme, and a ballet, *Uncle Remus*, written for the Vic-Wells company in 1934. He wrote in what was for the time a conservative idiom, heavily influenced by the Tudor Revival, and there were those who thought that he might emerge as a champion of traditional musical values. He continued to teach at the RCM throughout the war. Arnold Cooke (1906–2005) was making a name for himself as a promising composer of chamber music. Having studied in Berlin and taught for a period at the Royal Manchester College of Music, he had just moved to London when the war intervened. And there was one other composer who, although only twenty-four when the war broke out, had already begun to attract attention with his *Simple Symphony* (1934), his scores for the documentaries *Coal Face* (1935) and *Night Mail* (1936), and *Variations on a Theme of Frank Bridge* (1937). That, of course, was Benjamin Britten.

The 1930s was a period of almost frenetic activity. Radio and gramophone meant that more people had the opportunity to hear classical music than ever before. New orchestras were created. New conductors, such as Sargent and Barbirolli, brought new ideas and interpretations. There were more concerts than ever before; and newspapers and magazines reviewed them in greater depth and detail than they would today. Above all, new composers came to the fore, writing new works. Some, as we have seen, were influenced by Schoenberg, Berg, and the Second Viennese School. Others took inspiration from Les Six and French music. Some saw jazz as offering a way forward. Others continued to cultivate their own versions of the English national-pastoral style. Still others remained in the grip of Celtic fever, while there were not a few who simply went off in their own direction. What is certain is that, whilst there was much co-operation and cross-fertilisation of ideas, British classical music had no settled style or direction. Despite the length of time that had passed, British music and British musicians were still trying to make sense of the cultural upheaval that followed in the wake of 1914. They were then faced with another in 1939.

100   Films, Musicals, and Light Music

In September 1928, just a year after its New York premiere, the film, *The Jazz Singer,* received its first European showing at London's Piccadilly Theatre. It was an occasion that has attained almost mythical significance as heralding the age of 'The Talkies'. In fact, the technology of a synchronised soundtrack for films had been developing for some time. In 1926, Warner Brothers had released a three-hour version of *Don Juan*, starring Charles Barrymore, which had a specially-composed and synchronised soundtrack, although it featured no recorded dialogue. *The Jazz Singer* was an advance in that, although it featured only two or three minutes of recorded dialogue – the rest was done on intertitles which flashed up during the action – it featured nine synchronised songs, six of them sung by Al Jolson and including 'Blue Skies' and 'Mammy'.

Other sound films followed and the technology improved. The soundtracks for *Don Juan* and *The Jazz Singer* were recorded onto discs that were synchronised with the film projector. This was soon superseded by the more familiar system having the soundtrack recorded on a strip along the edge of the film itself. Cinemas had to invest in the equipment to play sound films, so the changeover was not immediate – in some of the more remote regions of the United Kingdom silent films were still being screened in 1934 – but it was nonetheless a comparatively quick process, and its impact on cinema-going in the country as a whole was spectacular. In 1926, there were some 3,000 cinemas in Britain. By 1939, there were 5,000. The growth in numbers is impressive in itself, and made more so by the fact that many early cinemas were replaced during those years by huge, custom-built, art deco 'picture palaces' capable of seating anything up to 4,000 people. In 1935, when the population stood at some 46.8 million, the number of cinema tickets issued each week averaged 17.6 million. By 1939, that figure had risen to 20 million; and during the war it would continue to rise until in 1946 it reached an all-time high of over 31 million per week.

Thus with the arrival of sound film, cinema-going suddenly became a mass movement on an unprecedented scale. As music was an essential part of the cinematographic experience, it is important to understand what kind of music such a large proportion of the population was exposed to. The live accompaniment provided by pianists, organists or cinema bands naturally ceased and the majority of the musicians thus employed found themselves out of a job. In some of the larger and more elaborately-themed cinemas, however, the organs survived. Originally installed because they could imitate an orchestra and thus provide suitable accompaniment for almost any silent film, they were now employed as virtuoso instruments, used for recitals before film screenings and during intervals. There were a number of manufacturers of theatre organs (as they were known), but only two of any significance were British: Robert Hope-Jones, and Hill, Norman & Beard. Almost all the others were American and by far the biggest and most prestigious supplier was Wurlitzer, whose products were characterised by their sweeping contours and glitzy, Hollywood appearance. Despite the cost – a 1926 list shows prices ranging between £3,000 and £22,000,[1] at a time when the average British house was valued at £619 – such organs became a popular and expected feature in larger cinemas, and were also installed in theatres, ballrooms and town halls. Several London cinemas still have working Wurlitzers from the 1930s. The Wurlitzer installed at the Glasgow Picture House in 1925 – only the fifth to arrive in the country – remained in use until 1957. One particularly splendid instrument with a fretwork and Bakelite façade and internal lights was installed in the Stockport Ritz in 1937 and remained there until 1998 when it was removed to Pollokshaws Burgh Hall in Glasgow for restoration and preservation. In Britain, the particular, vibrant tone of the theatre organ was associated for many years with the figure of Reginald Dixon (1904–85). Dixon played the Wurlitzer amid the late Victorian splendour of the

Blackpool Tower Ballroom for forty years between 1930 and 1970. At the height of his fame in the 1950s and 1960s, his dances and recitals could attract daily audiences of up to 7,000. His pre-war BBC broadcasts were so popular that he was given a forty-five-minute slot five times a week, and he continued to broadcast regularly right up to his retirement.

Cinema organs were the exception. Recorded music was the norm and it was overwhelmingly American. The film industry had been dominated by American studios almost from the beginning. By 1926, before the arrival of sound film, British films accounted for only five per cent of those screened in the country. In 1927, the government passed legislation requiring seven-point-five percent of films shown in British cinemas to be British productions (the 'quota'). By 1935, that figure had risen to twenty per cent. In theory, the legislation worked – although it did lead to a large number of low quality 'quota quickies' – but it did not alter the fact that the films the public wanted to see and went to see were American, and a high proportion of these were musicals. Precise figures are hard to come by, but during the 1930s the American film industry probably produced some eight hundred films that can be described as musicals or musical comedies. Many were adaptations of revues or stage musicals; some were based on stories from opera or operetta; some were effectively revues produced for film; others were narrative-based films into which songs were interpolated. How many of these crossed the Atlantic to Britain is again hard to determine with any accuracy, but there were certainly enough to have a major impact on the musical taste of the general public. A few examples must suffice to give an indication of the many names and many songs that became common currency in Britain, and in parts of Europe, during the decade.

Ginger Rogers had her first successful stage role in *Girl Crazy*, which opened on Broadway in 1930. The main female lead was Ethel Merman and the hit songs were 'Embraceable You' and 'I Got Rhythm' both by George and Ira Gershwin. Two film versions followed, one in 1932 and a second in 1943, starring Judy Garland and Mickey Rooney, both of which kept the songs but sought to strengthen the rather weak storyline. Rogers' first film success came in 1933 with *42nd Street*, a musical about a musical. The cast also included four other thirties musical stalwarts – Bebe Daniels, Ruby Keeler, Dick Powell and Warren Baxter – and among the songs, with music by Harry Warren and lyrics by Al Dubin, were classics such as 'Shuffle Off to Buffalo', 'You're Getting To Be a Habit With Me' and, of course, the title song itself. *Forty-second Street* was the first really big success for the choreographer Busby Berkeley. He went on to make some fifty films, sometimes as choreographer, sometimes also directing, but more often than not featuring the extensive, elaborate and spectacular dance scenes that were his trademark. One sequence in *Golddiggers of 1933* featured Ginger Rogers singing the Dubin-Warren song 'We're in the Money' surrounded by giant coins; while *Footlight Parade* (1933) is remembered for the swimming-pool production number, 'By a Waterfall', which featured three hundred choreographed swimmers and some remarkably innovative photography; and *Dames* (1934) used equally novel cinematic techniques so that 'I Only Have Eyes for You' is sung by a whole chorus of Ruby Keelers. Berkeley's choreography and production took the presentation of popular music to new levels and had an impact on contemporary audiences similar to that which the advent of the music video had on compact disc buyers in the 1990s. Ginger Rogers, of course, went on from her early successes to partner Fred Astaire in films such as *Top Hat* (1935), featuring the Irving Berlin song 'Cheek to Cheek'; *Swing Time* (1936), with Jerome Kern's 'A Fine Romance'; and *Shall We Dance* (1937) with George and Ira Gershwin's 'Let's Call the Whole Thing Off'.

The 1930s saw Jeanette MacDonald become a star. She partnered Maurice Chevalier in films such as *Love Me Tonight* (1932), with songs by Richard Rodgers and Lorenz Hart, and *The Merry Widow* (1934), an adaptation of Franz Léhar's operetta. She then joined Nelson Eddy in a series of films, again mainly adaptations of operettas and musicals – *Naughty Marietta* (1935); *Rose-Marie* (1936); *Maytime* (1937) – and also in one very odd attempt to reconstruct Puccini's opera *La fanciulla del West* as *The Golden Girl of the West* (1938). Bing Crosby's reputation had been growing in the United States for some time, but it was in the mid-1930s that he became known in Britain, co-starring with Ethel Merman in *Anything Goes*, with Frances Farmer in *Rhythm of the Range*, and with Louis Armstrong in *Pennies from Heaven* (all three released in 1936). The first of the famous 'Road' films in which Crosby worked with Bob Hope and Dorothy Lamour was *The Road to Singapore*, released in 1940. 'White Christmas' was first heard on American radio on Christmas Day 1941 and was then featured in the 1942 film, *Holiday Inn*. Judy Garland was only fifteen when she sang 'You Made Me Love You (I Didn't Want to Do It')' in *Broadway Melody of 1938* (actually released in 1937) but she stole the show from the official box office attractions, Robert Taylor and Eleanor Powell. MGM Studios paired her with Mickey Rooney for *Thoroughbreds Don't*

Cry (1938), the first of nine films they made together. Then in 1939 came *The Wizard of Oz*; 'Over the Rainbow' became her theme tune, and an anthem for American troops in the Second World War. It stands alongside 'White Christmas' as one of the best known and most popular songs of all time. Not all Hollywood musical films featured new music. *Alexander's Ragtime Band* (1938) was built round a storyline tracing the development of jazz from its early days to the point where swing and dance-band music became respectable musical genres. This provided a perfect vehicle for recycling some twenty-six of Irving Berlin's greatest hits – including the title song, 'Easter Parade', 'Blue Skies' and 'Heat Wave'. These were the stars, songs and production values that Hollywood exported; and they became the standards by which British audiences judged British productions, whether on stage or on screen.

None of this diminished the popularity of the stage musical, whether in London or in provincial centres such as Manchester, Edinburgh and Belfast. The 1930s saw three hundred new musicals open in London, with many of the more successful productions being given a run in theatres outside the capital. American productions were very much in evidence. Richard Rodgers and Lorenz Hart, Jerome Kern and Oscar Hammerstein, Fred Astaire and Vincent Youmans were just some of the composer-lyricist teams that had musicals running in London during the decade. Another name that was becoming known was that of Cole Porter. *The Gay Divorce* opened in London in 1933, a year after its Broadway premiere, featuring the song 'Night and Day'. Two years later, *Anything Goes* included some of what have become Porter's best-known compositions: the title song, 'I Get a Kick Out of You', and 'You're the Top'.

New British musicals also continued to be written and produced in large numbers, with André Charlot and C. B. Cochran maintaining their position as the leading impresarios. The British style was, on the whole, less obviously sophisticated and less given to spectacle than the American, but the resulting productions were not necessarily less successful. Billy Mayerl (1902–59) was a London-born, classically-trained pianist who, in 1925, gave the first British concert performance of Gershwin's *Rhapsody in Blue*. He went on to become one of the leading British show composers of the period. He wrote a dozen musicals during the 1930s, unknown today but moderately successful at the time, including several – *Sporting Love* (1934), *Twenty to One* (1935) and *Over She Goes* (1936) – with plots centring on horse-racing. A particularly successful British team was Joseph Tunbridge and lyricist Jack Waller. They were responsible for ten new shows during the 1930s – among them *Silver Wings* (1930), *For the Love of Mike* (1931), *Tell Her the Truth* (1932), *Mr Whittington* (1934), *Yes Madam* (1934), *Please Teacher!* (1935), *Certainly Sir!* (1936) and *Big Business* (1937) – some of them starring the elegant Scots singer, Jack Buchanan, who was given the unhelpful publicity label 'the British Fred Astaire'. Such shows were undoubtedly formulaic and contained few songs that are remembered now, but they produced solid, reliable returns. A British oddity – but nonetheless a profitable one – was the *Scout Gang Show* formula hit upon by the actor, author and producer, Ralph Reader. Scouting embodied healthy values. Gang shows were good, clean fun. Mix scouting with some good, singable tunes, with some quick fire crosstalk and a lot of silly jokes, and the result was not just a nationwide success, but a format that has since spread across the globe wherever there is a scout movement.

Noel Coward, as we have seen, began the decade with his historical spectacular *Cavalcade*, which was then turned into a film in 1933, one of a distinctly limited number of British films to generate a major box-office return in the United States. During the rest of the decade, however, his musical offerings were less successful than his straight plays. *Bitter Sweet* (1929) had been extremely popular, but, although Coward was a sufficiently important figure to have an American production of his works assured, neither *Conversation Piece* (1933) nor *Operette* (1938), which includes the witty and popular 'The Stately Homes of England', were successful.

Ivor Novello, by contrast, ended the decade in a blaze of glory. Having returned from Hollywood and then appeared in a series of straight plays, he was approached by the management of the Theatre Royal in Drury Lane, which was facing a financial crisis and feared they might have to turn the theatre into a cinema. The result was *Glamorous Night* (1935), a Ruritanian romance with a modern twist, featuring – among other things – a horse and carriage on stage, a skating scene, a shipwreck and a gypsy wedding. It was a huge success, both in London, on tour in the provinces, and subsequently as a film. *Glamorous Night* was followed by *Careless Rapture* (1936), which went one better and featured an earthquake. *Crest of the Wave* (1937) included a train crash. *The Dancing Years* (1939) was slightly different in that it was set in Vienna with the spectre of Nazi persecution in the background. All these shows had lyrics by Christopher Hassall and all were tremendously popular throughout the country. *The Dancing Years* became the most popular musical of the Second World War and is reported to have grossed over £1,000,000, an astonishing amount in those days. Novello obviously did not shy away from spectacle, yet nor did he seek to imitate the Broadway style. His musicals were set in Europe (or, in the case of *Careless Rapture*, Asia); they made use of classical dance and ballet styles; and musically they owed more to the central European tradition of operetta than to Broadway. They may have had an old-fashioned flavour but they were not run-of-the-mill. His series of successful productions at the Theatre Royal was interrupted only briefly in 1936. Just after *Glamorous Night*, the theatre's management decided to mount a huge, Broadway-style spectacular called *Rise and Shine*, with songs by Fred Astaire, Johnny Mercer and Vincent Youmans. It was a disaster, exacerbating the theatre's financial problems. *Careless Rapture* saved the day.

When sound film first hit British screens, it was musicals that initially attracted attention because of their sheer novelty. They offered the illusion of live performance to millions of cinema-goers who might only rarely experience live music. However, non-musical films, both comedy and serious drama, rapidly gained popularity. These films required soundtracks and that requirement began to provide opportunities for 'serious' composers. Bliss and Walton were among the first to take advantage of film commissions, both writing their first film music in 1934. During and after the Second World War, they were followed, as we have seen, by Vaughan Williams, Bax and Berners. Yet for none of them did writing for films ever become more than an occasional, interesting and profitable sideline.

In the career of William Alwyn (1905–85), by contrast, film music came to assume a much greater importance. Born William Alwyn Smith, he came from a Northampton family with no claim to musical talent beyond an uncle and aunt who topped the bill at the local music hall. He always said that his interest in music was stimulated by seeing a uniformed band playing in the local park on Sunday afternoons. However it came about, his commitment to a musical career led to him entering the RAM at fifteen and teaching composition there at the age of just twenty-one. His orchestral work *Five Preludes* was given by Henry Wood at a Prom in 1927 and, by the time 1939 came, he had written a Piano Concerto, a Violin Concerto and a number of other works that were generally considered promising, if somewhat conservative in style when compared to Bliss or Walton. He had also written his first film scores: he wrote eight between 1937 and 1939, all for short documentaries of promotional or patriotic intent: *The Future's in the Air*, *New Worlds for Old*, *Wings over the Empire*.

During the war, Alwyn continued teaching at the RAM and also wrote over forty film scores. The majority were documentary or propaganda films about Britain or the war effort – *Trinity House, The Western Isles, Desert Victory, Lift Your Heads* – but by 1942 he was also writing for feature films, again mainly those intended to boost morale and extol British heroism, such as *Fires Were Started, Wing Commander X* and *The Rake's Progress*. This, as it turned out, was just the beginning. Alwyn never lost the sense of himself as a serious composer – during the 1950s, encouraged by John Barbirolli, he composed a cycle of four symphonies, as well as a symphonic prelude called *The Magic Island* and a radio opera – but he was best known as one of Britain's leading composers of film music. Between the end of the war and his retirement, another eighty scores came from his pen, including classics such as the 1948 adaptation of Terence Rattigan's *Winslow Boy*; the 1949 version of *The History of Mr Polly*, starring John Mills; and *The Ship that Died of Shame* (1955), starring Richard Attenborough. Towards the end of his career, Alwyn was taken up by the Walt Disney organisation and wrote the music for *Swiss Family Robinson* (1960) and *In Search of the Castaways* (1962), but he resisted repeated invitations to move to Hollywood.

Alwyn's classical compositions are highly competent in technique, broadly late or neo-romantic in style, and marked by moments of strongly dissonant emphasis, but he struggled to find his own voice. His First Symphony (1949) sounds like Sibelius; his Third plays unconvincingly with his own version of twelve-note serialism; *The Magic Island* sounds like Bax. In his film music, however, he was able to bring his technical skills to the task of illustrating and developing whatever scenario was provided by the film. In doing so successfully over some thirty years, he was among those who led the way in turning film music into an art form in its own right.

Interestingly, only after he ceased writing for films – his last score was for Carol Reed's *Running Man* in 1963 – did Alwyn's other works assume a more individual character. His *Sinfonietta* (1970) is an impressive, highly chromatic work, apparently owing much to Berg; while the Fifth Symphony (1973), to which he gave the name *Hydriotaphia*, a reference to the seventeenth-century writer Sir Thomas Browne, is a powerful and compressed, one-movement work. Alwyn's late opera *Miss Julie* (1977; recorded that year, but not performed in public until 1997), based on the Strindberg play, is both curious and ambitious. It blends a range of influences from jazz to Strauss and Janáček, as if the composer was working his way towards an alternative vision for British opera that did not take into account the work of Britten and Tippett that was dominant at the time.

'The film', Vaughan Williams wrote in 1945, 'contains possibilities for the combination of all the arts such as Wagner never dreamed of,'[2] but not everyone agreed. Some critics, and some of the more committed modernists of the post-war period, liked to look down upon the kind of crossover represented by Alwyn's career, rather as criticism was directed at Sullivan for writing the Savoy Operas instead of concentrating on 'serious' music. It would be some years before film music was universally accepted as a genre in its own right. Nonetheless, it was profitable and the composers themselves found it fascinating: Alwyn claimed that it allowed him write for a greater range of emotion than any other form.

Arthur Benjamin (1893–1960) was less prolific than Alwyn, but his career followed a similar pattern. Born in Sydney, he arrived in London in 1911, having won a scholarship to the RCM, where he became friends with Howells, Gurney and Goossens. During the First World War he was in the Royal Flying Corps, but was shot down over German lines and found himself in the same prison camp as Edgar Bainton. A String Quartet (1924) and a Piano Concertino (1926) attracted some attention and, in 1926, he was appointed to the RCM staff as a piano teacher. He remained there for nearly fourteen years, counting Benjamin Britten and the Welsh composer, Alan Hodinott, among his students. His first and greatest popular success came in 1938 with *Two Jamaican Pieces*, originally written for two pianos, but later orchestrated. It was inspired by local tunes heard during a trip to Jamaica as part of his work as an examiner for the Associated Board of the Royal Schools of Music, and one of the pieces was called *Jamaican Rumba*. The rumba was already a dance hall craze in the United States, helped by a 1935 film called simply *Rumba*. It may in part have been a case of being in the right place at the right time, but Benjamin's *Jamaican Rumba* became a worldwide hit. It generated so much publicity that the Jamaican government actually decided to give Benjamin a barrel of rum every year for his, albeit inadvertent, contribution to promoting the island.

Benjamin always wanted to write for the stage and in 1931 wrote a light, humorous one-act opera, *The Devil Take Her*, which was taken up by Beecham, but it was film music that really suited his talents. Like Bliss and Walton, he started writing for films early. In 1934, he composed scores for *The Scarlet Pimpernel* and for the Hitchcock thriller, *The Man Who Knew Too Much*, some of the music for which was later recycled in his *Storm*

Clouds Cantata. With the coming of the Second World War, he moved to Vancouver where he taught, gave radio talks, and conducted both the Canadian Broadcasting Corporation Radio Symphony and the Vancouver Symphony Orchestras, but composed very little. After the war, he completed two more operas: *The Tale of Two Cities* (1950), produced during the 1951 Festival of Britain, and *Mañana*, which was the first opera commissioned by BBC television. *The Tale of Two Cities* was the more successful of the two, but both were criticised for lacking an individual voice. As with Alwyn, it was film music that really suited his talents. He produced scores for twenty major films, including classics such as Alexander Korda's *Ideal Husband* (1947), the documentary *The Conquest of Everest* (1953), and a series of major feature films: *Above Us the Waves* (1955), *Fire Down Below* (1957) and *Naked Earth* (1958).

Benjamin was less successful as a serious composer than Alwyn, although he too continued to compose in classical genres throughout his life. His fifth opera, *Tartuffe*, was left unfinished on his death. It was orchestrated by the conductor Alan Boustead and given at Sadler's Wells in 1964, but it has not been revived since. Works such as the Violin Concerto (1932) and his adaptation of Domenico Cimarosa's Oboe Concerto (1942) retain their interest, but it is his film music, uncomplicated, direct and always apposite, that really deserves recognition.

A third and somewhat different version of a classical crossover is demonstrated by the career of Eric Coates (1886–1957), whose works defined 'light music' for many people growing up in the post-1945 world. (Ethel Smyth actually called him 'the man who writes tunes.') We have met Coates briefly before, playing viola in the Beecham Symphony Orchestra's first concert in 1909. RAM-trained, having studied composition under Corder and viola with Lionel Tertis, Coates was already writing songs in large numbers before and during the First World War. Shakespeare settings were more or less obligatory for a young songwriter at the time and he wrote several, including 'It Was a Lover and His Lass', 'Who is Sylvia?', and 'Sigh No More, Ladies'. He also wrote a number of songs to words by the eccentric lawyer and writer Frederic Weatherly, who is reputed to have written over three thousand lyrics, including 'Danny Boy', 'Roses of Picardy' and 'The Holy City'. Coates's early compositions were modestly successful – four of the Shakespeare settings, under the title *Old English Songs*, were given at the Proms in 1909, and an orchestral piece, *Miniature Suite*, was given in 1911. Despite this, he continued to work as an orchestral player in order to maintain a regular income, becoming principal violist of Henry Wood's Queen's Hall Orchestra in 1912.

It was only in 1919, when he came into conflict with Wood over the deputy system and his contract was not renewed, that he gave up the viola and concentrated on composing. The main thing that differentiated Coates from so many of his peers was that he was not troubled by the desire to become a great composer: he was happy writing the kind of light, popular music that he knew people would like. At a fundamental level, his music looked back to Sullivan and Edward German, but he was capable of assimilating jazz, swing and almost any other current trend without apparent effort. He wrote songs, ballads, marches, waltzes, serenades and short orchestral suites. These were carefully constructed to come within the technical compass of a seaside pier or provincial hotel orchestra; and they were also tailored to the length and reproduction qualities of a gramophone record. The 1927 *Four Ways Suite*, for example, came in four short movements – 'Northwards – March'; 'Southwards – Valse'; 'Eastwards – Eastern Dance'; and 'Westwards – Rhythm' – which made it eminently suited to recording on the four sides of two 78 rpm records. It also avoided extended *piano* passages that might be less than fully audible over the surface hiss of a 78. Coates's decision in 1914 to become one of the founding members of the Performing Rights Society (PRS) was vindicated when he began to derive a significant proportion of his income from royalties. Ketèlby, who joined in PRS in 1918, similarly benefitted.

Coates's popularity grew throughout the 1920s, not least because the formula he had evolved to suit recording was equally suited to broadcasting. However, it was the 1930s that was Coates's big decade. His music was heard everywhere. The 1932 *London Suite* included a march section called *Knightsbridge* that was adopted as the signature tune for the BBC's *In Town Tonight*, an early chat show that ran from 1933 until 1960. It also featured in at least three feature films. The *London Bridge March* (1934) and the *Seven Seas March* (1938) struck an appropriately patriotic tone and were broadcast regularly. *By a Sleepy Lagoon*, a gentle serenade written in 1930, has kept Coates's music on the radio right up to the present day. In 1940, with words added by Jack Lawrence, it became a hit and was used in several films, including one that took the title *Sleepy Lagoon*; and in 1942 it was chosen as the signature tune for a new BBC programme called *Desert Island Discs*. Both the programme and its signature tune are still heard every week. When war broke out Coates employed his ability to come up with bright, hummable, but at the same time stirring tunes in the service of the war effort. The march *Calling All Workers* (1940) featured in several films, but, more significantly, it opened and closed *Music While You Work*, a fifteen-minute sequence of uninterrupted light music, originally designed to boost the morale of factory workers, that was broadcast on the BBC's Light Programme from 1940 to 1967. Another wartime march, *Eighth Army* (1942), was featured in the wartime drama *Nine Men* and then later in the documentary *Tunisian Victory*.

Coates's relationship with the film industry was different from that of Alwyn or Benjamin. He disliked writing film music and refused to write full soundtrack scores. He might provide a theme tune or allow one of his songs to be used in a scene within the film, but that was all: he never wrote anything on an extended scale. Even when, in the 1950s, he was pressed to provide the score for what he was assured was a film of national importance, Coates's reaction was to offer the producers a march he had finished the previous week. It was *The Dambusters*, an anthemic theme tune and one of his most famous compositions; it has since been heard everywhere from quiz shows and adverts to the stands at football grounds.

Coates's neat orchestral suites, his waltzes and marches all appealed to, and in a way came to represent, a section of 1930s society that was (or liked to think it was) at a distance from the dance halls and picture palaces. His music was played at hunt balls, at polite *thés dansants* up and down the country, among the potted palms in seaside hotels, and in village halls where the brass band practised. It was a large constituency, and, like every other section of society, it wanted to hear more of the music it liked. Across the country, this surge in demand for all forms of light or popular music had far-reaching implications. The gramophone at home and weekly or often twice-weekly attendance at the cinema had led to a decline in the membership of choirs and choral societies. This meant that the whole provincial festival circuit – and, with it, the oratorio which had always been its mainstay – also went into decline. And within the BBC, the role and purpose of the organisation in promoting music on the radio suddenly became a matter of concern and debate.

Early BBC broadcasts of recorded music had mixed classical pieces, light music and popular song on an almost random basis. Now, Percy Pitt, the BBC's first Director of Music, and Percy Scholes, the influential writer on music and music critic of *Radio Times*, managed to introduce a classification system for programme planning that favoured serious music. Such a system reflected Sir John Reith's known view that the Corporation existed in order to raise standards among its audience. And this view was taken to a rather odd extreme when Scholes, in a supposedly light-hearted article for *Radio Times,* actually criticised British audiences for their inability to appreciate modern composers, such as Bartok. Yet, at the same time as Pitt and Scholes were promoting serious music, the BBC was actually broadcasting more dance-band and light-orchestral music than ever before. In part, this was because outside broadcasts now presented fewer technical problems and were cheap to produce, but the fact that the Corporation had also taken the decision to appoint a Director of Dance Music, Jack Payne, and to form its own dance orchestra seems to suggest that a more popularist approach was favoured in some quarters.

There was a lull when Pitt retired and Adrian Boult was appointed Director of Music in 1930, but by 1933 the debate was in the open again. A series of articles, whether coordinated or not is unclear, in *The Times*, the *Daily Telegraph*, the *Observer* and other journals, accused the BBC of neglecting its role as an educator, and of taking the easy route by scheduling so many outside broadcasts from dance halls, hotels and cinemas to the detriment of serious music.[3] Such strictures were rejected by a growing number of commentators, many of them politically-motivated, who took the opposite view, believing that it was the purpose, even the duty, of the BBC to give its audience what that audience wanted. It was a debate that would be temporarily suspended during the collective effort of the Second World War, but would surface again immediately afterwards, intensified by the surge of democratic feeling generated by the war. Indeed, in a subtly but not essentially different form, it is a debate that continues in the twenty-first century.

101   The Second World War

The impact of the Second World War on British music was very different from that of the First. To start with, it was expected. Although many hoped right up to the last moment that war could be avoided, there was no surprise when it came, and the implications of at least some of Hitler's policies were already understood. In 1936, when taking the LPO on what came to be seen as a controversial tour of Germany, Beecham had found himself faced with the application of Nazi doctrine in practice when he was requested not to play Mendelssohn's *Scottish Symphony* on the grounds that the composer was Jewish. In 1938, Donald Tovey invented a role with the Reid Orchestra for the Austrian composer Hans Gál, who had had to flee Vienna on account of his Jewish ancestry. The same year Vaughan Williams visited Germany to accept a prize administered by Hamburg University supposedly intended strengthen cultural ties between Britain and Germany. Shocked by what he saw, he made his views known publicly. The German authorities responded by branding him a Communist sympathiser and banning his music. Vaughan Williams went on to play an active part in helping Jewish refugees, among them the German composer Robert Müller-Hartmann. This time, when war came, there would be no composers caught taking a holiday at Bayreuth.

Nor did the declaration of war in 1939 entail the kind of radical cultural realignment forced on the musical community in 1914. Germany had ceased to be regarded as the fount of musical culture. Vienna and Paris were more likely to attract young composers than Leipzig or Berlin. More broadly, as we have seen, American influence had been growing ever since the First World War, and this continued during the Second, particularly after 1941 when large numbers of GIs began to arrive. American influence was most obvious in popular culture, but it extended to classical music as well. Gershwin had died in 1937, but his music in particular and jazz in general were influences that British (and, indeed, European) composers were struggling to assimilate. And it was no accident that both Bliss's Piano Concerto and Bax's Seventh Symphony were commissioned for and premiered at the 1939 World's Fair in New York.

The beginning of the First World War saw a falling off in demand for classical music. The Second did not. Possibly because radio had created a new level of interest, audiences for classical music and classical concerts remained large and generally enthusiastic throughout the war. The attitude of the Government was different, too. The First World War had seen the somewhat ineffectual Music in Wartime Committee set up by musicians themselves, with Sir Frederick Cowen in the chair. The Second saw the establishment of a government committee – the Council for the Encouragement of Music and the Arts (CEMA) – which, in 1946, became the Arts Council. CEMA represented a recognition by the government that, in what was now known as 'total war', it was necessary to acknowledge and encourage – and, where possible, fund – those aspects of culture that were connected with or representative of national identity.

However, it was not immediately realized that the demand for classical music would remain high, and, with the beginning of the war, decisions were taken which in retrospect might not have been necessary. We have already seen Covent Garden turned into a dance hall and the Three Choirs cancelled for the duration. The BBC was particularly cautious. It disbanded the BBC Northern Ireland Orchestra that had evolved out of the Belfast Wireless Symphony Orchestra and had grown, under the direction of Godfrey Brown, into a respectable orchestra of forty players. It also gave up its sponsorship of the Proms, and moved the BBC Symphony Orchestra to Bristol where it was considered less likely to be bombed. Some forty players were released for war service, reducing the playing complement to seventy. Although Ireland had been independent since 1922 and remained neutral during the war, it too saw changes in the musical establishment. The Dublin Philharmonic Orchestra disbanded in 1939, having been in existence for nearly two hundred years. Its role was gradually taken over by a chamber ensemble of musicians recruited by the new Irish national broadcaster, Radio Éireann. The 'Station Orchestra' (as it was known) gave public concerts as well as studio broadcasts and grew in size and reputation during the war years. In 1948, it was renamed the Radio Éireann Symphony Orchestra, becoming, in effect, a national orchestra in much the same way that the BBC Symphony was, and is, often seen as representing the United Kingdom.

The number and scale of German air raids on Britain meant that there was more physical destruction and disruption than during the 1914–18 war. Herbert Howells' house in Barnes on the edge of London was bombed and many of his manuscripts lost. Walton's London house was also bombed. But the most significant loss was the Queen's Hall which, since its opening in 1893, had become a kind of symbol of British classical music. When the BBC decamped to Bristol in 1939, Sir Henry Wood obtained private sponsorship and the support of the LPO to keep the Proms going and the Queen's Hall open. During the 1940 season, these concerts became a symbol of defiance, often continuing throughout air raids; then in May 1941, an incendiary bomb gutted the auditorium and reduced the building to an unsafe, smouldering shell. Wood was seen weeping amid the ruins. The LPO, which had given *Gerontius* there the evening before the fire, lost most of its instruments – although these were replaced quickly as a result of an appeal broadcast on the BBC. The Proms then shifted to the Royal Albert Hall where they remain to this day. For the 1942 season, the BBC returned to its role as sponsor with the BBC Symphony Orchestra, which by that time had been bombed out of Bristol and moved to Bedford, taking up temporary residence in London during the Proms season. The 1944 season, which marked the Proms' fiftieth anniversary, was also disrupted. The season began at the Albert Hall with Wood conducting, but concerts were relocated to Bedford when the German V1 flying bombs began targeting London. Wood was due to conduct the fiftieth anniversary concert on 10 August, but was too ill to do so. He died just nine days later. More than seventy years later the Proms are still officially known as 'The Henry Wood Promenade Concerts'; and every year his bronze bust is placed on the stage of the Royal Albert Hall at the beginning of the season and ceremonially crowned with a chaplet of laurel leaves on the Last Night.

The conductor for that last Queen's Hall concert in 1941 was Malcolm Sargent (1895–1967). Brought up in Stamford, where his father was a clerk in a firm of coal merchants and a church organist, Sargent's early years were marked by an absolute determination to make a career in music. It was Wood who gave him his first big chance when the Queen's Hall Orchestra visited Leicester in February 1921. The concert organisers had commissioned a piece – *An Impression on a Windy Day* – from Sargent who was something of a local hero. Wood had no time to learn it so Sargent conducted. Wood was sufficiently impressed to offer him the chance to conduct the piece at one of that year's Proms. Four years later, he was on tour with the British National Opera Company and revelling in *Die Meistersinger*. The following year, 1926, he was conducting Gilbert and Sullivan for the D'Oyly Carte Opera Company. Although Sargent was acknowledged as a great choral conductor, his relationship with orchestral players could be stormy, but during the war he worked tirelessly to keep orchestras going and to keep classical music before the public. He worked with the Hallé, the LPO and the Liverpool Philharmonic – often making one orchestra jealous because of the amount of time he spent with another. He travelled constantly, taking his orchestras to bomb-damaged cities, particularly in the north of England, conducting through air raids, and dragging reluctant players to towns that had never previously seen a symphony orchestra. His hard work, defiance of danger and cheerful persona gave him an almost unassailable public reputation.

The other young British conductor of the period was John Barbirolli (1899–1970). His father was Italian and his mother was French, but Barbirolli was born in London, within the sound of Bow bells, and always considered himself a Cockney. He studied at Trinity College of Music and the RAM and came to prominence in the 1920s conducting the British National Opera Company and Covent Garden's touring opera company. He worked with the RPO, the LSO and the Hallé and, in 1936, was appointed to succeed Toscanini as conductor of the New York Philharmonic. As a consequence, he was in New York when war broke out.[1] He returned in 1942 and spent ten weeks conducting the LPO and the LSO without taking a fee in order to help the orchestras and the war effort. After another brief period in the United States to honour contractual obligations, he returned permanently to Britain – and to Manchester where he worked with the Hallé, rebuilding it almost from scratch, saving it from bankruptcy, and inspiring great devotion from its players and its public. The Hallé became *his* orchestra, and, despite later offers to become chief conductor of the BBC Symphony and at the Royal Opera House, he remained with them for the rest of his life.

Beecham, by contrast, did not come out of the war so well. He left Britain in the spring of 1940 and spent much of the war in the United States, commuting between the Metropolitan Opera in New York and the Seattle Symphony on the other side of the Continent, as well as acting as guest conductor with some eighteen different orchestras. His work there was undoubtedly legitimate and he worked hard to keep Britain and British music in the forefront of American minds, but his absence was noted. When he finally returned in September 1944, his concerts were well attended but he himself did not receive the rapturous applause he had become used to in the past. His American exploits appeared less than glorious when compared with Malcolm Sargent's odysseys through battered industrial towns, or the efforts of the pianist Myra Hess, who organised the now famous lunchtime concerts at London's National Gallery, over 2,000 of them, beginning during the Blitz and lasting until April 1946.

Other reputations also suffered during the war, not always justly. Noël Coward travelled widely, particularly in America, during the early years of the war. In fact, he was working on behalf of British intelligence, although this, of course, could not be revealed and his reputation suffered as a result. He was also fined £200 in 1941 for breaching the currency regulations. At the suggestion of Winston Churchill, who appears to have disliked him, Coward spent the next four years entertaining the troops and rebuilding his public image. Ivor Novello, too, suffered during the war. In 1944, he was convicted of fraudulently acquiring petrol coupons and sentenced to eight weeks in prison.[2] He re-established his public profile quickly – *Perchance to Dream*, which opened in 1945, ran for over a thousand performances at the Hippodrome – but the incident left a psychological scar from which he never fully recovered. Both Benjamin Britten and Michael Tippett, whose careers we shall consider in Chapters 103 and 104, registered as conscientious objectors. 'Conchies', as they were known, were extremely unpopular with both press and public. Britten spent the first three years of the war in the United States, which also attracted adverse comment at the time. Returning in 1942, he faced a tribunal which ordered him to do non-combatant work in the military, but he won an exemption on appeal. Tippett was also ordered to do non-combatant work, but his attitude was more confrontational than Britten's and, despite strong support from the musical community, he was jailed for three months in Wormwood Scrubs. Yet it was Britten and Tippet who produced *Peter Grimes* (1945) and *A Child of our Time* (1944), the two greatest works by British composers to come out of the war.

The role of CEMA was to protect music and the arts during the war. The role of the Entertainments National Service Association (ENSA) was to provide live entertainment for service personnel – a remit later extended to include factory workers involved in war-related production. ENSA was started in 1939 by the actor Basil Dean and the comedian Leslie Henson, both of them also experienced directors and producers, and the scale of its operations soon became so great that it, too, became a means of protecting and promoting British culture. The fact that its target audience was ordinary soldiers, sailors and airmen (who called it 'Every Night Something Awful') meant that its main focus was on popular entertainment: singers, jazz and dance bands, comedians, variety acts. Indeed, it is scarcely possible to think of a popular star from the 1930s and 40s who did not perform for ENSA: everyone from Billy Cotton and Joe Loss to Mantovani; Al Bowlly and Gracie Fields to Vera Lynn; and Arthur Askey to Tommy Trinder. ENSA also promoted serious drama, featuring actors such as Laurence Olivier, Ralph Richardson, Peggy Ashcroft and Edith Evans, and there was even a small classical music division. ENSA's classical performances might consist of anything from a tenor and piano recital to a string quartet playing in a factory canteen, where such music was not appreciated, or Malcolm Sargent dragging a reduced Liverpool Philharmonic to remote halls in blacked-out Lancashire to play Delibes, Schubert and Suppé.

ENSA performers travelled all over the world – Gracie Fields once found herself in Papua New Guinea en route for the Pacific islands – often in difficult and dangerous conditions; some were killed when planes crashed or were shot down. Whether wartime concerts were responsible for bringing large numbers of working people to appreciate classical music for the first time – a claim enthusiastically endorsed by Malcolm Sargent – may be arguable, but the concerts and performances given by ENSA artists to audiences of different races and nationalities all around the world undoubtedly gave British popular culture and British popular music a greater international profile than it had previously enjoyed.

The Second World War produced fewer memorable popular songs than the First. The one everyone knows, 'Lili Marlene', was, of course, German. The words had been written by Hans Leip during the First World War, out of longing for his girlfriend, Lili, a grocer's daughter from his home town. Only in 1939 was it set to music by the well-known German songwriter Norbert Schulze, and recorded by the singer Lale Andersen. Although the song was initially banned by the German authorities – Andersen was suspected of sympathising with the Jews – it was eventually played on German army radio in North Africa where it became an immediate hit. British soldiers listening to the German radio began singing it. An English version was recorded by Anne Shelton backed by Ambrose and his Orchestra, and numerous later recordings were also made – by Vera Lynn, Bing Crosby and Edith Piaf, among others. Marlene Dietrich's famous recording was made in 1944 for propaganda purposes.

Having begun her career singing with Ambrose at the Café de Paris before the war, Vera Lynn went on to become known as 'the Forces' Sweetheart', achieving a string of hits with emotional yet optimistic songs, such as 'The White Cliffs of Dover', 'There'll Always Be an England', 'A Nightingale Sang in Berkeley Square' and 'We'll Meet Again'. Noël Coward captured the same mood with his 1941 song 'London Pride'. However, many British songs of the period had a jokey, even facetious quality, exemplified by Coward's 'Could You Please Oblige Us with a Bren Gun', by Flanagan and Allen's 'Run, Rabbit, Run', or by 'We're Going to Hang Out the Washing on the Siegfried Line', first performed by Mantovani and his Orchestra in the early months of the war. This may in part have been a response to official encouragement to maintain morale and lift the nation's spirits, but it was more probably because of the ever-increasing presence of American popular music, whether on screen, on radio or on record. This was the era of Glen Miller, Benny Goodman, Duke Ellington, the Andrews Sisters, the Ink Spots and innumerable other acts that have since taken their place in the pantheon of what was an exceptionally fertile period in American popular music. Unable to compete with American music played and sung by Americans, British performers fell back on a style that hinted at music hall and displayed the famous British sense of humour.

Complaints about the amount of non-British music being played on the BBC were heard in 1940 when ten composers – among them Bantock, Ireland, Lambert, Ethel Smyth and Vaughan Williams – wrote to *The Author*, the voice of The Society of Authors. Their letter, entitled 'The BBC and British Composers', pressed for more broadcasting time to be allocated to British music, both light and classical. Sir Adrian Boult, the Corporation's Director of Music, vigorously maintained that British music was fairly represented and produced statistics to prove it. The argument would continue.

One piece of British music that was heard regularly on the BBC throughout the war was *Warsaw Concerto* by Richard Addinsell (1904–77). It was not an actual concerto, but a ten-minute tone poem for piano and orchestra, originally written for the 1941 film, *Dangerous Moonlight*. Released at what was just about the lowest point of the war for the British population, the film tells the story of a Polish concert pianist who becomes a fighter pilot in order to defend his country. The director had wanted to use Rachmaninoff's Second Piano Concerto, but copyright costs made this impossible, so Addinsell was commissioned to write a piece of emotionally-charged piano music as much like Rachmaninoff as possible. The film was a moderate success with the public on both sides of the Atlantic, although not with critics, but Addinsell's music was a massive and immediate hit, selling several million copies – the kind of number more usually associated with the big singing stars. As the film historian, John Huntley, has pointed out, its success was assisted by the fact that, like Eric Coates's orchestral suites, its length allowed it to fit neatly on two sides of a 78 rpm record.[3] *Warsaw Concerto*, with its surging romanticism, rapidly became a symbol of Polish resistance (Addinsell was honoured by the Polish government after the war) and of anti-Nazi defiance generally. Over seventy years later, it is still seen as one of the most evocative and iconic compositions of the war years.

With the exception of Al Bowlly, killed in a bombing raid on London in 1941, and Glen Miller, lost over the Channel on a flight to Normandy in 1944, most of the leading stars of popular music survived the war. In the classical world, by contrast, the deaths were more numerous, the result of natural causes, however, rather than enemy action: Donald Tovey, William Wallace, Frank Bridge, Hamilton Harty, Walford Davies, Leslie Heward, Henry Wood and Ethel Smyth all died of old age or illness between 1940 and 1944. Popular music, dominated by American styles and performers, had boomed during the war; so, too, had classical music but in a particular manner adapted to wartime. Popular music needed only to adjust to a peacetime commercial environment, but classical music lacked the essential infrastructure that had existed before the war and needed to reconstruct itself in a much more fundamental way.

British classical music had survived, but, for wholly understandable reasons, it had stagnated. There were, as we shall see, two or three composers who would lead the way forward, but any sense of an English Musical Renaissance had been lost. The years after the war were filled with projects and initiatives designed to get the world of British classical music back on its feet again. One of the earliest was the Cheltenham Festival, which was held for the first time in June 1945, just six weeks after VE Day. In terms of timing, it was a brave initiative, but musically the Festival appeared to look back to the pre-war world, rather than seek out new musical styles. In the immediate aftermath of the war, this was understandable, but it was an approach that characterised Cheltenham for many years. John Barbirolli became one of the Festival's leading supporters and began to use it to give first performances of works by British composers, but rarely of works which could be described as challenging. The term 'Cheltenham symphony' was later coined to describe the kind of traditional, late romantic work that he favoured – and which, it has to be added, evidently appealed to Cheltenham audiences.[1]

The Three Choirs was revived in 1946, in large measure due to the efforts of the Hereford Cathedral organist, Percy Hull. For generations, the Three Choirs had been a focal point for British classical music and its return was naturally welcomed, but this new incarnation was distinctly conservative in character, with little apparent appetite for the kind of premieres that had marked the early decades of the twentieth century. The Edinburgh International Festival, inaugurated in 1947, tried hard to be more innovative. It was the brainchild of Rudolf Bing, at the time manager of Glyndebourne Opera, and the musical cast for its first year was impressive: the Liverpool Philharmonic, the Hallé, Sadler's Wells Ballet and Glyndebourne Opera all took part. In reality, however progressive they tried to be, the underlying theme of all these post-war festivals was reassurance and rebuilding. Again, this was understandable in the context of the time – Britain was exhausted after the war and needed reassurance and stability – but the immediate post-war period was also marked by a barrage of self-congratulatory, even chauvinistic commentary. 'Britain is now leading the world in every branch of serious music-making,' wrote Russell Palmer in 1947.[2] The same note was struck by Alan Frank, a few years later: 'It is permissible to ask, without being chauvinistic, whether any other single country can claim so strong a school of native composers.'[3] Such sentiments had little to do with reality. They may have reflected a residual sense of triumph – Britain had, after all, won the war – but they were neither accurate nor helpful in understanding the true state of British music or helping it move forward.

One aspect of the rebuilding process was new orchestras. In 1945, Walter Legge founded the Philharmonia Orchestra. Legge was an experienced record producer working for EMI, but before the war he had been Assistant Artistic Director at Covent Garden under Beecham. He believed that London needed a first-class orchestra capable of working with equal ease in the opera house, the concert hall and the recording studio; and he believed Beecham was the obvious choice to be principal conductor. Beecham did conduct the first concert – claiming a single cigar as his fee – but, autocratic as ever, he expected to be given full control of the orchestra and its work schedule. This, Legge would not concede; so Beecham refused to have any further dealings with the Philharmonia and went off to found another orchestra, the Royal Philharmonic (which got its 'Royal' not from the King, but by associating itself with the Royal Philharmonic Society). The Royal Philharmonic made its debut in 1946 at Croydon and was soon a force to be reckoned with both in concert and on record. Within four years of its foundation, it was touring the United States, giving fifty-two concerts in forty-five cities. Legge, meanwhile, had taken a trip to India on behalf of the Philharmonia. He persuaded the Maharajah of Mysore to give £10,000 per year for three years to put the new orchestra and its associated concert series on a sound financial footing. He contacted Toscanini, Richard Strauss, Furtwängler and Herbert von Karajan, all of whom conducted the Philharmonia in its early years, but it was von Karajan who became most closely associated with the orchestra. Only when he was appointed Music Director of the Berlin Philharmonic, in 1954, did von Karajan disengage from the Philharmonia, his role then being taken by Otto Klemperer.

In 1851, Prince Albert's Great Exhibition had given London the Crystal Palace, a venue that played a major part in the capital's, and indeed the nation's, musical life for many years. In 1951, the Festival of Britain, designed to celebrate national recovery after the war, gave London the Royal Festival Hall. With a seating capacity of 3,000, it more than compensated for the loss of the Queen's Hall ten years earlier. It not only gave an actual boost to orchestral music in London, but also served as a symbol to the country as a whole of the importance placed on music in national life. The inaugural concert took place on 3 May 1951 in the presence of King George VI and Queen Elizabeth. Sargent conducted and the programme was solidly and powerfully English, with works by Elgar, Purcell, Arne and Vaughan Williams. This was no doubt appropriate in view of the national and patriotic nature of the event, but the lack of even one post-war work was an indication that the British musical establishment remained essentially risk-averse.

Financing opera had always been a problem in Britain, but the post-war world seemed to promise a fresh start – and, as we shall see, it was opera that was to lead British classical music forward over the next two decades. The Carl Rosa Opera Company had had to disband its ballet troop, but despite immense difficulties the opera company had managed to carry on throughout the war, giving seasons in London and in provincial centres such as Liverpool, Manchester, Leeds, and Edinburgh. With the end of the war, the Austrian conductor, Vilém Tauský, became its musical director and during a four-year period led the rebuilding of both the company and the repertoire. Then in 1950, the company's owner, the impresario Henry Bettesworth Phillips, died. Financial troubles loomed, but the Opera Company managed to keep going and eventually, in 1953, the Arts Council agreed to provide a subsidy. This made it possible to give seasons at Sadler's Wells Theatre in 1955 and 1956, but in 1960 the Arts Council withdrew its funding and the company finally closed after eighty-seven years.[4]

In 1951, Tauský became musical director of Welsh National Opera. This was an amateur company that relied on the BBC Welsh Orchestra for its orchestral players. It had given its first performance – the familiar double bill of *Cavalleria Rusticana* and *Pagliacci* – at Cardiff's Prince of Wales Theatre just five years earlier, and its early repertoire included nothing more challenging than Smetana's *Bartered Bride*, but, as one might have expected in Wales, it soon developed a reputation for the quality of its chorus singing. Tauský's tenure lasted five years and saw several major practical developments: the company moved its performances to Cardiff's New Theatre, which would remain its home for the next fifty years, and it struck an agreement with the Bournemouth Symphony, which became its regular orchestra.

A more unusual project – it was regarded as startling at the time – was the idea of staging opera in the middle of the Sussex countryside. Glyndebourne Manor and the 10,000 acre (4,000 hectare) estate which went with it had been in the Christie family since the mid-nineteenth century. In 1920, it passed to the thirty-eight-year-old John Christie. He had been a teacher at Eton and had served with distinction in the trenches during the First World War. Turning his attention to music, he installed a cathedral organ in the house and, at the same time, bought the British organ company, Hill, Norman & Beard. He held recitals and musical evenings, but it was not until 1931, when he married Audrey Mildmay, a soprano with the Carl Rosa Opera Company, that he had the idea of producing full-scale professional opera at Glyndebourne. By 1934, a three-hundred-seat opera house had been built, the German conductor Fritz Busch had been engaged, and the first performances were given. The repertoire was almost exclusively Mozart, with occasional excursions into Verdi, Donizetti and, in 1940 just before the house closed for the duration of the war, Pepusch's *Beggar's Opera*. The productions were professional but not particularly exciting. It was only after the war that Glyndebourne Opera began to make an impact on the national scene. The company reformed and took an active role in the first Edinburgh Festival. It also mounted a number of occasional productions at Glyndebourne, including the premieres of Britten's *Rape of Lucretia* (1946) and *Albert Herring* (1947). Then, in 1950, Christie obtained commercial sponsorship to supplement his own money and the annual Glyndebourne Festival was restarted, gradually establishing the format of five or six productions each year, including at least one by Mozart, which continues to this day.

Carl Rosa, Welsh National Opera, and Glyndebourne were all important in their way, but more central to post-war operatic restructuring was the fate of the Royal Opera House in Covent Garden. The financial risks involved made its future very uncertain, and there was a distinct possibility it would actually remain a dance hall. Eventually, the music publishers Boosey & Hawkes took a lease on the building, with the aim of installing a resident opera and ballet company. They offered the role of Chief Executive to David Webster, a former businessman who had been Chairman of the Liverpool Philharmonic throughout the war. It was an inspired choice. Webster persuaded Sadler's Wells Ballet to make Covent Garden their home – they reopened the theatre with *The Sleeping Beauty* in February 1946 – but finding a suitable opera company proved more difficult. The solution was to create one. The Austrian-born conductor, Karl Rankl, was appointed musical director. Singers and players were recruited; a chorus trained; and the new company's first production was Purcell's *Fairy Queen*, in association with the Sadler's Wells Ballet, at the end of 1946. Its first fully independent production was *Carmen* in January 1947. Initially, the policy was that all operas should be sung in English. This idea was supported by Rankl and his successor, Rafael Kubelik, but it proved difficult to recruit leading singers who were willing to relearn familiar roles in English and the policy was eventually dropped. As ever, promoting opera in Britain proved an uphill task, but Webster showed immense skill. He obtained an Arts Council grant; he managed the business aspects of the theatre; and he soothed the infighting and jealousies which opera inevitably seemed to provoke. The early years of the new company saw many standard works being performed – *Il Trovatore, Der Rosenkavalier, La Bohème, Aida, Die Meistersinger* – but there was also a genuine effort to include British composers. Bliss's *Olympians*, Vaughan Williams's *Pilgrim's Progress*, Britten's *Billy Budd* and *Gloriana*, Walton's *Troilus and Cressida*, and Tippett's *Midsummer Marriage* were all premiered at Covent Garden during Rankl's tenure as musical director.

Gradually, the Covent Garden company began to attract international attention. Kubelik was musical director from 1955 to 1958 and had a number of successes. With John Gielgud as director, he was responsible for what was claimed to be the first complete staging of Berlioz's massive opera *Les Troyens*. He also introduced the Covent Garden audience to Janáček's *Jenufa*. Guest conductor Carlo Maria Giulini, with Luchino Visconti as director, revived Verdi's *Don Carlos*, which was all but unknown at the time. In 1961, George Solti took over and during his ten years in charge, Covent Garden's operatic reputation soared. In 1968, the company was formally granted the title 'The Royal Opera'; and in 1970 David Webster retired after twenty-five years in charge, having seen the opera house he managed and the opera company he helped create recognised as among the finest in the world.

When looking for an opera company to take up residence at Covent Garden in 1945, Webster rejected Sadler's Wells Opera. He thought it too inward-looking, too set in its ways, and unlikely to attain the standard of performance he wanted. At the time, Sadler's Wells was going through an extended period of crisis so the decision was not a major surprise. Throughout the war, although much reduced in size, the company had toured constantly, performing in over eighty different venues and mounting a series of popular works, such as Puccini's *Madame Butterfly*, Smetana's *Bartered Bride* and Humperdinck's *Hansel and Gretel*. It was Joan Cross, a noted soprano and the company's wartime director, who decided that they should mark their return to London and the reopening of the Sadler's Wells Theatre with something entirely different. This was the world premiere of Britten's *Peter Grimes*. Joan Cross and Peter Pears took the lead roles; the critics loved it; so did the public; but there was a great deal of opposition to the opera in the company. In the end, Cross and Pears felt they had to leave – which is why Britten's next four operas were premiered either at Glyndebourne or at Covent Garden – and shortly afterwards, as mentioned above, Sadler's Wells Ballet departed for Covent Garden. Urgent and radical measures were required if the opera company was to survive. Clive Carey, a baritone and singing teacher who had been involved with the Sadler's Wells before the war, was brought back as director. The conductor James Robertson, who had worked with the Carl Rosa Company and at Glyndebourne, was recruited as musical director. It was an experienced team, but not one with the international profile that Webster wanted.

In the end, having two opera companies was probably better than one, but for Sadler's Wells the next few years were a struggle. By the 1951 season, however, some critics were suggesting that Sadler's Wells Opera was showing more spark and more innovation than Covent Garden. One major reason for this was the presence of the young Charles Mackerras. Mackerras had joined the orchestra at Sadler's Wells in 1947 as an oboist and cor anglais player. Then just a year later, after a spell in Prague, he returned as assistant conductor, beginning a relationship that ended only with his death in 2010. A lifelong champion of Janáček, he conducted the

British premiere of *Katya Kabanová* in 1951. He also conducted the premiere of *Turn of the Screw* when Britten returned to Sadler's Wells in 1954. He advocated a policy of staging lesser-known operas by, among others, Gluck, Handel and Donizetti. Working with the choreographer John Cranko, he created several ballets – including *Pineapple Poll*, made up of extracts from Sullivan's music for the Savoy Operas, and the innovative *Lady and the Fool* for which he arranged music by Verdi. Other new British works produced at Sadler's Wells during this period were Lennox Berkeley's opera *Nelson* (1954) and Arthur Benjamin's *Tale of Two Cities* (1957). After Mackerras, Alexander Gibson served as musical director for four years, resigning in 1961 to return to Scotland and found Scottish Opera. Colin Davis then took over, introducing, among many other things, Richard Rodney Bennett's first opera, *Mines of Sulphur*, in 1965. In 1968, the company moved to the 2,300-seat Coliseum Theatre and, in 1970, Mackerras returned in the role of musical director. During his tenure the company attracted huge praise for their English-language *Ring* cycle, conducted by Reginald Goodall. By the time the name was changed from Sadler's Wells to English National Opera in 1974, British opera had two world-class companies and had come a very long way from the uncertainties of 1945.

The twenty-five years following the end of the Second World War saw a complete transformation of infrastructure supporting classical music in Britain. New orchestras, new concert halls, new festivals, the emergence of revitalised opera and ballet companies were all part of the process, but in the long term the most significant change was probably in the role and importance of the BBC. By the end of the war, those who argued for more popular music on the radio appeared to winning. In the week beginning 6 May 1945, the amount of classical music heard on the Home Service and the General Forces Programme amounted to just twenty hours, although the fact that it attracted 3.5 million listeners demonstrated that there was still a large and receptive audience. And on VE Day, a thirty-minute broadcast by the BBC Symphony Orchestra and Chorus attracted 3.3 million listeners.[5] Then in 1946, the Third Programme was launched. The idea for the new network was based, as we have already noted, on a policy paper written by Arthur Bliss when he was Director of Music during the war, and it was given practical impetus by the Director General William Haley. In part, the Third Programme was an attempt to maintain the audience for classical music that had developed during the war years, but its remit was the arts in general, not just music. Indeed, for many years, classical music was also heard on the BBC's two other domestic networks. The Home Service carried news, drama and information-based programmes, but continued to broadcast concerts by the BBC Symphony and other orchestras; while the Light Programme, dedicated – as the name suggests – to light entertainment, also broadcast programmes of less demanding classical works.

The concept of the Third Programme marked a move away from the Reithian principle that the BBC should educate its audience – at least in that it separated 'the arts' from general programming and was thereby immediately open to accusations of elitism, which dogged its progress for many years. These reproaches were matched by others which accused the new network of conservatism, particularly in its choice of music, and it is certainly true that contemporary music by Continental composers did not feature largely – although it could easily be argued that in this respect the Third Programme was only reflecting what we have seen to be the national mood. On the other hand, a clear emphasis was placed on British composers and British music, which had been one of the demands made by the composers themselves just a few years previously. Contemporary figures such as Berkeley, Britten, Rawsthorne, Rubbra and Tippett were all heard regularly during the early years of the network; and the policy continued into the next generation, with special recognition given to women composers, including Elisabeth Lutyens, Elizabeth Maconchy, and Thea Musgrave.

British composers could be supported by programming their works. They could also be helped by receiving commissions. The BBC had begun commissioning new works in the 1930s. During wartime, commissions were seen as an extension of propaganda work and expected to amount to a 'new and healthy brand of patriotic music ... [giving] expression to our aims in the war and afterwards,'[6] which was somewhat limiting, if understandable in the circumstances. If composers hoped for major changes after 1945, they were to be disappointed. Commissioning policy was the preserve of the Director (later Controller) of Music and during the late 1940s and the 50s it remained essentially conservative. This was at least partly the result of administrative difficulties within the Corporation: there were no less than five Directors of Music between 1945 and 1952. Richard Howgill's appointment in 1952 seemed to offer more stability, but even under Howgill commissions were given to composers such as Alwyn,

Bliss and Rubbra who were regarded as safe. Only after 1959, when the determined and not always popular figure of William Glock became Controller did things change. Glock commissioned works from the likes of Elisabeth Lutyens, Malcolm Arnold, Peter Maxwell Davies and Harrison Birtwistle. Indeed, he went much further, arranging commissions and performances for genuinely avant-garde musicians: Oliver Messiaen, Hans Werner Henze, Luciano Berio, György Ligeti, Karlheinz Stockhausen. For once, the BBC appeared to be accepting contemporary music on its own terms and taking the risk of presenting it to the listening public. Yet the long-standing argument about the Corporation's role could not be so easily settled. Glock's policy aroused opposition both inside and outside the Corporation and when his successor, Robert Ponsonby, took over in 1972, he noted that the presentation of contemporary music remained a central problem.[7]

Some BBC commissions were given a broadcast first performance, but more often they were premiered at the Proms, which gained in stature significantly during the post-war decades. One crucial factor was the appointment of Sir Malcolm Sargent as Chief Conductor in 1948. Sargent could be a difficult character – both his orchestras and the BBC management could attest to his stubbornness and occasional bursts of temper – but the public loved him. He used his charm to reach out to the audience, and particularly to the young, boisterous promenaders. He turned the whole season, and especially the Last Night, which was now televised, into a national institution. There were many in the musical community who did not approve of what they saw as his showy, self-publicising antics, but for those watching on television or coming to music for the first time, Sargent was refreshing and unstuffy. These diverging attitudes were summed up in his nickname. Among disapproving orchestral players he was known as 'Flash Harry'. The young promenaders shortened this to 'Flash' and turned it into a term of affection. By the 1960s, Sargent was for many not just the public face of the Proms, but of classical music as a whole. His presence allowed the BBC management to drive the process of change. The Proms season was extended and the range of music greatly expanded. Glock, who from 1960 was Controller of the Proms as well as Controller of Music, was responsible for some much more adventurous programming. Participation by international artists and orchestras greatly increased. Solti, Stokowski, Giulini, Kubelik, Haitink and many others made Proms appearances. By the time Sargent stepped down in 1966, making way for

Colin Davis, the Proms had gone from a being national institution to an international one.

Sargent was too ill to conduct the 1967 Proms season, but appeared at the end of the Last Night to give a short speech which was rapturously received. He died two weeks later. Just three days before his death, BBC radio was transformed when a new network was added and the existing ones renamed and reconfigured. Radio 1 was given over to the new pop music which had become a phenomenon of the 1960s. Radio 2, the old Light Programme, continued to offer light entertainment. The Third Programme became Radio 3 and was able to devote itself almost entirely to what the BBC liked to call 'serious' music; while the Home Service became Radio 4 and concentrated on news, information, talk shows and drama as before, but dropped its musical component. That same summer, the BBC had also opened up its second television channel, BBC2, and begun broadcasting in colour. When Sir Adrian Boult conducted *The Dream of Gerontius* in Canterbury Cathedral in 1968, it became the first classical concert to be broadcast in colour on the BBC. Suddenly, it was a different world.

103   Benjamin Britten

The difference – one might even say the distance – between British composers and their Continental counterparts was again in evidence in their responses to the Second World War. Arguably, the two most iconic pieces of music to emerge from Continental Europe during World War Two were Olivier Messiaen's *Quartet for the End of Time*, written in 1940 when the composer was in a prisoner-of-war camp in Silesia, and Shostakovich's Seventh (*Leningrad*) Symphony, begun in July 1941 when he heard the news of the German invasion, and finished that December when Leningrad was already a city besieged. In a British context, the equivalent works would be Michael Tippett's secular oratorio *A Child of Our Time*, first performed in 1944, and Britten's *Peter Grimes*, premiered just a month after VE Day on 7 June 1945. Apart from the fact that both are vocal works and heavily dependent on a combination of words and music to convey their full message, they are also significantly more oblique in their approach to the idea and consequences of war. In one sense, this was inevitable: Britain had not been invaded and the composers' experience of war was that much less direct. Yet in both Britten and Tippett, that obliqueness is part of their style and personal idiom. Depending on context, it can convey certainty or doubt, but above all it conveys a strong sense of moral purpose behind the music.

Although Britten (1913–76) was the younger by eight years, his career took off first. The son of a dentist in the Suffolk town of Lowestoft, he grew up in a house overlooking the sea. His childhood appears to have been a happy one, although with tensions in the background. His father was an enigmatic figure, affectionate – particularly in letters when his son was away from home – but also daunting, and, perhaps because he was not musical himself, wanting to take a harder line on his son's upbringing than did his wife. There may have been love between the two of them, but there was not much understanding. Britten's mother, by contrast, was a talented amateur singer, understood her son's talents and was determined that he should succeed. She was undoubtedly the dominant influence in his early life. Britten himself, caught between the two, was a sensitive child, prone to anxiety.

He began piano lessons at seven, viola lessons at ten, and had reached the standard of piano playing usually required for college entrance by the age of twelve. Indeed, it was thought in the family that he might become a concert pianist, but Britten had already begun composing. By the age of fourteen he had a suitcase full of compositions. In 1927, while he was still at the local prep school, South Lodge, Mrs Britten engineered an introduction to Frank Bridge, who was sufficiently impressed to agree to take Britten as a pupil. This involved Britten and his mother taking day or overnight trips to London and Britten's latest juvenile compositions being subjected to rigorous dissection and criticism. In 1928, having won a musical scholarship worth £30 a year, Britten went to the supposedly progressive Gresham's School in Holt, Norfolk. For him, it was not a happy experience. He felt that the music teacher, Walter Greatorex – composer of the hymn tune *Woodlands* ('Lift Up Your Hearts') – was discouraging, even hostile. But lessons with Bridge continued, and that same year Britten wrote *Quatre Chansons Françaises*, orchestral settings of two poems by Victor Hugo and two by Verlaine, in honour of his parents' twenty-seventh wedding anniversary. For a fifteen-year-old boy, it was an astonishing work.

Britten endured two years at Gresham's and then, in 1930, won a scholarship to the RCM. Frank Bridge continued to take an interest in his progress, but his composition teacher was now John Ireland. It was not a happy relationship: Ireland was moody and often drunk, while Britten was going through a phase of adolescent self-assertion. He was highly critical of much British music – Elgar, Bax, Moeran, Bliss and Vaughan Williams were all dismissed. He preferred Richard Strauss, Mahler, Stravinsky and Berg, although he did admire Walton's work, particularly the Viola Concerto; and Beethoven, his first great musical love, remained matchless.

In 1931, the violinist Anne Macnaghten, the conductor Iris Lemare and the composer Elisabeth Lutyens began a concert series with the aim of promoting contemporary classical music. Based at the Mercury Theatre in London's Notting Hill, the Macnaghten-Lemare concerts, as they became known, ran for six years and gave many young composers, including Britten, an early opportunity to hear their work performed. Britten had several pieces programmed, including his *Sinfonietta* for ten instruments – an early work but one that already showed a characteristic mixture of contemporary European music influence and English lyricism. In 1933, he had his first experience of hearing his work on the radio when the BBC took up his *Phantasy Quartet* for oboe and strings. As well as writing, he was thinking hard about his mental approach to music and decided that technical excellence was the root of musical achievement. He won a £100 travel scholarship and proposed using it to study with Berg in Vienna. This was vetoed, probably by Sir Hugh Allen, the RCM's Director, who regarded Berg's music as unacceptably modern. In February 1934, the BBC broadcast another work, *A Boy Was Born*, a setting of ten fifteenth- and sixteenth-century texts relating to Christmas, ingeniously structured as a theme and variations and successfully mixing modernity with echoes of Elizabethan choral writing. It was Britten's first major choral work and his first to deal with religious themes. When his father died that April, extracts were played at his funeral in Lowestoft. *A Boy Was Born* was immediately followed by the neo-classical *Simple Symphony*, a highly accessible and still popular (although not actually simple) piece, based on themes taken from compositions found in his childhood suitcase. He conducted its first performance in Norwich in March, and Oxford University Press agreed to publish it. He eventually spent his scholarship money on a musical journey to Basel, Salzburg and Vienna, accompanied by his mother. They arrived back in November 1934. Britten was twenty-one and no longer a student. His music had certainly attracted interest, as well as a certain amount of criticism. He was poised on the brink of a musical career, but at that moment what he needed most was a job.

The period between 1935 and 1939, when he left for the United States, was crucial to Britten's development, both as a composer and as an individual. On the recommendation on the RCM, he was offered a job in the General Post Office (GPO) Film Unit, headed by John Grierson. The Unit made documentaries on topics related to the GPO and its activities. Although in later life Britten was reluctant to attribute too much importance to this period, it is clear that it was a formative one. His first score was for a short film called *The King's Stamp*, and Grierson was impressed by his ability to work quickly and effectively, and to create sound effects using instruments, electronic gadgets or even household objects. Nineteen more films followed, including *The Savings Bank, Sorting Office*, and the most often-quoted examples, *Coal Face* and *Night Mail*, both of which featured texts by W. H. Auden. The experience alerted Britten to the possibility of writing other forms of incidental music and, between 1935 and 1937, he wrote a total of forty scores for short films, radio programmes and theatre productions.

Britten was also wrestling with two important personal issues at this time: pacifism and homosexuality. Even at school, he had held broadly pacifist views, and these were no doubt strengthened by his association with Bridge, himself a determined, although not militant, pacifist. The extent of Bridge's influence is manifested in the work Britten wrote for the Salzburg Festival in 1937, *Variations on a Theme of Frank Bridge*. Each of the ten variations was intended to represent a particular aspect of Bridge's personality – energy, charm, humour, skill, and so on – and, despite being written at high speed, the work was immensely successful, bringing Britten to international attention for the first time. A less successful work was *Our Hunting Fathers*, an orchestral song cycle, first performed the previous year. Written for 'high voice' and orchestra, it made what were then considered unusual demands on both, and was held to be aggressively modern in style. The text, by W. H. Auden, was both broadly pacifist in intent and clearly an attack on the state of European politics, the final moments clearly identifying Germans as the hunters and Jews as the hunted. It was not the last time a new work by Britten would leave an audience bewildered.

The death of Britten's mother in January 1937 was devastating, but it was also liberating. She had believed in him, encouraged him, mapped out his life for him. In return, he had focussed his attention on her. Friends commented that her death allowed him to have a personal life of his own for the first time. It was just a month later that he met Peter Pears (1910–86) and for the next two years the two of them were edging towards to a permanent relationship. It took that long because Britten was still exploring his own nature, and still uncertain where emotional and sexual matters were concerned. Their partnership, when it eventually came about, was both musical and personal and lasted forty years.

Another life-changing event of 1937 was the discovery of the village of Snape in Suffolk, where Britten used the money he inherited from his mother to buy the Old Mill. At the time, it seemed that Lennox Berkeley might be the partner Britten was looking for. Berkeley moved into the Old Mill and collaborated on a suite of Catalan dances, *Mont Juic*; and he was the dedicatee of Britten's Piano Concerto, written in 1938. The Concerto was premiered at that year's Proms at the Queen's Hall with Wood conducting and Britten himself as soloist. The virtuosic qualities and technical brilliance of the piece were appreciated, but H. C. Colles, the influential, if somewhat stuffy music critic of *The Times*, identified a sense of mockery, even satire, in the work, which made him wonder if the composer was actually serious.[1] But it was Peter Pears, not Berkeley, who accompanied Britten when he set off for the United States in April 1939.

W. H. Auden had been a powerful influence on Britten ever since their first meeting in 1935, during Britten's time with the GPO Film Unit. They had worked together on *Our Hunting Fathers*, on a number of settings of Auden's poetry, and on incidental music for the Auden-Isherwood plays, *The Ascent of F6* and *On the Frontier*. It was more than just collaboration. Auden was a mentor to Britten. He encouraged his pacifism, edged him towards left-wing political views, and pressed him to acknowledge his homosexuality. So when Auden and Christopher Isherwood left for North America, there was a sense that it was an example for Britten to follow. Britten and Pears went first to Canada, then to Amityville in Massachusetts where they stayed with a rich, cultured German émigré family, the Mayers. For a short period they shared a house in Brooklyn with, among others, Auden and the writers Paul and Jane Bowles. They spent a summer in California. When the war broke out, they approached the British Embassy in Washington for advice and were told that, as they were not technically qualified to help the war effort, it was better for them to stay in the United States as representatives of British culture. It was advice they accepted, although not without some reluctance, and the fact that they did not return was misunderstood and criticised in Britain.

If Britten was hoping for generous commissions or film work in the

United States, he was to be disappointed. There was some work and there were some commissions, but they were not generous ones. Pears was offered a number of singing engagements which kept him afloat financially, but riches did not come their way. Nonetheless, for Britten it was a productive period musically. He completed the vivid, if troubled Rimbaud song cycle, *Les Illuminations*, which was premiered by the soprano Sophie Wyss in London in January 1940 – although it can also be sung by a tenor and was often sung by Pears. He finished the Violin Concerto, premiered by Antonio Brosa with Barbirolli and the New York Philharmonic also in 1940. He wrote a second song cycle, *Seven Sonnets of Michelangelo,* for tenor and piano. Each song dealt with a different aspect of love, and Britten dedicated the cycle to Pears. He also wrote the *Sinfonia da Requiem* in response to a commission from the Japanese Government for a work to celebrate the 2,600th anniversary of the Japanese Empire. Quite how Britten thought an ostensibly Christian work would suit such an occasion is a matter for conjecture. It is divided into three movements, each of which takes its title from the Catholic Mass for the Dead ('Lacrymosa', 'Dies Irae', 'Requiem Aeternam') and was, on his own admission, intended to express his anti-war sentiments. Unsurprisingly, the Japanese Government rejected it; Britten kept the money; and the whole issue evaporated when the Japanese attacked Pearl Harbour. *Sinfonia da Requiem* was premiered in 1941, again by Barbirolli and the New York Philharmonic, and received a generally positive critical response.

The one other large-scale work Britten completed while in North America was the operetta, *Paul Bunyan*, commissioned for a student production at Columbia University in 1941. The obvious collaborator was Auden, and together they chose Bunyan, a legendary lumberjack and pioneer of the American West, as the subject. The work may have been written with half an eye on Broadway, but Auden's libretto – and particularly the decision that Bunyan himself should not appear on stage – reduced the dramatic potential of the piece. Critical reception was at best mixed, although some reviews took a more positive view of Britten's music. The real significance of the piece was that it whetted Britten's appetite for the operatic stage.

Britten and Pears left New York on the Swedish cargo ship, *Axel Johnson*, in March 1942. They were bound for Liverpool, but it was a slow and uncomfortable voyage that lasted nearly a month. Britten's last months in North America had been marked by a creative block. Once on board, he found he could compose again. He worked on his *Hymn to Saint Cecilia*, again to a text by Auden,[2] and *A Ceremony of Carols*, for harp and treble voices, which has since become a popular Christmas work. To understand what was driving Britten at this stage of his career, these two pieces need to be seen together with the 1943 cantata *Rejoice in the Lamb*, based on the poem *Jubilate Agno* by the eighteenth-century poet, gardener and eccentric, Christopher Smart. All three are choral works in the English tradition and they marked his re-engagement with England – a musical parallel to his physical return to the country of his birth. The decision to celebrate Saint Cecilia placed him in a line of composers stretching back to Purcell and beyond (although it should not be forgotten that St Cecilia's Day was also his birthday); the boys' (that is, treble) voices used in *A Ceremony of Carols* created a characteristically English sound; while *Rejoice in the Lamb* with its idiosyncratic text and musical references to Purcell was again squarely in the English or British choral tradition. Moreover, all three in their different ways addressed the issue of innocence – its original purity, its loss, the suffering and oppression of man resulting from that loss, and the possibility of restoring or re-creating innocence. This concern was perhaps partly personal, but it was certainly also a response to the war and the state of the world, and it was central to Britten's thinking at this time. It would be one of the starting points for *Peter Grimes*.

One of the main reasons Britten returned to Britain was homesickness, and one contributory factor to that homesickness was reading an article by E. M. Forster about the work of the Suffolk poet George Crabbe. He went on to read Crabbe's poem *The Borough*, based on life in Aldeburgh, just down the road from Snape; one section of it tells the story of a fisherman called Peter Grimes. Britten claimed that he knew at once that Suffolk was where he really belonged and that Peter Grimes was the perfect subject for an opera. Once back in London, he approached the writer Montagu Slater, with whom he had worked in the GPO Film Unit, about a libretto. Britten received financial help from the Koussevitzky Music Foundation, but there were still many trials and tribulations – including a certain amount of trouble with the company at Sadler's Wells Opera, which we touched on earlier. In the end, however, *Peter Grimes* came to the stage in June 1945.

Peter Grimes is a consciously enigmatic work: the isolated, determined, old misfit; the death of two of his apprentices; the community that becomes a persecuting mob. Guilt joins innocence as one of Britten's themes. Is Grimes the victim of his own character, of fate, or of society? It is left to the audience to decide. That *Peter Grimes* is a great work is without question. Frequently acclaimed as the first great British opera since Purcell, it marked Britten's transition from a promising young composer to an established and respected one. It is grimly pessimistic about the human condition and the world in general – some early commentators, Frank Howes and John Ireland among them, saw it as having a diabolic or Satanic quality – and the tragedy unfolds with an inevitability that does not depend on operatic coincidence or plot devices. In that sense, it can fairly be seen as the composer's response to the Second World War. There have been other more personal interpretations, including a suggestion that the work should be seen as a parable of the oppression or persecution of homosexuals. Given the nature of Britten's later operas, such an interpretation is certainly plausible, but that does not necessarily contradict the idea that *Peter Grimes* represents the world as Britten saw it at that time.

The music is of European descent, but there are moments when the English lyric tradition is not far away. The four 'Sea Interludes' in particular stand in a long British tradition of representing the sea in musical terms which includes Purcell, Stanford, Ethel Smyth, Delius and, of course, Frank Bridge. In 1941, Britten wrote an article for the American journal, *Modern Music*, entitled 'England and the Folk-Art Problem'.[3] In it, he attacked English (while probably meaning British) cultural insularity. He dismissed folk song as the basis of English musical tradition and denied the validity of the idea of English national music. The article probably reflects the influence of Auden, for within two or thee years Britten had changed his position. He never became a paid-up pastoralist, but once back in Britain his output clearly suggested a belief in some kind of national identity expressed through music. There were two volumes of English folk songs (1943 and 1947), and the *Serenade for Tenor, Horn and Strings* (1943), effectively a song cycle for Peter Pears based on English lyric poetry. Around the time of the two-hundred-and-fiftieth anniversary of Purcell's death in 1945, he produced a number of Purcell-related works: realisations of some thirty of Purcell's songs; the ever-popular *Young Person's Guide to the Orchestra* (1945), based on a theme by Purcell; and in 1951 his own arrangement of *Dido and Aeneas*. Moreover, Britten committed himself to his own part of rural England. In 1948, he set up the Aldeburgh Festival, which soon involved a lot of what we would now call outreach, and, in 1951, he accepted the freedom of Lowestoft, in his speech for the occasion presenting himself as an artist whose role was to serve the community.[4] *Peter*

Grimes was an integral part of this repositioning. It was a modern master-piece; it was challenging; but it was rooted in England, in English literature, and in English history. Critics and audiences recognised and respected that.

Britten's next opera, *The Rape of Lucretia*, which was premiered at Glyndebourne in July 1946, showed that he was not afraid to change and to experiment. In the first place, it was chamber opera, requiring only eight singers and thirteen musicians. The expansiveness of *Peter Grimes* was replaced with a taut, economical score, and the narrative was carried not only by the action on stage, but also by description and commentary from a male and a female chorus – in each case an individual singer: Peter Pears and Joan Cross in the original production. The enigma of Grimes is paral-leled by ambiguity in the character of Lucretia who, it is implied, actually secretly desires Tarquinius, her rapist. And there is a significant develop-ment also in the ending of the work. Grimes' suicide is simply escape: he is offered no chance of redemption. Lucretia's suicide, having told her husband of the rape, is followed by an explicitly Christian epilogue, emphasising the possibility of redemption through the suffering of Christ. The libretto, written by Ronald Duncan, who had provided the words for a *Pacifist March* composed by Britten for the Peace Pledge Union before the war, did not originally include this last section. Humphrey Carpenter states that Britten himself asked for it to be added.[5] It is true that without the epilogue, the ending of *Lucretia* would be bleak indeed, but Britten's request may have had a personal as well as an artistic explanation.

A month after the premier of *Peter Grimes*, Britten went to Germany as accompanist to Yehudi Menuhin. They gave recitals to survivors of the concentration camps and visited the hospital at Belsen. It was a harrowing experience. On his return, Britten immediately embarked on a new song cycle, *The Holy Sonnets of John Donne*, a modernistic, even angry work, which concentrates on the poet's efforts to believe that despite man, and man's evil, salvation might still be possible. Carpenter has suggested that *The Holy Sonnets* could even be seen as a kind of epilogue to *Peter Grimes*. He quotes Pears as saying that for many years Britten would never talk about Belsen. Only at the end of his life did he say that the experience had influenced everything he had written since.[6]

Lucretia's fourteen performances at Glyndebourne were well attended, but on tour it played to half-empty houses and lost money. *Albert Herring* was premiered in June 1947, just eleven months after *Lucretia*, again at Glyndebourne, although by this time relations between John Christie and

Britten had soured and this was their last co-operation. In some ways, it is a complete contrast to *Peter Grimes* and *Lucretia*. It is a comic piece, based on a story by Guy de Maupassant, with an excellent, genuinely funny libretto by Eric Crozier, who had directed *Peter Grimes*. Britten's score is lively and brilliant, full of caricature, parody and a lots of witty references to well-known pieces of English music. Looked at in another way, however, it repeats *Peter Grimes* in a different context. Loxford is a version of the Borough. Albert is an outsider – the son of a greengrocer, dominated by his mother and hopelessly unassertive – but an innocent. The society around him is class-ridden and corrupt – at least in that there are no female virgins to be found who can be crowned May Queen. Through a combination of circumstances and alcohol, Albert breaks free. In doing so, he establishes a moral distance between himself and Loxford society. Whether he will maintain that distance is not absolutely clear, although – this being a comic opera – there are indications in both the libretto and the score that he will.

Although John Christie famously told friends attending the first night that 'this isn't our kind of thing, you know',[7] and despite a degree of critical carping, *Albert Herring* was, and has remained, popular with the opera-going public. Following the short run at Glyndebourne, Britten and Pears took the new opera, together with *Lucretia*, on tour to Holland and Switzerland. Performances were sold out, but the tour still lost money. It was at this point that Pears suggested it would be better to stage operas on their home ground and proposed an Aldeburgh Festival. Despite the logistical difficulties, a combination of dedication, hard work and enthusiastic local co-operation meant that they were able to hold the first Festival in 1948. It opened with the premiere of Britten's cantata, *Saint Nicholas*, and featured revivals of both *Lucretia* and *Albert Herring*. The 1949 Festival saw the premiere of *Let's Make an Opera!*, a continuation of Britten's concern to demystify classical music that had been evident in *A Young Person's Guide to the Orchestra* four years previously. The first part is a play about writing an opera, while the second consists of the short, three-scene opera, *The Little Sweep*. The insistence on audience participation – the audience provide the chorus – was considered daring at the time but has contributed to the work's lasting popularity with both children and adults.

Even before *Let's Make an Opera!* was completed, Britten was thinking about another full-scale, serious work. With E. M. Forster as principal librettist and Crozier as technical adviser, he embarked on *Billy Budd*, based on Herman Melville's last and posthumously-published novella. In its original four-act form – it was later revised and restructured to be two acts framed by a prologue and an epilogue – it received its premiere at Covent Garden in December 1951. Set on a nineteenth-century warship, the plot once again centres on an outsider, Billy Budd, whose innocence incurs the hatred of Claggart, the Master-at-Arms, and leads to his downfall and death. Once again, the central figure is faced with a moral dilemma. In this case, Captain de Vere, the tenor role sung by Pears, must decide whether to respond to his humanitarian feelings or obey the rules. And once again, the opera ends with a clear message that redemption is possible. Yet it was not an easy story to shape into operatic form. Melville's novella had obvious homosexual overtones – indeed, in the early stages Forster wanted the opera to be about the redemptive qualities of homosexual love – whereas Britten wanted a work with a universal application. There was also the problem of writing a full-scale opera with an all-male cast. In the end, however, the plot took on classical proportions – innocence and hubris leading to nemesis and eventual redemption – and the enclosed setting on board a warship is so credible that the absence of female roles goes unquestioned. Some critics have cast doubt on Billy's role as a Christ figure; others have found the motives for Claggart's evil insufficient; but there is no doubt that on stage the opera works. Although Britten uses a large orchestra, his music remains within the world of the ship. He makes no attempt to describe or characterise the sea as he did in *Peter Grimes*. Instead, there is an enhanced concentration on, and sensitivity to, individuals. He uses his orchestral resources to realise their constantly changing moods, shifting almost restlessly between virtuoso solo passages, different combinations of instruments, different rhythms, and the power of full orchestral passages.

Billy Budd took Britten to a new level of success. There were tears among the first night audience when the curtain fell, and even the usually reserved Frank Howes felt that this was the opera that Britten's followers had been waiting for. It was ten years since he and Pears had returned from the United States, and it is almost impossible to overestimate what he had achieved in that time. 'Uncle Ralph', now eighty, might remain the Grand Old Man, but Britten, not yet forty, was the composer in whom hopes for the future of British music were now vested. He had achieved the impossible: an English composer, he had written operas that were accepted and acknowledged as the equal of Continental operas. He had, in fact, written five operas, a cantata, several orchestral works, and several song cycles; he had given innumerable recitals as Pears' accompanist; and, in addition, he had helped to set up a major music festival. Of course, he was not universally popular. As ever when any public figure reaches new heights of popularity, there were those ready and waiting to drag him down – and sometimes Britten himself helped them.

Gloriana was written for, and first performed as part of the celebrations surrounding Queen Elizabeth II's Coronation in 1953. The libretto, by the poet Christopher Plomer, was based largely on Lytton Strachey's book *Elizabeth and Essex* and, in consequence, is a warts-and-all portrayal of an ageing queen, forced by her public position to make difficult decisions and frequently thrown back on her awareness of mortality. To complement this, Britten not only evolved a musical style that alluded to the rhythms and harmonies of Elizabethan music, but also included a masque, lute songs and period dances on stage as part of the action. The whole thing was clever and it was original, but it was a misjudgement. It was not what was expected for a major royal occasion. The first night audience was described as bewildered.[8] *Gloriana* itself was criticised for being inappropriate, for showing a lack of respect towards the monarchy, for being boring, for being too much of a pageant, for being a musical pastiche, and for being generally unsatisfactory. That the critics contradicted themselves did not matter. The poor reception contributed to Britten's growing resentment against them.

In the wake of *Gloriana*, Britten took a break from opera and wrote *Winter Words*, a song cycle for tenor and piano, based on eight poems by Thomas Hardy. He and Pears gave the first performance at the 1953 Leeds Festival. But the break was a short one, and he soon determined that his next opera would be based on Henry James's *Turn of the Screw*, although he did not even start composition until just five months before the premiere, which took place at La Fenice in Venice in September 1954. Like *Lucretia*, *The Turn of the Screw* is a chamber opera, but it is a much more complex work. The plot is a psychological thriller, which turns on two ghosts returning to 'reclaim' the children of the house where they once worked; and with whom, it is hinted, they may have had inappropriately close relationships. Britten gives an almost sinister prominence to W. B. Yeats's line, 'The ceremony of innocence is drowned.' Musically, too, there is a complexity which is necessary to carry the twists and turns of the plot. Britten mixes straightforward tonality and savage dissonance; and at the beginning of each scene there is a variation on a particular twelve-note motif, which seems to grow more threatening as the opera progresses. *The Turn of the Screw* received a much warmer welcome than *Gloriana* and is revived regularly.

In concentrating on Britten's major works, it is easy to forget or under-estimate the importance of his performing career. Although he was frequently nervous before a performance – even to the point of being physically sick – he was not only a conductor to whom orchestral players felt they could relate, he was also a brilliant accompanist. In 1955, he and Peter Pears set off on an extended journey, a mixture of concert tour and holiday, which took them to Austria and Yugoslavia, on to India, Singapore, Java, Bali, and Japan, before turning back to Thailand and what was then Ceylon. The trip offered Britten a break after an intense period of composition – three new operas in four years; it also offered the chance to explore some unfamiliar musical traditions. Bali provided the inspiration for *Prince of the Pagodas*, a ballet, choreographed by John Cranko, that was given at Covent Garden on New Year's Day 1957. It was Britten's first major work following his return, and his longest ever orchestral score, notable for the use of tuned percussion and clever orchestral scoring to imitate Balinese gamelan music. Japan, in due course, was to prove equally influential.

There is no doubt that the rate at which Britten composed did slow as he grew older, but it was still formidable. *The Prince of the Pagodas* was followed by *Noye's Fludde* (1958), a one-act opera taking its text from one of the fifteenth-century Chester mystery plays. Written for amateur performance, the piece clearly harks back to *Let's Make an Opera!* and Britten's belief in communal music-making. Children provide the chorus of animals and birds entering and leaving the ark, while the audience is required to sing two hymns; and there are some remarkable sound effects, made using cups, saucers and plates, as well as hand bells – the latter again reflecting Britten's new interest in gamelan music. Then came *A Midsummer Night's Dream*, which was premiered at the 1960 Aldeburgh Festival. It is Britten's most relaxed opera in that the story is familiar and the music less intense than *Albert Herring*, his only other comic work. Shakespeare's plot is altered only slightly in order to place more emphasis on the opposition between innocence and experience, but the opera is unusual in that the lead role, that of Oberon, is given to a counter-tenor. The role was created specifically for Alfred Deller (1912–79), the English singer who had done more than anyone else to revive the counter-tenor style of singing. Peter Pears, who usually played the lead role in Britten's operas, was given the comic role of Flute, one of the mechanicals, and was then required to dress as a woman to play Thisbe. All those who saw it remember his performance as hysterically funny.

Britten's *War Requiem* was composed for the reconsecration of Coventry Cathedral in 1962. It is a big work which, as we have seen, eclipsed Bliss's *Beatitudes*, written for the same occasion, and is generally regarded as his non-operatic masterpiece. A soprano solo, a mixed chorus and a choir of boys' voices sing the six movements of the Latin Requiem Mass accompanied by a full orchestra. These movements are broken up by settings of nine of Wilfred Owen's war poems, sung by tenor and baritone soloists and accompanied by a chamber orchestra. Only at the end do all these musical forces join up for the work's climactic conclusion. It was broadcast live on the BBC and, for once, critical reaction was unanimously positive. Even the listening public, usually sceptical where contemporary music was concerned, was overwhelmed. In 1963, when the *Requiem*, with Britten conducting, was recorded and issued on two LPs, it sold over 200,000 sets.

Even then, in the face of such unprecedented praise, Britten would not be tied down to a particular style or approach. *Curlew River* (1964) was the first of three 'Parables for the Church' – in practice, one-act chamber operas – that appeared during the mid-1960s. A Madwoman and a Traveller wish to cross Curlew River in the Ferryman's boat. The Ferryman tells them the story of a boy who died and is buried on the far bank. The boy turns out to be the son of the Madwoman. Once she knows that his soul is at peace, her madness departs. The most obvious dramatic source was the Japanese Noh play, *Sumida River*, which Britten had seen in Tokyo, but librettist Christopher Plomer turned the piece into a Christian parable, its starkness and simplicity suggesting the atmosphere of medieval mystery plays on which Britten had drawn in the past. Similarly, the musical style seems to derive from Japanese *Gagku* or court music, using oriental heterophonic techniques,[9] but Britten adds a western and medieval dimension by taking the ancient hymn *Te lucis ante terminum* as the source of most of the work's musical motifs. The result is a unique fusion of east and west, and of ancient and modern, which he repeated and extended in the other two parables: *The Burning Fiery Furnace* (1966), telling the story of the three Israelites who refuse to worship Nebuchadnezzar's golden statue, and *The Prodigal Son* (1968).

In 1966, Britten and Pears came up with the idea of providing a permanent home for the Aldeburgh Festival in the old malt house complex at Snape. They moved with impressive speed and the following year the Maltings Concert Hall was formally opened by the Queen. Other buildings in the complex were gradually reclaimed and fitted out as performance or rehearsal spaces and, despite a major fire in 1969 that entailed extensive rebuilding, the Maltings have remained the home of the Festival ever since. Britten's last two operas both had their first performance there, although in the case of *Owen Wingrave*, this was in front of television cameras rather than an audience. The opera was commissioned by the BBC, filmed at Snape in November 1970, and broadcast on BBC2 the following year. Like *The Turn of the Screw*, the opera was based on a story by Henry James and the libretto was by Myfanwy Piper, wife of John Piper, the artist and designer of stained-glass windows, who designed the sets for a number of Britten's operas. *Owen Wingrave* is not one of Britten's better operas. The plot contains a number of familiar elements – pacifism, an outsider oppressed by the expectations of others (in this case of family and tradition), self-realisation in death – and it is innovative in that it allows for television cross-cutting techniques to move the narrative forward, but the work as a whole seems somehow obvious, and the characterisation lacks subtlety. What is noticeable, however, is that Britten chose to continue his experimentation with gamelan-style tuned percussion in one of his mainstream operas.

It is always tempting to read extra significance into a last work. Britten was only sixty when *Death in Venice* was given its first performance at Snape in 1973, but he had known almost from the start of composition that he would need a major heart operation, and there are aspects of the opera which differ significantly from its predecessors. The idea of adapting Thomas Mann's novel came from Pears originally, but Britten was closely involved with librettist Myfanwy Piper in shaping the story. Aschenbach, an ageing novelist, arrives in Venice, but is revolted by the beggars, the filth and in particular by the outrageous, unrestrained campness of an Elderly Fop. He becomes fascinated by Tadzio, a beautiful young Polish boy, but is forced to face the fact that his interest, which he wanted to believe was detached and aesthetic, has both an obsessive and a sexual quality to it. Yet Aschenbach never even speaks to the boy. He watches from a distance until he dies, sitting on the beach, still watching. *Death in Venice* was the first, indeed the only, Britten opera in which the homosexual implications of the plot were not buried or disguised, but that does not make it any less enigmatic. Did Britten see himself as Aschenbach – caught between the crude antics and expectations of the overtly homosexual community, and an attraction, conditioned by his nature, on which he could never act? And what of Aschenbach's death? Does he somehow recapture lost innocence? Or is his physical death a metaphor for spiritual death?

Britten's music for *Death in Venice* is both simple in texture and complex in application. He uses a standard orchestra with the addition of Balinese gamelans, yet there are only three full-orchestra passages in two-and-a-half hours of opera. The rest is contained within chamber music textures, but, as Humphrey Carpenter points out, the music seems to hark back to moments and styles from previous operas – a sea interlude transferred to the Adriatic; a *Billy Budd* shanty as the boat approaches Venice; Tadzio's gamelan theme echoing *Curlew River*; the choral dances recalling *Gloriana*. Was Britten consciously looking back over his career? Or was he, as a mature composer, simply displaying his mastery of different styles?

Britten died in 1976, aged sixty-two. He was an incredibly prolific composer and there are many works that cannot be given proper consideration in these pages – his *Five Canticles*, for example, written between 1947 and 1974 and not based on religious texts, but nonetheless giving expression to his deep religious feelings; or the series of cello works he wrote for Mstislav Rostropovich in the 1960s and 70s. In the end, however, Britten is defined by his operas and one or two other works, such as the *War Requiem*. He saw himself as an outsider, expressing through music ideas which challenged the establishment, although – like so many others before him – it was an establishment he eventually joined: the year before his death he became the first composer to accept a life peerage. His music challenged audiences, too, and even today there is a sizeable community of music lovers who find his work unpalatable or incomprehensible. Others claim that he is a musician's composer; that singing or playing his work, or involvement in things like *Let's Make an Opera!* or *Noye's Fludde*, leads to a greater understanding of what he is trying to do. Forty years after his death, Britten is still capable of arousing argument and controversy, but few would dispute that in the decades after the Second World War, he did more than anyone else to raise the profile and reputation of British music.

Michael Tippett (1905–98) was Britain's other great post-war composer. The word *other* is chosen deliberately. Britten was gifted and precocious. He did not really choose to become a composer: he just followed his very obvious talent. With Tippett, it was different. There was a piano in the family home in Suffolk; he took piano lessons with local teachers; his mother sang songs by Quilter and Somervell and other Victorian song-writers; but it was not a particularly musical home and Tippet himself did not appear especially musical. What precocity he displayed was for reading and literature.

His school years were difficult. At prep school in Dorset, he got into trouble for writing an essay which denied the existence of God. At Fettes College in Edinburgh, he had a homosexual relationship with another boy, and his parents moved him to Stamford Grammar School, where Malcolm Sargent had studied. For three or four years, things went well. He took piano lessons with Mrs Tinkler (who had taught Sargent), and it was when he attended a concert in Leicester, with Sargent conducting, that he made up his mind that he wanted to be a composer. Then his rebellious streak kicked in. He refused to join the school cadet corps, boycotted house prayers, and was duly expelled. By this time his parents, in financial diffi-culties after the First World War, had moved to France. Tippett decided to stay in Stamford. He continued piano lessons with Mrs Tinkler, took organ lessons with the church organist and bought a copy of *Musical Composition* by Stanford. Eventually, in 1923, after much effort and despite a lack of formal qualifications, he was accepted by the RCM. Nothing could be further from the smooth progress of Britten's early years.

Tippett's time at the RCM was undistinguished. He studied composition with Hugh Allen, and conducting with Boult and Sargent, but he was not one of those whose student compositions were performed to great acclaim. When he graduated – at the second attempt – he went to live in Oxted in Surrey, conducting local choirs and teaching French at a prep school. By 1930, he felt able to arrange a concert of his own music. The critics were sympathetic, but Tippet himself was disappointed and went back to the RCM on a part-time basis, taking counterpoint lessons with R. O. Morris.

The 1930s were a troubled but formative time for Tippett. The impact of the depression strengthened his left-wing views. He wrote a ballad opera,

Robin Hood, for a work camp of unemployed miners in Yorkshire. He conducted the South London Orchestra, which was made up of unemployed musicians. His socialist ballet scenarios for Alan Bush also belong to this period. For a few months, he even joined the Communist Party, but he soon realised that political activity got in the way of composing. On a personal level, he had a passionate six-year affair with a young painter, Wilfred Franks. It was the break-up of this relationship in 1938 that led Tippett to undertake Jungian dream analysis. His compositions during these years show him maturing slowly. His First String Quartet (1935), the Piano Sonata (1938), and the attractive and melodic Concerto for Double String Orchestra (1939) all combine a strong sense of rhythm with folk-derived motifs. The Concerto, in particular, shows Tippett's willingness to fuse different musical genres, mixing Renaissance-style antiphonal effects with echoes of the blues and a tune originally written for the Northumbrian smallpipes. He also began sketching out ideas for *A Child of Our Time*, but it was only when he came out of analysis – in fact on the day Britain declared war of Germany – that he began writing with new confidence and authority. He said later that Jungian analysis helped him accept his homosexuality and understand how it could feed into his creativity.

A Child of Our Time was initially inspired by the story of Herschel Grynszpan, a Polish refugee who murdered a Nazi diplomat in Paris and thus sparked Hitler's *Kristallnacht* pogrom. It grew into a secular and pacifist oratorio, highlighting the sufferings of oppressed people throughout the world. Tippett acknowledges tradition by basing the work's three-part structure on Handel's *Messiah*: he begins with exposition and prophecy, moves on to a central narrative, and concludes with metaphysical speculation on how man can achieve healing. He asked T. S. Eliot to write the text, but Eliot refused – on the grounds that the kind of poetic language he used would get in the way of the music – so Tippett wrote it himself, constructing a central opposition between light and shade, which has clear Jungian overtones. Tippett's musical language is tonal and accessible. The orchestral writing is strongly rhythmic, while the choral and solo parts are recognisably English in style, characterised by a strong sense of the natural pace and rhythm of the English language. His main innovation was to integrate five Negro spirituals into the fabric of the work. These are carefully placed at those points where in a Bach Passion there would have been a chorale or a hymn. Tippett saw this as a way of emphasising the universality of suffering and oppression; early critics accused him of bad taste.

A Child of Our Time was finished in 1941, but not performed until 1944, when it was given under the baton of Walter Goehr at London's Adelphi Theatre, with Peter Pears and Joan Cross taking two of the solo parts. Public and critical reaction was generally positive. Arthur Bliss at the BBC agreed to arrange a broadcast performance at the beginning of 1945, and shortly after that Tippett himself conducted a full-scale performance at the Royal Albert Hall. The success of *A Child of Our Time* certainly propelled him to public notice, but in musical circles his reputation had been growing for some time. Since 1940, he had been working as Director of Music at Morley College and had achieved some success in reconstructing the College's musical life after the buildings had been hit by a bomb and the staff and students dispersed to safer premises. In 1942, his Second String Quartet and a pair of madrigals ('The Source' and 'The Windhover' to texts by Edward Thomas and Gerald Manley Hopkins) had been well received, and then in 1943 he had written *Boyhood's End*, an unusual, almost baroque-style cantata for tenor and piano, intended for Pears and Britten, whom he had met when they returned from the United States. And, of course, he had attracted attention and sympathy for his principled pacifist stance, which led to him spending three months in Wormwood Scrubs.

While in prison, Tippett had begun thinking about a symphony. He finished it in 1945 and it was given its first hearing by Malcolm Sargent and the Liverpool Philharmonic. Highly rhythmic and contrapuntal – characteristics of much of Tippett's instrumental music – it deserves to be called a war symphony, but not in an obvious descriptive or emotional sense. There is plenty of emotion there, but it is controlled. Tippet argues his way through the four movements, as if his thematic material represented the human spirit and he was determined to see it survive and win through. And it does – in a way. The work ends with a remarkable musical collapse which manages to suggest both finality and continuity.

Tippett's work at Morley College included some landmark events – including the first performance in modern times (and first ever British performance) of Monteverdi's 1610 *Vespers* – but in 1951 he resigned. He knew it was not a financially prudent decision, but he wanted to concentrate on composition and felt that teaching and other commitments were simply getting in the way. He went to live at Tidebrook Manor in East Sussex, which he shared with his mother, intending to finish his opera, *The Midsummer Marriage*. As it happened, another work claimed his attention first. Since the early 1930s, Tippett had enjoyed an emotional, even passionate, but non-sexual relationship with Francesca ('Fresca') Allinson, a musician, choral director and expert on folk song. The war meant that they saw less of each other, but they remained in close touch, sharing the details of their lives in letters. When she committed suicide in the spring of 1945, Tippett was profoundly moved. Only five years later could he bring himself to write a memorial piece for her. This was *The Heart's Assurance* (1951), a song cycle based on the work of Sidney Keyes and Alun Lewis, two young poets killed during the Second World War. Peter Pears gave the first performance with Britten as accompanist.

The Midsummer Marriage was conceived in 1941, begun in 1946, completed in 1952, and not performed until 1955. During those years, Tippett's stature as a composer had grown steadily, and when the premiere finally took place it was at Covent Garden with John Pritchard conducting and Joan Sutherland as Jenifer, the female lead. The first night audience was baffled, and it is not difficult to see why. The libretto, which Tippett wrote himself, tries to be poetic and profound, but is frequently awkward and embarrassingly 'new age'. He employed Jungian concepts of confronting the shadow in oneself and attaining spiritual maturity through a marriage of innocence and experience. These have the capacity to work in opera, but the plot, which takes the idea of parallel couples reaching self-knowledge through ritual from *The Magic Flute* – adding a dash of T.S. Eliot (in the character of Madame Sosostris), J.G. Fraser's *Golden Bough* (in King Fisher), and Shakespeare's *Midsummer Night's Dream* – is fundamentally undramatic. Set in an undefined, mystical world, and working through concepts and symbols rather than character and motivation, *The Midsummer Marriage* is more masque than opera – and in the early stages of planning Tippett did actually call it a masque. Yet somehow it works. It is saved by Tippett's rich, energetic, ebullient and melodic score: by the 'March of the Ancients' in Act I, the 'Ritual Dances' from Act II, Madame Sosostris' long aria in Act III, and the brilliant choral writing throughout. And it is saved also by the fact that, for all its faults, it is an optimistic, life-affirming work – much more so, in fact, than any of Britten's operas. It took time for audiences and musicians to come to terms with *The Midsummer Marriage*, but its appeal has grown and, over the years, there have been productions in the United States, Germany, Sweden and Australia, as well as in Britain. Today it is recognised as a great, if flawed, British opera.

After completing *The Midsummer Marriage*, Tippett returned to orchestral music. The lyrical *Fantasia Concertante on a Theme of Corelli* was commissioned by the Edinburgh Festival to celebrate the three hundredth anniversary of Corelli's birth in 1953. The equally lyrical *Divertimento on Sellinger's Round* (1954) was first played at the Collegium Musicum Zürich, an indication of Tippett's growing international reputation. The interesting, if uneven, Piano Concerto (1955) was premiered by pianist Louis Kentner with the Birmingham Symphony Orchestra. Then came the controversial Second Symphony (1957). Broadly neo-classical in form, it is a tense, driven, and (like the First Symphony) closely-argued work. Ian Kemp has suggested that Tippett had been searching almost desperately for his own alternative symphonic structure, but, having failed to find it, he decided to write what amounted to an impassioned justification of the traditional, four-movement form.[1] Now recognised as an important contribution to the British symphonic repertoire, it was unfortunate that the first performance should have been given by the ageing and conservative Sir Adrian Boult and the BBC Symphony Orchestra – within which a number of players distrusted Tippett's music. The performance, a live broadcast, broke down a few minutes into the first movement. Boult apologised and restarted the piece, but the incident – whatever its real cause, which has been much debated[2] – added to suspicion that Tippett's music was intentionally and unnecessarily difficult.

In fact, it was only after the Second Symphony that Tippett adopted a markedly more radical musical style; the change of direction, which commentators seized on and criticised at the time, was first evident in *King Priam*, his second opera, completed in 1961. It is clear, as Ian Kemp has shown, that Tippet chose to make *King Priam* contrast with its predecessor in almost every way.[3] *The Midsummer Marriage* is a comedy with a story invented by Tippett, full of symbolism, and told in just a few scenes through lyrical arias, big choruses and plenty of extended orchestral passages. *King Priam* is a tragedy based on a familiar story, consisting of numerous, short, juxtaposed scenes. It is realistic in manner, and it works through declamatory statements rather than arias. It is atonal and dissonant, drawing on solo instruments and small groupings of instruments within the orchestra to illustrate and express character and the events of the story. There were ten years between the completion of *The Midsummer Marriage* and *King Priam,* so some degree of change was to be expected, especially in a composer of Tippett's intellectual restlessness, but this was radical change. Having developed slowly over twenty years to the point where he could produce a work of the stature of *The Midsummer Marriage,* he clearly felt he now had the musical and intellectual confidence to go further and faster. The rest of his career would be characterised by attempts – some more successful than others – to explore new forms, techniques and styles, which would allow him to say what he wanted to say about the human condition. If *King Priam* was unexpected, that was because it was the first time this new Tippett had been revealed.

The premiere of *King Priam* was part of the 1962 Coventry Festival, that week of celebrations surrounding the reconsecration of Coventry Cathedral which also saw the first performance of Britten's *War Requiem*. No one would accuse the *War Requiem* of lacking feeling or intensity, but one can suggest that *King Priam*, which also carries an anti-war message, analyses the issues involved more deeply; that it considers causes, not just effects. Tippett shows the disasters of the Trojan War as stemming from the restrictive social codes of honour and heroism that apply equally to the Greeks and the Trojans. And he goes further. These codes and their conse-quences, he implies, mask a series of failures: a failure to understand, or even know, the basic facts; a failure to understand what motivates other people; and an essential failure of self-knowledge.

When Britten died in 1976, Tippett wrote that he was 'the most purely musical person I have ever known', a claim he repeated in his autobiogra-phy.[4] The compliment was real, but behind it lies an important truth about Tippett, because he was not a 'purely musical' person. He was an intellec-tual, who used music to express and communicate his ideas about life. His approach to composition was in the British tradition in that it was prag-matic, not an expression of a particular theory of how music should be written. In expressing his ideas and personal philosophy through music, he was, in fact, doing nothing more radical than Parry had done in his 'ethical oratorios' at the beginning of the century. It was just a question of degree. However, in Tippett's work, music and ideas were so closely interwoven that some of those who did not share his philosophical interests – or perhaps did not have the mental equipment to follow them – felt threat-ened and became hostile. Presented with Tippett's *Fantasia Concertante on a Theme of Corelli* at the 1953 Edinburgh Festival, Malcolm Sargent famously said that he intended to 'get all the intellectuals out of music.'[5]

Gradually, however, the musical establishment came to accept him – he was awarded a CBE in 1959, an Honorary Fellowship by the RCM in 1961, an Honorary Doctorate by Cambridge University in 1964, and a knight-hood in 1966. The early 60s saw a series of works continuing and consolidating the style he had established in *King Priam*. *Words for Music Perhaps* was a setting of a poem by Yeats, whose work Tippet loved – not surprisingly given their common interest in symbols and the unconscious. His incidental music for *The Tempest*, written in 1962, would influence his next opera. There was a Second Piano Sonata, and this period culminated in the vivid and energetic Concerto for Orchestra. His next major work, however, was *The Vision of Saint Augustine*, for baritone solo, chorus and orchestra. It was written in response to a BBC commission and given its first performance at the beginning of 1966 by Dietrich Fischer-Dieskau and the BBC Symphony Orchestra, with Tippett himself conducting. The first movement is one of spiritual exposition, preparing the way for the ecstatic vision itself, which is the subject of the central movement. The shorter, concluding third movement suggests that eternal life may be an indefinite extension of the moment of epiphany, but that the human mind cannot sustain comprehension of such a moment. The text, assembled by Tippett from the words of St Augustine, the Vulgate and other sources, is of characteristic complexity. The music is very much post-*Priam* Tippett: it is percussive, questioning, serene and mystical by turns, reaching an orchestral climax when words fail at the moment of vision, then falling away at the end with the acceptance of the true fallibility of human nature. It is certainly not an easy work, but it shows again the intensity of Tippett's personal vision and the intensity with which he could pursue it.

Tippett now embarked on a process of questioning established forms and conventions, fusing musical genres, and blending his humanist vision with a modernist – but by no means brutalist – musical agenda. An important element in this was his discovery of, and fascination with, the diverse culture he discovered in the United States. He made his first visit in 1965 and returned frequently, finding that he was often better understood and more appreciated there than in Britain or Europe. His third opera, *The Knot Garden* (1969), seems to suffer as well as benefit from his new discoveries. Like *The Tempest*, on which it is based, *The Knot Garden* is a parable of creativity and reconciliation. It follows the fortunes of seven characters: a married couple, their ward, a freedom fighter, a gay couple and a psychoanalyst. The titles of the three acts – 'Confrontation', 'Labyrinth', 'Charade' – indicate the stages of the process through which the characters achieve their individual and collective reconciliation. The trouble is that none of them really engage our sympathies, and, unusually for Tippett, it is not really clear what the final reconciliation amounts to. There are some wonderful moments, including a blues septet at the end of Act I, lots of jazz and blues influence, and even quotations from the rhythm-and-blues singer Bobby 'Blue' Bland. Elsewhere, however, Tippett's inclusion of elements of 1960s culture merely becomes awkward. The freedom fighter's language of oppression (which includes the orchestra quoting 'We Shall Overcome') has dated; so, too, has the period slang of 'Sure, baby', 'Play it cool', and 'Honey, make love to me.' Or perhaps we are still too close. Perhaps a future generation will find the opera's period overlay less intrusive and jarring.

Similar problems dog *The Ice Break* (1976), the title of which is drawn from an expression, common to Russia, Canada and Alaska, for the coming of spring. A pacifist political activist returns home after twenty years in a prison camp to find his country racked by violence and racial tension. His son and his son's girlfriend are committed to direct action, not pacifism, but when the son is injured in a major race riot, he and his father achieve a measure of mutual understanding. That much offers the basis for an opera. But Tippett also includes a black boxing champion to speak for the racially oppressed and an extraterrestrial being with an environmental message. The music, by contrast, has much to recommend it. It drives the work forward with great energy. Powerful choral writing, driving strings, a recurrent motif on wood blocks, electric guitar and percussion riffs, all create a sound world and an atmosphere appropriate for a society which is tearing itself apart. But, as an opera, *The Ice Break* has neither credible characters nor a coherent plot.

The fact that *New Year*, Tippett's last opera, was premiered at Houston Grand Opera in 1989 – being performed at Glyndebourne only later – is a further indication of the extent of his popularity in the United States. *New Year* is more masque than opera and consequently, because it works on a symbolic level, set in the worlds of Somewhere and Today and Nowhere and Tomorrow, it can escape at least some of the strictures applied to *The Knot Garden* and *Ice Break*. Yet even here, in the central act, when the Shaman figure is enacting the New Year rituals, he is interrupted by the arrival of a spaceship. Of course, one can point to the artificiality of all opera, but such scenes, however much one sympathises with Tippett's aim and however carefully they are produced and directed, are wide open to ridicule. The fact that Tippett appears not to have realised this must call his judgement into question. Again, however, his music breaks new ground. Electronics, electric guitars, saxophones, horns and percussion all blend to create a new kind of lyricism. Meirion Bowen, who was Tippett's companion in his last years, has suggested that the extensive dance and song-and-dance routines take *New Year* close to the realm of the musical.[6] The trouble is that Tippett tries too hard to be modern, to be accessible; and the result is that to present-day audiences the whole thing appears almost a parody – unless, as with *The Knot Garden*, we are actually still too close to make a proper judgement. Time will tell.

One other late work requires notice: Tippett's massive oratorio, *The Mask of Time*, completed in 1982 and premiered in 1984. It was the largest work he ever wrote, and the central idea could scarcely have been more ambitious. In his own words, he wanted to 'confront and consider fundamental matters bearing upon man, his relationship with time, his place in the world as we know it and in the universe at large'.[7] Although he claimed that *The Mask of Time* was neither an oratorio nor a stage work,[8] it must be said that Tippet is better at assembling the libretto for a concert work than creating the characters and dramatic situations necessary for a successful opera. *The Mask of Time* is an intensely literary work. Its two parts, each divided into five scenes, draw on a lifetime of reading. Poetry, philosophy, sociology, and fiction are all thrown into the mix; and the resulting text examines huge mystical, metaphysical and existential concepts in a way no opera could. The sudden juxtapositions of ideas, so characteristic of Tippett, are matched by contrasting musical styles and textures. In fact, *The Mask of Time* expresses Tippett's ideas in a mixture of musical styles that are as complex and varied as the ideas themselves. A large orchestra is supplemented by an electric organ and Tippett's own battery of strange percussion (which includes brake-drums being hit with coke hammers). There are sections of calm and beauty – the harp introduction to 'The Icecap Moves South North'; the chamber music textures of 'The Dream of the Paradise Garden'. There are quotations from Monteverdi, Dowland, Handel and Beethoven. The chorus hisses, hums and shouts, then sings in the manner of a Victorian oratorio. There are African influences; a sound like the brass section of a soul band; an onomatopoeic representation of a buffalo stampede; an incredible musical sunrise; a fanfare which sounds like Shostakovich; Tippett's own sea interlude describing the death of Shelley; and a driving, contrapuntal conclusion. Tippett saw *The Mask of Time* in a tradition that included Haydn's *Creation*, the *Missa Solemnis*, and Mahler's Eighth Symphony, but the work has none of the triumphant certainties of its progenitors. Tippett is clearly uneasy and uncertain about the future of a human race that has the capacity to destroy itself. Yet the title of Part Two – 'The Triumph of Life', taken from Shelley's poem of the same name – and that of the last section – 'The Singing Is Never Done' – both point to an essential, albeit qualified, optimism that underlies almost everything he wrote. It would be difficult for any work on the scale of *The Mask of Time* to be flawless. Tippett's almost reckless inclusiveness and the work's consequent diversity are enough to guarantee moments of structural and musical awkwardness. Its scale also means that it is rarely performed. Nonetheless, we may one day find that *The Mask of Time* comes to be regarded as one of the defining works of its period.

Tippett went on composing right to the end of his life. His last major composition – the orchestral piece *Rose Lake* – was first given in 1995 at a concert to celebrate his ninetieth birthday. During the last two decades of his life, after the death of Britten, with whom he was inevitably and regularly compared, his unorthodox approach seemed to become more generally accepted. He took on the mantle of the Grand Old Man of British music; his premieres (that of *The Mask of Time* particularly) became media events; and he gained a worldwide following. Since his death, his reputation has declined, though time will almost inevitably lead to a reassessment. Tippett was slow to mature as a composer, but once he reached maturity he stuck to the ideas and principles he had espoused. As a young man, he was interested enough in Vaughan Williams's work to conduct *The Shepherds of the Delectable Mountains* with his amateur choir in Oxted, but wise enough to see that Vaughan Williams was not a suitable teacher. By the time he died, forty years after Vaughan Williams, his restless, intellectual approach had played a major role in driving British music, and particularly British opera, forward to a point certainly beyond Vaughan Williams's comprehension and quite possibly beyond that of Britten as well. Sometimes, as we have seen, his experiments could misfire, but the accusation that British music was insular and conservative was no longer heard.

105   Technology, Trad, and Skiffle

By 1945, the importance of popular music as a cultural force had been growing steadily for over a century. In the nineteenth century, that growth had been fuelled by urbanisation, improved physical communications and improvements in printing technology. In the first half of the twentieth century, it was based on the advent of recorded and broadcast sound – the gramophone, radio, sound film – and on a gradual increase in living standards that made such technologies more accessible to more people. In the post-1945 decades, the trend continued and accelerated. Popular music reached new levels of cultural and economic importance. This was partly the result of rapid technological innovation; partly because from 1948 onwards disposable incomes began to grow steadily – a rise which continued uninterrupted until 1972; but also because music became closely identified with a number of socio-cultural movements affecting young people in particular. Of course, the link between musical styles and social identity was nothing new – sailors sang sea shanties; young Victorian men-on-the-make identified with 'The Swells', George Leybourne, and 'Champagne Charlie'; the Bright Young Things of the 1920s danced the Charleston and the Black Bottom – but the speed and effectiveness of post-war communications meant that such identifications ceased to be just local or regional. They rapidly became national and even international.

During the 1930s and the war years that followed, the United States was, as we have seen, the largest single influence on British popular music. After the war – unsurprisingly, given the parlous state of Britain, both materially and financially – that influence not only continued, but grew. Up to the end of the 1950s, almost all the technological improvements and all the new musical fashions that affected British music were, in one form or another, American imports. In terms of technology, the changes principally concerned the quality of sound reproduction. The first ten- and twelve-inch long-playing, or LP, records were released in the United States by Columbia in 1948; and the first seven-inch 'singles' followed in 1949. These discs played at 33⅓ and 45 rpm respectively, slower speeds than the then market-standard 78s, which allowed for greatly extended playing times, and they were made of vinyl, which was less brittle and generated significantly less surface noise. The new formats were introduced in Britain almost at once. By 1958, sales of 45s had overtaken those of 78s, and, after 1960, the old 78 discs were rapidly phased out. With new technology came new terminology. What had previously been a 'gramophone' now became a 'record player', many of them equipped with automatic record changers, but these early record players soon proved to be an intermediate phase. Nineteen fifty-eight also saw Pye Records issuing Britain's first stereo LPs. Within a few years, the novelty of stereo sound had sparked popular demand for high-fidelity, or hi-fi, equipment – a craze memorably satirised by Flanders and Swann in their 'Song of Reproduction' as a kind of musical one-upmanship – which in turn led to the 1960s and 70s fashion for separate hi-fi components.

A significant improvement in the quality of broadcast sound came in 1955 when the BBC began using frequency modulation (FM) technology for its broadcasts. For the next eighteen years, the Light and Third Programmes, and the Home Service – from 1967, Radios 2, 3 and 4 – were the only FM stations in the United Kingdom. Only in 1973, when the BBC's monopoly was lifted and commercial broadcasting became legal, was a network of local and regional FM stations set up. From 1966, the BBC also broadcast music and drama regularly in stereo, giving a further boost to sound quality. Such improvements naturally affected listeners to classical and popular music equally, but by this time the consumer demand for popular music, whether on record or on radio, was so much greater than that for classical music that new developments were presented with significantly greater emphasis on the popular end of the market.

The other major development was, of course, television. The BBC had run a limited service in the London area between 1936 and 1939, when it was suspended because of the war. It restarted in June 1946, but initially it was again confined to London and the surrounding area. Over the next few years, it spread gradually northwards, reaching Scotland in 1952 and Northern Ireland in 1953. The 1954 Television Act led to the creation of Independent Television (ITV), a network of regionally-based commercial stations funded by advertising and designed to compete with and challenge the BBC's monopoly. The first ITV station, Associated Rediffusion, was launched to serve the London area in 1955 and by 1962 the ITV network covered the whole of the United Kingdom.

There were some programmes of classical music, mainly on the BBC – the Last Night of the Proms has been was televised every year since 1947 – but for the most part the emphasis was on middle-of-the-road, family-oriented programming. The term 'easy listening' was coined. *Café Continental* was the first televised variety show, broadcast live from the BBC studios in Alexandra Palace from 1947 to 1953. The programme's format mimicked attending a nightclub. Viewers were greeted by a maître d'hôtel, and ushered to a 'table' from where they could watch Sydney Jerome and his Orchestra and a series of guest appearances by well-known singers and dancers. *The Billy Cotton Band Show*, which ran on the BBC from 1956 to 1965, adopted a simpler, presenter-to-camera format. Cotton himself fronted the show and directed his big band and the popular vocal-ist Alan Breeze. There were regular guest slots for the singer Kathie Kay and the pianist Russ Conway. An even greater success was *The Black and White Minstrel Show* which ran for twenty years from 1958 to 1978. The Mitchell Minstrels, a group of white singers wearing blackface, performed a range of familiar songs in a kind of sing-along format, accompanied by a group of high-stepping female dancers, the Television Toppers, and inter-spersed with comedy interludes, among them the Scottish trombonist, George Chisholm. ITV's flagship variety programme was *Sunday Night at the London Palladium*, which mixed quiz and comedy acts with appear-ances by the leading singers and groups of the moment.

Big band and swing music continued to be popular into the 1950s. Geraldo (real name, Gerald Bright; 1904–74) had begun musical life as a silent film accompanist. He enjoyed some success in the 1930s, but his 'Orchestra' – which was really a dance band, although it did occasionally add a string section – reached the height of its popularity in the ten years after 1945. Jazz musicians such as Ronnie Scott, John Dankworth and Stan Tracey all played in Geraldo's Orchestra at some time during the early part of their careers. Another favourite bandleader of the period was Ted Heath (1902–69). He played in a number of bands, including Geraldo's, before forming Ted Heath and His Music, which played in a style that was some-times compared with the Count Basie Orchestra. Heath's popularity peaked in the 1950s – in 1958 alone, he recorded nine LPs – and he was one of the few British jazz or big band musicians to become popular in the United States. His 1956 American tour, during which Nat King Cole sang with the band, was an outstanding success. Edmundo Ros (1910–2011) was a bandleader of mixed Trinidadian and Venezuelan parentage. His Rumba Band offered a variation on the standard dance music of the time by intro-ducing Latin-American rhythms. Ros became a club owner, started a dance school and a management agency. The Rumba Band became an Orchestra, and their 1958 album, *Rhythms of the South*, one of the first to exploit stereo sound technology, sold over a million copies. Other band leaders of the period included Victor Silvester (1900–78), who gradually moved away from jazz towards ballroom dancing; Joe Loss (1909–90), whose big hit was 'In the Mood'; and Ray Ellington (1916–85), who famously appeared regularly on *The Goon Show*.

As the big band sound matured, it became slightly tamer and more respectable – although this change was probably more marked among

British bands than their American counterparts – perhaps reflecting the less fraught atmosphere of the post-war world. A corresponding development was a growth in the popularity of big romantic ballads. Individual singers rather than bands and bandleaders now became the major stars. American singers were naturally the most popular. Male vocalists such as Frank Sinatra, Perry Como, and Frankie Lane, and female singers like Doris Day, Jo Stafford and Patti Page were promoted in films and on record. They also visited Britain on tour, giving concerts and making guest appearances on radio and television. Most leading British singers of the period began by imitating American styles and covering American songs, often adopting a more British approach once their reputations were established. Among them were crooners such as Frankie Vaughan, Clinton Ford, Dickie Valentine, David Whitfield and Jimmy Young (later to become a radio and television personality); while the female vocalists, who were on the whole more successful, included names such as Dorothy Squires, Anne Shelton, Alma Cogan, Ruby Murray and Kathy Kirby.

In the United States, one part of the broad spectrum of swing and dance-band music evolved into be-bop. Although it never achieved mainstream popularity, be-bop was musically a step forward. It was a form of art music, rhythmically and harmonically complex, based on small groups, improvisation, and great instrumental virtuosity. Its figureheads were musicians such as Charlie Parker and Dizzy Gillespie. Be-bop then spun off cool jazz, a mixture of different styles, less intense and more obviously melodic, bringing to the fore musicians like Miles Davis, Thelonius Monk and Chet Baker. This kind of advanced jazz crossed the Atlantic to the extent of becoming a cult among jazz aficionados, but it attracted relatively few British players. In Britain, by contrast, the popularity of swing and dance-band music began to be challenged by a revival of traditional or 'trad' jazz. Based around Dixieland and variants of ragtime, with a dash of blues, the music of these trad jazz bands featured clarinet, trumpet and trombone as their lead instruments, and frequently included a banjo as part of the rhythm section. The saxophone, which had become essential to American jazz, was something of an optional extra. The British trad jazz revival was essentially a conservative movement, offering fast 2/4 or 4/4 tempos, improvisation on clearly identifiable themes, and stylised polyphonic interaction among the lead instruments. It placed the emphasis on lively entertainment, rather than depth of feeling or the kind of innovation that characterised be-bop.

The trad jazz revival had its origins in 1943, when George Webb (1917–2010) formed his band, the Dixielanders, playing regularly in a pub called The Red Barn in Barnehurst on the south-eastern outskirts of London. Among the graduates of Webb's band was one of the most famous British jazz musicians of the late twentieth century, the trumpeter Humphrey Littleton – although Littleton moved away from trad jazz, adopting a more mainstream, American-style approach. Another trad revival pioneer was Ken Colyer (1928–88), who in the early stages of his career alternated playing jazz with serving in the Merchant Navy. On one occasion, he jumped ship in the United States and made his way to New Orleans where he joined a band led by his hero, the clarinettist George Lewis. The adventure was cut short when he was arrested for working without a permit and deported. For a decade or more from the early 1950s, trad jazz was a significant driving force in British popular music. It also generated a following in a number of northern European countries, particularly Germany and Denmark. Ken Colyer's 1953 band, for example, made their first recordings not in London but in Copenhagen. One characteristic of the early stages of the trad jazz revival – even more marked than with the dance bands of the pre-war period – was the way in which personnel constantly combined and recombined to form different bands with different leaders. Following every twist and turn is neither possible nor, in the end, instructive, but we can note the contributions made by some of the most important names.

Perhaps the high point of the trad jazz boom came in January 1963, when just about everyone who was anyone took part in an All Night Carnival of Jazz at the Alexandra Palace.[1] It was billed as the biggest trad jazz event ever staged in Britain, and among those taking part were the clarinettist Monty Sunshine; the Scottish trumpeter and cornet player Alex Welsh; and the singer George Melly, later to become a writer, art critic, enthusiast for surrealism, and general media personality. Topping the bill, however, were the three giants of British trad jazz – Kenny Ball (1930–2013), Chris Barber (b.1930) and Acker Bilk (1929–2014) – all three of whom had had a number one album during the previous year. Kenny Ball was a trumpeter. He and his Jazzmen based their style on Dixieland jazz, and enjoyed a string of hits between 1961 and 1964, the biggest being 'Midnight in Moscow'. Chris Barber, a trombonist, was more blues-oriented, and played an important role in bringing American blues artists such as Big Bill Broonzy and Muddy Waters across to the United Kingdom for the first time. His band's biggest hit was their 1959 version of 'Petite Fleur', a tribute to its writer, Sidney Bechet, the first great jazz saxophone soloist, who had just died in Paris. Acker Bilk and his Paramount Jazz Band appeared on the now televised Royal Variety Performance in 1961. Bilk's appearance, with silk waistcoat, goatee beard and bowler hat was as instantly recognisable as his clarinet style. 'Stranger on the Shore', released in 1961, took him to the top of the charts both in the Britain and the United States. But the trad boom was not to last. Just two days before the Alexandra Palace all-nighter, the Beatles' second single, 'Please Please Me' entered the charts. It did not reach no. 1, being kept from the top spot by Frank Ifield's 'The Wayward Wind', but it was a sign of the times. Within less than two years the trad jazz bubble had burst.

British trad jazz, as we have noted, was not homogenous. It was a mixture of different styles reinvented for its era, and contained within it many of the features that would characterise the other genres and revivals of the 1950s. The influential 1953 Ken Colyer Band, for example, included the young Lonnie Donegan on banjo, and despite Colyer's reputation as something of a New Orleans' jazz purist, their set would usually include a 'skiffle break' of one or two numbers. Skiffle drew on jazz, but it also drew on American folk and blues, on country and western, gospel, and on early rock'n'roll. It was fast, highly rhythmic and repetitive, and based on a twelve-bar structure derived from the blues. Typically, a vocalist – often adopting an American accent – would be backed by some combination of guitar, banjo, mandolin, drums, washboard and bass. Some skiffle bands used a tea-chest bass. While this may not have been as common as popularly supposed, it does point to the essential informality of skiffle as a genre. It was one of the first manifestations of the youth culture that emerged in the 1950s, appealing particularly to working class youths for whom jazz held little interest, and – crucially – demanding participation and commitment as much as skill.

In July 1954, Lonnie Donegan recorded an up-tempo version of 'Rock Island Line', an American traditional song, originally recorded by the blues singer Lead Belly in 1936. There had been other recordings, both in the Unites States and in Britain, but Donegan's skiffle version caught the mood of the time. It was not released until late 1955, when it sold three million copies in six months. It marked the beginning of the skiffle craze. Donegan had hits with songs like 'Cumberland Gap' and 'The Battle of New Orleans'. In an attempt to get away from his dependence on American material, he then recorded a number of songs that seemed to look back to music hall, such as 'Does Your Chewing Gum Lose its Flavour on the Bedpost Overnight?' and 'My Old Man's a Dustman'. The nearest rival to Donegan was the British group, the Vipers, including the singer and guitarist Wally Whyton, who went on to be a children's television presenter. Skiffle groups sprang up all over the country, including in Liverpool where, in 1956, the sixteen-year-old John Lennon and some of his friends formed the Quarrymen, taking the name from the Quarry Bank School which they attended. Skiffle was a genuinely popular movement. Its origins were American, but it was a British blend of styles and its popularity did not extend beyond Britain – although that did not prevent American artists from joining in: Johnny Duncan had a huge hit with 'Last Train To San Fernando'. The problem was that skiffle was not backed by any of the major record or film companies. As a result, its period of glory was even shorter-lived than the craze for trad jazz. By 1958, it had peaked, been challenged, and then quickly overwhelmed by rock'n'roll – which, by contrast, began in United States but soon became an international phenomenon, while at the same time enjoying huge commercial backing.

106   Post-War Men and Women

The ten or twelve years that followed 1945 were a particularly difficult time for Britain. The war had been won, but the financial burden and cost to life and property had all been enormous. The population sought familiarity and reassurance. Faced with such a situation, serious composers tended to divide into those whose music met that need, offering some kind of comfort or relief, and those whose work sought to express the need, and thus the spirit, of the times. The music of the second group might be appreciated intellectually, but was less likely to achieve immediate popularity. Two events acted as a focus for the spirit of national recovery: the Festival of Britain in 1951, and the Coronation of Queen Elizabeth II in June 1953. They were the occasion for an outpouring of hope and patriotism that had a psychological and cultural impact on the whole country, and within just a few years the cultural climate had begun to change.

Britten and Tippett were the composers who led British classical music through the years of post-war austerity and into the consumer decades of the 1960s and 70s. Although both were well on the way to establishing their reputations by the end of the war, their leadership role did not emerge at once. The post-war period was a time when there were many prominent musical figures jostling for public and critical attention, but, as in the 30s, there was no settled or shared direction. Vaughan Williams, Dyson, Ireland, Bliss, Howells, Rubbra and Walton were still composing and still highly regarded by many. Their place in the musical firmament was secure, but for all their undoubted talent, they did not represent the future. Even Rubbra and Walton, though only four and three years younger than Tippett, clearly belonged to an earlier musical generation.

In the late 1950s, with the economy and national confidence both showing signs of revival, familiarity became less important. Critics and audiences alike became more willing to accept challenge and experimentation – although, as ever in Britain, such developments took place against a solidly conservative background. The growing importance of the Arts Council in promoting new music, the appointment of William Glock as Controller of Music at the BBC and Controller of the Proms, and, to a lesser extent, the spread of television, all contributed to greater interest in more advanced or even avant-garde music. Such a change – in British terms, a radical change – had a major effect on the careers of those composers, some of whom we met earlier, who had begun but not fully established their careers before the war. Although they were talented, and although many of them went on to enjoy extended careers in music, their ability to develop and to respond to change determined whether or not they fulfilled the promise and the expectations of their pre-war years.

Alan Rawsthorne emerged from the war considered by many as among the most promising composers of his generation. After he was demobbed, he embarked on a particularly productive period. There was a lyrical Oboe Concerto (1947), a *Concerto for String Orchestra* (1949), and a Second Piano Concerto, commissioned by the Arts Council for the Festival of Britain in 1951. Clifford Curzon was the soloist for the first performance of the Piano Concerto, and went on to become closely associated with the work, taking it on tour all over the world with both Beecham and the RPO and with Barbirolli and the Hallé. Rawsthorne's approach at this stage of his career was hard to pin down. The Quartet for Clarinet and Strings (1948) and the superb Sonata for Cello and Piano (1949) both suggest he was moving towards a warm, even neo-romantic style; but by the time of the Second String Quartet (1954), which is among his finest works, we find him adopting a terse, disciplined, economical approach to his material. The same period also saw him devoting more and more time and energy to writing for films: he produced over twenty scores, including those for *Where No Vultures Fly* (1951), *The Cruel Sea* (1953) and *The Man Who Never Was* (1956). Unmoved by fashion or novelty, Rawsthorne was a composer with a strong individual voice. Nonetheless, during the latter part of his career, there is a sense that he was unsure in which direction he was moving. His Second (*Pastoral*) Symphony (1959) reflected the English pastoral tradition that he had previously and pointedly turned away from; while the Third Symphony (1964) was decidedly unpastoral, with a turbulent opening, a haunting second movement and a quite unusual use of twelve-note technique bringing the work to a powerful resolution. Between these two symphonies, he produced two entirely different works, his only large-scale choral compositions: *Medieval Diptych* (1962) for baritone and orchestra, and *Carmen Vitale* (1963) for soprano, chorus and orchestra. Both use medieval texts and show something of a historian's capacity to enter into the medieval mind. *Medieval Diptych* in particular is a fascinating work, built on a complex interaction of serial technique and harmonic units. All reports of Rawsthorne as an individual describe him as educated, intelligent, witty and engaging. His music shares those qualities, but perhaps lacks that extra, driven, compelling quality one finds in Britten, Tippett, or in the work of some of the other composers of the period whose music has maintained its position on concert programmes and with the musical public.

Alan Bush's determined attempts to mix music and hard-line, left-wing politics continued throughout the war – during which he served as a private in the Royal Army Medical Corps – and beyond. He wrote four symphonies between 1940 and 1983. The second these, known as *The Nottingham Symphony,* was commissioned by the Nottingham Cooperative Society to celebrate the city's five hundredth anniversary. Over the course of his career, he also wrote a large number of piano pieces and chamber works, but his real interest was in vocal and choral works that could carry a didactic, political message. Opera was the obvious vehicle and, in 1951, *Wat Tyler*, telling the story of the 1381 Peasants' revolt, won an Arts Council prize during the Festival of Britain. It was the first of four operas, but the only one to receive a professional production – and that was in Communist East Germany. In 1952, Peter Pears commissioned a work from Bush. The result was the four-part cantata *Voices of the Prophets,* to texts from the Bible, Milton, Blake, and the Barbados-born poet Peter Blackman. This was Bush's home territory and the work he produced is committed, authoritative and on a grand scale. His commitment to left-wing politics never flagged and his music barely altered. In 1985, at the age of eighty-five, he completed *Mandela Speaking*, for baritone, chorus and orchestra, and conducted it himself at a concert organised by the African National Congress. In East Germany, he was honoured by both the City of Halle and the Akademie der Künste. In Britain, however, apart from a couple of honorary doctorates, he was regarded as a harmless and rather outdated eccentric and largely ignored – although it is worth noting that among his students was the minimalist composer, Michael Nyman.

In the difficult years after the war, Gordon Jacob's tonal clarity and concentration on melody above all else offered just that degree of familiarity and reassurance that audiences seemed to require. His popularity reached its highest point during the 1950s when he was invited to produce work for both the Festival of Britain and the Coronation. In the 60s and 70s, however, his conservative style lost its relevance, overtaken by a more assertively modern musical world, so that what had seemed reassuring was now merely quaint. He never became the force in British music that some had predicted before the war. Arnold Cooke, whose style, like that of Jacob, was essentially conservative, was just beginning to make his way as a young composer in the 1930s. After serving in the Navy during the war, he became Professor of Composition at Trinity College in London, a position he held from 1947 until 1978. Although he wrote some interesting chamber works – particularly for his own instrument, the cello – his career as a composer never really revived after the war.

Lennox Berkeley stands out against this general pattern. Although firmly embedded in the musical establishment – from 1946 to 1968 he was Professor of Composition at the RAM – he showed more awareness of changing tastes and a greater willingness to adapt than many of his contemporaries. Berkeley composed in most genres, yet, true to his English roots if not his French training, he was happiest in choral and vocal music. Two works from the immediate post-war period – *Four Poems of St Teresa of Avila* and *Stabat Mater*, both written in 1947, and both reflecting his Catholicism – are among his best, showing a definite sensitivity to language and word-setting. During the 1950s, quite possibly influenced by Britten's operatic success, he wrote three operas. *A Dinner Engagement* (1954) is a compact, almost surreal work about an aristocratic family's attempt to avoid financial ruin by marrying off their daughter. *Nelson* (also 1954) is in a more traditional, heroic mould, but suffered at the time by comparison with Britten's more challenging and more enigmatic works. *Ruth* (1956), in just three scenes, and scored for a small ensemble including a piano, is biblical in subject matter, detached in manner and post-romantic in style, extending the musical language of his earlier choral works. In a sense, these works sum up Berkeley and his place in British music. They are varied and versatile; they show solid technical ability, and they have probably received less attention than they deserve, at least in part because there is a persistent feeling of emotional reserve: he never quite lets go.

As the 1950s progressed, Berkeley's style continued to evolve. He began to experiment with twelve-note and serial techniques. It was an evolutionary rather than a revolutionary process: serial techniques never replaced the broadly tonal style that had characterised his work since the 1920s, but they did extend the possibilities open to him. His compact Third Symphony (1969) – it lasts only fifteen minutes – derives much of its undoubted power from his manipulation of two six-note chords. *The Hill of Graces* (1975), an eight-part setting of words by the Elizabethan poet Edmund Spenser for unaccompanied choir, is again heavily dependent on serial compositional methods. By contrast, two other works – *Five Poems of W. H. Auden* (1959) and *Five Chinese Songs* (1971) – depend for their effectiveness on the juxtaposition of tonal and atonal passages.

The sense of reserve in Berkeley's music seems to have been a reflection of his personality. In an interview with *The Times* in 1959, Berkeley said, 'I know quite well I'm a minor composer, and I don't mind that.'[1] Those who knew him suggest that he did not seek the limelight and was reluctant to assert himself personally unless roused. Such judgements may be accurate, but they do not do justice to the influence he exerted during his lifetime. Within the limits that he set himself, he had an ability to adapt, innovate and reflect the musical developments of his time. He was appreciated, even loved, by his students – who included David Bedford, Richard Rodney Bennett, William Mathias and John Tavener; and he was held in great respect by the wider musical community. He was honoured, not just in Britain – where he received a knighthood and numerous fellowships, doctorates and professorships – but by the Vatican, and by national institutions in Monaco, Belgium and the United States.

One important change in the post-war musical world was the way in which women composers could achieve the recognition denied to previous generations. We have noted the difficulties faced by a talented composer like Alice Mary Smith in the 1860s and 70s; and we have seen that the success enjoyed by Ethel Smyth was due in no small measure to her absolute determination to face down the obstacles placed in her way. There were, of course, many others who might have achieved more than they did. A number of women born in the Victorian era had the talent and the ability, but, for a variety of reasons, some educational, some social, some family-related, some based on sheer prejudice, never quite got to the point where they could enjoy a career as a composer.

Mary Grant Carmichael (1851–1935), for example, was born in Liverpool, probably to an Irish family. Although better known as a pianist and accompanist, she wrote songs with an Irish feel to them (*An Album of Six Songs*, 1890), and an ambitious Mass in E flat for unaccompanied male voices. Dora Bright (1862–1951) trained at the RAM, where she was a member of a student group that also included Edward German. She became a concert pianist, and also a composer. Several of her works were performed at Philharmonic Society concerts, and in the years leading up to the First World War she worked closely with the dancer Adeline Genée. In the Edwardian period, Emma Lomax (1873–1963) wrote a number of small-scale works for the stage that are now lost, but they were appreciated at the time. She went on to teach composition at the RAM between the wars. Rebecca Clarke (1886–1979) was a violist and the first female player in Henry Wood's Queen's Hall orchestra. She also wrote some interesting chamber music, often under a male pseudonym, and was the only female composer to be financially helped by Elizabeth Sprague Coolidge. She enjoyed a brief period of recognition just after the First World War, but it did not last. Someone who nearly got there was Ina Boyle (1889–1967). Born in County Wicklow, she studied in Dublin and also took lessons by letter from her cousin Charles Wood, at that time teaching at Cambridge. *Soldiers at Peace* (1916), a setting of a poem by Herbert Asquith, son of the Prime Minister, was published by Novello and performed in Dublin's Christ Church Cathedral. *The Magic Harp: Rhapsody for Orchestra* (1919), which attempts the same kind of evocation of Ireland as Stanford's *Irish Rhapsodies* and Hamilton Harty's *With the Wild Geese*, was performed in London and won a Carnegie Award. Encouraged by her success, she began travelling to London to take lessons with Vaughan Williams, who thought highly of her work, but somehow she never made the breakthrough. With the coming of the Second World War, she ceased travelling and remained in her native Enniskerry, continuing to compose but becoming increasingly detached from the musical world. One of her finest works is her setting of Edith Sitwell's war poem, *Still Falls the Rain* (1948), for solo voice and string quartet.

The movement towards equal status for women in British society had progressed only slowly during the inter-war years – the most significant moment being the advent of equal voting rights in 1928. The Second World War accelerated things. By 1945, there were six-and-a-half million women in civilian war work and nearly half a million in the armed forces. Recognition of the role they had played in winning the war led to greater prominence for women in all walks of life, including music. There had, of course, always been female singers, and female instrumental soloists had long been accepted. The inter-war years had seen the Royal Colleges and the universities offering much greater support to women students. Now there emerged a generation of women composers who not only had the talent and the education necessary for success, but also the support of the BBC and access to new commercial and career opportunities.

Not that the life or the career of Elisabeth Lutyens (1906–83) was easy. Her father was the architect, Sir Edwin Lutyens, while her mother was a noted theosophist who, during Elisabeth's childhood, had invited the Indian thinker and philosopher, Krishnamurti, to share the family home. Lutyens' family were largely indifferent to her musical ambitions and, at the age of fifteen, she sought escape by moving to Paris and enrolling in the École Normale de Musique, but then her mother turned up and disrupted her studies by whisking her off to India. On her return to London, she studied briefly with John Foulds, and then spent the four years from 1926 to 1930 at the RCM, where her teachers included Vaughan Williams, Gordon Jacob, and Harold Darke. It was obvious from an early stage that she was not happy with the contemporary musical orthodoxy, disliking the emphasis placed on Brahms and Mahler, but it took some years for her to find her own style.

Lutyens' Chamber Concerto no. 1, which appeared in 1939, just before the Second World War, seemed to indicate the way ahead. It was a taut, highly chromatic work, pointing to the serialism she would later adopt. At the time, however, her first marriage was breaking up, and her mental state was such that she felt unsure of her direction. During the war, she experimented with neo-classical ideas, but then in 1946 she produced *O saisons, O châteaux!*, a setting of Rimbaud that showed that she had developed an individual twelve-note technique capable of harmonic variation and of expressing her emotional response to the words. That was the beginning.

During the early 1950s, she wrote a number of works that confirmed her position as Britain's first true serialist composer: *Concertante for Five Players* (1950); the String Quartet no. 6 (1952), which demonstrated a new command of rhythmical writing; and the austerely beautiful *Wittgenstein Motet* (1953), which set words from the *Tractatus Logico-Philosophicus*. These were highly original works. The BBC played them on the new Third Programme, but twelve-tone music was still beyond the comprehension of most audiences and, indeed, many critics.

Lutyens' second husband was the conductor and radio producer Edward Clark. He was a musical intellectual with ideas that often proved to be ahead of their time, but he was not good at bringing in a regular income, so much of the burden fell on Lutyens. She was not one of those commissioned to write for the Festival of Britain – understandably, given the prevailing attitude to the kind of music she was writing – but with help from William Walton she began to receive commissions for film scores. This was not work she enjoyed but it kept the family afloat financially. In the end, she wrote over a hundred scores and gained a reputation for writing remarkably effective music for horror movies.

Lutyens' approach to composition, like Tippett's, was a highly intellectual one, but she stands apart from other British composers in that she worked on a mathematical and theoretical basis. *Quincunx* (1959), based on Sir Thomas Browne's *Garden of Cyrus*, represents one of the high points of her achievement. Premiered at the 1962 Cheltenham Festival, it is essentially a lament. The mood is dark and controlled, but at the same time passionate, while the theme slowly evolves, changing in density and texture as it moves across the surface of the orchestra. The mid-1960s saw a change of style. The two song cycles *Akapotik Rose* and *Suddenly It's Evening* (both 1966) are both structurally and harmonically simpler than much of her previous work. There is greater emphasis on repeated patterns, suggesting a nod in the direction of minimalism. She went on to write three operas. *Time Off? Not a Ghost of a Chance!* (1968) was a highly idiosyncratic, and at times parodic, exploration of the concepts of time and chance. *The Numbered* (1967) was a musically direct and powerful piece set in a society where everyone knows the time of his or her own death but may not reveal it. *Isis and Osiris* (1969–70), based on the Egyptian Book of the Dead, returned to an austere, repetitive, block-like method of construction. She continued to write into her eighties but *Isis and Osiris* represented the final major achievement of thirty years of frequently unappreciated musical exploration which had certainly extended the technical boundaries of British music.

Grace Mary Williams (1906–77) took a degree in music at Cardiff University before attending the RCM, where she was a student at the same time as Lutyens, also studying with Gordon Jacob and Vaughan Williams. She went on to finish her formal studies in Vienna with the Austrian Jewish composer, Egon Wellesz. On her return to London, she had a series of teaching jobs, and, on the basis of a recommendation from Benjamin Britten, was offered the chance to write music for documentaries produced by the Strand Film Company. Only when the school where she was teaching was evacuated to Grantham at the beginning of the war did she begin working on her own compositions. Her *Fantasia on Welsh Nursery Tunes* (1940), which is still played regularly, could not be further from Lutyens' work of the same period. It shows no sign of the influence of Wellesz, who studied with Schoenberg, but clearly derives from Vaughan Williams and Elgar. Her five-movement *Sea Sketches* (1944) is a more personal and emotional piece, with some strong chromatic writing evoking the different moods of the sea. It actually pre-dates Britten's *Sea Interludes*.

In 1947, following a period of illness, Williams returned to her native Barry in South Wales and remained there for the rest of her life. The symphonic poem *Penillion*, written in 1955 for the National Youth Orchestra of Wales, marked a step forward. Taking its title from the traditional Welsh method of improvising words over a folk melody (mentioned on p.228), it showed both a more individual style and the increased identification with Wales and Welsh culture that was to characterise her later work. During the 1960s, she wrote a Trumpet Concerto (1963); *Carillons* (1965), an imaginative four-movement suite for oboe, string orchestra and brass, inspired by the sound of bells; and *Ballads for Orchestra*, written for the 1968 National Eisteddfod which was held in Barry. By that time, she had established herself as one of Wales's leading composers, something that was recognised when her orchestral fanfare, *Castell Caernarfon*, was played during the inauguration of the Prince of Wales in 1969. Perhaps oddly, given the Welsh tradition of choral music, Williams's output was more orchestral than vocal, although two choral works should be noticed: the Welsh-language *Missa Cambrensis* (1971), and the beautiful *Ave Stella Maris* (1973), emphasising the connection with the sea that was important in much of her work.

When Lutyens and Williams entered the RCM in 1926, Elizabeth

Maconchy (1907–94) was already there, having joined the College in 1923, aged just sixteen. The three of them, together with Imogen Holst, formed the core of the most powerful and talented generation of women composers yet to emerge in Britain. It was Maconchy in whom the RCM teaching staff – which included Charles Wood, Vaughan Williams, and Hugh Allen – saw the greatest promise. They encouraged her to pursue a career as a composer and, initially at least, she was the most successful. Nineteen thirty was her breakthrough year. Her Piano Concerto was performed in Prague, where she had studied briefly on a travelling scholarship; her orchestral suite *The Land*, inspired by Vita Sackville-West's poem of the same name, was given by Henry Wood at a Promenade Concert; and three of her songs – settings of Shakespeare, Ben Jonson, and Rossetti – were published. The following year saw the first performance of *Two Motets for Double Chorus*, remarkably rich and intense settings of John Donne's 'A Hymn to Christ' and 'A Hymn to God the Father'. Then, in 1932, she was diagnosed with tuberculosis and left London to live in the Kent countryside. She continued to compose and eventually, after four years of serious illness, recovered, but she never again lived in a city and never again became fully involved in the business of musical life.

During the 1930s, despite her illness, Maconchy's reputation continued to grow. The Macnaghten-Lemare concerts programmed more of her compositions than of any other composer, and her music began to be heard in Germany, the United States and Australia. It was her chamber music that attracted most attention at this stage. The Quintet for Oboe and Strings (1932) won a *Daily Telegraph* prize and was recorded by His Master's Voice. She wrote her first three string quartets (1933, 1936, and 1938), and also the *Prelude, Interlude and Fugue for Two Violins* (1934). These are single-minded pieces, based on short, often simple themes, developed with great intensity and economy of means, owing much to Bartok, whose music she had admired since her student days.

The war years were a quiet period for Maconchy, although she did have a ballet, *Puck Fair*, staged in Dublin in 1941; its lyrical qualities, coupled with the careful use of the harp, suggest an attempt to reconnect with her Irish roots. The 1950s, however, saw her regain her previous popularity. In 1953, the overture *Proud Thames* won a Coronation Year prize offered by London County Council, and was performed at a gala concert in the Royal Festival Hall. In fact, the piece was somewhat uncharacteristic in that it was programme music, a depiction of the Thames from its source to its arrival in London (perhaps recalling Smetana's *Vltava*). However, its reception confirmed that she was now regarded as a leading composer: her work might be modern, but not unacceptably so. In 1955, the BBC broadcast the six string quartets she had written up to that date (the Fifth and Sixth had both won prizes) as part of a series of programmes celebrating her contribution to British music – a signal honour for a woman composer.

For a few years, Maconchy's focus shifted to the stage, and she composed three one-act operas – *The Sofa* (1957), *The Three Strangers* (1958), and *The Departure* (1961) – all of which are colourful and dramatic but do not feature her best music. Then, at the beginning of the 1960s, when the BBC and the musical establishment in general were becoming more accepting of atonality and avant-garde musical styles, she seemed to move in the opposite direction. The change can best be seen in the string quartets. In all, she wrote thirteen between 1933 and 1983, and they probably represent the heart of her achievement as a composer. The later quartets, particularly those from no. 8 (1967) onwards, have a freedom and an openness of expression, even a lyricism, that is not there is the earlier ones. The same qualities are also evident in other later compositions, such as *Four Shakespeare Songs* (1965); *Ariadne* (1970), for soprano and orchestra; the extraordinary solo cello piece *Epyllion* (1975); and the setting of J. M. Synge's translation of Petrarch's sonnets, *My Dark Heart* (1981).

Although never as radical as Lutyens, Maconchy's work still expresses a powerful individuality. Bartok was the strongest and most consistent influence on her work, yet she also learned a lot from Vaughan Williams, who remained her friend and mentor until his death. He influenced her style less than her attitude to being a composer. She believed wholeheartedly in the need for music to express the absolute convictions of the composer; but she also understood the value of remaining in contact with tradition. Her *Symphony for Double String Orchestra* (1953) is a strongly contrapuntal and occasionally rhythmically difficult work. She called it a *symphony* in order to distinguish it from Tippett's 1939 *Concerto for Double String Orchestra,* and it certainly has more drive and less lyricism than Tippett's work, though its structure bears little relation to a traditional symphony. It shows the influence of Bartok and Janaček, yet it is still recognisably within a British tradition of writing for strings that stretches back to the *Fantasia on a Theme of Thomas Tallis* and Elgar's *Introduction and Allegro*. Maconchy also shared with Vaughan Williams a belief in the role of music in society, and spent much time working with children – for whom she wrote *The*

Birds (based on Aristophanes, 1968) and *The King of the Golden River* (based on a story by John Ruskin, 1975) – and with amateur performers.

The fourth member of this RCM generation, Imogen Holst, is not generally regarded as a composer. In fact, she composed throughout her life: she wrote for everything from handbells, recorders, and brass bands to choirs and full orchestra – but the first commercial recording devoted to her work was issued only in 2009. Not unnaturally, her early compositions seem to reflect her father's style and interests, while her later works show more originality. She herself considered her 1982 String Quintet her best work.

Her career was an immensely varied one. Even while still at the RCM in the 1920s, her ability to control and direct an orchestra was noticed; and when her student years were over, she worked as a freelance conductor before joining the staff of the English Folk Dance and Song Society. She went on to teach at Roedean Girls' School. Her arrangement of carols was sung at Chichester Cathedral. Her Concerto for Violin and Strings was given by the RPO. She made recorder arrangements of works by Pelham Humphrey. She published a biography of her father. During the war, she supported refugee musicians from Germany and Austria, and worked with CEMA to support music in rural areas. She established Dartington Hall in Devon as a musical centre. For twelve years, from 1952 to 1964, she acted as Benjamin Britten's amanuensis, working on the scores of his operas and helping to organise the Aldeburgh Festival. She became the Artistic Director of the Festival, instituting – among other things – early music concerts in the parish church. She published books on Bach, Byrd, Purcell and Britten. And when Snape Maltings was opened in 1967, she shared the podium with Britten. Even summarised thus briefly and baldly, it is a formidable record of activity. In terms of her generation of women in music, however, Holst's importance is that she did not become a noted composer, nor a soloist, nor a full-time teacher. Yet she enjoyed a career at the very heart of British music, exerting an influence few, if any, women had been able to exercise before; and, in the end, she collected a clutch of fellowships and memberships (RCM and RAM), honorary doctorates and honours (CBE) in recognition of her achievements.

It would be too much to suggest that there are no difficulties facing women who wish to pursue a musical career today, but we can at least say that many obstacles were removed or overcome between the 1930s and the 1970s; that the generation represented by Lutyens, Grace Williams, Maconchy and Imogen Holst paved the way for those female composers who have flourished since – composers such as Nicola LeFanu (Elizabeth Maconchy's daughter, b. 1947); Judith Bingham (b. 1952); Judith Weir (b. 1954); and Sally Beamish (b. 1956). Even so, the pace of change might be too slow for some. It was 1922 when Ethel Smyth became the first woman composer to be made a Dame; it was 1987 when Elizabeth Maconchy became the second. It was 2013 before the American conductor Marin Alsop became the first woman to preside over the Last Night of the Proms, and 2014 before Judith Weir became the first female Master of the Queen's Music.

107   Folk Revived Again

Managements, film and record companies were quick to exploit the commercial, mass-market potential of trad jazz and, when it arrived, of rock'n'roll, too. Skiffle, as we have seen, attracted less attention from promoters and backers, although it, too, became a mass market phenomenon, however briefly. Folk music, by contrast, never achieved the same mass market status and, until the late 1960s, attracted far less commercial interest, but it nonetheless exercised a considerable cultural influence. The Folk Revival of the early-twentieth century had concerned itself principally with collecting and arranging traditional folk songs. The second revival of interest in folk music, which began in the 1950s and continued into the 1970s, was a more complex movement: it naturally continued to take inspiration from traditional music, but it also gave birth to an entirely new genre, contemporary folk music, and it was closely associated with left-wing politics.

Albert Lancaster Lloyd (1908–82) – known usually as A. L. Lloyd or simply Bert – was brought up in London, but shipped off to Australia as an assisted immigrant at the age of fifteen. For nearly ten years he worked on sheep stations in New South Wales, picking up songs from the other farm hands and educating himself as best he could in music and in art. He returned to London in the early 1930s when unemployment was at its worst. Unable to find a job, he spent a lot of time in the British Museum researching folklore and folk music. He also fell in with a group of left-wing intellectuals, including the Marxist historian, A. L. Morton, who was an important influence on Lloyd's later writings. Lloyd joined the Communist Party at this time, remaining a loyal member for the rest of his life. Still unable to find work, he signed up on a whaling ship and made a trip to the Antarctic. Journalism – with *Picture Post* – military service, and work with the BBC sustained him through the war years and into the 1950s, by which time his status as an expert on folk music and folk customs was sufficiently widely recognised to earn him a living.

Lloyd wrote two books about folk music which had an impact in their day. *The Singing Englishman* (1944) was an attempt to define folk song in relation to the people whose lives it portrayed and sustained. *Folk Song in England* (1967) took the process a stage further, analysing the development of folk song in relation to socio-historical changes and the move from a rural to an industrial society. Lloyd's essentially Marxist interpretations are often poorly supported in terms of evidence, and today can seem simplistic, even naïve; but, by putting folk music in a political context, the books appealed to the audience of their time and alerted a whole new generation to its existence and importance. More influential, however, were Lloyd's albums of traditional British and Australian songs, such as *Australian Bush Songs* (1956), *Thar She Blows!* (1957), *Outback Ballads* (1958), and *English Drinking Songs* (1961) – some of them recorded in collaboration with Ewan MacColl, another singer, writer and activist, whom we shall meet again shortly. Although he occasionally incurred criticism by collating different variants of the same song to produce his own version – a practice regarded by folk purists of the day as little short of desecration – it was Lloyd's style that attracted attention. His range was limited and his voice was croaky. He sang unaccompanied or with simple banjo, concertina or accordion accompaniment. He sounded like a singer in a pub. This was the antithesis of the approach taken by everyone from Cecil Sharp to Benjamin Britten, where traditional songs had to be carefully arranged and performed in the manner of the classical tradition. Yet it was the very simplicity of Lloyd's approach that made it effective. In this sense, the impact was like that of skiffle. Anyone who was interested could have a go – and they did. Folk clubs sprang up across the country. MacColl's claim that there were 1,500 of them in Britain by 1957 was almost certainly exaggerated, but there were certainly enough for the Folk Revival to have become a movement.

Lloyd was a folk purist in that he sang only traditional British and Australian songs. He neither wrote songs himself nor performed songs by contemporary writers; and he also chose to distance himself from the growing influence of American folk and blues music. In this, however, he was swimming against the tide. The original Folk Revival had been an essentially British affair, although some of the ideas behind it had come from central Europe. The Second Folk Revival, like so much else in British music in the post-war decades, had a strong American component, which can best be illustrated in the career of Alan Lomax (1915–2002), variously described as a folk-song collector, ethnomusicologist, archivist, editor, film-maker and crucially – like so many others involved in the Second Folk Revival – a political activist.

By the time he arrived in Britain in 1950, Lomax had already had a distinguished career, including a period in charge of the folk-song archive in Washington's Library of Congress. He had produced albums by Woody Guthrie and Lead Belly. He had written and produced an American ballad opera, *The Martins and the Coys*, about feuding families who put aside their differences to help win the war against Hitler. It was broadcast on the BBC in 1944 with what now seems a legendary cast, including Burl Ives, Woody Guthrie, Sonny Terry and Pete Seeger. He had come to London to edit the *Columbia World Library of Folk and Primitive Music*, but he soon had a much broader impact. Visiting Scotland in 1951, he worked with the Scottish poet, songwriter and communist intellectual, Hamish Henderson (1919–2002). With Henderson as guide and adviser, Lomax recorded some two hundred and fifty Gaelic work songs sung by women in the Western Isles. The resulting collection was a significant factor in the decision to establish a School of Scottish Studies at Edinburgh University. In 1953, he appeared on BBC television hosting a series called *The Song Hunter* which presented traditional singers and instrumentalists from various parts of the United Kingdom. (The commissioning editor was the twenty-seven-year-old David Attenborough.) From 1953 to 1958, he worked with the BBC and with the English folklorist Peter Kennedy on a Sunday morning radio series, *As I Roved Out*, which featured traditional singers, looking at their lives as well as their music. In 1955, his second ballad opera, *Big Rock Candy Mountain*, was produced at the Theatre Workshop, run by the actress Joan Littlewood, former wife of Ewan MacColl. Lomax even formed a skiffle group, which had among its members MacColl, Peggy Seeger, and the English folk singer Shirley Collins, with whom he was at that time romantically involved. Lomax may have had little influence as a performer, but his knowledge and experience had a significant impact on the people he worked with – and one of those was Ewan MacColl.

MacColl (1915–89) was born Jimmie Miller to a working-class family living in Salford in Lancashire. His parents were Scottish and passed on to him an extensive repertoire of Scottish folk songs. They were also active socialists. His father was a particularly militant trade unionist and member of the Communist Party. Young Miller shared his father's politics and, on leaving school and being faced with unemployment, joined the Young Communist League. He showed a talent for writing satirical poems and articles and soon became involved with the local Workers' Theatre. Finding it insufficiently radical, he set up his own street theatre group, Red Megaphone. It was during this period that he wrote one of his best-known songs, 'The Manchester Rambler', in support of ramblers fighting for the right to walk in open countryside (the 'mass trespass movement'). He met and married the actress Joan Littlewood and together they established Theatre of Action and Theatre Union. After the war, they formed Theatre Workshop, with Littlewood as producer and MacColl (as he had by that time become) as playwright. He wrote eleven plays between 1945 and 1952, many of them featuring songs he had written himself – including 'The Asphalter's Song' and the famous and much-recorded 'Dirty Old Town'.

Only in 1952, after Theatre Workshop had moved to London and he and Littlewood had divorced (although they continued to work together), did MacColl become seriously involved in traditional music and the Folk Revival. Even then, his motivation was as much political as musical. Folk music became an extension of his political work, and he approached it with the same commitment and intensity. He began working with Bert Lloyd and Alan Lomax on a 1953 radio series, *Ballads and Blues,* which mixed a range of British and American folk and blues styles. The same trio, with the addition of the uilleann-pipes-player and Irish folk-song-collector Seamus Ennis, then opened a club in London's Soho district also called Ballads and Blues, although the emphasis in the club was more strongly on folk music. MacColl's insistence that singers should sing from their own tradition – which meant that British singers had to stop trying to sound like Lead Belly or Woody Guthrie – has been credited with accelerating the revival of interest in traditional British folk.[1]

In 1956, MacColl met Peggy Seeger – sister of the American singer and activist, Pete Seeger, and a friend of Lomax – and they formed a personal and professional partnership that lasted for the rest of their lives. Although they performed, wrote and recorded together for thirty years, MacColl and Seeger are probably best known today for the eight, innovative radio ballads that were recorded for the BBC between 1957 and 1964. Each one-hour programme took an everyday topic – building Britain's first motor-way, herring fishing, mining, teenagers, gypsy travellers – and told the story of the people involved in their own words, cut and edited to create a radio montage, with the addition of songs and music in the folk idiom written and performed by MacColl and Seeger. The radio ballads contained some of MacColl's most memorable songs: 'Shoals of Herring' and 'North Sea Holes' from *Singing the Fishing*; 'The Big Hewer' from the programme of the same name; 'The Moving On Song' and 'The Thirty-Foot Trailer' from *Travelling People*.

Both as a songwriter and a recording artist, MacColl was remarkably prolific. He recorded nearly thirty albums of traditional English and Scottish material, many of them in collaboration with Peggy Seeger; he also worked with Bert Lloyd on a series featuring selections from the so-called Child Ballads, collected and published by Professor Francis Child at the end of the nineteenth century. Then there were numerous albums of his own songs – with titles like *Scots Street Songs* (1956), *Shuttle and Cage* (1957), *Bad Lads and Hard Cases* (1959), *Four Pence a Day* (1963) and *British Industrial Folk Songs* (1963). Because he regarded folk music as the expression of working class culture, MacColl saw his own songs, describing that culture in a modern context, as belonging to the folk tradition. He was writing ballads for the modern age. In doing so, he gave shape to the modern idea of a folk singer, who may choose to use traditional instruments and traditional styles, but is not necessarily bound to traditional material. This was to make possible the careers of later folk-style singer-songwriters in the 1960s and 70s – people such as Nick Drake, Richard Thompson, Brian McNeill, Dougie MacLean, Andy Irving, Christy Moore, and many others.

By the mid-1960s, a decade after the first LP recordings by Lloyd and MacColl, folk music was booming. It would never challenge rock'n'roll or pop, but it was no longer an exclusive minority interest. Singers and instrumentalists who would remain leading figures on the British folk scene for the next thirty or forty years made their first appearances. The Ian Campbell Folk Group broke new ground with their *Ceilidh at the Crown* (1962). It was their first release, and it was also the first record to feature a live recording from a folk club. The same year, the young guitarist Davey Graham (1940–2008) came out with the guitar instrumental 'Angi', that rapidly became a folk club standard. In 1964, Anne Briggs (b.1944), who has been credited with inspiring a generation of female singers – among

them June Tabor, Maddy Prior and Sandy Denny – made her first recording, *The Hazards of Love*. Nineteen sixty-five was something of a bumper
year. The Yorkshire group, the Watersons, released their first album, *Frost
and Fire*, featuring some remarkable and original close harmony singing.
Martin Carthy (b. 1941) released his eponymous first album – the first in a
series of five that would also feature Dave Swarbrick (1941–2016) on violin.
Bert Jansch (1943–2011) and John Renbourn (1944–2015), both of whom
would go on to form the idiosyncratic group, Pentangle, also released
eponymous first albums. And in 1966, contemporary folk music joined
with the psychedelic counterculture when Robin Williamson, Clive Palmer
and Mike Heron recorded their first album as the Incredible String Band.

It was the 1950s that made this transformation possible. Lloyd, Lomax,
MacColl and Seeger all regarded pop music as something like a conspiracy,
fundamentally manufactured and ungenuine. Yet, in one sense at least,
they took the first steps along the road that has since connected folk music
far more closely with pop and rock than with classical music. Seen with
hindsight, one of the most radical developments of the period was the
introduction of the banjo and the guitar into folk instrumentation. The
banjo is of African origin, but came to prominence in black American
music during the second half of the nineteenth century. It was adopted by
sailors to accompany singing on board ship and spread not only to Britain
but also to Australia. In Britain, it was used by music hall 'minstrels' and
then, as we have seen, in trad jazz and skiffle. In the 1950s, the banjo was
frequently used to accompany folk songs, although its popularity declined
during the 1960s – unlike the guitar.

The Spanish or classical guitar was, of course, a familiar and respected
instrument, and classical guitar music was sufficiently popular for concerts
by the great Spanish guitarist Andrés Segovia to sell out when he visited
London in 1949. But it was through American blues and jazz, particularly
in the post-war years, that the potential of the guitar as an instrument in
popular music came to be recognised and realised. In the context of folk
music, the acoustic guitar rapidly overtook the violin, the concertina, the
accordion and the banjo to become the accompanying instrument of
choice. This spurred criticism from purists at the time, but by the 1960s,
the image of the folk singer and his guitar had become firmly established,
and that association has been so completely successful that it is now almost
impossible to think of folk music without the guitar.

Then, in the mid-60s, everything changed again. The electric guitar had emerged from the United States during the 1930s. The guitar was an essential rhythm instrument in dance bands, but as bands grew bigger and brass sections grew louder, it required amplification if it was to be heard. Blues singers in United States quickly saw the possibilities of the electric guitar and so did the early rock'n'rollers. Indeed, without the electric guitar rock'n'roll would not have been possible. Then in 1965, Bob Dylan played an electric set at the Newport Folk Festival, creating a storm of outrage among traditionalists. His new, electrified version of contemporary folk music was heard in Britain during his 1966 tour when he played in twelve cities, beginning with Dublin and ending at the Royal Albert Hall. During the Manchester concert, he was famously called 'Judas' by a member of the audience for betraying the true nature of folk music. Dylan's experiment made it almost natural for folk music to attach itself to and merge into pop and rock – which is what happened in Britain when musicians like Martin Carthy, Ashley Hutchings, Dick Gaughan, Richard Thompson and John Martyn began to play folk music on electric rather than acoustic guitars. They added bass, drums, and often an electric violin, thus creating the explosion of folk-rock groups like Fairport Convention, Steeleye Span, the Albion Band, Horslips, Five Hand Reel, the Oyster Band, and Lindisfarne, during the 1970s.

This Second Folk Revival spread to all parts of the United Kingdom, but, as before, in Scotland and Ireland folk music was closer to the surface of national consciousness than in England. This meant that the process of revival was less about educating and encouraging a new generation than about bringing out and publicising performers who were already there. In Scotland, Hamish Henderson was a key figure. Henderson's decision to stage a ceilidh during the Edinburgh People's Festival in 1951 – something strongly encouraged by Lomax – was a landmark moment in bringing Scottish traditional music, performed in a broadly traditional manner, to a public stage. Also important were the recordings made by Lomax and Henderson of Jeannie Robertson, a Scottish traveller from Aberdeen. Lomax persuaded her to come south to appear on television in London, and many of her songs appeared on an album, *Scottish Ballads and Folk Songs* (1960) – among them 'I'm a Man You Don't Meet Every Day', which has been recorded many times in recent years. Perhaps because folk music was better known and understood in Scotland, it was often a less serious business than in England. Hamish Imlach (1940–96) became known for his gospel parody, 'The Cod Liver Oil and the Orange Juice', while Robin

Hall (1936–98) and Jimmy MacGregor (b. 1930) mixed folk songs with comedy numbers such as 'Football Crazy' and 'Donald, Where's Your Troosers'. These and other artists like the Glaswegian singer and storyteller Alex Campbell (1925–87) brought Scottish music to a wider audience. And they in turn prepared the way for groups such as the McCalmans and the Corries which emerged in the early 1960s; for instrumentalists like the Shetland fiddler Aly Bain (b. 1946), singers such as Dick Gaughan (b. 1948), and songwriters like Brian McNeill (b. 1950). From the 1970s onwards, Scottish folk music has enjoyed a number of highly successful champions, including the Battlefield Band, Boys of the Lough, Capercaillie, and the internationally popular folk-rock group, Runrig.

In Ireland in the 1950s, traditional music remained popular and widespread, but it was dominated by ceilidh bands, which meant that while it was frequently heard in bars and at local dances, with a concentration on jigs, reels, hornpipes, polkas, slip-jigs and waltzes, it featured less prominently at major public events or on radio or television. Seamus Ennis worked hard to preserve Ireland's folk heritage, collecting well over 2,000 songs and tunes, but much of the stimulus for the revival of interest in Irish traditional music came from outside the country. There was Margaret Barry (1917–89), another singer recorded by Lomax, known particularly for her singing of 'She Moves Through the Fair' and 'The Turfman from Ardee'. She was an Irish traveller – although she referred to herself as a 'tinker' – who sang regularly and successfully at Irish street fairs. Lomax brought her across to London where she recorded several albums and sang to an audience of 3,600 at the Royal Festival Hall. Only after her success in England did she go back and make her debut at Dublin's Theatre Royal. The Clancy Brothers and Tommy Makem, probably the most popular of the Irish groups of the 1960s, began their career in the United States, where they recorded their first album, a collection of Irish rebel songs, *The Rising of the Moon* (1956), and their second, a collection of drinking songs, *Come Fill Up Your Glass with Us* (1959). The success of these records led them to be invited onto the *Ed Sullivan Show*. Hearing of savage winter weather in New York, the mother of the Clancy Brothers sent Aran sweaters for the whole group. The subsequent television appearance sent sales of both records and sweaters soaring and created an association between Aran sweaters and folk singers that still persists in some quarters. In Ireland, as elsewhere, the 1960s were marked by a sudden flowering of new folk-music talent. Nineteen sixty-two saw the formation of two groups that would carry Irish traditional music around the world – the Dubliners and the Chieftains – and they were soon followed by the Wolfe Tones and the Irish Rovers. These, in their turn, paved the way for a new generation of bands and musicians that would open up Irish music during the 1970s: Planxty and Christy Moore, the Bothy Band, De Dannan, and the folk-rock group Horslips.

108   Malcolm Arnold

On 24 September 1969, the composer and conductor Malcolm Arnold took the rostrum at the Royal Albert Hall to conduct the Royal Philharmonic Orchestra and the rock band Deep Purple in the Concerto for Group and Orchestra by the Deep Purple keyboard player, Jon Lord. It was a ground-breaking project and the culmination of a long and difficult process. Malcolm Arnold had leapt at the chance to become involved in the project, but Lord's idea did not have the wholehearted support of the rest of the band, and some members of the RPO were prejudiced and obstructive. It took all the considerable force of Arnold's personality to bring them into line.[1] In the end, the performance was a success. The audience loved it, although the mainstream musical press was stuffy about the experiment. Fifty years on, the weaknesses of the piece show. The first movement, with its intense guitar solo and some fine orchestral writing, remains impressive, but the second movement is let down by weak lyrics and bland vocals, while the finale, which begins with some good percussion playing and a good drum solo, is only just strong enough to bring the work to a conclusion. Nonetheless, it was a symbolic night. It marked the first major public outing for symphonic rock – a genre that was developed and extended by bands such as Procol Harum, Yes, and Pink Floyd; and it showed just how far music had progressed since the end of the war.

Malcolm Arnold (1921–2006) was the ideal figure to champion Jon Lord's idea. He was born in Northampton, where his father owned a shoe manufacturing business; the family background was respectable, middle class and Methodist. From his early childhood, his mother encouraged his musical talent, and then, when he was twelve, came a musical epiphany. The family were on holiday in Bournemouth when he heard Louis Armstrong play in a hotel ballroom. The experience fed into the contrary or rebellious streak that was fundamental to Arnold's character. He became an avid collector of jazz and blues records; he took up the trumpet in preference to the violin which he was learning at the time; and it was as a student of the trumpet that in 1937, at the age of sixteen, he won a scholarship to the RCM.

The young Arnold was constantly challenging discipline. On one occasion, he ran away to Plymouth with a beautiful Welsh girl from the Royal College of Art and got a job in a dance band. His parents had to hire private detectives to track him down. George Dyson was Director of the RCM at the time. A lesser man than he would have expelled Arnold, but Dyson actually persuaded him to come back and continue his studies. When the war came, Arnold left the RCM – without any formal qualifications – to play trumpet with the LPO and, despite the uncertainties of the times, married Sheila Nicholson, a young violinist. When he was called up, he registered as a conscientious objector, but later changed his mind and volunteered. Posted to a military band instead of a combat role, he shot himself in the foot in order to be returned to civilian life, somehow managing to avoid being court-martialled. At this stage, he still thought of himself as an instrumentalist rather than a composer. He joined the BBC Symphony Orchestra for a short while, before returning to the LPO in 1946 as principal trumpet. Then the Society for the Promotion of New Music organised a performance of *Larch Trees*, a tone poem he had written during the war. This led to a Mendelssohn Scholarship, a year in Italy, and the decision, in 1949, to become a full-time composer.

That decision having been made, Arnold threw himself into composition with an energy that was both prodigious and self-destructive. He had a serious breakdown in 1950 and was in hospital for three months. He recovered, but alcohol continued to be a problem, and there were numerous affairs which put his marriage under strain. He won an Oscar for the music for David Lean's *Bridge on the River Kwai* in 1958, but the following year, writing the score for Joseph Mankiewicz's *Suddenly, Last Summer* in which issues of mental illness feature strongly, he had another serious collapse. His first marriage broke up in 1962. A second marriage followed, but, after a happy period in Cornwall, things grew steadily worse and it, too, broke up amid alcoholism, affairs, domestic violence and depression. Surrounded by family tragedies – one brother was killed in the war, another died in a suicide pact, his sister died of cancer – Arnold himself tried to commit suicide twice. His family took out a court order and he was confined to a psychiatric hospital for over two years. Only in 1984 did some stability return to his life when a young man called Anthony Day was recruited as Arnold's carer. He stayed twenty-two years, until the composer's death at the age of eighty-five.

And yet, despite his demons and the tragedies surrounding his life, Arnold produced a vast amount of fascinating music, some of it profound, some eccentric, some light-hearted, much of it entertaining, and much of it misunderstood. In 1956, for example, he composed *A Grand, Grand Overture* for the celebrated cartoonist and musical comedian Gerard Hoffnung. It required an orchestra, three vacuum cleaners, a floor polisher and four rifles. It was dedicated to President Hoover, and Arnold even gave it an opus number. The public laughed, but the critics felt challenged and therefore threatened. How did such a work relate to the sombre-toned Third Symphony, written the following year at a time when Arnold was grieving for the death of his mother and had just met Shostakovich in Prague? And how did the seriousness of the Third Symphony relate to the alternately jaunty and emotional patriotism of *The Bridge on the River Kwai*? Or *The Bridge on the River Kwai* to the slapstick comedy of his scores for the *St Trinian's* films? With Britten or Tippett, the critics knew where they were, but which was the real Malcolm Arnold? Was he a serious composer or was it all just a game?

In fact, versatility was an essential part of Arnold's musical personality. It stemmed from a refusal to conform, and a refusal to regard any one musical form or genre as superior to another – something which itself probably stemmed from his early encounter with the jazz of Louis Armstrong. He composed scores for sixty-four full-length feature films, and at least the same number for shorter films, television programmes and documentaries. In part, these may have been undertaken because the money was welcome, but he is on record as saying that composers should not take on film work if they do not feel themselves in sympathy with the film for which they are providing the music.[2] His scores were often written at speed – he was given just ten days to write the music for *The Bridge on the River Kwai* – but they demonstrate both his understanding of the medium itself, what it could and could not achieve, and of the increasingly sophisticated, even cosmopolitan, expectations of cinema audiences. His technical versatility and his sympathy with different musical traditions allowed him to move with apparent ease between a range of different styles. The contrast between *The Bridge on the River Kwai* and the girls' school comedies of the *St Trinian's* series has already been mentioned. Caribbean sounds and rhythms feature in *Island in the Sun* (1955). There are oriental flavours (not particularly original ones, it has to be said) mixed in with the rich romanticism of *The Inn of the Sixth Happiness* (1958). The score for *Nine Hours to Rama* (1963), about the assassination of Ghandi, introduces Indian modes, while *Tunes of Glory* (1960), a story about a Scottish regiment, leans heavily on Scottish rhythms and the bagpipes. He could move easily between the heroic strains necessary for *The Heroes of Telemark* (1965), and the echoes of folk song and 'We Three Kings' which feature in *Whistle Down the Wind* (1961), a film telling the story of three children who find a fugitive murderer in a barn and believe him to be Jesus.

Because he did not distinguish in compositional terms between different genres, this level of versatility is also evident in his symphonies. He wrote nine between 1946 and 1986. The First (1949), clearly influenced by Sibelius, was written in the aftermath of the Second World War, and has something of a war symphony about it: melodic passages are overwhelmed by the intrusion of heavy brass; and there is an odd, almost parodic military march. The Second (1953) moves from a pastoral opening, through a burst of extrovert self-expression, to a very Mahlerian funeral march and a brilliantly-scored fugal finale. The Third (1957) is more consistently sombre, but in the Fourth (1960) Arnold's true nature as a symphonist broke through. Commissioned by Glock at the BBC, it was written in the wake of the 1959 Notting Hill race riots, and has been interpreted as a picture of British society at the time. A rather ordinary dance tune is disrupted by loud, threatening passages based around Caribbean percussion and Caribbean rhythms. A light scherzo is followed by a dream-like, sensual, even sleazy slow movement, which is then blown away by an explosive finale, with a fugue, a march, loud dissonance and more Caribbean percussion. The Fifth Symphony (1960) plays elaborate cipher games with the initials of Arnold's friend, Gerard Hoffnung, who had recently died aged just thirty-four, and those of his bereaved wife, Annetta. It is also a memorial to another friend, the brilliant, young French horn player, Dennis Brain, who had been killed in a car crash. It has a big, romantic central tune, a blues-based interlude over string chords, and ends with bells suggesting a funeral. The Sixth Symphony (1967) has echoes of saxophonist Charlie Parker and be-bop; it has a section where the orchestra seems to imitate a pop group; and it ends with more bells, apparently – but not certainly – triumphant. The Seventh (1973) makes a reference to the Irish folk group, The Chieftains. And so it went on, with each symphony throwing up new ideas and new influences.

New music in Europe during the late 1950s and early 60s was heavily influenced by the Darmstadt School, a group of composers, musicians and musical theorists who attended the International Summer Course for New Music held annually in the German city. Darmstadt represented the post-war avant-garde. It included composers such as Luigi Nono (1924–90), Luciano Berio (1925–2003), Pierre Boulez (1925–2006) and Karlheinz Stockhausen (1928–2007), and became synonymous with uncompromising modernism and twelve-note serial techniques, although such a perception was not strictly correct: not all those who attended were outright serialists, and only a few extremists attempted to impose a serialist orthodoxy. In the end, there was sufficient friction between different factions for the school to dissolve in disagreement and acrimony, but what Darmstadt did, in the broader scheme of things, was to create an expectation, even a belief, that new music should *sound* modern, however 'modern' was defined.

Of course, neither Britten and Tippett were Darmstadt disciples, but they sounded more obviously and consciously modern than Arnold, and they did not ignore, or poke fun at, the musical establishment in the way that he did. Whatever its virtues, the Darmstadt School had little room for humour, so a man who could revel in the idea of a comic overture called *Beckus the Dandiprat* or write a *Grand Concerto Gastronomique for Eater, Waiter, Food and Orchestra* was never going to sympathise with its aims. Indeed, Arnold never sympathised with modernism at all, regarding it as prescriptive and limiting. His music could be dissonant and aggressive, but it was essentially diatonic, tonal and full of melody. It was immensely varied and inclusive, crossing boundaries with great versatility, conforming to nobody's expectations, and, in the case of his film music, making a lot of money. All this continued to upset those critics of the 50s and 60s who saw modernity as an end in itself. It also alienated the British musical establishment – although, to be fair, Arnold's erratic, drunken and often aggressive behaviour certainly helped in this respect. As time progressed, it became increasingly difficult for his 'serious' music to get a hearing, even when it was popular with both players and the public.

Arnold's championing of Jon Lord's Concerto for Group and Orchestra in the autumn of 1969 came at the end of twenty years during which he had worked and composed with incredible but damaging intensity. Shortly afterwards, his health collapsed again. He gave up writing for films, the sheer volume of which had been part of the problem: at one stage he was producing six film scores a year in addition to other work. He did not cease composing altogether – over the course of the next thirty years there would be three more symphonies, a fine Second String Quartet, the *John Field Fantasy* for piano and orchestra, and some settings of John Donne, all produced at times when illness receded for a while – but the bulk of his composing was done, and he began to slip out of the public eye. His involvement with Deep Purple was the culmination of his commitment to working across musical genres. It also showed how he had managed to remain abreast of, and in sympathy with, fashions in popular music – jazz, blues, pop, rock – which had succeeded one another with immense rapidity during those twenty intense years. Tippett, as we have seen, also integrated aspects of popular music into his work, but with Tippett it was an intellectual process: he incorporated popular genres into his musical language as a means of expressing the ideas he wanted to communicate. With Arnold, the process was more visceral. Both his attitude and his music pointed not to some higher musical unity, but to the rapidly widening gap between contemporary classical music – which he saw as elitist and exclusive – and the rest of the musical world. It was a gap he wanted to bridge. Arnold was not a great composer in the sense that he changed the direction of music, but he was a highly individual one, and he wrote a lot of varied and entertaining music. If proof were required that, in the second half of the twentieth century, British music still retained the capacity to go its own way, heedless of theories, he provided it.

For all his adaptability, his willingness to respond to and integrate other musical genres into his work, Arnold's music remains rooted in the pre-1945 world – probably the last composer of any real significance of whom this is true. Even the much-neglected symphonist Robert Simpson (1921–97), who was the same age as Arnold, did not start composing until the 1950s. The contrast between 1939 and 1945 was in many ways greater than between 1914 and 1918. Those composers who came to musical maturity or were born after 1945 found themselves in a social, political and physical environment that was wholly different from that of their predecessors. Moreover, that environment was evolving at an unprecedented speed. Naturally enough, taken as a whole, their music reflects these changes.

Since 1945, Britain has produced a succession of talented and original composers, pursuing many different – and often contrasting – approaches to the idea of what constitutes classical music in the modern world. A rapidly-assembled and far from comprehensive list would include names such as Malcolm Williamson (1931–2003), Harrison Birtwistle (b.1934), Peter Maxwell Davies (1934–2016), Richard Rodney Bennett (1936–2012), John McCabe (1939–2015), John Tavener (1944–2013), Michael Nyman (b.1944), Oliver Knussen (b.1952), Judith Weir (b.1954), Sally Beamish (b.1956), James MacMillan (b.1959), George Benjamin (b.1960), and Gabriel Jackson (b.1962). It is not possible, in these pages, to enter into any assessment of their work – or that of their many contemporaries who would also deserve inclusion. In part, this is simply a question of space. But there is also a sense in which much of their music is still too close, too contemporary, to be considered with the level of objectivity that is possible for the music of earlier generations.

109   Rock'n'Roll and After

The term 'rock-and-roll' (soon contracted to 'rock'n'roll') was first used as early as 1951 by the extrovert American disc jockey, Alan Freed, to describe the kind of black rhythm-and-blues music that he played on his show on Radio WJW in Cleveland, Ohio. The following year, Freed was responsible for organising the Moondog Coronation Ball, the first ever rock'n'roll concert of any size, which was devoted to the music he had been promoting. It was staged in the Cleveland Arena, a hockey and baseball stadium that could hold up to 10,000 people. On the day, however, 20,000 turned up, and, after the first song, sung by Paul 'Hucklebuck' Williams, the authorities closed the concert down, fearing that such a large crowd might become uncontrollable – and thus, incidentally, creating the association between rock'n'roll, teenagers and social disorder, which was to persist on both sides of the Atlantic for many years. Despite the size of the Cleveland audience, rock'n'roll remained a minority interest until 1954, when Bill Haley and His Comets released 'Shake, Rattle and Roll'. Shortly afterwards, their recording of 'Rock Around the Clock' was chosen as the theme song for the 1955 film Blackboard Jungle. Suddenly, rock'n'roll was a marketable commodity, and what is remarkable is how quickly and successfully it was marketed outside the United States.

'Shake, Rattle and Roll' was issued in Britain in December 1954. 'Rock

Around the Clock' followed in January 1955. Elvis Presley's first British singles 'Heartbreak Hotel' and 'Blue Suede Shoes' both came out that May. Before the end of the year, the film *Rock Around the Clock* was on general release in cinemas around Britain. The floodgates were open. A wave of new American singers was launched upon the British market, singing songs specifically directed at young people and immediately seized upon by the new generation of young consumers. These were songs that would later be recognised as rock'n'roll classics, many of them still regularly revived on British radio. Gene Vincent released 'Be-Bop-A-Lula' in July 1956. Little Richard's 'Rip It Up' (December 1956) was followed by 'Long Tall Sally' and 'Tutti Frutti' (both February 1957). Chuck Berry's first British hit was 'School Days' (June 1957), followed by 'Sweet Little Sixteen' (May 1958). Buddy Holly was immediately successful with 'Peggy Sue' (December 1957) and 'Rave On' (June 1958). Eddie Cochran's classic 'Summertime Blues' (November 1958) was followed by 'C'mon Everybody' (March 1959). And, of course, Elvis Presley continued to enjoy a string of hits, including 'Hound Dog' (November 1956), 'All Shook Up' (May 1957), 'Jailhouse Rock' (February 1958) and 'King Creole' (October 1958), many of them linked to the series of formulaic, music-and-romance films – one or even two a year up to 1970 – that served to promote the star and his music.

The British music industry quickly sought to find and groom its own rock'n'roll stars. One of the first was Tommy Steele (real name Thomas Hicks; b. 1936). Steele was a merchant seaman, who had played guitar and banjo in skiffle groups, including the Vipers, but, hearing the music of Buddy Holly when his ship docked in Norfolk, Virginia, he became a convert to rock'n'roll. Tommy Steele and the Steelmen released 'Rock with the Caveman', a not entirely serious song with lyrics by Lionel Bart, at the end of 1956. It sold well, and was rapidly followed by a series of hits, mostly covers of American songs – the most successful being 'Singing the Blues', which reached no. 1 in January 1957. In the end, however, Steele was never quite convincing as a rock'n'roll star. Within two or three years, he was recording comic singles such as 'Little White Bull' and 'What a Mouth'. Like Lonnie Donegan, when he sought to move away from American material and establish a British image, he fell back on songs that suggested music hall and the kind of light entertainment featured on television variety shows. Steele quickly made the transition to that world, becoming a well-loved entertainer and star of West End musicals. Then came Marty Wilde (real name Reginald Smith; b. 1939). With his backing band the

Wildcats, Marty Wilde had five top-ten hits – all covers of successful American songs – between 1958 and 1959. These included 'Endless Sleep', 'Donna', and 'Teenager in Love'. Although considered by some to be one of the best of British rock'n'roll singers, he gradually lost popularity, becoming more successful as a songwriter than a performer.

A more durable and successful attempt to emulate the success of American stars was Cliff Richard (real name Harry Webb; b. 1940). Born in India but brought up in South London, he was playing in skiffle bands by the age of sixteen; then, under his real name, he became lead singer with a local rock'n'roll group, the Drifters. Under the influence of the promoter and theatre owner Harry Greatorex, Harry Webb became Cliff Richard (the first half of the name intended to suggest rock, the second a tribute to Little Richard). Record producer Norrie Paramor presided over their first recording session. The song 'Move It', written by Ian Samwell, a member of the Drifters, was narrowly preferred to an American cover for a first single. It was released in September 1958 and rapidly reached no. 2 in the charts. A string of rock'n'roll hits followed – 'Mean Streak' (May 1959), 'Living Doll' (July 1959), 'Please Don't Tease' (July 1960), 'It'll Be Me' (September 1962). Following a change of personnel and a legal challenge from the American vocal group of the same name, the Drifters became the Shadows. Although they continued to be Cliff Richard's backing band, the Shadows also released a long series of instrumental hits in their own right – among them 'Apache' (July 1960), 'Wonderful Land' (March 1962), 'Foot Tapper' (March 1963), and 'Atlantis' (June 1963). In fact, before the coming of the Beatles, the Shadows were undoubtedly Britain's leading 'beat group', to use the terminology of the time.

Initially presented to the public as a slightly rebellious champion of youth and youthful music, very much in the mould of Elvis Presley, Richard rapidly matured into a singer of melodic popular songs with a broader appeal. The change is reflected in the sequence of films that were created as vehicles for him. *Espresso Bongo* (1959) was about a young bongo player making his way to rock'n'roll stardom. Though certainly not gritty realism, it is set in a world of coffee bars, strip clubs and unscrupulous agents. *The Young Ones* (1961), about a young singer who wants to save his youth club from a property developer, is much closer to mainstream light entertainment; while *Summer Holiday* (1963) is a traditional light-hearted musical with no realism and no rebellion in sight. Songs taken from the last two of these films for release as singles – 'The Young Ones' (January

1962), 'Bachelor Boy' (December 1962), and 'Summer Holiday' (February 1963) – were all no. 1 hits.

There were, of course, numerous other British attempts at rock'n'roll. Johnny Kidd and the Pirates' 1960 hit, 'Shakin' all Over', was one of the most successful, but many of the other singers who appeared during the late 1950s and very early 1960s – Adam Faith, Billy Fury, John Leyton, Helen Shapiro – were happier singing songs that, while less aggressive than rock'n'roll, were still distinct from the romantic ballads of an earlier generation of singers. These songs, which became known as 'beat ballads', marked a dilution of the intensity of the initial phase of rock'n'roll, and an attempt by managements and record companies to broaden the appeal of their young artists.

More than trad jazz or skiffle, rock'n'roll became a movement, driven by a combination of music and extra-musical factors. For reasons too complex to be more than touched on here, young people wanted to assert their difference. That they should seek to differentiate themselves from the rest of society by age rather than by professional status or social class was an entirely new idea. The often-quoted fact that until the late 50s, children and young people dressed like miniature versions of their parents is important. The generation to which rock'n'roll appealed wanted to look different, dance differently, and listen to different music. Money was part of it, but so, too, was the fact that, unlike their parents, they did not have adult experience of the war and post-war austerity to restrain them. 'Rock Around the Clock' may have started things off, but Bill Haley himself did not embody the spirit of rock'n'roll. When he toured Britain in 1957, he was regarded by many as a fat, middle-aged man (he was over forty) in a tartan jacket. Rock'n'roll was not about changing the world: the association between popular music and political change, a connection reflecting the influence of both folk music and the psychedelic counter culture, would come later. Rock'n'roll was about a generation creating an identity for itself.

Rock'n'roll was simple enough: a solo singer (sometimes with backing vocalists), lead guitar, rhythm guitar, bass and drums, sometimes a piano. Songs were up tempo, in 4/4 rhythm, with blues-style harmonic progressions, and verses and choruses usually consisting of three four-bar phrases. And yet it created something approaching a moral panic. Parents, town councils, the Church – all felt threatened. The rhythms were seen as primitive, even sexual. So, too, were the gyrations of some of the singers. And there was added suspicion because rock'n'roll derived from black

American music. The Bishop of Woolwich called for the film *Rock Around the Clock* to be banned because it incited depravity,[1] and a number of local councils followed his advice. The *Daily Mail* even dubbed rock'n'roll 'the Negro's revenge'.[2] It is certainly true that there were occasions when young cinema-goers danced in the aisles rather than sitting through the film, and ripped up seats in wild excitement. It is also true that rock'n'roll became associated with Teddy Boys, a youth subculture that began in the East End of London and spread rapidly to the rest of the country, characterised by long, pseudo-Edwardian jackets, 'drainpipe' trousers and heavily greased hair with extravagant quiffs. In fact, the vandalism of cinemas associated with rock'n'roll probably began not with rock'n'roll itself but with a Teddy Boy audience watching *Blackboard Jungle*, which is about juvenile delinquency, in London in 1956. However, it is worth noting that only a proportion, even a small proportion, of British youth were involved or significantly affected by rock'n'roll; and the numbers involved in violence and disorder were even smaller. That did not stop some of the media indulging in a frenzy of disapproval, which from a twenty-first-century perspective seems disproportionate, even quaint. Even *Melody Maker*, the music industry weekly, came out against rock'n'roll, although the folly of such an attitude was demonstrated when its circulation dropped sharply, while that of the pro-rock'n'roll *New Musical Express* soared.

Yet while much of the printed media were convincing themselves that rock'n'roll constituted an attack on civilised values, the broadcast media were – albeit very slowly – making popular music in general and rock'n'roll in particular more accessible. On the Light Programme, the BBC offered *Saturday Club*, hosted by Brian Matthew, which ran from 1957 until 1969, usually for two hours on a Saturday morning. This was almost the only radio programme to present the new styles of popular music – it included jazz, skiffle, rock'n'roll and beat ballads – until the arrival of *Easybeat* in 1960. This added another hour of popular music, this time on a Sunday morning, hosted initially by Brian Matthew, then later by Keith Fordyce. Even then, given the explosion of popular music that had taken place since the mid-1950s, three hours was a pitifully small allocation. The BBC's failure to reflect audience demand in this respect explains the immense popularity of both Radio Luxembourg and of pirate radio stations. Radio Luxembourg – known as 'Big L' – was a Luxembourg-based commercial radio station. From the mid-1950s, right through the 1960s and 1970s, its English-language service famously broadcast on 208 metres in the medium-wave band. This meant that it could be picked up on the new, small, portable, transistor radios now owned by many teenagers. It offered a range of popular music shows, including a weekly chart show on Saturday evenings, hosted by Barry Alldis. Pirate radio stations began to appear at the beginning of the 1960s. Broadcasting from ships anchored just outside the three-mile limit, they were beyond the reach of British jurisdiction, which did not allow private or commercial broadcasting. The most popular were Radio Caroline and Radio London – although there were many others, including Radio City, Radio Solent, Radio Sutch (funded by Screaming Lord Sutch), and Radio North Sea International – and they broadcast non-stop pop and rock music. Both Radio Luxembourg and the pirate stations broadcast programmes that went beyond popular trends and chart music, championing Motown, American soul or the new psychedelic music. John Peel's late-night *Perfumed Garden* on Radio London became famous for introducing audiences to music by 'underground' artists like the Grateful Dead, Jefferson Airplane, Captain Beefheart – to take three names almost at random – which was otherwise all but inaccessible. By 1965, it was reported that pirate radio stations were attracting weekly audiences of up to fifteen million. That such large audiences did not, apparently, impact upon the numbers listening to the Light Programme is an indication of the immense demand that existed for the kind of pop and rock music programming the pirates offered. In 1966, the government – perhaps moved less by audience figures than by the fact that the pirates were attracting advertising revenue in excess of £2.5 million – determined to act. The 1967 Marine Offences Broadcasting Act made it illegal to supply the pirate ships from the United Kingdom, making it impossible for them to function. One or two, supplied from Continental Europe, continued to broadcast for a while, but their day was over. The demand for popular music broadcasting was largely filled by the advent of Radio 1 that same year, featuring many disc jockeys – such as Tony Blackburn, Kenny Everett, Dave Cash, Emperor Rosko and John Peel – who had made their names on the pirate ships.

The first attempt to put teenage music on television was an uninspired fifteen-minute show called *Cool for Cats*. First transmitted in December 1956 and produced by the ITV company Associated Rediffusion, it featured new single releases, often to the accompaniment of dance routines which did their best to make use of the new visual possibilities of television. Better known and more memorable was the BBC's *Six-Five Special*, which ran for a year from February 1957. Although it suffered from heavy-handed banter on the part of its hosts ('Time to jive on the old Six-Five'), it was the first attempt at a live milieu – a studio without sets, simply filled with an audience listening and dancing to live performances from the resident group, Don Lang and the Frantic Five, and guest performers like Tommy Steele, Petula Clark, Lonnie Donegan and visiting American artists. The BBC was not keen on the format and pressed the producer, Jack Good, to include magazine-style features or an educational component instead of concentrating on the music. Good went off to ABC Television, another part of the ITV network, to produce *Oh, Boy!*, an improved version of the same format; it ran from 1958 to 1959. Resident *Oh, Boy!* performers included Cliff Richard, the Shadows, and Marty Wilde, while guests included Billy Fury, Lonnie Donegan, Shirley Bassey, and touring American artists such as the Ink Spots and Brenda Lee. The BBC came up with a new format in *Juke Box Jury*, where four guest panellists – usually, but not always from the music industry – listened to new releases and gave their verdict as to whether each song was likely to be a 'hit' or a 'miss'. Although comparatively tame by comparison with *Six-Five Special* and *Oh, Boy!*, the format proved durable and the show ran from 1959 until 1967. Nonetheless, it was ITV that seemed to understand, or perhaps accept, how the younger generation wanted its music presented. *Thank Your Lucky Stars* (ABC Television; 1961–66) and *Ready Steady Go!* (Associated Rediffusion; 1963–66) became compulsory viewing for teenage music fans. *Ready Steady Go!* was the more fashionable and exciting of the two, and had a discernible influence on fashion as well as music. The show's female host, Cathy McGowan, with her long dark fringe, heavy makeup, and mini dresses, became a style icon for thousands of teenage girls. Then, in 1964, the BBC combined the live studio format with the kind of chart rundown show already familiar from Radio Luxembourg and the pirate stations. *Top of the Pops* was first transmitted in January 1964 and, although it became increasingly formulaic and mainstream (and was criticised for it) it ran for forty-two years and 2,206 editions. The programme ceased in 2006, but the BBC continues to rebroadcast old episodes.

Records, films, radio and television all contributed to the boom in popular music. So, too, did the coming of transistor radios and car radios, meaning that music was accessible on the move. And then there were juke boxes in coffee bars, youth clubs, pubs and other venues. There was music everywhere. Social commentators noted that teenagers used music in a different way from previous generations. It could be listened to in an active manner, or it could be just background, left on while they did other tasks. Attitudes to music were changing in other ways, too. The growth of television meant that there were more programmes needing signature tunes and soundtracks; and the advent of commercial television meant that there were adverts requiring themes and jingles. Music was increasingly being used to fill a space. In this way, the 1950s and 60s prepared the way for the all-enveloping musical environment of today, where music is piped into every public space, from pubs, restaurants and hotels to shopping malls, supermarkets and dentists' waiting rooms; where call centres play tinny pop songs while you wait to be connected; and where fruit machines and computer games greet success or failure with a blast of musical cliché.

The next great change can be dated to 1963. It saw rock'n'roll and its derivatives give way to what the media initially dubbed 'Merseybeat' – a reference to its Liverpool origins – in order to distinguish it from the more general term 'beat music', which by the early 1960s was being applied to almost any guitar-based music. The terms have no connection with the American 'Beat Generation' and are little used these days, although they remain present in the name of the group that made the initial breakthrough. The Beatles' first single, 'Love Me Do', had been issued in October 1962 on Parlophone Records and had reached no. 17 in the charts. Of the next four singles – 'Please Please Me', 'From Me To You', 'She Loves You' and 'I Want To Hold Your Hand' – all released in 1963, only 'Please Please Me' failed to get to no. 1, although it did reach no. 2. The Beatles were not an overnight success. They had existed as a group since 1960, gone through a couple of personnel changes, built a reputation in Liverpool – notably in the famous Cavern Club – and also in Hamburg; and they had been carefully moulded into a professional ensemble by their manager, Brian Epstein. Their music derived from many existing styles. There was rock-'n'roll; there was rhythm-and-blues; there was country and western; there was skiffle (all four Beatles had played in skiffle bands); and there was trad jazz, too – the Beatles actually released the trad jazz standard 'Ain't She Sweet' as a single in 1964. But the resulting mixture was new; and as well as being new, beat music as played by the Beatles was distinctly British. Unlike every other post-war fashion in popular music, it did not require performers to look or sound American. The Beatles were not the only group of young British musicians playing beat music, but, through a mixture of talent, luck and good management, they were the ones who broke through. And their success opened the door to a hundred competitors and imitators.

The Rolling Stones, whose music was more aggressive and rhythm-and-blues-oriented than that of the Beatles, were formed in 1962. They entered the charts with 'Come On' in 1963, and between 64 and 65 had five consecutive no. 1 hits. The Dave Clark Five promoted 'The Tottenham Sound' as an alternative to Merseybeat, and their single, 'Glad All Over' (1964), knocked the Beatles' 'I Want To Hold Your Hand' from the top of the charts. The Kinks, a very English and idiosyncratic group who later specialised in witty, ironic lyrics, came from Muswell Hill in London and had their first hit with 'You Really Got Me' in 1964. The Animals, a more blues-orientated group fronted by Eric Burden, came from Newcastle-upon-Tyne, and enjoyed hits with 'House of the Rising Sun' (1964) and 'We Got To Get Out of This Place' (1965). There were softer bands, such as Gerry and the Pacemakers, the Searchers, Herman's Hermits and Freddie and the Dreamers. There were harder bands, such as the strongly rhythm-and-blues-flavoured Yardbirds and Pretty Things, or the Who, originally known as the High Numbers, formed in 1964, whose songs were closer to what we now consider rock music. These are just a few of the groups that emerged during the early 1960s – another fifty could be added without exhausting the list, many of them enjoying some degree of commercial success.

The Beatles, however, were the first – and they had soon sold more records and made more money than anyone else in the history of music. In numerical and financial terms their achievements have long since been surpassed, but they are probably the most influential and iconic pop musicians of all time. What made them so special? To begin with, it was the sound. Carefully produced by George Martin – who, like Epstein, made a crucial contribution to the group's success – the Beatles' early releases were engineered to sound like live recordings; they had a rawness and an immediacy that matched early rock'n'roll, and reflected the simple, direct appeal of the music. Driven by the writing partnership of John Lennon and Paul McCartney, the Beatles matured rapidly, refining and developing the three-minute song – some of their best, like 'Taxman', 'Dr Robert', and 'And Your Bird Can Sing', were on the 1966 album, *Revolver*. Their unprecedented success enabled them to take more control over their own development than other groups, allowing them to become more genuinely experimental. *Sergeant Pepper's Lonely Hearts Club Band* (1967), one of the first concept albums, was partly inspired by the Beach Boys' album *Pet Sounds* and the new psychedelic music coming from America's west coast. It also reflected the band's flirtation with drugs and Indian philosophy. At the same time, it is a profoundly British work: Sergeant Pepper himself is an Edwardian figure and there are clear echoes of music hall and circus music. *Sergeant Pepper* was followed by the double album, *The Beatles* (1968; also known as *The White Album*), which is far less coherent and disciplined. It contains some fine songs, but also much that is self-indulgent and of lesser quality. Both *Sergeant Pepper* and *The Beatles* are now widely regarded as iconic productions of the 1960s. *Abbey Road* (1969) and *Let It Be* (1970) feature a number of songs which suggest that the Beatles might have returned to a simpler, more rhythm-and-blues-oriented style, but in 1970 the group broke up in acrimony.

Like rock'n'roll but in reverse, beat music was rapidly and successfully exported to the United States. The success was so sudden and so complete that it became known as the 'British Invasion'. The Beatles' first tour of America began in February 1964. Immediately they arrived, they appeared on the *Ed Sullivan Show,* and it was estimated at the time that forty-five per cent of all United States television viewers watched the programme. By the beginning of April, Beatles singles held the top five places in the Billboard Top 100 chart, a feat never equalled before or since. The Dave Clark Five followed the Beatles on the show just a month later. The Rolling Stones arrived that June. Billy J. Kramer and the Dakotas also appeared with Ed Sullivan and on several other television shows. Dusty Springfield was a huge hit in the Unites States, being described as a white soul singer. The Merseybeats were another band which toured successfully. The Who did not make it across the Atlantic until 1966 when, bizarrely, they were the support act to Herman's Hermits. That same year also saw the Belfast-based group Them on tour. With Van Morrison as lead singer, they played at Los Angeles' famous venue Whisky-A-Go-Go, where their support act was Jim Morrison and the Doors. Only the Kinks were excluded, having been banned from entering the United States, for reasons which never became clear, but possibly because of their rowdy stage act.

The new music of the 1960s changed everything. It needed to be loud, so groups had to have bigger and better amplifiers. It required more complex equipment in the recording studios to meet new production values. It demanded longer tours and bigger venues so that the tide of teenage fans who flocked to their local town hall or ballroom could hear their idols play live (often a disappointing experience as live performance could rarely replicate the quality of studio recordings). The one thing it did not do was stand still. It evolved rapidly.

Many artists – the Hollies, Brian Poole and the Tremeloes, the Searchers, Cilla Black, Lulu – spun off into mainstream pop. Others evolved with the times. In 1967, the Rolling Stones, like the Beatles, briefly jumped on the bandwagon of psychedelic music with *Their Satanic Majesties Request*, but love and peace did not suit the Stones: their next album was *Beggar's Banquet*, which included songs like 'Sympathy for the Devil' and 'Street Fighting Man'. The real exponents of psychedelic rock were bands such as Traffic, who recorded songs with titles like '40,000 Headmen' and 'Shanghai Noodle Factory'; Procol Harum, whose first release was 'A Whiter Shade of Pale'; and Pink Floyd, whose early albums included *Piper at the Gates of Dawn* (1967), *A Saucerful of Secrets* (1968), and *Atom Heart Mother* (1970). By the early 1970s, one strand of psychedelic rock was evolving into 'glam rock', making stars of David Bowie (*Hunk Dory*, 1971; *Ziggy Stardust*, 1972), Elton John (*Goodbye Yellow Brick Road*, 1973) and Queen (*Sheer Heart Attack*, 1974; *A Night at the Opera*, 1975). Another strand developed into progressive rock with concept albums from bands such as the Moody Blues (*In Search of the Lost Chord*, 1968), King Crimson (*In the Court of the Crimson King*, 1969), Yes (*Fragile*, 1971), Genesis (*Nursery Crime*, 1971; *Foxtrot*, 1972) and Pink Floyd, whose 1973 concept album *Dark Side of the Moon* became one of the best selling records of all time. Progressive rock often showed classical influences: the title track of Yes's 1972 album, *Close to the Edge*, was actually based on sonata form. In a parallel development, the harder, more aggressive and blues-influenced strain of 1960s pop music rapidly evolved into hard or heavy rock. Deep Purple was essentially a hard-rock band, Jon Lord's Concerto for Group and Orchestra representing an excursion into progressive or symphonic rock that was uncharacteristic of the band's music as a whole. Other hard rock bands that evolved out of 1960s beat groups included names such as Cream (*Wheels of Fire*, 1968), Led Zeppelin (*Led Zeppelin I* and *II*, both 1969), Black Sabbath (*Paranoid*, 1970), and the Who (*Live at Leeds*, 1970; *Who's Next*, 1971). The Who also recorded a concept album, *Tommy*, in 1969, which remains arguably the most successful attempt to blend rock music and opera. When the self-indulgence and heavy superstructure of the big 1970s bands became too much to bear, punk rock in the mid-1970s was a reversion to the simplicity and everyone-can-do-it approach of skiffle. And Britpop in the 1990s represented another turn of the same wheel.

To follow in detail the twists and turns of these different sub-genres would not only be time consuming and potentially tedious, it would also, again, bring us too close to the present day, making it necessary to offer judgements on music and musicians that cannot yet be seen in their full historical and cultural context. It is sufficient to say that the so-called 'beat revolution' started a chain reaction in music which is still continuing. From the time of the pleasure gardens, through the music halls and into the twenty-first century, Britain has always had a healthy and creative popular-music sector. The beat revolution of the 1960s was further evidence of that creativity. The difference was that it spread like no previous musical trend or fashion.

Epilogue

What conclusions can we draw from the story of British music down the centuries?

British composers have shown themselves resistant to schools, isms, and abstract or theoretical models of composition. They may have studied together, socialised together, swapped ideas and helped with each other's compositions; they may have had shared interests; but their approach to their music was always individual rather than collective. They certainly never formed groups or issued manifestos. Yet such a characterisation is not confined to music. It is there, to a greater or lesser extent, in the British approach to all forms of art – painting, drama, literature, even film.

One recurrent characteristic of British music is a sense of yearning, a sense of transcendental longing sometimes verging on mysticism. It is something that is difficult to define with any precision, and is not unique to British music. It may well have Celtic origins, but it is not limited to Celtic music. It is present in the works of the great Tudor composers of church music, in Sebastian Wesley's anthems, and in Stanford's settings of the Anglican Service. It is not limited to the expression of religious belief; it is there in Bantock, Vaughan Williams, Dyson and Finzi – to take a few names almost at random – and it goes beyond responses to the natural world or English pastoralism. It can be found in the work of folk and folk-rock artists like Kathryn Tickell, Moving Hearts or Runrig, and in some of the progressive rock bands of the 1970s, particularly those, like Pink Floyd, Yes, King Crimson, and Renaissance, that leaned towards symphonic rock. This aspiration towards the transcendental may have been what led so many composers from the late-nineteenth and early-twentieth centuries, and rock and pop groups of the 1960s and 70s, to seek inspiration in the stories of Persia and the philosophies of the Indian subcontinent. Perhaps all that one can say in the end is that it demonstrates an enduring need, somewhere at the heart of British music, to evoke and affirm the spiritual qualities of life, art, and humanity.

Then there is the British genius for word-setting. Again, the ability to set words imaginatively, so that the music complements and enhances their meaning is not uniquely British – one has only to look at the French-Burgundian songwriters, from Machaut and Dufay to Ockeghem and Josquin des Prez; or at the great German lieder writers, from Schubert and Schumann to Wolf, Strauss and Mahler. Yet, whether in Latin or in English, word-setting has been a consistent strength of British composers. The soaring expressiveness of Taverner, Tallis and Byrd; the carefully-wrought artifice of the madrigalists; the absolute clarity of Purcell, even when faced with bad verse; Sullivan's precision in transforming Gilbert's lyrics into unforgettable songs; the intense response to poetry we find in Gurney, Warlock, Ireland and Finzi and others – all this points to a special relationship between composers and the words they set.

Except perhaps in the shadowy days of Dunstable, British music has never been a leader in terms of exploring new styles and techniques; and certainly since the Reformation it has been slow to adopt new ideas, genres and fashions originating on the Continent. This certainly reflects an innate conservatism on the part of the British musical community – and an equally deep-seated feeling, which is not confined to music, that what suits Continental European tastes does not necessarily suit the British. But from the late-seventeenth century onwards that conservatism was rooted in a social and commercial reality. Long before Continental nations, Britain began to move away from traditional patronage as represented by the Church, the monarchy and the aristocracy. Britain became a mercantile society with a rich and influential middle class. Music became increasingly subject to the disciplines of the market place. Promoters, composers and players grew ever more dependent on income from the public – whether from ticket sales, subscriptions, or sales of sheet music. In Britain more than anywhere else, therefore, it became necessary to accommodate and respond to public taste – and public taste was essentially conservative. Yet the lessons learned about the market, and the need to satisfy popular taste, did lead to innovation at the popular end of the musical spectrum, with the pleasure gardens, promenade concerts, music hall, and then pop and rock music.

There is, then, no single characteristic that makes British music unique, just as no British composer has changed the face of music in the manner of Haydn, Beethoven or Wagner. Yet much British music is recognisably British, just as much as German music is recognisably German and Italian music recognisably Italian. Why should that be? It is – it must be – a combination of all the various musical and extra-musical factors that this book has tried to address. British music has a rich history, closely integrated with the religious, political and social history of these islands. It has an equally rich back catalogue of works, much richer than is often realised. There are more than a few British works that merit the title of 'masterpiece' – from Dunstable's motets and Tye's *Euge bone* all the way down to *Peter Grimes* and the Who's rock opera *Tommy*.

If this book does not follow developments right up to the present day, it is not because I do not feel enthusiasm for George Benjamin's *Ringed by the Flat Horizon* or James Macmillan's *Strathclyde Motets*, for the songs of Richard Thompson, Liane Carroll or June Tabor. It is rather because the story still continues and, for all we know, could be at some crucial turning point at the very moment of writing. Judgements made too close to the event are hostages to fortune – and my assessment of *Tommy* may well be one of them. Birtwistle *may* rank alongside Boulez, Maxwell Davies with Sibelius, and MacMillan with Byrd or Tallis, but surely it is too early to tell. To some extent, this principle has already been breached by following Lutyens, Maconchy, Tippett, Arnold and others through to their deaths in the later years of the twentieth or the beginning of our current century. In such cases, all one can say is that it would have been even less satisfactory to end a composer's story midway through his or her life.

If I were to make predictions – which are equally hostages to fortune – I would say that much will depend on the way in which we consume music in the future. From rock'n'roll and its successors to grunge and garage and hip-hop and rap, popular music in all its diverse forms has been far and away the most commercially successful and culturally influential music of the past sixty years – and British groups and British artists have often led the way in terms of creativity and inventiveness. During that time, popular music has often been associated with new ways of experiencing music – the car radio, the portable cassette player, the walkman, the music video, and now information technology in its various manifestations. But the age of downloads, YouTube, Spotify and sharing on social media affects popular music, folk music and classical music equally: it allows a level of access inconceivable to previous generations and will surely lead to an increased blurring of the boundaries between different types and genres of music. The traditional concert or gig format seems unlikely to disappear – indeed, it may even be strengthened by the growth in the popularity of festivals for all kinds of music, but there will be a growing middle ground where different traditions meet and mix. Quite how this will affect popular music and folk music is hard to predict – although the close relationship between pop and rock music and technology will surely continue, spinning off new musical genres along the way – but one can at least see new classical music becoming less rigid, allowing more room for improvisation, drawing on electronics and jazz, but also on older improvisatory traditions, such as those based on the viol and the harpsichord. And social media has already altered the way in which issues and events surrounding classical music are communicated, something which has the potential to attract a new and younger audience.

Whatever happens in the future, this book is an attempt to describe how we got to where we are today.

Notes

54   *The Land without Music*, Clementi, Cramer and Field   pp. 1-10

1   Oskar A. H. Schmitz, *Das Land ohne Musik: englische Gesellschaftsprobleme*, Georg Müller, Munich, 3rd edition 1914, p.30.

2   Heinrich Heine, *Pariser Berichte*, 29 July 1840.

3   Peter Beckford was the cousin of William Beckford, author of the Gothic novel, *Vathek*, and builder of the enormous Gothic Fonthill Abbey in Wiltshire.

4   The nickname 'Glorious John' reappeared in the twentieth century applied to Sir John Barbirolli.

5   Some musicologists classify his works differently and come up with a figure of twenty.

55   Songs and Dances of the Napoleonic Wars   pp. 10-20

1   *Oracle and Daily Advertiser*, 21 April 1802, quoted in *Europe, Empire and Spectacle in British Music*, ed. Rachel Cowgill & Julian Rushton, Ashgate, 2006, p.18.

2   Colin Martin & Geoffrey Parker, *The Spanish Armada*, revised edition, Manchester UP, 1999, p.243.

3   http://www.bl.uk/collection-items/a-new-patriotic-song-from-a-collection-of-mate-rial-relating-to-the-fear-of-a-french-invasion;
http://www.staggernation.com/msb/battle_of_waterloo.php;
http://ballads.bodleian.ox.ac.uk/static/images/sheets/10000/07340.gif
Consulted 20.11.2015.

4   Queen Victoria did not come to the throne until 1837.

5   Technically, the Regency lasted only from 1811, when King George III was declared insane, until his death in 1820. In practice, however, and particu-larly where the arts are concerned, the term Regency is usually employed to cover a period from, say, 1790 until George IV's accession.

6   *The Times*, 16 July 1816.

56   The Philharmonic Society, and the Royal Academy of Music   pp.20-28

1   'The Philharmonic Society', *Quarterly Musical Magazine and Review*, Vol. 1., 1818, pp.340-56 (p.346).

2   'The Philharmonic Society', *Quarterly Musical Magazine and Review*, Vol. 1, p.348.

3   *The Spectator*, 1813, quoted in Charles Knight, *London*, Vols 5–6, Charles Knight & Co, 1843, p.190.

4   George Marek, *Beethoven: Biography of a Genius*, Funk & Wagnalls, 1969, p.533.

5   Kenneth M.Craig Jr, 'The Beethoven Symphonies in London: Initial Decades',
http://symposium.music.org/index.php?option=com_k2&view=item&id=1991:the-beethoven-symphonies-in-london-initial-decades&Itemid=124.

6   *The Times*, 3 February 1825.

7   *Harmonicon*, April 1825.

8   'The Philharmonic Society', *Quarterly Musical Magazine and Review*, Vol. 1, p.349.

9   The numbers used here are based on the generally accepted chronological order of composition. See http://www.unsungcomposers.com/forum/index.php?topic=445.0. Consulted 30.11.2015.

10 Percy Young, *A History of British Music*, p.444.

11 Collet Dobson, 'State of the Royal Academy of Music', *The Musical World*, J. Alfred Novello, 1837, pp.18–21 (p.20).

57   Oratorios and Festivals   pp.28-35

1   'Shetland Notes and Queries', *The Shetland Times*, 14 May 1887. Courtesy of the Shetland Museum and Archives.

2   Ernest Walker, *A History of Music in England*, p.281.

3   Ernest Walker, *A History of Music in England*, p.299.

4   H. R. Haweis, *My Musical Life*, pp.208–9, Longmans Green, 1898.

5   *The Annual Biography and Obituary*, Longman, Rees, Orme, Brown, Green & Longman, 1832, pp.381–90.

6   http://admin.concertprogrammes.org.uk/html/search/verb/ListIdentifiers/set/agentName/26477. Consulted 5 December 2015.

7   Dr Pippa Drummond, *The Provincial Music Festival in England 1784–1914*, Ashgate, 2013, p.189.

8   Quoted in *The Oxford Dictionary of Music*, OUP, 2013, p.189.

58   Foreign Oratorios, Spohr, and Mendelssohn   pp.35-41

1   *The Spectator*, 25 September 1830, p.15.

2   'The Musician About Town', *The Analyst*, Vol. 10, Simpkin & Marshall, 1840, pp.483–491 (pp.485–6).

3   Ronald Pearsall, *Victorian Popular Music*, David & Charles, 1973, p.145.

1   *Harmonicon*, 11 June 1824.

2   The Royal Society of Musicians was previously the Society for the Support of Decayed Musicians so beloved of Handel.

3   *The Musical Times*, Vol. 27, no.519, May 1, 1886, pp. 253–9.

4   *The Musical World*, 17 March 1855.

5   Ernest Newman, *The Life of Richard Wagner*, 4 Vols. CUP, 1976, Vol. II, p.463.

6   *Harmonicon 1828*, Samuel Leigh, 1828, p.155.

7   Letter from Berlioz to Liszt, 23 July 1848.

8   *Journal des Débats*, 29 July 1851, p.2.

9   Letter from Berlioz to Louis-Joseph Duc, 26 May 1848.

1   'An Englishman', 'The Present State of Vocal Art in England', *Quarterly Musical Magazine and Review*, 1824, pp.1–17; 'An Observer', 'The Present State of Music in England', *Quarterly Musical Magazine and Review*, 1824, pp.281–92.

2   'Sketch of the State of Music in London', *Quarterly Musical Magazine and Review*, 1829, pp.275–310 (p.275).

3   Some sources suggest that he chose the pension in preference to a knighthood.

4   Statistically, the popularity of Wesley's services actually peaked in 1938. Nicholas Temperley, *Music and the Wesleys*, U of Illinois P, 2010, p.221.

1   Christopher Fifield, *The German Symphony between Beethoven and Brahms*, Ashgate, 2015, pp.137–8.

2   A special note should be added to recognise 'The Carol Singers', tune by Bennett, words by Charles Haynes, a comic song about a group of carol singers who are arrested for making too much noise and greet the happy morn inside a police station.

3   G. A. Macfarren, 'Jerusalem', *The Musical Times*, Vol. 5, no.100, 1852. p.59.

4   *The Times*, 25 September 1852, p.8.

5   This self-aggrandisement ignored the fact that Willsbridge, a crenellated Gothic monstrosity, did not originally belong to his part of the family. His mother bought it from a bankrupt uncle when he was eighteen.

6   Percy Young, *A History of British Music*, p.472.

62   George Macfarren   pp.65-70

1   *The Musical World*, 1840, p.328.

2   Richard Wagner, *My Life*. http://www.wagneropera.net/MyLife/RW-My-Life-Part-3-1850-1860.htm. Consulted 8 January 2016.

3   *The World*, 4 February 1891, pp.16–20.

63   Early Nineteenth-Century Opera   pp.70-77

1   Hermann Pückler-Muskau, *Tour in England, Ireland, and France in the Years 1828, 1829*, trans. Sarah Austin, Carey and Lea, 1833, pp.59–60.

2   Ann Rigney, *The Afterlives of Walter Scott: Memory on the Move*, OUP, 2012, p.62.

3   Quoted in Eric Walter White, *A History of English Opera*, p.262.

4   *Quarterly Music Magazine and Review*, Vol. VII, 1825, pp.402–3; Vol. VIII, 1826, p.115.

5   *La Sylphide* should not be confused with the better-known *Les Sylphides* (1909), which has music by Chopin orchestrated by Glazunov.

6   George Macfarren, 'Barnett, John', *The Imperial Dictionary of Universal Biography*, ed. John F. Waller. Vol. 1, William Mackenzie, 1863. p.389.

7   *The Spectator*, 5 March 1837, p.14.

64   Balfe, Wallace, and Benedict   pp.77-90

1   *The Literary Gazette 1837*, H. Colburn, 1837, p.771.

2   Eric Walter White, *A History of English Opera*, p.278.

3   *Nabucco* was initially staged under the title *Nino* because the promoters would not allow a biblical name to be used in the publicity.

4   *Sydney Gazette*, 16 February 1836.

5   Catherine Mackerras, 'Wallace, William Vincent (1812–1865)', *Australian Dictionary of Biography*, National Centre of Biography, Australian National University. Consulted 17 January 2016.

6   Carl Rosa's real name was Karl August Nikolaus Rose.

65   Industrial Ballads, and Sea Shanties   pp.91-98

1   'The Cricketers' Song' (1850); 'Song of the Railroads' (1865).

2   Quoted in A.L. Lloyd, *Folk Song in England*, p.320.

3   http://mudcat.org/@displaysong.cfm?SongID=6014. Consulted 22 January 2016.

4   www.traditionalmusic.co.uk/folk-song-lyrics/Weaver_and_the_Factory_Maid.htm Consulted 22 January 2016.

5   A. L. Lloyd, *Folk Song in England*, p.339.

66   Song-&-Supper Rooms, Ballet, and Promenade Concerts   pp.98-109

1   If I had but a thousand a year / What a man would I be / And what sights could I see / If I had but a thousand a year.

2   Dave Russell, *Popular Music in England 1840–1914*, Manchester UP, 1997, p.78.

3   Dr Roy Johnston, Dr Declan Plummer, *The Musical Life of Nineteenth Century Belfast*, Ashgate, 2015, p.189.

67   Pianos, Parlour Ballads, and the Great Exhibition   pp.109-15

1   Cyril Ehrlich, *The Piano: A History*, Dent, 1976, p.97.

2   David Starkey, *Music and Monarchy*, p.298; https://www.royalcollection.org.uk/sites/default/files/Music%20and%20Theatre.pdf Consulted 30 January 2016.

3   *The Times*, 8 May 1883.

68   Early Sullivan   pp.115-21

1   *The Times*, 8 May 1883.

2   As an adult Sullivan dropped his middle name, not liking the effect it had on his initials.

3   Percy Young, *Sir Arthur Sullivan*, Dent, 1971, p.10.

69   Grove, Manns, and Sullivan   pp.121-28

1   Quoted in Samuel Midgley, *My 70 Year's Musical Memories*, Novello, 1934, pp.21–22.

70   Sullivan and Gilbert   pp.128-37

1   Several sources state that *Thespis* was taken off at the end of January, but if the figure of sixty-four performances given in Terence Rees' *Thespis – A Gilbert & Sullivan Enigma*, (Dillon's University Bookshop, 1964, p.78, note 7) is correct, this cannot the case. Gilbert himself claimed there were about seventy performances.

2   The often-quoted idea that Gilbert got his inspiration from a Japanese Exhibition in London's Knightsbridge, which was dramatised in the film *Topsey Turvy*, is not correct. The exhibition opened in January 1885. *The Mikado* opened in March.

3   *The World*, 4 February 1891.

4   *Allgemeine Musik-Zeitung*, 24 November & 1 December 1891.

5   *The Times*, 23 November 1900.

71   The Golden Age of Music Hall   pp. 137-47

1   Hence the children's rhyme 'Up and down the City Road / In and out of the Eagle / That's the way the money goes / Pop goes the weasel.' The last line apparently refers to pawning a kind of iron used by tailors.

2   In fact, the two-shows-a-night system was actually pioneered at Barnard's in Chatham, but only because the military authorities considered it necessary to have one show for officers and one for other ranks.

3   Marie Lloyd claimed that her debut was in June 1884 and she was fourteen. Her sister Alice stated that it was May 1885, when she was fifteen. There is no conclusive evidence either way.

72   Musical Education, and the Anglican Revival   pp. 147-57

1   *The Musical Times*, Vol. 24, 1883, p.309.

2   The second verse runs:
'Sleep and rest, sleep and rest / Father will come to thee soon; / Rest, rest, on mother's breast, / Father will come to thee soon; / Father will come to his babe in the nest, / Silver sails all out of the west, / Under the silver moon, / Sleep my little one, sleep, / My pretty one, sleep.'

3   These days, sadly, the hymn is often recast as 'Onward! Christian pilgrims!'

4   *St Nathaniel* was originally entitled *St Luke* but the name was changed to avoid confusion with another hymn tune of the same name.

5   Edward Greenfield, 'Sullivan (The) Golden Legend', *The Gramophone*, Awards Issue, 2001, p.6.

73   Alexander Mackenzie   pp. 157-65

1   *Monthly Music Record*, Vol. 14, 1884, p.249.

2   Pablo Sarasate's full name was Pablo Martín Melitón de Sarasate y Navascués.

74   Hubert Parry   pp. 166-76

1   J. R. Sterndale Bennett, *The Life of William Sterndale Bennett*, Cambridge University Press, 1907, p.399.

2   J. A. Fuller Maitland, *English Music in the XIXth Century*, Grant Richards, 1902, p.199.

3   Ernest Walker, *A History of Music in England*, p.330.

4   Meirion Hughes & Robert Stradling, *The English Musical Renaissance 1840–1940*, Manchester University Press, 2001, p.220.

5   Quoted in Nicholas Tarling, *Choral Masterpieces: Major and Minor*, Rowman & Littlefield, 2014, p.117.

| 75 | Charles Villiers Stanford | pp.176-87 |

1 Walford Davies *et al*, 'Charles Villiers Stanford', *Music & Letters*, Vol. V, no.3, July 1924, pp. 193–207.

2 Quite why Stanford authorised German and Italian translations, which would inevitably alter – and damage – the balance of the whole piece, is a complete mystery.

3 Edward Fellowes, *English Cathedral Music*, Methuen, 1946, p.238; Eric Routley, *A Short History of English Church Music*, p.84.

4 Charles Villiers Stanford, *Interludes, Records and Reflections*, John Murray, 1922, p.65.

| 76 | Parratt, Lloyd, Alcock, Corder, and Cowen | pp.187-96 |

1 George Bernard Shaw (Cornetto di Basso), '*Eden*', *The Nation*, 14 October 1891.

2 'Walter Parratt, February 10, 1841 – March 27, 1924', *The Musical Times*, Vol. 65, no.975, 1924, pp. 401–3.

| 77 | The Idea of a Renaissance | pp.196-200 |

1 *Daily Telegraph*, 4 September 1882.

2 Frank Howes, *The English Musical Renaissance*, Secker & Warburg, 1966; Peter J. Pirie, *The English Musical Renaissance*, Gollancz, 1979; Michael Trend, *The Music Makers*, Macmillan, 1985.

3 This William Wallace is not to be confused with the operatic composer William Vincent Wallace.

| 78 | Edward Elgar | pp.200-212 |

1 Charles Villiers Stanford and Cecil Forsyth, *A History of Music*, Macmillan, New York, 1916, pp.316–17.

2 *Salut d'Amour* was originally entitled *Liebesgruss* because Caroline was fluent in German.

3 Talk given by Stephen Johnson at the Hereford Three Choirs Festival, 2012.

4 Michael J. Kennedy, *Portrait of Elgar*, OUP, 1987, p.23.

| 79 | Frederick Delius | pp.212-19 |

1 Don C. Gillespie, *The Search for Thomas Ward, Teacher of Frederick Delius*, U Florida P, 1996, p.xi.

80   Ethel Smyth, and Edward German   pp.220-24

1   Eugene Gates, 'Dame Ethel Smyth: Pioneer of English Opera.' *Kapralova Society Journal*, Vol. 11, no.1, 2013, pp 1–9.

2   Thomas Beecham, 'Dame Ethel Smyth', *Musical Times*, Vo.99, no.1385, July 1958, pp.363–5.

81   Scotland, Ireland, and Wales   pp.224-30

1   No relation to Hubert Parry.

2   In later hymnals, the words are frequently revised to 'Guide me, O thou great Redeemer'.

82   National Music   pp.230-33

1   The numbering of Dvořák's symphonies has a long and complicated history. The accepted, modern numbering – by order of composition – is used here.

83   The Folk Revival, and the Tudor Revival   pp.233-41

1   John Broadwood and Geoffrey Dusart, *Old English Songs, as now sung by the Peasantry of Surrey and Sussex*, Betts & Co, 1847 (not 1843 as frequently stated).

2   G. Peter Winnington, *Walter Fuller: The Man Who Had Ideas*, Letterworth, 2014, pp.65–104.

3   See David Harker, *Fakesong*, Open UP, 1985; C. J Bearman, 'Who Were the Folk? The Demography of Cecil Sharp's Somerset Folk Singers', *Historical Journal*, no.43, 2000, pp.751–75; C. J. Bearman, 'Cecil Sharp in Somerset: Some Reflections on the Work of David Harker', *Folklore*, no.113, 2002, pp.11–34.

4   It is important to distinguish Richard Runciman Terry from Charles Sanford Terry (1864–1936), who wrote a detailed biography of Bach and was awarded an honorary doctorate by Leipzig University.

84   Exoticism, Bantock, and Foulds   pp.241-47

1   *A Gaiety Girl*, first performed in 1893, with music by Sidney Jones and lyrics by Owen Hall and Harry Greenbank; *In Town*, 1892, music Frank Osmond Carr, lyrics Adrian Ross *The Shop Girl*, 1894, music Ivan Caryll, lyrics H.J.W. Dam and Adrian Ross; *Gentleman Joe*, 1895, music Walter Slaughter, lyrics Basil Hood.

2   Notes by Michael Hurd to *Bantock*, Hyperion CDA66450, 1991, p.3.

3   Quoted in Imogen Holst, *Gustav Holst: A Biography*, Oxford, 1988, p.31.

4   This was an amateur performance. The first professional performance did not take place until 1921.

85   Celtic Connections, Bax, and Boughton   pp.247-53

1   Arnold Bax, Farewell, My Youth, Longmans, 1943, pp.47–48.
2   Arthur Bliss, William Walton *et al.*, 'Arnold Bax 1883–1953', *Music & Letters*, Vol. 35, no.1, January 1954, pp.1–14 (p.14).
3   Lewis Foreman, *Bax*, Scholar, 1983, p.282.
4   Colin Scott-Sutherland, *Arnold Bax*, Dent, 1973, p.75.

86   Gustav (von) Holst   pp.254-59

1   The Scottish Orchestra is today known as the Royal Scottish National Orchestra.

87   Somervell, Quilter, Ireland, and Dyson   pp.259-66

1   *Sarnia* is the Latin name for Guernsey.
2   Letter from George Dyson to Geoffrey Bickersteth, 5 December 1915, quoted in Paul Spicer, *Sir George Dyson: His Life and Music*, Boydell and Brewer, 2014, p.96.
3   Lewis Foreman, notes to *Dyson: The Canterbury Pilgrims*, Chandos, CHAN 9531(2), 1997, p.8.
4   The *Agincourt Hymn* is also sometimes known as the *Agincourt Carol*.

88   Coleridge-Taylor, Bridge, Scott, and Grainger   pp.266-74

1   *The Musical Times*, 1 December 1927.
2   Quoted in David Tame, *The Secret Power of Music*, Destiny (Rochester, Vermont), 1984, p.264.
3   Philip R. Buttall, notes to *Frank Bridge, Cyril Scott, Piano Quintets*, NAXOS 8.571355, 2015.

89   Vaughan Williams   pp.274-91

1   Also 'Potipher', 'Potiphar' and 'Potiffer' depending on the source. The spelling here follows Ursula Vaughan Williams.
2   *The Times*, 7 September 1910, p.7.
3   The 1920 premiere was of the original violin and piano version. The orchestral version was heard for the first time in 1921. Marie Hall was the soloist on both occasions.
4   Meirion Hughes & Robert Stradling, *The English Musical Renaissance 1840–1940*, p.161.
5   Stephen Johnson, *Vaughan Williams and the Lost Generation*, Radio 3, 11 May 2014.
6   Ursula Vaughan Williams, *RVW*, OUP, 1988, p.138.
7   *The Cambridge Companion to Vaughan Williams*, ed. Alain Frogley and Aidan Thomson, CUP, 2013, p.137.

90   The Proms, Henry Wood, and Thomas Beecham   pp.285-91
1   In 1929, the LSO was finally obliged to issue its own ruling against the use of deputies.
2   Charles Reid, *Thomas Beecham*, Gollancz (Readers Union), 1962, pp.98–111.
3   Rimsky-Korsakov's *Ivan the Terrible* is also sometimes known as *The Maid of Pskov*.

92   Wartime Melodies   pp.297-303
1   John Sant, *Albert Ketèlbey: From the Sanctuary of His Heart*, Manifold, 2001, p.11.

93   War Damage   pp.303-314
1   Georges Auric (1899–1983), Louis Durey (1888–1979), Arthur Honegger (1892–1955), Darius Milhaud (1892–1974), Francis Poulenc (1899–1963), Germaine Tailleferre (1892–1983).
2   http://www.warcomposers.co.uk/bliss.html. Consulted 10 Janury 2016.
3   Anthony Boden, *Three Choirs: A History of the Festival*, Alan Sutton, 1992, p.166.
4   Li Bo is more commonly known these days as Li Bai.
5   Geoffrey Self, *The Music of E. J. Moeran*, Toccata, 1986, pp.19–20.
6   Geoffrey Self, *The Music of E. J. Moeran*, p.221.
7   Herbert Howells, 'Ivor Gurney: The Musician', *Music and Letters*, Vol. 19, no.1, January 1938, p.14.

94   Howells, and Warlock   pp.314-22
1   Warlock appears, thinly disguised, as Halliday in *Women in Love*.
2   In recent years, it has been revealed that Warlock was the father of the art critic Brian Sewell.
3   Constant Lambert, 'Master of English song', Radio Times, 1 July 1938, pp.12–13.

95   Musicals, Noel Coward, and the Dance Bands   pp.323-32
1   *The Star*, 19 April 1919.
2   Noel Coward, Introduction, *Noel Coward Songbook*, Michael Joseph, 1953.
3   Gordon Bathgate, *Voices from the Ether*, Lulu.com, 2012, p.33.

96   William Walton   pp.332-38
1   The Sengerphone is said to have been invented by the Swiss bass Alexander Senger to amplify his voice when singing the part of Fafner the dragon in *Siegfried*.

2   Michael Kennedy, *Portrait of Walton*, Oxford, 1990, p.16.

3   Michael Kennedy, *Portrait of Walton*, p.50.

4   In fact, all three composers produced works which required much larger musical forces than specified in the original commission.

5   Michael Kennedy, *Portrait of Walton*, p.212.

98   Lambert and Berners, Ballet, and Opera   pp.342-49

1   Gerald Hugh Tyrwhitt-Wilson, often referred to as Gerald Tyrwhitt, became Lord Berners in 1918. I find it simpler to use this name throughout.

2   They sacked the ships of London town,
They burned the ships of Rye and Cadiz,
They burned full many a city down;
A bloody trade the pirate's is.
But Theodore,
Though dripping gore,
Was always courteous to the ladies.

99   Between the Wars   pp.349-56

1   Berkeley's *Serenade* is sometimes called *Serenade for Strings*.

100   Films, Musicals, and Light Music   pp.356-68

1   http://stories-of-london.org/the-theatre-organ-part-two-builders-of-the-theatre-organs/. Consulted 9 January 2017.

2   Vaughan Williams, 'Director's Report', *Royal College of Music Magazine*, Vol. 40. no.1, 1945, p.7.

3   Meirion Hughes & Robert Stradling, *The English Musical Renaissance 1840–1940*, p.106.

101   The Second World War   pp.368-75

1   In fact, Barbirolli was a second choice. Wilhelm Furtwängler was originally chosen, but as a German continuing to work in Germany under Nazi rule, he was politically unacceptable.

2   Some versions of the story suggest that the judge was motivated by homophobia; others suggest that Novello tried to bribe the arresting officer.

3   John Huntley, *British Film Music*, Skelton Robinson, 1947, p.54.

102   Post-War Transformation   pp.376-85

1   For the last twenty years or more, the situation has been reversed and Cheltenham is noted for its premieres of contemporary music.

2   Russell Palmer, *British Music*, Skelton Robinson, 1947, p.10.

3   Alan Frank, *Modern British Composers*, Denis Dobson, 1953, p.8.

4   A new Carl Rosa Opera Company was started in 1997.

5   Tony Stoller, *Classical Music on UK Radio 1945–1995*, Ph.D thesis,
    U Bournemouth, 2015, p.55.

6   BBC Internal Circulating Memo, Peter Montgomery, 'Music for the
    National Effort', 4 August 1942, BBC WAC R27/121/5, quoted in John Morris,
    Ph.D. thesis, *Music and British Wartime Propaganda 1935–1945*, U Exeter,
    2011.

7   Humphrey Carpenter, *The Envy of the World*, Weidenfeld & Nicolson, 1996.
    p.283.

103   Benjamin Britten   pp.385-400

1   *The Times*, 12 August 1938.

2   Britten's original MS was confiscated by US customs on the grounds that it
    was in code. Britten rewrote it from memory during the voyage.

3   Reprinted in *Britten on Music*, ed. Paul Kildea, Oxford University Press,
    pp.31–35.

4   Heather Weibe, *Britten's Unquiet Pasts: Sound and memory in Postwar
    Reconstruction*, Cambridge University Press, 2012, p.20.

5   Humphrey Carpenter, *Benjamin Britten*, Faber and Faber, 1993, p.235.

6   Humphrey Carpenter, *Benjamin Britten*, pp.227–8.

7   Quoted in Humphrey Carpenter, *Benjamin Britten*, p.252.

8   David Kynaston, *Family Britain*, Bloomsbury, 2009, p.308.

9   Heterophony involves two players playing the same melodic line varying it
    simultaneously but independently.

104   Michael Tippett   pp.401-10

1   Ian Kemp, *Tippett: The Composer and his Music*, Oxford, 1987, p.313.

2   Ian Kemp, *Tippett: The Composer and his Music*, pp.53–54.

3   Ian Kemp, *Tippett: The Composer and his Music*, p.322.

4   'Obituary', *Tippett on Music*, ed. Meirion Bowen, Clarendon, 1995, pp.70–72
    (p.71).

5   Quoted in Michel Tippett, *Those Twentieth Century Blues*, Pimlico, 1994,
    p.207.

6   http://www.meirion-bowen.com/mbartnewyear.htm. Consulted 13.02.2017.

7   Michael Tippett, '*The Mask of Time*: Work in Progress', *Comparative
    Criticism, Volume 4: The Language of the Arts*, ed. E. S. Shaffer, CUP, 1982,
    pp.19–29 (p.19).

8   Michael Tippett, '*The Mask of Time*: Work in Progress', *Comparative
    Criticism, Volume 4: The Language of the Arts*, p.29.

| 105 | Technology, Trad, and Skiffle | pp.410-17 |

1   Bob Stanley, 'Acker Bilk: the hitmaker who symbolised the generation gap', *The Guardian*, 4 November 2014.

| 106 | Post-War Men and Women | pp.417-29 |

1   *The Times*, 2 April 1959.

| 107 | Folk Revived Again | pp.429-37 |

1   'Ewan MacColl: the godfather of folk who was adored – and feared', *The Guardian*, 25 January 2015.

| 108 | Malcolm Arnold | pp.437-443 |

1   After one rehearsal he is reported as having told them they were playing 'like a bunch of cunts'. https://brendanball.com/2012/09/13/jon-lord-concerto-for-group-and-orchestra/. Consulted 18.02.2017.

2   Mervyn Cooke, *A History of Film Music*, CUP, 2008.

| 109 | Rock'n'Roll and After | pp.443-54 |

1   *The Times*, 13 September 1956.

2   *Daily Mail*, 5 September 1956.

Printed Sources

Abraham, Gerald, *The Concise Oxford History of Music*. Reader's Union, 1979.

Adams, Martin, *Henry Purcell: The Origins and Development of his Musical Style*. CUP, 1995.

Anon, 'Shetland Notes and Queries'. *The Shetland Times*, 14 May 1887.

Anon, 'The Philharmonic Society'. *Quarterly Musical Magazine and Review*, Vol. 1, 1818.

Anon, 'The Present State of Music in England'. *Quarterly Musical Magazine and Review*, 1824, pp.281–292.

Anon, 'The Present State of Vocal Art in England', *Quarterly Musical Magazine and Review*, 1824, pp.1–17.

Anon, 'Walter Parratt, February 10, 1841 – March 27, 1924'. *Musical Times*, Vol. 65, No. 975, 1924, pp.401–403.

Archer, Jayne Elisabeth, Elizabeth Goldrin, and Sarah Knight, *The Progresses, Pageants, and Entertainments of Queen Elizabeth I*. OUP, 2009.

Auden, W. H., Kallman, Chester, and Nora Greenberg, eds., *An Elizabethan Song Book*. Faber & Faber, 1957.

Bacharach, A. L., *British Music in Our Time*. Pelican, 1946.

Bailey, Leslie, *The Gilbert and Sullivan Book*. Cassell, 1952.

Baker, Richard Anthony, *British Music Hall: An Illustrated History*. Pen and Sword, 2014.

Baldwin, David, *Royal Prayer: A Surprising History*. A & C Black, 2010.

Banfield, Stephen, *Gerald Finzi*. Faber & Faber, 1997.

Barlow, Michael, *Whom the Gods Love: the Life and Music of George Butterworth*. Toccata P, 1997.

Bathgate, Gordon, *Voices from the Ether*. Lulu.com, 2012.

Bax, Arnold, *Farewell, My Youth*. Longmans, 1943.

Bearman, C. J., 'Cecil Sharp in Somerset: Some Reflections on the Work of David Harker'. *Folklore*, No. 113, 2002, pp.11–34.

Beecham, Thomas, 'Dame Ethel Smyth'. *Musical Times*, Vol. 99, No. 1385, July 1958, pp.363–5.

Bicknell, Stephen, *The History of the English Organ*. CUP, 1996.

Bliss, Arthur, *et al.*, 'Arnold Bax 1883–1953'. *Music & Letters*, Vol. 35, No. 1, January 1954, pp.1–14.

Boden, Anthony, *Three Choirs: A History of the Festival*. Alan Sutton, 1992.

Boeringer, James, *Organa Britannica: Organs in Great Britain, 1660–1860.* Bucknell UP, 1989.

Bowen, Meirion ed., *Tippett on Music.* Clarendon, 1995.

Bowers, Jane & Tick, Judith, *Women Making Music: The Western Tradition, 1150–1950.* U of Illinois P, 1987.

Broadwood, John & Dusart, Geoffrey, *Old English Songs, as now sung by the Peasantry of Surrey and Sussex.* Betts, 1847.

Brown, Clive, *Louis Spohr: A Critical Biography.* CUP, 2006.

Budd, Vincent, *An Introduction to the Life and Work of Sir Granville Bantock.* Gnosis, 2000.

Burgh, Allatson, *Anecdotes of Music.* Longman, Hurst, Rees, Orme & Brown, 1814.

Burke, John, *Musical Landscapes.* Webb & Bower, 1983.

Burney, Charles, *A General History of Music,* 1789.

Burrows, Donald, *Handel.* Oxford, 1994.

Burton, Humphrey, *Menuhin.* Faber & Faber, 2000.

Bush, Douglas and Richard Kassel, eds. *The Organ: An Encyclopedia.* Routledge, 2006.

Buttall, Philip R., notes to *Frank Bridge, Cyril Scott, Piano Quintets.* NAXOS 8.571355, 2015.

Carley, Lionel, *Edvard Grieg in England.* Boydell, 2006.

Carley, Lionel, *Grieg and Delius.* Marion Boyars, 1993.

Carpenter, Humphrey, *Benjamin Britten.* Faber & Faber, 1993.

Carpenter, Humphrey, *The Envy of the World.* Weidenfeld & Nicolson, 1996.

Cartellieri, Otto, *The Court of Burgundy.* Taylor & Francis, 1972.

Carwood, Andrew, notes to *Byrd: the Great Service.* Hyperion, CDA65573, 2005.

Chappell, William, *Popular Music of the Olden Time.* Cramer, Beale, & Chappell, 1859.

Chivers, Richard William, *The Hymns and Responds of John Sheppard.* M.A. thesis, U of Durham, 1997.

Clark, Bunker, 'Adrian Batten and John Barnard: Colleagues and Collaborators'. *Musica Disciplina,* Vol. 22, 1968, pp.207–29.

Coles, John M., 'Irish Bronze-Age Horns and their Relations with Northern Europe'. *Proceedings of the Prehistoric Society,* 1963, Vol. XXIX, pp.326–56.

Collinson, Francis M., *The Bagpipe: The History of a Musical Instrument.* Routledge, 1975.

Collis, Louise, *Impetuous Heart: the Story of Ethel Smyth.* William Kimber, 1984.

Cooke, Mervyn, *A History of Film Music.* CUP, 2008.

Copper, Bob, *A Song for Every Season.* Heinemann, 1971.

Cowgill, Rachel & Peter Holman, eds. *Music in the British Provinces, 1690–1914*. Routledge, 2007.

Cowgill, Rachel & Julian Rushton, eds. *Europe, Empire and Spectacle in British Music*. Ashgate, 2006.

Cummings, William Hayman, *Dr Arne and Rule Britannia*. Novello, 1912.

Cunningham, John Patrick, *The Consort Music of William Lawes, 1602–1645*. Boydell & Brewer, 2010.

Davies, Norman, *The Isles*. Macmillan, 1999.

Davies, Walford *et al.*, 'Charles Villiers Stanford'. *Music & Letters*, Vol. V, No. 3, July 1924, pp. 193–207.

de Chabannes, James Grier Ademar, 'Carolingian Musical Practices and 'Nota Romana'. *Journal of the American Musicological Society*, Vol. 56, No. 1, Spring 2003.

de Sola Pinto, Vivian and A. E. Rodway, eds., *The Common Muse*. Penguin, 1965.

Denton, Jeffrey Howard, *English Royal Chapels 1100–1300*. Manchester U P, 1970.

Dobson, Collet, 'State of the Royal Academy of Music'. *The Musical World*, J. Alfred Novello, 1837, pp.18–21.

Downing, Sarah Jane, *The English Pleasure Garden*. Shire, 2009.

Drummond, Pippa, *The Provincial Music Festival in England 1784–1914*. Ashgate, 2013.

Duckles, Vincent, 'Sir William Herschel as a Composer'. *Publications of the Astronomical Society of the Pacific*, Vol. 74, No. 436, 1961, p.55–9.

Elliott, Kenneth & Frederick Rimmer, *A History of Scottish Music*. BBC, 1973.

Fawkes, Richard, *The Classical Music Map of Britain*. Elliot & Thompson, 2010.

Fellowes, Edmund H., *English Cathedral Music*. Methuen, 1941.

Fifield, Christopher, *The German Symphony between Beethoven and Brahms*. Ashgate, 2015.

Foreman, Lewis, *Bax*. Scholar, 1983.

Foreman, Lewis, *From Parry to Britten*. Batsford, 1987.

Foreman, Lewis, notes to *Dyson: The Canterbury Pilgrims*. Chandos, CHAN 9531(2), 1997.

Foreman, Lewis, 'The Canterbury Pilgrims'. *Three Choirs Festival Hereford 2012*, Three Choirs, 2012.

Frank, Alan, *Modern British Composers*. Denis Dobson, 1953.

Frogley, Alain & Aidan Thomson, eds., *The Cambridge Companion to Vaughan Williams*. CUP, 2013.

Fry, Helen, *Music & Men*. History P, 2008.

Fuller Maitland, J. A., *English Music in the XIXth Century*. Grant Richards, 1902.

Fuller Maitland, J. A, ed. *Grove's Dictionary of Music and Musicians*. Macmillan, 1922.

Gant, Andrew, *O Sing unto the Lord*. Profile Books, 2015.

Gates, Eugene, 'Dame Ethel Smyth: Pioneer of English Opera'. *Kapralova Society Journal*, Vol. 11, No. 1, 2013, pp 1–9.

Gaul, Liam, *Masters of Irish Music*. Nonsuch, 1976.

Gibson, James M., *Kent: Diocese of Canterbury*, Vol. 3. U of Toronto P, 2002.

Gilbert, W. S., *The Savoy Operas*. Macmillan, 1926.

Gillespie, Don. C., *The Search for Thomas Ward, Teacher of Frederick Delius*. U of Florida P, 1996.

Gillies, Midge, *Marie Lloyd: the One and Only*. Gollancz, 1999.

Gollancz, Victor, *Journey Towards Music*. Gollancz, 1964.

Grattan Flood, W. H., 'New Facts about John Dowland'. *The Gentleman's Magazine*, 1906, pp.287–91.

Greenfield, Edward, 'Sullivan (The) Golden Legend'. *The Gramophone*, Awards Issue, 2001.

Gregory, E. David, *The Late Victorian Folksong Revival: The Persistence of English Melody, 1878–1903*. Scarecrow Press, 2010.

Hadow, W. H., *English Music*. Longmans, Green, 1931.

Hand, Colin, *John Taverner: His Life and Music*. Eulenburg, 1978.

Harker, David, *Fakesong*. Open UP, 1985.

Harley, John, *The World of William Byrd: Musicians, Merchants and Magnates*. Ashgate, 2010.

Harman, Alec, and Wilfred Mellers, *Man and his Music*. Barrie & Rockliff, 1962.

Haskell, Harry, *The Early Music Revival*. Thames & Hudson, 1988.

Haweis, H. R., *My Musical Life*. Longmans Green, 1898.

Headington, Christopher, *Peter Pears*. Faber & Faber, 1992.

Henigan, Julie, *Literacy and Orality in Eighteenth-Century Irish Song*. Routledge, 2015.

Hoare, Philip, *Noel Coward*. Sinclair-Stevenson, 1995.

Hogwood, Christopher, notes to *Orlando Gibbons: Keyboard Music*. Decca Music Group, DSLO515, 1975.

Hold, Trevor, *Parry to Finzi*. Boydell, 2002.

Holland, A. K., *Henry Purcell*. Penguin, 1948.

Hollingworth, Robert, notes to *Thomas Tomkins: Music Divine*. Chandos, CHAN 0680, 2002.

Holst, Imogen, *Gustav Holst: A Biography*. OUP, 1988.

Hooker, John, *The Ancient History and Description of the City of Exeter*. Andrews & Trewman, 1765.

Howes, Frank, *The English Musical Renaissance*. Secker & Warburg, 1966.

Hughes, Meirion & Robert Stradling, *The English Musical Renaissance 1840–1940*. Manchester U P, 2001.

Huntley, John, *British Film Music*. Skelton Robinson, 1947.

Hurd, Michael, notes to *Bantock*. Hyperion, CDA66450, 1991.

Jacobs, Arthur ed., *Choral Music*. Penguin, 1963.

Johansen, Claes, *Procul Harum: Beyond the Pale*. SAF, 2000.

Johnson, Stephen, 'Darkness and Light'. *BBC Proms Festival Guide 2017*, BBC, 2017, pp.46–49.

Johnston, Roy & Declan Plummer, *The Musical Life of Nineteenth-Century Belfast*. Ashgate, 2015.

Kassler, Michael, *The Music Trade in Georgian England*. Ashgate, 2011.

Keates, Jonathan, *Handel: the Man and his Music*. Gollancz, 1992.

Keates, Jonathan, *Purcell*. Chatto & Windus, 1995.

Kemp, Ian, *Tippett: The Composer and his Music*. Oxford, 1987.

Kennedy, Michael, Joyce Kennedy and Tim Rutherford-Johnson, eds, *The Oxford Dictionary of Music*. OUP, 5th ed., 2013.

Kennedy, Michael, *Portrait of Walton*. OUP, 1990.

Kennedy, Michael J., *Portrait of Elgar*, OUP, 1987.

Kildea, Paul, ed., *Britten on Music*. OUP, 2003.

Klinck, Anne Lingard & Anne Marie Rasmussen, *Medieval Woman's Song: Cross-Cultural Approaches*. U of Pennsylvania P, 2002.

Kynaston, David, *Family Britain*. Bloomsbury, 2009.

Lambert, Constant, 'Master of English Song'. *Radio Times*, 1 July 1938.

Lambert, Constant, *Music Ho!* Pelican, 1948.

Lang, Paul Henry, *Music in Western Civilization*. Dent, 1963.

Le Huray, Peter, 'Towards a Definitive Study of Pre-Restoration Anglican Service Music'. *Musica Disciplina*, Vol. 14, 1960, pp.167–95.

Lee-Brown, Martin, & Paul Guinery, *Delius and his Music*. Boydell, 2014.

Linklater Thomson, C., *A Child's History of Great Britain*. Horace Marshall, [1910].

Littlejohn, J. H., *The Scottish Music Hall 1880–1990*. G. C. Books (Wigtown), 1990.

Lloyd, A. L., *Folk Song in England*. Panther, 1969.

Lloyd, Stephen, *H.Balfour Gardiner*. CUP, 1984.

Macfarren, G. A., 'Barnett, John'. *The Imperial Dictionary of Universal Biography*, Vol. 1, William Mackenzie, 1863, p.389.

Macfarren, G. A., 'Jerusalem'. *Musical Times*, Vol. 5, No. 100, 1852, pp.51–54 & 59.

Mackerness, E. D., *A Social History of English Music*. Routledge & Kegan Paul, 1964.

Mainwaring, John, *Memoirs of the Life of the Late George Frederic Handel: To which is Added a Catalogue of His Works and Observations Upon Them*. Dodsley, 1760.

Marek, George, *Beethoven: Biography of a Genius*. Funk & Wagnalls, 1969.

Martin, Colin & Parker, Geoffrey, *The Spanish Armada*. Manchester U P, 1999.

Matthews, Betty 'The Earliest English Organ-Builders'. *British Institute of Organ Studies Reporter*, January 1982, Vol. 1, VI, No. 1.

McLucas, Anne Dhu, 'Forbes' *Cantus: Songs & Fancies* Revisited'. *Defining Strains: The Musical Life of the Scots in the Seventeenth Century*, Lang, 2007.

McVeagh, Diana, *Gerald Finzi*. Boydell, 2005.

McVeigh, Simon, *Concert Life in London from Mozart to Haydn*. CUP, 2006.

Mellers, Wilfrid, *Vaughan Williams and the Vision of Albion*. Barrie & Jenkins, 1989.

Meyer, Ernst H., *English Chamber Music*. Lawrence & Wishart, 1946.

Midgley, Samuel, *My 70 Year's Musical Memories*. Novello, 1934.

Mole, John, *The Sultan's Organ*. Fortune, 2012.

Moore, Frank Ledlie ed., *The Handbook of Gilbert and Sullivan*. Barker, 1962.

Moore, Jerrold Northrop, *Edward Elgar: A Creative Life*. OUP, 1984.

Morley, Sheridan, *A Talent to Amuse*. Penguin, 1974.

Moroney, Davitt, notes to *William Byrd, the Complete Keyboard Music*. Hyperion, CDA66551/7, 1999.

Morris, John, *Music and British Wartime Propaganda 1935–1945*. Ph.D. thesis, U of Exeter, 2011.

Motion, Andrew, *The Lamberts*. Chatto & Windus, 1986.

Murdoch, Brian & Malcolm K. Read, *Early German Literature and Culture*. Boydell & Brewer, 2004.

Murray, Teresa Ann, *Thomas Morley and the Business of Music in Elizabethan England*. Ph.D. thesis, U of Birmingham, 2010.

Norwich, John Julius, *Fifty Years of Glyndebourne*. Cape, 1985.

O'Donovan, Matthew, notes to *John Sheppard, Media Vita*. Harmonia Mundi, HMU 807509, 2010.

Palmer, Christopher, *George Dyson: man and music*. Thames, 1996.

Palmer, Russell, *British Music*. Skelton Robinson, 1947.

Palmer, William, 'Gibbons's Verse Anthems'. *Music & Letters*, Vol. 35, No. 2, April 1954, pp.107–113.

Parry, C. Hubert, *The Art of Music*. Routledge & Kegan Paul, 1950.

Pearsall, Ronald, *Victorian Popular Music*. David & Charles, 1973.

Pearson, Hesketh, *Gilbert and Sullivan*. Penguin, 1950.

Percy, Thomas, *Reliques of Ancient English Poetry*. Frederick Warne, 1887.

Pilkinton, Mark Cartwright, *Bristol*, Vol. 8. U of Toronto P, 1997.

Pirie, Peter J., *The English Musical Renaissance*. Gollancz, 1979.

Poulton, Diana, *John Dowland*. U of California P, 1982.

Pückler-Muskau, Hermann, *Tour in England, Ireland, and France in the Years 1828, 1829*. Trans. Sarah Austin. Carey & Lea, 1833.

Pulling, Christopher, *They Were Singing*. Harrap, 1952.

Pulver, Jeffrey, *A Dictionary of Old English Music and Musical Instruments*. Kegan Paul, Trench, Trubner, 1923.

Rayborn, Tim, *A New English Music: Composers and Folk Traditions in England's Musical Renaissance from the Late 19th to the Mid-20th Century*. McFarland, 2016.

Raynor, Henry, *A Social History of Music from the Middle Ages to Beethoven*. Barrie & Jenkins, 1972.

Reece, Isobel, notes to *Robert Carver*. CORO COR16051, 2006.

Rees, Terence, *Thespis – A Gilbert & Sullivan Enigma*. Dillon's U Bookshop, 1964.

Reese, Gustave, *Music in the Renaissance*. Dent, 1954.

Reid, Charles, *John Barbirolli*. Hamish Hamilton, 1971.

Reid, Charles, *Malcolm Sargent*. Hamish Hamilton, 1968.

Reid, Charles, *Thomas Beecham*. Gollancz, 1962.

Rigney, Anne, *The Afterlives of Walter Scott: Memory on the Move*. OUP, 2012.

Rishton, Timothy 'William Smethergell, Organist'. *Musical Times*, Vol. 124, No. 1684, June 1983, pp.381–3.

Routley, Eric, *A Short History of English Church Music*. Mowbray, 1977.

Russell, Dave, *Popular Music in England 1840–1914: A Social History*. Manchester U P, 1997.

Sandon, Nicholas, notes to *Thomas Tallis, The Complete Works*. Brilliant Classics, 93612.

Sant, John, *Albert Ketèlbey: From the Sanctuary of his Heart*. Manifold, 2001.

Scarisbrick, J. J., *Henry VIII*. Folio Society, 2004.

Schmitz, Oskar A. H., *Das Land ohne Musik: englische Gesellschaftsprobleme*. Georg Müller, Munich, 1914.

Scholes, Percy, *The Great Dr Burney*. OUP, 1948.

Scott, Derek B., *Sounds of the Metropolis: The 19th Century Popular Music Revolution in London, New York, Paris and Vienna*. OUP, 2008.

Scott-Sutherland, Colin, *Arnold Bax*. Dent, 1973.

Self, Geoffrey, *The Music of E. J. Moeran*. Toccata, 1986.

Shaw, George Bernard (Cornetto di Basso), 'Eden'. *The Nation*, 14 October 1891.

Shead, Richard, *Constant Lambert*. Simon, 1973.

Simpson, Robert ed., *The Symphony 1: Haydn to Dvorak*. Pelican, 1966.

Simpson, Robert ed., *The Symphony 2: Elgar to the Present Day*. Pelican, 1966.

Smith, Bruce R., *The Acoustic World of Early Modern England*. U of Chicago P, 1999.

Smith, William, *The Reasonableness of Setting Forth the Most Worthy Praise of Almighty God.* T & J Swords, 1814.

Smither, Howard E., *A History of the Oratorio: The oratorio in the nineteenth and twentieth centuries.* UNC, 2000.

Sounes, Howard, *Down the Highway: the Life of Bob Dylan.* Black Swan, 2002.

Spencer, Charles, *The World of Sergei Diaghilev.* Penguin, 1979.

Spencer, Neil, 'Ewan MacColl: the godfather of folk who was adored – and feared'. *The Guardian*, 25 January 2015.

Spicer, Paul, *Herbert Howells*, Seren (Bridgend), 1998.

Spicer, Paul, *Sir George Dyson: His Life and Music.* Boydell & Brewer, 2014.

Stanford, Charles Villiers, *Interludes, Records and Reflections.* John Murray, 1922.

Stanley, Bob, 'Acker Bilk: the hitmaker who symbolised the generation gap'. *The Guardian*, 4 November 2014.

Starkey, David & Katie Greening, *Music and Monarchy.* BBC, 2103.

Stephens, G. M., 'The Waits of the City of Norwich'. *Proceedings of the Norfolk and Norwich Archaeological Society*, Norwich, 1933.

Sterndale Bennett, J. R., *The Life of William Sterndale Bennett*, CUP, 1907.

Stevens, Denis, *Tudor Church Music.* Faber & Faber, 1966.

Stoller, Tony, *Classical Music on UK Radio 1945–1995.* Ph.D thesis, U of Bournemouth, 2015.

Stone, George Winchester, *The Stage and the Page.* U of California P, 1981.

Strangways, A. H. Fox & Maud Karpeles, *Cecil Sharp.* OUP, 1955.

Strype, John, *Historical and Biographical Works*, Vol. 24. Clarendon, 1821.

Summerly, Jeremy, notes to *Tye: Missa Euge Bone & Western Wynde Mass.* Hyperion CDA677928, 2012.

Tame, David, *The Secret Power of Music.* Destiny, 1984.

Tarling, Nicholas, *Choral Masterpieces: Major and Minor.* Rowman & Littlefield, 2014.

Temperley, Nicholas, *Music and the Wesleys.* U of Illinois P, 2010.

The Annual Biography and Obituary. Longman, Rees, Orme, Brown, Green & Longman, 1832.

'The Musician About Town', *The Analyst*, Vol. 10. Simpkin & Marshall, 1840, pp.483–491.

Thompson, Wendy *et al*, 'A Sea Symphony'. *Three Choirs Festival Hereford 2012*, Three Choirs, 2012.

Tippett, Michael, 'The Mask of Time: Work in Progress'. *Comparative Criticism, Volume 4: The Language of the Arts*, CUP, 1982, pp.19–29.

Tippett, Michael, *Those Twentieth Century Blues.* Pimlico, 1994.

Trend, Michael, *The Music Makers.* Macmillan, 1985.

Vaughan Williams, Ralph and A. L. Lloyd, *English Folk Songs.* Penguin, 1959.

Vaughan Williams, Ursula, *RVW*. OUP, 1988.

Walker, Ernest, *A History of Music in England*. Oxford, 1952.

Walton, Susanna, *William Walton: Behind the Façade*. OUP, 1988.

Warlock, Peter, *Thomas Whythorne: An Unknown Elizabethan Composer*. OUP, 1925.

Weibe, Heather, *Britten's Unquiet Pasts: Sound and Memory in Postwar Reconstruction*. CUP, 2012.

Weir, Alison, *The Six Wives of Henry VIII*. Bodley Head, 1991.

Weir, Christopher, *Village and Town Bands*. Shire Publications, 1981.

Westrup, J. A., *Purcell*. Dent, 1947.

White, Eric Walter, *A History of English Opera*. Faber & Faber, 1983.

Whitehouse, Edmund, *London Lights*. This England Books, 2005.

Williams, Ralph, 'Director's Report'. *Royal College of Music Magazine*, Vol. 40. No. 1, 1945.

Winn, James Anderson, *Queen Anne, Patroness of the Arts*. OUP, 2014.

Winnington, G. Peter, *Walter Fuller: The Man Who Had Ideas*. Letterworth, 2014.

Wood, Henry J., *My Life of Music*. Victor Gollancz, 1938.

Wyatt, E. G. P., *St Gregory and the Gregorian Music*. Plainsong and Mediæval Music Society, 1904.

Young, Percy M., *A History of British Music*. Ernest Benn, 1967.

Young, Percy M., *George Grove 1820–1900*. Macmillan, 1980.

Young, Percy M., *Sir Arthur Sullivan*. Dent, 1971.

Young, Percy M., *The Choral Tradition*. Hutchinson, 1962.

Young, Rob, *Electric Eden: In Search of England's Visionary Music*. Faber & Faber, 2011.

Internet Sources

Australian Dictionary of Biography
http://adb.anu.edu.au/biography/wallace-william-vincent-2769/text3935

Bodelian Library, 'Battle of Trafalgar'
http://ballads.bodleian.ox.ac.uk/static/images/sheets/10000/07340.gif

Brendanball.com, 'Jon Lord - Concerto for group and Orchestra'
https://brendanball.com/2012/09/13/jon-lord-concerto-for-group-and-orchestra/

British Library, 'A New Patriotic Song'
http://www.bl.uk/collection-items/a-new-patriotic-song-from-a-collection-of-material-relating-to-the-fear-of-a-french-invasion

Concertprogrammes.org.uk
http://admin.concertprogrammes.org.uk/html/search/verb/ListIdentifiers/set/agentName/26477

Craig, Kenneth M., 'The Beethoven Symphonies in London: Initial Decades'
http://symposium.music.org/index.php?option=com_k2&view=item&id=1991:the-beethoven-symphonies-in-london-initial-decades&Itemid=124

Folk and Traditonal Song Lyrics, 'The Weaver and the Factory Maid'
http://www.traditionalmusic.co.uk/folk-song-lyrics/Weaver_and_the_Factory_Maid.htm

Meirion-bowen.com
http://www.meirion-bowen.com/mbartnewyear.htm

Mudcat.org, 'The Bury New Loom'
http://mudcat.org/@displaysong.cfm?SongID=6014

Officialcharts.com
http://www.officialcharts.com/charts/singles-chart/

Oxford Dictionary of National Biography
http://www.oxforddnb.com/

Oxford Music Online
http://www.oxfordmusiconline.com

Staggernation.com, 'Battle of Waterloo'
http://www.staggernation.com/msb/battle_of_waterloo.php

Storiesoflondon.org
http://stories-of-london.org/the-theatre-organ-part-two-builders-of-the-theatre-organs/

The Royal Collection
https://www.royalcollection.org.uk/sites/default/files/Music%20and%20Theatre.pdf

Unsungcomposers.com
http://www.unsungcomposers.com/forum/index.php?topic=445.0

Vauxhall Gardens 1661–1859
www.vauxhall gardens.com

Wagner, Richard, *My Life*
http://www.wagneropera.net/MyLife/RW-My-Life-Part-3-1850-1860.ht

Warcomposers.com
http://www.warcomposers.co.uk/bliss.html

Horton, Peter, 'The Church Music of Samuel Sebastian Wesley'
http://www.church-music.org.uk/articles/samuel-sebastian-wesley.asp

Index

I = Volume One; II = Volume Two

Main entry in **bold**

Lightning Source UK Ltd.
Milton Keynes UK
UKOW04n1412120118
316029UK00002B/40/P